ALSO BY MATTHEW J. BRUCCOLI

The Composition of *Tender Is the Night*
As Ever, Scott Fitz (editor, with Jennifer Atkinson)
Profile of F. Scott Fitzgerald (editor)
F. Scott Fitzgerald in His Own Time
(editor, with Jackson Bryer)
F. Scott Fitzgerald: A Descriptive Bibliography
F. Scott Fitzgerald's Ledger (editor)
The Great Gatsby: A Facsimile of the Manuscript (editor)
Apparatus for a Definitive Edition of *The Great Gatsby*
Bits of Paradise: 21 Uncollected Stories by F. Scott and Zelda
Fitzgerald (editor, with Scottie Fitzgerald Smith)
The Romantic Egoists (editor, with
Scottie Fitzgerald Smith and Joan P. Kerr)
"The Last of the Novelists": F. Scott Fitzgerald and
The Last Tycoon
Fitzgerald Newsletter (editor)
Ernest Hemingway, Cub Reporter (editor)
Ernest Hemingway's Apprenticeship (editor)
Hemingway at Auction (editor, with C. E. Frazer Clark, Jr.)
Fitzgerald/Hemingway Annual
(editor, with C. E. Frazer Clark, Jr.)
Raymond Chandler: A Checklist
Kenneth Millar/Ross Macdonald: A Checklist
Chandler Before Marlowe (editor)
Ring Lardner: A Descriptive Bibliography
(with Richard Layman)
Some Champions: Sketches & Fiction by Ring Lardner
(editor, with Richard Layman)
Lost American Fiction (series editor)
Screenplay Library (series editor)
Pittsburgh Series in Bibliography (series editor)
First Printings of American Authors (series editor)
John O'Hara: A Checklist
The O'Hara Concern: A Biography of John O'Hara
"An Artist Is His Own Fault": John O'Hara on Writers
and Writing (editor)
John O'Hara: A Descriptive Bibliography
Scott and Ernest: The Authority of Failure and the
Authority of Success

Selected
Letters *of*
JOHN
O'HARA

Selected
Letters of
JOHN
O'HARA

edited by

Matthew J. Bruccoli

RANDOM HOUSE
NEW YORK

Grateful acknowledgment is made to the Newberry Library for
permission to use a letter from John O'Hara to
Malcolm Cowley of February 9, 1962, from The
Malcolm Cowley Papers.

Library of Congress Cataloging in Publication Data

O'Hara, John, 1905–1970.
The selected letters of John O'Hara.

Includes index.
1. O'Hara, John, 1905–1970—Correspondence.
2. Novelists, American—20th century—Correspondence.
I. Bruccoli, Matthew Joseph, 1931–
PS3529.H29Z48   1978   813'.5'2   [B]   77-90249
ISBN 0-394-42133-7

Manufactured in the United States of America

2 4 6 8 9 7 5 3

FIRST EDITION

Acknowledgments

I could not have edited this volume without the cooperation of my old friend Charles W. Mann, Curator of Rare Books and Manuscripts at the Pennsylvania State University Library. John O'Hara's widow, the late Katharine Barnes O'Hara, gave this project her approval. A bonus in working on John O'Hara was Mrs. O'Hara's generous friendship. Albert Erskine of Random House many times proved himself a good friend and a superb editor. Angelic Marisa Erskine always pretended to be delighted when I arrived with a suitcase of typescript. Silvia Erskine and Alexander Erskine also submitted to my violation of their privacy. I am fortunate to have had the help of Lynn Strong, the perfect copy editor.

I am heavily indebted to: Jo August (Kennedy Library), Carlos Baker, Jeanne Bennett, B. A. Bergman, Mrs. Gerald Bramwell, David Brown, John Chamberlain, Alexander Clark (Princeton University Library), Malcolm Cowley, James Gould Cozzens, David Crosson (University of Wyoming Library), Honoria Murphy Donnelly, Felicia Geffen (National Institute of Arts and Letters), Harcourt, Brace, Jovanovich, Mary Hemingway, John Hersey, William Hogan, Kenneth Lohf (Columbia University Library) Fletcher Markle, William Maxwell, Robert Moses, Hoke Norris, Joseph O'Hara, Martin O'Hara, Joseph W. Outerbridge, Ruth Sato Reinhardt, J. Albert Robbins, R. L. Samsell, Don Schanche, Edgar Scott, Scottie Fitzgerald Smith, Mrs. John Steinbeck, Robert Stocking (Kennedy Library), Mrs. Gilbert Troxell, Theodore Wagner, Graham Watson, Glenway Wescott, Katharine Angell White.

I am obligated to the staff of the Reference and Interlibrary Loan Department at the Thomas Cooper Library, University of South Carolina, particularly to Claudia Drum, Virginia Ashley, and Joyce Werner. I am also indebted to Professor William Nolte, Head, Department of English, University of South Carolina.

Special acknowledgment goes to my assistants: Glenda Fedricci, Karen Rood, Frances Ponick, and—especially—Cara White.

To
Albert Erskine

Contents

Introduction

—◆◆—

The Letters of John O'Hara is an obligatory development from *The O'Hara Concern* (New York: Random House, 1975). Most of the letters printed here were assembled for the biography. In addition to their availability, these letters require publication because they document aspects of O'Hara's career and character that a biographer can only summarize. Moreover, a number of O'Hara's letters give the impression that he was writing them for the record. This is particularly true in the Sixties, when he expanded business letters into autobiography. In addition to their value as supplementary biography, the letters are highly readable: John O'Hara wrote them.

O'Hara was not a saver. Nor were some of his closest friends. Consequently, this volume has some of the same lacunae as *The O'Hara Concern*. There are no located letters to Robert Benchley, Dorothy Parker, John McClain, or Philip Barry. Only business letters to Wolcott Gibbs survive. The files for Duell, Sloan and Pearce cannot be found. There are no located letters to O'Hara's first two wives, Helen Petit O'Hara and Belle Wylie O'Hara. Belle is known to have organized O'Hara's papers; but this material disappeared after her death in 1954. There are no letters to his third wife, Katharine ("Sister") Barnes O'Hara—but they were rarely separated. No letters to his mother have been found. Fortunately, O'Hara's daughter Wylie preserved his letters to her.

Editorial Policy

This volume is not a definitive edition of John O'Hara's letters, and the letters are not presented in diplomatic transcription. Obvious pen slips have been silently corrected; O'Hara's deletions have not been preserved; and his placement of insertions or corrections has not been indicated. Most of the letters were typewritten, and typing errors (spacing, strike-overs, and obvious transpositions) have been silently emended; otherwise, misspellings have been preserved. Missing terminal periods have been supplied, and the first letter of a sentence has been capitalized where required. The editor has used [*sic*] to call attention to ambiguities when an error or a possible error has been preserved.

When it has been necessary for the editor to omit a name, the deletion is indicated by dashes. Most of the letters are printed in their entirety; but in cases where material has been omitted a word count is provided in the notes. There are no concealed deletions or omissions.

The format for the headings of the letters is:

Recipient   Description. Location of original
Assigned date   Place of writing

When a letter was dated by O'Hara, that date is included as part of the letter. Dates assigned by the editor appear in the headings. If O'Hara's address appeared on the letter, it is stipulated in the heading; otherwise, the editor has supplied the city O'Hara was writing from.

Most of O'Hara's located letters are at the Pennsylvania State University Library, which is identified with the symbol PSt. Letters of Harcourt, Brace editors Sloan and Pearce are in the files of Harcourt, Brace, Jovanovich, which is identified by the symbol HBJ. No other location symbols are used. All of O'Hara's letters to his daughter Wylie O'Hara Doughty are in the possession of Mrs. Doughty.

ALS means autograph letter signed. TLS means typed letter signed. AL or TL indicates that the letter was not signed.

John O'Hara's letters are full of names and the sociohistorical details that characterize his fiction. Their density of reference is so great that it was not feasible to footnote everything. More notes meant fewer letters. The policy on footnoting is to identify: (1) all of O'Hara's writings; (2) people who were important in his life; (3) references required for readers to understand the letters. When O'Hara uses the last name only for people who are not footnoted, the full name is provided in the index. O'Hara's own footnotes are indicated by asterisks.

Chronology

---

31 January 1905	Birth of John Henry O'Hara at 125 Mahantongo Street, Pottsville, Pa., son of Dr. Patrick H. and Katharine Delaney O'Hara.
1912–1920	Attends Miss Carpenter's School and St. Patrick's School.
February 1920–June 1921	Attends Fordham Preparatory School, Bronx, N.Y.; dismissed.
September 1921–June 1922	Attends Keystone State Normal School, Kutztown; dismissed.
Summer 1922–Summer 1923	Works at various jobs, including stint with White Engineering Co.
September 1923–June 1924	Attends Niagara Preparatory School, Niagara, N.Y.; chosen as valedictorian but not allowed to graduate. Falls in love with Margaretta Archibald.
July? 1924–late 1926	Reporter and columnist on *Pottsville Journal.*
18 March 1925	Death of Dr. Patrick H. O'Hara.
January–March 1927	Reporter on *Tamaqua Courier.*
June–July 1927	First trip to Europe, as waiter on *George Washington.*
October 1927	Hitchhikes to Chicago in unsuccessful search of newspaper work.
February 1928	Leaves Pottsville for New York City.
March–August 1928	Reporter and rewrite man on *New York Herald Tribune.*
5 May 1928	First *New Yorker* sketch, "Alumnae Bulletin," published. Becomes regular contributor.

August 1928–March 1929	Reporter on *Time,* covering sports, religion, theater; also checker.
Spring 1929	Reporter on *Editor & Publisher.*
July 1929	Rewrite man on *New York Daily Mirror.*
Early 1930	Works for Heywood Broun.
May–July 1930	Movie critic and radio columnist ("Franey Delaney") for *New York Morning Telegraph.*
28 February 1931	Marries Helen Ritchie Petit ("Pet") in New York.
April–June 1931	Works for New York publicity department of Warner Brothers.
Summer 1931	Bermuda. Writes "The Hofman Estate" and plans novel.
Fall 1931	Reporter for *The New Yorker.*
1932	Works for New York publicity department of RKO.
Spring 1933	Separates from Pet.
May–August 1933	Managing editor of *Pittsburgh Bulletin-Index.*
15 August 1933	Helen O'Hara obtains divorce in Reno.
August 1933	Returns to New York and begins writing *Appointment in Samarra.* Friendship with F. Scott Fitzgerald.
March 1934	Editor of ship's paper during Caribbean cruise of *Kungsholm.*
9 April 1934	Completes *Appointment in Samarra.*
June–August 1934	Hollywood. Works for Paramount.
16 August 1934	Publication of *Appointment in Samarra* by Harcourt, Brace.
September 1934	Returns to New York.
21 February 1935	Publication of *The Doctor's Son* by Harcourt, Brace. Florida trip.

April 1935	Works on *Butterfield 8* in East Sandwich, Mass. Meets Barbara Kibler.
July–August 1935	Visits Italy and France. Completes *Butterfield 8* in Paris.
17 October 1935	Publication of *Butterfield 8* by Harcourt, Brace.
Early 1936	Engagement to Barbara Kibler terminated.
April 1936–Spring 1937	Hollywood. Appears in *The General Died at Dawn*. Works for Goldwyn and MGM. Writing "So Far, So Good" (*Hope of Heaven*). Plans dramatization of *In Dubious Battle*.
Spring 1936	Meets Belle Mulford Wylie.
Spring 1937	Returns to New York; summers at Quogue.
3 December 1937	Marries Belle Wylie in Elkton, Md.
17 March 1938	Publication of *Hope of Heaven* by Harcourt, Brace.
April–August 1938	Visit to France and residence in London.
22 October 1938	"Pal Joey" appears in *The New Yorker*.
March–April; September–December 1939	Hollywood. Works for RKO and Twentieth Century–Fox.
21 September 1939	Publication of *Files on Parade* by Harcourt, Brace.
January–April 1940	Hollywood. Works for Twentieth Century–Fox.
July 1940–February 1942	Writes "Entertainment Week" column for *Newsweek*.
Fall 1940	Writes book for *Pal Joey* musical in New York.
October 1940	Publication of *Pal Joey* stories by Duell, Sloan & Pearce.
25 December 1940	*Pal Joey* opens on Broadway.
March–July 1941	Hollywood. Writes *Moontide* screenplay for Twentieth Century–Fox.

1941–1943	Attempts to join armed forces; works for Office of Inter-American Affairs; OSS training. Works on unproduced plays.
Summer 1944	*Liberty* correspondent attached to Task Force 38 in Pacific, aboard *Intrepid*.
24 March 1945	Publication of *Pipe Night* by Duell, Sloan & Pearce.
14 June 1945	Birth of Wylie Delaney O'Hara in New York.
August 1945–January 1946	Hollywood. Works for MGM.
June 1946	Hollywood. Works on *A Miracle Can Happen* for United Artists.
9 August 1947	Publication of *Hellbox* by Random House.
1948–1949	Writing *A Rage to Live*.
16 August 1949	Publication of *A Rage to Live* by Random House. Break with *The New Yorker*.
September 1949	Moves to Princeton, N.J.
Summer 1950	Working on unpublished nonfiction book, "Observation Car."
8 November 1951	Publication of *The Farmers Hotel* by Random House.
January 1952	Broadway revival of *Pal Joey*.
May 1952	Production of *The Searching Sun* in Princeton.
4 August 1953	Publication of *Pal Joey* play by Random House.
20 August 1953	Hospitalized for ulcer hemorrhage; stops drinking permanently.
December 1953–June 1954	Writes "Sweet and Sour" column for *Trenton Sunday Times-Advertiser*.
9 January 1954	Death of Belle Wylie O'Hara at Princeton Hospital.
February 1954–September 1956	Writes "Appointment with O'Hara" column for *Collier's*.

18 October 1954	Publication of *Sweet and Sour* by Random House.
31 January 1955	Marriage to Katharine Barnes Bryan ("Sister").
Spring–Summer 1955	Hollywood. Writing screenplay for *The Best Things in Life Are Free* for Twentieth Century–Fox; completing *Ten North Frederick*.
24 November 1955	Publication of *Ten North Frederick* by Random House.
February 1956	*Ten North Frederick* receives National Book Award.
16 August 1956	Publication of *A Family Party* by Random House.
1956–1957	Writes two unproduced screenplays for Twentieth Century–Fox (*The Bravados* and *The Man Who Could Not Lose*).
January 1957	Detroit suppression of *Ten North Frederick*.
14 January 1957	Library of Congress lecture.
May 1957	Induction into National Institute of Arts and Letters.
Fall 1957	Completion of Princeton home, "Linebrook."
December 1957	Albany suppression of *Ten North Frederick*.
27 November 1958	Publication of *From the Terrace* by Random House.
September–November 1959	Commences regular trips to Britain.
27 February 1960	Publication of *Ourselves to Know* by Random House.
17 September 1960	Publication of "Imagine Kissing Pete" in *The New Yorker*.
24 November 1960	Publication of *Sermons and Soda-Water* by Random House.
11 August 1961	Publication of *Five Plays* by Random House.
November 1961	Resignation from National Institute of Arts and Letters.

23 November 1961	Publication of *Assembly* by Random House.
29 May 1962	Publication of *The Big Laugh* by Random House.
29 November 1962	Publication of *The Cape Cod Lighter* by Random House.
2 March 1963	Publication of "The Glendale People" in *The Saturday Evening Post*.
4 June 1963	Publication of *Elizabeth Appleton* by Random House.
28 November 1963	Publication of *The Hat on the Bed* by Random House.
20 May 1964	Presentation of Award of Merit for the Novel by American Academy of Arts and Letters.
26 November 1964	Publication of *The Horse Knows the Way* by Random House.
October 1964–October 1965	Writes "My Turn" column for *Newsday*.
December 1964	Hospitalized for jaw pains.
25 November 1965	Publication of *The Lockwood Concern* by Random House.
14 April 1966	Publication of *My Turn* by Random House.
10 September 1966	Marriage of Wylie Delaney O'Hara to Dennis Holahan in New York.
September 1966–May 1967	Writes "Whistle Stop" column for *Holiday*.
24 November 1966	Publication of *Waiting for Winter* by Random House.
May 1967	Speaks at Foyles book luncheon in London.
23 November 1967	Publication of *The Instrument* by Random House.
December 1967	Last visit to Pottsville.
26 October 1968	Birth of Nicholas Drew Holahan.
10 November 1968	Injured by fall in Philadelphia.

28 November 1968	Publication of *And Other Stories* by Random House.
September 1969	Hospitalized for throat problem; diabetic condition discovered.
30 September 1969	Birth of Belle Holahan.
27 November 1969	Publication of *Lovey Childs* by Random House.
9 February 1970	Finishes *The Ewings.*
13 February 1970	Starts sequel to *The Ewings.*
11 April 1970	Death of John O'Hara at "Linebrook."
28 February 1972	Publication of *The Ewings* by Random House.

Selected
Letters *of*
JOHN
O'HARA

John Henry O'Hara was born in Pottsville, Pennsylvania, on 31 January 1905, the first of the eight children of Dr. Patrick and Katharine Delaney O'Hara. Pottsville—one hundred miles northwest of Philadelphia—was the principal city in the anthracite fields (known as The Region). The leading surgeon in Pottsville, Dr. O'Hara was bitterly disappointed when John declined to prepare for a medical career.

After being dismissed from two schools, John was chosen valedictorian of the class of 1924 at Niagara Preparatory School but was not allowed to graduate because of an alcoholic celebration on the night before commencement.

Although John's greatest ambition was to attend Yale, the Doctor refused to send him to college until he had demonstrated his seriousness. In the summer of 1924 John went to work as a cub reporter on the Pottsville Journal. The death of Dr. O'Hara in March 1925 put an end to John's Yale plans, as the family went from prosperity to genteel poverty. Bitterly unhappy over his frustrated college hopes, John remained in Pottsville with a growing sense of failure.

TO: Robert Simonds[1]   ALS, 5 pp. PSt.
Early 1923   606 Mahantongo St.,
                                                            Pottsville, Pa.

Dear Bob:

Your most welcome epistle arrived today and strengthens my belief that some day you will either occupy the Chair in Philosophy or at least be the "power behind the throne." I admit of the latter possibility only because thru' extreme youth—as goes the age of philosophers—you may have to speak thru' the voice of another.

Your suggestion relative to the regulation and spirit of our correspondence meets with my august and enthusiastic approval. As you have doubtless observed, I have gradually broken away from enthusiastic descriptions of the fair Gladys,[2] or narrating accounts of booze parties, and have rather been inclined to reflect the spirit of your letters. It has been a gradual metamorphosis, but let us quote Dr. Coué: "day by day . . . etc." As to writing without waiting for an answer—well, I see no reason why we can't do that. If I carried a note-book and jotted down some of my thoughts, there'd be a continual stream of mail pouring into 305 Topliff, but some of the thoughts might land me into either Federal prison or a home for the violently insane—and inane. I'd likewise be excommunicated from the Catholic Church. (Pardon, I just saw E. Fox pass; he must be week-ending in town.) I have arrived at what amounts to a second childhood. Sounds ridiculous, but look: a child plays with a mechanical toy and after a time he will want to see what makes the wheels go around. After a time he destroys the toy in his eagerness to get at the spring. My toy has been about everything one can imagine: the study of behaviour; the change in lines of a Packard car; the loopholes in certain laws. Every damn thing imaginable has come in for a share of inspection by me, and this may sound queer, but one thing I blame it on is learning to arrive at the meaning of a word by recalling its Latin root. Bend that!

I'm so glad you mentioned my remark about working on a sort of outline for a constitution. I'll take you up on your suggestion immediately. For some time past I was going to ask you and Lem[3] to act as a committee to draw up a constitution but I was afraid you might think I was electing myself president pro tem, but now you have relieved me of what to me, was the hardest part of establishing ΣΛΛ[4] as a fact. Go right along old man, and thanks for the suggestion and offer of help. I do hereby rescind any prior right, so there! I picked out you and Lem because you two have one or two brains in your heads and have had experience in college fraternities, which, if I may say so, are the only real fraternities. A prep fraternity is usually basically wrong, being founded on the desire of a certain coterie to become exclusive. I know. But I digress. You could also write the boys and let them know that if the gang goes in in its entirety, then you're all for it. I'm not horse-shitting when I say that your influence means something. As I have often said, everyone is all for the idea. When Dan Boone has a serious thought about anything, there must be something to it. He's for it, Hummell, Reilly, etc., are for it and it only remains for you to spread the propaganda with Lem and Deac, who, upon seeing you're with the idea, will readily acquiesce.

I've been invited to a party at Doc Keeney's on Monday. Joe Devitt is going to furnish the oil, so I expect to take on something for a battle.

Now that you're bored to tears I'd better lay off for a time. Write soon again.

As ever

Doc

[1] Robert Thurlow Simonds was O'Hara's closest Pottsville friend. Both were members of a group sometimes ironically referred to as "The Purity League." The earliest letters to Simonds date from 1923, when Simonds was at Dartmouth and O'Hara was working in Pottsville between attendance at Keystone State Normal School and Niagara Prep.

[2] Gladys Suender of Frackville, a girl friend of O'Hara's. He referred to her as "The Creole," "The Mulatto," and "The Wonderful Wench."

[3] O'Hara's other Pottsville friends included Lem Platt, Ransloe ("Beanie") Boone, George ("Deacon") Deisher, Fred Hoefel, and Bob Root.

[4] Sigma Lambda Alpha was a nonacademic social fraternity O'Hara tried to organize among his friends in Pottsville.

TO: Robert Simonds
Postmarked 3 March 1923

ALS, 6 pp. PSt.
YMCA/AEF letterhead, Pottsville

Tuesday

Dear "Fishie,"

I'm trying to pen this amidst the clamour and tumult of the famished crowd at the Y.M.C.A., so please allow for my surroundings, and don't be too harsh in your judgment of this letter.

Before I go much farther, allow me to say that your letter was one of the best I've ever read. If those thoughts on sacrifice are original to you, you may push the button in your easy chair and sit back, recline etc., and spend the remainder of your natural days by propounding theories of philosophy to the youth of the nation. I am compelled to admit that I saw the same thought in "The Mother of All Living," but it was not clothed in language like yours. This fact compels me to believe that you were original; you were not only original, but you're damn right! A thing is not only made worth while by the sacrifices incident to its achievement, but there is an added satisfaction in knowing that sacrifice is the medium whereby the thing was accomplished. That's not so well worded and is apt to be a little cloudy, but I hope you get my point.

Relative to George, the Deicher, I must first announce that what I am about to say is to be taken in confidence. You will know why in a minute. The member of the gang who was most averse to having Deac on some of our parties, is our friend who is just undergoing the second stages of sophistication. I refer to Fred. Allow me to say that I don't plead complete innocence as regards giving the Deacon a razz occasionally, but I don't think I've been much more vehement in heaping invectives upon George than any other member of the gang. Further, Fred is having his first

5

taste of city life and the Deacon, I fear, is a little more provincial and less literary than the rest of us, which may explain why Fred waxes impatient with Deacon. The difference between Fred and me is that he is inclined to be a bit more outspoken at the possible expense of Deac's feelings. But Deacon *is* "seeing daylight." He showed signs of improvement at Xmas, and I think that before September rolls around, he'll be capable of being characterized as a *damn* good egg. Well, that's that for the present.

Thanks for the T.L.[1] about my latent ability, but as a matter of fact, my old man must undergo a radical change of heart if I am to start school again in September. All I crave is two years in college, but P.H.O'H. and son John are at swords-points at this writing; we have been that way for two years, as I told you and Lem. I'll agree that being kicked out of two schools[2] is not conducive to a companionable feeling between father and son, but I told him not to send me to Kutztown else I should be kicked out. At present I am considering an offer to sell Chevrolets. If I make good on that, I might clean up enough money to go to school—with a little assistance from Mother. But I haven't got the requisite winning personality, so perhaps I'd better not plan too far ahead.

Damn glad to hear that you're rating better with the Committee on Marks. Keep it up Fish, old keed.

I've had one can on since I last wrote. Jack Taylor, Alex, Bull Payson, Beck Ibach, Marg[3] and I celebrated Washington's birthday with a dinner at the club, whereupon I got nicely fried and no one knew it but Jack, in spite of the fact that I had a session with Marg after the others were dropped at their respective homes or resting-places.

Your fencing team is helping to make up for losses of the cage team. They will not be foiled!

Well, old man, keep up the good work. Write and study.

As always
Your friend
Doc

[1] Trade-last.

[2] O'Hara had been dismissed from Fordham Preparatory School in The Bronx (1921) and Keystone State Normal School in Kutztown, Pa. (1922).

[3] Margaretta Archbald, O'Hara's first serious love, whom he began dating when he was eighteen. Four years older than he, she had graduated from Bryn Mawr.

Dear Bob:

It would seem to the not very casual observer that I have not been very attentive in my correspondence with you, but the same observer might find the same to be true in regard to correspondence with about everyone who writes to me. In my coat pocket reposes positive proof that I have made two measly attempts at writing to you, but there's the rub; they were too measly. I have several other alibis to offer and you may choose your favorite or reject them all. Marg Archbald figures prominently; so does bridge and my job in the P&R freight office takes up a lot of the time I formerly devoted to staying on the plus side of "Letters Owed". Perhaps those excuses will appear pretty damn measly too.

The constitution was very well done and certainly is a fitting result of the time you put on it. I'm glad to see that *you* tho't enough of the embryo fraternity to knock off time that you could have spent in something else, to utilize said time in working on what, to my mind, is one of the three most difficult parts of organizing a club like ours would be. But I suppose by this that you have detected a note of two dimensions (flat) in my writing. Correct. I'm disgusted. Hereafter someone else may assume the position I have maintained. The reason for it all is Bob R.'s indifferent manner of acceptance of the whole affair. I have referred to the club in every letter and he answers without saying a word about said club. Probably afraid of hurting my feelings. Very likely he can see nothing but T.N.E.[1] in the whole thing. Everyone else has acquiesced with just about everything I could suggest. Some of the good "fratres" had about decided what orchestra to have for our first dance! Oh my ass, a singular lack of enthusiasm—accent on the "singular." I think Bob was pretty well disgusted because some of us went on a tear on Good Friday night, but tho' I can't blame him, he shouldn't forget that if *we* go to hell, he'll not burn. Another thing that Bob doesn't like, I *think,* is that the membership includes Reilly. I'm pretty sure he's not so crazy about Francis. He made a crack to me that didn't get by so big because Reill' and I are the only vestige of the "league" who are left in the town and we do quite a bit of running around together. Aw nuts!

Bob, I forgive you anything you ever said about the Mulatto—not that I held anything against you, but it did rankle temporarily, Why? Well, Since November Marg Arch and I have been knocking around quite some. —to such an extent as to cause Mrs. Diller to start the report that we're engaged. (Enjoy your laugh.) My record for a week is four dances—which really gives *Pottsville* sufficient cause for gossip. Last week I had three and this week two dates and two auto rides with her. Well, the Creole wasn't pleased when I "aired" her so ever since she has been quite obviously, but diplomatically trying to break up the affair.

Well Bob, I'll write soon again.

My school chances have taken a drop.

As ever
Doc

¹ The fraternity Theta Nu Epsilon.

TO: Robert Simonds   ALS, 7 pp. PSt.
Postmarked 28 April 1923   Pottsville

Dear Bob,

If I were you I'd write a series of imaginary letters, calling it "Letters of Bob to a Friend"; eliminating words like "ass," "horse-shit," etc., but following your usual custom of delving into philosophy, psychology, and similar Sciences. Methinks 'twould get by big. I find a great stimulus in your letters. I've often expressed a desire to write things—and still do—but you haven't, and yet your vocabulary has been developed to a far greater degree than mine. Apropos of vocabularies, here's something that may strike you as incongruous—tho' it's quite possible that you've discovered the same thing: I read Robert Benchley's criticisms of the drama in "Life" and while he writes in a semi-cynical,—sarcastic,—satirical vein, he nevertheless has helped my limited vocabulary immensely. For example, I can't recall ever having seen the word "protagonist" before, yet he used it last week and I knew what he meant. Too bad he's a Harvard man else I might suggest a cheer.

Your suggestion to let the club matter ride until summer meets with my hearty approval. Root was home last week-end and didn't bring the matter up, so I shall wax indifferent and allow the whole thing to slide as far as I'm concerned. Yes, there is visible a merger of two or possibly three gangs into one, yet our gang of last summer was constituted of factions. Perhaps a tolerant attitude extends only as far as there is no tangible form of organization. As to the drinking part, I'm going to continue to get drunk just as much as I can, club or clubless. The beauty of a drinking club is the identical spirit that actuated the first cave-dweller in opening up a bar. What I mean is that since drinking is patently a "social vice" (a man who drinks much alone is dangerous) there is always a feeling of comfort in knowing that there is at least one good frater in urbe who will respond to the call of one of his fellows and go out on a bat. I daresay I have boozed a little more than anyone else in the gang— tho' Fred seems to run me a close second this winter—and I know that

8

I don't get as much kick out of deciding to get boiled and *then* going to a saloon and making up with a bare acquaintance or even absolute stranger and getting fried as I did on our last summer's parties when someone would suggest something and we were off. Verily, ah, verily them was better days!

I have often felt like appealing to my grandmother to send me to school, but there's the hitch that you recognized in my make-up. For purposes of classification I have created a name for myself; it is "The ΨΥ Type." I say Psi U because almost invariable the Psi U's are snakes—they dance, drink, dress and dawdle, yet, tho' I never expect to strut with a ΦBK key dangling carelessly but ostentatiously from my chain, I mean it when I say that I'll do less dawdling than I would had I not worked this year. "When I get to college" I want to rate a good* national social, a drinking club, a minor varsity letter, varsity play, and "The Lit." I would also like to be a political boss. There's a peculiar attraction in politics for me. Perhaps in future years the wielding of my masterful pen will spell defeat for more than one seemingly likely candidate. (Opposing candidate, of course.) I would like the minor letter to show to my son as he matriculates at my college: I crave athletics for the fun I get out of them. I don't deny that I'd not refuse a tennis or golf cup, but I start out by liking tremendously both sports. I would like the place in a play or something because of the trips involved. I would like "The Lit" because it's an honor and because I like "Lit", and the only sincerely unselfish feeling I'd have would be fraternity spirit (in its campus sense). All the other "points" I have spoken of are inspired by a motive purely for "*me*" and not "for the good of the college." Frankly, I think that stuff is horse-shit and the man who flaunts *that* flag to the breezes is either old Joe Athlete who is sure of his letters and gold footballs or he's Joe's brother, Tom Politician who for himself or one of his clique is sending thrills thru' the freshmen's spines and incidentally thereby getting said frosh vote. (I don't claim that Juniors and Seniors are immune to that applesauce.) I hope I'm not being iconoclastic and smashing any cherished ideals of yours, but when one says "frankly", one feels that almost anything is permissible.

Bob, you're deserting me. I can see that I'll be the only genuine failure in the gang. The passing of your exams was the turning-point in your life and you can now sit back and decide what to call your three children while you cogitate over just how much a failure I'll turn out to be. Mark my words, Bob.

Well, old boy. I mustn't run out of material for my next letter. In the next I shall dwell on psycho-analyses I have made.

Always your friend
Doc

---

* This eliminates Bus Suender & Brethren ΣN.

Dear Bob,

At present I am too much concerned over things temporal to discuss with you matters pertaining to the spiritual. My father and I are off again. This time he has good and sufficient reason to become perturbed: someone has told him of my boozing. He told me about what he had heard and made several dire threats which aren't even interesting; he hasn't the nerve to carry them out, but nevertheless, life henceforth will be a veritable hell for me. He has made it so before and he'll use every means he can to make it hell, because of all things he hates, liquor receives double its share —he had a brother who, when drunk, fell down a flight of stairs and died from the effects of the fall. As I told you and Lem, our relations have been anything but amicable since August 1921. This discovery of my intemperance may eventually culminate matters. Anticipating such culmination, I have begun tentative bag-packing. I'll probably hang around for a month or so, but when Marg returns from the Vineyard on Labor Day, I think that she'll find one less persistent snake. (Very poorly put, but you know what I mean.) If war were to break out, matters would be simplified, but one can't order wars over-night.

Another thing that adds greatly to my discomfiture is the fact that I may lose my job. No job means no money and one can't go very far without money. I have made up my mind to get out of Pottsville but when, I can't say. If the Deacon is in earnest about going to Europe, he can count on me for a companion, but there is to be considered "the drama of the emergence of an idea." Perhaps *you* may feel the urge. A job as night clerk in a large hotel appeals to me. When I say large hotel I don't mean in New York especially, but some place the *size* of New Haven or Los Angeles. I don't think I'd crave New Haven because I might not like to take hooey from some half-boiled freshman and I'd probably reach over and tap him with the register. Los Angeles is quite the nice thing—but pardon me for raving on this way.

I'd better haul ass and get into a tub. Write soon. I always appreciate your letters a lot.

As always
Doc

TO: Robert Simonds   ALS, 8 pp. PSt.
1923   606 Mahantongo St.,
                                                      Pottsville, Pa.

Dear Bob:

You and Boone certainly possess one thing in common; I'll give you one guess what it is. Lem was, for a time, (. . . and I an embryo journalist!) a participant in the race for correspondence cutting, but he snapped to, so that there remains but one contestant—the Mercersburg lad, but he frankly admits that he has no qualms about neglecting to answer the sweat of my pen, therefore one can expect but little from such a wet smack, so that's them.

So you've been working off some ⊖NE credit? Well done and nobly, sir. You and me both. I shall be more explicit. Here's how. (This is the latest episode.) On Saturday, the tenth, the entertainment committee came out of their trance and gave a dance at the club. —— & I and Jack & —— went down for dinner. (DINNER) We had with us one (1) quart of lubricant. It was Dougherty, and just about as good as I've had for a heluva spell. Well, as the evening progressed our (editorial plural) pep began to wane, whereupon the bottle was brought forth. The women failed to function as regards absorption of the oil and Jack held out on me with the very natural result that I got drunk as a skunk. All well and good but as near as I can figure—and conservatively withal—I downed 1½ pints, which is noble, but is also ½ pint beyond my present capacity, so that at closing time I was though by no means raucous, still visibly moved. Jack had to take the wheel but unfortunately I had imbibed some White Rock but not at the same time as I inhaled the hootch. To this I attribute the later occurrences. Anyhow, Jack had to stop the car 5 (five) times between the C.C. and Pottsville so that I might get out and act seasick. It's the first time I've ever done that with women on the party and so help me, I hope it's the last. I think that it's disgusting, etc. Well, L'Envoi would be nothing more or less than I'm off until "the boys come home." Needless to say, there were two nice apologies to make. However, all is well.

I've finally and positively broken off with The Wonderful Wench. Was up there some weeks ago and cleared up one or two matters and left the house in a fine rage. I don't mind admitting that there's still a vestige of flame left for her, but "I gave her up just before she threw me down." I saw it coming and maybe I'm not glad I got the edge. "Lol" Richards is President of the House just now. It's beginning to look serious, too. He's a pretty good egg, but naturally, I hate to see him getting by so big with The Captivating Creole. Well, that is also that.

Now for something of a different character. About this club. You and Lem, and possibly the Deacon, are the doubtful prospects and your grievances, if I may say that, are basically identical. Although you and I have several faults in common, you possess a virtue to which I have never laid claim; said virtue is conscientiousness. The point of that is this: I personally, and I might say the four who seem to wax more enthusiastic about ΣΛΑ, did not notice any friction in the old gang at Xmas. I will concede that the Deacon palled a bit with Mr. Youngfleish, and that it was damn hard to get any enthusiasm about a meeting, but remember that between two parties to Reading, Joe Haight's visit, and numerous dates by individuals, it was a case of try and find a nite to get organized. As for the Deac, I don't know what to say. He was invited to Boone's on two occasions and turned down both bids. Likewise he had a chance for the assembly and one of the club dances, which also he turned down. Well one can't force him to go along. So I rest my part of the case with you. The others are writing to me and asking me about organizing and getting the keys. Well, I feel as you do; I want to see the gang go in en masse. Secondly, I have had Clawson send away for better estimates on the chain-weights. I've even drawn up a tentative constitution. Of course, we'll bear a greater resemblance to Κβφ or ΘΝΕ than to ΣΧ or φτΔ. It's a kick in the can to find that after spending a little time on this thing, the enthusiasm I tried to put into it has not touched *everyone*.

I suppose you've heard that good beer is now at a premium in the old tome hown. We'll soon have prohibition.

I've up and bought me a norfolk suit. A dark herringbone. Not really *very* dark, but it's darker than the run of norfolks. Cheaper too, but that's allright. (No, it's not whipcord.) I've also accumulated some Foulards and a dotted scarf, a suspicious cough and a tougher beard.

Did you ever read any of John Galsworthy's thrillers (?) I've finished "In Chancery." Liked it immensely. Also read two other English authors, —Beresford and Frances Hodgson Burnett. The more I read modern English authors, the more I think that we Americans are sadly lacking in pen-wielders. I've assayed Balzac and am compelled to admit that he held no interest for my temperamental nature. Christopher Morley amuses me with his one act plays. (Yes, I've acquired a taste for plays.) By the way, did you read "Brass"? If you didn't, don't. I saw something quoted from it and thought, 'Lord God, I gave up that book over a year ago; I must have missed something.' As a result, I've learned not to trust to my passions when in search of reading.

Well, old boy, enjoy yourself in Hanover and if you must drink White Rock, drink while drinking the stuff.

Write to

Your friend,
Doc

TO: Robert Simonds   TLS, 1 p. PSt.
Received 19 March 1925   Pottsville

Dear Bob:

Your very fine note came today and we, Mother and I, accepted it as a note of condolence and I want to thank you for it.

My father died early yesterday morning of Bright's Disease, which, as you know, is the result of kidney trouble—an O'Hara pet. The end came quite peacefully and suddenly, the seriousness of his illness notwithstanding. He returned from Florida a week ago and when I saw him get off the train I knew that he had few days remaining in this vale of tears. He went to bed and on Thursday he became less aware of what was going on around him. On Monday he recognized me for the last time. We had Beardsley, a Philadelphia specialist, here to see him on Monday night and he pronounced the case incurable.

On Tuesday we were gathered around the bed-side and the doctors told me to go to bed—I haven't been very well latterly—that my father would not die that night. This was at twelve. At one, just as the clock in the courtie struck, he opened his mouth as though to say something and then his head fell.

Your Journal will tell you all the rest. Beanie managed to write a very good story.

As you may have surmised, I'll be a busy man for a long time, what with settling affairs and the like. I'll write you a long letter, however, when I can get to it. My father's death has a great effect on my future plans and I'll probably have a lot to tell you ere you heer from me again.

Again, many thanks for your letter. I knew you'd come through.

Sincerely,
Doc

TO: Robert Simonds   TLS, 3 pp. PSt.
Postmarked 25 March 1925   Pottsville

Dear Bob,

I am going to accompany this letter with one I wrote on the day I received your long letter.[1] I forget all I said in it: I do know that I gave you as much advice as I could on the question of your affaire de coeur but I can't seem to recall whether or not I mentioned future plans. If I did, they are probably the kind that should now be given the blue pencil; if I did not mention plans, all the better. I remember the gist of what I said on the subject of your more or less amatory dalliance and I hold to all the words of wisdom which came to me at the time I wrote.

My father's death has had a sobering effect on me. I have given up all hope of seeing Europe or anything like that. In February I wrote but fortunately did not mail a letter to the editor of The Missoulian, Missoula, Montana. I asked him to tell how chances were for my getting a job on his estimable sheet. Of course my plan was to work in Missoula for a while and then repeat the old question to one M.T.A.[2] Marriage is now out of the question for at least two years.

I don't know much about the governor's estate.[3] I don't think that any of the children[4] will have to sell papers or have to rely upon my small stipend for sustenance, but I have, nevertheless, begun to plan to live economically. There may even be enough money on hand to send me to college but I shall wait for a time. If Joe, the next in line, wants to study for a profession—medicine, engineering, the law—I'd rather allow the money to be used for his education than to go to college myself. Aren't I the altruistic bastard?

It will take time for us O'Haras to adjust ourselves. The main thing is to give the younger idea some book-larnin. There are so many, many phases of the situation to consider. I would like to have *one* year at college, because I have always wanted to have the name behind me—and if the truth be told, I'd like to see what I'd rate in frat-club bids, but all this is ancillary to the education of the others.

Just now I am doing fairly well in my chosen career. On April 1st I open a colyum in The Journal, one after, 'way after the manner of F.P.A.'s.[5] I have written three days in advance and I hope that you will be a contributor to it. If it's a success,—in fact, whether it's a success or not—I shall go out for bigger and better things. My ambition is to get a job on The World. It's the very best paper and it would help immeasurably for me to get a job with the Pulitzer sheet. To be able to say, "Yes, I worked for the N.Y.W." is open sesame. One can go almost anywhere and say, "Give me a job on your desk; I want $75 hebdomadally."

I can indulge in one little dream. Why don't you, Robert Thurlow Simonds, get a job on a newspaper? That may or may not have occurred to you, but it's not bad dope. You have the intrinsic, or, shall I say, latent ability to write editorials. Your judgment, even at your present tender years, is sound. You know history—and Oh, how vital that is in writing editorials!—and you have had enough training and outside reading, or will have had, in philosophy and psychology to approach the subjects of your editorials scientifically. And you write in what I am pleased to call editorial style. A couple years of experience and a desk somewhere as city or news editor, then your own paper, OUR own paper! We could get a paper in some small town and see what a go we could make of it. Nanticoke, I hear, had a paper which has been defunct several times and it always comes back when someone else starts it. The only thing is this: how about money? Of course the idea would be to make money and lots of it. My smokiest dream would be to have you, Beanie and me run a paper: You, the editorials, Beanie, the news—for he has good news sense —and I the features; sports, humor and human interest stories, as well as a colyum. I shall take up the matter with the board.

Are you going to bum home for the Easter vacation? Looks to this unpracticed pair of eyes as though we're in for a spell of good weather and the bumming, therefore, would be good. That was one of the things which were upset by my father's death: I meant to take a bumming trip to see you graduated, then make you bum to Montreal with me. That was to be a surprise, of course—I to appear on your graduation day or thereabouts and force you into the Canuck trip by appealing to your sporting blood or something. "Now it can be told".

I had one pleasant surprise when the governor came home from the old Southland. He heard me cough and it prompted him to tell me or to reveal to me (I haven't found out which) that I have two spots in the pulmonary apparati. Since then I have been taking mighty good care of myself: No liquor and lots of milk, vegetables and the like, and even a cutting down of my lone vice, Madame Nicotine.

This death thing makes one think. After my father went I began to think—that all this about the immortality of the soul is worth the while of even the most cynical. No one knows better than I what sort of life the governor led. Hard work, a clean life and so little pleasure. No one can tell me that he derived a lot of satisfaction from the knowledge that he was doing good and that alone. It's all out of proportion. He never took vacations and he had very little real pleasure, and it's awfully upsetting to the predestination idea, my boy, is this death affair. I was inclined to believe in predestination but when it strikes like a thief in the night, when it strikes near YOU like a thief in the night you say, "This sort of thing can't be predestined; why does he linger until just this moment?" One can readily presuppose the argument which will follow these questions but in the calm hysteria of the moment one seems awfully close to God and God doesn't seem like the kind of man who would predestine that a man should die without having had some enjoyment in life, a proportionate enjoyment to the amount of hard, thankless work he has done.

Quite verbiose [sic] and rather maudlin have I grown in this letter and it's about time to call a halt. Write me very soon in answer to these fat letters.

Always your friend,
Doc

Didn't you say you knew somebody named Kane or something at Dartmouth from Missoula? Do you know him or them well enough to ask them about the town and its paper—and get an honest answer?

[1] The earlier letter has not been located.
[2] Margaretta Archbald was teaching at an Indian school near Missoula, Mont.
[3] Dr. O'Hara died intestate, leaving an estate that was appraised at $49,649.60.
[4] The seven other O'Hara children were Mary, Joseph, Thomas, Martin, James, Eugene, and Kathleen.
[5] O'Hara's column was called "After Four O'Clock." No example of it survives, and there are no located issues of the *Pottsville Journal* for O'Hara's period of employment during 1924–26. F.P.A. was Franklin P. Adams, who conducted the enormously popular "Conning Tower" column in the *New York World*.

TO: Robert Simonds   ALS, 3 pp. PSt.
Early 1927   Pottsville

All Alone
Mondee

Your Honor:

This is a preliminary skirmish and subsequent events may prove it to be futile and then again may not. However, I saw Silliman[1] again today and explained that I couldn't take the Shenandoah job because of Mother's objections and I then brought up the matter of the Allentown one.

It is the Call and not the Chronicle-News after all, that H.I.S. thinks he can put me on. If the job would pay upwards of $35 a week I'd take it, but not for less, not for $34.99. And even at $35 I'd demand a five-buck raise at the end of a month because I figure I'm worth that to a paper the size of the Call.

Anyhow, Silliman said he'd write this afternoon, which at best wouldn't mean an answer before Friday. The point of this letter is to ascertain whether or not there is another room vacant at 1413 Vinson. You might make tentative inquiries. I believe you said 11 bucks for room and two meals a day? Be sure and tell Mrs. W. that I'm a Catholic. There's so much prejudice in Allentown, you know, and there are people otherwise normal who feel that to harbor a Papist is to defy the great god Janus—wasn't he the home-god, or was it Lares and Penates? This, as I say, is tentative and may never materialize. In the event of my obtaining a job I would let you know definitely and immediately, but I *would* like to have the domicile question settled as soon after I get a job as practicable.

. . . .[2]

Hope I can be with you ere the Ides of May. Take good care of yourself and be careful of snuggling burns on the back of your neck.

Faithfully,
Ruth Flint
John Yolsborough
Henry R. Luce[3]

[1] Harry I. Silliman, publisher of the *Pottsville Journal*, fired O'Hara twice in 1926. After less than three months on the *Tamaqua Courier* in early 1927, O'Hara was again fired.

[2] Fifty words omitted by the editor.

[3] Ruth Flint and Laird Goldsborough were on the staff of *Time* magazine; Henry Luce was one of the founding editors.

TO: Robert Simonds   TLS, 2 pp. PSt.
July 1927   Pottsville

Dear Bob:

Back again, and doing business at the old stand. If you want to hear anything about my trip to Germany you'll have to ask me about it.[1] Damned if I'm going to bore you with stories that may not interest you in the slightest.

And logician that you are, you have assumed that this letter's purpose is not a travelog. Right you are, if you think you are, Mr. Pirandello. No, it's a question I have to ask you and an answer I'm damned soon expecting as you will soon realize.

Do you want to go to Central or South America with me?

There, in words of one syllable (for the most part) is the question.

To be more explicit: I think I can land a job with the United Fruit Company as overseer in one of their Latin American plantations. With the possibility of inducing you to come along I told my uncle, who is trying to get me the job, to make it for two.

The job, as I understand it from a man who was on the G. Washington and who held one of these United Fruit jobs, consists mainly of ducking malaria, drinking liquor, bossing natives and, if you're so inclined, laying the dusky wenches. The trip to the tropics is made at the expense of the company, of course, and you travel first class coming and going. The salary is about $125 a month and unless one gambles, he can save practically all of it.

There's always a hitch and here's the hitch to this prospect. While the plantations are made as liveable as possible, still they are not to be confused with the estate of T. Suffern Tailer at Newport. There is a constant stream of Americans going back and forth from the plantations; quitting, accepting jobs, dying, living and whatnot. The jobs are kept in circulation, and no mistake.

A year ago I don't think I'd have considered the possibility of taking such a job. Now, however, since I've made the original break, I'll go lots of places I would have passed up heretofore. For one thing, I've decided I'll roam the world (or as much of it as I can) over until I'm twenty-five. Three years on the high seas and in the low valleys doesn't seem to me to be a bad idea. It would be at least as good as college, I believe. Everyone goes to college; not everyone leaves the comparatively good old U.S.A.

Now just a second, old chap. Don't go dashing into print with your plans for a pedagogical career this fall, and thus forestalling me. Baar has told me you expect to land something in the teaching line. But how about learning a little more before you settle down to the cap and gown? I don't mean book larning. It's obvious, patent, palpable and apparent that travel "finishes" one and while I do not recommend that you hang with me for three years (for you would indeed be a patient man to last that long) I nevertheless would like to cut away from the conventional with you for as long as you can stand it.

I have one other iron in the fire at this writing. I almost got the job of assistant purser on the Leviathan but missed it by one day. I met the chief purser and favorably impressed him, so, with my uncle's aid, I shouldn't be surprised if I'd land *that* job before long. If there were a possibility, I'd take *it* and let the fruit job go for a while—perhaps even a year. I will not, rest assured, take another job as steward unless I am "left on the beach" somewhere. And take my advice; don't *you* think because you scrubbed your way through Dartmouth that you're qualified as an assistant steward. Not so.

There is still another possibility—and that's all it is. The Firestone people want men to go to Liberia, on the west coast of Africa, to take jobs as overseers on rubber plantations. They pay more money and offer a better trip, but God knows they ought to. The weather in Liberia is o-u-t as far as white men are concerned and the family has done a lot of putting-down-feet at the idea of my taking such a job. However, if worst comes to worst, it wouldn't be the *very* first time I didn't entirely acquiesce to the family's desires.

Quite a surprise to learn that I had passed my brother in mid-ocean and didn't know it, as you may well imagine. There were lots of other surprises, too, but I'll save them for a talk with you at the earliest opportunity. Let me know about the United Fruit chance and don't misbehave too much until I see you.

Faithfully,
Doc

[1] During June-July 1927 O'Hara worked his way to Germany as a waiter on the *Washington*.

Dear Vanzetti:

You couldn't have had more than half a package when you last wrote me, or else your tongue was hanging out a mile. Lord, man, how in the name of Alvan T. Fuller[1] do you chase the booze, pay your rent, buy clothes, get around and have enough for the strikes on your salary? You are almost as much a dilemma to me as I am to some people—unless, of course, you got yourself That Raise.

You missed a friendly little reunion on Sattidee night. . . .[2] I obtained two quarts of Dusel-oil (gin) and repaired to the country club where we did injustice to it. The occasion was more or less of a reunion for me also, I having been in Lykens[3] for two weeks. I got home Thursday with $10.55, which my grandmother had given me. After a vain attempt to get a ride to the lake I gave up and Jim Bailey and I proceeded to do the town. We did. After getting a good base of Scotch at Mart Motley's we went places, all places, until five a.m. An interesting feature of the proceedings was a high Mass which was sung at St. Joe Brennan's church,[4] corner Norwegian & Logan, by Father Bailey, Cardinal O'Hara, the Rev. Dr. McCarthy and one unidentified person. It must have been great. Fortunately we all knew the Latin. I went home in a taxi, with the 55 cents and one cigaret in my pocket and was greeted by the mater. The conversation:

Where have you been?

Nowhere.

What have you been doing?

Nothing.

Who was with you?

Nobody, now lemme go sleep.

Have you ever seen one of Al's two-quart flagons? If more than a quart is ordered he insists upon giving it to us in a half-gallon bottle that makes a loud noise when dropped at the railroad crossing near Lakewood.

The boys are saving their energy and money for Mr. Whiteman's appearance at Lakewood[5] tomorrow night. I am in hopes of seeing you there, but am inclined to be pessimistic on the chance, what with so many allurements in Das Vaterland.

You should see Root. He has a carbuncle or something, the result of an infected hair on the back of his neck and he goes around with a scarf, hat and topcoat with collar turned up, looking like an undertaker who has just lost a big sale. Instead of vacationing with his partner he is trying to get in some sleep credit on his belly and not succeeding. He said you told someone you are planning to go up to State next fall. My God, man! I tried admirably to get in Yale. Had A'chie[6] write to the Dean, who was a classmate of his. The result was some very pleasant correspondence for all concerned and the information that my chance of going to Yale was about as good as my chance of going to heaven. So unless someone dies and leaves me a trillion my college years are not so bright. Hoefel is practically sure of going to Lafayette and it is Baar's idea that we have a get-together at the Lafayette–W.&J. game. We'll stay at the Sigma Nu house, where I know the king and to which we have been invited, and do the conventional football game stuff. In other words, that is one of the things we won't do this fall. Whenever we plan anything like that it always goes up the flue.

Had a letter from the purser of the Leviathan asking me to make formal application at 45 B'way for a job on that boat. That is the extent of my job-getting thus far. I'm mad at the world and if I had the guts I'd Take the Cowardly Course and jump in the lake. Disgusted and disillusioned at 22, that's me.

Misbehave yourself and when you're broke and tired of it all we'll hit the highways for the south. Friend of mine on the boat said he lived at Pinehurst for an entire winter and had a good time caddying and working in a store. If you're interested I know a place where I think we could get fair jobs.

It is called Yeoman's Island[7] or something like that and I daresay you never heard of it. That's the point; it's exclusive. Marg's uncle, Albright Archbald, the one from Buffalo who has made a couple million in gold mines, is one of about 50 men who have bought this island and developed it for themselves only. They all belong to a club and in order to live on the island one must belong to the club. Try and get in. My idea is, there must be at least two jobs at a place like that. Certainly there is a lot of dough. But this talk is off if I can get on the Levi or with the United Fruit. Bumming is the third alternative, but I really mean it. If you'll go, we'll be off whenever you say. A loaf of bread, a jug of wine, and how!

This is a pretty damned long letter to be written to a correspondent as desultory as you. I must be off to bed now. Don't give my love to Miss Williams. John speaks for himself.

Faithfully,
Ruth Flint

[1] Governor of Massachusetts at the time of the Sacco and Vanzetti trial.
[2] Eleven words omitted by the editor.
[3] Home of O'Hara's maternal grandparents, the Delaneys.
[4] Motley and Brennan were proprietors of Pottsville speakeasies.
[5] Lakewood dance pavilion. Paul Whiteman's orchestra was a favorite of O'Hara's.
[6] Col. James Archbald, Margaretta's father.
[7] Yeamans Hall Club, near Charleston, S.C.

TO: The Editor of *Scribner's Magazine*   TLS, 1 p. Princeton
                                                    606 Mahantongo St.,
                                                        Pottsville, Pa.

                                                    September 23, 1927

Sir:

I am preparing an article on next year's political fuss which is entirely distinctive, I believe, among the many articles published up to this time.

It is written from the standpoint of a rank outsider, an amateur and a citizen who will cast his first vote for one of next year's candidates. I am 22 years old.

The title of the article is (at present), "Why the Next President Will Be a Dark Horse."

Your first reaction to my youth and my standing will not be favorable, but if you care to encourage me, because of the differentness of the article, I shall write it as I believe Scribner's would have it written. The thoughts will be the same, no matter who takes the article, but I well realize that structurally and otherwise your requirements and those of other magazines differ.

Hoping, as I always have, to "make" Scribner's,[1] I am

                                                    Faithfully,
                                                    John H. O'Hara

[1] *Scribner's* did not commission the article.

TO: Robert Simonds   TLS, 2 pp. with 1 p.
Fall 1927   holograph calculations. PSt.
                                                    606 Mahantongo St.,
                                                        Pottsville, Pa.

Dear Rob:

Can you manage to come home this weekend? There are several things I want to talk about, notably, plans for the winter, and since it will be more conversational than dissertative, it would solve the problem of communication if you were to come home. As is, a proper conveyance of thoughts and plans would require too much exchange of letters, phone calls and whatnot.

I can say at this time, however, that I am all set to go anywhere. Purposely I have delayed writing you about your statement that if you didn't get a raise by the 15th, you'd be ready to light out for parts unknown. Inasmuchas you haven't written, I am at a loss to know *your* plans.

There are several things we can do. I prefer going south with the birdies, who show excellent judgment. Now how to go? Shall we go to N.Y. and sign on a coastal steamer as super-cargo; shall we bum it, or shall we buy a Ford? Each has its advantages and disadvantages. The best plan, of course, is the least feasible financially, meaning, of course, the Ford. We could pick one up for about $35—$17.50 apiece and take our own good time about getting down. Signing on a boat has its disadvantages. There would be difficulty getting a one-way job, super-cargo, in other words. Bumming it doesn't particularly appeal except as a last resort, in the event everything else fails. Getting on a boat would mean going to New York, which is one thing I'm not particularly anxious to do, strange though it may seem.

I think we could make it, via the Ford, on $50 apiece, and bumming it wouldn't be a hell of a lot cheaper.

After we got down? Well, you might ask Tom Beddall for a job. I couldn't honorably work for him . . . I'd try Dick Coogan or someone like that.

The thing to do is to go, no matter how. I simply must get out of Pottsville or I'll buy a gun and use it. Yes, it's come to that. I've never been so unhappy, so little enthusiastic about life, and it's all the fault of this place, or of myself. If I had some objective, something tangible to look forward to, it wouldn't be quite so lethal, but as is—

The idea of having an apartment in N.Y. for you, Baar and me, is the nuts every way you look at it except that we haven't got jobs. I delved into the mathematical side of it and have figured that if each of us earned $30 a week, he could have $16.25 a week over and above the apartment rent, cook, etc. I enclose the calculations, but of course that's what we Latin students call a future less vivid condition.

You must not fail me, Young Simonds. If you do you'll be cheating yourself. Once we've made the break we'll be better off. We'll at least have the satisfaction of knowing we did make the break. One winter won't mean much now, and you might as well face the fact that you're getting closer to the age where you won't be able to step around blithely and debonairly as you can at present.

If you can't come home this weekend, call me Friday night and if I'm not at home, leave word with someone, saying you can or can't come over. Then I'll bum over Saturday.

Now is the time for all good men to come to the aid of this certain party.

Faithfully,
Hockaday

$30.00 a week each
$$3\overline{)100.00}$$ a month rent
$$33\frac{1}{3}$$

$3\overline{)48\ 00}$ nigger cook for dinner & cleaning
16

$3\overline{)8.00}$ laundry (sheets, pillowcases, etc.)
$2.33\frac{1}{3}$

$3\overline{)90}$ food (raw material—groceries)
30

$\left. \begin{array}{l} 30. \\ 2.33\frac{1}{3} \\ 16. \\ 33,33\frac{1}{3} \end{array} \right\}$ apartment expenses.

$81.66\frac{2}{3}$ total pro rata share

120 — salary
$81.66\frac{2}{3}$ — expense

$4\overline{)38.33\frac{1}{3}}$

$9 + for cigarets, carfare, liquor, etc. each week

$///\equiv///\equiv///\equiv///\equiv$

but $\quad 3\overline{)50. a month}$
$16\frac{2}{3}$ — rent
$16\frac{3}{}$ cook
$2\frac{1}{3}$ — laundry
30 — food
$4\overline{)65}$
16.25 a week

23

ALS, 2 pp. PSt.
Pittsburgh

Dear Judge—

(Quite *some* water has gone over the bridgework since you've had an opportunity to decode the cuneiform which is my handwriting.)

Well, I've made the break, as you see. When you didn't 'phone Friday night I definitely decided to go up to State[1] with Root, who was home to see the doctor about his neck. I went with him Saturday, loafed around and left Monday, yesterday. Got to Pittsburgh, 160 miles from State, in one ride and immediately made for Carnegie Tech and Ned Dolan. I left State with six bucks, of which I now have three. On the morrow I leave for Columbus. There I'm going to try to get a job. I'll save some (if I get said job) then hit for Chicago and another job, *then* points South or West, depending on how much dough I'll have by that time. My ultimate aim is Missoula, Montana and I'm going to try to make the Mardi Gras in New Orleans in February. I know how tough the going will be, but it will be only physical and not the mental torture I've been entertaining since I came back from Europe and previous to that jaunt.

I wish you were with me and I wish I belonged to some Greek lodge. It helps to be able to drop in somewhere and get free tick-pounding.[2] At State I stayed at the φτΔ house. At any rate I'm going to try to make the colleges as much as possible. Bumming a bed (on a davenport) ought not to be too difficult. It's food that will give me my worst moments, I have no doubt.

I have with me only the clothes on my back, shaving kit and one toothbrush and a towel. I also have a Penn State banner for my back, which is wet,[3] of course, but helps with the rides no end.

If I get a job in Columbus, I'll wire you and you wire me whether I shall wait for you there. If not in Columbus, I'll let you know from "Chi." If I get a really good job I'll stick for a while but having tried my hand in Pittsburgh I can see it's not so easy picking up work.

Au revoir, Bob, and so to bed on the eve of the third lap of the glorious adventure.

As ever
Doc

P.S.: Save up all the interesting comment you hear and write it to me when I give you an address.
P.P.S.: Ned sends his best and said he'd see you Thanksgiving.

d.

---

[1] Pennsylvania State University.
[2] A place to sleep.
[3] Fresh or corny.

TLS, 3 pp. PSt.
606 Mahantongo St.,
Pottsville, Pa.

My dear Schopenhauer:

So old man Mammon has got you, eh? In other words, I hear you've been given That Raise and have decided to stick. Well, congratulations is the least (and the most) I can offer you.

As you see I'm back from d.o. Chicago, land of the free criminals and home of the brave bandicks. Some other time I'll tell you about it all—the way I told you about my European junket. Suffice it to say I couldn't get a job, or I'd have stayed long enough to have saved sufficient dough to grubstake myself on a trip farther west. Lord knows how long I'll remain in this adorable hamlet. Not long, I assure you.

I wish you could get home this w.e., but I suppose after the past one you've been having to go easy on the exchequer, notwithstanding even your raise.

I must admit I'm a little disappointed in you, young Simonds. After our many arguments in which you upheld the anti-materialistic side I am almost amazed that mere money could lure you into smugness. Yes, I'm accusing you of that. I wouldn't accuse anyone else of it under the circumstances. If you were anyone else I'd say you were bowing to the inevitable. Beyerle, for instance, is planning his remaining days to be spent right here in prosaic Pottsville. But I thought that any man who deliberately would stick his hand through a pane of glass would be at heart always a non-conformist.

I can see it all clearly. You've gone Rosenberg.[1] If the Purity League is to have a soldier of fortune (one of, shall I say, Mr. Fortune's Maggots?), it will have to be my own improvident self. Pretty soon, Simonds, you'll be agreeing with Harry Silliman if you don't watch out. God forbid! But the way you're headed now is the road straight to respectability, security. You have always been a comfort to me when I was threatened with an acute attack of clothes-pressing, water-waggoning, conventionality. If I haven't you to depend on, what on earth is to become of me?

My next imitation will be of Eugene O'Neill—in my subconscious I suppose he always has been an influence in my life. Well, I'm going to try for another sea job. Want to come along? Anything but a whaleboat and any job but coal-passer. (Birsie Richards[2] passed coal for eight hours in one stretch, when usually they don't work more than four.) First I must get laid, then I'll be all set again. Just between us I haven't had any poongtang since I was in Germany.

While in Chicago I spent $1.65 to hear Richard Halliburton give a lecture on his travels. He's the bird, you recall, who wrote The Royal Road to Romance and The Glorious Adventure. He is disillusioning, so I'm not going to pattern my Career after his. Worse yet, he talks in English—different from talking English.

I've broken with Marg again. It might take, this time. There's nothing like a good jolt in an affaire de coeur to throw a man off balance. I celebrated last night by drinking 13 steams in less than an hour—Sam Marquardt was mighty poor company, drinking only one beer!

Don't mind me, boy. At my present rate I'll end up in a joint in Tia Juana with a bullet in my left ventricle. And when that time comes you'll know that someone else did what I haven't the courage to do myself.

Drop me a line, and don't tell me what movies you've been seeing.

As ever—and worse,
Doc

[1] A collegiate tailor; for O'Hara a symbol of respectability.
[2] William ("Birsie") Richards committed suicide in February 1933. O'Hara used him as the model for Julian English of *Appointment in Samarra*.

TO: Robert Simonds   TLS, 1 p. PSt.
Postmarked 12 December 1927   Pottsville

My dear Hockaday:

If you think you can write a letter about superficialities, prepare yourself for a rude come-down, because this is going to be a masterpiece of twaddle.

In the first place, I have to report that I am about to go Mammon. That is to say, I am about to go to work, perhaps. The Yale Club wired me last week, asking me if I wanted a job on The New Yorker—[1] "Manhattan smart-chart," Time calls it—at $35 a week. The job is reporter. So I wired the Y. club for an appointment, then received a letter telling me to write a letter of application to a Mr. Ingersoll and ask him for an appointment. It is too early yet to make any positive predictions, but it looks as though I will be drafted into the great army of the employed.

But have no fears, my boy. What I will write will be the type of thing I like—impressionistic, satirical, "interesting", and not humdrum. The New Yorker is frankly pro-Semitic, clever, ultra-modern. It is, you might say, a weekly Vanity Fair. I say have no fears, because I will merely be getting paid for writing stuff that I now write for nothing.

And here is another funny bit. I have fallen in love again. It all happened this way—strengthening my alarming tendency to accept Determinism: Mary O'Hara, Fred, Reilly and I went to Reading last night to a Junior League show and dance. I didn't want to go but the family practically insisted. We got all lushed up on the way down and were in fine shape when we got to the Rajah Temple. Well, whom did I see but a girl I met only once, years ago, but who always has been an inhibition of mine. To

26

wit, Edith Quier, the golfer. She's beautiful and I fell. I danced with her no less than 10 times times and when the thing was over she invited me to a dance at her house on the 29th. The Quiers are Mr. and Mrs. Reading —the kind of people who give $10,000 to community chest drives. In other words, if my feelings are requited I will be just where I was but 35 miles away![2] Apropos, wouldn't it be fate-freighted if I were to work in New York and Marg there and me calling her up once a week or so and saving my pennies for visits to Reading! Thank God I still can laugh, for I'd otherwise go crazier.

If I get this New York job, you simply must get working on the Dartmouth Club or the SX club. I'll be famous in two years—not world-famous, of course, but at least well-known—but I'll need you to prod me along and laugh at me and keep me from getting to be too much of a prick. There are a hundred schools in the Met. district and if you went out for it, you could get a job. Plan to go to Columbia next summer and brush up. I promise to be a bad moral influence and to help you enjoy life.

More later.

Juan

[1] O'Hara did not get the *New Yorker* job. The Yale Club of New York City had a placement service that O'Hara was using through a Yale friend.

[2] O'Hara's feelings were presumably unrequited, and the romance did not develop.

TO: *Time* (23 January 1928), 1[1]

Sirs:

Says Grace Gordon Cox, of Boston, under LETTERS in the Jan. 9 issue of TIME:

". . . There will never be a man on your staff big enough to 'stand in Lindy's shoes.'"

Why not give Robert Emmet Sherwood a job?

JOHN H. O'HARA

New York City

[1] *Time* printed O'Hara's letter with an editorial comment: "Robert Emmet Sherwood's feet fill size 13 shoes. He is editor and cinema critic of *Life*, and author of *The Road to Rome*, highly successful comedy."

———— ◆ ◆ ————

In March 1928 John O'Hara was hired as a reporter and rewrite man by the New York Herald Tribune. Fired in August, for drunkenness and tardi-

ness, he worked for Time as a reporter and checker until March 1929, when he was again fired.

As soon as he arrived in New York, O'Hara sought a connection with The New Yorker. His first fiction piece appeared in May 1928, and he became a regular contributor, with thirty-seven appearances in 1928–29.

TO: Robert Simonds   ALS, 4 pp. PSt.
Postmarked 8 March 1928   538 Central Ave.[1]
                                            East Orange, N.J.

Dear Judge—

You asked me to write "if anything turned up." I am writing.

Tomorrow, almost without doubt, I shall become a member of the staff of the N.Y. Evening Post on the strength of a "very unusually high recommendation, young man" from—guess! One F.P.A., none other.

Wednesday I shall return two books ("Robert Louis Stevenson" by G. K. Chesterton, and "The Legion of the Damned" by Bennett Doty) to Time, when I hand in the reviews of those books.[2]

So things have begun to happen.

It came about this way. I left Povie[3] Tuesday after week-ending at Bucknell. I fussed around N.Y. and the Yale Club, which sent me to Time. There I met Noel Busch and Newton Hockaday. They're about my age and occupy an office together. I was chatting with Busch, telling him my record and yes I read Time and have had letters printed in it and yes I understand Time-style. Hockaday, whom I hadn't met said, "Say didn't you write about Sherwood? I called Sherwood and asked him point-blank what size shoe he wore." So we were a pleasant trio for a few minutes. Busch then suggested I do these books and bring in my reviews Wednesday.

Next day—I had been gathering nerve—I phoned F.P.A.[4] and had a lengthy chat. He sent me to the W.[5] but said there wasn't much chance but to go ahead anyhow and let him know next day how I made out. No soap, so I went to see Adams next day, at his office in the W.

He was editing the weekly diary and said as I entered "Hello. Sit down." Then forgot about me in the excitement of editing. Suddenly he began to read aloud, that stuff about the power of print. We discussed that and then he said "How'd you make out." I told him no soap. He said "Sunnavabitch! Isn't it hell?" So we talked some more and abruptly he halted, picked up the phone and demanded a connection with a Mr. Mason or Mr. Renault at the Post.

His Side of the Conversation

"Julian? this is Frank Adams. Say Julian I'm sending a boy down to you and I want you to put him on, hear? He's probably better than anyone you have there now anyway . . . Oh, a perfect gentleman . . . Can he *write*? What a question! Very well, three-thirty. Thanks." Then he turned to me and described Mason: Yale, about 40 and inclined to be snobbish but a good fellow really. So he asked me more questions: where do I send my stuff? Where *is* Pottsville? Had I tried the New Yorker? What? Oh, hell! (every other word is damn or hell) *I'll* talk to Harold Ross.[6] Don't worry. *I'll* get you somewhere. Now get the hell out of here and come back Monday. I'll see Ross tomorrow and Sunday. So I saw Mason and he told me he wants me on, but doesn't do the actual hiring himself. "Come back Monday and I'll take you to Renault. I'm sure everything will be all right." So this time tomorrow I may be. . . .

How about F.P.A., huh? Never saw me before and did more for me than anyone but you would do. With him cheering for me I'll get along. Remember what I told you about 1928 vs. 1927? This time next year I'll *be* somebody.

Now plan to come to N.Y., Fisher. I'll need your snicker to keep me from getting a swelled head and I'll need your solace when things break not to my liking. Why not be a newspaper man? You have a better supply of gray matter than most and the rest isn't hard if you can learn to feel that way. To *that* degree Harry Silliman was right.

The above address is O.K.

Doc

Sunday

START TOMORROW ON THE HERALD-TRIBUNE, thanks to F.P.A.[7]

[1] O'Hara was living with his uncle and aunt, the John McKees (his mother's sister and brother-in-law).
[2] O'Hara's reviews were not published.
[3] Pottsville.
[4] O'Hara's earliest identified contributions to Adams' "Conning Tower" column appeared in 1927.
[5] *New York World.*
[6] Editor of *The New Yorker.*
[7] Postscript on envelope.

TO: Harold Ross

TLS, 1 p. PSt.
Herald Tribune
letterhead

April 7, 1928

Dear Harold Ross:

Here are the Stories from a Distorted Mind I told you about.[1] Rather, two of them. When the others come back from The Bookman I'll send them on. I regret to say that *they* are better, but you know The Bookman. I, frankly, don't.

I'm glad you introduced me to Miss X. (I didn't get her name.) Really it will be a pleasure to have manuscripts turned down by her, which is a compliment if ever I gave one.

Faithfully,
John H. O'Hara

¹ These pieces submitted by O'Hara were not accepted. His first appearance in the magazine was "Alumnae Bulletin," 5 May 1928.

TO: Thomas O'Hara¹   TLS, 1 p. with holograph
Postmarked 10 April 1928   postscript. Mrs. O'Hara
                                 Herald Tribune letterhead

Dear Tom:

I suppose I owe you more letters than I owe anyone else, so here goes. Watch the splash.

I am feeling rather vague at this writing. Last night I was on a party with Dick Watts, the movie critic; Frank Sullivan, The World humorist, Don Skene, the boxing writer for the H.T. and later, Noel Busch, of Time, Lynn Segal, of Time (a girl) and many others. We started at the Artists & Writers club, which is really a speakeasy near the H.T. and then went to Tony's, another speakeasy where all the celebrities go. There I met Frank Sullivan, whose stuff you may have seen in The World. He gave me a big howdedoo and congratulated me on my stuff, etc. From there we went to Chez Florence, a night club, and had much fun. I met lots of celebrities, near-celebrities and people like myself. Among the former was Tommy Guinan, Texas Guinan's brother and Charles Brackett, who does theatre reviews for the New Yorker. It was great fun and I had a lovely time. Only a few venial sins, too.

I have sold a piece, at last, to The New Yorker. I mentioned it in Ma's letter so you've probably heard about it by this. I don't know how much money I'll get for it and as a matter of fact I don't really care an awful lot. The point is that I've broken in. The idea in this willitch is to get yourself known; the rest will follow after that. I had a long interview with Harold Ross, editor of the N.Y.-er on Friday and he sounded very encouraging. He's a queer duck. Funny stiff German hair and a long gap between his two front teeth. Like F.P.A. he swears all the time and when I say swear I mean swear. I saw F.P.A. the other day. We had a nice chat about this and that. Needless to say I think he's quite the boy.

Well, this must come to an end. Not long, of course, but it's something.

Be a good boy and don't forget your morning prayers and don't ever kick your mother.

With love
John

Why not send some of your best stuff to F.P.A. c/o The World, 53 Park Row, New York?

¹ O'Hara's brother Tom became a political reporter for the *New York Herald Tribune*.

TO: Robert Simonds   TLS, 1 p. PSt.
Postmarked 25 April 1928   *Herald Tribune* letterhead

Rob:

Many maudlin thanks for your letter which came today. But did I sense faint sarcasm in your being glad to know the great O'Hara? I grow cynical as the number of my days decreases, being now 23 years old and so forth.

Of course I'm going ahead. A year from now people will be glad to have loaned me money and proud to have insulted me and, a few, rewarded for calling me friend. Right now I am a little happy. My pay check was for nine dollars above the salary agreed upon. Shall the morrow bring an adjustment and disillusionment? I have got drunk, slightly, with the city editor and the asst. c.e. went to the trouble of coming down from his desk to congratulate me on a story, but nine dollars!

TIME is still experimenting with me. I saw Luce the other day. When I walked into his office he said, "Well Mr. O'Hara, after all these years of letter-writing!" He wants me to do a fiction book as a specimen of my reviewing that type, but he was pleased (although) did not accept) with the two already written. I am fairly certain I will do that work as a regular thing, which would mean, I understand an additional $20 a week to my income.

Through F.P.A.'s kindness I am a potential contributor to the New Yorker once more. This time I have more to base my hopes upon. I have been told to write a Profile of Al Smith, jr., and asked to contribute other stuff. It will be at least a month before I will be able to call myself settled, as far as selling stuff is concerned. But I keep prodding myself by a remark the city ed. made the other night; "In this town the sky's the limit for you." Please pass the size 10 Herbert Johnson.¹

I am hoping hard that you will do something about coming to New York. This amounts to a call to quarters, Rob.

My love to those that love me and let the rest of the world go fie!

The same
Doc

¹ Hat brand.

TO: Robert Simonds
Spring 1928

ALS, 7 pp. PSt.
538 Central Ave.,
East Orange, N.J.

Send me your address again. I lost the other.   J.

Dear Judge—

The best explantion of my dereliction that I can make is that I have been doing so many other things that I haven't even had a chance to read "Time"! As a matter of fact much of my playing-periods has been spent with Noel Busch and Lin Segal. Lin, strangely, is a girl. A rather attractive Jewess. She was with Wm. Beebe on the Sargasso Sea trip and now does the Medicine & Science stuff for Time. I have been out several times with both of them.

Does it sound horse's-assy to say I've had such a busy life lately? Here is an idea of the people I've met and spoken to either on assignments or socially: F.P.A.*, Frank Sullivan*, Herbert Asbury, W. O. McGeehan*, Dick Watts*, Clare Briggs*, Belle Livingstone*, Walter Winchell*, Charles Brackett, Don Skene*, Frank Getty*, Arthur Caesar*, Harold Lloyd* and wife*, father* and daughter; Howard Dietz*, and spouse*, Tommy Guinan*, Senator George, Denis Tilden Lynch*, McKay Morris*, George de Zayas*, Mrs. Harry Houdini*, John Haynes Holmes, Wm. Lloyd Garrison—to name but a gross. Then there are the purely office celebrities and local big and semi-big shots whose names would mean nothing to you. I have marked with a star the names of the people who I think would remember me if they were to see me tomorrow. (None of them will. It's my day off.)

Now all this has left my head quite the same. Why shouldn't it?—and yet—these people are easier to meet than pastors of Reformed Churches in Schuylkill Haven. Probably my best impression was made on the most famous of the horde: Clare Briggs. I met him quite accidentally. (He never comes to the office, altho' the paper publishes his cartoons.) This Belle Livingstone is a 4-times-divorced woman of about 52. She conducts what is said to be the only true salon in America. She bet $10,000 that she could climb the Woolworth stairs in 90 minutes. I was sent on the story and interviewed her alone. At the conclusion she insisted I join the crowd upstairs and Briggs was one of said crowd. He's a funny little duck. Wears, duckily enough, a wing collar and bat-wing tie. After many drinks and conversation he whispered to me a tip on a heluva swell theatre story. It's confidential: Helen Mencken, McKay Morris and a couple of other Theatre Guild actors are going to hire an old-fashioned show-boat this summer and give the natives of the Ohio valley a treat. Good, eh?

I am not going to do Time's book reviews. Luce told me they have given someone else the job. We had a little fight about it. I accused him of stalling and he rather lamely excused himself by saying he thought Noel Busch had told me about the other person's appointment. Luce, however, is a pretty good guy regardless, although he probably thinks I have all the crust in the world. I have sold one piece to the New Yorker. I'll send a copy when it appears.

I am now compelled once more to get out that old bunch of type that reads: Marg and I have agreed, amicably, to disagree.[1] You'll get a snicker out of that but hold your ur-reen until you've learned the rest. It started three weeks ago when I got drunk as hell before taking her out, and she got just tight enough later to enjoy the inevitable fight. I was entirely wrong, terribly so. Didn't see her for more than a week and *then* I took Dougie—you remember her from 78th Street: the one who drank quite well—to a night club and merely chatted with Marg while waiting for Dougie. I've had a few dates with Dougie and none with Marg since then. I started this system as a reprisal. . . .[2] But I've become "interested in" Dougie beyond that and in the future I'll probably see as much of her as of M.

But the *big*, important part is that I am in a fair way to having the compassionate mistress I used to talk to you about. I met her two weeks ago down in the Village. . . .[3] After seeing her the first time I wanted to see her again but was actually afraid to ask her for a date. . . .[4] This time I clicked and on Thursday for the first time—having seen her just three times previously—I slept with her. God! What a body! And what a brain!

This is Sunday. I had tea with her today, not having seen her since Thursday nite—or Friday morning. She announced the restrictions under which she would continue to see me. The principal one is that if I ever *think* of wanting to marry her, I am bound in honor (☺) never to see her again. There is to be positively *no* claim on the other by either of us, except that when one of us needs the other he is to call up, whether it's four in the morning or one in the afternoon. Both of us may be unfaithful and have entire freedom. There is to be an absolute Dutch Treat idea as regards the theatre, meals, taxis, etc. Do you blame me for being slightly gaga? We are not to live together, as her mother is living in New York, although not with this girl, whose name is not Elizabeth—but that's a good handle. Elizabeth gets about $200 a week, I daresay. She scorns doing pieces for the New Yorker, which pays only $150 for a Profile!

It may not be Love, but it's much easier on the metabolism. We *call* it Love for want of a better word.

So you see, Rob, I am set for a long stay in New York. Elizabeth and I are going to collaborate on some stuff for magazines: she has the entree and,—she thinks,—I have the ability to take an equal part in a couple of articles. Watch us go! She has a much better education than mine, both from college and what she has taught herself, and she has, I'll concede, a better brain except for versatility of information and an interest in trifles.

Well, a year ago I told myself I would be on a N.Y. paper and have A Woman. This time next year my name will mean something in the field of journalism and, possibly, in the more general literary world.

Only as far as you're concerned—

—As ever
Doc

[1] Marg Archbald was living in New York City.
[2] Twelve words omitted by the editor.
[3] Twenty-one words omitted by the editor.
[4] Fifteen words omitted by the editor.

TO: Harold Ross
1928

TLS, 1 p. PSt.
538 Central Ave.,
East Orange, N.J.

Dear Harold Ross:

I am pregnant with what I think is a good idea. We spoke, you and I, of the advisability of doing a Profile of Betty Compton. She is a good type and probably excellent copy, but my idea is, how about a twin-Profile of Betty Compton and Bobby Arnst,[1] who are almost without a doubt the leading Tiny Tots of New York?

"As every (prep)school boy knows", this Bobby Arnst has had a Meteoric Rise, more so even than Betty Compton's. The idea would be, of course, to give them equal space and more or less subtly to contrast their careers. Incidentally I believe this plan would remove any trace of press-agentry that might dullen (?) a Profile of either one.[2]

I shall await, etc.

Faithfully
John H. O'Hara

[1] Betty Compton and Bobbe Arnst were musical comedy stars.
[2] This profile plan was not accepted. Ross's note on the letter reads in part: "Too airy, not enough substance. . . ."

TO: Harold Ross   TLS, 1 p. PSt.
Summer 1928   *Herald Tribune* letterhead

Dear Harold Ross—

Under separate cover I am sending you the Profile of young Al Smith.[1]
I have tried to avoid obvious repetitions of common knowledge and instead
I have tried subtly to convey a sense of the boy's father's influence. Young
Al is *not* intrinsically good copy. When he has *made* good copy he has
received so much notoriety that everyone knows about it.

Herewith are two pieces which I believe are in the New Yorker manner.[2]
I hope these pieces will find favor.

John H. O'Hara

[1] This profile was not accepted.
[2] Unidentified.

TO: Harold Ross   TLS, 1 p. PSt.
Summer 1928   538 Central Ave.,
                                               East Orange, N.J.

Dear Harold Ross:

If your objection to the enclosed should, by any chance, be on the
grounds of unwillingness to offend, you may take my word for it that the
stuff that is being said and written about the Pennsylvania coal fields is
liberal poppycock.[1] I suppose in your career you have done some knocking
around strike camps. In that case you need not be told that "conditions"
are invariably exaggerated and heightened for journalistic expediency.

Faithfully,
John O'Hara

[1] "The Coal Fields," *The New Yorker* (20 October 1928), one of a series of eleven
pieces about the Orange County Afternoon Delphian Society.

TO: Katharine Angell[1]   TLS, 1 p. PSt.
Late 1928   *Time* letterhead[2]

Dear Mrs. Angell:

Here is another piece in the same vein.

A suggestion for a short Talk piece:[3] In a fog (which is the only way
I can explain it) I wandered the other night into Schrafft's, 42d Street, to
be dined. A girl waited on us, and while she was gone to fetch the food,
a most impressive sight was presented. About ten or twelve young men,

attired in dinner jackets, wearing striped waistcoats, trooped in in semi-military fashion. It was but the work of a moment to observe that each carried a napkin, to realize, Mrs. Angell, that they were the male waiters. They looked so much like a Shubert chorus (neuter) that I expected any moment to see Adele Astaire come frolicking out and hear the chorus singing "Oh, Kay you're O.K. with me," or something.

Another idea which I am Working On. A series of pieces to be called Speakeasy Knights, about such people as Prince Romanoff, the illegitimate son of the Tsar; Jeff Harris, the remittance man, and other characters who are to be found in almost any bar in New York. I will submit a few in the Near Future.[4]

Faithfully,
OLD DOG TRAY
(John O'Hara)

[1] Fiction editor of *The New Yorker*.

[2] O'Hara was fired by the *Herald Tribune* in August 1928 and was employed by *Time* as a reporter and checker from that date to March 1929.

[3] O'Hara probably wrote many pieces for the "Talk of the Town" section of *The New Yorker*, but only two of his published pieces have been identified.

[4] None of these projected pieces was published.

TO: Robert Simonds   TLS, 2 pp. PSt.
December 1928   *Time* letterhead

Dear Bob:

This soul-unburdening letter is under the hat, hear?

I've been doing some proselytizing for you. At Time there is no chance of your getting a job. Fred gave you an inaccurate account of the way things are done here. The research-and-check people are little girls, one of whom, by the way, knows your sister Marion from Connecticut College. There isn't any chance of your getting a clerical job, because a guy who used to take care of the mail and do things for Boss Luce has been ousted and a girl put in his place. I myself am only a part-Timer at this point. For a while I was doing these fucking Newscastings but I had to work under Roy Larsen,[1] who is a —— if ever there was one, so I quit. I did not entirely sever my connection with Time, however. I am nominally the second string theatre critic—on space rates, which is barely enough to live on. I am on the make for a newspaper job and expect to have one between now and the first of the year. At any rate, I have to fix up some cock and bull story to the family, telling them why I won't be home for Xmas. The real reason is I'm flat broke. I'll probably tell the family I've lost money in the stock exchange. You can tell them, if you see them, that you heard from me and the last you heard was I was making dough on the market. If it hadn't been for The New Yorker I'd be on my ass good and proper.

Here's what little I've been able to do for you. I saw Stanley Walker, city editor of the Herald Tribune. I told him about you. Told him you were a Dartmouthist, age 27 or 28. I told him you have done stories for me while I was an editor of the Pottsville Journal. I told him that your stories were good. I told him that you are steady, reliable, will not cover a story from a speakeasy phone. I was fired from the Trib by this same Stanley Walker, because I was drunk most of the time and never was punctual, but we are still friends. He's young—about 30—and very intelligent. He can't be bluffed. He's a Texan and inclined to be querulous, but don't let that frighten you.

Now here's what Stanley said. He agreed with me that the inevitable first-of-the-year shakeup will be stirred at the Trib and that there will be openings among the younger generation of reporters. That means $25 a week at the least—and probably at the most! But it's a spot in New York, which, I take it, is what you want. It's much less than you're getting now, but as I see it, you're thoroughly disgusted with Pennsylvania and want to do things before it's too late. Well, come to New York if you can, and between us we'll eke out a living and some fun of the worse sort.

This is what your next step must be. Write to Stanley, mentioning that I told you he and I had been conversing about you. Confirm (within whatever modest bounds you like) the nice things I said about you. Tell him you've done a little reporting with me (he thinks I'm swell and had tears in his eyes when he fired me) and that you've lived off and on in New York, know the streets, location of important and semi-important places. (They're sick and tired of kids who don't know where the police station is.) Be brief, but not too brief. Be snappy, but not too snappy. Above all, just merely dash off the fact that you went to Dartmouth. (They're griped with nice young Rosenbergers-Frankers[2] who made D.K.E. at Yale.)

In the meanwhile, read the Trib. Notice that instead of saying 14 W. 46th St. it says 14 West Forty-sixth Street. Although it *does* say 14 West 146th Street. Notice the absence of Mr. except on the editorial page or in dealing with Coolidge or some other personage. Notice that you don't say secure when you mean obtain—all things which I shall point out to you if Stanley says come ahead. Stanley knows that I couldn't have a friend who would be dull or nit-witted, and I really would not be a bit surprised if you get a job. But don't expect any money. $25 is what you may count on. $30, if you're lucky. We can live together and keep down expenses.

I have just come off a three-weeks' bender, during which I fell down a flight of stairs, was punched in the face, had a mild attack of d.t.'s although maintaining a residence (if such it may be called) at 107 West 43. I expect little difficulty in getting a job and if I should land somewhere this week, I'll try to rope you in too. Things aren't at the best for me just now, but I'm hoping that I'll land this week on some daily rag so that I can tell the family the reason I won't be home for Xmas is because I'm a new man on a paper and will have to usher in the newborn in back of a typewriter. I am expecting a New Yorker check this week, which will carry me over until—

I'm writing all this in a big hurry and I hope nothing's been left out. You can write or wire me at Time, noting the new address, and I'll get it, as I come here every day. I may be working full-Time after the first of the year, when Brit Hadden, who is a better friend of mine than Harry Luce, becomes editor and hands over the business end to Luce, as is done semi-annually.[3] This, however, is something I'm not counting on.

My best to Coaldale[4] and always to you. I told Stanley you're my best friend.

Doc

---

[1] "Newscastings" was a daily news rewrite service for radio stations. Larsen became president of *Time*.
[2] Rosenberg and Frank Brothers were clothing stores.
[3] Briton Hadden died in February 1929, and O'Hara was fired by *Time*.
[4] Hometown of Simonds' future wife, Catherine Melley.

TO: Thomas O'Hara   TLS, 1 p. Mrs. O'Hara
Postmarked 15 January 1929   *Time* letterhead

Dear Tom:

When that pair of bucks fluttered out of that envelope I couldn't believe my ears. You could have heard a stock drop. It was a very neat deal you made with John Mootz and I congratulate you upon your perspicacity. Things of that sort seem to indicate that you will be not a litterateur but a financial giant, like Charley Ponzi—although you're probably too young to know who he was.[1]

Be that as it may, have no fear for your book nor for your two books. I have a copy of 10,000 Copperfields Under the League.[2] The thing that is holding up the execution of your commission is none other than Grover Whalen. Grover, as you may have heard, is sending policemen about the city, closing speakeasies with reckless and ill-becoming abandon. He happened to choose one of the places—the place—where Robert Benchley hangs out, and to which I paid occasional visits. It is known as Tony's and is one of our toniest places of easy speech. What with that closed, I am temporarily at a loss as to how to find Benchley. He has an office somewhere on Broadway. On the door is painted a sign that reads ACME STOVE & FOUNDRY CO.: KEEP OUT. Of course that sign (that's not it exactly but it's something like it) is to keep out people like myself who come around asking him to autograph books. But I'll run into him, never fear. I had a copy—autographed to me—of F.P.A.'s Column Book, and somebody lower than a dry agent stole it out of my desk, or I'd have sent it home for a conspicuous corner.

Meanwhile, will you tell Mother that I could use that ill-fated suit which was sent to 50th Street while I was living with Larry Brown,[3] and which the Post Office Department bollixed. Tell her to send it to Time, because there's at least an even chance that the P.O.D. will keep that address straight.

Speaking of the Post—I was only a minute ago. Look up there. See?—I may be getting myself a job on the Evening Post.[4] I went down there last week and talked to the city editor and managing editor. I told them I would like to work on their nice paper and at the same time keep my job on Time and continue doing stuff for the New Yorker. They were amenable to the idea and said they would put me on at the first vacancy. The pay will be ample and help me in my business.

Tell Joe that I have a chance to buy a Baby Peugot cheap—$500. Our Foreign News editor—Laird Goldsborough—bought one from Tommy Milton, the racing driver, for $1500. Goldy (no Kike, he) is a cripple and doesn't like to use a car around N.Y. so he has had it jacked up for a year. He has driven it about 2,000 miles, mostly when Time was in Cleveland, and Milton drove it about 3,000. Milton did something extra to it, I forget just what. It is smaller than a Ford and will go about 45 miles an hour, using very little gas—about 30 miles to the gallon. Of course I couldn't be bother [*sic*], nor could I afford to buy it until Spring, but it's something worth bearing in mind. I could sell it for what I pay for it—possibly more. And I would have a car more distinctive than a Pierce Arrow, more economical than a Chevrolet and costing only about as much as a Ford.

Well, keep the faith.

Love to all
John

---

[1] A swindler of the Twenties.
[2] Robert Benchley's 20,000 *Leagues Under the Sea, or, David Copperfield* (1928).
[3] Unidentified.
[4] O'Hara was not hired by the *New York Evening Post.*

TO: Robert Simonds   TLS, 1 p. PSt.
Postmarked 18 January 1929   *Time* letterhead

Rob:

I judge from your silence that you've heard nothing from Stanley Walker and the Herald Tribune—by the way, there's no hyphen between Herald and Tribune. If you've heard nothing it's because Stanley is on his vacation, down in Texas, and won't be back until, I believe, next week. So keep the faith.

In the old days didn't you used to talk about one Halsey Mills, of Dartmouth? I'm pretty sure you did. Anyhow the name was very familiar. I went to see Brit Hadden the other day in a hospital in Brooklyn. Brit's a very sick young man. During my visit this guy Mills, a dapper little gent if ever I saw one, came in with a girl. I didn't want to go in for Do You Know This Person and That, so I didn't. But the first thing he said to *me* was, "Say, didn't you go to Dartmouth?" I asked him what class he was in and he told me '23, which was a year earlier than your original class, wasn't it? He used to work on Time.

I have taken up my abode with the little girl I told you about at Christmas, but I'm afraid it won't last much longer. Too bad, too, because we have a very comfortable place. Well, if you come to N.Y. we'll get ourselves one just as comfortable. I got very very drunk last night on a party out at Kew Gardens with some friends of my sister's, to which the little girl was not, of course, invited. When I came barging in about five-thirty this morning her only comment was, You can sleep in the other room. Which I did. When I called her this afternoon . . .[1] she was very polite and aloof and told me she couldn't go to the theatre with me tonight. Has a date. Well, that's O.K. with me, except that she's probably going out with a guy whom she likes and whom she doesn't lay but whom she wants to lay because he's been so nice to her. Just can't bring herself to it, she says, but if she lays him tonight, I'll leave. (Not exactly fair, inasmuch as I laid one of the girls on the Kew Gardens party last night, but my mate doesn't know that—altho she probably suspected something of the sort.) So much for affaires de cock.

Let me hear from you as soon as Stanley writes. I'll run in to see him when he gets back and prod him along.

Meanwhile, to hell with Harvard.

'S ever
Jawn

[1] Five words omitted by the editor.

TO: Katharine Angell   TLS, 1 p. PSt.
Early 1929   *Time* letterhead

Dear Mrs. Angell:

I have lots of spare time and interesting thoughts and ideas and I am not going to California for just years and years, if at all. So what do you think of the interesting thought and idea of letting me do The Wayward Press? Pending, of course, Mr. B.'s[1] return. From my cello stand I might well do a Toscanini and do it all the time—but of course you'll have to see about that.

I've worked on almost as many papers as Mr. Ross, so I know pretty much what it's all about. Other dope on myself are: my father was a doctor, I am just 24 years old and my favorite word (not that Charles Shaw[2] or you asked me) is *inevitable*.

Breathlessly,
John O'Hara

[1] Robert Benchley. O'Hara did not get this assignment.
[2] Shaw wrote articles about authors for *Vanity Fair, The Bookman,* and *The New Yorker* which were collected in *The Low-Down* (1928).

TO: Katharine Angell   TLS, 2 pp. PSt.
October 1929   New York

Dear Mrs. Angell:

We laid dear grandmother away,[1] with her first g'son an amused spectator, thanks to you (the good father's sermon sounded so much like a Delphian piece that my mother kept pinching me all through it). It was grand of you and many thanks.

Old Good Will O'Hara has put on his thinking cap for Profile ideas and here are some of the results:

General Borden is a swell one. At 60 or so he learned to play the saxophone, plays polo, flies, speedboats, hunts, generals in the N.J. national guard. His Interesting Career began at Yale, where, briefly, he was everything. His boy is the onetime Princeton polo captain. The objection is, Charm, Bamberger's magazine, had a piece about him a year ago that was fairly exhaustive. It was suburbanly written, however, and I see no reason why you shouldn't do something more, including the best that Charm had.

Surely in your files there is something about Col. Archibald A. Anderson, who lives atop the Beaux Arts bldg. on W. 40th St. The colonel (I seem to be running to military titles) is about 70, an artist who studied under I don't daresay who, someone we've all heard about. He is immensely wealthy. I wrote a swell piece about his apartment for the Herald Tribune while I was there.[2] Even his car is distinctive. It's a Cadillac with an Amesbury body, designed by himself. I can't bother you with all the details about the cunnel but may I assure you he is an almost ideal Profile. Better get him before he dies.

Charley Hand, the mayor's personable secretary, is a possibility. Mr. Ross probably knows him. Perhaps you do.

In that section of the city also is City Clerk Michael J. Cruise. It is he, you'll recall, who marries those of us who are satisfied with the legal passes. He has gone prima donna latterly and marries only celebrities. There's a lot of stuff on him, not hard to get.

I think an exception might be made some time against The New Yorker's no-writers policy so that Deems Taylor[3] could be told about. I hate to think that the world will have to wait for his obituary to learn what a versatile, able guy is Taylor.

Did you ever hear of Waldo Peirce? Artist by profession. He's about 76 inches tall and terribly broad. Played football at Harvard. His father's a plute, made his money in Maine lumber. Peirce is pretty good professionally and in addition has done such things as jumping off a boat in the harbor, swimming back to shore when he decided he didn't want to go abroad after all. He lives at 77 Rue Lille, Paris, but is here frequently.

Jack Thomas[4] and I once decided that there is a Meade Minnegerode[5] for every room at the Yale Club. Go to the lounge, he's there; go to the bar, he's there; take a shower, a nude Minnegerode is drying itself; go to the grill, Minnegerode is eating. Of course he's a writer and that probably lets him out.

A Profile I'd like to do, jointly with a boy on Time, is that of Fletcher Henderson. Harlem thinks he's God and I can't prove anything different. You're not by any chance one of us unfortunates who forget time and space and sex when we hear really good oomba-dada music? Henderson at the piano seems to be doing nothing but sneering at the dancers; his fingers don't seem to move. But if you get close enough to the piano. . . . Words! Words!

Does a day go by without at least one little paragraph in the Times, dated some island you never heard of, telling about a slight earthquake, and under it a note from the Fordham seismographist, a Mr. Tynan, S.J. who tells the Times it was 5,438 miles from New York? Tynan might be a dull subject, but if he were found to be so, a Talk piece on the seismograph might result. I wish somebody would clear it up for me. It's an open secret that I went to Fordham Preparatory School for two, not quite two, years and someone might ask me some time about 'quakes.

Cole Porter is a pretty able guy who hasn't been described for the public.

Either a Profile or a Talk piece might be written about this Agutter fellow, the tennis pro at Forest Hills. He's the best in his line.

That's enough to give you sleepless nights until Christmas. If I think of any more I won't let my natural reticence keep me from writing about them.

Best wishes.

Faithfully,
John O'Hara

Mrs. A.: Apropos of the seismograph, I think it must be a racket of some kind. Every Jesuit college in the country seems to have one.

[1] Liza Delaney, O'Hara's maternal grandmother, died in October 1929.
[2] This article was not published.
[3] Composer and music critic.
[4] Novelist, author of *Dry Martini* (1926).
[5] Biographer and novelist; coauthor of Yale's "Whiffenpoof Song."

TO: Katharine Angell   TLS, 1 p. PSt.
1929   New York City

Dear Mrs. Angell:

Here are some articles for your paper.

I went to see Colonel Baines at the Peck Advertising Agency, regarding the Crescent A.C.'s *Crescent*. I don't seem to have much competition for the job, so apparently I get it.[1] Sell F-R short.[2] They want me to pep it up or at least make it readable, which it certainly is not at this point.

What an old silly I was about football. Of course Bob Kelley does it for you, doesn't he? Be that as it maaaay, I still am in a receptive mood, in case anything turns up at 25 west 45. Going from the ridiculous to the ridiculous, what ever happened to victrola-record listening department? I am an authority on records. To prove it: my friendship with Howard Dietz[3] dates from the night in Tony's when I hummed and sang the Whiteman orchestration of "Washboard Blues", errorlessly.

Judge[4] has asked me to write stuff for them. . . . Why am I telling you all these things? Ah, well. You are a mother, and you will understand.

Very gratefully,
John O'Hara

[1] O'Hara never held this job.
[2] *The New Yorker* was owned by the F-R Publishing Co.
[3] Lyricist who wrote "Dancing in the Dark."
[4] Humor magazine.

TO: Katharine Angell White[1]   TLS, 1 p. PSt.
Early 1930   New York City

Dear Mrs. White:

Here is ON HIS HANDS[2] again, and we shall see what we shall see.

I am afraid I've been, latterly, more of a liability than an asset to The New Yorker, what with revised pieces, and advances. About the former, I shall try to be more careful in the future; about the latter, it won't happen again.

Please know that I appreciate the many kind things you have done for me, I really do. Right now I am In a State about various things, not the least of which is My Work, which is having a transitional (though not left-bank) period. If anything good comes of it, I'll owe a lot to you for your kindness and patience. I do anyhow.

Sincerely,
John O'Hara

[1] Katharine Angell and E. B. White were married in November 1929.
[2] 22 March 1930.

TO: Kyle Crichton[1]   TLS, 1 p. Princeton
February 1931   606 Mahantongo St.,
                                     Pottsville, Pa.

Dear Mr. Crichton:

Here is that piano piece again which, thanks to your encouraging note (and thanks *for* it) I did over again.[2] I hope you like it, because I'd rather be in Scribner's than in any place else.

. . . What am I doing in Pottsville? I'm writing a lot of potboilers for The New Yorker and other markets, I'm riding a borrowed horse and trying to make the owner's girl, I'm drinking enough to keep the franchise, and I'm suffering horrible nostalgia for 21 west 52nd and New York generally. I was in New York for the past three years but the going was too tough. Job trouble. My family live here, so I am playing Artist In The Family.

How, really, is David Burnham's THIS OUR EXILE?[3] David is quite a nice boy but why do the sons of railroad presidents think they have to write books and deprive us country doctors' sons (like Sinclair Lewis and yr. correspondent) of a place on Scribner's lists?

Faithfully,
John O'Hara

[1] Editor at *Scribner's Magazine*. Under the pen name Robert Forsythe, Crichton was also an editor of *The New Masses*. He became an editor of *Collier's* and wrote biographies.
[2] Unpublished.
[3] A novel published by Scribners in 1931.

◆•◆

After being fired by Time O'Hara held a series of jobs: movie critic and radio columnist on the New York Morning Telegraph, *publicity agent for*

Warner Brothers and RKO. In 1930 he met Helen Ritchie Petit ("Pet"), a Wellesley-educated aspiring actress from Brooklyn. They were married in New York on 28 February 1931. In the summer of 1931, while on a delayed honeymoon in Bermuda, O'Hara wrote his first extended fiction, a novelette called "The Hofman Estate," which was not published.

TO: Robert Simonds

March 1931

TLS, 2 pp. PSt.

41 W. 52nd St., New York City

Dear Rob:

We got the books fine and thank you fine. They were fine, and when Pet gets around to it she'll write you. Maybe she already has. We have few secrets—in common. Anyhow I'm having fun reading the Decameron again, and I never read any of the France.[1] The problem of cutting the leaves almost broke up our menage, but we compromised: I assumed ownership of the Decameron, or control of it, and decided against cutting the leaves: Pet assumed supervision of the France and probably will cut the leaves. You and Kate[2] have the distinction of being the first of my friends to send us a present, which, all things considered, is as it should be. I wouldn't have had it otherwise.

Pet is anxious to meet you both and we fairly reckoned you'd be with us on one of the weekends after your initial telegram. We're still hoping. But meanwhile, here is a plan for something in the more remote future, a plan, by the way, which I know has been lurking in the back of your mind and mine for a couple of years, and which now approaches fulfillment. I mean, Judge, Bermuda. Ah, Bermuda! The fragrance of it . . . the long passionate nights on the lagoons, if any. The Furness-Bermuda Line . . . Anyhow, last night Helen and I (let it be explained that she is known to Wellesley friends as Petie, to me as Pet, to her mother as Stubby, to a few as Helen, so I call her everything but Petie) anyhow we had dinner at her home. Her mother is quite a pal, and has given me a couple of cheques to buy things for myself and all that sort of thing. Her mother and uncle live together in Brooklyn. The uncle is an inventor and is partner in a firm that builds naval equipment like gyroscopes (a rival of the Sperry crowd in a smaller way). He is a nervous, slight fellow of about 40 and is crazy about Pet. Well, he already has crashed through with some money, perfunctorily, but last night he got Pet's mother to tell us of a new proposition: he wants to give us a thousand bucks and wants to know whether we want a bond, the cash, or in the form of an allowance. We decided we want the cash so that we can take half of it and go on a wedding trip, and use the rest as a Rainy Day Fund. We could go to Bermuda in practically luxurious fashion for $500. I know that's what it cost Wolcott Gibbs when he got married and went to Bermuda, and he stayed at a pretty expensive hotel and did the social thing. We figure on being less extravagant and staying longer. Or staying about two weeks and not spending so much as $500.

Now then, why don't you and Kate plan to come with us? It wouldn't cost a whole hell of a lot more than your Canadian trip. The difference would be worth it to both of you: the old sea voyage and that sort of thing. We'd be going out of season, and it's much cheaper. The weather is warm in the daytime but cool at night. Pet and I were thinking of taking Eugene O'Neill's old place, a small house on the non-tourist side of the island, a picture of which we have (an old beau of Pet's did a water color of it). Pet's been there and she thinks it's swell. Of course that's all in the tentative stage, but how about it, old fella. How about it? Doesn't your blood tingle at the thought? You could go swimming for white-bellied shark, we could play golf and ride a bicycle. Kate and Pet could play games like categories (of which she is very fond) and we all could get royally boiled.

While the thought's in mind, ask Ned Dolan where Esther lives and ask him her name (dare him to remember it). Start saving your money or hope for a Packard boom or something. We're young only once, and I can think of no more pleasant time than we four together on a desert island, alone with forty well-chosen books and four cases of Bacardi. And some pemmican.

Give my love to Kate and get her all steamed up about this. You simply must plan to go . . . Of course we haven't got the money yet, but we'll get it. Of that I'm pretty sure.

My best to your family and say hello to Hoefel and Ned for me. (I haven't heard from my family as I am still without the Roman fold, entirely through my own fault as Pet has urged me to come around but I haven't quite got to it.)

As ever
John

¹ Anatole France.
² Catherine Melley.

TO: Robert Simonds   TLS, 3 pp. PSt.
Postmarked 3 July 1931   "Greenway," Paget East,
                                                                     Bermuda

Dear Rob:

It is a far cry from Paris, France, to Paget Parish, Bermuda. A very far cry. Pet and I have just been out on the porch of our little dream cottage, trying to get Paris with a cry, but it's too far.

You see Finance reared its ugly head, and when all things were taken into consideration, we decided to come here for a longer stay than we'd have been able to afford in Europe. Another thing that we have learned since we came here: these horrid Amurricans pass right by our door, but they do pass. In Europe they'd have lingered. So far we have had social intercourse only with the local champion cricketer and his wife, and that very slight, and that slight bit only because their dog was either so exuberant or so unfriendly as to take a piece out of my leg. I was biking peacefully along, hurrying home to the little woman, when the son of a bitch yapped at me, plunging his incisors into that sinful flesh of mine. Fortunately there never has been a case of hydro—oh, call it rabies for short, so the leg remains and the only foaming at the mouth comes, so far as I'm concerned, from good old Bass's.

We have a swell cottage. Living room, two mahster's bedrooms, maid's room, dining room, kitchen, electric refrigerator, and about 1/3 of an acre of woodsy ground, all for $50 a month. Food is comparatively inexpensive (although we haven't got the bills yet). The drinking question is by way of being an exclamation: we just don't drink. No resolutions or anything of the kind. It just doesn't seem to occur to us. We bought a bottle of gin when we got here, and we still have it, two weeks and one day later. Pet reads, and I have done a lot of writing. We eat and smoke, and at night we sometimes knock off a bottle of ale and a bottle of porter, and that's just about our life. I bike to Hamilton (about twelve minutes going, fifteen coming back on account of a hillock) once or twice a day to mail letters and buy the papers and magazines and cigarettes. I haven't even got a sunburn. I'm not pale, but if you remember what I looked like after my nautical experience—well, I *am* pale compared with that.

So far I have resisted the impulse to buy a pith helmet, but I do wear linens or flannels all the time. The only possible objection to the place is the insects, which are quite harmless but annoying, and will, I am told, decrease in number soon. Otherwise the place is perfect, and I'd like to be able to buy this place and live here always. Go to NYC twice a year for the theatre and new ideas, etc., but have my home here. The Mrs. doesn't cotton to that idea, but as I said to her the other day: "Sweetheart this is so heavenly that we must spend most of our time here, and if you don't like it I'll knock your God damn block off, sweetheart." So we are not going to stay. We are going to remain here until September 15, however, so it looks pretty much as though you two'll have to spend your vacations with us. Remember, we're chaperons now. The boat fare is $60 return, I said return. Tips and things bring that to about $75, but no more. You'd have no gasoline, no hotel, damn small liquor and just about no other bills to foot. I'd look into it seriously, folks. That extra room is entirely idle. We have a swell maid who is a dandy cook.

I am writing a play,[1] among other things, which keeps me thinking I'm not entirely loafing. Already I can tell you that it isn't a good play, but it's my first, and I suppose we've all got to write a first if we expect to make money writing plays. (The man thinks so clearly, like Coolidge.) I also am yawning, it being close to nine o'clock, and I suppose you are, no matter what time it is, so this is this.

. . . .[2]

Now start figuring on Bermuda. Why not plan to come in August?

As ever
J. O'H.

[1] Unidentified.
[2] Seventy-six words omitted by the editor.

TO: Robert Simonds   ALS, 4 pp. PSt.
Received 21 July 1931   "Greenway," Paget East,
                                                              Bermuda

Rob—

A hasty note and hasty urging to come here.

(a) You don't need passports.

(b) The best lines are the Furness and the Munson.

(c) Any date is fine, up to September. We're returning in September.

(d) Bring only summer clothes as it's warm though not so warm as N.Y., according to the Press.

(e) Tennis racquets are in order and so are golf clubs and bathing suits. White clothes really don't get very dirty, but blue shirts and dresses are of course better (I sound like a boarding school prospectus). You won't need much clothes as we're *very* informal. Gentlemen, by the way, may wear only the trunks of their bathing suits. With ladies that's optional. We use a private beach.

Let me see now, if there's anything else. Two dollars apiece is enough for your bedroom steward's tip, and one dollar for your dining room steward.

The less luggage you bring the more you'll enjoy the actual trip. Bob don't bring a dinner coat; Kit may bring a semi-formal dress if she likes. White flannels are plenty formal on a man.

Get your deck chairs together as soon as possible after getting on the boat. A quarter apiece is enough to tip the deck steward, although the chairs cost a dollar. Don't bother to buy or rent chair cushions: you'll probably be playing ping pong anyhow and won't use your chairs.

If you like you can cable me the name of the boat the day before sailing. I'll know when it arrives.

There is no cure for seasickness, but you aren't likely to get it this time of year.

I will meet you at Hamilton. Be sure not to get off at St. George's. The reason it's better to come via Furness or Munson is that you come all the way in to Hamilton (except on the Franconia, which brings you in on a tender). Just remember that you want to go to Hamilton.

I apologize if I've given you a lot of useless information, but you know how it is.

Pet and I are anxious to see you and already have some ale on the ice for you.

Be seeing you.

John—

TO: Kyle Crichton
August 1931

TLS, 1 p. Princeton
"Greenway," Paget East,
Bermuda

Dear Mr. Crichton:

Having rotten time. Wish you were here.

You, I gather from various impressions (such as the Hugh O'Connell piece in The New Yorker, and one or two other things that I can't place) are a Southwestern boy. You will, therefore, understand the odd state of mind I was in just prior to writing the accompanying piece.[1] You may not know it, but for the first time in history Bermuda is finding itself facing a definite Negro problem: the dinges are beginning to rape white girls with alarming frequency, to such an extent as to call for an editorial in today's Royal Gazette & Colonist Daily. Tonight a scion of the oldest Bermuda family told me that among the well-bred folks they are getting together a Vigilante society, hinted at my joining it, and said in these words: "We're going to put some of our cedar trees to good usage."

These facts, and the honest-to-God thrill and encouragement I got out of selling my first piece to Scribner's,[2] embolden me to send you the piece, which I wrote a week ago and which I have really been afraid to submit. I certainly won't be offended if you don't buy it, because there are so many obvious reasons for your steering clear of it. Still it is a good story (I hope you will agree with me on that) and I am eager to see what you think of it.

We now enter August, the hottest month here, wit flying cockroaches, wit rain, wit O'Hara working like hell on his one-fifth Minor American Novel (one-fifth finished), which by an odd coincidence will come within

49

the conditions of the Scribner's Five Grand Contest.³ See you in September, and thanks for your note.

Faithfully,
John O'Hara

¹ Unidentified.
² "Alone," December 1931.
³ *Scribner's* short novel contest. O'Hara submitted "The Hofman Estate," which was not published but which later developed into *Appointment in Samarra*.

TO: Kyle Crichton

TLS, 1 p. Princeton
"Greenway," Paget East,
Bermuda

August 18, 1931

Dear Crichton:

Here is the short novel by that amazing young genius, O'Hara, who will be hurled into the literary spotlight by winning the Scribner's contest, and who will be promptly hurled into durance vile by his many creditors who will attach the five-grand prize.

Anyhow, here it is for you to look at. There seems to be nothing like a public stenographer here, so it has to go as is. If you want to keep it, I'll have it retyped when I arrive in New York, circa September 18. If you don't want to keep it—that's something else again. This is the only copy.

The piece, you will find, moves fast. As you will guess, it is based to some extent on a true story—obviously not autobiographical. I have used dialogue sparingly, but, I trust, effectively. As for "Influences" you can detect Hemingway, Fitzgerald, Sinclair Lewis (you know, the fellow that Harcourt used to publish?), S. V. Benet, Hergesheimer and almost anyone you look for. On the other hand, the pace is mine and the piece has been written so fast (it's really journalistic) that there hasn't been much time for Influences. I leave it in your tender care.

If there are any moneys accruing to the author at this point, please see that he gets them pretty soon, for during the writing of this The Hofman Estate I have done no New Yorker or other stuff, and I am quite broke. I hope you understand that sort of thing.

One last request: please let me know as soon as possible when you have accepted or rejected it?

Thank you for your encouragement and kindnesses. I hope they are justified.

Faithfully,
John O'Hara

My next address in New York will be 24 Monroe Place, Brooklyn, after Sept. and The New Yorker always knows where I am.

TO: Kyle Crichton
August 1931

TLS, 1 p. Princeton
"Greenway," Paget East,
Bermuda

Dear Crichton:

I suppose you have read op. 1 by this time, and have made up your own mind about it, and perhaps this letter is exceedingly ill-timed and unpropitious, but I think I know you well enough by letter to ask you some questions, and ask for your comment.

It is my understanding that Scribner's buy a group of the short novels which they consider the best, and pay for them at your regular rates, and then pick the best from that group to win the five grand. (Stop me if I'm wrong). Now I've been casting accounts and I find that in theory I would have to leave Bermuda on September 16 owing close to $300, and I am looking about here and there on the magazine and newspaper horizon for ships that might come in ere the 16th. Is there, really, any point in my looking for any of that space-rates dough before the 16th? (You see I think my story is probably good enough for that, but I don't think it's a prize winner.)

To complicate matters: Nash[1] wrote me today again and said Farrar & Rinehart want to see the thing as soon as possible. They don't know that since they first wrote I decided to send it to Scribner's (and I wish you wouldn't mention that if you see Nash, because if you-all don't like it, they might, as Larry Barretto[2] told me that Johnnie Farrar[3] has suddenly gone daft on the subject of journalistic writing, and he might like The Hofman Estate). Also, there is this complication: I could stay on here a little while longer, probably writing myself out of debt, except for the fact that I have a good chance of a good job in New York beginning with the football season, and I don't want to miss out on it. There is still another complication: I could borrow from the in-laws, but I don't want to so long as I can possibly avoid it. And there—or, more exactly, here—I am.

I seem to have written myself out for the time being and now am more than a little eager to get back to New York and See How Things Are. I will, therefore, await with some trepidation your reply. I suppose it'll all come out all right in the end, but at the nonce I am jittery and inclined to snap at little children and throw bottles at my wife. You, I hope not, know how it is.

> Sincerely,
> John O'Hara

[1] Poet Ogden Nash, then an editor for Farrar & Rinehart.
[2] Novelist and war correspondent.
[3] Co-founder of Farrar & Rinehart.

TO: Kyle Crichton
TLS, 1 p. Princeton
Bermuda

Dear Crichton:

I'm still a bit groggy, having just received The Hofman Estate and your note, which, I must say, broke it as gently as possible, and thanks for so doing. Anyhow, here are some pieces.

I received a mysterious cable dated Sept. 2 about holding the MS. Tell me more.

I leave here Sept. 16 and thenceforth will be at 24 Monroe Place, Brooklyn. If you buy these pieces or one of them please send the cheque to the Bklyn address unless you're sure it would reach here before the 16th. I plan to send this to you through my sister, who is coming here for the week-end, so disregard the postmark if it's New York. I've still almost two weeks here. And now I think I shall get quietly drunk.

> Faithfully,
> O'Hara

Sept. 4 [1931]

TO: Thomas O'Hara
Postmarked 8 October 1931
TLS, 1 p. Mrs. O'Hara
New Yorker letterhead

Dear Tom:

Thanks for your note, and you're right about the switch from Bermuda to noisy New York. I would like to live in the country, say Connecticut, always; not too far from the New York literary market, but out where it's quiet. But my wife, poor wretch, is a city girl. Guess what we're going to do. . . .

As you infer, I am working here, at least for the time being. It is a fluke job. I have a drawing account, against my pieces. Markey is to be gone for a couple of months, so I am to take a shot at The Reporter At

Large stuff.[1] I am not too optimistic about it, but at least it's a stop-gap. Ross is a hard guy to write for. I've done some Talk of the Town stuff for him, but not a hell of a lot.

As to getting on the Journal. Do approach Walter.[2] You will get little or no money for the start, but mention your Herald Tribune experience. Walter will, I am sure, do what he can, but of course the ultimate decision rests with Silliman. Journalism is a tough racket always. There is no money in it at boom times, even (how Dutch I remain yet!), but at least it can be steady if the man himself is steady. I speak from experience. The best course in journalism is to read Alva Johnston's[3] stuff in the Herald Tribune. The Trib, by the way, is now the best paper in the country, aside from its political shibboleths. Read it. Avoid dullness, but don't on the other hand get wordy. A new reporter always has that tendency. Tell Silliman you will start as I did, for nothing the first month, and then $6 a week, and on up. Then after you've had six months experience I'll speak to Stanley Walker about you. Pay attention to everything about the paper. On a small paper you learn things about typography that you never do on a big sheet. Tell Fred Hohman, the linotyper, who you are, and that I said to ask him to tell you things about type, etc. (I assume that you will get a job.) I wish you all luck and I know you have the stuff, so go to it without delay.

The mighty tome[4] will have to be rewritten, according to Ogden Nash and Scribner's, so I guess it will have to be rewritten. We saw Joe last night. He's looking well, I thought. Best wishes and love to all who want it.

John

[1] Morris Markey; none of O'Hara's work for this department was published.
[2] Walter S. Farquhar, sportswriter and columnist on the *Pottsville Journal*.
[3] Writer who later became known for his profiles in *The New Yorker*.
[4] "The Hofman Estate."

TO: Robert Simonds   TLS, 3 pp. PSt.
November 1931   19 W. 55th St., New York City

Monday
Dear Fisher:

Candor, and all that, compels me to admit that I got your first letter. I then was in the throes of something which, I daresay, was a bit more immediatately troublesome than your own problem in Coaldale. I was having mother-in-law trouble, which can be all that the comic supplements reveal. You see, Pet's mother found out from a tactless friend of Pet's that I was not on leave of absence, as she had been given to believe, but that I had quit my job, and would have none when I returned to New

York. The result was simply hell. We had to live in Brooklyn with her family until I got together enough dollars to take an apartment in Manhattan, which we finally did a fortnight ago. But between the time of landing and the moment of apartment-taking there was enough on my mind to heighten my native neuroticism. On at least one occasion I got so drunk that I passed the evening in a speakeasy and did not return home to Brooklyn. But first I got some sort of half-assed job on The New Yorker: a drawing account of $75 a week, to be charged against whatever I wrote for them. That lasted exactly two weeks, until an officious son of a bitch decided to be efficient and call a halt to that. Had I not last week sold a piece[1] to Vanity Fair for $100 Mrs. O'Hara and I might well be worse off, by a week, than we are now. I have no job, and no source of income. I have written a lot of stuff for various publications, but The New Yorker particularly seems to be having manuscript trouble (excusitplease, this "trouble" trouble). Right now, however, they seem to be on the verge—on the verge, my dear Simonds—of buying a piece which I called Screendoor,[2] and if they do buy it I shall consider that the O'Haras are eating on R.T.S. this week. I told it in the first person, combining the character and the dog part of the Screendoor anecdote with an experience I once had in Llewellyn,[3] which happened while I was wearing that state police raincoat.

Ah, the novel! Nash read it (Scribner's having turned it down insofar as giving me money while I rewrote it was concerned) and liked it. His words were that there was no monkey business to it, but that it seemed a shame to keep it so short, to overlook the opportunities for writing about a swell, small-town aristocracy. He told me to write him a synopsis and hand it to him so that he could take up with the Farrar & Rinehart part of the firm the matter of paying me so-much a week while I rewrote it (which is the only way it ever will be rewritten). I did the synopsis today, and he will have it tomorrow. Then the prosecution rests, so far as the novel is concerned, except that I am going to see one other publisher, William Morrow & Co., this week. Meanwhile I have taken a ride in the Goodyear dirigible Columbia, getting dope for a New Yorker piece, and I have tossed off various other pieces against the December 1 wolf.

Keep on with your novel, for Christ's sake. I find that my coal region memory is slipping in favor of new information on more recent visitations and abodes. I bought a Republican[4] the other day, and there was a list of schoolteachers arranged by townships. I find that I forget where Hubley Twp. is, and things like that. I have to stop to remember where Duncannon is, and Rock. I forget many important facts about some of the County's most important people, such as Dory Sands and Puss and the Bolicks and the Mosolinos. Write a novel while you're more or less on the ground, and rewrite it when we go to Nassau next summer or before that. Read your Scribner's which I humbly believe has the best short stories now being published in magazines. I don't like all their stories, and if I hadn't written it I probably wouldn't like the story I have coming out in the December issue.[5] Nevertheless, it's the only place I can think of where they are giving us newcomers a break, and publication in Scribner's does give some sort of stamp of approval. I like to think so. . . . Keep writing, no matter how badly or how bad you think it is, because you'll never forget what you set down in writing or on a type-writer (that, and my old declaration that a girl who lies will lay, are my two lone axioms). Make it your own, as an old English teacher of mine used to say. Or file and forget, as Ross of The New Yorker says. But write like hell all of the good copy you can think of. Between us we might make Winesburg, Ohio, take a back seat. Imagine the vote of thanks we'll get from the Chambers of Commerce at Pottsville and Shenandoah! People like the half breed and so on, if written about in intelligent fashion, can be made to fit in with the brolies and the Irish and dirty black Protestant Welsh of Sch. Co., and we'll create our own market. I don't know the principles of a good essay: vaguely in my mind has always been a theory, perhaps inaccurate, that a good easy [sic] form is the syllogism. This, I truly believe, is a little too conclusive a form for the modern novel or short story. My half-baked theories on these forms of literature arrive at the ultimate opinion that life goes on, and for the sake of verisimilitude and realism, you cannot positively give the impression of an ending: you must let something hang. A cheap interpretation of that would be to say that you must always leave a chance for a sequel. People die, love dies, but life does not die, and so long as people live, stories must have life at the end. When there is no longer life, then is time for the Happy Ending, or any ending in the narrowest sense. . . . Horseshit yourself, Simonds.

I cannot entirely resist the temptation to stick my snoot into your trouble with Kate. I think you are now where Marg and I were several points in our lengthy battle. That is, you have arrived at a sort of cul de sac, with two ways out: you can get married, or you call it quits. But I sincerely feel that you ought to do one or the other and spare yourselves the anguish I had with Miss Arch, and which I undoubtedly caused. If I had had sense enough to break it off early in 1928, or if she had had sense enough to have let me alone in 1929, we'd have been spared 1930, the worst year in my life.

I mentioned you to F.P.A. the other day. I told him about that Bible instructor at Daatmuth who used to refer to Joe and his blazer. Adams laughed loudly. He wanted to know who you are. Send him some more stuff. It won't do any harm.

My luck in picking Columbia's good spots continues, although with no monetary gain. I picked her when she beat Cornell a couple of years ago, and I picked her against that big Green team. I now pick Cornell to knock her off this week, and Cornell to knock off that big Green team the following week. Do I hear takers? I picked fourteen out of fifteen last Saturday, which is the old O'Hara pickin's. Remember the Journal days? I'm afraid it's going to be something awful when the Green meets Yale. And the best they can do is to save the carfare to Stanford and give it to the unemployed alumni.

Mrs. O'Hara and I have done a good deal of drinking since Bermuda, you will not be interested to know. We have a nice enough apartment; very likely will look very lupine when the rent comes due, which is Dec. 1, thus leaving me flat on my ass for Christmas, which is as it should be. It will be something not to have to be sorry about not giving Christmas presents this year. I've been sorry so many years that it almost spoiled my holidays. Come and see us.

John O

¹ Unpublished.
² Unpublished.
³ "Screendoor" was a Schuylkill County character, so named because his face was pockmarked, who had trained his dog to urinate on people at his command. Llewellyn was a town in the coal region of Pennsylvania.
⁴ The *Pottsville Republican*.
⁵ "Alone."

TO: Katharine Angell White   TLS, 1 p. PSt.
1931–32   New York City

Dear Mrs. White:

I've just finished writing the most difficult letter I've ever attempted, but I think I got the idea across to Wolcott¹ about the necessity for his keeping on writing.

I am sending you a piece. It goes by the name of "JUST A TWIRP".² May you like it.

I have a list of dates of issues in which appeared pieces I would like to take to Harrison Smith.³ What is the procedure about buying back copies? Is that Editorial or Circulation Department at The New Yorker?

Faithfully,
John O'Hara

¹ Wolcott Gibbs, an assistant to Mrs. White, became O'Hara's closest friend at *The New Yorker*. O'Hara named Gibbsville for him.
² Unpublished.
³ Editor and publisher. A collection of O'Hara's stories was not published until *The Doctor's Son* (1935).

TO: Robert Simonds
Postmarked 17 January 1932

TLS, 2 pp. with holograph
postscript. PSt.
19 W. 55th St., New York City

Letter II, to be read first, however.[1]

Robert:

We caught our colds on New Years Eve and have had them since; just the amount of time that has passed since I lost my most recent job.[2] Well anyhow, the rent was taken care of by Mrs. P. (and I don't by any chance mean Mrs. P. H. O'Hara), and day before yesterday Helen's uncle decided we needed a change of air to help us get rid of colds, and supplied the funds necessary for a weekend in Atlantic City. We left yesterday, Friday, and this afternoon I began figuring: $14 a day hotel bill, and dollars here and there for incidentals, and said: "Look here, you, who the hell are we to spend this money this way, even if it was intended to be spent this way?" So we checked out and came home on the next train, thereby saving $14. Of course we pretend we are there for the whole weekend. So when we got home there was a large box marked glass, postmarked Allentown; and I figured it was from Joe, who asked us what we needed besides money, and I had said glass (we have thirty-two ten-cent cocktail glasses for parties, but only about half a dozen other presentable ones). And then when we opened the boxes—honestly, Robert, I am embarrassed by the kindness of you two. We have been home only ten minutes, and our conversation has consisted of "beautiful" and "oh, now really" and "they shouldn't have done that" and other such banalities that quite inadequately attempt to cover up the inadequacy of our ability to express grateful surprise. The set really is the loveliest thing in our apartment, in the best of all possible taste, and the only thing lacking is the occasion when it shall be filled with the best obtainable liquor to be drunk *a quatre* by donors and donees; an occasion which cannot come too soon, and will come very soon, may we hope?

It really is a good thing the depression is so catholic—the happiest catholicity I have come upon in quite some time! For since the depression *is* so universal the state of mind of the individual depressed is less morbid than it might be. And thus roundaboutedly I come to my comment on the irony of It All: we, who are so broke, are supposed to pass the weekend in the style of the still-affluent, and come home to find a gift fit for a Mellon. The telephone has been disconnected—and a press agent gives me a $20 hat for Christmas. That sort of thing. We eat a cheap table d'hote dinner . . . and proceed to a first-night. We buy two "quarts" of cordial shop gin . . . and four people drop in (one of them, an artist named Strater[3] a boxing companion of Hemingway's) and the evening turns into a swell party. I try without success to get a $50 a week job, and a few minutes later am promised tickets for the Beaux-Arts Ball.

Maybe this isn't a depression at all. Maybe it's just L-i-f-e. Of course I say that with all awareness of my sympathetic interest in, and vicarious knowledge of, the waywardness of Packard shares.

My habit of posting my letters in my inside coat pocket is getting to be unforgiveable. I haven't yet mailed a letter to Tom which I wrote two weeks ago. Among, by the way, a thousand other things I am grateful to you for is your interest in, and intellectual stimulus of, Tom. It is not at all embarrassing to me to confess that I know you do it so much better than I would be able. Mary and Joe have told me about it and about how Tom appreciates it. You must know this, even though he may be inarticulate in expressing it. I am so glad that he is not going to be wasted, which he might have been had it not been for you. He has too much stuff on the ball to let him bury himself in Pottsville, and in addition he needs college as you and I needed it. I don't know what your current attitude toward the system is, but I am sure that you got out of college many of the things that make life bearable for you. I, of course, am less unreconciled to having missed it; or I think I am; but it keeps cropping up in the oddest ways: on the train tonight in the washroom an old gent made some wise-crack about walking away from a hotel with his roomkey in his pocket, and believe it or not, I said to him: "Well, that's a hell of a thing for a Phi Bete to do." His key registered that quickly, you see . . . . And I'm the guy that called Harve Batdorf[4] the perennial collegian.

It's bad luck to talk about it, and all that, but I have submitted a second, totally different (except as to locale) short novel to Scribner's.[5] It has passed the first reader and is now going the rounds. It is, of course, a candidate for the $5,000 prize, which it can't conceivably get; but if it is bought as one of the twelve best it means $500 and a boost in my literary stock. Tell Kate to light a candle for me. The first opus reposes in a manila envelope right in this desk, and probably will for many a day, as I can't afford to work on it right now. I am dallying, mentally, with the seductive idea of a College Humor contest,[6] which pays $3,000 for the first prize, exclusive of movie rights, etc. I have no definite idea in mind, but am discarding a couple every day. Why not try it yourself? The contest closes June 30.

If I get any kind of money within the next six months I am going to return to Pennsylvania, Pet notwithstanding. My plan on that is this: I have quite forgotten altogether too much of what I once knew. For instance the other night I was writing a gruesome little piece about the South Penn explosion, and I discovered that the word "slope" made me wonder. I never was a mining engineer, exactly, but Lord! I knew more about a mine than, say, my father. Tonight I honestly can't define a drift. Of course on the other hand I can describe the Breakfast Club at Delmonico's, but . . . . I want to go somewhere in The Region—Schuylkill

Haven, Tamaqua—and be able to find out by telephone accurate information about mining, local history, geography, etc.

I am now going out before the drugstore closes and get toothpaste so I can enter a radio contest and win $200. If I win it I'll fill that lovely decanter and then you and Kate come and drink up . . . but for God's sake don't wait for that! Pet sends love and many, many thanks, and that makes it unanimous.

Johno

The other letter is just to show I wrote months ago.

[1] The letter enclosed with this one may have been the November 1931 letter to "Dear Fisher."

[2] Probably either as a *New Yorker* reporter or with Benjamin Sonnenberg's public relations firm.

[3] Henry Strater.

[4] A friend from Lykens, Pa.

[5] Probably an early version of "The Doctor's Son," which was not published until 1935.

[6] It is not known whether O'Hara entered this magazine contest.

TO: Thomas O'Hara   TLS, 2 pp. Mrs. O'Hara
Postmarked 17 January 1932   19 W. 55th St., New York City

Pardon the delay![1]

Dear Tom:

I have been enjoying a dandy cold, which, with a sprained shoulder (the result of wrestling with Joe) has had me abed for a couple of days. Hence the delay.

Howard Barnes,[2] who went to Yale, is my chief consultant on matters pertaining thereto, and these are his suggestions. You should get four years of Latin, English, History cold. It is my understanding that you have had four years of these subjects. In addition, if you can get four years of French (you've had two, haven't you?), you should do so. Your next move is to write to Yale and find out, or let the sisters find out, how you can buy second-hand copies of old College Board exams in Latin, English, History and French; also whatever else you have, like Mathematics or Sciences. You will not need a Science to enter, but if you haven't one, you'll have to take one while at Yale. You plan, of course, to enter Yale College and not Sheffield Scientific School. My advice is to write to the Dean of Admissions, whose name is Corwin and who is a classmate and friend of Mr. Archbald's, and tell him just what you have in the way of completed work, and ask him to check over what you will need to get in; then when he has checked your list, study the Old College Board exams for the past three or four years and get those subjects and those questions cold. Then you will be ready to take the actual examinations in June, and if you flunk them then you will have another chance in, I believe, September. But don't think of September; it is decidedly to your advantage to pass in June, inasmuch as Daddy was not a Yale man, because the September exams usually are understood to be held as the last chance for sons of alumni to get in. If I were you I would also try to enter Harvard, so that that will be in reserve if you can't get into Yale; and also make application to enter Dartmouth.

As to working your way through: if you are going to have a thousand dollars for your freshman year, Howard Barnes, who had only that much for freshman year, advises you to go out for the Yale Daily News for this reason: if you get on the News you will eventually get a "cut" of what the News makes; probably not freshman year, but in senior year if you are on the board you can make as much as $3,000, which would enable you to pay off a student loan. Also, meanwhile you could use your name and experience here as a means of getting the correspondent's job for the Herald Tribune. For this reason Howard believes you ought not to wait on table, even though it would mean getting your meals free. He believes it would take too much time off your News activities, and since you will have $1,000, you will have enough to get by. I might point out that $1,000 must mean a lot more now than when Howard was in college, which was six years ago.

You are fortunate in having enough to get you through freshman year, because you will be able to devote more time to your studies and make yourself eligible for scholarships. I would begin now to work for a scholarship. Examine the list. I recall that the Yale Club of Philadelphia gives several for Pennsylvania boys, and there also are other tricky ones. For example, there is one scholarship which is awarded to the boy who shows the most improvement in freshman year. I imagine also that you ought to be able to pick out various prizes to concentrate upon. There will be lots of competition, but I have every confidence in your ability.

I would also suggest that you read The New Yorker carefully and even send them pieces when you have good ideas. Send them to Wolcott Gibbs, The New Yorker, 25 West 45. You probably won't sell many—maybe not any—but they will criticize what you *do* send in a way that will enable you to discover, ultimately, what they like and don't like. Don't hesitate to use my name in writing to Gibbs, but don't bother sending them anything that mentions the name of a celebrity, like F.P.A.; don't send them anything pertaining to journalism or advertising, no puns, no Greenwich Village stuff, nothing with a trick ending. I am giving you this advice because if you could sell them a piece now and then while you are at Yale it would help your journalistic standing there, and they pay so well that you could have money for extra furniture, clothes, proms, games, etc., and you would have swell writing practice. Be careful not to send them stuff that is too long, and don't send them too many pieces. Write every day if you can, and send The New Yorker your best. (I'm a swell one to talk, who just got back two pieces.) My best advice is to concentrate on your typewriter; it's the most pleasant—and if you have the knack—the easiest way to work your way through. It's also quite the most dignified, and the way which will help most when you get out of college. By the way; a minor point: sign your name simply Thomas O'Hara when you write pieces. No middle initial.

These are the main points upon which I can pass on advice at this time. Later on, if and when you have more definite plans, I will be able to tell you some Yale lore, tradition, social custom and legend. But right now that isn't necessary. Concentrate now upon study and writing. If you like any minor sport, keep in practice in it, because there are prizes—very good ones—which are awarded for boys who are best in all-around activities, which includes studies and all extra-curricular activities: sport, leadership, cultural activities other than those you take "in course". You might even be a Rhodes scholar if you're a very good boy.

The best of luck. Don't let anything get in your way. I wish I'd had sense enough to take advantage of the chance you're giving yourself.

Love,
John

[1] Holograph.
[2] Drama critic.

TO: Robert Simonds   TLS, 1 p. with holograph footnote. PSt.
Postmarked 31 January 1932   19 W. 55 St., New York City

Dear Judge:

Many thanks for your note. I almost got a jag on, and I certainly got a healthy thirst when you told me about your supply. It's a good thing we have nothing like that here. I haven't had a drink in exactly one week (the longest spell, and quite unintentional, since you know when[1]). We've been so broke that we haven't dared, and I've been slaving away at the rewriting of The Hofman Estate, which suddenly began the other night.

I am writing to tell you it's a smart idea to let us know when you and Kate plan to come over, and this is why: embarrassing as it is to confess it, our phone's been disconnected (like my conversation), and I don't know when I'll have enough dough to pay the bill. I'm hoping either The New Yorker or Scribner's will come through next week, but . . . Anyhow, there is absolutely no likelihood of our being out of town, but tomorrow, for instance, we are going to Helen's mother's for dinner and then to the Philharmonic Concert, which we do every month or so, and if we didn't know in advance we might be in Brooklyn when you arrived. But we are planning no out-of-town trips, mon cher.

Next time you see Tom tell him Gibbs told me he'd had to reject a piece of his, but that Gibbs said it was intrinsically a good piece, and its chief fault was not in the writing but in the fact that it was a not unfamiliar idea. Tell him to read the magazine carefully and to keep sending stuff. (Can he write dialogue? They need that kind.)[1]

As to F.P.A., he annoys me at times, but I am very much in his debt, as you know. I would have guessed about the Bonwit Teller boner; he isn't on the World any more, and the Trib is run from the business department (and, of course, The White House), and no paper is getting too free with advertisers these days, believe you me.*

I wish I had some of your stuff right now. About a pint of it. I am twenty-seven years, three hours, old; and God! I hate it.

Come soon and stay long. Oh. Here's an idea. When you come, plan to take a small room for yourself at an inexpensive hotel, and I can sleep with you, and Kate can sleep here. Even if you take a double room you'll save money that way. A damn smart Jew, this O'Hara. My woman sends her love to you and your woman and so do I.

Johno

*As to Stackpole;[2] if you send him any more pieces you'll have a fight on your hands. . . .[3]

[1] Parenthetical material in holograph.
[2] Unidentified.
[3] Six words omitted by the editor.

TO: Thomas O'Hara   TLS, 3 pp. Mrs. O'Hara
Postmarked 20 May 1932   19 W. 55th St., New York City

Friday

Dear Tom:

This is to be a literary letter rather than one of guidance in pre-collegiate matters. I was at a guy's apartment last night, and he is a Yale man. I meant to ask him a lot of questions, but somehow the chance didn't present itself; his wife got scared of a mouse, and we played games, etc., etc.

And so, at the very outset I will say I was most agreeably surprised by your writing, which, of course, was the first specimen of your work I've seen. They are definitely mature pieces; far, far superior to many I've seen by older young men who regarded themselves with a great deal of seriousness in literary aptitude. I am not handing you any horseshit (I wonder if the modern young people know what that means. In these days of motor cars . . .) when I say you have a fine mind and a definite talent. Stick to it.

Now I will tell you what Gibbs told me Sunday night. We were having dinner in a speakeasy. Helen, another girl, Gibbs, and I. Gibbs was very drunk, and as sometimes happens when he gets like that, he got one of his Brutally Frank moods, in which the idea is to tell people that I know more about him than anyone else in the world; that I never take advantage of his friendship; that I am the God damn best writer The New Yorker has, but that I am stupid because I don't know what they want; that I am too obscure, and forget that The New Yorker is read by pretty dull people. Then he said: "And that's the trouble with your kid brother. You O'Haras simply refuse to recognize the fact that The New Yorker isn't for clever people. The New Yorker's for people who live on Riverside Drive. But you're stubborn," etc., etc. Well, he had just returned a piece of mine for that reason. The ending was too subtle. That's something to bear in mind when writing for that magazine. You must be subtly obvious, but not subtle, and not obvious.

I consider these pieces, and I will tell you why they were turned down (according to my guess, which is as good as any). The piece called "The Balcony" is, of course, patterned after Alice Frankforter and Patricia Collinge in the beginning.[1] That will never do. You're not allowed to do it. It's almost impossible to kid Jews in the magazine—not strange when you consider that Raoul Fleischmann owns it. You can't be very snobbish about them either. Another thing about the whole piece is that it is what is called the "stream of consciousness" type of thing. That is, you set down impressions and observations and thoughts as they come to you, as though you had a stenographer in your brain. This is an important development in modern literature; Marcel Proust is the acknowledged master of it (although personally I think Proust is heavy, dull, overrated, and sometimes ludicrous), but there are others among the young moderns who do it very well. You, I see, are among them. The piece I had in Scribner's was a sample. Incidentally, I never told you that Dorothy Parker[2] told me I would never be happy because I am a genius, and that she'd bet if Hemingway saw the Scribner's story[3] he wanted to cut his throat. I am sorry to be compelled to add that Mrs. Parker was tight, but I understand she has told other people the same thing about me. Pardon the digression, but you know how it is, uh? Say, that's great. Well, anyhow, to get back to your piece The Balcony. The final and chief reason The New Yorker rejected that one is (still according to my personal little guessy-wessy) that in New York everyone has been to the theater so often that any such piece as yours would not be acceptable to the would-be smart readers of The New Yorker, no matter how well written. The idea is

63

that people would say: "All right, what of it? People come to the theater drunk, so what?" But I maintain it is a swell piece of writing, and the fact that it did not make The New Yorker is unimportant right now. You'll make The New Yorker and take it in stride before you're much older.

The other piece is out, I believe, because they don't like to accept pieces that are not New Yorkish. By that I mean the piece either must be laid in New York, or in a place that would be familiar to the smart New Yorker. You must bear this in mind always. Pennsylvania mining country is not good copy in a magazine read by people who don't know the difference between anthracite and bituminous. In that connection I recall an experience which should give you The New Yorker's attitude. A couple of years ago I wrote some college satires. They said they'd take one or two, but insisted that the satires had to be Yale, Harvard or Princeton lads. You see the staff aren't kidding themselves, not by any means. They are kidding the wealthy Jews and others who read The New Yorker, and it is they who kid themselves.

Another thing in connection with that piece, and you might as well put this in your pipe and smoke it: kidding Rotary clubs went out with Mencken. It is passe. I suppose I was one of the last to do that successfully, and I haven't done it for a couple of years.

To summarize, I will be doing you no favor by urging you any longer to whip your style into New Yorker eligibility. I think you are too good for that. You might go over The Expert again and send it to F.P.A. just to see what'd happen. He might not use it, but you have something new and, at the moment, undefinably so, which might attract his attention. Mention me. My wife read your pieces and her conclusion was that you today have a better mind than I have. I bopped her on the snout and let it go at that. I know I can praise you without doing any harm, holding you back, or making you believe you are a finished writer. God knows writing can be the most discouraging form of expression in the world, but it's also the most exhilarating. When you sell an oil-burner you are only, after all, a sort of clerk; but when you sell a piece, one lousy measly little piece, you've sold something only you can manufacture. It's out of yourself, and its very lack of intrinsic value makes it all the more gratifying.

You must have misunderstood my letter if you gather that I have a contract at my job.[4] All I have is assurance that I can stay as long as I do the work (which is horrible drudgery) and Bob Sisk,[5] who has the contract, is in authority.

I will get down to brass tacks about the other matters when I see George Burgess, the Yale man, with whom I plan to have lunch one day next week. Meanwhile, follow Bob's advice and when you drink, drink pure apple or drug store alcohol-gin, etc. Give your stomach a break when you're starting. I'd probably be dead now if I hadn't started with old man Hoefel's pre-war stuff, which Fred and I used to steal. As it is I can't even trounce Gibbs at ping-pong without being stiff the next day.

Cherrio,
John

[1] Contributors to *The New Yorker*.
[2] In subsequent letters O'Hara refers to Mrs. Parker as "Dottie" or "Dot."
[3] Either "Alone," December 1931, or "Early Afternoon," July 1932.
[4] With RKO publicity.
[5] Public relations and advertising executive.

TO: Kyle Crichton   Wire. Princeton
23 May 1932   New York City

PLEASE READ LIBERTY MAY 21 STOP[1] MY STORY SUPERIOR BUT IF YOU DISAGREE BURN MANUSCRIPT BECAUSE DASHIELL WEBER BRIGHTON[2] THOUGHT MINE DECENT PIECE AND IF THEY WERE WRONG I MAY BE WRONG STOP I THINK STORY IS WORTH DECENT BREAK STOP IF YOU THINK NOT ITS TIME TO DECIDE

OHARA

[1] *Liberty* had published "Her People of the Patch," a story by Conrad Richter set in Pottsville. O'Hara's story was probably an early version of "The Doctor's Son," which was not published until 1935.
[2] Alfred Dashiell and William C. Weber were editors at Scribners; Brighton has not been identified.

TO: Harold Ross   TLS, 1 p. PSt.
1932   19 W. 55th St., New York City

Dear Ross:

I would like to write one of those "blind" profiles, or Character Sketches, or Portraits (by this time you've got the idea) of a chorine.[1] Specifically, a shaker; one of the burlesque chorines. They have a language all their own; a lot of it too rough for New Yorker consumption, but some of it pretty funny and printable. (I must tell you some time what they mean when they say "There's a couple of newspaper men out front".) The piece, of course, would be lovingly handled with that incisive attention to detail which has made me The New Yorker's most popular, best loved, oftenest demanded writer.

It would be a longish piece, and I don't want to go ahead with it unless you'd be interested in buying it. I understand, to be sure, that The New Yorker orders nothing except on speculation.

Faithfully,
John O'Hara

[1] "Of Thee I Sing, Baby" O'Hara's profile of a chorus girl, appeared in the 15 October 1932 issue. He subsequently collected it as a short story.

TO: Harold Ross
September 1932

TLS, 1 p. PSt.
RKO Distributing
Corp. letterhead

Thursday

Dear Ross:

I had dinner with Alva Johnston last night, and he told me (I hope I violate no confidence) that you are distrait over the lack of writers to do long pieces, meaning Profiles and Reporter pieces. He then suggested that I might talk to you about the Ed Wynn Profile, which had come up in a yesterday's meeting. I would like to do it.[1] I know a few things about Wynn, and can find out a lot more from Bob Sisk, who was Wynn's press agent just before coming to RKO. Can I have it?

Gibbs tells me there is a very good chance of your buying the chorus girl Profile, because he and Mrs. White liked it and thought you would too. If you do like it, I'd like to try one or two more of the same. I'd like to do one of a cop.[2] The material for that is readily available through my friend Arthur Chamberlin, assistant to the Commissioner and former newspaper man, as well as through my own various experiences with law-enforcing agencies.

Meanwhile I am getting together material on Father Hogan, president of Fordham University, whose Profile was assigned me a long time ago.[3]

I think the general tone of the book has picked up considerably in the last month or so. Johnston, of course, is always perfect, but I also liked Josephson's[4] piece about the Communist headquarters (and I've never liked Josephson before). The casuals,[5] too, have been better. Frank Sullivan's Parisian memoirs was the funniest thing he has written, and White's Theatre piece was so good that it must have been slightly embarrassing to the regular incumbent. And while the logs are rolling, I hope you never again get Tunis[6] to write tennis so long as Gibbs is handy. Oddly enough, Gibbs really knows tennis, which Tunis just doesn't.

Faithfully,
John O'Hara

There must be a postscript: Coates' "Self Portrait"[7] was swell, and I think you were very wise to forget, at least once, your dislike of pat endings.

[1] O'Hara apparently did not receive the assignment.
[2] Not published.
[3] Not published.
[4] Matthew Josephson.
[5] "Casual" was the *New Yorker* term for anything not written for a department—including fiction.
[6] Sportswriter John R. Tunis.
[7] Robert Coates' story was published 3 September 1932.

TO: Wolcott Gibbs   TLS, 1 p. PSt.
Fall–Winter 1932   New York City

Dear Wolc:

This is, as you will learn, the second of what could be a pretty funny series—not to mention a pretty lucrative one.[1] As a matter of fact I think it could go for about six pieces if Ross likes the idea. They will not be timely. That is, not depending on news events to carry them, and, be [*sic*] the same token, they need not be ruined by a subsequent news event. Unless, of course, Hoover and Roosevelt die, in which case I think you ought to buy them anyhow so people wouldn't forget Franklin and Herbert. I can get out enough of them within a week so you can arrange dates for the whole series, if you like (on speculation, of course).

Fitfully,
John

[1] The series has not been identified

TO: Robert Simonds   TLS, 3 pp. PSt.
October 1932   19 W. 55th St.,
                                                     New York City

Dear Robert:

The skimpy little telegram was meant to be expanded, this long time, into more words as well as into something a little more tangible, a little more material.[1] The words are beginning to pour forth, the rest will surely follow, and meanwhile, please forgive us if we seemed 150 miles away. On the other hand, if you hadn't noticed it, you can go plumb to hell, Young Simonds, and who do you think *you* are?

Today was my last under the happy sign of RKO, or the sign of the viscera. They fired me, pardner; they ousted me, and only because I missed, on the average, a day a week from hangover trouble. My boss is an old pal, and whatnot; but he insisted that pal or no pal, opal or diamond in the rough, I didn't belong in that p'ticular setting. I always was the last in the office, insisting on that as the prerogative of late-sleeping (albeit not latent) genius. But the others couldn't see it that way, and there was Talk; there were mumblings and murmurings about special privilege and teacher's pet. So today was my last as a publicity man for RKO. And am I glad! Now I have no excuse for not doing some decent work, and really I do feel a writing jag coming on. I don't know whether I have anything much, or important, to say, but I'm going to do a deal of writing, friend. I have two plays[2] to write, which have been sithering (how's that for a word?) within me for some time past. One of the ideas you'll be liking. Do you remember the old Christmas tree parties at the Boones'? Well, I would start my play with a sort of reunion of such: a wealthy guy decides to get the old bunch together, after ten years, just as they were in 1922; that is, the same people, the same furniture. The play would be an exposition of what had happened to them all in the intervening decade, and what would happen the night of the reunion. I think it's a hot idea—and a lousy one if it doesn't come off. But we must watch and pray. The other play is much in the Philip Barry tradition, and is too New Yorky for words. I don't want to start it till I've spoken for Katharine Hepburn and Pat O'Brien, whom I see in the leading roles, and no one else do I see. In addition, there is the item known as Novel, which I do want to get over and done with. I still may go to Hollywood for RKO, as a dialogroller (awful!), and I'd like to get an awful lot done before that happy day.

OLD LADY: I like it when you write about love.[3]

AUTHOR: I must say your marriage came as a complete shock. The breath of scandal had not singed the wings of either of you. I understood on fairly good authority that you were seeing quite a good deal of Miss Melley (I hope I have the name right), and that yours was one of those too, too rare friendships, based on a mutual love of literature, painting, apple, and punching people on the nose. Indignantly I denied, some months ago, that any such perversion as is implied in matrimony had ever reared its ugly head in the lovely companionship between you. But, alas (alas in wonderland; read it; a rather good book), how you let me, your arch-defender, down. As a result my wife and I have had little left to do but to make calculations, based on the normal period of gestation, and to agree on the thought that we wish you whatever solace may come to you in the sinful knowledge that by wallowing in the sordid pastime of connubial bliss, you may be forgetting your plain, however painful, duty. I mean, sir and madam, that as good citizens you must register, or you can't vote. And I hope you have fourteen small children, all crying for beer.

We remain at 19 West 55, not by reason of any unusual tolerance on the part of our landlords, but by grace of my having written and sold a Profile for The New Yorker,[4] which netted me the still incredible sum of

$175 ($175). The sum, in turn, was handed over to the proper person, and as a result I was able to hold up my head, practically erect (just $40 short of totally erect) and to sign a lease without so much as a bend. Which means that the same old Johns Manville will be our shelter for another twelvemonth, and if luck is with us, you kids will be, ere next October, so familiar with the layout that you will be able to find your way to us in the dark. I had rather hoped that finances would enable us to add a wing to our already spacious diggings, so that boys would not have to sleep with boys and girls with girls. However, there has been some talk about a depression, and in view of the fact that I have just received that 100% cut in salary, it is just as well we took no more roomy quarters. The owners voluntarily knocked $20 a month off our rent, so we have had as much as we could ask for. The only trouble is that while Helen's maw formerly paid $25 a month toward the rent, now that we had the cut she no longer contributes. A pity. A great pity. But we shall somehow weather it all.

As you may have heard, I went up to Providence with Tom in Joe's automobile. A pleasant little trip, and judging from the tenor of Tom's letters, he likes it pretty good there. He is out for the college daily, and I wouldn't be atall surprised if he were a success. I gave him the standard pep talk about college activities, fraternities, etc., which he later admited was about the same thing you previously had told him. I urged him to spurn invitations to Catholic frat-clubs, and to take the bid from the house he liked best at Brown, and not the one which has the big national rating. Dick Watts, a Sigma Chi if ever there was one, has written up about him; so has a DU friend of mine, and two Psi U's in the local newspaper racket. I have a hunch that you also wrote to Alpha Chi Rho—or do I mean Phi Doodle? At any rate, he'll come through all right. I only wish I had the stuff he's going to have on the w.k.[5] ball. I'm pretty well fed up on myself at this juncture. I wish I could take a vacation from myself. I have, of course, taken quite a number of overnight vacations; getting so cockeyed drunk that twenty hours elapse before I recover. But that's just the trouble. A change of scene is what I need more than anything else. Even so short a trip as the one to Providence made me realize that New York is licking me. I couldn't help thinking that the other day in a street car. A few years ago—say seven or eight—I could go to a town like Philadelphia, stay at a hotel, and get a swell kick out of listening to the city noises. I could get a kick out of uniformed delivery boys, and electric motor trucks, and elevated trains and orchestras unobtrusively playing at luncheon in the hotel diningrooms; mounted police and shops that sell $20 shoes. Maybe I could recapture that swell feeling in another city. Chicago still seems to me more of a city than New York, because I now know New York so well. God, to think that I recognize the faces of scores of cops and doormen between 42nd and 59th! Waiters in speakeasies and the Algonquin and Sardi's and B-G sandwich shops know me by name better than the same craftsmen at

George's or the Plaza—and in essence I don't like it. Perhaps that's the reason I liked Chicago. It was so completely foreign and strange, and I was so completely an outsider. And yet it isn't that I am really an *insider* here. I have few enough friends, and a lot of people who speak to me, really hate my guts. The spurious attentions, if you can call them that, of waiters and the like are entirely the result of 15% tips. . . . All this is rather familiar stuff, I am aware.

Well, when I write like that it certainly is time to call a halt. I am very glad youse guys got married and are off to a good start, for I don't know any two people who have the good wishes of so many, and such good, people. And much as we like to reminisce, you two are off to a start. From the old Manila[6] days down to the present was dandy fun for us, but in your case it was only a preparation for not a bad thing called the habit of matrimony. You two will thank God you did it. I thank God you did.

J. O'H.

[1] Simonds and Catherine Melley had been married on 2 September 1932.
[2] The plays were not written.
[3] O'Hara is parodying Hemingway's *Death in the Afternoon.*
[4] "Of Thee I Sing, Baby."
[5] Well-known.
[6] Manila Grove, a dance pavilion near Tamaqua, Pa.

TO: Robert Simonds   TLS, 4 pp. PSt.
c. December 1932   New York City

Dear Robert:

I don't go off half-cocked about things. For instance, when I write a letter, I don't just rush right out and post it without considering everything. I parse the sentences, criticize the *decor*, examine the philosophical content, re-discover the nuances—and then file the letter to think it over some more. Thus, you see, my few correspondents are almost always sure of two letters instead of one. As for instance.

I have just re-read the enclosed, and it's really quite a newsy letter.[1] It was written in October, to be sure, but nothing much has occurred to alter the statements. They are practically as though up-to-date (now there's a nice construction for you to wrinkle your brow over). I still am among the idle. I still plan to do some writing (of which, you may be sure, more anon), and so forth and so on. Money continues to circulate in our vicinity, but not on our premises. Life, as Vicki Baum[2] has it, goes on. The only remarkable event in my life has been staying on the wagon for a week.

Beyerle dropped in last night, and Robert, he can't take it any more. He had not more than six shots of gin, and when he left he was talking loud and—you know—confidentially. How the mighty have fallen! Hoefel dropped in a couple of weeks ago, and I got tight and finally let him have it. Not with my fist, but with words of abuse. I told him all the things, or at least quite a few of the things, that I have been wanting to tell him for a couple of years. I scored his social climbing, his attitude toward his old playmates, etc., etc. When he left I refused to shake hands. But he called up the next day, and he and Lesher and two girls and Pet went out to dinner together. I was absent. Otherwise I have seen no one we know. I survive. To show how things are really going, I went to a party at Emily Hahn's[3] a couple of weeks ago, and there saw some people I knew named Stephens. Stephens used to be Mary O'H's boss. I was introduced to his wife, and she said, "Are you *John* O'Hara?" I thought to myself, Good God, another New Yorker reader who is going to ask me who writes Talk of the Town (they all do, you know). But this one said: "You're not at all like I expected you to be. Mary was at our house for dinner the other night, and I gathered that you always needed a shave and a haircut. Why, you're really very—nice-looking!" That's the kind of thing Mary has been doing, apparently. So I got tight and called Mary up and gave her small-sized bawling out for it, but you can't intimidate Mary. The hell with her.

Which gets me around to something of a problem. You remember The Hofman Estate and The Doctor's Son, the two pieces I submitted in Scribner's contest? Well, I now have an idea about them which sounds sound. I showed the Doctor's Son to Howard and Betty Dietz, and I hear, from other sources, that they have gone around praising it to pretty influential people, among them Guinzburg, of the Viking Press. My idea is this: make a few changes in both stories; that is, give them a definite common locale (such as referring to Pottsville by a fictitious name, but using the same name in both stories), and writing a third story, also with the same locale, and putting them in one book together. I would write a third story, about someone like Puss or Furdummt, to complete what might inaccurately be called a trilogy. It would be a post-war picture of The Region, from the standpoint of the three classes: the Sheafer aristocrats,[4] the middle class O'Haras, and the Schwackie[5] gangster type. You'd have the three classes and the predominating races in just about the right periods. Don't you think it sounds good? All I'd have to do would be to make the simple changes in the stories I have, and write the third. Which is where you come in.

As soon as I get some money, and we can arrange it, I want to see you. It would be nice of you to invite Pet and me for a weekend. The girls could talk about their spinning and tatting, and we could talk about Letters (or is that a sore point, an unfortunate word?). Pet gets bored when I talk about The Region, and I get sore when she gets bored, and so on. We could have a nice get-together as a foursome, and also as a pair of two-somes. Or am I protruding, as Beatrice Lillie would say? You see, I would like to sit around and chew the fat, sort of to refresh my memory about the roundheader boys, and to Study Conditions. You and I might even go for a spin in the general direction of Pottsville, although not in it, to be sure. I honestly think there is a good book out of such a "trilogy" and I'm pretty sure I could get it published. I have plenty of time on my hands, and the will to do, and so forth. Also, I could use the money. I could use any money, down to, and including, a dollar. I have a lot of work to do. I have an assignment for a two-part Profile of a typical New York cop, and when it's accepted (which, of course, will be some time after it's written) I'll get about $400 for it; not to mention one other Profile, and also some fictional pieces. I have one at Scribner's now, which, if they buy (there's always the chance that they might, you know) it, you'll enjoy. I won't tell you about it now. So, as is always the case with me, prosperity is just around a couple of corners. I'm not even looking for a job. What's the use, when shoe leather costs so much? And why go out and deliberately put myself in a position which ultimately will be only disheartening?

Getting back to the book (never very far away from it, I'll agree), what do you think of this idea? In the book about the Sheafers, I brought them up to about the time of the crash, but, of course, did not refer to it. The Doctor's Son was left hanging, as it were, at about the age of 14, just after the war. Now the third story, about the Schuylkill County gangster, could be built around a guy like that Malloy[6] (if that's the name), but not an Irishman. He would have to be a Schwackie. The gangster might be a sort of hanger-on at a roadhouse which was occasionally visited by the Pottsville country club set. I would bring the doctor's son up to date, as of 1930; a drinker, roustabout, etc., playing around with the Sheafers. The roadhouse could be either a place like Turin's, or like the Log Cabin. The third story most likely would be told through the eyes of the gangster, whose job would be that of assistant manager (at a place like Turin's), or, if we decided on a lower-scale dump, the gangster could be just one of those mysterious pimps or bootleggers, whose source of income is never very definite, so far as you and I can be sure. He would be attractive, in a common way, and we could have Polly falling for him, the doctor's son either picking a fight or being a pal, and Clint being friendly but superior. In the first two stories there would be only slight relationship between the two: a common locale, and names of towns and streets and people would appear now and then in both stories, but in the third story the people would really get together in the same roadhouse barroom. It might be effective to have the whole story take place over a period of one night; from the time the gangster comes around, early in the evening, to "go to work", until dawn the next morning, when the night's festivities had ended. This would give me an opportunity to give a complete picture of the roadhouse, with a lot of behind-the-scenes stuff, such as the arrival of the liquor in a Reo speed-wagon (Turin's, I really think, would be the best place), and a few unimportant people having dinner, and Papa[7] and the gangster talking business, and a small orchestra setting up their instruments, getting ready for the nightly brawl, etc., etc. If you and Kate could have us for a week-end, or even if I could come over alone, and you could tell Papa in advance what I have in mind, I think the atmosphere would be all set. You and I could go up there early in the evening, or late in the afternoon, and just hang around and watch things. You could assure Papa that I have no designs on his place, that I'm not a Prohi agent, and that I would not libel him.

I'm really enthusiastic about this whole idea. It would combine pleasure with pleasure to come to Allentown. It doesn't seem as if you two plan to come to New York soon, and we're eager to see you. For instance, although you've been married more than four months, I'm sure there are things you must learn. I could show you how to administer a punch in the jaw without inflicting an embarrassing bruise on your wife's chin, and my Mrs. could show your Mrs. how to place crackers in a husband's bed with a maximum of effectiveness. These things take at least a year to master, and no marriage can be a success without them. We would guarantee not to be expensive guests, because through lack of wherewithal, we have forgotten how to spend money. As a matter of fact, if you *should* decide to have us, the trip would have to wait until I get enough money to cover the rock-bottom expenses, such as railroad fare. We have felt lousy about not crashing through with a wedding present, but if you knew the sales talks I've been giving the landlord, you'd understand. I'm sure you do anyhow. The truth is, we've been living on Pet's allowance of $100 a month, and just not paying the rent. We pay "something on it" when I sell a piece. I've rewritten one piece three times, which The New Yorker is now considering, and in the last seven weeks I've sold two, for a total of $95. Well, I never expected to own a yacht. Our love and the seasonal humbug go with this screed. And so, leaving you a large amount of scratch paper, I beg to remain, your New York correspondent.

Johno

[1] The preceding letter to Simonds.

[2] German novelist, author of *And Life Goes On* (1931).

[3] Contributor to *The New Yorker*.

[4] Clinton and Polly Sheafer, a wealthy Pottsville couple. O'Hara's character Whit Hofman was based on Sheafer.

[5] "Schwackie" was a Pottsville term for people of Eastern European descent.

[6] Jimmy Malloy became a persona for O'Hara in "The Doctor's Son" and other stories.

[7] Papa Turin, the proprietor of the roadhouse.

———◆◆———

O'Hara and Pet separated in the spring of 1933. In May of that year O'Hara went to Pittsburgh as managing editor (without title) of the Bulletin Index, a weekly news and social magazine. He was deeply unhappy in Pittsburgh and suffered guilt over the collapse of his marriage. On 15 August Pet obtained a Reno divorce on the grounds of extreme cruelty. During the same month O'Hara was fired by the owners of the magazine and returned to New York.

TO: Kyle Crichton   ALS, 2 pp. Princeton
May 1933   Letterhead of William Penn
                                                             Hotel, Pittsburgh

Dear Kyle—

This is what happens to minor talents. They become outland celebrities, live on due bills, and park their asses at University Clubs and talk about what they said to Tallulah Bankhead.

If there is anything to be done about either of those stories will you let me know what? With the sport-writer one you can do as you like. That is, make any changes you deem essential to a sale. The other (the long-short one) will take more of a bit of doing, and I wish when you return it you'd go into some detail as to what changes should be made—if they still want to order a rewritten version.

I shall be here, barring assassination by the hand of an outraged father of a contented calf, for at least a couple of months. I am not making much in the way of actual cash, but I can run up a $50-a-week bill here under the terms of my agreement. It's nice to know where your next 180 meals are coming from.

The next story you get will be for Scribner's, and it will be another "Alone." I now fully realize that I love my wife, and you'll see a story with plenty of depth, kid.

Yrs.
Mr. O'Hara

TO: Kyle Crichton   TLS, 2 pp. Princeton
June 1933   Letterhead of William Penn
                                                             Hotel, Pittsburgh

Dear Kyle:

Here is a little jewel, a fine bit of bitterness without laying it on too thick. I wouldn't be at all surprised if you boys broke down and bought this one.

Notice O'Hara in O'Brien's "Distinctive" list?[1] Five of them, boy. Only two other writers (F. Scott Fitzgerald and Kay Boyle) in the world had more stories on the list. They each had six. And did you notice that my annual Scribner's story[2] got **? I tell you, boy, all you have to do is buy them. They get noticed.

I have a swell idea for a collection of pieces, if some foolhardy publisher would care to publish it: print all the stories (13, I think) which have received O'Brien rating, under the title, "O'Brien Liked Them" (with his permission, of course). It would make a nice little book, and if all my creditors bought a copy, I'd be able to pay one of them.

I'm still here, as you see. I rather liked your piece on Lehigh, but not that Open Letter, boy. Not that Open Letter. When you write pieces of that kind don't spell Synge, Singe, etc. You have some others, too. And for gosh sakes, will you buy some good pieces for Scribner's? Not necessarily mine, boy. But some good ones. I am a cash reader of the magazine, besides a worthy contributor, and when I buy the mag I want my 50¢ worth. Did anybody read that story of Wolfe's?[3] The dialog was so incredibly bad that it should have embarrassed everyone, beginning with Woofie himself. Look Around, Angel.

Give all the voluptuous gals (like Noel) a pat on the behind for me, and in your less libidinous moments remember me to the Mrs. and to Weber. No telling, I may be ousted here, but so far no signs of it. Doing a good job of it, boy.

Now go ahead and encourage a young writer, 28 years old, now editing The Bulletin Index.

Chee-ro
Mr. O'Hara

Are you going to make old Billy Phelps As I Like It Emeritus?[4]

[1] Edward J. O'Brien edited an annual collection of *The Best Short Stories*.
[2] "Early Afternoon."
[3] Probably Thomas Wolfe's "A Portrait of Bascom Hawke," *Scribner's Magazine* (April 1932), which won the short-novel prize contest O'Hara had entered.
[4] William Lyon Phelps wrote a department for *Scribner's* called "As I Like It."

TO: F. Scott Fitzgerald[1]   TLS, 1 p. Princeton
                                                      Letterhead of William Penn
                                                              Hotel, Pittsburgh

June 25 [1933]

Well;

You've written another swell piece, doing again several of the things you do so well, and doing them in a single piece.[2] Miss Jean Gunther, of the More Than Just a House Gunthers, was one of those girls for the writing about of whom you hold the exclusive franchise, if you can puzzle out that sentence. It was really all told when she told Lew Lowrie, "Well, at least you've kissed one Gunther girl." Not to get too autobiographical about it, she's the type that the Lowries and O'Haras never have been able to cope with, and in my experience I've encountered a complete set of them. Have right here, in this really Fitzgeraldian city, where I am editing a magazine for the upper crust.[3]

And that easily we get to the second thing you've done so well: Lowrie, the climber; and I wonder why you do the climber so well. Is it the Irish in you? *Must* the Irish always have a lot of climber in them? Good God! I am the son of a black Irish doctor (gone to his eternal reward) and a mother who was a Sacred Heart girl, whose father was born Israel Delaney (Pennsylvania Quaker who turned Catholic to marry an immigrant girl, Liza Roarke). My old man was the first doctor in the U.S. to use oxygen in pneumonia, was recognized by Deaver[4] as being one of the best trephiners and appendix men in the world. But do I have to tell you which side of the family impresses me most? I doubt it. You've guessed it: because Grandfather Delaney's connections included some Haarmons from Holland and a Gray who was an a.d.c. to Washington, and I have some remote kinship with those N.Y. Pells, I go through cheap shame when the O'Hara side gets too close for comfort. If you've had the same trouble, at least you've turned it into a gift, but I suspect that Al Smith is the only Irishman who isn't a climber at heart. Anyhow in Lowrie you've done a sort of minor Gatsby. (By the way, I saw Warner Baxter in a pretty bad movie tonight.)

Another thing you did was to take a rather fantastic little detail—the girl wearing bedroom slippers with Jodhpurs—and put it across by timing it just right. You got the old man's madness with the detail of the $20 he borrowed in 1892, and once again you dabbled successfully in death. Oh, hell. A swell piece.

I read somewhere that you are in Maryland, and I hope things are breaking better for you than they were when I last heard from you, which was from Lausanne. Breaking fine for me. My pretty little wife is rolling out to Reno next week, and the girl I loved from the time I was 17 got married in Haiti last month,[5] to a Byronic lad whom she'd known about two months. And she was the shadow on the wall that broke up my marriage. Oh, my.

John O'Hara

---

[1] This is the earliest located letter from O'Hara to Fitzgerald, but he probably began writing to him in the Twenties. Fitzgerald wrote "Save" at the top of the letter.

[2] "More than Just a House," *The Saturday Evening Post* (24 June 1933).

[3] This letter prompted Fitzgerald's widely quoted letter of 18 July about his own social insecurity: "So if I were elected King of Scotland tomorrow after graduating from Eton, Magdalene to Guards, with an embryonic history which tied me to the plantagonists [sic], I would still be a parvenue."

[4] Dr. John B. Deaver, distinguished Philadelphia surgeon.

[5] Margaretta Archbald Kroll.

TLS, 1 p. Princeton
Letterhead of William Penn
Hotel, Pittsburgh

Dear Kyle:

Mr. O'Hara is your humble servant, Mr. O'Hara is mortified, ashamed, beholden, chagrined, embarrassed, apologetic, humiliated. Mr. O'Hara has found the MS. of The Hofman Estate, tucked away among other items in the Second Thought file.

I am sending you another piece,[1] by way of making up. You can reject this number, and then you'll feel better again. Unfortunately it is a pretty fair item, with some Depth, and you may like it; but it does not say anything about how lovely it is to be hungry in Vermont, or how terrible it is to see someone die in Amsterdam Avenue, so I suppose it can be turned down on the ground that the people written about are not worthy of a writer's talent, if any.

Still here, more than two months, and doing an excellent job, but making just about the same money. I'm being honorable, for a change, and paying off some debts, but along about football season I hope to be out of the red and maybe the owner of a third-hand Austin. I played 18 holes of golf yesterday, and boy, can I smack them! First time I played since Bermuda, but I had four drives more than 200 yards long.

Yrs.
J. O'H.

[1] Unidentified.

TLS, 1 p. Princeton
Letterhead of William Penn
Hotel, Pittsburgh

Dear Kyle:

I think a lot of what you said is a lot of crap, for the reason that I know so much better than anyone else that I have an inferior talent. The reason I think I have an inferior talent is that when I write I can't sustain an emotion. It isn't that I don't feel things, but when I begin to write out of hate, I find myself being diverted into tolerance; and when I write about love, or from love, I get critical and nasty. Only once in a while can I sustain either of the two, and the pieces in The New Yorker are the ones that start from hate, and here is one that started from love. I can't tell you, though, whether it's a good piece, but it has plenty of feeling in it. But I'm not important, and I never will be. The next best thing is to be facile and clever. But thank you for the analysis and the kind words. I get nothing of the kind here, and I miss them.

The University piece[1] is coming under separate cover. I wonder if Dashiell and Perkins know you used their name in a piece. . . .[2]

Yrs.
John

[1] Unidentified.
[2] Alfred Dashiell and Maxwell E. Perkins, editors at Scribners. Crichton's piece has not been identified.

TO: James Thurber?   TLS, 1 p. PSt.
September 1933   New York City

Jim:

I hear Niven Busch has resigned. What are the chances, therefore, of my doing football?[1] I know the game, have covered it, have played it, and I like to watch it. I've written some pieces for The New Yorker on football figures—Portrait of a Referee, of a Manager, satirical fight talks, etc., all of which are in the files of my stuff—and I know I would do at least as good a job as Busch did. I've covered both college and professional (which, of course, is infinitely more scientific football than the college game) games from Providence to Muhlenburg.

O'Hara

[1] O'Hara wrote four football articles for The New Yorker in November-December 1933.

TO: F. Scott Fitzgerald   TLS, 1 p. Princeton
                                              230 E. 51st. St., New York City[1]

October 14–15, 1933
Dear Mr. Fitzgerald:

A little story I have to tell you runs about like this: a bunch of the boys and girls were sitting around Tony's last night, and Jim Thurber began to rave about a piece you wrote in The New Republic. Dottie Parker, who knows about my admiration for your writing, said to me: "Did you hear that, John? Jim just said Scott has a beautiful piece about Lardner in The New Republic."[2] So on the way home I stopped at an all-night newsstand and bought a New Republic, blind, and went into a beanery to read your piece. But it was not the right issue, so I went to another newsstand across the street and said, "Have you got last week's New Republic?" The man said, with a smile: "Why yes, I have, but it's tied up in this bundle (indicating a tightly tied bundle of old magazines). You want it for the article on Lardner I guess." So he got it out for me. He said he had had a lot of requests for that issue of The New Republic, and wondered why, and made a point of finding out. "And so I read it," he said. "It's a wonderful article."

I read the piece over and over, and tonight I gave the magazine to Mrs. Parker. We stopped here, where I am living, while I went upstairs and got it, and then we went to a Baltimore Dairy Lunch (by a coincidence) and she read the piece, and she wept tears. The only thing I could think of to say was "Isn't it swell?" You know. The usual inarticulate O'Hara. Mrs. Parker said: "The Gettysburg Address was good too."

Last night I tried to write to you to tell you what I thought of the piece, but I gave it up, because I told myself that you'd rather not hear what anyone thought of what you thought. But tonight I write regardless. I think you ought to know that I do mean to tell you what I think of the piece. The only thing is, you'll have to guess by my incoherent words. If you never wrote anything else, if you never had written This Side of Paradise, "Ring" would have been a writing [career]³ enough for anyone. But then if you hadn't written This Side of [Para]dise you probably wouldn't be the man who did write "Ring". (I [don't] seem to have any consistent style about quotes and titles. Do [you] mind?) I only hope no one else tries to do a piece on Lardner. [You] have said all that should be said. Lardner must have made the [nine] First Fridays⁴ to get that piece—and I mean that as reverently [as I] can mean anything.

All this from one who has been a frank imitator of Lardner.

Regards.
John O'Hara

¹ After his return to New York from Pittsburgh, O'Hara lived at the Pickwick Arms Club Residence, the hotel where he wrote *Appointment in Samarra*.

² "Ring," 11 October 1933.

³ The lower right corner of this letter is missing; bracketed words are inferential.

⁴ A Catholic who takes Communion on nine consecutive first Fridays of the month is promised the opportunity to enter eternity with proper dispositions and grace.

TO: Thomas O'Hara

TLS, 3 pp. Mrs. O'Hara
230 E. 51st St., New York City
October 23, 1933

Dear Tom:

Are you a tall thin fellow by the name of O'Hara? I used to be a brother to someone who answered that description, and I was just wondering whether it was you or not. If it is, I'm very glad to renew the acquaintance and why don't we have lunch some time?

Gibbs forwarded your note as soon as he got it, and I was mighty pleased to get it. The trouble with that sentence is it hasn't any get to it. Anyhow, picking up the thread of the conversation where I left off to be self-conscious, I meant to write you right away, but I didn't, for no good reason. I am, as you see, back in New York. I am not working, but am getting by with pieces for The New Yorker, which have been selling well enough to keep my belly provided for, but not so well that I don't dread the coming of colder weather. I have an overcoat and a fur coat at Macy's, in storage, but I owe two years' storage on them, so I haven't tried to get them, and even so when I do try I may find that they have been sold. I have no plans except to live until I die, which may be for weeks, and may be (though God forbid) forever. As I daresay you know (though how, I cannot tell) that I was divorced in Reno in the first week in August. Pet and her mother went out there. Then I got thoroughly fed up with Pittsburgh and my job there, and quit. You may have heard some story to the effect that Pet went to Pittsburgh with me and did not get the divorce. It was untrue. She did not go to Pittsburgh with me. Well, I got fed up with the job at about the same time that Pet was to return from Reno, so I quit and came to New York and saw Pet the day she got back, and have been seeing her ever since. That was about August 12, when she got back. I want her to marry me again, and this time make a go of it, and she says she will if I get a job and make some money. The money is necessary, because in the first place, she is living with her mother and uncle, and they don't even know I'm in New York, let alone suspect that she is seeing me, and if she marries me again she'll never get a cent from them. So I am looking around for a good job. I dream of going to Hollywood and making large sums there, but I don't suppose that ever will come true, so I am on the make here. That really is a resumé of my life, except to add that since July 4 I have been a sober citizen. I got good and drunk, I mean good and drunk, the night of July 3, and then went on the wagon, and the most I have had in any one day since then has been a cocktail and a glass of wine at dinner. At no other time I have taken so much as a single cocktail. I am down to 174 lbs on the hoof, and while in Pittsburgh I took up golf in a surprisingly pleasing way. I shot pretty consistently in the 80's, and if I'd remained in that lovely city I might have been shooting par by this time. However I might also have been shooting myself, so my golf game would have been just about where it is now; non-existent.

I am leading what is called a life, but there isn't anything to it. I am staying at a place called the Pickwick Arms Club Residence, above address, Eldorado 5–0300, because my room costs $8 a week without bath. Still I don't miss the bath, as I am not in favor of pampering children the way these modern parents do. I usually sleep all day, get up and have breakfast, meet Pet and go to the movies or something, sneak her home, and then go to Tony's and talk with Dottie Parker, who is by way of being one of my best friends at this point. Or else I go to the Gershwins', Ira and wife, and play backgammon for a cent or a dime a game. I come home late— around three—and try to write something, and read the morning papers, and then take some aspirin for my cold and then go to sleep. I have a feeling that all this is time-out preparatory to something terrible happening to me, but I almost don't care. My little pieces in The New Yorker, unimportant though they are, are the only things that make the difference between my being dead and alive. I don't mean only that the money keeps me alive. I mean that I do nothing else, and except for them I might as well be dead. I turned out a beautiful story two weeks ago, got a note from one of the editors of Scribner's which I am too modest to quote— and then they finally rejected the piece. So I *accept* this mantle of mediocrity, from whatever source it came, without even bothering about whether it fits.

Obviously you did not go back to Brown, and I don't suppose it makes much difference, unless you wanted to go back. In a way it's a good thing you didn't go back, especially if you didn't want to. After all, you have a label if you need one. You can always say, "I went to Brown," which is much better than saying you went to a thousand other places I could name. And when you don't need a label, you don't wear one. You were not there long enough for it to influence you much in any but a superficial way. You know about the right kind of clothes, you have seen boys from strange parts of the U.S., you have been away from home and pretty much on your own, and you may even have captured some disillusionment. However, you are very intelligent anyway, and you might have got that, at least, without going to college. Still, it's better to acquire it at college I suppose. It sort of crystallizes it, which is much better than to have a lot of illusions and anaemic hopes bubbling around until you're twenty-eight years old. I would like to see you on a paper. I'm curious to know what you're doing anyhow. I don't think there's much future on a paper, but I don't think there's much future in anything right now. We're in the Darker Ages, with wars or rumors of wars, men flying like birds almost, and the people not ready to turn to God. But come, we mustn't get into that. Let it stand with I think journalism would be the most fun for you, and it may turn out also to be the most profitable, and what have you got to lose?

It is quate daylight now, quate, and I ought to get some sleep as I am going to two very dull parties tomorrow, and I want to be at my dullest. Write me at length. How tall is Genie?[1] I was wondering about him today, and according to my figures he ought to be 15 in March, and in freshman high school, the idol of the ladies and a hot-cha-cha. I suppose he never asks about the picture that's turned to the wall. Now spread yourself, son. At ten cents a word this is a valuable letter.

John

Have you any Simonds news? They have a baby yet or anything?

[1] O'Hara's youngest brother, Eugene.

In December 1933 O'Hara began writing the novel which would become Appointment in Samarra. *On 16 January 1934 he informed Simonds: "30,000 words done at this point, and 60,000 more to come." When he ran out of money, Harcourt, Brace provided a $400 advance for completion of the novel. The typescript was delivered on 9 April 1934.*

TO: Harold Ross

TLS, 1 p. PSt.
Letterhead of Pickwick Arms,
New York City

January 5, 1934

Dear Harold:

I have been going over my history, and I find that I am approaching a New Year, the seventh year of my association with The New Yorker. I have had dealings with The New Yorker in the years 1928, 1929, 1930, 1931, 1932, 1933. During that time I have done everything except to sell a drawing: I have written casuals, a column of Notes & Comment, several Talk items, newsbreaks, one department, one Profile, and two tips on pieces by Frank Sullivan and Robert Benchley. The association has been uniformly pleasant for me, and I hope satisfactory to you. I have resented very few rejections. The good pieces I wrote have been recognized by O'Brien and other collectors, or recommended by Winchell[1] or Russel Crouse,[2] and the bad pieces have been forgotten by my enemies. I have sold more than a hundred casuals, and so far as I know, caused only one cancellation of subscription (a football column brought that about). And so I think it would be nice if you were to have a medal struck, or did something else in the way of commemorating what I believe to be a fact: that in the period beginning 1928 I have contributed more pieces to The New Yorker than any other non-staff man. This year I hope not only to sell you a great many pieces, but also to round out my record with the sale of a drawing; thus establishing me as one who has done everything on The New Yorker.

With best wishes,

Faithfully,
John O'Hara

A dollar bonus on each casual—nice!

[1] Walter Winchell, gossip columnist and broadcaster.
[2] Journalist who later collaborated with Howard Lindsay in writing *Life with Father* (1939), among other successful theater works.

TO: Thomas O'Hara
Postmarked 12 February 1934

TLS, 4 pp. Mrs. O'Hara
Letterhead of Pickwick Arms,
New York City

Dear Tom:

I ought to wait, I guess, until I get into the right mood to write you, but what I usually recognize as the right mood hasn't come over me since your letter came, so I might as well write now. I keep forgetting that there is no way except by a letter from me by which you can hear what has been going on in this lovely life of mine, and that may be a good thing at this point, because without it I'd have little enough else to write about.

The most important news, so far as I'm concerned, is that I've sold a novel. An unfinished novel. Just before Christmas I started to work on it, and I did 25,000 words without taking time out to write a single magazine piece. Then I began to get little notes, then bigger notes, from the proprietors of this Work of Art,[1] reminding me that the most important rule of the place was Payable in Advance. So, with no money coming in, I did take time out to write to three publishers: Harcourt, Brace; Viking Press; Wm. Morrow & Co. I told them all the same thing; that I was doing a novel, and wanted to finish it without having to interrupt my writing streak, if you could call it that, to do stuff for The New Yorker. I told them I would show them what I had written, providing they would agree to read it with the thought in mind that if they liked it they would pay me a subsidy to live on while I finished it. I mailed the letters, and the next day all three publishers phoned me (at one time or another all three had asked me to do a novel). I took the one that phoned first. I showed Harcourt, Brace the MS., and they kept it over night and the next day phoned me to find out if I would come in and tell them what I was going to do with the characters, how long I expected the novel to be, what further action was to take place. I went in and told them these things, and they signed me a contract: $50 a week for eight weeks. That was three weeks ago, and the novel now is about half finished. The $400 counts as advance royalties, to be charged against the book if and when it begins to sell. It is to be completed by April 1, and will be published in the fall. Harcourt himself said it was the most promising part-manuscript he'd ever read, and so far we are all pleased. But now that it is half finished I am suffering from what Dorothy Parker says Ernest Hemingway calls "the artist's reward"—in other words, I think what I've written stinks, and I just can't seem to get going again. I gave the MS to Mrs. Parker, who took it away with her over the weekend, and has promised me an opinion. I have worked like hell on it when I've worked, and the two people who have read it (besides the Harcourt Brace people) like it. I refer to Mary March, whose family our parents met in Kentucky, and to Helen P. O'Hara, who has the best taste of anyone I know. What I am doing now is stalling. I work in jags. I work like the devil for days at a time, and then suddenly I dry up or get stale, or get physically too tired to go on.

The locale of the novel is Pottsville, called Gibbsville in the novel. Mahantongo Street is called Mantenengo Street.[2] All points in Schuylkill County are given fictitious names—Taqua, for instance. And others you will recognize. Points outside Schuylkill County—Hazleton, Easton, Reading, Wilkes-Barre—are mentioned by their right names. The plot of the novel, which is quite slight, is rather hard to tell, but it concerns a young man and his wife, members of the club set, and how the young man starts off the Christmas 1930 holidays by throwing a drink in the face of a man who has aided him financially. From then on I show how fear of retribution and the kind of life the young man has led and other things contribute to his demise. There are quite a few other characters, some drawn from life, others imaginary, who figure in the novel, but the story is essentially the story of a young married couple and their breakdown in the first year of the depression. I have no illusions about its being the great or the second-great American novel, but it's my first. And my second will be better. All I care about now is getting it finished, written. I'll be able to edit and to polish off etc. after I've done the labor of setting down what I have to tell. I have done no rewriting up to now and very little editing. From now on, when I get the MS back from Dottie, I will have to work much harder than I have done, but I know where I'm going, God help me.

I see I keep referring to Mrs. Parker. Right now I think she is the best friend I have in the world. You append a little note to your letter, a question asking how I got along without an overcoat. I couldn't have. Just before Christmas I was going to go away for a weekend with Helen and then I got a rejection from The New Yorker which put the kibosh on the weekend, and I mentioned it to Dottie. Without a word she got up and wrote a cheque for $50 so we could go away. I couldn't refuse it, even if I'd wanted to. Then Helen got afraid (her people think I'm still in Pittsburgh) and the weekend was put off, so I took the money and got my coats out of Macy's storage. I had the football job which kept me going all fall, and I sold a piece now and then by which I managed to keep going afterward. I sold a story to Harper's Bazaar,[3] for instance, for $125, which came in the nick of time, whatever the nick of time is. So I have not frozen. In between times, when I managed badly, I skipped a day now and then without a meal, I mean I had a day—*you* know.

About your writing, once again, Tom. If you're going to write, you're going to write. You probably read the profile of Sinclair Lewis. Well, that's the story of Sinclair Lewis. The stories of no two writers are the same. There is a guy like David Burnham, whom I used to know, whose father was a railroad president and very rich. On the other hand there is James T. Farrel. It happens that most of the guys I like to read have had newspaper experience, but some of them haven't. Scott Fitzgerald didn't. He came of a wealthy family, who lost a lot of money around wartime. I told Harold Ross I would like to have a job at $250 a week and he said what for and I said so I could do something for my relations, and he said, "Yes. And make them unhappy." He pointed out his own case and the case of his mother, who was happy in Aspen, Colorado, until son Harold made money and began to spend it on her. She came east, and hasn't been happy since then. I don't agree with Ross. If I ever amount to anything I'm going to owe a lot to a lot of people who paused to do me small favors—F.P.A., for instance to whom I am dedicating my novel. I say if I ever amount to anything as though I had all the time in the world, when I know nothing could be much farther from the truth. I have been on the wagon seven months, but even with that I don't give myself more than five years to live. I don't expect to drink again, by the way. Anyhow, for the moment the only encouragement I can give you is pretty intangible stuff, to wit, you know I'm for you. But don't bother your pretty head so much about how to write. *Write.* Keep a diary, for one thing. Set down in it such things as the feeling of Pottsville people about the CWA;[4] write in slang as much as you can. Write down the names of the tunes of the day and the girls you love. Write down the kind of clothes women are wearing. I kept a diary once, in 1922-23, and I'll never forget that year. That was a great year; I was home from school, between Kutztown and Niagara, and it was the first year Marg and I were in love. I haven't seen that diary for a long time, but I can remember movies, tunes, clothes, slang, parties—everything. I must have been a good reporter. Then. I wrote down what I thought of books and what I thought of my father, and I was embarrassingly honest about both. You, of course, are growing up in a different environment and an almost completely different set of circumstances. I don't know which I'd rather be in, but I guess my years were better for me, and yours are for you. I might point out, too, that I do not keep a diary now. I could use one, but these days I write pieces instead of a diary. And don't tell anyone you're keeping it. People, stupid people, kid you for it, because stupid people think you have to write "Dear Diary—" Well, there was a guy named Pepys who did pretty well for himself by keeping one. You don't remember who was king in that day, but you do remember Pepys.

Interesting fact I dug up. The name O'Hara used to be spelt: O'h-Eadhradh. If you can pronounce it you can have it.

To get to more tangible things, I told Stanley Walker about you, and he said he would keep his ears open for something. I also have written to a friend of mine named Gude, a publicity man with Columbia Broadcasting, who went to Brown and wanted to send up a letter about you to the Psi U's. He probably won't have anything, and Stanley Walker is a four-flusher, but we keep on trying. Keep on trying The New Yorker, but also keep on with magazines like Scribner's in mind. The man to send stuff to Scribner's to is Alfred Dashiell, who is no special friend of mine, but knows me. Why don't you try to write an article about your CWA experiences? An honest, reportorial piece, telling what you and all lads your age think. If you know the economic angles, spill them, but don't unless you're sure of your ground. I bought a couple of Pubs[5] a couple of weeks ago, and found that one of the most interesting men in Pottsville had died without my ever knowing him. I refer to one Wm. Garretson, who witnessed the kidnapping of Charlie Ross.[6] Boy, you don't have to go away from Pottsville to get people to write about. Write a piece about Squirrel Row. Get mother to tell you the histories of the Muirs, McClures, Chambers, Althouses, McCools. Why, Faulkner never had anyone like them to write about, and they're right at your doorstep. Write a novel about Charlie Snyder,[7] for God's sake. Or Claude Lord.[8] In my novel I am using characters whom I'm going to write about in my next novel. Write a novel about Grandpa.[9] There is a man worth writing about; how he carried the miners in I think it was the 1902 strike, how he practically taught them to speak English, did their banking. Or that fantastic character, Grandfather O'Hara. Find out things about them while there are still people alive who can tell you about them. Do you know anything about the Mansion House in Mount Carbon? Punk[10] will tell you about it. Or the history of George Street.[11] Or your friend Strangler Lewis.[12] I'd love to be back there for a while and refresh my memory on some of those people. By the way, I take good care of Mrs. Howell[13] in my novel, and I give her a fictitious name that ought to give you a laugh: Lydia Faunce Brown. Do you knowabout Albert Kear and Jack Lee? (Or maybe it was Tom Rickert.) Write a piece about a live bird match, and if you want a real one get Walter to tell you about the time Johnnie Clemens dropped dead at one. By the way, you'll never in your life meet a finer man than Walter Farquhar, and I hope you know that without my telling you. And what is more, my son, he's a gentleman.

I think I have held forth long enough for the moment. I don't make much sense, maybe. I'm twenty-nine years old now, and I don't see as good as I used to. I went all the way to New Philly the other day, thinking I was on the Minersvull car.[14] If I hear anything I'll let you know, but I probably won't hear anything but the banging of this noiseless portable (anyhow it's portable) and the 2nd Ave. L for the next couple of weeks. If I had a radio now I could turn off Father Coughlin.

John

[1] Sinclair Lewis's novel about a hotel, *Work of Art*, was published in 1934.
[2] Lantenengo Street in *Appointment in Samarra* and subsequent Gibbsville fiction.
[3] "All the Girls He Wanted," October 1934.
[4] The Civil Works Administration, a New Deal agency.
[5] The *Pottsville Republican*.
[6] A case of kidnapping in which the child was never found.
[7] One-time District Attorney of Schuylkill County.
[8] Mayor of Pottsville.
[9] Joseph I. Delaney, O'Hara's maternal grandfather.
[10] Walter S. Fraquhar.
[11] George Street, a once-fashionable street in Pottsville, became the model for O'Hara's North Frederick Street.
[12] Ed "Strangler" Lewis, champion professional wrestler.
[13] Perdita Pence Howell of the *Pottsville Journal*.
[14] Reference to an O'Hara family joke.

TO: Robert and Catherine Simonds   TLS, 2 pp. PSt.
Postmarked 21 February 1934   Letterhead of Pickwick Arms,
New York City

My dear good friends:

I am going to take a rain check, if I may, on your invitation. The simple unadorned truth of the matter is that I can't leave Pet—and I don't know whether you've been married long enough to know what I mean by that. Perhaps you do; certainly there is nothing that I can tell you two about love. I am so happy for you both. As I told you when you went and did it, I know of no two people who started out with the real good wishes of so many real people, and this time the good wishes seem to have done no harm. To return to my own case, if I were to leave New York—which is to say the vicinity of Pet—I wouldn't be able to work, and right now the only important thing in my life is work, this novel (our talk about hobbies, Robert). I think that if I came to stay with you now I should become jealous of your happiness—a lousy thing to admit, but I'm afraid it's true. I thought it over, and I told

87

myself I could get a girl in Allentown, to use her for an anodyne, but my real self told me how impossible that was—and I found out how completely impossible it was when I saw Pet last night.

I do think I am in for some unhappiness, a complete set of the same. She is opening in this damn revue[1] in a fortnight or so, and I hate the very thought of it. I think all actors are terrible people. As Benchley once said, Scratch an actor and get an actor. As Percy Hammond[2] said, The better you treat an actor, the more it hates you. The thing that makes actors of intelligent people is something I refuse to understand. However, there it is in Pet, one of the most intelligent people I've ever known, so I have to take it, and I am afraid it's going to cause trouble. I have many friends in show business, and if this revue closes soon, she'll get another job—a friend of mine offered her a job through me yesterday. So I think we'll have that to contend with. I have one chance of sanity, and that is to finish the novel and make it good. To have done that will enable me to keep my self-respect, and not only my self-respect, but Pet's respect; she still will believe that a good novel is better than the best performance an actor can give. In order to finish it, I've got to have conditions right in my mind: I don't want to be pining for her, worried about money, (I find that I have only three more payments coming in on my contract, not four as I'd hoped), wondering where my next lay is coming from, and feeling, as I inevitably would feel, that I was causing you inconvenience. What's worse, I suppose you both noticed that there have been changes in me, and the changes aren't entirely for the better; when I am in one of my moods (what Dottie Parker calls a Scotch Mist) I am unfit for human consumption, and it is best for me to be here in this two-by-four cubicle, alone, where I cannot snap at little children and aged couples, and can frighten my pet cobras, Audrey and Louise. (I had to mongoose Audrey last week.)

I say a rain check, and I hope you'll leave it at that, because I want to come and visit you when I've finished the novel—or before that; at the current glacier-like speed the novel will be ready for publication in the Spring of '38, although my contract calls for April 1. That's another thing: I'm going to try to put over a book of selected short pieces and get the advance on that, and that's going to mean I'll have to work on it the next week or two, drumming up trade and breaking down sales resistance.

Well, here I am. I thought on Saturday night when you invited me that that was an automatic solution of many of my problems, and late that night, when I missed Pet so horribly, I thought it would be all right in the morning, and it *was* all right in the morning and on Sunday night, but when I got back to New York and saw her I knew that missing her Saturday night was just a sample of what I could expect. So you see we rich people have our troubles, too. Just because we have yachts and racing stables and servants and cars—we're not any happier than you colored folks underneath it all.

I had a fine week-end, and no other two people in the world could make me forget for a minute that until something happens I am tied to New York. Please let me feel that I can come again when I can't stand it here (which occurs more frequently than you've any idea). I need not tell you that in my opinion you two ought to be President. In fact, *aren't* you President?

Here is the passage from Spectre and Emanation:[3]

> Let us agree to give up love
> And root up the infernal grove,
> Then shall we return and see
> The worlds of happy Eternity.
>
> And throughout all Eternity
> I forgive you, you forgive me.
> As our dear Redeemer said:
> This the wine and this the bread.

John

[1] *New Faces of 1934.*
[2] Drama critic for the *New York Herald Tribune.*
[3] Untitled poem from William Blake's notebook. "The Infernal Grove" was the working title for *Appointment in Samarra.*

TO: Thomas O'Hara   TLS, 3 pp. Mrs. O'Hara
Postmarked 9 April 1934   New York City

Dear Tom:

I've just written The End at the middle of a page, and that means The End of my novel. Finished. Of course there will be changes and fights and so on. I don't think the publisher will go for the title. I'm calling it Appointment in Samarra, which will be explained on the title page. If you can get a copy of a play by Somerset Maugham, called Sheppey, look on Page 112 of the play, where Death speaks and tells an anecdote. That explains the title.

I submit the MS. or the typescript, as the precise F.P.A. calls it, on Monday, and then the fun begins. I have exactly $5.55 in the world, so the O'Hara problem is shared even by the least of the O'Haras (you don't think I believe that, do you?).

I'm afraid I've muffed the story, but I can't do anything about it now. Oh, I know there'll be more work. I know it because I haven't got the sense of relief that I thought I'd have on finishing it. I've been working on it since December, and doing nothing else, and now I have to bat out some New Yorker stuff. I need a suit. I am also getting behind in the rent. I know where I can get some money. Scott Fitzgerald offered me some last week and I turned him down, or turned myself down, because he really needs money himself. I have an autographed copy of his book, by the way, which I will lend you provided you promise to guard it and return it. If you can get it in the library, do so. It's called, as you know, Tender Is the Night, and it's one of the great books of the world. I think of it and think of it, and the more I do, the more I'm beginning to believe it's the greatest book I've ever read, despite certain obvious failings. Who am I to talk? Well, I know what I like, as Zuleika Dobson said.

My trip to the West Indies was fine. I got out the ship's paper—more a magazine.[1] It meant about twenty minutes' work a day, for an average, and the rest of the time I devoted to study of nature's master-pieces—Woman Triumphant, the Atlantic Ocean, Old Sol. In Haiti I made an effort to see Marg Archbald, but she was away on a cruise, so I met her father-in-law, a pompous horse's ass who is Bishop of Haiti. We also went to Barbados, Trinidad, Caracas (Venezuela; so I've been in the Andes and set foot on South America), Curacao, Panama, Kingston, Nassau. I could have desired more money than I had, but I'd only have spent it. I rode in the Panama Canal—Gatun Lake—but not through a lock. I saw the Pacific Ocean and will say it is quite a thing. Saw the Panama jungles, and will say they are something to see. Saw not one, but two Southern Crosses, and whichever one is the real Southern Cross, I like it. Think the Caribbean Sea is perfectly darling, and the Andes foothills are too, too divine. But divine, and steep! Steeper than Gottschall's Hill, Tom, on my word of honor. We did not run into much English language, but my Spanish was adequate—a las siete y quince; para!; haga me Vd. el favor de— etc. Went to Simon Bolivar's house, but he is dead; however I did meet the *most* attractive girl from Detroit. (As a matter of fact I did, and she telephoned me this morning.)

I got the trip because a friend of mine, a Psi U. from Brown who wrote up about you, named John McClain, who does ship news for the Sun—couldn't go. So as a favor to him I went. I got my passage, which meant stateroom, meals, and shore excursions, for nothing. I had a swell room on B deck, alone. The Kungsholm is now my favorite boat, and I'd like to go on the North Cape cruise this summer (the Northernmost point of the Scandinavian peninsula), but it's a six-week thing and I'd need money in addition to free passage. It goes to Leningrad, among other places, and I want to go there, hoping to fly to Moscow. But I guess I won't make it. If there's a chance of selling the novel to the movies, I'll do that and go to Hollywood, if they want me. I want to go there and make some money, because I want almost more than anything I can think of to buy a Ford and tour the U.S. I have theories about the revolution that I want to check up on. I haven't thought about doing a book on it, but now that you mention it, Mr. Harcourt, that isn't a bad idea. I'm a good reporter, and I can put one word after another. I was thinking of buying a Rolls-Royce. You can get them for buttons, practically. A guy I know, Dudley Murphy, who is a movie director (Emperor Jones is one of the things he ought to be ashamed of), bought a Rolls town car for $75 and drove it to the coast and sold it at a profit. I could do that. I just want to own a Rolls-Royce once in my life, and to drive it a couple of hundred miles. I could drive it to the coast, sell it, and then buy a Ford for my tour of the country. I am going to tour incognito, of course. I will be just plain J. O'Hara, and I am not accepting invitations to address Delphian societies.

How are you coming? Don't pull your punches, Tom. It may be a long time coming (although I say three years), but the day will come when you or you or you or I will be more important than the Reading Company,[2] if that's what's worrying you. You will be important because you can write, or have it in you to write. Listen to Walter, but do your own writing. I worry about the influence of Walter and Mary—Mary O'Hara, I mean. Walter is tired, you know, and like everyone else at home, he is awed by the Reading Company, even though he may hate it for the octopus that it may be. As to Mary, she is charming, honest, and all that, but she is also ignorant. I saw that word "vile" which she used in connection with the James T. Farrell book, and I squirmed in my pew. Vile is not Mary's word; it's Mother's. She got that word from Mother. Now Mother is a fine woman and I love her, and she may be right, but I don't think she's always right. Give her the respect that you give anyone you disagree with; yessing isn't respectful. Her influence for good—decency, honor, and so on—is—well, it's good. But you're old enough to do your own thinking. Vile is too easy a word. In the case of the Farrell book, vile is not the word. It's an inferior piece of work, just as my novel is an inferior piece of work. Quarrel with any book on that ground, but never dismiss a book as vile. Vile has nothing to do with taste, and no book is vile because of a bedroom scene.

I once asked a priest, Father Wood (olav hasholem! he's dead) at Niagara, if a certain book (I forget what book) was on the Index. He said: "For you and me, O'Hara, no book is on the Index. The Index is in your mind and your heart. You can read an advertisement in the papers and your reading of that advertisement, the interpretation you put on it or the things you get out of it, may mean that that ad ought to be on the Index. For you and me there's no such thing as the Index. Don't let it bother you." That, of course, is what people like Mary don't know— but then the Index is for people like Mary.

Don't think a person is intelligent because he "gets" everything in The New Yorker.

Don't trust a writer because he's a radical. He must have more than that for me. Fourteenth Street is full of minor Mike Golds—[3]and that's plenty minor.

Don't throw yourself heart and soul into any school of writing or thought. Look at the Hemingway school. They work and work to try to get like Hemingway, but even when they do the same trick better, they're only bushleague Hemingways. That's metaphysical. And when they *are* better than Hemingway, what of it? Hemingway won't last. A Farewell to Arms is the greatest love story ever written, if you ask me, and that's enough for any man to have done, and that's when the writers who form a school make their mistake, I mean the writers who haven't enough in themselves, so they follow another, successful writer. Their mistake is in failing to see that they can't write A Farewell to Arms, because it's already been written. By Ernest Hemingway. Class over.

John

[1] O'Hara edited the *Kungsholm's* paper in March.
[2] The Philadelphia and Reading Coal and Iron Company, a financial and political power in Pottsville.
[3] Michael Gold was the author of *Jews Without Money*.

TO: F. Scott Fitzgerald   TLS, 1 p. Princeton
April 1934   New York City

Dear Scott:

Thank you, for myself and my bibliophile grandchildren, for the inscribed copy of Tender Is the Night.[1] The little bastards will have to be satisfied with cut leaves, because I am reading the novel once again, having read it in the magazine, in galley proof, and now. I will say now that Tender Is the Night is in the early stages of being my favorite book, even more than This Side of Paradise. As I told you once before, I don't read many books, but the same ones over again. Right now I can't think of any other book clearly enough to make a comparison between it and Tender Is the Night, and I guess in its way that is the most important thing I've ever said about any book.

You helped me finish my novel. I finished it yesterday. The little we talked when you were in New York did it. I reasoned that the best parts of my novel will be said to derive from Fitzgerald, and I think I have muffed my story, but I became reconciled to having done that after talking to you and reading Tender Is the Night in proof. No one else can write like that, and I haven't tried, but the best parts of my novel are facile pupils of The Beautiful and Damned and The Great Gatsby. I was bushed, as Dottie says, and the fact that I need money terribly was enough to make me say the hell with my book until you talked to me and seemed to accept me. So then I went ahead and finished my second-rate novel in peace. My message to the world is Fuck it![2] I know this is not the right, the classical (as Hergesheimer would punctuate it), attitude, but I can write better than Louis Bromfield, Tiffany Thayer, Kathleen Norris, Erskine Caldwell or Mike Gold, so I am not the worst writer there is. I never won anything, except a German helmet for writing an essay on Our Flag, and a couple of Father Lasance's My Prayer Book's for spelling bees.

Please look me up when you come to New York, and thank you for the book.

John O'Hara

[1] The inscription read: "Dear John: May we meet soon in equally Celtic but more communicable condition Scott Fitz."

[2] Fitzgerald blue-penciled the word "Fuck" when he pasted this letter in his scrapbook.

TO: Wolcott Gibbs   TLS, 1 p. PSt.
April 1934   Letterhead of Pickwick Arms,
                                                    New York City

Wolc:

I've finished the novel, turned in the MS., had the title (Appointment in Samarra) approved—and now begins the reign of terror for you boys and girl.

J. O'Ha

TO: Thomas O'Hara   TLS, 1 p. Mrs. O'Hara
Postmarked 4 June 1934   Letterhead of Pickwick Arms,
                                                    New York City

Dear Tom:

I leave Thursday for Hollywood, on a contract that calls for my services for at least ten weeks.[1] Thirty days before the ten weeks have elapsed they are to let me know whether they want me to stay on for another three months, so I may be out there until November 20, or maybe only till August 20. Dear, dear; that means I won't be home in time for Mary's birthday. Anyway, I'm going to work for Paramount. They read galley proofs of my novel, and they said they couldn't buy it, but they want me, so they got me. I'm so excited about the trip, and the prospect of being able to buy a Ford phaeton of my very own, and a new suit, and some razor blades. A week from today or tomorrow I'll be in greener pastures, pastures made green by exactly the fertilizer that I have to offer.

St. Clair McKelway is a tall, handsome guy with blond hair and a quiet, smooth way of talking. He came up from The World, and I asked him if he remembered you in '28, and he wasn't sure. He's a very nice guy. He quit the Trib and went out to Yokohoma and then to Bangkok, where he edited the paper owned by Prajadhipok (?) Rex until a year ago, when he returned to the U.S. You probably don't know him, and he probably was being polite in saying he remembered you. But he's okay. He is taking Gibbs' place, Gibbs having had a nervous breakdown and gone away for a rest cure. Like me. I'll write you from the coast. Best of luck.

John

<hr>

[1] O'Hara was hired as a dialogue writer by Paramount. He worked in Hollywood through August, polishing scripts, but did not earn a screen credit.

TO: Thomas O'Hara   TLS, 3 pp. Mrs. O'Hara
                                          570 N. Rossmore,
                                          Hollywood, Cal.

August 16 [1934]

Dear Tom:

By the time you get this the fat'll be in the fire and I'll be officially the promising young novelist. The book is published today, and so far I've seen reviews by Kyle Crichton (a friend of mine, a Communist), who said my talent was too big for my theme; by Donald Gordon, who does the SEPost and American News Co. bulletin reviews. Gordon praised the book and regretted the sex passages, one or two of them, because it would keep it out of small public libraries, but said "the man has what it takes"; and the third review, which I enclose, appears in all Hearst-owned morning papers, including the Los Angeles Examiner. I'm very much afraid of Isabel Paterson[1] and the likes of her, but a few good reviews, which I expect, will offset the bad ones. I'll believe the good things they say about me, and assure myself that the bad ones are written by people who Missed the Point. I expect the book will have the curtains drawn at 606, but why should it? I certainly have been repudiated there as thoroughly as possible, and what I do is on my own head and has been for 3½ years, so elp me. The advance sales are very encouraging, especially here, and tonight Helen and Herbert Asbury[2] gave a party for me out in Beverly Hills. I'll try to think of some names: Dorothy Peterson represented the acting business; Nunnally Johnson, Joseph Moncure March, Douglas MacLean (who used to be an actor; you probably wouldn't remember), and a lot of other people whose names don't mean anything outside of Hollywood were there. Oh, S.J. Perelman, who is a good friend of mine and a Brunonian,[3] he was there. It was a nice party, at which only Nunnally Johnson got stewed. The book has had good sales here, as I said, and the total advance sale is about 3500 copies, as far as can be estimated, and if the reviews are fairly uniformly good the thing ought to top 5000. I hope so. The League of Decency probably will scare off the movie producers who might be tempted to buy the book, which makes me no happier. I'm glad you didn't sign that thing.[4] The L. of D. is something that a few half assed laymen and publicity-seeking priests put over. Cardinal Hayes, I happen to know, was against it, and so, I hear was Dougherty. What they wanted was for Warner Bros. to stop writing those dirty ads, and WB ignored the clergy, so the clergy said Very Well, Don't Say We Didn't Warn You. The result was the Philadelphia boycott. Watts has been fine. I congratulated him on his pieces.

I am no happier here than ever. I bought a new car; traded in my Ford roadster for a new 1934 V-8 phaeton, sand color. I got $355 for the roadster, and the rest I am paying off $50 a week. The insurance, etc., run into money, but what doesn't? Buy now, kid. Inflation aplenty is just around the corner, and not the corner where prosperity has been taking that long squirt. Paramount has taken up my option, which freely translated means I stay here another three months at the same salary. Then I go back to New York to get to work on my next novel, some more defamation of character. I have another book coming out either late fall or winter; a collection of short ones, most of them from The New Yorker. It'll probably sell like hotcakes in a cemetery, but I mustn't get bitter.

I am going nuts with a headache, which has lasted just one week. I've had to go to the doctor about it, and am going again tomorrow. It may be sinus, and it may be Brights, and it may be that concussion I got tobogganing years ago. I'll know more after x-rays etc. and washing my hands, as the saying goes, in a bottle. Heart and lungs are okay, so it isn't thrombosis. Whatever it is I hate it, and it isn't helping me with my crocheting. They wanted to send me to El Paso to get atmospheric dialog on the story I'm working on for Carole Lombard, Cary Grant and Richard Arlen, an army cavalry post story,[5] but thank God that's apparently too expensive a trip or something, so instead I may go up to San Francisco to the Praesidio cavalry post, and I do want to go to Frisco, especially at the expense of Paramount. So far I haven't done a picture, but they say they like my work. What they really like is that a novelist is content to work for what I'm getting.

I don't suppose anything any Older Person ever said affected, to any important degree, the love life of any younger person. However, just a few comments, if not advice: to begin with, I think you are fundamentally decent. I think I was fundamentally decent, too, but on the other hand I was—am—a weak character, and no one ever will know the number of ladies I enjoyed life with—and suffered various kinds of remorse and fear afterward. Anyway, I assume that you know all about Sex, or anyway you have a working knowledge of it. Get yourself, then, a good girl and stick to her. Don't ever fall for this line about Freedom. Freedom is a lot of crap. Two people in love—and that's all you can ask of life. Just about everything in the world, with the possible exception of the South African locust plague, was part of the great conspiracy to keep me away from Margaretta Archbald. Don't let anything like that keep you away from your girl, whoever it is. When you meet her you'll know it's the one. Marg was the one for me; Pet I love actively and deeply, and she fills my waking hours, but all those years with Marg, no matter how much I cheated on her, haven't erased the handwriting on the wall of love, and you may have ten such metaphors for a quarter by writing to Drawer B, Emporia Kansas. It isn't that Pet is second best. It's just that she's second, that's all. So what I am leading up to is, go for Miss Smith if she's the one. Turn detective if necessary. Do anything to get her that will not jeopardize your own integrity. What your own integrity is, you know, without my wasting a lot of time trying to tell you. Anyway I couldn't tell you. Don't be too cerebral with a girl. I'm sure now that an hour's conversation with Marg would make me want to run screaming for a Jewish intellectual from Union Square, but in three months I'd forget the intellectual and still be pining for Marg. Not that I pine for Marg; Pet is the one I pine for, because she was my wife, and still is, really. I will add a few thoughts. The most successful chaser in the world is far less happy than the man who never knew anyone but his wife. The chaser, as a matter of fact, is only a poor guy who is looking for just that one woman, and hasn't sense enough to wait and see if this one or that one isn't The one. Also, your name is O'Hara, and there is the congenital tendency in you to dominate your wife or your girl. Here is the only piece of straight advice: never forget that your girl or your wife is every damn bit as much a person as you are. She regards you as another person, just as you regard her as another person. She thinks the world revolves around her just as you do around yourself, just as anyone does. She has a vote in life as well as in politics, she eats and sleeps and suffers and loves and thinks (regardless of how badly you or I may think she thinks) like you and me. She was born, she lives, she's got to die; and for you to attempt to dominate her, to pinch her personality, is some kind of sin. And it won't make you any happier. I speak of conscious domination. Inevitably the man will dominate in the right ways. The woman will dominate by influence and suggestion; the man by being a man. I hope you are in love, but if you're not you will be. Be slightly critical, very discriminating, and extremely fastidious at the beginning of your friendship with every girl, even those you are strongly drawn to at first sight, and if you love her you'll most certainly know it and be unable to stop it no matter how carefully you check your brakes.

You, as I say, are fundamentally decent. What's more, you are rightly cynical, and awfully intelligent. You'll know the girl when she comes along, or if she has come along; and don't let any remarks of your betters or your inferiors keep you away from that girl. If you want to get married, stall a while until you're fairly sure, and by that time maybe I'll be able to give you a start. Not a hell of a lot; but a couple of hundred bucks anyway. Maybe some movie company will buy the rights to my novel; never can tell.

Write a piece about Auntie[6] and let me see it. I tried to do it last night, but failed miserably. (This letter is written in two sittings.) You write a good long piece about her, show it to me, I'll make any changes that are necessary, and I'll sign your name to it and (one hopes) sell it.

Pet told me you wrote her a nice note. Thanks for that.

John

Do you like money? Here is some for you.

[1] Reviewer and book columnist for the *New York Herald Tribune*.
[2] A *New Yorker* writer who wrote books about sin and crime, including *The Gangs of New York* (1928). His 1926 story "Hatrack" led to the banning of *The American Mercury* in Boston.
[3] Brown University alumnus.
[4] Probably a League of Decency pledge.
[5] The movie was not made.
[6] O'Hara's great-aunt Mary Roarke, who lived with the family.

TO: Katharine Angell White

TLS, 3 pp. PSt.
Letterhead of Pickwick Arms,
New York City

September 11, 1934

Dear Mrs. White:

As I see the sports job,[1] its disadvantages, the chief disadvantage will be that the reader, seeing a football game, a tennis match, and a whippet race covered in one piece, and then a separate department devoted to horse racing, will ask himself, "Why racing by itself?" That will be the thing that will be asked more than anything else. Well, the only answer, the only way to overcome that, I think, is by making the sports job, as you said, pretty much of a column kind of thing, very personal; leaving the inference that the man who is doing sport is not interested in racing—not that The New Yorker isn't, but that the sports writer isn't. And that's the whole secret of a successful general sports department, if there is to be one—to make it a personal thing in the sense that the Theatre as done by Benchley is really Benchley on the Theatre, and not the Theatre by Benchley. You may not agree with Benchley's opinions and prejudices, but at least you know what *he* thinks about the plays he sees. The department would have to have that, so far as "policy" is concerned, *and* it would also have to have, of course, the factual quality of good Reporter pieces. So far what I have said will be true no matter who does the job, me or Ralph Paladino or Gretta Palmer.

So then it's really up to you to decide whether you think *my* opinions *and* observations are good enough, interesting enough, to warrant your giving me the—well, freedom that I think the department would have to have. All right, assume that you give me that freedom. Well, so we take a week, any week, in which there are four or more or less sports events. It doesn't make a lot of difference what they are; just any four. I go to all of them, and in writing my piece I hold forth at great length on one, write a little about another, and put the other two in the Trivia class. That may occur one week; the next week there may be only one thing I think worth writing about, and the week after that there may be three events that get equal space in the department, maybe with the "lead" devoted to the one that's most important, or just as likely the three events will have something in common—luck, or color, or last-minute-finish—that I feel is the thought to get across in the first paragraph.

For my money there is no such thing as a sports event too dull to write about. There are, of course, very dull sports events, but the fact that they are that is something to write about. I mention this because a game of donkey baseball[2] sounds pretty dull, but people who have seen them tell me different, and I might be able to write a very good piece proving that they are or aren't. I would like that kind of freedom, too; that is, to be able to drive up to Wellesley to cover the inter-class crew races, to go to Placid for the curling tournament, or to the Penn Palestra for the basketball tournament, or to Harlem for a cockroach race—assuming, of course, that that would be a week in which there was no first-rate event to be looked at and reported on.

Now all I have to do is write a sample piece, if you want me to. I just wanted to get it straight in your minds that it would be as personal as I have indicated, and would be always and not just for the sample piece. Also, I think you will understand that no two departments will be exactly alike, and that the sample piece is a sample only of that department as of that week. A week later I might write a completely different kind of piece.

We spoke of my being paid to write the sample. We didn't talk terms on that. How about paying me my casual rate? You arbitrarily set the length of the piece in advance, so I won't write too long. My guess is somewhere between 1500 and 2000 words would be the usual department, but that may be longish, although of course 2000 words is only a full page and two columns carried over.

I just happened to think of something else. I seem to be doing football again this year, in any case, and I am going to do two pieces about football before I do one that covers a game.[3] I am going up to Cambridge and to New Haven and Princeton, to do an early-season-dope piece that will end early-season-dope pieces. Well, the two non-game pieces will be of necessity more personal than game pieces hitherto have been, and I was thinking they might easily work into, be followed by, a general sports piece by me. In other words, about three weeks hence, if you like my sample department, I could be doing the first department.

I have a handsome new Ford phaeton now, and all paid for, so I am ready to go.

Faithfully,
John O'Hara

[1] O'Hara did not get this job at *The New Yorker*.
[2] Baseball played on donkeys.
[3] Only one football piece by O'Hara, "The Coming Boom in Stadiums," 29 September 1934, appeared in *The New Yorker* that fall.

TO: Walter S. Farquhar   ALS, 2 pp. PSt.
Fall 1934   New York City

Dear Walter—

You are a gentleman and a scholar. I hope you're also a good judge of writers. I think that there isn't another soul in Pottsville who knows and understands as you do what that piece did for me.[1] I think that because you know and understand, you wrote the piece. I think I'm good, and Pottsville will think so eventually. But between my conviction and that day when Pottsville realizes my ability, I'll know—as I've always suspected —that the brain behind the Sportitorial[2] is calculating my progress; and the heart that feeds that brain is wishing me well. And by God that means I'm successful already.

And how could it be otherwise? Who wrote Joe Dark's obit?[3]

Gratefully
John O'Hara

[1] Farquhar had reviewed *Appointment in Samarra* in the *Pottsville Journal*.
[2] Farquhar wrote a column called "Sportitorial."
[3] Possible reference to the obituary of a local bootlegger.

TO: Dr. Percy Fridenberg   TLS, 1 p. Univ. of Colorado
                                                        New York City

                                                          12–4–34
Dear Doctor Fridenberg:
    "Copacetic" is a Harlem and gangster corruption of an Italian word.[1]
I don't know how to spell the Italian, but it's something like copasetti.
In American it means all right. Bill Robinson, whose favorite word it is,
has an expression: "Everything is copacetic, everything is rosy and the
goose hangs high . . ."
    "A fig"—that's just the old saying: "He has a fig up his ass," meaning
he is peevish, petulant, upset, worried, hypersensitive, vexed, etc.
    If you will reread the context you will see what Beech Nut kiss, not
Beech Nut bacon kiss, means. Caroline's mother has been chewing Beech
Nut gum, and her daughter simply asks her for a kiss, which inevitably
will be flavored with Beech Nut. Nothing esoteric, erotic, or anything
else about that, Doctor.
    Rx—My next book, The Doctor's Son and Other Stories, and thank you
for the kind words about A. in S.

                                                        Faithfully,
                                                        John O'Hara

    [1] The Oxford English Dictionary supplement gives no origin for this word but cites
Appointment in Samarra.

TO: Ruth Sato[1]   TLS, 3 pp. Bruccoli
Postmarked 10 February 1935   Letterhead of Ricks Hotel,
                                                 Rocky Mount, N.C.
Ruth:
    So here I am, and who'd ever think old democratic man-of-the-people
John would ever be found putting on the Ricks? Oh, well, it's Saturday
night, so why can't I stay up till ten o'clock if I want to? I do my work the
rest of the week, and I don't see why I can't have a few minutes relaxation
same as other folks.
    My best advice to you, after thinking it over—let me see: 9:44, 9:45—
one minute, is, when you are looking for an all-year-round vacation spot,
with boating, bathing, fishing, golf, polo, tennis, dancing, horseback riding,
scenery unsurpassed and carefully selected clientele—don't come to Rocky
Mount, beautiful Rocky Mount, North C'lina. I am going to be out of
here so early tomorrow morning that the honest proprietors of this swank
hostelry probably will be running after me with $1.25, or half the price
of this room. Last night I stopped at the Willard, but at least I saw Huey

Long, accompanied by a bodyguard of four gangsters and three southern crackers. That was worth the price of admission. I got up at noon today and drove like hell to get here, and could have continued tonight, but I'd heard this was a good hotel. Wait till I go back and meet the man that told me so.

I have an amusing bit to mention. You remember meeting Mary March. Well, she went to Boston as press agent for "The Eldest", and while there she met your friend Mr. Holland. In conversation she mentioned, ". . . as John O'Hara would say." Holland said, "John O'Hara. Do you know him? What kind of a guy is he?" She said, "I love him. One of my dearest friends." Holland wanted to know if she was having an affair with me, and my reputation in that respect, and she assured him it was platonic. Then he said, "I wanted to know because he's my rival." And I guess we know who he said was the girl I'm his rival for. When do you go to Boston, Peril?

Tomorrow night I hope to be in Savannah. That's not hoping for much, to be sure. I could hope to be in Johannesburg. But it's more likely I'll be in Savannah, so I'll settle for that. At my time of my life (30) you only hope for the things you're purty sure will come to pass. It's when you're younger that you waste good time hopin' for big, fancy stuff. I think I shall get a lasso and some chewing gum.[2]

It is warm. From now on it will be getting warmer. I miss you. I'll miss you more, too, because the names of the places are getting more and more Japanese. It's a good thing you are the only Jap I know. Think of the confusion. Ah, but confusion was Chinese! The hell with it. I must be getting sick. I wonder what I have now. I think I have a fever. Yes. I'm sure I have a fever. Put a fever on Equipoise, to win. That dog is ready, I hear. I have it right from the horse's mouth, which is not where I usually—I see by Ed Sullivan's column that John Steinberg[3] is at Miami. I am going to Key West.

Oh, yes. I forgot to tell you. The reason I am making this trip is to interview Hemingway. I'd rather you didn't mention that for the time being. He is in Key West, and I think there is a good interview to be written about him. So I went to The New Yorker and got some dough out of them on advance against two or three pieces. It puts me horribly in debt but if I write a couple of good pieces I'll have paid for the trip. And this trip is pretty important, because I've been stalling around with my second novel, and I decided I had to get away in order to get a proper perspective. The other novel, about a small town, was written in New York. The next, mostly about New York, probably should be written in a small town, except that I can't live in a small town for more than a week at a time. New York is just the best place for me because it takes longer for me to get tired of New York than any other place. So I am letting The New Yorker pay for my relaxation and thinking-out process.

I wish you were here to rub my back. My front, too. But one never speaks of that in polite society, at least I never heard it in a Metro-Goldwyn society picture, which is all I have to go by.

If I knew an address to give you I'd ask you to write me, but maybe Hemingway will be in Cuba when I get to Key West. I don't want to frighten him off, so I am not telling him I'm coming. I am going straight to Key West, maybe spend a couple of days there, and then stop in Miami for the races and a look at the night life for two days. Then home and to work. That will be about two weeks hence. I'll write again when I can make more sense. I hope you miss me, Sato San (?). Don't become a blonde while I'm away.

John

[1] Japanese showgirl who was one of O'Hara's steady dates in 1935.
[2] Reference to Will Rogers.
[3] Maître d'hôtel at the Casino-de-Paree night club in New York.

TO: Charles A. Pearce[1]   Wire HBJ
14 February 1935   Miami, Fla.

YOU CAN REACH ME IF NECESSARY AT HOTEL CORTEZ MIAMI UNTIL TUESDAY
STOP PLANS VAGUE BUT NORTHERLY THENCEFORTH STOP KEYWEST LOOKS
DOUBTFUL BECAUSE OF PEOPLE VISITING HEMINGWAY STOP ANYTHING NEW
STOP REGARDS=

JOHN OHARA.

[1] "Cap" Pearce and Samuel Sloan were the editors at Harcourt, Brace who worked with O'Hara. They later became partners in the firm of Duell, Sloan and Pearce, which published O'Hara commencing in 1940.

TO: Wolcott Gibbs   TLS, 1 p. PSt.
Early 1935   103 E. 55th St.,
                                                        New York City

Wolc:

Here is a story[1] which I am sending you only because I know it is a waste of time. You will reject it, but you are such nice people at The New Yorker that I am giving you first crack at it.

As you may know, the thing I have avoided saying is that the man has paresis. The story is sound medically, as I know a medical history exactly like it, which occurred when I covered compensation hearings in Pennsylvania. As literature it belongs in the same genre with THE PUBLIC

CAREER OF MR. SEYMOUR HARRISBURG, which you so kindly admitted liking and which Mr. Mosher rejected.[2] It is long, but I rewrote it, boiled it down to its present length, which is the least wordage it can be told in. I do wish you would buy it and I will be sad when you reject it, but one must expect them things when they are a creative artist.

Or perhaps it is too New Yorkerish?

J. O'Ha

[1] Unidentified.
[2] *Brooklyn Daily Eagle* (5 November 1933).

TO: Wolcott Gibbs   TLS, 1 p. PSt.
1935   New York City

Wolc:

This[1] is submitted with fear & trembling. I must refuse at the very outset to put a date-line on it, or tell what time of year it is, or the names of the parties involved, or anything else about it. It is so slight a piece that it has to be read in its entirety for it to have any point, and if Ross wants to make what is only a mood read like a Reporter piece, he can send it back.

The title is in quotes because it is a quote from a line in "I Get a Kick Out of You," a song by Cole Porter.

Otherwise I am starting a novel.[2] Otherwise is put in there to confuse you.

Jack

[1] Unidentified.
[2] *Butterfield 8.*

TO: Charles A. Pearce   TLS, 2 pp. HBJ
March–April 1935   Letterhead of Oceanside Inn,
                                                             East Sandwich, Mass.

Dear Cap:

I am not telling you this to cheer you up or anything, but despite a cold, and a good old fashioned Cape Cod cold it is, I have passed the 15,000 word mark in Novel No. II, which shall be nameless. I am working like hell, and maybe I have something. It is, of course, a little too early to tell, but I am going ahead and finishing a first draft.

It would appear that this one will be longer than A. in S., although not much, and maybe not at all, but I have a few more things to say than I had then. I will get damned to hell by some people, but I'll try not to care. *I'm* writing this.

I hardly think I will come to New York when I have 25,000 words finished. The novel is full of "holes", that is, matters of fact which I must check up on, but I am keeping a list of them. Don't be upset by the speed of the moment. There is nothing else to do but write, here, and I decided against doing the short stories I'd planned to do. Unless the cold gets worse I should be finished the first draft in two months.

Please lay off any publicity for the time being, that is, lit notes stuff.

I may need some money. I did not sublet my flat in N.Y., but am carrying it. I am a little short, that is, I will be when the first of the month comes 'round. Up here I can live on the $50 remittance and to spare, but comes May 1 there will be bills in N.Y. I'll let you know then.

Did you ever try to write a novel? It's hard work.

My room has two windows facing the sea, and a third looking out on the long beach. I am less than 50 yards from the surf. The food is good and plain, and I am the only guest. I pay $25 a week. There is no sex, no nothin'. I work in the afternoon and in the evening, and quit at one a.m. It is now after that.

J. O'Hara

TLS, 1 p. HBJ

TO: Charles A. Pearce
April 1935

East Sandwich, Mass.

Dear Cap:

Thank you and Harcourt for the cheque, which arrived today. Its immediate effect was to cure my cold, put a new light in my eyes, spur me to new efforts, and enable me to announce that the processing tax on cotton is a good thing after all.

It now appears most likely that I shall have finished 25,000 words of the novel by the end of the week, and I am not coming to New York with them. If, however, the average continues, I shall in all probability come to New York the week-end after this, or some time within the octave of that week-end, as I shall have to begin having more retyping done, and it will have to be done practically in my presence. Don't tell this to Harcourt, of course. I haven't made carbons.

One whole "Part" of a chapter is being left out at this time, as I'll have to do some more research in New York on it.

You should see my beard. I'll send you some of it for a davenport.

Did you ever try to write a novel and break in two new pipes at the same time? And grow a beard? And live ascetically?

J. O'H.

Dear Walter:

I'm sorry about this long silence. The best way I can explain it is to tell you that today I got a letter from my mother asking me what I had been doing since Christmas. So you see.

I am up here writing a novel, doing a job which I found impossible to do in New York. But before I left New York I spoke to the only man left in the sports end of the newspaper business whom I can talk sense with. Harry Cross, of the Herald Tribune. I said, "Harry, I have a friend, one of the best sports writers in the country, and he wants a job."

"Ooh, Jesus. Tell him he's lucky to be out of it," he said, without even asking who it was. So then I told him, told him who you are, all about you, and I asked him the best way to go about getting a job on the Trib. He said the only chance, and that remote, is to write to George Daley, a full, complete account of yourself, being careful to spell it Daley, and ask him to keep you in mind. I don't know Daley, and I think he is a shit from the things I know about him. He writes crap, and he is a stuck-up, ass-kissing, mean old man. You wouldn't like him, but write him just in case.

Here is the rest of the line-up. Dan Parker of the Mirror is, I hope, still a friend of mine. Joe Williams, of the World-Telegram, I never met, but he knows who I am and you can write to him and mention that I can back up anything you care to say about yourself. Kieran (not Kiernan) of the Times, another one I don't know. The Sun is a closed book to me, a lousy sport sheet anyway. Bill Corum is a guy I've met. He likes my writing and the same for him as with Williams and Parker. The Evening Post, don't know anyone and their top salary is $50 a week. Gallico knows who I am but I don't think my name would mean anything with him, but I'd write to him if I were you. He's no longer sports editor of the News, and I don't know who is, but he carries a lot of weight. About 200 pounds. So you see even if I had been prompter I wouldn't have been much help.

I can't be too pessimistic about your chances. Not because it's you, but because it's anybody. Stanley Woodward I suppose is about as good a sports reporter as there is. He writes intelligently and really knows sport. Well, he used to work in Boston, top man in New England, with a college following at Harvard and all other New England colleges (an Amherst man himself). He was so good that Daley decided he wanted him. Know what he offered Woodward? Sixty bucks. Of course Woodward told him to stick it up his ass, but he finally came down for around a hundred, figuring on the New York prestige for magazine stuff. Rud Rennie, a swell baseball reporter, gets no more than $75 a week, and he has been at it about ten years, writing stuff that is used as models for cub reporters on the Trib, and I don't mean sports reporters. I'll be frank and tell you I don't think you have a chance in a hundred, Walter. The papers take on a Columbia

Journalism student or two once a year to do copy boy work, then get him to cover a few pork and bean fights—two sticks. Then put him on high school sports, then the C.C.N.Y. football games, and by that time he either gets wise to himself or else he's in it, and may count on spending the rest of his career in the odor of sweat. Joel Sayre, a top-notch writer, has been in it for the Trib, World-Telegram, and one of the Boston papers. He loves sporting characters and writes beautifully about them, but he thinks it's the ass-hole job of the world. And he is a guy who would be expected to give it a good sendoff, but he told me he'd rather have his wife and daughter starve than go back. Now that's from a guy who made good, whose stories are still remembered, in the big league. I know I'm not telling you anything new about sport, but I am about how they feel in New York.

If you have written that legal-baseball book I'll help you market it, or if you write a movie plot I'll get you dough for it, a novel I'll help you sell it, a poem I'll help you sell it, I'll give you a send-in that will count with any publisher in New York, and if you've got a marketable book I'll help you make money. But I couldn't get you a job with Harcourt, Brace, my publishers. I know, Walter, I've been trying for two years to get Tom a job, and I know the job situation. The same with the better magazines. I'm known to them, and I will help you sell a good article or story to almost any mag you mention, if it's one of the better magazines—quality or quantity; Harper's or the Post, etc. If you're going to get out of that God awful town, for God's sake write something that will *make* you get out of it. Write something that automatically will sever your connection with the town, that will help you get rid of the bitterness you must have stored up against all those patronizing cheap bastards in that dry-fucked excresence on Sharp Mountain. Stick it out for another year, but in that year go home at night knowing that you've done a thousand words a day toward showing them what you really think of them. You don't love them, any more than I do. You couldn't. You are a snob, but a snob not the way Ed Luther is, but the way I am. The Ed Luther kind can be bought—and lost in Wall Street. I was a snob when I was starving on 43rd Street. I give you the Sheafer Estate. I give you the Bannons, Weinkoops, Thompsons, DeFrehns, Halberstadts, Beddalls, Brighams—go to it, boy. But I warn you, the Atkinses won't ask you to their tea dance next Christmas.

John

TO: Ernest Hemingway
May 1935

TLS, 1 p. Kennedy Library
Oceanside Inn,
East Sandwich, Mass.

Dear Mr. Hemingway:

(I suppose you know there is a group of cute ones in New York who always refer to you as Hemingstein?)

I just want to say that your first instalment in Scribner's is magnificent.[1] Swell. The nuts. Magnificent. It is what they mean by good writing. It is what I mean by the best writing. Any writing has to be my idea of damn good before I read it through, and not only did I read that through, but I wrote letters to people about it and resumed work myself. I am writing a novel, or what is called sticking my chin out, leading with my puss. The boys and girls will go to work on it next fall and then I will go back to the newspaper business in time to cover the bombardment of Paris.

I went to Florida this past winter with the idea of calling on you, but when I heard who were visiting you I was glad enough of the excuse to spend my time working on one of Earl Carroll's[2] problem children. It took me a week to find out that she was Lesbian. They have to wear suits and smoke cigars before I recognize them.

A couple of years ago a very swell guy named Mike Strater (?) called on my wife and me one night and before the night was over we left to join you on a big-game hunt. We got as far as 52nd Street, and that was the last I saw of Strater and practically the last my P.O.M.[3] saw of me. That was probably what she meant by mental cruelty. Strater and Scudder Middleton and I. That was a big night.

About a year ago Dottie Parker and Mr. Campbell[4] and I waited four hours for you at Sara Murphy's.[5] I think there was some sort of skullduggery going on that night. I think it turned out that you were getting stewed with Mrs. Payne Whitney, but I had the pleasure of watching first one dog, then another taking a squirt on Mrs. Murphy's expensive rugs.

I'd like to see you some time, but I guess I never will if it rests with people like Sara Murphy and Max Perkins. They don't like me, and I don't like them, in spades. But I certainly do like the first instalment of "Green Hills of Africa".

Faithfully,
John O'Hara

[1] *Green Hills of Africa* began appearing in the May 1935 issue of *Scribner's*.
[2] Producer of *Earl Carroll's Vanities*.
[3] Hemingway's wife Pauline is referred to as P.O.M. (poor old mama) in *Green Hills of Africa*.
[4] Dorothy Parker's husband, Alan Campbell.
[5] Gerald and Sara Murphy were close friends of the Hemingways.

Aug 4 [1935]

Dear Cap:

At the moment of writing I am a dead man. I am in the last chapter of Butterfield 8, and will be finished tomorrow in time for the Berengaria.[1] I am later in finishing it than I said I would be, but actually will be getting it to you before the time I set, as the Berengaria gets to New York before the Conte di Savoia, which is what the MS would have gone on if I'd mailed it in Genoa.

I went from Genoa to Florence for a few days, and arrived here today. I had a bad night on the Roma-Parigi express, so I went straight to bed, then got up at five and worked until now. I worked on the boat, too, like a good boy; every day. I don't know how it is. Sometimes I think it's good, sometimes I think it stinks. Right now I am too full of it, as authors say; too close to it.

I wrote Morley[2] a note and told him I would go to London if there was enough royalties there to pay for the side trip. I plan to stay here till around the 14th, then home. I probably will be sending a desperate cable for $100 to get out of France. If you don't like Butterfield 8, don't send the hundred. I am supposed to be getting a rate here, but the letter hasn't come from the press agent in New York.

I have only seen Paris from the taxi window, from the station to the hotel. I am not seeing it until I can write Finis to the novel. I am not leaving this room. So far I've had all my meals sent up.

Don't do the title page finally till I tell you. I want to quote the phone company announcement of the change from Butterfield to Butterfield 8, and I didn't bring the announcement with me. Also I am thinking of quoting, instead of a bit of verse, Jimmy Walker's remark in the Assembly that "no girl was ever ruined by a book," but I want the quote to be exact.[3] There will be no dedication.

I hope you like the revised MS better than the first. I think it's better, if I'm any judge, which I sometimes doubt.

My next novel is to be about 50,000 words long, on one of three hitherto unmentioned subjects, if a novel has a subject. Mine will have anyway a lot of predicates.

You may be pleased to know that on the Conte di Savoia I won the rifle shooting contest with a score of 57 out of a possible 60. Only one passenger ever has made a 60; that was last year when the weather must have been a great deal smoother. For Mr. Sloan's benefit, the arm used was a Remington hammerless pump gun, a better weapon I'm afraid than the Winchesters I've been using. I got a cup as a trophy. I think there is about as much silver in it as in a 10-lira piece, but of course. . . .

I have not booked return passage. I shall do that Tuesday, I hope.

Best to you and Sam and the partners, and I promise you a better novel next time. I will be here until I leave Paris. You will have had a cable when you get this.

At this point I collapse.

O'Hara

[1] The last page of the typescript of *Butterfield 8* is dated: "Exactly 2 o'clock p.m., August 5, 1935/Paris France."

[2] Frank Morley of Faber & Faber, O'Hara's first English publisher.

[3] O'Hara did not use the Walker remark in the novel.

TO: F. Scott Fitzgerald   TLS, 2 pp. Princeton
October 1935   103 E. 55th St.,
                                 New York City

Dear Scott:

Thanks of course. I've been thinking about you ever since this book[1] came out, and wondering if you were reading the reviews, and wondering if they reminded you of fourteen years ago, when "The Beautiful and Damned" came out. Tunes lasted longer then, and so did books, and I remember how angry I was at the time, et seq., because people thought the story of the collapse of Anthony Patch was sordid. Unnecessary, that was the word they used then, and now. I don't like metaphorical speech from me, but writing an honest book is like suddenly closing your fist when you've been sparring with someone for fun. In its effect, I mean. The readers being the ones who are on the receiving end of the surprise punch. They like to fool around with an idea, and take it lightly, but if you give it to them the way you want to give it to them, you are a shit, and they get sore. All of which, of course, is to say that I am not so far from the first excitement of being a writer that I don't feel it when I am put on the pan. They've all said the same thing about the book and about me, and I hope I can write a play before I write another novel, as I don't want to be affected by the critics, professional and amateur. This is a lot of crap, but now I can't ever deny having said it.

I was hoping you could make Adele's[2] party. I am in love with a 19-year-old, a sophomore at Wellesley. Her name is Barbara Kibler, and she is 5'3, dark, beautiful figure, and looks younger than she is. She is from Columbus, and her family are nouveau riche and Protestant. You would like her. Dottie will hate her, unless Dottie has changed more than I believe she has (not having seen her in more than a year). Barbara and I are most likely going to get wed the minute I sign a Hollywood contract. I have no money, and her family are against me, so I have to take the Hollywood thing and will work at it until we have a good stake, then we will leave there. I may leave for the Pacific littoral in a fortnight, accompanied by my bride. The party Saturday night will *really* be "to meet Miss Barbara Kibler". The guests will be my friends almost exclusively, with a few of Adele's, and Barbara knows hardly any of them, and I want her to meet the people I like, a lot of them at once so she will get an impression before it's too late.[3] She is pretty wide-eyed now, but she has good Ohio common sense. I wish you could see her, but I guess you won't. I also wish that you could be there so I could get a chance to talk to you, to hear what you have to say that you won't say in a letter. Come on, Scott, what won't you say in a letter?

What are you doing?

Yrs.
John

P.S.: In Who's Who 1934-35 they use what I suppose was a tentative title of Doctor's Diver's Holiday instead of T.I.T.N.

P.P.S.: At one time I planned to have you for a father-in-law, as I fell in love with Scotty last year, but I couldn't wait, and I couldn't very well ask her to.[4]

Please write, and forgive this shitty letter.

[1] *Butterfield* 8.
[2] Adele Lovett, wife of banker Robert M. Lovett.
[3] The party for O'Hara and Barbara Kibler took place 28 October. The engagement was terminated early in 1936.
[4] This is a joke; Scottie Fitzgerald was fourteen years old.

TO: Harold Ross

TLS, 1 p. PSt.
103 E. 55th St.,
New York City

Dec. 5, 1935

Dear Ross:

I am planning a trip in my Ford, to take me South, then West on the Santa Fe trail, then to the Pacific Northwest. Would you be interested in more than one piece on it? I will finance myself, of course, but I would like to have some assurance that it is not going to leave me entirely in the red. If I were sure that you would be interested in, say, six pieces, that would be fine. It could be a consecutive series, or every now and then. It would be a Footloose and a Reporter piece each time. I would write about whatever I thought was interesting, and the chances are that at least once I would happen on something of timely interest; not necessarily of immediate topical interest in the sense that is used at The New Yorker, but say a follow story on something that would have occurred around the time

I arrive at a given place. I have no doubt you have had this idea put to you before, but you never have run any such pieces, except one Reporter piece, so you may still be interested. All I want is the word to go ahead, assured that you will not think the saturation point will have been reached with one piece.[1]

Well, that's all. Best regards.

John O'Hara

[1] O'Hara did not write this series of articles.

TO: Wolcott Gibbs   TLS, 2 pp. PSt.
Early 1936   New York City

Wolc:

The points:[1]

1. Real names out.

2. Crude. Killed.

3. Killed.

4. Fixed.

5. "Doing the Dutch" is not particularly new or gun moll talk and I think ought to stand. It certainly is in character.

6. Oh. Well, aren't there thousands of Blumies taking thousands of movie queens to Mayfair?

As to the unnumbered point: She herself was embarrassed etc. because she thought the doc thought she was a souse, and that explains her anger. Actually (and I think this is fairly clear, really) all the doc came for was a genuine, sincere, on the up and up appeal to her to help his friend. It was a scene of cross purposes, and I really don't think it ought to be explained at greater length. Pet and McClain read it all right.

As to Eddie's being in love with her, I have inserted (3A) "He was very depressed and all, but . . ." which I hope shows the man loved her. He certainly knew she wasn't much good, but he loved her.

Of course the real reason the man knocked himself off is that he wanted to die before inflation, when we'll all be dying like flies. He wanted to die like a man.

I never can remember: Do you feed a cold and starve a fever, or what?

Yrs.
JOH

(over)

Wolc:[2]

If it looks like a rush of pieces, it is. The reason for it is that I don't think I'll be very happy driving to the Coast with the hangover of a cold

111

and in weather in which it is freezing in Oklahoma, so I want to make the dough to ship the car and my carcass by train. I regard this as extravagance and will not pay for such extravagance out of my Harcourt, Brace screw.

Yrs.
JOHn

¹ "Most Gorgeous Thing," 7 March 1936.
² On verso of preceding letter.

———————◆◆◆———————

After the success of Appointment in Samarra *O'Hara began working as a screenwriter when he needed money. In 1936 he saw Belle Mulford Wylie, the daughter of a prominent New York obstetrician, on a plane to California. They met at a dinner party in Hollywood and were married in December 1937.*

TO: Charles A. Pearce   TLS, 1 p. HBJ
Received 28 February 1936   Los Angeles

Dear Cap:

Shortly after you receive this I shall have moved into permanent quarters. The address will be: 10735 Ohio Avenue, West Los Angeles. Please send my remittance there (and you might as well get it off now, as I am running short, what with unforeseen expenses incident to baggage transfer and moving and tips, etc.). I have been living with the Alan Campbells (Dorothy Parker), thank goodness, as it has cost nothing or next to it. Had it not been for them I'd have had to put the touch on you for a dollar or so for a cup of coffee.

Please also send me the amount of my earnings from Harcourt, Brace for the year 1935, as it is income tax time.¹ I guess I'll have to pay New York State tax, too, won't I? Anyway, the federal is due any minute, and if you recall our conversations, we agreed that you would let me have an additional $500 at Tax Time, over and above the monthly remittance. You could save the price of a tax on one cheque by sending me a cheque covering the $300 and the $500, for a total of $800. But suit yourself about that.

I haven't seen Sam. I called his hotel, or what was going to be his hotel, and there was a Sloan there, but an N. H. Sloan. Then the other day I went to the Roosevelt to pick up my mail and there was a note from him, he having been there one day last week. I almost accepted his invitation to join him in Mesa, but the truth is I have not altogether got over that touch of flu I had in New York. I have not been well, and I've been resting a lot and going to the doctor. My cold does not seem to leave me, and I am trying out for Camille. Be that as i. m., I have decided not to join Sam in Arizona, but to stay here and sit in the sun, whenever there is any, and to get big and vigorous before tackling any real work. I have a feeling I'm going to get a lot of work done this year. There isn't anything else for me to do. That little girl in Ohio[2] has had a far worse effect on me than I expected her to have, so there is nothing left for me but work. I hope *that's* left, but I guess it is. I think it is. I may do some movie work for the quick touch. I talked to Clark Gable the other day about an idea I have for him, and had lunch with Merle Oberon about an idea for her, and Gable would be a good guy to work for and with, judging by our talk.[3] Dottie had done some good work beforehand, and he was highly receptive. But that isn't very imprtant. I have an idea for a play, which I think can be done in a shortish time,[4] and the novel is always in my mind.[5] When I move I'll start to work. I am also planning to take a course in the French tongue and in the American History at the U.C.L.A.,[6] which is only a few blocks from my new digs. I am on the wagon, not even wine or beer, again. I am also getting radical again, more so than I was before.

I was surprised in a bookstore today to find that A. in S. has been published by Grosset & Dunlap. Nobody ever tells me anything. And what is the Albatross edition?[7] Regards to Wade and the Partners and everyone, and I hope you are happy. You may tell a certain someone that one of the nicest people out here is Mrs. Kendall Lee Glaenzer Milestone,[8] sister of a Mrs. Kent.

Yrs.
John O'Hara

[1] The figure $8,502.52 is noted in the margin.
[2] Barbara Kibler.
[3] O'Hara hoped to write a screenplay of *The Great Gatsby* for Clark Gable, but the project did not develop.
[4] A play based on Steinbeck's *In Dubious Battle*, which O'Hara dropped.
[5] O'Hara was working on a Hollywood novel, which became *Hope of Heaven* (1938).
[6] These educational plans were not pursued.
[7] An English-language paperback edition of *Appointment in Samarra* published on the Continent.
[8] Wife of director Lewis Milestone.

TO: Charles A. Pearce and Samuel Sloan   TLS, 1 p. HBJ
Spring 1936   10735 Ohio Ave.,
                                               West Los Angeles

Dear Fellows:

Thank you for the kind and encouraging words and I hope I can do something for the team!

All I can say now is that SO FAR, SO GOOD looks from here like a matter of maybe 20,000, maybe 25,000 words. Somewhere between the length of THE DOCTOR'S SON and A LOST LADY,[1] and bearing very very little resemblance to either. The story, such as it is right now, has to do with three.young persons; that is, under thirty all three; two males, one female. The background is California, and the time, of course, is the present. In the first draught on the first page and the pages immediately following we discover one of the young men counting a large sum of money and then hiding it in various places throughout his abode. One of the males is a Pennsylvania Dutchman, the other a Jew, and the girl is a Californian. The story is romantic, middle class to a low degree, and there is a slight, but only slight, touch of plot. Not enough to raise my temperature in the Pacific sun. I set August 1 as the date for delivery of the typescript. And I guess that's all I better tell you for the present. I will write it long and then shorten it.

I hope this is enough to cause endless confusion and to make you realize how well off you were before I spoke. Then when I turn in the script you will be so glad to have the confusion ended that the script will look better than it is. Now I must to bed and dream. Regards and regards

                                               J. O'H.

[1] By Willa Cather.

TO: Wolcott Gibbs   TLS, 1 p. PSt.
March 1936   10735 Ohio Avenue,
                                               West Los Angeles

Dear Gib:

In spite of what looked suspiciously like a paid ad in Mr. Winchell's column (t.f.[1]), I was—let's be downright conservative about it—not altogether pleased with the way MOST GORGEOUS THING came out.[2] The editing, I mean. It reminded me of the proofroom's botches in a piece called THE GENTLEMAN IN THE TAN SUIT.[3] So please send me proofs? And oblige. (I mean in future please send me proofs, of course.)

I seem to be having a rush of New Yorker contributions. It must be spring. Or else it may be the competitive spirit. Kober[4] tells me has been promised a 25% bonus for a certain number of pieces in a certain time, and I sure do hope I win *my* little gold Rea Irvin[5] New Yorker for my watch chain. Dad and Mother would be really proud and so would that certain someone.

How would The New Yorker like a Wayward Press piece by Benedict Arnold (me) on the L.A. papers?[6] It would be a bore, I'm sure.

Well, guess will close.

John

[1] Possibly "to follow."
[2] 7 March 1936.
[3] 7 September 1935.
[4] Arthur Kober, a writer for *The New Yorker*.
[5] Artist who created the "Eustace Tilley cover for *The New Yorker*.
[6] O'Hara did not write this article.

TO: F. Scott Fitzgerald   TLS, 2 pp. Princeton
April 1936   10735 Ohio Ave.,
West Los Angeles

April . . .

Dear Scott:

I suppose you get comparatively little mail these days that does not dwell at greater or less length on your Esquire pieces, and I guess few of the writers resist, as I am resisting, the temptation to go into their own troubles for purposes of contrast. However, I am not very good at analyzing myself, and especially now. I was in love with a girl, as I wrote you; she gave me the air, and on the rebound I got a dose of clap. I apparently suffer more in the head than in the cock, and much more than most men. So if I went into my own troubles I couldn't tell you much except abundant detail, all getting back to the genito-urinary tract.

I have been out here two months, not working for the movies, but living comfortably on a $75 a week subsidy from Harcourt, Brace. Very comfortably, except for the emotional life. I have two Fords. I have an incompetent but adequate Negro servant. I am out of the New York cold, which I could not stop taking as a personal affront. The movies will not give me $1000 a week, and I have refused to work for less. I write little pieces for The New Yorker, some of them so vague that when I send them away I almost include a plea to the editors that if they can understand them, please to let me in on the secret. And of course I regard the intelligible ones as hack stuff. I keep hoping I will get well, because there are some lovely dishes out here which I have to pass up. A curious thing about me, which may be universal: me, in my Condition, I meet a dame, I like her, and I want to be friends with her in a tentative way—for future. But their instinct warns them, or else it is that my subconscious and my conscience keep me from throwing in the old Sunday punch. The result is I have no relationship with these exciting creatures. And I am lonely. I have no social grace, either. I lack the Princeton touch. People do not invite me out much, and the only way I can climb is down.

How I happen to be writing to you this particular night is that I was reading Thomas Mann's "Early Sorrow",[1] which I like; and especially I like the idea of that length. It reminded me of what you wrote me after Butterfield 8 was published. I have the letter right here so I quote: "Your effects might show to good advantage through a very quiet theme just for a change—I mean practically a bucolic idyl interrupted by the high pitched mood which you handle so well—but to make it effective remember that you would have to believe in the bucolic idyl." I wish you would tell me more about that. There is something I want to do of a length somewhere between "Early Sorrow", and "The Great Gatsby". It is about freshmen and their girls and cars, in California, now. It is young love. But I would thank you for information, criticism, that might save me nights of work while doing this thing.

For two years now I've been trying to get some company to let me do a movie script of "The Great Gatsby" for Clark Gable and Miriam Hopkins. Contractual difficulties always set in. I even talked to Gable about it, and he was enthusiastic, but apparently has too many commitments not of his own doing. Paramount owns the picture rights; Gable is with Metro; Hopkins with Sam Goldwyn. Hopkins is out of town just now, and I hear she is going to marry an unknown artist who lives here. She likes me, or rather she thinks she ought to approve of me, so when she gets back I am going to work on her, as I understand Paramount would sell their rights, and if Hopkins got hopped up enough about it, Sam Goldwyn probably could be persuaded to buy the rights and borrow Gable from Metro. And also give me a grand a week to work on it. It's the only thing I want to do out here. I've never done a movie script, and I'd like to do one good one, if for no other reason than that I would get over my secret awe of people who can turn out good movie scripts.

I stayed with Dottie and her husband when I first came out here. They have a large white house, Southern style, and live in luxury, including a brand new Picasso, a Packard convertible phaeton, a couple of Negroes, and dinner at the very best Beverly Hills homes. Dottie occasionally voices a great discontent, but I think her aversion to movie-writing is as much lazy as intellectual. She likes the life. She and Alan are with Paramount, writing a courtroom picture for Claudette Colbert. Don Stewart,[2] who is full of shit, has converted himself to radical thought, and goes to all the parties for the Scottsboro boys. His wife, who is more honest and whom I don't like either, stays home from them. Don talked to me for an hour one afternoon about how he makes a much better radical than— well, than I. Because, he pointed out, he'd *had* Skull & Bones, he'd *had* the Whitney plantation, he'd *had* big Hollywood money. He is certainly scared about something, and it isn't only the Revolution. But he is such a horse's ass that it doesn't matter much. Benchley arrives tomorrow by plane, I am told. I will miss his cheery absence. Archie and Ada MacLeish and Adele Lovett are in Japan. Archie went there to do a piece for Fortune, and I went to San Francisco to see them off. I quarreled with Adele the night before and did not see them sail. I'm wonderful. What other friends of yours have I news of? Your man Nathanael West, of whom I am mildly jealous for your plug in the Modern Library edition of The G. G., is working for Republic, an independent studio, on a picture for, I believe, Marion Talley, the cornfed opera singer. Dos Passos is not here just now. Norma Shearer and her husband[3] are rumored not to be hitting it off too well. It's the first time I ever heard that, so they have two more chances.

Will you write to me?

Ever your friend
John O'Hara

1 *Disorder and Early Sorrow.*
2 Donald Ogden Stewart, humorist and screenwriter.
3 Producer Irving Thalberg, who became the model for the hero of Fitzgerald's novel *The Last Tycoon*.

TO: Wolcott Gibbs
Spring 1936

TLS, 1 p. PSt.[1]
10735 Ohio Ave.,
West Los Angeles

Dear Wolc:

Thank you for your letter. The pieces which you have just rejected, the one about the kid and his father, called FIFTEEN DOLLARS, and the other one, PRETTY LITTLE MRS. HARPER, are cases in point.[2] When I have paid off the money I owe The New Yorker I will write no more pieces for it.[3] You and Mrs. White, as it happens, were right about FIFTEEN DOLLARS. The father was only and simply glad his son had a good girl. The other one was just as obvious, but you happened not to like it.

You can tell Ross about my decision, and also tell him not to bother

117

about answering my letter. My only regret now is that I have to give you pieces to pay off what I owe.

Yrs.
John

Please don't use my name in any advertising.

¹ An office note on this letter reads "9 rejects 4 acceptances. Since July."
² "Fifteen Dollars" remained unpublished; "Pretty Little Mrs. Harper" appeared in *Scribner's* for August 1936.
³ O'Hara was somehow placated; he continued to write for *The New Yorker*.

TO: Charles A. Pearce   TLS, 3 pp. HBJ
Spring 1936   10735 Ohio Ave.,
                                          West Los Angeles

Dear Cap:

Nothing much to report, but I thought I would report. I have a lot of work to do, but I am not doing much of it. There is the matter of a play which is an adaptation of John Steinbeck's novel, In Dubious Battle, for Herman Shumlin.¹ But at the moment what has been holding my attention is a novelette. How would you like to publish a nice little novelette for $1.50 next fall, latish? I mean, would you publish it at all? It's not a Hollywood story, but it is Californian. It would be about the size of Early Sorrow, Mario & the Magician, and those other Mann books. I want to do it because I want to do it. Butterfield 8 (remember?) made money, but you weren't really behind it, now were you? But anyway, a piece of advice Scott Fitzgerald gave me after he read it, and has repeated since, is that I ought to do a book that is practically a bucolic idyll, only I must believe in the bucolic idyll, and the reason for doing it is that the staccato stuff ought to be saved for an effect, rather than used throughout a novel. Badly quoted, but the idea is somewhere around there. One more fast-moving, realistic novel, and nobody will listen to anything else I have to say; they'll be too sure of what to expect, etc. This would be a good stop-gap, so far as the critics are concerned, and it would be good exercise, so far as I'm concerned. Anyway, I am trying to justify something that may not need justification. I have a good idea, I am working on it, and if you don't want to publish it, well, maybe someone else will. I do not say that threateningly or angrily. Because of the size, it would not affect our basic agreement, our contract. At least I don't think it would. I have two more novels to deliver, and I think the contract says full-length novels. Anyway, this is what I am really interested in now. I have a title for it: So Far, So Good. So you see it is not in the ABC sequence of novels, no more than was The Doctor's Son.

What's new, for instance in England, and what ever happened to good old Sam Sloan, and how is your life, and do you really honestly think Transgressor[2] was a good book for Christ's sake? I mean, disregarding the Baker & Taylor[3] angle. I don't want you boys to make *too* much money. You'll forget all about us artists.

Regards to 1 & all.

Yrs.
John

[1] Broadway producer.
[2] Negley Farson, *The Way of a Transgressor* (N.Y.: Harcourt, Brace, 1936).
[3] Book distributors.

TO: Wolcott Gibbs   TL, 1 p. with holograph
Spring 1936   postscript. PSt.
                                                 10735 Ohio Ave.,
                                                 West Los Angeles

Dear Wolcott:

Here is a little different piece.[1] If you love it I could do some more like it. All the anecdotes are true. The first is about Whiteman and Junior Laemmle;[2] the second, obvious; the third, Joan Bennett and Walter Wanger.[3]

I may come storming in one of these days. I am very discontented. I want more money and a lot of it. I also want Fleischmann fired and Fadiman[4] transferred to As To Men and the signature, The New Yorkers, restored to Talk. I also want The New Yorker to send for me, paying all expenses, to talk things over. This way we are not getting anywhere and I have not seen Idiot's Delight[5] and On Your Toes.[6] (I don't think you ought to say Dick Rodgers in a review, either, Wolcott. Otherwise I like your pieces.) Write soon.

Scribner's took the "experimental" piece I sent them.[7]

[1] Unidentified.
[2] Orchestra leader Paul Whiteman; movie executive Carl Laemmle, Jr., of Universal Studios.
[3] Actress Joan Bennett was married to movie producer Walter Wanger.
[4] Clifton Fadiman, book reviewer for *The New Yorker*, whose review of *Butterfield 8* had offended O'Hara.
[5] Play by Robert E. Sherwood.
[6] Rodgers and Hart musical.
[7] "Pretty Little Mrs. Harper," August 1936.

Dear Cap:

I am keeping the two copies of the contract for SO FAR, SO GOOD (so what?) until I clear up a little matter.

The matter is this: in the contracts you have stated "about 35,000 words." The novelette I am sure will not be within 10,000 words of it. I hope to keep it around 20,000. I already have told you this, in substance, and I am only repeating it for the record. I don't want any misunderstandings. The Mann books I am using more or less as models are 20,000 or under. Goodbye, Mr. Chips! is not much more. The story is much too slight for more words, and as now planned (and written) there is only one real love scene. I hope this does not spoil the encouraging enthusiasm you and Sam have shown.

I might say that I do not expect the book to sell. Also, about the bucolic idyll part, I think that in order not to mislead you, I ought to state that the difference between this and the other novels (by the same author) is in the fact that there is some Hope for the characters in this, unlike English in A. in S., or Gloria or even Liggett in Butterfield 8. I am not going to try to write poetry, and there will be plenty of realism; of detail, dialog, and so forth. Just don't expect too much, my friends. Just expect a MS about August 1.

Faithfully yrs. in Xto.,
J. H. O'Hara

Dear Fellas:

I regret to report that since returning to California I have been living at the bottom of a bottle. This, however, seems to have been ended by, of all things, a yachting trip, and I now can give you what you asked for. Or approximately. And with apologies.

I believe it is bad luck to spill too much of a book before it is written, but this is what I am trying to do: Quote: I am going to try to tell a good story, that is, write a good if short novel, which can stand or fall on its own merits, but which also will have a complete second meaning. Much as Thomas Mann's Mario & the Magician. That was a good story on its own, but as almost every Mann reader knows now, the story had a complete allegorical value. I think the short form is the best for this kind of work, because I think it is impossible for the writer to sustain the effectiveness of this kind of work in a piece that runs into bulk. I may be wrong in this, but I think it is dangerous to write a great many words in this kind of writing, and not only dangerous but unnecessary. The secondary, or allegorical, meaning of SO FAR, SO GOOD is simple and will be apparent, probably more so than was the case with MARIO & THE MAGICIAN.

I will not put myself in the position of explaining the allegory until after the book has been published, if then. Right now the book is simply a short novel dealing in the main with three young persons; a girl, a California girl; a Pennsylvanian of Pennsylvania Dutch background, and a young New York Jew. The locale is Southern California. The time: the present.

I will write to each of you in a minute or two.

Kind thoughts from
J. O'H.

TO: Charles A. Pearce and Samuel Sloan
Received 19 September 1936

TLS, 2 pp. HBJ
10735 Ohio Ave.,
West Los Angeles

Dear Friends:
First I have to force myself to tell you about So Far, So Good. When it will be along I don't know. I may hit it tonight, but if what has become almost precedent means anything, it will be many more nights before you get a MS., and this is why: as I told you, the book is first of all a book on its own, and the allegory business is ancillary to the obvious tale. Two of the characters, the girl and the young Jewish lad, come out all right. But the third character, the young Pennsylvanian, just doesn't sound like anyone I want to be known as the creator of. He is a tough one for these reasons: he is discovered on the first pages of the book in a thoroughly dishonest act. Now I have been able to justify this act (to some extent) and to reconcile it with certain other things he does later in the story—but the horrible part is that I find myself writing about two (and sometimes three) different persons. I find myself writing about one person who does the dishonest thing, and then writing about a totally different guy who does something pretty darn good. To bring it pretty close to (my) home I read over the stuff and I discover that I am writing about two of my brothers. That's bad, because the character is supposed to be only one person. If it isn't one person the story's no good. This guy has to start out (in the book) as a pretty ruthless guy, to be able to do what he does. Then later he has to do this good altruistic thing—without there being any great regeneration, since I distrust great regenerations based on any

one important incident in anyone's life. So I have two thirds of a good thing, but only two thirds. So I have to give it more thought.

As to my own character, if any, I am working for Samuel Goldwyn. I took the job because I had to for the money, and because the offer, while not giving me the kind of money I'd held out for, did give me a chance to work on a story I like—Murder in Massachusetts, the story of the Millen case by Joseph Dinneen, which appeared in Harper's last winter. I am now on the third week of a three-week guarantee. If they like my treatment, I will be signed to do the screen play, which will take probably six weeks.[1] I have let it be understood that between finishing the treatment and starting on the screenplay, I shall have a week to work on the novelette. As it happens, the research on the picture is happily the same as I have been doing on the novelette, so there will be no trouble about that, I mean about picking up the novelette again. But if I can't make sense on the novelette and they want me to do the screenplay, I'll do the screenplay and then come back to the novelette. Me, Detective,[2] by the way, came along at a good time for my purposes.

So this time next week I'll be working again on the novelette, and of course I may finish it the way I want it. In any case, my plans are to remain here until November or December and then drive back to New York via the southern route, and take up residence somewhere in NY and begin writing the Hollywood novel; that is, assuming that the novelette has been finished. The novel will take about six months, I imagine.[3] Maybe less. I'm afraid NY is the only place to write it. I wanted to go to Ireland or some place, but there will be times in the writing of it when I will want to consult a Film Daily Yearbook or back files, etc., and NY is the only place besides Hollywood where that kind of dope will be readily available, so it's a hole in some Greenwich Village wall for me this winter and next spring, I suppose.

Now here is a headache which I hate to visit upon you, and if you can't arrange it please let me know and I'll get Mrs. Lovett or someone to do it. I am not signing up for my 103E55 flat again, and I have to get the furniture out of there before the end of the month. Will you tell Peniston or Jennison or whatever his name is that he will have to move out and will you see to the storing of the furniture? I will send you a cheque to cover the moving and storage if you will let me know the amount. Ordinarily I would ask Mrs. Lovett who likes to do this sort of chore, but she will be moving to town from Long Island just about this time, and she has a lot more to move than I ever will have. Under no circumstances will I have any dealings with Wade, and I don't know the other guy, but I should think he might conceivably have tipped me off regarding the arrears that have had to be made up.

I am good and bored with Hollywood and the temptation is strong upon me to lam the hell out, but this is the only way I can make enough money to pay off certain debts and commitments. I could write a serial for Cosmopolitan, I suppose, but between their kind of crap at one price and this kind of crap at a higher price, I choose this kind. At least this is anonymous crap, and it also is part of the business of finding out about Hollywood. Once before I was as fed up with a place as I am with Hollywood, and the result of that was Appointment in Samarra, the most readable book since Steps Going Down,[4] Fadiman, New Yorker.

By the way, here is one for the trade: Fadiman, you know, is on the payroll of Goldwyn, and in a letter to the story editor he talked about Steps Going Down, saying it was not picture material, and ending up his letter with ". . . and of course it's a lot of crap." At least that's what the story editor told me before the New Yorker review.

I notice I get no fan mail for my acting.[5]

Yrs. in Xto,
J. O'Hara

[1] O'Hara's treatment was not used.
[2] By L. T. White (N.Y.: Harcourt, Brace, 1936).
[3] The Hollywood novel was never written.
[4] By John T. McIntyre (N.Y.: Farrar & Rinehart, 1936).
[5] Clifford Odets and Lewis Milestone gave O'Hara a small part in *The General Died at Dawn*.

TO: Joseph Bryan III[1]   TLS, 1 p. PSt.
                                           New York City

May 3 or 4, circa [1937]

Dear Joe:

I finished a Winchell profile for The New Yorker, and they turned it down for rewriting. Well, I have refused to rewrite it. They said it was too Broadway for the average reader, and they didn't like it when, almost as a P.S. to the rather severe appreciation I accorded Winchell, I gave him a slight break from the philological-slang student's point of view. They themselves liked it, but not for their readers.

Now I have a lot of stuff on the guy, and I hate to see it go to waste. If it is not true that Alva Johnston is doing a piece on Winchell, would the Post be interested in my doing one? It would be a one-part job, of course, and around 5000 words long. I think it ought to be agreed that I get a grand for it, if the Post should take it.[2]

I am at work on the novelette and have got off to a good start, I think; but I am anxious to get into the non-fiction world. I'd like do four or five a year, not necessarily for the Post, but in the same genre, if not in the same class, as Alva's marvelous job on Goldwyn. So far as I could detect (and I worked for Sam) Alva had only one error. He had Ben Kahane's name spelt wrong.

Tell Stout[3] Bob Lovett is full of respect and admiration for the way the Post handled Gilt-Edged Insecurity.[4]

I'll buy you a powder at the crib soon, I trust.

Regards,
The Candy Kid

[1] Editor at *The Saturday Evening Post.* Bryan was married to the former Katharine Barnes, who became O'Hara's third wife in 1955.
[2] *The Saturday Evening Post* did not take O'Hara's profile of Walter Winchell.
[3] W. W. Stout, editor of *The Saturday Evening Post.*
[4] Lovett wrote "Gilt-Edged Insecurity," which appeared 3 April 1937.

TO: Wolcott Gibbs
Summer 1937

TLS, 1 p. with holograph
postscript. PSt.
Dunes Rd., Quogue,
Long Island[1]

Dear Wolc:

If you think you've heard the end of my pathetic plea for an advance, you are v.m.m.[2] As you see. I still want and need the money, even in spite of the picture I have of a terrified Ross and a timid Shuman,[3] throwing their hats into Fleischmann's office, and waiting to see if they'll be thrown back. Next is the picture, after they've Gained Entrance, of Fleischmann et al. holding forth to Proctors Ross and Shuman about the profligacy of writers, etc., etc. I would not urge upon them that they take all these chances if I didn't really need the dough.

Now I know a few people with an extra five, who would let me have the money without even so much as a note. But I prefer to be business-like. Me! I am doing business at The New Yorker, and it is only a 50% credit business, the other 50% being cash. So long as I continue to contribute, what difference does it make if I owe The New Yorker a couple of hundred bucks. (Of course I ignore the possibility of my dying in debt to the F-R people.)

I challenge the reasonableness of the statement that I have not contributed anything in the past three months. I have contributed but I have had rejections, as you well know. Furthermore, in the months from, roughly, January to June I *sold* enough pieces to make my bonus—in other words, nine pieces. So if I do have a lazy period, I do make up for it. Just count up the number of pieces I've sold the magazine, and divide by the number of years I've been contributing.

Finally (for the moment), it is pleasant to see The New Yorker spending so much money to advertise one, isn't it? It's flattering. Well, if

The New Yorker thinks it does any good, or gets any good out of advertising a piece by me, it must think I am worth a slight financial risk. And for God's sake if it doesn't think advertising me does any good, then for God's sake give me the money you spend on advertising. Or, just stop buying the pieces. There's always that alternative.

How are you? I am working hard.

Regards.

John

(over)

Tell Shuman I'm sure I signed and mailed that bonus agreement.

J.[4]

[1] Belle Wylie's family had a summer home at Quogue; O'Hara rented a cottage there in 1937.

[2] Very much mistaken.

[3] Ik Shuman, a *New Yorker* editor.

[4] On verso of letter.

TO: *Time* (6 September 1937), 8

Sirs:

On Ernest Hemingway's forehead there are two scars. They were there long before Hemingway's recent encounter with this Mr. Max Eastman.[1] They were there prior to a night two years ago, when Hemingway and James J. Tunney put on a friendly bout in the dining room of a New York apartment. Moreover, I was with Hemingway the night before he sailed, which was three days after the Eastman encounter, and I saw no new scars. I was with him for several hours in Manhattan's Stork Club. TIME's heavy implication that the Hemingway scars resulted from the Eastman encounter is misleading. I certainly would like to see Mr. Eastman after a friendly bout with Mr. Tunney. I certainly would.

JOHN O'HARA

Quogue, L.I., N.Y.

[1] Hemingway and critic Eastman had engaged in a well-publicized scuffle at Charles Scribner's Sons.

TO: Stanley Woodward, *New York Herald Tribune*
(16 January 1938), III, 3

Don't you think it's about time to blow the whistle on Mr. Okeson[1] and all others who are trying to gadgetize sport? I view with alarm this Lehigh man's suggestion that an electric-light ray be substituted for goal-line crossbars. Of course it can be done (probably by a Lehigh man), but it is just one more instance of what happens when Tau Beta Pi's and Sigma Xi's begin to brood over things that are none of their business. The inalienable right of the American fan to kill the ref, or at least to threaten to, is in grave danger; and if you care anything about American institutions, you will give the matter your best thought and some of your strongest words.

I have long watched the light at hockey games, and resented it for the symbol it is. Electric timing at track meets may have been all right for the ticker-tape boys of the Curb Exchange, but I have resented that. The photo-finish in horse-racing still requires explanation—"perspective," they always say. But even if it were good, I wouldn't care for it. They've all led up to such suggestions as Mr. Okeson's, which in turn will result in light rays along the foul line in baseball, and magnetized niblicks to catch you heeling your club in the sand, and nasty hidden contrivances on pool tables to prove that you (a) are, or (b) are not frozen, always at the wrong time.

All those gadgets tend to take away whatever human qualities a chronic official may possess, and yet at the same time they tend to make him absolute. You are just about to let fly with a cushion or a beer bottle, and along comes a fat ex-athlete with a piece of cross-section paper on which is drawn a graph, which for all you know may represent what happened to car-loadings from 1927 to 1937, but he says Don Lash has kicked the goal, just barely nosing out Gehrig (a good trick, at that). Well, there is no fun in wasting a cushion on a Log Co-sine. You can't even argue with it.

Mark you, the Saturday will come when you will find yourself filing: Referee, Dr. E.J. O'Brian, Tufts, and New England Electric Company; umpire, W.G. Crowell, Swarthmore, and Cutler-Hammer; field judge, Larner Conover, Penn State, and Bristol Recording Meter; head linesman, Richards Vidmer, St. Luke's and Western Electric.

Yours,

JOHN O'HARA

[1] Walter R. Okeson, football official.

TO: William Maxwell[1]   TLS, 1 p. PSt.
February 1938   New York City

Dear Maxwell:

I had a note from K.S.W.,[2] in which she said she was going to Bermuda. She didn't say when, but I suppose tomorrow, Saturday, which is when people usually go to Bermuda. Anyway, I am sending this piece[3] now because it is semi-topical, and if accepted it ought to run either in March or early April (that is, unless you buy it for next year, in which case a change or two). As you will see, the time and place are, in reverse, a summer home in late winter or early spring, quite out of season.

I would like to sell it for this month or next, because I am getting out a book of short stories in the early fall.[4] For that reason, too, I wish you would contrive to schedule the pieces on the bank. As Gibbs will tell you, Nash once got out a book with a lot of pieces in it that The New Yorker had bought but hadn't printed, and I don't want to do that. After all The dear New Yorker has been terribly kind to me, etc. The piece called Are We Leaving Tomorrow,[5] for instance, is almost timely.

I'll be in early next week to see about polishing off Days. Also to find out whether you'll be buying while Mrs. White is on her holiday, etc.

Yrs.

J. O'Hara

[1] William Maxwell, *New Yorker* editor, who was filling in for Mrs. White. Maxwell later became O'Hara's editor, and a close working relationship developed.
[2] Mrs. White.
[3] "Days," 30 April 1938.
[4] *Files on Parade* did not appear until September 1939.
[5] 19 March 1938.

TO: Ik Shuman   TLS, 1 p. PSt.
March 1938   Quogue, Long Island

Dear Ik:

I am selling again, to the F-R Pub. Co., and in less than a fortnight I am having another book.[1] It is my theory that this enhances my value to The New Yorker. It is Ross's idea that it neither enhances nor lowers my value to The New Yorker; but since Ross no longer has anything to do with the fiscal details (a likely story, but his), we can safely and consistently leave him out of this. This being, how about getting me a raise in word rate? I haven't had one for several years, and in the ordinary course it's about time, book or no book. Will you get up off your pratt and pound Fleischmann's desk and tell him you want a straight 20¢ a word for good old faithful O'Hara, the meat of the magazine, the punch, the charm, the elegance, the malarkey? Because if you don't do it, I will, and when I do it it only sends people to Dr. Ford's.[2]

Yrs.
John O'Hara

[1] *Hope of Heaven*, published 17 March 1938.
[2] Possible reference to Dr. Frank R. Ford, neurologist at Johns Hopkins.

TO: Joseph Bryan III   TLS, 1 p. PSt.
March 1938   Quogue, Long Island

Dear Sholem:

I'm sorry I missed you last week, sorry in more ways than a & b; *a* being that we could have had lunch (courtesy Curtis),[1] and *b* being that we could have had lunch (courtesy Curtis).

We could have had it legitimately, too, because we could have talked some business. I have banged out about 3000 words of what could turn into a serial.[2] I am writing it as a straight, magazine type novel (I mean by that I don't say f—— or s——. I make a few references to that prique Calvin Coolidge, but I know the Post wouldn't care about that). Anyway, it's so long since I've read a Post serial that I don't know how demanding they are about putting a teaser near the end of each instalment, and all that mechanical stuff. This thing has six principal characters, all, so far, nice people. To be honest, I only know what the ending is going to be, as distinguished from how I am going to end it. The suspense, as planned, hangs on character and character development, rather than on plot. It probably would be four parts.

If you're in town this week, how's for wasting the price of a drink on a message to Quogue 4247, and if I'm not here, I may be in town, where messages can be left at Atwater 9-1101, Belle's home. I don't know that anything will come of this, because there is a job imminent. A job certainly is indicated after the reviews I've seen of Hope of Heaven, possibly a job writing ads for Brooks. But if the job isn't what I am dickering for (not Hollywood), I may yet take some of that Post gold. Heaven knows I haven't tried very hard.

Yrs respy
O'Hara, Bart.

[1] *The Saturday Evening Post* was published by the Curtis Publishing Company.
[2] The serial was not published and was presumably never completed.

TO: Samuel Sloan
April 1938

TLS, 3 pp. HBJ
Letterhead of Hotel Scribe,
Paris[1]

Dear Sam:

So here we are in Paris the beautiful, without a chestnut in blossom, and with ski trains coming down from St. Moritz to take advantage of the wonderful skiing weather, which also has been good for ducks. As a pleasant change we are going to be in England beginning next Tuesday, the 26th. We go to Almond's Hotel, which is a new one on me, and then we expect to take a flat. I have asked Morley[2] to see that I get any mail addressed me at Faber & Faber, and also I have given Brown, Shipley as a forwarding address. Belle's mother and sister are in London now, hence that curious hotel.

The trip across was made without incident. Rats in the hold caused an outbreak of bubonic plague, which was quickly stamped out. A time bomb exploded in the foc's'le head, but the loss of life was slight. Indeed, many passengers were not aware of the accident, for which two German spies were drumhead court-martialed and shot. A lady on B Deck was seasick all the way, and the commandant was buried at sea, with traditional honors. Belle had twins, back to back, and the bodies of Nungesser and Coli were picked up in an advanced state of decomposition, having been in the water just eleven years.[3] But nothing really happened except a Miss Fenstermacher, of Davenport, Iowa, won the ping-pong tournament with a furious, slashing forehand. It was an exciting exhibition, and from the first serve onward the issue was never seriously in doubt. Mike Romanoff was unable to make the trip.

I am in serious doubt as to the advisability of your not publishing a book of short stories unless Hope of Heaven sells 30,000. Of course there is about a 15–1 chance that Hope of Heaven will sell 30,000, in which case I am wasting my valuable time and yours. But I think that on a basis of the three weeks sale that I know about (or know approximately about) the showing of H o H justifies a short book or a book of shorts. I don't for a minute delude myself into thinking I could go to England and buy a Bentley on the unrealized profits of a book of short pieces; but neither do I think you would lose money. The Dr's Son made money, a little, and the pieces in it, except for the title piece, were uniformly inferior to what I've been doing since. If it were brought out in time for Xmas it ought to be acceptable on Xmas lists, and then there is always that thing I keep harping on about its being good advertising. I know there are people who like my short stories who cannot abide my novels . . . There are no new points I can bring up, I suppose, but I do hope you reconsider this decision.

I suppose Hanna[4] told you that he has withdrawn both as agent for my end of H o H and as my agent for personal services. There doesn't seem to be much likelihood of a book sale, but I just wanted to tell you how things are. In other words, you are sole agent for the movie rights to the book.

Why don't you and Peggy come over and sell some H-B books to Korda?[5] There's an idea.

Best always,
J. O'Hara

[1] The O'Haras spent spring-summer 1938 in France and England.
[2] Frank Morley or Morley Kennerley, editors at Faber & Faber.
[3] Charles Nungesser and François Coli disappeared on a flight from Paris to New York in 1927.
[4] Mark Hanna.
[5] British film producer Alexander Korda.

TO: Harold Ross   TLS, 1 p. PSt.
April 1938   Paris

Dear Harold:

Why don't you just buy this piece[1] and never bother me any more? How the hell did you pull that fast one about owning all the reprint rights? Is that my old H W Ross of Aspen Colo or is that my old Harrison Cady Ross?[2]

Well, Rossie, either buy the God damn piece or send it to God damn F PA of Information Please?[3]

How are you and Dixie Tighe[4] getting along very well? Because she would smother both you and me?

Yrs very truly?
Your faithful Comtriburtor
John O'Hara
Clarence Budington Kelland
In a pig's ass
19, Rue Blondel
Arondissement 25
Paris, R.F.

Send cheque to above care of Morgain, Harjes, et Cie.
quatorze Place Vendome
Paris, R.F.
that et Cie is purely shitte

[1] Unidentified.
[2] Walter Harrison Cady, author and illustrator of children's books.
[3] Radio quiz panel show.
[4] Reporter who specialized in crime stories.

TO: William Maxwell   TLS, 3 pp. PSt.
                                    Letterhead of Almond's Hotel,
                                                    London

                                          April 30 [1938]

Dear Maxwell:

For the most part we have been doing a lot of footless scampering, if such be possible, since coming over here. But now we have taken a flat and will settle down, more or less. The address of the flat is

> 52, Chesil Court
> Manor Street
> London, S.W.3

We have taken a three-months lease on the place, and are going to buy a jaloppy so that I can take my first gander at the English countryside; also get some work done.

I now want to ask you what may be a series of favors. Faber & Faber, my English publishers, have had a brainwave, and they are going to bring out a book called Hope of Heaven & Other Stories. The others include The Doctor's Son, plus the pick of the pieces in the book of that name, plus the pick of the New Yorker pieces that have appeared since that time, or will have appeared by September. And this is where you come in: will you get one of the office boys to make a list of all my pieces since March 1935, then clip all the pieces from the magazine as they have appeared, then send me the batch of clippings care of

> Faber & Faber
> 24 Russell Square
> London, W.C.1

I realize, of course, that buying up the old copies of the magazine will cost me money, but tell Ralph Paladino to discredit me with whatever it costs. I wish you could arrange this as soon as possible so that I can make the selections and get the book into shape.

So much for that. Now, Favor 2. Will you write me a letter or something, giving me a blanket reassignment of copyright covering all pieces up to December, 1938? This is a mere technicality, but it is better to have it before proceeding. The New Yorker, of course, has copyright on the pieces until they appear, but you reassign copyright on request. To cover everything I set the date at December 31, 1938, a purely arbitrary selection.

It looks like a pretty good book, or does from this point. Faber & Faber are a good house. They did all right by and with my first book, and now they want to catch up with Harcourt, Brace in point of stuff published, and they think I ought to make some money out of this.

I am sorry not to have been in before I left, but my days were numbered and so were my hours, and when I had time to drop in I just seemed to be in the wrong part of town. There was also a bit of farewell boozing to be done.

Will you tell McKelway—this is another one of those technicalities, without which business would get along just as well as ever—that I, John O'Hara, hereby relinquish all claim on the Winchell profile, and he can assign it to anyone he likes, or hates, or who will have the patience to do the God damn thing.[1] In return, I wonder if he would be interested in my doing a reporter piece on Scotland Yard?[2] If he would, I wish he would write me a note to that effect. I also wish I could get a New Yorker police card, which would come in handy now and then. I don't want to conflict with Janet Flanner[3] in any way, of course, but I think there is room for her, and Thurber, and me. If not, they must go!

I am picking op a Breetish axunt.

I am, &c.,
O'Hara, Bart.

[1] St. Clair McKelway's six-part profile of Walter Winchell appeared in *The New Yorker*, June–July 1940.
[2] This piece was never written.
[3] London and Paris correspondent for *The New Yorker* under the pseudonym "Genet."

TO: Charles A. Pearce and Samuel Sloan

TL, 2 pp. HBJ
52 Chesil Court,
Manor St., London

May 3 [1938]

Dear Cheps:

The above is, and will be for three months, our address. We have taken a flet, my dear old cheps, in Chelsea. Last year I lived in Old Chelsea, and this year I am living in just plain Chelsea Chelsea. I like this better, although it's a little early to say so. Paris was a bit too much for me. It wasn't so much that most French people speak French; it was that so few of them converse in English. I don't mind their French (half so much as they mind mine), but they are a useless race, and should learn English. The least they could do. I am now conducting an insidious and entirely unsuccessful one-man campaign to win the English over to the American language. The movies are not very helpful, because in language as in everything else, these etrangers copy the wrong things from us. For instance, they say scram. Do you ever hear anyone saying scram? A mille no's. Next week we are going up to Oxford, and I suppose I shall be called upon for a few words. After a conversation the other day with Geoffrey Faber, I think the few words will be in double talk. There is nothing takes the starch out of an Englishman like a good bout of double talk.

By this time I suppose you have heard the Plans, or rather, that the Plans are going through. I mean, that Faber is going to publish H o H and the Dr's Son and about two dozen other stories, all in one book.[1] Some of the stories will be from the Dr's Son, and the rest from The New Yorker, stories that I wanted you to publish. It seems to me to be a very good idea. Anything that makes money for me is a good idea, and they think this will make money for me. My wife, poor wretch, has been haunting the Guaranty Trust to consult the N.Y. Times on Monday, and apparently H o H is taking its rightful place on the best seller lists.[2] This is no more than right, in my opinion. Of course when I occasionally see THE NEWS FROM HARCOURT BRACE I ask myself, "O'Hara, old boy, how does it feel to be a Doubleday, Doran author?" but I always answer myself, "Listen, O'Hara old boy, don't be sarcastic. They *did* take an ad for you. Don't you remember?" And, with difficulty, I do. But don't infer that I am complaining. I think it is sound business psychology to make the reading public think a book is hard to get. A book prospect says to another, "Say, didn't that O'Hara have a book published this year?" and his friend in the know says, "Yes, sure. You can get one. You just have to know how to go about it, that's all. Ask around, and find out who published it, then drop in at your favorite bookseller's, take him out to lunch, and gradually bring the conversation around to O'Hara's book. I wish I could remember who published it. If I knew I'd tell you, then you could write to them and they might send you one. In a plain envelope." I was thinking along these lines the other day, when we were having a drink at the Savoy with Frank Morley, Morley Kennerley, and Dick Simon. I thought how lucky I was not to be identified with a house like Simon & Schuster. No dignity. Put over all their books by advertising. It must be terribly embarrassing to fellows like MacLeish and Mumford to find their books advertised all over the place, like Bell-Ans. However, it was nice to see Simon. He said Hope of Heaven is going very well, which, in a way *is* NEWS FROM HARCOURT, BRACE.

Partly on the strength of which we are going to buy a jaloppy and see England through a windshield. Beg pardon; windscreen. We don't know what we're going to buy. Probably what they call a Ford 10, which looks the way an ordinary American Ford would look if you suddenly became nearsighted. It would make a nice tender for a Rolls-Royce. We went down to Kent Sunday in one, and they can bang out the miles, without burning up petrol, which is quite an item. Our lease is until August 2, and I am sort of hoping to be invited to Scotland for August, when J. P. Morgan will be there, too. Unless Canada and Mexico united and declare war on *you* people, we expect to be home in time for the World Series. The plan to stay over here a year is never mentioned any more. Not after one cold snap in sunny France, sans central heating. England has been having the longest drought in 160 years or thereabouts, until we came. I wonder about that. I get a little messianic when I think of it. Or mosaic. Up to now my divining-rod has been used for other purposes. I never made a living by it.

Random observation: I'm glad I didn't bring my .22. Those chimney pots . . .

Thank you for cabling my allowance. I wonder if you would do that for June, July, and August, too? The same way as you did the May one. This is why: Belle received a dividend cheque in the mail yesterday and took it to the Guaranty, where we have an account. The nice mans there told her not to deposit it, as His Majesty would immediately take out ¼ for taxes. Apparently cabled things are not subject to that tax, probably on the theory that they do not represent income; whereas cheques do. Funny world.

Alec Waugh[3] has taken me up and is giving a cocktail party for me Thursday. Last week he gave a supper party for me, and naturally he invited Mrs. O'Hara I[4] as well as Mrs. O'Hara II, not to mention the curator of reptiles at the London Zoo, a Lesbian who loved Butterfield 8 and didn't know anything else I'd written, an illegitimate son of Oscar Wilde (!!!), a lady journalist, and other interesting folk. Beebe[5] would have loved it. I didn't. We went to someone's flat, and the Lesbian asked all the girls to dance with her. Most of them did. Oh, and Mrs. —— —— ——, who wanted everybody to get drunk and start fucking. The Lesbian's hubby wrote —— — —— ——. In France we went out to Senlis, to Bromfield's[6] house, and there was a huge luncheon party, consisting of some of the prize pricks of three continents. Only two prize cunts: third prize. Oh-ho say can you see?

Best to Chet

---

[1] In 1938 Faber & Faber published an English edition of *Hope of Heaven* with thirty-six stories.
[2] *Hope of Heaven* appeared once on the *Times* best-seller list, as #2 on 1 May 1938.
[3] English novelist.
[4] Helen Petit O'Hara was in London.
[5] Society reporter Lucius Beebe.
[6] Novelist Louis Bromfield.

TO: William Maxwell   TLS, 1 p. PSt.
July 1938   London

Dear Maxwell:

Here, posthaste, is a piece which I am reasonably certain will go through.[1] If it does, and the other one I sent you last week also, I will have made the bonus.

In any case, whatever I make—one piece, without bonus, or two pieces with bonus—will you send the cheque to me at the Guaranty Trust Co., 50 Pall Mall, London S.W.1? We leave this address at the end of the month, when our lease expires, and our plans are rather vague after that. We'll do some touring here, and then to France, returning to N.Y. on Sept. 7. The book is coming out here after I leave, in the middle of September.

I wish you would let me know how I could have fixed that piece so Ross would like it. I refer to the one about the ex-footballer who wanted to get up a memorial for a fraternity brother, and slapped another frat.bro. who said the footballer wasn't as good a friend of the dead guy, etc. etc.[2] You said Ross said the ending made him unhappy or something, and something about fixing it, but you didn't say how. I know you didn't like the piece, but don't forget that when there is a chance of fixing these numbers I have to do it, because The New Yorker is the only market for this kind of thing. The length, and frequently the treatment, preclude the possibility of peddling the pieces elsewhere.

                                                            Yrs.
                                                            J. O'Hara

[1] Unidentified.
[2] Unpublished.

TO: William Maxwell   TLS, 4 pp. PSt.
July 1938   52, Chesil Court,
                                                       Manor St., London

Dear Maxwell:

I have numbered your marginal notes on proof[1] on the probably wrong theory that that is the only way we can make any sense at this distance. Anyway, let's try, and for God's sake give Ross the enclosed bill. It seems to me there is a very bad case of editis at The New Yorker, and it's contagious.

1. Okay. They don't sweat.
2. Okay. Say: "Ask Mischa. That's what he gets paid for, writing songs."
3. Make it waxed moustache.

4. Make it ". . . said Mischa. He got up and went to the director."

5. Should be do, I guess. Probably a stylographical error.

6. Make it ". . . to write you a little number."

7, 8. "Smile, Brother," was a tune which was popular circa 1927. As a matter of fact it was called "It Won't Be Long Now," and there was a record of it made by Paul Whiteman with vocal by the Rhythm Boys, who were Bing Crosby, Harry Barris, and two other guys whose names I forget.[2] The lyric was: "Smile, brother, smile brother, let's congratulate each other—oh, boy—it won't be long now. Laugh, sister, laugh, sister, etc." It was a very popular record among people like me, and it reposes in my vast and valuable collection at 606 Mahantongo Street, Pottsville, Pa., unless one of my God damn brothers left it at Brown or Lafayette, or at camp or at Princeton, or my sister left it at Eden Hall or my other sister left it at the Convent of the Immaculate Conception. Or Mother hit one of them over the head with it. I would not worry about the libel. There is no libel. Go to the Gramophone Shop and have them play the record and then the Fire Music. The only thing you have to look out for in a case like this is reprinting too much of the lyric, in which case ASCAP gets after you and makes you (or me, to be exact) pay up to $150. These are things which, as a jazzophile, I know, probably as well as Gene Buck,[3] and in future please remind Ross in future to take my word for it. I might and shall mention, by the way, that I am not risking any $150 of my own money. Fleischmann's, yes; gladly. He can risk 900 G's—but, alas, I guess that's another story. Anyway, Gibbs and McKelway, among others, will tell you that Jazz is one of my specialties. I once corrected George Gershwin on a Gershwin tune, and he had to admit I was right. So there. P.S.: It should be Smile, Brother. Richard Wagner: R.I.P.

Thus we come to A DAY LIKE THIS

(I mean, of course, A DAY LIKE TODAY.[4])

There must be a lot of riveting going on in your neighborhood, because this piece was read in London by others than me without undue brow-wrinkling. In fact I thought it went off very well. However, here, as the saying goes, goes.

1. Okay. Make it: (third line) ". . . but the girl, who was named Sallie, remembered etc."

2. See 1.

3. Schoolgirl wit.

4. In the language of the kerb, the gentleman had fucked her. You could get Galbraith to do you a drawing of what occurred, but since that is against Policy, I will now rewrite a paragraph for you: "What do you think I remember about last night? I'm sorry about the way it happened. I mean, I'm sorry about the *way* it happened. I'm not sorry it happened." Then pick up with She chewed her lower lip.

5. Don't worry is like saying, Oh, don't you worry, I'm not going to tell everybody I laid you, and *her* saying don't worry is an ex-virgin's worrying about getting pregnant, getting the clap, losing her reputation— all that. But my God, does that have to be explained? Please, boys, remember that the people who read The New Yorker read only six or seven casuals a week, plus Talk, departments and captions.

6. Transposition not needed, in my opinion, but transpose it if you think necessary. And I give you leave to make those changes, that kind of change, without hurting my feelings.

7. You are right and I thank you.

We are having lovely weather, and the sun will shine like a bat out of hell when I get that bonus. In your letter you said you probably wouldn't be using these pieces before September. One piece is slugged Summer (Day Like Today), and should run in July or August because it is what used to be called Timely. There is a mystifying disparity between July 10, 1938, and June 10, 1938, on the slugs of the two pieces, but I suppose that is a typesetter's error. When you next write will you let me know, through Ralph's calculations, how much I owe the F-R Pub Co.? I may want to put the touch on them again. We are leaving England early in August, as our lease is up Aug. 1 and we are taking ourselves and my car to La Belle France, unless Hitler gets out of hand and there is another Serajevo.

Also, is there anyone from The New Yorker besides Thurber and me (I mean boys) abroad right now. Some fairy in London is telling people he is a big New Yorker guy. My informant didn't remember the name but whoever it is didn't answer the description of any of The New Yorker's fairies. Flanner, Thurber and I racked our brains, but could not figure out who it might be.

Now try and make sense out of those proofs. I dare you to.

Regards,
J. O'Hara

[1] "Richard Wagner: Public Domain," 3 September 1938.
[2] There were only three Rhythm Boys; the third member was Al Rinker.
[3] Songwriter.
[4] 6 August 1938.

TLS, 2 pp. PSt.
52 Chesil Court,
Manor St., London

Dear Maxwell:

Herewith an item[1] to bring forth a lot of patronizing letters from your Catholic readers. I think I have them, this time. They can't really Take Exception to anything; but neither can they adopt me.

Did I write you our final plans? I think I did, but here they are again. We sail August 10, on the Normandie. From August 1 to August 8 we are touring, and our address will be the Guaranty Trust, 50, Pall Mall, London S.W.1.

Yrs.
J. O'Hara
p.t.o.

I am a little shaky on the spelling of dolmatic. It may be dalmatic. It is a vestment worn by deacons and subdeacons at solemn high mass. I also am shaky about *ideo praecor*. The proofroom can check that easily by asking one of the Catholic office boys to bring in a prayer book that has the Ordinary of the Mass in it. Ideo praecor will be found in the Confiteor, which is in the beginning of the mass. Or, you can always call Benziger Brothers, Barclay Street, for any information like that. By the way, there is a good Talk piece in Benziger Brothers, the biggest Catholic supply house in the U.S. and probably in the world. You're welcome.

[1] "No Mistakes," 17 September 1938.

To dear John Hayward

1115, 5TH AVE

GREAT CIRCLE

ATLANTIC OCEAN

22, B INA

RAND, McNALLY O'H.

(see page 319)

am running out of
space. But how the
hell can I do anything
else when Th is telling
us this story?

John O'Hara
Bill O'Hara

---

[1] English editor and scholar. The page reference in the inscription is to the back end paper, which has a list of page numbers with material regarded as censorable in England and a drawing of a dog by James Thurber (identified above as "Th").

TO: John Hayward
Received 22 November 1938

TLS, 2 pp. King's College
Library, Cambridge
196 N. Carmelina Dr.,
Brentwood Heights, Los Angeles

Dear John:

Me and the girl friend were about to say, "Well, old Hayward and Spenser and the Faerie Queene are in that certain place," but the old woman couldn't pronounce place. I gave her a try-out. I says to her, place, it rhymes with bouillabaisse. She says balls. I say go take a flying fuck at a galloping r—ster. The end result is that me and the old lady are in Hollywood. We need money. If you have any, keep it. She'll only squander it.

A lot of things have occurred since Dirty Old Nev became Dirty Old Nev.[1] Naturally we are glad that you are a new neighbor of ours. That you took such a God damn long time to be one is an insult which we shall take up at another time. Like 1952. When a friend of mine takes as long as you did to become a near neighbor (by that I mean neighbour, a hourse of another colour) I naturally suspect that he has been waiting till I get the hell out of the neighborhood. It is nice, in a way, to know that you have moved over with the solvent group, at long last, but I do wish (and the old woman joins me in this, at least) that you could have made the Swanns Way while I was there to observe your own little blowings of the Moncrieffian[2] trumpet. I daresay you didn't know I could write so flowery, and neither did I. Well, there you are, with those dopes waking you up with the Lambeth Walk, and here I am, with Belle and Joan Crawford and Ginger Rogers and Joan Blondell and Gertie Lawrence tickling my feet, and I would rather be where *I* am, in my gold bath-tub, than In England, even if England meant being with you, dear John. At least our mob knows that the fixeroo is in, and if we want to copper our dime we can still do it before the flag is up. The mouse and me give one another the office, and I give you the tiperoo: lay it off from here to Chi, if you are on that dog the Admiral.[3] Admiral aint got a play. I give it to you once again, Kiddie: you're on the Admiral and the bruise will be but terrific. But terrific.

This Hollywood is not much different from the Hollywood I have come to know. A little bit of Broadway, a little bit of California, a little bit of England (played by C. Aubrey Smith), and a liberal portion of the Ghetto. I flew out, having the worst trip I ever had in a plane. I am temporarily ensconced with Belle's sister and brother in law.[4] He is a director, H. C. Potter by name. They are what is called well off and all that goes with it. I have not signed with a picture company or any other company, but I will if they think I'm not too repulsive. The news of my success as an actor in The General Died at Dawn has, apparently, not reached Hollywood, so I am branded as a writer when of course acting is my real forte, my life blood. Of course there is a lot of jealousy here too.

We plan to remain here about six months. That will about bring us up to the arrival of Their Majesties, at which point I plan have [*sic*] my bomb perfected and expect to be in Washington only overnight. After that a short period in hiding and then—who knows? Life grows tedious, John. We left Long Island two days before the hurricane and missed all the fun. Bodies of *total strangers* were being washed up constantly at our beach club. The Sette of Odd Necrophiles had a splendid fortnight, although there was a bit of ill feeling over the prior rights to a genuine blonde female in a fairly good state of preservation. They saved me a lock of her pubic hair.

From time to time I grow mildly curious as to the publication and reception, if any, of Hope of Heaven & Others Stories. It has all been kept a deep dark secret from me, and I'm not even sure that dear old Geoffrey went ahead with publication. They wrote me and said they'd sent you galleys, and were sending me some too, but I left Long Island about that time and so I don't know what happened to them (that's my story). The conspiracy of silence now in effect at Faber & Faber naturally whets my curiosity (cf. O'Hara on Mixed Metaphors), but all things notwithstanding I am not so un-English as to inquire of Morley K. and F. Morley . . .

We had an evening with the Kennerleys before they returned to their special paradise, and we sent you card after card, which I suppose are just about rounding the Horn. You will get them by the April packet.

Waal, pardner, it is time for me to finish dressing and go downstairs and get drunk. Belle asks me to send her love, but I say to her she can send her own love. Having gone to such trouble and expense to teach her to read and write I think she ought to make some use of it, don't you? And so, all out for A.R.P.[5]

With love,
J. O'Hara

[1] Prime Minister Neville Chamberlain.
[2] C. K. Scott Moncrieff, translator of Proust.
[3] Possible reference to Adm. Russell Grenfell, who in 1938 was urging a build-up of the British armed forces.
[4] Lucilla and Henry Potter.
[5] Air Raid Precautions.

TO: Harold Ross   TLS, 1 p. PSt.
January 1939   471½ Landfair,
                                              Westwood, Los Angeles

Dear Harold:

I have decided to reject your rejection of this piece[1] and to give you a chance to read it over again. I think you often are unduly influenced by bulk—that is, when you get three pieces at a time you think they can't all be good, and then you go beyond that and think none of them can be good. The result: three rejections, which, of course, are unsalable elsewhere.

As a matter of fact when a writer writes in spurts, as I do, there is just as good a chance that everything he produces in a spurt will be good. In this case I happen to agree with you that one of the three pieces you just rejected is not the best I ever wrote, and that another of them could stand some rewriting. However you too frequently reject flatly when a piece could easily be salvaged. That is my squawk about some pieces. In the case of the enclosed I honestly think you ought to read it again. It is better than its predecessor, and even Mother Woollcott wrote a fan letter about that one. He called it "pure gold" and told Gibbs he had read it twice. (Winchell, whose standards are probably less haughty, called it "a literary toy for the mind," a statement which partly baffles me but at least shows Winchell's heart is in the right place.) Anyway, if Woollcott can read "Invite"[2] twice, you can read this one twice, and I trust you will and will see the light.

You must occasionally remind yourself that, having written probably more than 200 pieces that have appeared in your magazine, I have some idea of your requirements. I don't send you junk.

                                                        Love,
                                                        O'Hara

[1] Unidentified; probably "that college piece" mentioned in 8 February letter to Maxwell.
[2] 10 December 1938.

TO: William Maxwell   TLS, 1 p. PSt.
Received 8 February 1939   Los Angeles

Dear Bill:

About Adventure on the Set,[1] it has been used over and over again. It is a corny plot by now, and therefore safe. Leave it. As to the weak remark in next to last paragraph, don't forget that it is "Don" doing the reporting, not me. The weak remark is in character for that kind of letter writer, who would understate at one point and exaggerate at another.

Okay, kill the old ending in Ideal Man.[2] If the ending hadn't been there Ross would have suggested it. It's there, so he doesn't want it. Ross wants to be a writer.

Other corrections have been made in proof on Like It Here.[3]

Tell Shuman I think it's pretty cheesy to hold up a check this way. Tell him also that I have not made up my mind about the Agreement, because this year's agreement does what no other has done, namely, it fixes a word rate for a year. That means I would not be entitled to a raise until 1940, and I am going to spend a lot of time in 1939 getting the raise to which I am entitled, to which I have been entitled for more than two years, if only on a basis of number of pieces sold since 1928. The 25% bonus is a sop, welcome enough it is true, but the conditions are burdensome. It pays on a basis of selling a piece in every month but two, but still does nothing about that old and tiresome problem of rejections which simply are not saleable anywhere else. Every time I write a piece for The New Yorker I write it so that The New Yorker will buy it. It won't go anywhere else. Now that is not true of non-casuals. Fact pieces, etc., can find other markets, but not my stuff. All this has been covered before, but I know I face the dreary prospect of saying it again.

I thought we were going to have an earthquake yesterday, but we didn't. I was wrong.

Yrs,
John

Why do I get my New Yorker exactly a week later than everyone else? What the hell's the matter with the Circulation dep't?

PPS: I rejected a rejection. I sent back that college piece,[4] the one about plans for the summer, to Ross, registered mail, telling him I thought he ought to read it again and buy it. I'm sure it infuriated him but I gotta have some fun.

[1] 15 November 1941.
[2] 29 April 1939.
[3] "Do You Like It Here?" 18 February 1939.
[4] Unidentified.

TO: William Maxwell   TL, 1 p. PSt.
Early 1939   471½ Landfair,
                                          Westwood, Los Angeles

Dear William:

These pieces, and a slice of raw onion, will bring tears to your eyes. I want all three to be purchased immediately and cheque in full sent airmail special delivery, and no two ways about it. I want no nonsense about obscurity, etc. All that is OUT for 1939. In fact I am commencing a campaign the result of which will be that I can put my own pieces through and the hell with Ross.

I may be going to work soon on the next Cagney picture. Practically set.[1] That means that if you get any pieces they will be on Warner Bros. time.

Will you tell Ralph that I would like to subscribe to The New Yorker? 471½ Landfair, Westwood, Los Angeles. Be sure of the Los Angeles, as there is another Westwood Up No'th.

Random thought: could you learn to hate Mr. Fadiman as I do? I'll give you some help: listen to him on Information Pl.

Happy new happy new happy new YEAR!

> PUREGOLD O'HARA,
> A Literary Toy
> for the Mind

---

[1] O'Hara did not work on a movie for James Cagney.

TO: William Maxwell
Received 14 March 1939

TLS, 1 p. PSt.
Los Angeles

Dear Bill:

Let's have a little consistency here. Ross objects to a reference which is a quote from a highly popular radio program—the Why Daddy reference in the Numbers piece.[1] The program is "spotted" on the second most desirable spot on the radio, and has been for more than a year. But Ross thinks people won't get it.

Then the next proof has a query about cribs. Now how many people know that a crib meant a kind of whorehouse? They exist in only a few places—Reno, New Orleans. On the other hand, Ross ought to know that crib is a derogatory term for a night club, like flea-bag for hotel. I wish to hell there would be an end to this quibbling about my use of the vernacular. Even if people don't get it at first, they will. I was the first person ever to do a piece about double talk,[2] and God knows a lot of people still don't know what it is, but that was several years ago that I did the piece (in The New Yorker), and several things in that piece have become established slang. It is a point of artistry with me. I like being first in those things, but you-all make me nervous. I'm afraid to put in anything more recent than you tell em casket, I'm coffin. There is a piece I've been wanting to do, or rather a kind of talk called ski talk, but I know it would be no use because the queries would drive me crazy—if it ever got to the query stage. I also have been unable to use the verb to make in the sense of recognizing and/or identifying. Detectives are always saying "I made him the minute I sore him," meaning "I recognized him . . ." But Ross would think the detective was a fairy, I suppose. I remember Miss Fishback[3] had a poem in which she said something about somebody's on the up and up, as tho it meant the person was being increasingly successful in business. It doesn't mean that at all, yet Ross passed it.

This is a biennial squawk, but I do wish there were more liberality at your shop. People after all don't blame The New Yorker. They blame me, and I've written enough pieces so that those who read me at all know what to expect.

Nothing happens here. I suppose I did tell you Hedy Lamarr now recognizes me and speaks to me. Nothing else, except that I cancelled my subscription to Time, and apropos of that, tell Gibbs that of late the resemblance between his stuff and the Hearst editorials is embarrassing— apparently more embarrassing to me than to him.

So once again, I have to read much of Kay Boyle's stuff three times to find out who she's talking about. I've been abroad five or six times, but I don't always get the place references in Janet Flanner's columns, and— time out for a deep breath—have you ever tried to unscramble the metaphors in Fadiman's reviews? Leave me be.

Love

J. O'Ha

---

[1] "The Magical Numbers," 8 January 1941. "Why, Daddy?" was a question repeated by Fanny Brice on her *Baby Snooks* radio program.
[2] "Portistan on the Portis," 23 November 1935.
[3] Margaret Fishback, prolific contributor to *The New Yorker*.

TO: William Maxwell   TLS, 1 p. PSt.
Received 3 April 1939   Los Angeles

Dear Bill:

I have one[1] here for you that I think everybody ought to like. It is about a boy that came to a new school and stole a watch. At least we think he stole the watch. Maybe that isn't what the author intended. The author is very vague.

I am working for RKO now, on a picture for Carole Lombard.[2] If you want to know why it is because The New Yorker doesn't pay me that kind of money, and anyway Lombard is much prettier than Ross and I'm not saying anything behind his back. If I have anything to say to a man I say it to his face. Lombard is prettier than you, too. Out of sight, out of mind.

I wish you would start using up some of my pieces. I don't like the look in people's eyes when they ask me what I think of Irwin Shaw.

y. v. t.
John

[1] "Do You Like It Here?" 18 February 1939.
[2] The Carole Lombard movie was not made.

TO: William Maxwell   TLS, 1 p. PSt.
Received 12 May 1939   Los Angeles

Dear Will:

Back in the new routine; which is hangovers without any fun the nite be4. I tho't I would have a studio job waiting for me but no. Either they got tired waiting or nothing was there in the 1 place. Do you think I ought to start working on Shuman et al on the financial situation? I managed to scatter about $1000 as a result of the tremor in my tummy, and apparently that is only the beginning. I do think I thought to get a raise, and Belle thinks I have just about earned a new bonus. Of course there is the infinitesimal matter of what I owe the F-R Co., but who would bring that up at a time like this?

We are moving out of here June 1 and taking a tent somewhere, unknown at this point.

Don't ever get an ulcer. I suppose you went through this with McKelway. First you can't sleep because of going on the wagon, then you (I) get horrible melancholia because you can't eat what you want to and when you want to. I imagine it's like being put in jail. By God, sir, this isn't The American Way! Is this why I labored so hard for repeal? Is it for this that I taught three headwaiters how to make my favorite meat sauce? Etc.

Tell McK our cook is gleaning Robinsoniana.[1] Also tell him I would appreciate a word of thanks for sending in the tip that Barclay Street[2] was worth a piece. I ought to get 10%.

I drew a negative Wassermann. I feel like a Phi Beta Kappa.

J. O'H

[1] Reference to dancer and actor Bill ("Bojangles") Robinson.
[2] O'Hara had suggested a "Talk of the Town" piece on Benziger Brothers.

TO: Harold Ross   TLS, 1 p. PSt.
                                                   Los Angeles
                                                   May 15, 1939
Dear Harold,
    Today I got an idea for a Profile, and I've started to work on it. I've done
about 2000 words on it, but it occurs to me that I might be luxuriating in
a terrific waste of time unless I have a little talk with you. Believing that
you would find it impractical to fly here to chat with me, I take pen in
hand to give you the substance of the idea.
    How about a three-part Profile of a 1939—for want of a better word—
Babbitt? I *mean* 1939. A guy, 41 years old, with all the differences in his
history, outlook, etc., that a '39 Babbitt would have. I have started with
two incidents which occur in his college days, which I think tell all you
want to know about that phase, and right now he is out of college and
sneaking up on matrimony. He of course would not be a New Yorker, but
neither is Heh-Ven.[1] The next part would find him a young married man
in the beginning of the boom days, taking him up to 1930. The third part
would bring him up to the trylon and perisphere, off which I would drop
him with a sickening thud.[2]
    Well?

                                                   Love
                                                   J. O'Hara

Did you ever have an ulcer? I guess not. I guess if you survive the Aspen
food nothing can harm you ever after.

[1] Possible reference to Fred Astaire's pronunciation of "heaven" in "Cheek to Cheek."
[2] This profile was not written.

TO: Samuel Sloan   TLS, 1 p. HBJ
May 1939   471½ Landfair,
                                                   Westwood, Los Angeles
Dear Sam'l,
    I hope that old NY Central did not keep you standing anxiously at Har-
mon. It kept us standing anxiously at 91st Street and then again at Mor-
risania, for an hour and 20 minutes. Broken air coupling. We were mad to
have missed you both, and don't think your telegram made up for it, thank
you.
    I am finding this a sorry life, what with just beginning to be able to
sleep, a result of so abruptly going on the wagon; and I am as melancholy
as a pregnant woman around mealtime, hating the discipline, and suddenly
losing all appetite when I remember that I have to think before I eat

147

instead of just pouring on the hot mustard and Escoffier and going to it. Parenthetically it was gracious of you to let me prepare at the St Regis for the subsequent nights of sleeplessness. I am very embarrassed about that and will thank you not to mention it until next fall. Then I'll mention it. Maybe intolerant Peggy[1] will mention it first. Give her my love.

As to the enclosed, I think the Foreword[2] is practically self-explanatory, tho not self-justifying. If you object to it I won't put up a fight, but it just possibly might annoy some of the boys like Fadiman enough to cause a tiny controversy, which would keep the book alive. The dedication, of course, was inevitable, and I can't think of anyone at H-B who has anything against my mother.[3]

As Mark Hanna says,

Cheers
John

[1] Mrs. Sloan.
[2] To *Files on Parade* (1939), in which O'Hara attacked the critics.
[3] O'Hara dedicated *Files on Parade* to his mother.

TO: William Maxwell   TLS, 1 p. PSt.
May 1939

Moving next week; new address after May 31 will be

542 Midvale Avenue
Westwood
Los Angeles

Plenty of room if you care to visit us

Dear Bill:

It is hard for me to think of the rejection of the previous Pal Joey piece,[1] so hard that I am not going to bother, save only to say that of the two objections you cited, one of them could have been fixed with a pencilled one-word change in the office, and the other was just so damned ununderstanding of the whole Pal Joey series that I wonder how any of them could have been bought. Joey on the surface was looking for advice, but isn't it obvious (what a weak word) that he wasn't asking for advice, but only using that form as an excuse to brag? Oh, hell. Well, here's another one. If you don't like this one, the series ends—and maybe if you do like it. You just might pass this on to Ross, though, with this reminder: that he said to me in 21[2] last Fall, when both of us were sober, that if I wrote him ten Pal Joey pieces I could say the hell with Hollywood. You might also let him know that until recently I have allowed myself to consider Shuman a temporary measure, and that it is pretty damn distressing to have such a flat turndown on the money question. As you probably know, I got some money from the radio for letting them butcher THE IDEAL MAN, "the lovely story John O'Hara wrote for The New Yorker"—played by Don Ameche and Rosalind Russell! But those velvety godsends come (exactly) once in a lifetime.

Just what giant intellects determine the value of my words and decide upon a 13½ cent limit?

Here Lies
John O'Hara

---

[1] Probably either "A Bit of a Shock" or "Reminiss?"—first published in *Pal Joey* (1940).
[2] "21" was one of O'Hara's favorite New York restaurants.

TO: William Maxwell   TLS, 1 p. PSt.
Received 11 August 1939   Los Angeles

Dear Will:

Just get the Goslings out of your head until next Spring and settle down to a quiet ten minutes with Joey, a real American, who doesn't know a sixpence from a dime (but I'll bet it wouldn't take him long to find out).

Do you do the scheduling? I believe my short story book[1] emerges on Sept. 21, so will you be jolly and run what you think is my nicest composition in the issue of the 23rd of Sept.?[2] In that way you may embarrass Fadiman if he pans the book, and if it is at all possible to embarrass anyone with such self-assurance, I want to be the boy to do it.[3] I once figured out that the only way to put Jed Harris[4] in his place was to slap a custard pie in his kisser, and I guess the only way to fix Clifton ("Kip") would be to hang a KICK ME sign on him.

Please remind Ross that in the enclosed piece I violate still another O'Hara-New Yorker tradition: I numbered the pages as a result of his plea.

j o'hn

[1] *Files on Parade.*
[2] "Bread Alone" appeared in this issue.
[3] *The New Yorker* gave it only a brief mention on 23 September.
[4] Broadway producer.

TO: William Maxwell   TLS, 1 p. PSt.
Summer 1939   Los Angeles

Dear Wm.:

Here we have a little item for hammock reading.[1] I will be the first to admit that the first part is kept pretty dull, but I think it's more effective that way. For your information, the cop vs girl part actually occurred in Palm Beach four years ago the day before I got there. A friend of mine saw it happen and I nearly went insane. For months I wanted to kill every cop I saw, and as you see I never have forgotten it. The nice thing is that the woman told me about it has a daughter of her own, just then reaching the age when a girl might possibly become indiscreet with a handsome cop.

Wuddia hippum the mob?

                                                                Jack

   [1] "Too Young," 9 September 1939.

TO: William Maxwell   TLS, 2 pp. PSt.
Summer 1939

                                                        John O'Hara
                                                        542 midvale
                                                        westwood
                                                        los angeles
                                                        john held jr.
                                                        e. e. cummings

Dear Will:

Ask me no questions I'll tell you no lies. Ask me questions you get answers. My gut acted up once or twice when I ate wrong things (that sounds like Lenny in Mice & Men), but has been behaving pretty well, thank you. Better than Dempsey's[1] anyway, and he keeps a fucking restaurant.

About that piece[2] which Ross liked the ending of but not the refugee stuff, I like the refugee stuff. I slightly know a refugee on that order, and I really think I had a good point in that piece. Now that the n. y.er is running Mencken, of course, we can't have any bolshy propaganda, and I am thinking of writing a piece for the new masses[3] on Not Enough[4] and calling Mr. Ross a Harold, because he has all the other qualifications.

Yes, I had word that Cap was with you. In what capacity? I would like to see him replace Fadiman, but that is not to be taken as a token of love. I would like to see Fadiman replaced, and I don't care whom by. Dick Simon or Max Schuster might be a good choice. Or the man who wrote Steps Going Down.

Tell Gibbs hereafter to pull his punches when he writes Wayward Press, as I am secretly counting on that to pay my rent when I return in the Fall, toothless, teetotaler, and trembling.

I was a little worried about Thurber when he got out here, but he is all right now. We went to a big cocktail party for him, and when we saw him later that night he already had checked the invitation list and knew what big shots had failed to show up. Thurber's well.

By the same token, how are you and your double life, my friend?

John

[1] Jack Dempsey.
[2] Unidentified.
[3] Left-wing weekly.
[4] Unidentified.

TO: William Maxwell   TL, 2 pp. PSt.
September 1939   542 Midvale,
                                              Westwood, Los Angeles

Dear Bill:

Boss Ross must be feeling his old self again, judging by the queries on Bread Alone.[1] Splendid! And now let us to business, for the moment.

I will go along with most of the small queries, and in fact anticipated Ross' wanting me to draw a picture of a coal black pappy. That is the penalty of trying to write decently and with some respect for the possible reader, figuring, as I occasionally do, that anyone who can read can get what I am saying. I therefore was a little surprised that Boss Ross wanted me to draw a picture of a man with a Roman schnozz and a circumcised whang, with a social security number etc., also a driver's licence saying he was Morton Ginsburg, 34, 1166 Decatur Ave., The Bronx, employed as a bookkeeper at the Elbee garage because he had a cousin who knew one of the owners, etc. Well, Ginsburg is clear, I do trust. I also added some details about how Mr. Hart could bum a ride home, because Ross wouldn't believe me if I told him how easy it is to bum rides to Harlem, me having had a valet once who did just that, nearly every day. My ex-valet is now a doorman at the Mad. ave. translux, if you care to have a look at him. His name is Harris and he whistles while he works, or did when McClain and I had him.

However I refuse to explain further about why Hart was worried about spending some of the 10 bucks. I mean I won't chop up the piece any more. Isn't it apparent that keeping the money a secret, and, further, spending any of it, is something to worry about?

The second thing I won't go into in proof is that about his not having seen a ball game for 15 yrs. There are thousands of men (and women) in this country who never saw a big league game, who know offhand the batting averages, fielding averages, etc., of every player on the Boston Red Sox of 1938. I happen to know that Ross has an old hate on baseball, claiming that New Yorker readers don't know or care anything about it. But I also happen to know that Ross is so wrong in that. I can be just as snobbish as he and say that an Aspen, Colo. boy is less likely to know what a Racquet & Tennis boy is interested in than I am. The boys I grew up with went to good prep schools and colleges, the same ones that N.Y.ers go to. Andover, Yale, Hill, Princeton, same difference. Anyway I *expected* trouble because the piece was partly about baseball.

On the Joey piece,[2] Al Rinker was one of the Rhythm Boys, with Bing Crosby and Harry Barris. He is now, I believe, some big shot in radio or Music Corp. of America. I have decided that it should be Brooks John, as being the kind of error Joey would make. The fellow's real name was Brooke Johns. Played banjo for Ann Pennington, and is now, I understand, running a chicken farm in Maryland. You will find me never making the errors I occasionally come upon in New Yorker reviews of "swing" records.

No bowling in summer? Wish I had the money bowling turns over in summer.

I don't think we ought to worry too much about Joey's observing any style rule on titles of songs.

I don't think we ought to worry about anything else! We were coming home from the Troc,[3] the Sidney Skolskys[4] and the O'Haras in my car, when we were taken to 10, Downing street and heard Chamberlain's announcement of the state of war. For the last few nights I have been working on a piece about my recollections of 1914–18, which I thought might go to The New Yorker. I haven't been able to write anything else, because I haven't thought of much else. When I finish the piece I'll send it along; if you buy it, okay, if you don't, read it, show it to Gibbs, and throw it away.[5] I'm going to get a chance to check up on the accuracy of some of my (unwritten) observations of the war. I'd rather be unsure. One trouble is that since the days of my wartime patriotism I have seen several men who have been shot and several who have been stabbed and quite a few who had been in mine explosions. That sort of takes a few decibels out of your voice when you join in Tipperary and Over There.
God save Roosevelt!

Have you at this moment a literary agent? If so, who? I choose to be vague at this point about why I'm asking. I will write you in a week or so if and when I have something to say to follow up that question.

[1] 23 September 1939.
[2] "Joey in Herta," 25 November 1939.
[3] The Trocadero, Hollywood night club.
[4] Hollywood columnist.
[5] Unpublished.

TO: William Maxwell   TLS, 1 p. PSt.
Fall 1939   Los Angeles

Dear Will:

Here I am still writing about Christmas and it's practically Hallowe'en. We writers lead such a topsy-turvy life. I think I will say that this is about last Christmas and then maybe get straightened out. I think—I'm not sure, but I *think*—Santa's going to bring me a whole new set of teeth this year. If I'm good. If I don't disobey Darryl F. Zanuck[1] or talk back to Will H. Hays,[2] and be polite to Uncle Harold.

I saw Thurber's play[3] last night. It's very spotty and has, I think, too much Nugent and not enough Thurber, which means that it goes from one Thurber point of view to another Thurber point of view, and in between, no point of view but indecision between farce and gentle comedy. If ever there was a play that needed a certain collaborator this is the play. And the collaborator, Mr. Maxwell, is you! I know what's wrong with it, too, and if Thurber asked (and followed) my advice, he would have the Pulitzer Prize play, and a good P. P. play. As is I think he has a good chance of a hit, but the hands and the kitchen sink of the trouping Nugents make me uncomfortable.

                                                       Yrs truly
                                                       John

[1] Head of production at Twentieth Century–Fox.
[2] Motion-picture censor.
[3] *The Male Animal* by James Thurber and Elliot Nugent.

TO: William Maxwell   TLS, 1 p. PSt.
Late 1939   Los Angeles

Dear Will:

What was it I wanted to say to you? Oh, yes. I infer that you bought Cake-Line, although no cheque came. I therefore wrote this one to fill in the hiatus between Cake Line and Calcutta Club.[1] If I bollixed up the intent of your note, just put in a Life with Father[2] or a Mr. North[3] and vamp till ready.

So Ross is getting bored with Joey too. I shudder to think of what they (meaning *I*) must have done to your nervous system and digestion in the past year. It was bad enough for me, although as easy money as you can get without actually inheriting it or being home when Horace Heidt calls you on Tuesday night. But I got pretty fucking bored. There is an idea for a master's thesis at a bad university on series like Joey and the other serieses I did for The New Yorker and other people did for The New Yorker. The

                                153

first time I heard Guy Lombardo I liked him (it was a recording, of course). The second time, the second record of his, made me want to smash the phonograph. But not the dear readers of the Joey series, any more than the listeners to Lombardo, who I am afraid may be pretty much the same people. Not altogether, but pretty much. Well the Joey stuff got readers and I got applause and easy money and now I'll have to think up another idea for a series. I am marking time until I evolve a Dere Mabel.[4]

I'm still working in the films, the writing end, you know. I never work more than 3 hrs a day but I am so much faster than they are accustomed to that my boss laughs at me. "You'll catch on," he said the other day. "I hope you don't," I said to myself.

> Hold tight
> John

[1] "Joey on the Cake Line," 23 December 1939; "The Erloff," 3 February 1940; "Even the Greeks," 2 March 1940; "Joey and the Calcutta Club," 30 March 1940.
[2] *New Yorker* series by Clarence Day.
[3] *New Yorker* series by Richard and Frances Lockridge.
[4] Edward Streeter's *Dere Mable* (1918), a series of vernacular letters from a soldier.

TO: Joseph Bryan III   TLS, 2 pp. PSt.
November 1939   Twentieth Century–Fox
                                                              letterhead

Dear Cap'n Suh:

The unidentified body of Robert Wallace was found in Cutting Room B at the Fox Lot yesterday. Mr. Wallace, who refused to give his name, died of Leica poisoning said to have been administered in his Doctah Peppah etc . . . And if that was the good one you sent me, Bryan, I don't know what form of libel you're up to, showing people the other one.

Unlike you, I write letters with a purpose. My purpose is to find out what became of my RBBB cap and coat? You have my cap size, you and North,[1] and the coat size is 44. I haven't a thing to wear and I've been holding off shopping until I see what will go with my uniform. The tennis club I belong to had a circus ball, and I would have been the hit of it had John sent me my circus suit. As it was I was the hit anyway. I and ——— and a couple of girls from Casting gave a circus that will top anything a Ringling ever thought up. I ended with my own foot in my kisser, and never knew before what fun that could be. Now every time I open my mouth I *try* to put my foot in it. If you want to ring any more changes in that gag you can jollywell hand it over to Farr,[2] with my love.

The news here is that David Niven has declared war on Unity Mitford,[3] My Dream Girl of the Thyroid Eyes. Otherwise I am working for Zanuck and every week I dream of Hanna and the $75 he would be getting if he'd left me alone with Stradner for two minutes one day. But Hanna is a dog in or out of a manger and so I had to let him go—with Stradner. And you saw what happened to Stradner, she wound up with a dreadful mankiewicz,[4] which you can also get from too much polished rice.

Belle, once again on her feet after her horrible siege as a result of being a good sport about it all, is fine and the Bantam[5] is fine. Sloan was out here for a minute and we gave him a party, dismally failing in our pathetic effort to find in all Hollywood a match for his Peggy. The Troc folded right after you were there, which of course may not necessarily be cause and effect. It leaves us with nothing to do but take in the show at Grauman's Chinese and Werba's Jamaica. I am pale again as a result of often going to the studio and my friends would recognize me once more. I am sending teasing little sums to various people whom I owe money to, and am toothmarking a certain sum each week for the dental work and will soon have a smile like Paul V. McNutt's.[6] Exactly like Paul V. McNutt's to you.

I think you went all out on the Ranger piece,[7] and liked it better than the Benchleys, which of course was not your fault. I know Bob too well, and got no surprises, and the big piece on Benchley would have to be privately printed anyway. Sloan and I were as one on the Ranger article. I suppose you couldn't have told more of Benchley's leftist philosophy and action without making him, at least in the eyes of the Post and Post-average-families, a public enemy, and of course Bob's so-called private life is something I only hope I am capable of when I reach his age. Or now. I hear you are leaving the Post, and I can't for the Life of me remember where I heard it. But I heard you got a Big Offer. Could Sloan have told me?

I trust you saw Joel Sayre's valentine to me in the Eve. Ledger.[8] I have the Ledger in the palm of my hand, what with Joel and my kid brother Tom working there.

Morton Downey[9] told me a filthy story today but it makes me laugh. About a Cockney who for years had been working in the London sewers. At long last they gave him a holiday and he went down to Brighton, got in his swim suit, went out on the beach and took one, two, three deep breaths of the sea air. "Ah, the sea air," he said, and fainted. And they had to throw three bucketfuls of shit on him to bring him to.

With that thought, so delightfully reminiscent of dear old Dr. Arthur Twining Van Dyke,[10] I will close.

Closing,
The Pride of the Palomar[11]

155

Tell North that if the Bedaux[12] system is keeping him from sending me my uniform I'll have a little talk with John L. Lewis. And if he wants to make up for the delay by sending me a pair of boots, Peal[13] has my size.[14]

[1] John Ringling North, president of Ringling Brothers and Barnum & Bailey Circus.
[2] Finis Farr, who later wrote a biography of O'Hara.
[3] Englishwoman known for her association with leading Nazis.
[4] Actress Rosa Stradner married producer-director Joseph L. Mankiewicz.
[5] An English car O'Hara owned.
[6] Government official and diplomat.
[7] "Hi-Yo, Silver!" *The Saturday Evening Post* (14 October 1939).
[8] The *Philadelphia Evening Ledger.*
[9] Singer.
[10] Arthur Twining Hadley, President of Yale; Henry Van Dyke, author and clergyman.
[11] The Palomar was a ballroom in Los Angeles noted for its swing bands.
[12] Charles E. Bedaux, an efficiency expert.
[13] London custom shoemaker.
[14] Final sentence in holograph.

TO: William Maxwell   TLS, 1 p. PSt.
January 1940   Los Angeles

Dear Bill:

Have a nice Xmas? Well.

In spite hell and high Harold, here is another Joey. It unwound itself in about an hour, so I tho't what the hell. I have my own personal and private reasons for wanting you to buy this, plus a few more, the personal and private reasons being (a) a book of them and (b) a play based on Joey. As I have told you before, but do not object to telling you again, these damn things are the most successful things I've ever done for The NYer. I beat my brains out writing fine, sensitive prose, careful streams of consciousness, lean spare sharp exposition, accurate shot of dialog and what do I get yet? * in O'Brien. Then one morning at the Pierre, with a roaring hangover and no sleep and a wife thinking I am in Philadelphia, I knock out a bit of autobiography and the literary people discover me. Well, Life With Father is a success and if somebody would write a play about Joey, the way I figure Life With Father would send them hurrying across the street to see my baby. Or it would me.

Well, have a nice Xmas.

                                                       John

TO: *The New Republic*, CII (15 January 1940), 88

SIR: Except for the fact that I worked for him and saw him every day during the Give-a-Job campaign and for one precious moment in "21" when he came over and told me he liked a book I wrote, I think I am very well qualified to write about Heywood Broun.[1] The period of the daily association, and the few minutes in the restaurant almost disqualify me because they put me apart from the hundreds whom he so easily convinced that they were his pals.

"Hello, Heywood," in the thick accent of Broadway, unreproducible in print, and undisguisable in utterance.

"Hello, there. How *ah-h-h* yuh?"

It didn't make a great deal of difference to the Broadway heel that he knew Broun did not know his name, and probably did not remember his face. The heel knew that Broun's heart was in the right place. He very likely did not expect anything from Broun—nothing more than the most superb courtesy that man ever gets from man. Incurable, helpless bores would fly at him, often despising themselves for what they were doing; but when he brushed them off they came away from him with their self-respect and often more than that.

He was a gentleman. He was what *I* mean by a gentleman, and what my father and mother meant when they tried to bring me up to be one. He was kind, courteous and square. Generous, considerate and big. I would hear some of his fellow members of the Racquet Club putting the knock on him, and I would always be reminded of the fascist bastards who like to say that Roosevelt is a traitor to his class—meaning, of course, *their* class, a class, however, to which they had only very recently transferred from some exceedingly cow college, and in senior year at that.

There are some men who are everything they are for no other reason than that they have about them or attached to them the right things: a Richard Whitney, who naturally went to Harvard and was a member of the Pork and the crew, and hunted, and did this and that. Not so Broun. Broun honored Harvard by going there, continued to keep it respectable by continuing to like it. He gave the imprimatur to basketball because he had played it at Horace Mann. He gave the horse laugh to the food-and-wine purists by simply tossing off a stinger and following it with a whiskey sour. I know I still have a raccoon coat for the excellent reason that at my age Heywood Broun had one too. He made a lot of people seem right by letting it be known they were his friends. He honored me, by God, by letting me sit with him, work for him, drink to him.

Hello, Heywood.

Los Angeles, Calif. JOHN O'HARA

[1] Columnist Broun died 18 December 1939.

TO: William Maxwell   TLS, 1 p. PSt.
Early 1940   542 Midvale Ave.,
                                                           Los Angeles

Dear Will:
   Here is an unimportant problem which you can turn over to whoever.
   A couple of years ago, or more, there was a Talk piece about how to get
a foreign decoration. According to the piece, as I recall it, you wrote to some
consulate or legation and for something like $35 they gave you an Order
which gave you a medal, rosette, etc., and the right to wear it. Can you
ask one of the boys to look in the files, find the piece, clip it, and send it
to me? I'm sorry I have to be so vague about when it appeared, but perhaps
it will be filed under some classification that will make it easy.
   Marc Connelly[1] wears a ribbon which is a symbol of, I think, the
American Academy of Arts and Sciences or something. It drives everybody
crazy, and some night I would like to appear at a dinner with Marc,
wearing a much more impressive and apparently authentic decoration. Yes,
it might even be worth $35. I've spent more for much less pleasure.
   Here it's raining.

                                                              Yrs
                                                              John

[1] Playwright, author of *The Green Pastures*.

TO: Richard Rodgers[1]   TLS, 1 p. PM (22 December 1940), 50
Early 1940   Los Angeles
                              Thursday
Dear Dick:
   I don't know whether you happened to see any of a series of pieces I've
been doing for The New Yorker in the past year or so.[2] They're about a
guy who is master of ceremonies in cheap night clubs, and the pieces are
in the form of letters from him to a successful band leader. Anyway, I got
the idea that the pieces, or at least the character and the life in general
could be made into a book show, and I wonder if you and Larry[3] would be
interested in working on it with me. I read that you two have a commit-
ment with Dwight Wiman for a show this Spring but if and when you
get through with that I do hope you like my idea.[4]
   . . . .[5]

                                  158

All the best to you always. Please remember me to the beautiful Dorothy[6] and say hello to Larry for me. Say more than hello, too.

Faithfully,
John

[1] Composer who wrote the songs for *Pal Joey* with lyricist Lorenz Hart. The show opened on Broadway Christmas 1940 and ran for 374 performances.
[2] The Pal Joey stories.
[3] Lorenz Hart.
[4] Rodgers responded favorably, and O'Hara came east to work on his book for *Pal Joey*.
[5] Part of this letter was excised in the facsimile published in *PM*.
[6] Mrs. Rodgers.

TO: Virginia Schulberg[1]   TLS, 2 pp. Budd Schulberg
Early 1940   27 Sutton Pl South
                                            NYC

Dear Jige Honey:

Any number of people have written in and asked me why I didn't take a few minutes off to give you some instructions on how to bring up Gretchen. In answer to this spontaneous and timely request I shall jot down a few hints that may save you many's the heartache later on.

TEETHING

I am against teething. Teething a ickle baby only meanth it will have a bad temper when it gwowth up.

PICKING THEM UP WHEN THEY CRY

With me it has always been just the reverse. I stop the car on Fairfax, pick them up, spend $35 on them, and it's on the way to my villa that they begin to cry. I can't help you on this.

FEEDING

There is no doubt whatever in my mind that babies should be fed.

FRESH AIR

How, indeed, would this old world get along without fresh air? Without it history certainly never would have recorded the names of Wilbur and Orville Wright, Glenn Curtiss, Bleriot, Charles A. Lindbergh, General Mitchell, Leland Hayward—to name but a few. It is excellent also for drying diapers and one's own hair if one has just had a home shampoo. Lazy but lovable Old Glory needs it if l. but l. O. G. is in triumph to wave. How would that smoke from the power plant across the river get to this room as I write were it not for fresh air? What else provides the chaps with such innocent enjoyment at Wilshire & Rodeo after lunch? In the case of Gretchen and sailboats, I recommend a spanking breeze, which leads me, however awkwardly, to the next Hint.

159

ON SPANKING

When I was in prep school—and probably when Winston Churchill was in prep school—there used to be a brain twister that went like this: Q. How do you keep a baby from crying? A. Give it a bust in the mouth. That, however, is a measure which is for the little mother herself to determine. Nevertheless, I have a few thoughts on spanking. When I was a child someone apparently put a fist in the parcel post and send it to my dear beloved Daddy. At least it always felt like he was using a mailed fist. I do not approve of that. I do not approve of any spanking at all before the child is two weeks old, except when necessary. Authorities disagree, but according to the best available opinion a child does not begin to recognize either parent, nurse, Adohr[2] man, Ring Lardner, Collier and/or Valerie Young, or anybody else before it has reached the age of three months. Therefore if one of the parents—or, for that matter, any of the afore-mentioned persons—wishes to spank the child, it is better to do it before the child begins to recognize people. Otherwise the child is liable to harbor a grudge, grow up to be Mildred Didrikson,[3] and beat the livin shit out of the spanker.

PETS

I found very interesting the results of a recent poll to which I subscribed. It appears that on the question of Pets children are divided. Some children love them. Some hate them. Still others have not given the matter a great deal of thought, and one little moppet residing at the home of its parents in Bismarck, N.D., refused to answer any questions. This, of course, simply proves two things: that the matter should be put squarely up to the child, and (b) that there is a stubborn child in Bismarck. However, having had some little experience in the matter, I feel free to make certain recommendations: A pterodactyl around children is likely to become irritable, doubtless because of the difference in their ages; I know of no children today to whom I would entrust the care of a valuable gorilla; the best pet for a child is another child which has been chained to the bedside. That gives Child A a distinct advantage in eye-gouging, hair-pulling, nuts-kicking and other juvenile sport.

HOW SOON SHOULD MY BABY BEGIN TO WALK, HUH?

On this question the really progressive mother should have no hesitation. No modern child should be taught to walk. What with the automobile, the airplane, the escalator, the lift (ascenseur), scooter, burro, roller skates, ice skates, skis, and St. Christopher himself, the Trend is obvious. To fight the atrophication of the lower limbs is to fight progress itself, and I won't have it. Walking on the hands is permissible if the parents intend to send the child to college. The child may become a cheer-leader and thus make contacts that will be invaluable in later life. But leg-walking, or foot-walking, is, in the literary term, pedestrian.

In the case of Gretchen, I would say let her decide that for herself. Nursing is all right, but she might like to be a stenographer or a railway mail clerk.

SEX EDUCATION

It's better with your shoes off.

****

****

I have of course not covered everything fully, dear Jige but please feel free to ask me anything. Your answer will be mailed in a plain wrapper which I always kept as a souvenir of a raid in the old Times Square hotel. Hope you are well and happy.

J(ohn) O'H.

[1] This letter was written to novelist Budd Schulberg's wife before the birth of her daughter, Victoria. Schulberg was a close friend of O'Hara's in Hollywood.

[2] Los Angeles dairy.

[3] Athlete Babe Didrikson.

TO: Walter S. Farquhar   TLS, 4 pp. PSt.
Early 1940   542 Midvale Ave.,
                                            Westwood, Los Angeles

Dear Walter:

It sounds as though you had reached the serious stage in extra-curricular endeavor, and I hope my surmise is correct. For what it's worth, here is a sort of round-up of my thoughts on agents.

First of all, to be specific, I never have heard of either of the three agents whom you mention. However, you did not say whether they were individuals, in business for themselves, or persons working for agencies. I could have been more helpful if you had added that detail. But I repeat, I never heard of either one of them.

My opinion of agents is frankly low. I do not use a literary agent, and never have. Neither does Hemingway. Neither does Dorothy Parker. (I will first discuss literary agents. Movie agents in a minute.) The best an agent does for an unpublished writer is to make up his mind to try to sell the writer to a publisher, then to take the material around to various publishers (frequently the wrong ones) and save the writer the trouble of mailing and remailing the stuff himself. A writer living abroad probably needs an agent—although as I said, Hemingway has none—and/or a writer to whom New York is inaccessible. But I honestly believe that no agent ever sold a piece that would not have been sold without the agent. Book and magazine publishers are, believe it or not, always on the lookout for a new author, and I believe there is a rule at the Satevepost that every editor has to find a brand new author, at least one such a year, simply by picking him out of the mailbasket—and you should see a Satevepost mailbasket. Much the same system is in vogue in some other magazines, although Cosmopolitan, for instance, is chary of unpublished writers, and maybe that's where an agent does some good.

It is difficult to declare that all agents are honest or dishonest. A crooked agent is usually found out, and when he is the Authors League gets after him and occasionally puts him behind bars. On the other hand, a lot of sharp practice, legally okay, does go on. I think it's probably analogous to a man going to a strange city and picking out a lawyer. A matter of luck.

However, here are a few agents or agencies of repute. George T. Bye, probably the best known—but he very rarely handles an unpublished author. O. K. Liveright seems okay. The Curtis Brown agency is big and wellknown. Harold Ober handles some people I know. I think they are about all I would even mention and I will not take the responsibility of recommending any of them.

Maybe I am being obvious, but at that risk I will say First, be careful what kind of letter you write to any agent. You studied law, so you know how far you commit yourself. Don't touch any agent who wants more than 10% commission. Don't advance any money whatever for typing and mailing expenses, or for "expert criticism". Don't sign any long-term agreement without letting me know who is handling you. (They all ask you to sign a seven-year agreement, but don't do it.) Be extremely careful what rights you sign away. An agent is entitled only to 10% of what he gets for you, and that goes for first American rights (book or magazine publication), movie rights, television, dramatic, radio, etc. Any time you are in doubt get in touch with me or with the Authors League. The League, by the way, has a list of reputable agents. You might ask them for a list, although since you are not a member I am not sure they will give it to you. If an agent wants you to sign an agreement, ask him if it is a standard Authors League agreement or contract, and get his answer in writing.

All the big magazines are reputable and honest. That is not true of the book publishers. The best of them will try to cut in on your rights as listed above, and the League is now fighting a winning battle to take all dramatic, etc. rights away from the publishers. Anyway, there isn't a publisher in the book business who won't try to get you to sign away at least a part of your extra rights.

The belief by which agents continue to exist is that they have some Masonic power by which they charm editors into buying. That's crap. The reason they continue to function is that once they have sold an author (who really sells himself by his writing), the agents can hold up publishers for more money, and can do it more effectively than most authors can.

If you have a book in mind, these are the usual terms for an unpublished writer: 10% of the retail price on all copies up to 2500 copies; 12½% on the second 2500, and 15% straight on all copies more than 5000. I get more, for obvious reasons, but those are the terms of my first deal with Harcourt, Brace & Co. To make it plain and unmistakable, on a book retailing at $2 a copy, the author's cut is 20 cents, 25 cents, and 30 cents, in the 10, 12½, 15% order. (But I need not add that if you have an agent, he takes 10% of your 20 cents, etc.)

I said I would go into the movie agent situation, but I've written enough and I don't want to confuse you, if I haven't already. I wish you had seen fit to tell me more about the material you have, and your problem. I probably could have been briefer and far more helpful.

One more thought: always distrust an agent's optimism. Authors are pathetic the way they believe agents when they say that "Viking Press are terribly excited about your book. We oughta hear any day now," or "Wes Stout is in Miami but I happen to know your story will be on his desk when he gets back. Both Sommers and Bryan said it was a swell story. May need a few changes, but essentially it's great." I know, baby. I believe it when I endorse the cheque. And after you've become reconciled to agents and their little white lies, never forget that beside an Editor the weather is mathematically constant.

Good luck.

John

TO: Gustave Lobrano[1]   TLS, 2 pp. PSt.
c. March 1940   New York

Dear Mr. Lobrano:

If I were you I'd howl for a raise, if my inference is correct and you are to "handle" my contributions and me. You saw what I did to Maxwell, and he was a wiry fellow.

Well, to start off, there's this, and it's got some m. or l.[2] confidential information in it. I am going to write the book for a musical comedy to be produced next fall in New York, and the book is to be based on my character Joey, Pal Joey. Also, probably at the same time I am going to bring out a collection of the pieces, in a book. So would be so kindly and ask Miss Schmidlap, which is my name for your secretary, if she will find out how many Joey pieces I have sold, including those not yet published. Later on, of course, I will write you a very formal note asking you to reassign copyright so that I can do the musical and the book, but first I want Miss Schmidlap to get me the dope on the pieces. In fact, just to give her something extra to do, she might even clip those pieces that have already appeared, and have extra proofs pulled of those on the bank, and sent to me.

This is the kind of thing you get asked to do, which is entirely out of the line of duty and for which the most you get out of it is an occasional drink at 21, and maybe, when I get to know you better, an abusive little philippic now and then.

Yrs,
J. O'Hara

[1] Fiction editor at *The New Yorker*.
[2] More or less.

TO: Edmund Wilson[1]

TLS, 1 p. Yale
8 East 52nd St
New York City

Jan. 20, 1940 [1941]

Dear Mr. Wilson:

Please forgive my delay in answering yours of Jan. 7. The trouble is I read my mail in the morning, then go back to sleep, and when awake think I must have dreamt the letters.

I would be very glad to reply in kind or in any other way to the disgusting hostility of some of Scott's obits.[2] If you will tell me more about the kind of thing you want, I'll do my best. This, however, is only an armistice between The NR[3] and me. I'm still annoyed about the Luce piece that you wouldn't print.[4]

Faithfully,
John O'Hara

[1] Critic who was at that time an editor of *The New Republic*.
[2] Wilson had invited O'Hara to contribute to a series of tributes to F. Scott Fitzgerald in *The New Republic*. O'Hara's "Some Aspects" appeared on 3 March 1941.
[3] *The New Republic*.
[4] *The New Republic* had rejected O'Hara's article "Luce Talk."

TO: Budd Schulberg

Inscription in
Appointment in Samarra.[1]
Schulberg

To Buddy (Sally Joe) Schulberg
In fond appreciation of.
some tender and knowing
hand-holding at the Forrest
Theatre, Philadelphia, and
the Ethel Barrymore, New York.
Actually
John O'Hara
Beverly Hills,
April 16, 1941

[1] The inscription refers to the tryout of *Pal Joey* in Philadelphia and the opening in New York.

TO: James V. Forrestal[1]   TLS, 1 p. Princeton
                                            Letterhead of Garden
                                             of Allah, Hollywood

                                               7 February 1942
                                                 (Navy style)

Dear Jim:

I am still slacking,[2] writing letters to Joe Barnes of the Donovan Committee and getting nowhere; hearing that physicals have been waived for
this man and that one to get commissions; boiling over at the actions and
some of the Acts of Congress but with no journalistic valve to pop off;
fuming at incompetence and complacency—but a very vulnerable guy for
counter-attacks on just those bases, because after all, what the hell am I
doing? I am earning money that will go for big taxes, but that's a Hollywood cliche. Even the Screen Actors Guild has come out with a statement
that it didn't think Hollywood people should get preferment, as advocated
by Mellett, or deferment. The result of all this? A strong sense of guilt
and futility, and on the fiscal side, impulsive, unplanned, and sometimes
extravagant donations to various Causes. I'm reading a hell of a war.

When I wrote you early in December and offered the Duesenberg to the
Navy for one buck I was not kidding. It is still in storage, still for sale to
the Navy for one buck. What do you think I ought to do about it?[3]

                                                    Yrs,
                                                    J. O'Ha

  [1] Former partner in Brown Brothers, Harriman who was Assistant Secretary of the
Navy in 1942. Forrestal became Secretary of the Navy in 1944 and Secretary of Defense
in 1947.
  [2] O'Hara was trying to obtain a Navy commission. After being rejected by the Navy
and the Army, he was accepted for OSS training in 1943, but resigned for health
reasons.
  [3] O'Hara thought the Navy could use his Duesenberg Speedster as a VIP car, but his
offer was declined.

TO: Folkestone[1]   TL, 3 pp. PSt.
                                             17 W. 54th St.,
                                             New York City

                                               May 31, 1942

Dear Folkestone:

If you feel that you have anything to say to me, anything worth a piece
of my valuable time, here is how you do it: you buckle on your sword, you
don your fore-and-aft hat, you ask for permission to come aboard, you
salute my flag, you get piped aboard, and in due course you are ushered

into the presence of the Chief Story Editor, Motion Picture Division, Office of the Coordinator of Inter-American Affairs. That will be me.[2]

We got back here on a Friday. The following Monday I lunched with P. Dunne and Jock Whitney—[3]and went to work that afternoon. I am serving "without compensation", which means that I'm not even a dollar a year man. I get a per diem allowance when I am out of town, but that amounts to somewhat less than I usually drop for a pleasant dinner for three at Mike's. I figured I would make that contribution to Uncle Sam while I am able, then when I am broke I will put in for a salary. My duties never have been accurately or completely defined, but I work mostly with Dunne. We discuss ideas for films—usually one or two reelers—then assign subjects to writers, then harry them until their scripts come in, then I butcher the scripts until we get something we can shoot (at not more than $2500 a film). I also am supposed to assist Dunne in planning and cutting short subjects which are made up of newsreel clips and stock shots, and write or rewrite the commentaries in English, which then are translated into Spanish and Portuguese, and possibly, in some cases, into English. I had to fill out some questionnaires for the FBI which gave me a tinge of inferiority complex. There wasn't room for all the schools I've gone to, and space enough for only eight jobs. Inasmuch as my employment career runs to something like 60 jobs of all sorts, I solved that by saying See Attached. This questionnaire was necessary in order that I can hire a secretary which will turn out, I am sure, to be a young lady who left Smith in junior year due to an exhibition she and a classmate gave at a Psi U party at Wesleyan, and which became so popular that she and her classmate were booked solid over the college circuit.

The job means New York, with occasional trips to Washington. Kenneth Macgowan[4] asked me right off if I would go to Washington and I said I hoped not and he said well I'd have to go for six weeks because after a guy has been down there a while he grows one big callous all over himself and doesn't know if an idea is good or bad, so since I had no callous I eventually would have to go there. My only reaction to that was to go straight to Brooks and buy three seersucker suits. I have been in bed all week with a touch of flu but will resume tomorrow. Unfortunately Whitney has or is about to quit and go in the Army. I say unfortunately because he is a good man besides being a nice guy, and being in his corner was going to mean big things politically. I don't know enough about it, but strictly Fence Club[5] it was something like this: our division has been the most efficient in the Office and also we have made the best pictures, so Jock has been trying to wangle it so that our division becomes an autonomous unit making all government propaganda films. A big job, to be sure, but certainly that doesn't make it any less attractive. I have had no trouble with Dunne as he seems to regard me as his best friend and Amanda feels the same about Belle. But tomorrow I am going to take a few stands when I go back refreshed from my illness. I am going to ask that my powers, authority and duties be defined or redefined, not only for my vanity's sake but also for the sake of efficiency. One or two little projects would have had a flat no from me from the very beginning, and I'd have saved the division from at least part of a snide attack on it last Monday by John O'Donnell in the News. They were sending films on orchids, California fashions, American jade, etc., to South America when they knew or should have known that the most successful stuff has been basketball, aviation, etc. The ability, or the habit, of saying no has been one of my most laudable characteristics, professionally speaking, so I don't see why it should be wasted when I am working for Uncle Sam.

We went out with Major Rex Smith of the Army Air Corps last night and he got me all steamed up about a specialist's job, with captaincy or majority, but along came another guy who said, as I have heard several times before, that one thing they will not waive is an ulcer history. Bob Wylie[6] told me if you've had an ulcer in the last five years they just won't look at you. It seems that some patriots already have snuck in the army or navy, developed illnesses such as ulcers after they had been waived, and now said patriots will be taken care of by the government for the rest of their lives. I of course am in no condition to take over a B-25 or to campaign with an infantry regiment. If I didn't have milk I would die, and that is no exaggeration self-pity. Nevertheless I don't feel any less a jerk when I go to 21 and have a toddy with Major Sy Bartlett, Major Rex Smith, Captain Bob Wylie, et al., all duked out in their zoot suits. Although I gave Bob Lovett as one of my references, which resulted in my getting past the FBI in six days, a new record, I am going to be embarrassed when I see him and Forrestal, because I won't be able to disguise my resentment. After all I wasn't one of the crowd that first flocked to Washington *after* Pearl Harbor. I started working on both Lovett and Forrestal almost two years ago, when their Wall Street pals regarded them as traitors to their class,[7] so the only conclusion I can come to is that they just plain didn't want me, and that's something to resent, isn't it? Oh, well.

I hope you will be able to see New York soon, under dim-out conditions. We had a pretty good blackout last week, and an air raid alarm rehearsal yesterday, but I'd like you to see the town, Times Square for instance, under present conditions. It's just a historical phenomenon I don't want you to miss. There's a kind of dark holiday spirit in the town. I now think the Nazis intend to bomb the shit out of New York before the summer is out, even though at the moment the Interceptor Commands seem to think the west coast is going to get it sooner. I base that, of course, on the report on the radio that cops from San Diego to Portland have been given tin hats and gas masks. If they do come over here with their eggs I know a great many lovable characters who ought to be treated to a few slivers of shrapnel. I refer to the ladies in their chauffeur-driven town cars who continue to double-park at Saks 5th Ave, and to the gas bootleggers and the sunburned young geese in convertible coupes who get their gas from God knows where, who were threading through the 3d avenue L pillars yesterday just as they always have. I am very much afraid that the youth who frequent or at least patronize 21 are acquitting themselves better than those who visit Leon & Eddie's,[8] if you know what I mean. I would like to know from you some time what you have been thinking about this past year and especially these past six months. It is important that you tell me because you don't get headaches when you think and you are articulate. Your generation are probably thinking the same things you are, but I'm sure they'll never get it into words. One of my brothers, who is in the Army Air Corps (radio man, now up for OCS) enlisted a year ago, more or less out of boredom. His best friend was killed on the Arizona, but before that happened Jimmy's attitude was that he didn't hate Hitler or anybody else; that if they came at him he would be glad to give them a fight. Then when Burnsie, his pal, was killed his attitude changed. The funny thing is, he wants to stay in the army for the rest of his life—a guy whose interests in college and since then have consisted chiefly of the more recondite forms of jazz music, foreign movies, the French language, and whiskey. He is a peculiar individual and much too individual to be typical of his age, which is the same as yours. I couldn't ask him what you are thinking because I know he never has given a thought or a damn what anyone else thinks. I ask you because you belong to your generation in age only, but because of that fact you are thrown with your contemporaries and are able to observe them without putting on a false face. Next to us last night at 21 was a large party of the jeunesse doree. All the lads except two were aviation ensigns; the other two were OCS. A year ago the proximity would have made me nervous; there'd have been a loudmouthed drunk, an amorous couple, and a lot of too loud talking. I watched them last night, and while there was an unmistakable scent of amorous doings ahead, the boys and the girls were clearly subdued. Disciplined was the word Belle used, and as usual she is right. But now that I think it over there was something else, the woman's angle. A year ago Joe X, who is now Ensign X, would be sitting there, putting away one or two too many Scotches, and wondering if since last night he actually got his hand on some of the hair, *maybe* tonight he might get a finger in, or better. But this year, last night, I am quite sure there wasn't a virgin in the crowd (average age 18 or less). Each girl and her boy knew that when the party broke up they would go home and very quietly stretch out on the living-room couch. I am sure I'm right because not a single girl on this party felt it necessary to scream or show off in any way or be flirtatious with anyone but the guy she was with. That, you'll agree, is very uncharacteristic behavior for young ladies of that set.

—— time-out ——

¹ "Folkestone"—probably a nickname—has not been identified. The letter was not finished or sent; it was found in a book in O'Hara's study after his death.
² O'Hara resigned this position after a couple of months.
³ Screenwriter Philip Dunne; financier John Hay (Jock) Whitney.
⁴ Broadway and Hollywood producer.
⁵ A Yale fraternity, i.e., secret.
⁶ O'Hara's brother-in-law, Dr. Robert Wylie.
⁷ For joining the Roosevelt administration.
⁸ New York night club.

TO: Gilbert Roland¹   TLS, 2 pp. Roland
                                                    Quogue, Long Island

                                                    July 13, 1942

Dear Amigo:

It was La Belle who first told me she read in Louella's² column or some place that you were in the Army. Then I myself saw that you were the most popular guy in your outfit, so I knew it was somebody masquerading under your name . . .

When we got back to NY I was here three days when I took a job with the Rockefeller Committee, or, if you want to address me by my full title, here it is: Chief Story Editor, Motion Picture Division, Office of the Coordinator of Inter-American Affairs. I was there a week or two, then got flu, and was bedded for a couple of weeks. Then when I licked the flu bug I got a sty on my eye, then when that disappeared I got your trouble, but good. A little alligator pear that I had been keeping warm for lo these many years suddenly began acting up. I couldn't sit down, I couldn't lie on my back. I went to the doctor and he prodded me and took other liberties, but he said he thought it was getting better and to let it go for a few days. That was on a Friday and for a day it did seem to get better, but on Sunday it got worse than ever—so bad that I was ready to cut the thing out with a rusty razor blade. Fortunately this was not necessary as I caught the doctor at home and he cut it out that day. He gave me novocaine, five shots, which hurt worse than anything up to that time, but then it began to work and I thought this was nothing, pure heaven as long as he didn't accidentally snip off my left nut (which was hanging in his way). Then I said something about this not being bad at all, and he said "Wait till the novocaine wears off." "When'll that be?" "In about an hour from now," he said. But he was wrong. It began to wear off in the taxi on the way home, and brother, I know how you must have been feeling the night we played gin rummy and anagrams. The doctor said it would feel as though somebody had given me a surprise kick in the ass, but that doctor is no slave to hyperbole. However in a week's time I was able to sit up or sit down, or just sit. I went for the final examination last week, and he said this was going to hurt a little. Of course it did, but not as much as I expected, but when he told me I could get off the table and get dressed and I saw an instrument in the washbowl I said, "You mean to say you had that thing inside me?" He said yes, and now it hurts when I think of it. But I'm glad it's over. Rather superfluously the doctor said on parting, "Don't let it happen again."

I submitted a resignation from my job but they asked me to withdraw it and to take a leave for as long as I liked. Jock Whitney, who was at the head of our division, resigned and is a captain in the Air Corps intelligence, due to go to London. I was sorry to see him go because I get along okay with him. My plans now are to get some health down here (it's about 85 miles from NY on the south shore, about 18 miles from Southhampton), get my teeth yanked out, and try for a commission in the Army Specialist Corps, or anywhere else.[3] Frankly I don't feel very much at home in the job I took, principally because I lack final authority, but probably that would have been worked out if I'd not had a more or less general physical crackup right after taking the job. I feel like a jerk being out of uniform when I go to 21 and places like that, and at the Field Club here the kids I used to play tennis and golf with are all gone—or come home on leave. Right here on the property I have two brothers-in-law, one a captain in the Medical Corps, the other a lieutenant in the artillery. The fact that I am as close to 40 as I am to 35 doesn't quite square me with myself, so I have my eye out for something or other all the time. I am starting flying lessons tomorrow, and that may be the answer. They have a Civil Air Patrol here which makes sense, and especially in recent weeks. The place where four of those saboteurs were picked up—Amagansett—is quite near here, and in about two weeks they are going to have a Civil Pilot Training Course which I hope to get in, but meanwhile I'll try to get some dual flying time and maybe even solo.

It's strange down here now. I've been coming to Quogue for five years. This is my sixth summer. You're not allowed to go on the beach at night; only the parking lights of your car are permitted in the village and along the Dune Road. Windows on the ocean side of the houses are blacked out, and if you forget about it you're reminded by the soldiers. The beach is patrolled 24 hours a day, as it should be, and field telephone lines are strung along the sand at the Beach Club. We have that Bantam down here, so the gas problem has not yet hit us seriously. I could probably trade the Bantam for the snappiest Darrin Packard on Long Island. Bikes are everywhere, but on account of my ass and my legs I haven't been able to ride more than a mile at a time. A few people have horses, but of course in recent years most of the people converted their stables into garages. When you go visiting you're supposed to bring your own sugar. Most of the gas dealers simply close up their pumps over the weekend, and they've taken the club cars off the trains between here and NY. In spite of all these little reminders there's still a great deal of silly talk about Washington and the Administration but it comes from the same greedy ones as ever, the unthinking, unseeing dopes who for nine years have been unable to get it through their thick skulls that the President was trying to retain and not to snatch away the way of life to which they had become accustomed. There was plenty of the same greed and stupidity in Wilson's time, as in Lincoln's, but never, I'm sure, so much of it in so many phases as now. There again is a reason for wishing I were in uniform; I'm so sick and tired of the civilian point of view, especially as one hears it on Long Island.

I am serving "without compensation" in my job, which enables me to do my own writing—when I get something to write. Right now I want to do a serious play first, then a musical. The latter, however, will have to wait as I'm afraid I'll have to go to the coast for a few days to get in some research on the idea for the musical (that's the one Constance[4] and I discussed). It seems impossible for me to think in terms of another novel at this point. The best I can do is observe and store up impressions for a novel to come later. It's a hell of a time to be a writer or at any rate a writer who is 37 years old and very likely 4-F.

We send our love to you both, and I'd like to hear from you about what you are doing and thinking. When we go to NY we intend to send rosaries and prayer books to our Godchildren so don't think we aren't as conscientious as we were complimented. Anyway, let me have a word from you, Amigo. Our NY address is 17 West 54, but we'll be here for most of the summer.

All the best,
John O'H

1 Actor and close Hollywood friend of O'Hara's.
2 Louella Parsons, Hollywood gossip columnist.
3 O'Hara never succeeded in getting a commission. The closest he came to involvement in the war was as a Navy correspondent for *Liberty* in 1944.
4 Actress Constance Bennett, Roland's wife.

TO: James V. Forrestal   TL (copy). Princeton
                                          Quogue, Long Island
                                          July 28, 1942
Dear Jim:

I hope and think that you are the guy who best can handle this for me. This, by the way, is strictly Psi U, Cottage Club, Masonic, etc.

I want to do a musical show, with Rodgers & Hart, based on the "swing shift" in an airplane factory.[1] Sort of an answer to the Berlin show,[2] but with no conflict. Mostly civilians, mostly women.

Naturally I have asked around and find that Sam Goldwyn has three scripts built around the name Swing Shift, but I don't know what those scripts are all about, nor does my informant.

What I want from you is a letter introducing me, or letters introducing me to important guys out on the coast, like Ki——berger[3] at North American, etc., et al., which will enable me to do just this: I want to go to Vultee or any and all plants and see just what happens to a woman who goes to work for an airplane plant. Employment office. Various examinations. Basic training. Qualified worker. Recreation and rest rooms. Fiscal data such as if she had a husband in service and a kid at home. Penalties and punishments. Etc., etc.

I have my own ideas as to characters, but these might easily be added to or enlarged upon. As you already have seen, if the show's a success it has great value as propaganda over and above its immediate and apparent morale value. Dick Rodgers and I have discussed it in some detail, and if you give me the light you'll see a show. I'm writing to you about this because I am under the impression you are somewhat concerned with just this "E" kind of thing.

To change the subject a little, two more requests will be going from me to you: (1) I shortly am going to be put up for that lively mausoleum on the west side of Park Avenue somewhere in the Fifties;[4] and (2) I am learning to fly so's to get in the CAP, and need a letter to guarantee that I like this country.[5] These requests will be sent separately so you won't write a letter to the Racquet club saying I am a good citizen. That, if I remember correctly, might amount to a blackball.

Well, anyway, the important thing is the send-in out on the coast, and I may say I'll leave almost the minute I hear from you. With the kindest to Josie and you.

                                          Yrs,
                                          /S/ JOHN

[1] The play was never completed.
[2] Irving Berlin's *This Is the Army*.
[3] Name appears thus in letter.
[4] The Racquet & Tennis Club in New York; O'Hara was not elected to membership.
[5] O'Hara took flying lessons, but did not join the Civil Air Patrol.

TO: Harold Ross   TLS, 1 p. PSt.
c. April 1943   Letterhead of Harkness Pavilion,
                                                        New York

Dear Harold:

I am up here with an infected jaw, swollen to pomegranate size, and before the week is out a lot of teeth will be, so I am taking a lot of sulfa stuff, etc.

I called Gibbs today and he is coming up probably Tuesday to discuss the piece called RADIO.[1] Here is another (a good one, I think) which ought to cause no mystery.[2] I told Maxwell on Friday to give you another which I had written on the 20th floor. I just want you to know that my theory of having an office is working out to the degree of industry I promised it would, and I want to keep that office. Three casuals in two weeks of occupancy ought to give me squatter's rights on the section.

I'll be here for a week anyway, Room 1134, so if you want to write, phone, or call in person, you know where to find me. I can guarantee you strained carrots, etc., if you want to trek up here for lunch.

                                                   Truly truly,
                                                   John O'Hara

[1] 22 May 1943.
[2] An office note has identified this story as "Cardinal Sin," which was not published. A six-page typescript for this story is among the O'Hara papers.

TO: Harold Ross   TLS, 1 p. PSt.
Summer 1943   Quogue, Long Island

Dear Harold:

This[1] would have to run in the Labor Day issue, so let's have a little action, pal.

You will, I know, be happy to learn that your favorite writer just sold a short short[2] to Collier's: three pages, $750.00! Wow! About a dollar a word. Who is this Calvin Coolidge?

                                                   Love
                                                   John

[1] Possibly "The Next-to-Last Dance of the Season," 18 September 1943.
[2] "Revenge," 25 September 1943.

TLS, 3 pp. PSt.
Quogue, Long Island

August 16, 1943

Dear Cameo (those big watch chains and fancy waistcoats you used to affect, and now the moustache, justify my being reminded of Cameo Kirby,[1] and notice I'm not saying don't they):

(Also you are known as a man who carries his own deck)

Well, just returned from a busy day at the beach in time to dodge the gentle rain, which droppeth as the quality of mercy on the sweet peas, hydrangeas, rambler roses, forsythias and catheters. I thought of you at the beach today, not because of anything unpleasant but probably because there's an old Richmond celebrity at Quogue. Penelope Anderson Mac-Bride. I like her. I guess she's almost the only celebrity from Richmond as Doug Freeman[2] is known only to the Pulitzer Prize Committee, and Ulysses Simpson Grant was really only an honorary citizen of Richmond, and youse-all can't properly claim him. There was an article in the Post by Pete Martin about the Tredegar plant.[3] Pete, since he has taken to doing pieces about iron-man truck drivers and pig boats and pig-iron and other such rough, tough & nasty subjects, no longer is to be known as W. Thornton Martin. Jus' call me Pete, implies W. Thornton. Anyway Penelope and I talked about the article and I finally was able to drag in the fact that my connection therewith was rather remote: that I only knew Lady Tredegar.[4] It was she, you recall, who lifted the diamond gardenia off Beebe's lapel a few years ago, resulting in her being slightly arrested which in turn resulted in rumors that the Royal Navy had a gunboat lying off New Dorp. The Sea Scouts from Our Lady Help of Christians Parish sank the craft, having mistaken her for a blockade runner, and thus neatly do I round out the paragraph.

I don't know about you, Bryan. Are you a sly one? Anyway don't think I didn't notice that you gave your address as Gleet P.O., San Francisco. Gleet, brother, is a horrid word, but it's worse on the end of your cigar,[5] take it from one who knows. It was a rather profitable accident so far as —— ——, M.D., was concerned, but I went elsewhere for treatment when he got romantic. One day as he was about to put the finger to me he said, "Have you been true to me, dear?" I've often wondered since then just how many times it was his finger. Once in a while it did feel more like a long thumb. However I shall desist as I understand the Navy might regard this as provocative talk. (I tried to get in the Navy for other reasons.)

Until I have the word of a more competent authority I am not accepting your ideograph of my name in Japanese. For one thing, you did not dot your *sh*, and you spelt San with three ///s. You forget—if you ever knew—that I once had quite a thing with —— ——. Since you affect to know so God damn much, have you learned what my name means? Well, it means happy valley, *but*, the interesting part is that by extension it also means that happy valley between a woman's breasts, and if I had my choice I would claim squatter's rights on Lana Turner, or settle for Joan Blondell. Settle for, settle on—who counts?

I don't know if you are on Mary Lord's mailing list. Probably you are, as I shall never forget who it was I found putting a Willkie button on my topcoat while accepting my hospitality. I don't think even old unreconstructed (and couldn't they do a reconstruction job on him!) Carter Glass[6] would do a thing like that. So I guess you were in the pay of Mary Lord then and are on her mailing list now. But in case you have proved as faithless to her as you have to a Brother in Right Wing[7] (Hon. '27), here is what news I have picked up. Toots Shor[8] is in a jam with the OPA. Seems he bought meat he didn't have points for and apparently can't ever save enough points to get even, so he'll probably have to close if he hasn't already, and okay by me, bro . . . 2d Lt Farr's address is Hotel Burlington, Vermont Avenue, Washington . . . I talked to someone who must have been his old lady and she gave me the address. He is writing radio as far as the old dame seemed to know, but recalling that Finis never was afflicted with silver cordee, I can't be positive. Matter of fact I should have written to Farr but never have, and after the war I expect he will slap me across the kisser with his hunting crop and push me off the sidewalk for the slacker I am . . . Went down to East Hampton last week for lunch and tennis with the Bill Lords. Others around were the Hugh Chisolms, the Phil Barrys, Buffy Harkness, the Johnny Haneses, Bob McCormick, Mrs. MacAldrich, and Mrs. John Cole. I guess they all hate you as your name never came up, and when I saw that I was afraid to bring it up myself as I didn't want to cause a scene. I remember they talked about Jo Forrestal, and plans for the dance Sat. night, and they said Di Gates and Dan Caulkins and Babs would be up this week, and Betsey Whitney and Mrs. Cushing were staying at the Sea Spray. But they never once mentioned your name. This is interesting as Belle and I went down to my Mother's a couple of weeks ago. My aunt and my two sisters and two young people from Pottsville were there, and they didn't mention your name either. Looks to me like some sort of conspiracy of silence. Whatever it is they won't tell me anything about it and I'm dying to know. Are you any particular friend of Douglass Montgomery's or something? Today at the beach Penelope MacBride did say she knew you, but she hasn't seen you for ages, she said, so I guess she aint hep, or "in on it", whatever it is.

Hanna was down for the weekend latterly, with Lily Emmet, a girl he can look up to and he don't have to put her on no God damn pedestal either. Reminds me of what Howard Dietz said to Johnny Martin one night after dancing with Mimi: "I've just had the great pleasure of going up on your wife." . . . I had to go to NY last week. I have a bum shoulder from overdoing the tennis. It's at least a couple of ligaments or tendons pulled, and may even be slightly cracked. I am also spavined, a victim of thrush and am foundered . . . Lucilla Potter, my sisterinlaw, dropped a 9½ lb. colt yesterday . . . We have not seen or heard from Catherine, so she may be carrying on the feud between the O'Haras and the Barneses, which I declared when Needle-Nose, as Buddy North calls Janet, stood me up for a thé dansant in Washington last Spring . . . Good old Payson is running a defense plant somewhere in Massachusetts, but I understand they are hiding all the bandages and powdered glass in the vicinage . . . Saw Hope and Edgar Scott at the Barrys' two weeks ago. They are fine. Edgar stood on his hands for us . . . No word so far about my waiver for the Army so it don't look like I will be a major and get saluted by certain two-stripers in a brother service . . . Al Wright,[9] who is on a Certain Carrier out your way, saw this painted on a PB4Y: "The Hottest Tail in Town." He also relays an Army one: "Shoot, Jerry, You're Faded." . . . Sam and Peggy Sloan are in charge of the Travelers Aid at Grand Central every Sat. from 00:01 to 08:00 in case that's a handy fact . . . Alan Campbell is exec officer at some hideaway field in Connecticut . . . Tommy Manville proposed, was accepted, and last week entered the holy bonds of matrimony . . . Well, side boy, pipe me over as here is where I shove off in the old man's pinnace.

And remember, if you don't write—you're wrong!

God

p t o

Why were you surprised when I knew you'd changed your address? Don't you know my slant-eyed cousins never sleep?

[1] *Cameo Kirby* was a 1908 play by Booth Tarkington and Harry Leon Wilson about a gambler; it was twice made into movies.

[2] Historian Douglas Southall Freeman.

[3] "Century Plant," *The Saturday Evening Post* (24 July 1943), an article about the Tredegar Iron Works in Richmond, Va.

[4] Reference to practical joke played on Lucius Beebe when a diamond gardenia was removed from his lapel and hidden in Lois Tredegar's purse.

[5] Fleet Post Office was the mailing address for Navy personnel. "Gleet" was a colloquialism for gonorrhea. O'Hara is referring to the Cremo cigar advertisement: "Spit is a horrid word, but it's worse on your cigar."

[6] Virginia senator.

[7] Undergraduate club at Princeton.

[8] New York restaurateur.

[9] Alfred Wright, Jr., former *Time* writer who was now a Navy flier.

TO: Joseph Bryan III

TLS, 4 pp. PSt.
27 E. 79 St., New York City
Stationery with O'Hara
coat of arms

Oct about 20 1943

censored by Matt O'Hara

Dear Sideboy:

Yours dated Sept. 30 came to me as I was wondering what shoestore to go to to mooch a shoebox in which to send you the hairnets, tampans, [*sic*] suppositories and other little things I have planned to shoot you for Xmas. In view of the fact that I now get my shoes at Peal's (a piece of vulgarity matched only by this paper) and in view of the fact that my shoe coupons go to the Mrs., who probably turns them over to Tony de Marco,[1] I don't know where to turn; and in view of the fact that I have been in sick bay for five days (just a Presidential cold, old sport) I don't think I'll turn at all. Azzaamttrafact what I really was doing when your letter came was I was sitting here writing out my sketch for the next Who's Who, and this time I was trying my hand at a little fiction. When I first was asked in I was pretty God damn impressed, even if you weren't, and I followed their style to the comma. I gave them, to the best of my knowledge, the names of my parents, the last of my schools, publications, journalistic record (within numerical reason), club, and address. Next time out I inserted as a club the Hook & Bullet, which you may recall as that moribund organization to which I contributed $150 annually for three years and all I got out of it was three dinners at the Racquet Club and a dubious piece of a probably non-existent birchbark canoe. Today, though, I put in a few extras. For instance, I said I was a member of Phi Upsilon. Phi Upsilon, not to be confused, or rather *to* be confused with Psi Upsilon, is an organization of which I am founder and sole member. I therefore feel that I won't get into any trouble with the brethren by letting you in on the secret that Phi Upsilon means Fuck You. I am having a pin made up. It will resemble the Psi U badge in that it will have a Phi and an Upsilon in the right places and between them will be clasped hands, only in this case both hands will be mine. I am having a picture of my hands shaking hands with themselves and I can hardly wait for McClain and Lovett and a few others to get a hinge at the badge. For Who's Who I also said I was a member of the Quogue-Southhampton Tuesday Lunch Club. As it happens I am not the only member of that Club. The other members are my wife and Peggy Potter Marvel (Hank's sister, Bill's wife). We had several pleasant lunches this summer and in token I bought three small silver cups on which I had engraved the name of the club and each member's name. There was some confusion at the jeweler's as he phoned and said, "But Mr. O'Hara, I notice you have 'President 1943' after each name. Is that right?" I also put in Quogue Field Club. That, of course, is an actual club. As to its exclusiveness, the only person I can think of in Quogue who doesn't belong to it is Jerry Wimpfheimer. Jerry is the local Jew and wine merchant. I was thinking of putting in "Right Wing, Princeton" but you never can tell where you will find a Right Wing. Might be one reading copy on Who's Who. After all, you worked for the Journal of Commerce or whatever the hell it's called in Chicago. I also thought of putting in M.A. (hon.), Plainfield Teachers, but the Little Lady said no on that. Her very words were: "Oh, no." I contemplate toying with my sketch a little every volume so that by, say, 1950 (unless I am in Necrology) I ought to have it fucked up but good. Yale, by which I mean Chauncey Brewster Tinker, has asked me for my original MSS and I have said yes and I may get an honorary out of it (rumor has it) (on dit) (fat chance),[2] so that future historians will have a picture of a well rounded character if Who's Who is their source material. I used to know a —— named George Morris who did one good thing: he got his dog in the Social Register. This particular bitch got in as a Junior.

I am working on a plan which, with the cooperation of John L. Lewis and a few other superior intellects, may enable me to assume my rightful place in the current unpleasantness. Naturally Lewis (I seem to have trouble typing the cox ucker's name) was my second choice as I bridle at lunching with a fellow whose eyebrows would be continually getting in my soup, but it's got to be somebody. You see, old sport, I got the final No from the Army about three weeks ago. Not only was I turned down; I was turned down for waivers for limited service! When they gave me that one I was almost afraid to test my strength in crushing a grape, but I finally took on a brioche single-handed and tore it to pieces, so I don't feel so unmanly now. Indeed, since I could not wheedle my way into the Army, where as a captain or a major I might earn the Pour le Merite or at least the Iron Cross second class, I now feel I can do some mighty good work with Lewis or at the very worst I can muscle in on the black market. The Bonneville Dam is too far away. Some other smarties already have thought up wrecking the Congressional and the 20th Century, and the Welland Canal is old hat. And anyway a man of my brains ought not to concern himself with acts of violence. I shall devote myself to strikes, the nylon and roast beef enterprises, with now and then an occasional quart of deadly microbes in the ventilating system of the Interboro . . . If you think I'm kidding you're only about 98% right. I am so God damn mad I didn't get my commission that I never will forgive four guys. Two of them are obvious: Lovett and Forrestal; the others are Jack Ford and Bill Donovan.[3]

I have two more plans. One is the Red Cross, the other the Maritime Service. If Jack Miley can get a commission in the Maritime Service I should be a breeze, Breeze. As to the Red Cross, I saw Ward and Frankie Cheney the night Ward got back, and since Frankie's old man used to be chairman of the A.R.C. I figured she might still have an in there. Well, I figured good. She knows Norman Davis. So I am getting them to have Davis and me to dinner together, at which point I will outline to him what I think is a hell of a good idea. If he goes for it you can give that pape priest a hot seat to make room for me in your wardroom. Meanwhile I have been reasonably industrious for good old JO'H. I have made not only my regular bonus at The NYer, but also sold two short shorts to Collier's (through high-priced Hanna, who got me the most dough ever paid for that type of creation), and the big news is that I am to get a $2000 bonus from The NYer because I have been so good about turning out the lights and flushing the can for 16 years. Just think! Four hash marks! Just think! Two g's.

You ask about McClain. Well, I saw Hank Fonda (j.g., and I think the Navy handled the knock-up situation manfully[4]) about ten days ago. He had seen someone who wandered into a crib in Sicily, and sitting there over a bottle of the finest were McClain, Steinbeck, Ernie Pyle, Bruce Cabot and two others whom I forget. I think I told you his old lady died, which is tough on the old man who is all alone out in Ohio. Alan Campbell was stationed at Westhampton and had received the usual list of what to take abroad. Dottie came down and stayed with us for about a week. That was two weeks ago. We haven't any later information, but Alan seemed to think he'd be going toward the perfidious island any minute now.

Say, dog robber, do you wear an aigulette?

Now let me see. News . . . .[5] Gibbs, with whom I am lunching today, is in his fourth month on the wagon, and a mighty fine thing. Young Bobby Benchley got wed in Detroit to a very nice girl two weeks ago. Bob Senior in town looking more and more like Mike Romanoff, who also was in town last week. Jock Whitney's Ma almost got wrapped in the flag but according to today's paper she has rallied and still breathing. The Phil Barrys have taken a house in 69th Street as Ellen thought it would be cheaper than Hampshire House. Lucilla Potter's newborn has been named

Earl Wylie Potter. The John O'Haras took the Penelope Anderson Mc-Brides for $4 at bridge. Winchell has declared war on the Argentine and Louis Sobol[6] has declared war on me. Nat Benchley is stationed here temporarily while his new ship is having the chintzes put in. Bill Marvel in Italy. My brother busted from staff sgt to pvt. Bea Tolstoy[7] in town last week. By the way we are all palsy again, and really so. She was with Benchley and I asked her why she didn't ditch him and go with me, Belle being in the hospital for a 48-hour check-up at the time. Buddy North[8] is a hero in either the Sicilian or Italian invasion. We saw John a week ago and he told us about it but I was being a scofflaw that night and don't remember much about it. Belle just came in: the story on Buddy is that he was the first to land at Amalfi and capture-rescued Mussolini's would-be assassin. Farr hasn't answered the letter I didn't finish so I guess he's sulking. My Mother still maintains a significant silence about you and so does my Aunt Verna. Haven't seen Reynolds[9] as he and I had a slight contretemps a while back but apparently he is booked for a lecture tour and Hanna got him $1500 a week on a new radio program. The Sam Sloans moving in to town this fall as Peggy just couldn't take that country rap again, which is understandable and also pleasant. I am writing a play.[10] Perelman's show[11] got pretty good notices, but he didn't, which suits me right down to the earth as he said when Pal Joey opened that "it just proves that only a Frenchman can write about that situation." The Harry Hopkinses have moved, so I no longer can call the White House "the place where Louie dwells" (Yale song).[12] LATER. Had a drink with Norris.[13] He said to tell you something but I forget what. Let him tell you himself. Who does he think I am, a God damn messenger boy? Busch is back from some of the wars but I haven't seen him. Joel Sayre[14] in Iran and none too happy with his assignment except that at least he retains civilian status. I may throw in my lot with Norris if I don't work for the Trib.[15] I'd kind of like to do feature stories for the trib, always with the weather eye on a correspondent's job, but the dough Norris has offered me is also pretty inviting too, especially in view of the fact that I am down to buttons as a result of that fucking Army thing. I turned down $40,000 worth of Hollywood work while trying to get my commission—and could have done the work anyway, which is what's infuriating. We never see Sister[16] so I can't tell you any news of her or how she looks.

Well brother that's enough for you. Anybody you want me to fuck or anything you want me to eat or drink for you just send me the word and I'll be in the saddle or at the table as quick as you can say Katharine Hepburn.

Phi Upsilon!

O'Hara p.t.o.

I enclose a cutting from today's *Journal American*.¹⁷ What I want to know, Mandel, is how did you ever get in the Vine?¹⁸

¹ Ballroom dancer.
² O'Hara eventually donated the typescripts for *Butterfield 8* and the proofs for *Appointment in Samarra* to Yale, but did not receive an honorary degree.
³ Robert A. Lovett, Assistant Secretary of War for Air; James V. Forrestal, Secretary of the Navy; probably director John Ford, who headed a Navy movie unit; Gen. William Donovan, head of the O.S.S.
⁴ Actor Henry Fonda was named in a paternity suit in July 1943.
⁵ Nine words omitted by the editor.
⁶ Newspaper columnist for King Features syndicate.
⁷ Former wife of Donald Ogden Stewart.
⁸ Henry Ringling North and his group took part in the capture of islands off Naples in October 1943 and rescued political prisoners opposed to Mussolini.
⁹ Reporter and war correspondent Quentin Reynolds.
¹⁰ Possibly an unfinished play about a country doctor or an unfinished musical play for Rodgers and Hart about an airplane factory swing shift.
¹¹ *One Touch of Venus*.
¹² Mrs. Hopkins was known as "Louie."
¹³ Frank Norris, editor at *Time*.
¹⁴ Sayre had become a *New Yorker* war correspondent.
¹⁵ O'Hara did not go to work for the *Herald Tribune*.
¹⁶ Mrs. Bryan.
¹⁷ Probably Bill Corum's "Sports" column, which printed a letter from Alfred Wright on 20 October 1943.
¹⁸ Possibly a reference to the Princeton University Ivy Club.

TO: Stanley Woodward, *New York Herald Tribune*
(8 January 1944), 13

This dispatch doesn't properly belong with your current collection of great feats in sport, but I was happy to see that your Greenwich contributor, Mr. Henry L. Maxwell, included Red Grange's four touchdowns against Penn among his favorites.¹ In recent years I have been getting my entertainment and my living less and less from sports and more and more from the movies and the theater. Nevertheless, I never saw anything in the theater so dramatic as the closing seconds of the first half of that Penn-Illinois game, with Grange the actor and Zuppke the director.

I was covering football then, as many as three games a week end. I had asked my boss, Walter Southhall Farquhar, of Pottsville, Pa., to excuse me that one Saturday so that I could see that Penn-Illinois game.

The chances are that I pointed out to Mr. Farquhar, who was a Penn man, the sentimental fact that my father and my uncles were Penn men, and that I belonged at that game. This, of course, was fraudulent, since I always, from the time I was able to sit on my father's lap at old Franklin Field, have rooted against Penn.

And so with my new coonskin coat covering my guilty heart, and a large shakerful of orange blossoms and a quart of Golden Wedding to keep me in good voice and to ward off any possible ill effects of the muddy day, I went to the new stadium to get my first look at a Big Ten team and the man who was, and remains, with the possible exception of Tony Latone, my favorite football player. Tony Latone, of course, was the greatest line-bucker that ever lived, and any one who wants to argue that point will have to look elsewhere, since I can't waste my time debating facts with ignorant persons. I can waste my time writing you letters, but it's a pleasure.

Of Grange's performance that day I need say nothing in addition to what has been said by experts, including even Charles Parker, who failed to put Grange on his All-America team. But to Bob Zuppke, who a short time later was to denounce Grange for turning pro, goes the credit for intentionally or accidentally providing us with the real thrill of the day.

Get the picture, Rufus. We in the East had been hearing about this Grange until he had become something between a legend and a bore. The brand new Franklin Stadium was the football capital of the East that day, and there wasn't room in the place for another pack of cigarettes. Everybody had come to see Grange, but not everybody had come in the hope of seeing him triumph. Well, triumph he did, as you know. Then, with about a minute left of the first half, Zuppke pulled him out.

Grange went over to the bench, leaned over and spoke to Zuppke, who put his hand on Red's shoulder while thirty-two assistant managers tried to bundle him up. Grange nodded, and then he began his jog trot to the dressing room.

All alone, the slow trot down the seventy-five yards to the exit, and there wasn't a man or woman not standing in the whole stadium. And if I was any judge, there wasn't a dry eye, either. There he was, the boy who had come through when the chips really were down, dragging his blanket behind him, and it was wonderful. The men on the field could have pulled pistols and shot it out and no one in the stand would have noticed, because we were all looking at Grange, and we couldn't have heard the shots for hearing ourselves cheer him. Somehow or other I felt that the eyes of the whole East were on that solitary figure, and for some reason or other I was proud of him.

I could hardly believe it later on when I read that Zuppke had denounced Red when Red tried to make a few bucks out of the game. It was hard to believe that this was the same Zup who had had the grace and the superb sense of timing that made him yank Grange those few seconds before the half was over, and let Red take his bow. I've never met Zuppke, so I can't say that he did it deliberately, but I have heard that the two men became friends again, so I give Zuppke the benefit of the doubt, and anyway wasn't Zuppke an artist of sorts?

By the way, Grange was. He appeared in one movie, and he turned out to be a damn good actor. Maybe that October matinee had given him confidence.

¹ Woodward's 3 January column had included Maxwell's choice of the four greatest feats in sport.

TO: Gilbert Troxell¹   TLS, 1 p. with holograph
                                                        footnotes. Princeton

My address is 27 East Seventy-ninth Street. The phone number, which is not in the book, is Regent 4-7559.

Wednesday January 19, 1944
Dear Mr. Troxell:

This is to offer my thanks for an afternoon that was one of the pleasantest I've ever had, thanks entirely to you. I know I fucked up your afternoon schedule, and because of that I returned to New York with a guilty conscience; but it is easy to reconcile conscience and schedule when the conscience-stricken has had as fine a time as I had today. I dub you the perfect host, and I do hope you will be in New York soon so that I can repay you in kind.

My compliments to Mrs. Troxell and please tell her that the only reason I was unable to exert my charm on her was that her husband is a second-guessing, late-inviting man. *Hello to Knollenberg, Babb, Lohmann, Gee, Lewis, Tomms, Eli, bones, snakes, heads of wolves, keys and books,² all of which & whom made for my fine afternoon. An essex to Bess³ and those who keep her memory alive, and tell Tinker I've had a much, much better reception at Bryn Mawr, no thanks, I am sure, to him.

Seriously, Mr. Troxell, I didn't think there was a Yale any more, but you showed me there is. I don't know whether to be sorry or glad.**

*Please correct names.
**Glad (Ed.)

Yrs,
John O'Hara

¹ Curator of American Literature at Yale.
² References to members of the Yale community and to the Yale senior societies.
³ Reference to the Elizabethan Club at Yale.

TO: Gilbert Troxell

TLS, 1 p. Princeton

27 E. 79th St.,
New York City

January 24, 1944

Dear Mr. Troxell:

The parcel containing the Yale seal and the 1942 souvenir has just put in its appearance and I am delighted and appreciative. The seal is hanging in its proper place, that is, eye-height where it will stare back at our non-Yale friends. As a matter of fact a Harvard girl (wife to one, sister to another) was having lunch when the parcel arrived. She owns a bulldog which she and her husband promptly called John Harvard to irritate their Yale friends, so I tossed her the tobacco[1] with no comment except, "John Harvard. Hmmph." If you will let me know how much you are out of pocket I will send you a cheque almost any day.

Probably sticking to your fingers as you read this are half a dozen bookplates and two for good measure; six because six is the number of books I've had published, and two extra because I expect to have a book of short stories this Spring and a novel next year, and I don't dare plan beyond that. You will, of course, get the MS of the novel. (I keep saying MS when I suppose I should say TS for typescript, but nobody seems to notice.) If you like I will send you the copy for the book of short stories, but it'll consist mostly of New Yorker galley proofs unless I can wangle the original stuff out of The New Yorker. As I told you last week I have applied for a writing fellowship at the University of Minnesota, which I'll know about on April 1, and I expect to have the novel finished by June 1, 1945, provided, naturally, I'm still around.[2] By the way, Dean Lohmann would find a heraldic error on the bookplate, but my sister, who gave me the plates, doesn't know about such things and I couldn't, it you'll excuse the pun, look a gift plate in the mouth.

Tell Babb I haven't forgotten about the Hemingway letter.[3] It's in Quogue, which is not a place I visit much in the winter, but when I do go down again I'll send it to him.

Again, thank you, and I hope to see you very soon.

Faithfully,
John O'Hara

[1] Probably a reference to Handsome Dan pipe tobacco, a brand named for the Yale bulldog mascot.

[2] O'Hara did not receive the fellowship. A Rage to Live was published in 1949.

[3] James T. Babb, Yale Librarian, had asked O'Hara to donate his Hemingway correspondence.

Dear Jim:

I am back with an idea which I briefly submit in the belief that it's good enough for further discussion between us.

The quality that impressed me most is the Enormity of what is going on in the Pacific. I didn't know about it, and not many people at home do. So my contribution can be the telling about that quality; the enormous things that already have been done, at Pearl and elsewhere, and the enormity of merely operating out there.

Well, I figured out a way of doing it, of telling about a Pacific operation. I propose to write a book (the forms are down; the concrete is to be laid) which I tentatively call HOW TO TAKE AN ISLAND.[1] I start out with the meeting of the chiefs of staff, when they decide that X Island is strategically attractive. We then go to the various phases: staging, softening up, assault, occupation. It will be the logistics story without, I trust, my ever mentioning that word.

Meanwhile, to humanize the story, I have invented a marine, who goes to boot camp (by a manufactured coincidence) the very day the chiefs of staff decide to take the island, say eight months before D-Day. As he progresses so do we progress with the business of supply, etc. It is sort of movie technique: cutting in and out between the gyrene and the operation for which he is being trained without knowing it. If you ever read a fine book called STORM, by George R. Stewart, you know what I mean.

The approach is this: it will be told plain, by a man (me) who knows nothing about strategy, but will be learning a hell of a lot about what it takes to take an island. As I learn from the Navy, I put it down. By using the device of the marine I constantly check myself from letting the bigness get away from me.

You come in at the very beginning, because I would have to have access to a lot of stuff that has not been available, or anyway printed. Access, and, of course, permission to use same. As you know, I have been security-checked to the last follicle, so there won't be any worry on that score. It will be a matter of getting send-ins from you and Admiral Merrill or whoever is necessary as I progress.

If I do the job I hope to do the book will have enormous value for indoctrination purposes, and I will have earned at least the Letter of Commendation. The only hitch that I can see is that there may be a feeling that it is late in the day for this book. But I happen not to think so. I think there will be plenty of time for the book to do good, and I am not only thinking now in post-war terms.

I worked out the form in some detail while I was away, and I have been waiting till I heard you were back before taking it to anyone in authority. If you would like someone else to do the work I am perfectly willing to turn over what I have done.

I am coming to Washington Wednesday 11 October and will go to the Mayflower if I can get a room, but will call you or Duffield[2] when I get in. I am going to New York Tuesday morning. The address there is 27 East 79th Street, the phone Regent 4-7559.

I insist upon one condition: if you don't like the idea or the book you can call it bilge. But I don't want it called Billingsgate, in or out of the presence of an admiral.

Kindest regards,
John

[1] The book was not written; O'Hara was a Navy correspondent for *Liberty* in the Pacific during the summer of 1944.
[2] Eugene Duffield, Forrestal's assistant.

TO: Frank Sullivan[1]

TLS, 2 pp. Cornell
New York City
16 Nov. 1944

Dear Franchot:

I am, as freely predicted by me and probably anyone else who gave it a thought, back. Back, and convinced with a certain finality that this, and not that, is where I belong, or beslong, as Dan Parker would say back in the pre-Dewey days when he was funny. The first question everyone asks is where did I get, and giving you credit for no more originality than the next one, I'll answer it for you: I got as far as the Philippines. I saw the Philippines, that's how close our carrier got.[2] I didn't go on any sweeps or strikes, because on account of Ray Clapper's[3] death correspondents are not supposed to, but I very much doubt if I'd have gone anyway unless I'd been shamed into it by my roommate, that sterling lovable liberal character Emmet Crozier.[4] We were not attacked but the task group next to ours was and at four one morning I had the pleasure of seeing a jap bomber knocked down. Otherwise it was mostly psychological warfare for me. I was scared most of the time—what time I was not admiring the kids who fly our planes. In spite of eating three and four big meals a day I lost 20 pounds, which I am rapidly putting on again, and I had to go to the boys' dept at Brooks for a new suit when I came home. It was a fine experience, all told, but the brass hats are right about this being a young man's war. I guess any war is. Too many decks to climb too many times a day (and night). When you come to town again I will get you at the point of a gun some night and tell you more and in detail. Professionally I did myself no good, selling only one piece to Liberty and ending up with them on my prick list, but of that too more another time.

The Navy, meaning Forrestal, wanted me to go out again, this time for the Navy, but I said no, being coy. But I don't know; if they ask me again I may do it, because what they want me to do is all right and I might as well be doing it. I don't seem to be able to write anything more than 2000 words long, in spite of several good ideas. And I am going to need money. I am going to need a lot of money—hold your breath—along about next June. Yes, Belle is going to have a baby. We'll have been married seven years in December and I had ceased to care about progeny (the other brothers are doing only too well in that respect), and as I believe I once told you, Belle's brother didn't think she ought, as doctors say, to undertake a pregnancy because her ticker is peculiar. But she always wanted one, and now she's going to. I don't know what the hell is proven. More than two months of the wagon (nothing available in the Pacific) and sweating everything out of me and no sex life probably did it. We are going to call it Wylie O'Hara, boy or girl, which I think is a good name. The notion of calling it Sullivan O'Hara never entered my head until just this second, and whee! it's already gone. Well, life begins at 40, which I'll be in Jan. I suppose it's a little early to be telling people, but I haven't been able to keep my big mouth shut. Now I suppose it'll be turning up in Joe Cummiskey's[5] column, you spy.

Clarence Knapp sent me the state manual and a note telling me you had diverticulosis, by which I guess he meant diverticulitis. You had gone home by that time or we'd have gone up to Presbyterian and held your large intestine. I don't imagine we'll be going to the Spa this winter, and indeed I may even go to Hollywood if Hollywood'll have me. I don't regard what I do in Hollywood as an honorable way of making money, but at least the law does not call it a felony, so if they beckon, I'll go. Maybe Hollywood'll take my mind off the war.

I saw Mac[6] at the Pipe Night[7] the week before he died. He was what happens when you start on old fashioneds at one o'clock and switch to martinis at five (this, when I first saw him, was about 7.30), but he was fine, I thought. He looked fine. Later in the evening he asked me to join him in outsinging the Protestants Vir Den[8] and others, who were hymnizing. I have no inside dope, but I do question Cagney's wisdom in letting Mac do that job of bringing the horses to California. I question it even though Mac may have insisted on doing it. Certainly no one knew better than Cagney that Mac had had a scare. Well, Mac had a couple of good nights at the club and the pleasure of seeing FDR win before he died. I had a great love for that man, and you never forget people you love. It is indeed always the wrong man.

Not that this has any connection with the last remark, but don't you think Ethel Barrymore went out of her way to avoid Clayton Hamilton?[9]

Dial Regent 4-7559 when you hit town again. Speaking for the two of us I'm sure Belle would like to see you.

Yrs,
Nimitz[10]

[1] Humorist and *New Yorker* contributor, a friend of O'Hara's from his earliest days in New York.

[2] O'Hara was on the *Intrepid*.

[3] Clapper was killed in a plane crash while covering the Marshall Islands invasion.

[4] New York *Herald Tribune* reporter.

[5] Sports editor of *PM*.

[6] Edward McNamara, actor and singer, died while transporting actor James Cagney's race horses.

[7] At the Players Club. A "pipe night" is a meeting at which entertainment is provided by club members.

[8] Publisher Ray Vir Den.

[9] Playwright and drama critic.

[10] Reference to Adm. Chester W. Nimitz.

TO: Katharine Angell White   TLS, 1 p. PSt.
                                                      New York City

                                                      2 March 1945

Dear Katharine:

Supplementing our telephone conversation:[1]

In answer to Query 1: The word transient is Navy talk. A correspondent is not actually a member of the ship's company or of the Air Group, and is therefore regarded as a visitor, even though he may stay aboard as long as three months. Some of these poker and bridge games last as long as a year. Also, at some places in the Pacific correspondents and visiting officers, lumped together as transients, are not allowed to join the local officers' club.

Query 2: You ask about a small "d"; I think you probably meant small "g" for God damnedest. Okay.

As to the radar stuff, if necessary I'll take this up with Forrestal personally. He is a friend of mine, and in fact I stayed at his house this week as I always do in Washington. References to radar, using the word, are made constantly and nowadays there are even permitted pictures of radar equipment on ships and on night fighters. The radar ban was put on like the mention of submarine rescue of pilots (just to show I know what I'm talking about), and this has been lifted too. Also, this is a fiction piece, and the Navy makes a big distinction between fiction and fact pieces. If I take out the early reference to the Betty on the radar screen the subsequent alarm becomes a deus ex machina, a form of writing of which neither I nor The New Yorker approves.

This is thrown in to save another letter: I have been leading The New Yorker for more than ten years, and I am not going to be eased into the back of the book again, not even to help out with a gerrymandering makeup.[2]

Yrs,
J. O'Ha

[1] The conversation was about "War Aims," 17 March 1945.
[2] "The Pretty Daughters," 3 March 1945, followed an S. J. Perelman humor piece and a poem by Vladimir Nabokov. Mrs. White unsuccessfully tried to persuade O'Hara that the lead piece in The New Yorker had no special significance. "War Aims" occupied the lead position.

TO: Belle Wylie O'Hara
March 1945

Inscription in *Pipe Night*.[1]
PSt.

To Belle

who somehow got
home from the Tango
after observing a man
in Wichita and seeing
and again seeing the man
from Newark airport who
loves her in 1945

The Man
27 East 79

[1] Refers to O'Hara's first meeting with Belle Wylie at the Wichita, Kans., airport in 1936 and their first date in California, when he took her to the gambling ship *Tango*.

191

To Jim Thurber, from
one middle-aged
man on the very same
trapeze
to another owl in an
attic
—— and welcome
John O'Hara
16 March 1945 ΦΚΨ
New York

TO: James V. Forrestal
TLS, 1 p. Princeton
New York City

20 March 1945

Dear Jim:

It was friendly and considerate of you to take the trouble to write me about the Times review.[1] I appreciate it.

Last week, when I got my allowance of books I inscribed one for you, but I have been too much of a goldbricker to wrap it and put it in the mail. My out is that I thought I might be in Washington this week and could deliver it in person. But you'll get it soon one way or another.

Some months ago Duffield told me he (which I imagine also means you) was interested in Navy pieces from the point of view of making those wonderful guys human beings. I thereupon wrote the enclosed, which appears in the current New Yorker.[2] I have another one in the typewriter, and I may do a brief series. I honestly if immodestly think pieces like this are worth a damned sight more than 100 columns of dispatches from Guam. It is, of course, possible that I am prejudiced.

Again, many thanks and good wishes.

Yrs,

J. O'Ha

[1] Lionel Trilling's receptive review of *Pipe Night* on 18 March.
[2] "War Aims."

TO: Katharine Angell White
TLS, 1 p. Bryn Mawr
Summer 1945
Quogue, Long Island

Saturday

Dear Katharine:

It was so nice of you to write, but we were sorry to hear about the sinus business, which at best is a damned nuisance, and I am told can be very painful.

Belle and the baby both are fine.[1] The baby has been averaging better than the conventional, or anyway desirable, ounce of added weight daily, and she has long since begun to look like her mother, although regrettably she has her father's ears.

The Exeter trip was fun, and if I had a son I now think I would want him to go there. I had no idea the meeting of the Lantern Club was going to be the size it was: 23 boys and four or five masters, but it went off easily after the first 20 minutes, when I had to ad lib.[2]

I haven't written anything since we've been down here but I'll get to work any minute now, after I've finished the Introduction to the Viking Portable Scott Fitzgerald. I wrote a review of Bunny Wilson's collection for the Times but that was hidden by the strike. Wilson and I are now even for The Boys in the Back Room.[3]

I understand there is no August casual hiatus this year, so you will be hearing from me. Our kindest and thanks to you.

Faithfully,
John

[1] Wylie Delaney O'Hara was born 14 June 1945.
[2] O'Hara had been invited to talk to the Lantern Club at Phillips Exeter Academy.
[3] Edmund Wilson had included an unfavorable essay on O'Hara in *The Boys in the Back Room* (1941). O'Hara's review of *The Crack-Up* appeared in the *New York Times* (8 July 1945).

TO: Katharine Angell White   TLS, 1 p. PSt.
Late 1945

Bel-Air Hotel
701 Stone Canyon
LA 24

Monday

Dear Katharine:

Glad you liked the Atomic Age number[1] and I am sending another. I have dedicated one night a week to New Yorker pieces, as of two weeks ago, so I can make another bonus and have a lot more babies, etc.

Queries: 1. I fixed it.

2. Inconsequential query. People of a same general background know each other or have mutual friends all over the U.S. I also might point out that the girl went to St. Margaret's, which is a good school in Waterbury even if Ross doesn't know about it.

3. Okay.

4. Okay.

After all these years the boys still try to punctuate my dialog, losing, for example, the effect of long breathless sentences. Also, this woman is not likely to quote exactly from the Oldsmobile ads, and in fact (I know about cars) the thing always is known to automobile people, mechanics, et al as the hydramatic shift. Always.

Dear Kate: Will you please have somebody airmail me The New Yorker to the above address every week? If that's asking too much, I'll pay the postage. It is simply impossible to obtain a copy from the newsstands out here, even newsstands where I have dealt for years. And regular subscriptions arrive sporadically, from four to eight days late. I do not want to lose touch. Kindest thoughts,

Faithfully,
J. O'Ha

---

[1] "Conversation in the Atomic Age," 12 January 1946.

TO: Katharine Angell White

TLS, 2 pp. PSt.
Los Angeles
17 December [1945]

Dear Kate:

For the moment I'll just go down the line with the queries:[1]

1. okay

2. okay I guess. Don't understand your query.

3. okay

4. I think the physical note is necessary.

5. I permit this change but I consider it one more example of the dreary, conventional changes that are inflicted on what is possibly my dreary style of writing, but is nevertheless *mine*. I learned about orthography, etymology, syntax, and prosody in school, but . . .

6. Here is meant that it's too soon after leaving the army; needs a vacation. It's cleared in the next paragraph.

7. Let Boss Ross stew.

8. See 7.

9. Gibbs is really asking for it: these ads are known in the small-town newspaper trade as "front-page locals". They are printed with such code letters as 3t (meaning three times), tf (till forbid, meaning till the ad is stopped by the advertiser) or with numbers like 13, 14, 15, 16 (meaning the ad is to be used on those dates). Maybe Gibbs' Mr. Griscom was more generous to the medical profession than the owners I've worked for, but in Pennsylvania, and oddly enough in Suffolk County N.Y. these items run as ads.

10 (mine). In a fiction piece, where the man is referred to by his title —Reverend Mr., or Doctor—I prefer it spelt out.

* * *

The words continue to trickle out, as you will see by the enclosed piece.[2] I anticipate a little trouble with it and you'll soon see why, but we can cross under that bridge when we come to it.

The New Yorker is arriving fine now, and I thank you for it. I found out while I was in the Pacific that I could do without the newspapers (I read all of them every day in NY), but I do require Ross' Folly. Now

I even get it a little ahead of the subscribers. The season's greetings to you and yours.

Faithfully,
John

1 "Doctor and Mrs. Parsons," 23 February 1946.
2 Unidentified.

TO: Katharine Angell White   TLS, 2 pp. PSt.
26 December 1945/3 January 1946   MGM letterhead

Boxing Day 1945

Dear Kate:

Boxing Day indeed. I couldn't box my very small daughter today, I never have been able to box the compass—and so on. Here is a piece,[1] and for the record, another one is half finished.[2] I say for the record because I think I have to submit one more before 31 Dec. 1945 to make my bonus. It's also about a night club, a colored girl saxophone player, and the Irish proprietor, so it can be considered in work, provided you want to stretch a point. Of course I may be wrong about the bonus deal and I begin to suspect that I am. As I understand it now, I qualify for some kind of bonus every time I submit six pieces and the unfinished one qualifies me for the second bonus this year. I am represented by Cadwalader, Wickersham, Ernst, Mead and White. First and third Thursdays.

I haven't seen Ross but I suppose if we stay out here long enough I'll run into him and tell him how a magazine should be run. For this advice, usually attended by a frozen grin, I charge nothing.

Remember: Ars gratia artis,[3] which I somehow suspect is bad Latin.

J. O'Ha

p.t.o.

3 Jan[4]

I fixed the ending of "Common Sense",[5] which I enclose. I also fixed the Jake query. The others can be fixed in proof. Happy New Year to you.

John

1 Unidentified.
2 Unidentified.
3 MGM slogan.
4 On verso of preceding letter.
5 "Common Sense Should Tell You," 9 February 1946.

TO: Katharine Angell White   TLS, 1 p. PSt.
January 1946   27 E. 79th St.,
                                           New York

Dear Katharine:

Sorry about the delay with this, but what with ten things and some others my attention was diverted.

The boy is waiting so this must go fast.[1]

1. Two non-pros read this and had no trouble with it.

2. Eddie Schmidt is the Wetzel[2] of the West, 200 bucks a suit.

3. Here is the girl's breast. The slip has to be either where a breast pocket would be or where the lower pockets of a jacket would be.

4. You have to allow me changes like that in dialog. It's easy to go from It, horse-racing, to Them horses.

5. A producer's trainer usually is a masseur mostly; masseur and body-guard. Not only peculiar to Hollywood producers, either. Is Ross pretending he doesn't know rich men like Bernie Gimbel?

6. Ross is right about the cigarette case and Louis B. Mayer and Hoover. This is taking liberties, of course.

I made it 20 instead of a dozen because I wanted to exaggerate, although it's hard to exaggerate the Christmas present situation in Hollywood.

I have written another piece but I guess it must be in my trunk on the way east.

Let's have lunch some day next week and I'll tell you why I have taken a vow never again to work for a motion picture studio.

As ever,
John

[1] "Common Sense Should Tell You."
[2] New York custom tailor.

TO: Katharine Angell White   TLS, 1 p. PSt.
                                     New York City

                                   1 May 1946
Dear Katharine:

I must say I reserve the right to go away for the week-end. Although your letter was dated 26 April it must have been posted very late in the day, and 27 April was a Saturday. In other words, it was not *handed* to me on the Friday.

The revisions about the money in the piece called THE DECISION[1] are the kind of thing which as a rule I figure out before ever a MS is submitted to The New Yorker.

But (and here you are on my side) when I present a fact like the closing hours of a drug store, I know what I am talking about. The other stuff may be mathematical; I might be doing card tricks to myself. But when I say a drug store is closed at certain times, or anything like that, I reject suggestion. I just won't have it. Indeed, if in a piece of fiction, I say the village drug store is closed from 11 a.m. to 4 p.m. I think that is permissible.

Changes like the five-dollar bill thing can, may, and should be done in the office. Semi-colon stuff, no, nor sequence of tenses stuff, since after all I have my own ignorant style—but then. . . . And then again, when my point is insufficiently clear to the Editors, you most certainly have a beef, the right to insist upon my making the point clear, a right which is implicit in the right to accept or reject.

I am trying like hell to be fair to all concerned. This, on May Day, is what the Commies consider a defeatist attitude, and maybe it is. I don't know. I don't know. (The hell I don't.)

Love,

John

[1] 18 May 1946.

TO: Gustave Lobrano
Summer 1946

TLS, 1 p. PSt.
Quogue, Long Island

Monday p.m.

Dear Gus:

I'll probably be demanding an opinion on the enclosed[1] before you've read it, a demand which I, at least, am happy to say will be made in person.

Be not dismayed by my Tchoupitoulas French,[2] as used in the title. I think in all the years I've been sending yellow paper to The NYer, this is the first use of *the belle lingua* except for a time in '30 when I employed the word *blase*. I call this piece what I call it because I think a little French now and then gives a writer class, and Boss Ross is impressed by class.

I am writing my next story on patent leather, with Pernod.

Yrs,
John

[1] Unidentified.
[2] Possible reference to Tchoupitoulas Street in New Orleans.

TO: Katharine Angell White
November 1946

TLS, 1 p.
Letterhead of "Horizons,"
Paget West, Bermuda
Thursday

Dear Katharine:

I have here a little article[1] about high society, written as only Henry James can write them, which I am offering for sale at a good price. I am doing this to raise the general tone of the magazine, which lately has seemed rather middle-class. Let us have more little articles about nice people and in so doing draw a better type advertiser. Who likes to read about people they would not have in their own home?

I shall return to NY a fortnight hence, 5 December. Will you kindly tell Gibbs that Trimingham's have no linen suits whatever and that Smith's have only size 38 stout. They are pre-war, and look it (name any war), but if Gibbs is planning to put on five stone between now and next summer I can still buy the garments—against, I may say, the advice of the clark.

Raining here. How's it there?

Love
John

[1] Unidentified. The stories mentioned in this and the following letter to Mrs. White may have been "Not Always," 11 January 1947, "The "Moccasins," 25 January 1947, or "Pardner," 22 February 1947.

TO: Frank Sullivan

TLS, 2 pp. Cornell
Letterhead of "Horizons,"
Paget West, Bermuda

Sullivan Travel Service Our Motto Hit the Road Ya Bum

1 December 1946

Dear Frank:

Thanks for the "info". When the Grange gets through tracking cowshit up the stately halls of the New Worden[1] I shall take over with my own brand, horseshit, more suitable to the traditions of the Spa.[2]

I'll write Mr. Bolster a couple of days in advance so he can turn on the hot water. The only time I've been to the Gideon was with you and Adele in '35, and that's a place like Aiken to me. A place to gaze at longingly from afar, or with my nose pressed against the window while the quality go through the intricacies of the quadrille. On the other side of the picture and of this piece of writing paper, I feel at home at the Worden.

I've done some good work on my play[3] and before I leave Saratoga I'll ask you to read it, or some of it, anyway. Your piece on the coming of winter, which I was glad you put in your book and which is one of my favorite pieces by anybody, is the kind of thing I am trying to get a holt of in the first act of my play. Saratoga's perfect for that atmosphere. Did you ever hear James J. Hill's remark, "I got no use for a man it don't snow on"?

I expect to keep awfully busy, but of course will be available if you want to arrange to have me judge a beauty contest at the Skidmore pool. I have certain interesting tests which the contestants must pass while the orchestra plays "Doin' What Comes Naturally."

Love to Belle yourself.

O'Hara

[1] Hotel in Saratoga Springs, N.Y.
[2] Sullivan had moved from New York City to Saratoga Springs.
[3] A play about the atomic bomb project, which O'Hara did not finish.

TO: James V. Forrestal   TLS, 1 p. (copy). Princeton

JOHN O'HARA
55 East 86th St.,
New York 28

17 December 1946

Dear Jim:

Your 13 December note just arrived today, this, as you know, being the time of year when a Certain Other Department isn't up to Navy standards; and the Navy itself used my old address. For the files, the above is correct, and my phone, unlisted, is Atwater 9-9193.

It was kind of you to remember my own personal Manhattan Project and I am sorry that I will not be able to come to Washington at least until after Christmas. As a matter of fact, Admiral Parsons is pretty high echelon for the kind of information I need, and as one who never mastered the use of the slide rule I am avoiding the technological in my mag. op. I never write about anything that I don't know cold, and in this case—well, suppose I give you a tell on what I am doing: it is a play based on the life of a man about my own age, who gets his education rather later in life than most men in his field, which is industrial chemistry. The play appears as a series of episodes from boyhood on, from the point of view of a man forty-two years old. He is a competent industrial chemist, but not of Nobel prize stature, and yet he is important enough in the atomic scheme of things to be inextricably tied up with it when he comes to make the most important decision of his life. From what I have been able to find out, Higinbotham[1] is the man for me to see. The questions I have to ask are of a non-scientific nature; they have to do with what is patronizingly called the human side. When I wrote Appointment in Samarra I established a dummy garage business, took my papers to a guy I know who is a v.p. at General Motors (who wanted to know when the hell I had run a garage), and he in turn passed me on to a fellow at the Automobile Chamber of Commerce. Not much of that appears in the book, but everything that does appear is accurate and sound. I also boned up on toxicology with the late Yandell Henderson[2] so that the carbon monoxide suicide would be all right. Coming, as I do, from a coal mining and steel mill town, I have known quite a few industrial chemists, and I've worked in a steel mill and a briquet plant so I've seen them at work. I don't need a very great deal of information, merely some "facts" to fill in on my principal character.

We just got back from three weeks in Bermuda, where I reconstructed the entire play and learned to my dismay that it will be impossible for me to finish up in time for a production this season. However I am on the right track now and I ought to get it on next September or October.

If you're still with me—Merry Christmas to you and Gene and Miss Foley.

As ever,
/s/ John

[1] William A. Higinbotham, atomic scientist who had been on the staff of the Manhattan Project.
[2] Professor of Applied Physiology at Yale, an authority on the physiology of respiration.

TO: Katharine Angell White   TLS, 1 p. PSt.
May 1947   *New Yorker* letterhead

Dear Katharine:
  My pieces don't run second.[1]

Yrs,
John (O'Hara)

[1] "Other Women's Households," 24 May 1947, followed a Ludwig Bemelmans story.

TO: Joseph Henry Jackson[1]   TLS, 1 p. Berkeley
                                          New Yorker letterhead

                                          1 September 1947

Dear Joe:
   I don't see why an author can't thank a critic. As a rule I don't, but
I do now. I thank you. As I might say to Jim Thurber: "Live ever, die
never . . ."*

                                          John O'Hara

   *I looked you up in Who's Who and learned you are Phi-Psi. You
probably don't even remember ki-yi-yi.

   [1] Jackson was book review editor of the *San Francisco Chronicle; Hellbox* had been
published in August.

TO: Katharine Angell White   TLS, 1 p. PSt.
1947   New York City

Dear Katharine:
   I am sending you the enclosed piece,[1] but in all candor I wish I had
some place else to send it. I am very unhappy about the rejection of
the one that came back yesterday.[2] I had no difficulty ticking off the
answers to the questions you raised, and for the second time in as many
pieces I have come up against that unfortunate comment "no story" (yes,
you will recall that was Gus' succinct comment on the last one you
bought and now it turns up again). What is more I certainly take a dim
view of bringing this last piece back to the office with an accompanying
sales talk. If some of my pieces do seem to be miniature novels that
isn't necessarily against them. Time and again the friendlier reviewers
say just that: that some of the pieces *are* novels in brief and that the
reader ends up knowing all there is to know about such pieces.
   But the really distressing thing is the waste, anywhere from a week
to three weeks gone out of my life, an occupational risk, to be sure, but
that doesn't make it any better. I really don't know what to do.

                                          John

   [1] Unidentified.
   [2] Unidentified.

TO: Herman Liebert[1] TLS, 1 p. Yale
55 E. 86th St.,
New York City

29 January 1948

Dear Mr. Liebert:

I have just within the hour returned from Hobe Sound, Florida, where I was the guest of, I imagine, an old Elizabethan Club member, Philip Barry. Your letter was one of several which had not been forwarded to me, and I apologize for the delay in acknowledging it.

I would be delighted to accept your invitation to meet with the Elizabethan Club, but a speaker I am not. The only other occasion similar to this in my career was a visit I once paid to the Lantern Club at Exeter, which I believe is a sort of junior Elizabethan Club. Young Michael Forrestal was then president of the Lantern, and he gave me a subject—I forget what it was—on which I held forth for about fifteen or twenty minutes, and the meeting then became general conversation, as you say. We gathered at Mr. Perry's house, around the fire, and I did not stand, which gives you an idea of the informality of the evening. The question-and-answer, open-forum part of the session lasted about an hour and a half, and I believe was mutually painless. If the Elizabethan Club would be willing to settle for that kind of get-together I would be glad to go to New Haven. Almost any time would be okay with me. If you like the idea of my more or less ad-libbing on a topic to be agreed upon, I will leave the date up to you. As to fee and expenses, if you know anything about me you know how I feel about Yale, and I certainly could not take any money from my friend Gilbert Troxell's club.

Thank you for thinking of me, and I hope we do meet.

Faithfully,
John O'Hara

[1] A member of the Yale Library staff.

TO: James V. Forrestal TLS, 1 p. Princeton
55 E. 86th St.,
New York City

16 March 1948

Dear Jim:

Greetings and salutations, and you don't have to read the rest, but will you kindly pass it on the proper authority?

An important character in my novel, which is coming along very well thank you, is a man who in 1917 is forty years old.[1] Through the governor of his State he has been making an effort to wangle a commission in the Navy, and I have a scene in which the governor tells my man that he thinks the commission (lieutenant commander) is coming through. I would like to know all the official steps: how he applies and to whom, and where he goes for his physical, etc. Since it is a Pennsylvania novel I suppose my man appears at League Island for the physical. I then want him turned down because of a heart condition, and I would like to know how that was done in 1917. Do they write him a letter? Do they say he cannot get a waiver? Who writes the letter, etc.? The governor is appealed to, and he knows somebody on the House Naval Affairs Committee, but the turn-down is final, and my character remains a civilian. (Hell, I know a fellow who knew a Secretary of the Navy and he couldn't get a snap commission.)

I'll be glad to send you an autographed first edition, although I don't anticipate your having much time to read it.

Kindest regards,

Yrs,
John

¹ Sidney Tate in A *Rage to Live*.

TO: James Cerruti¹
Spring 1948

TLS, 1 p. (not mailed). PSt.
55 E. 86th St.,
New York City

Dear Mr. Cerruti:

I was born at 125 Mahantongo Street, Pottsville, Schuylkill County, Pennsylvania, on January 31, 1905, son of Dr. and Mrs. Patrick H. O'Hara. My wife was born at 72 West 52nd Street, New York City, daughter of Dr. and Mrs. Robert H. Wylie, and the first time I had a date with her in New York I took her to the Onyx Club,² where she felt very much at home. Why not? It had been her home. The last time I saw my birthplace it had an A.&P. store on the ground floor. I didn't go in. We have a three-year-old daughter, Wylie O'Hara, who was born at the Harkness Pavilion, Presbyterian Hospital, which, as of early this afternoon, has not been turned into a crib or a foodmonger's.

My latest book is "Hellbox," a collection of short stories. At this writing I have passed the half-way mark in my new novel,³ my first in ten years. It is for late fall or 1948-49 winter publication.

The Stutz piece⁴ is my first for HOLIDAY, and with an appropriateness that I consider neat, it was written at the Hobe Sound, Florida, home of my friend Philip Barry, who is, of course, a "Holiday" author himself.⁵

I divide my time between New York City and Quogue, Long Island, and I seem to go in for unusual cars: a 1939 Bantam, a 1947 Standard "14", and a 1932 Duesenberg. Maybe if my father had bought me a Stutz Bearcat instead of a Buick I'd own a Buick now.

John O'Hara

[1] *Holiday* associate editor who had requested a biographical note from O'Hara.
[2] A jazz night club on West 52nd Street.
[3] A *Rage to Live* (1949).
[4] "The Stutz Bearcat," August 1948.
[5] Reference to Barry's play *Holiday*.

TO: Harold Ross   ALS, 1 p. PSt.
Received 7 June 1948   *New Yorker* letterhead

Dear Harold—

The enclosed, being a poem, does not mean that I have surrendered or yielded from my position.[1] As far as I know, we are just where we were in January, and our stalemate is not affected by my being compelled to express myself in verse.[2]

This poem was rejected by Film Fun, Modern Screen Classic, and The Journal of Naval Institute Proceedings.

Cordially
J. O'Ha

[1] In the late Forties O'Hara became increasingly upset by *The New Yorker's* rejection of his short stories. He felt that since the stories were written for that magazine, they were unpublishable elsewhere. Harold Ross refused to meet O'Hara's demand for a $500 payment for every rejected story. When *The New Yorker's* review of A *Rage to Live* appeared in 1949, O'Hara stopped writing stories for eleven years.
[2] O'Hara's poem was not published.

TO: Bennett Cerf[1]   TLS, 1 p. Columbia
                                            New Yorker letterhead

17 June 1948

Dear Bennett:

I have received a note from Littauer[2] of Collier's, asking to have a look at my novel. This, tentatively, is what I am going to say to him: Collier's can look at my novel for $15,000, half payable now and half on completion, when they get first look. If they want to buy it they can pay me $100,000, to which the $15,000 does not apply, and the purchase to be subject to our agreeing on cuts. If we can't agree on the cuts, the deal is off and no part of the look-at money is returnable by me.

Will you give that proposition your shrewdest appraisal and let me know what it is soon so I can reply to Littauer? I am fairly certain of getting the same request from Cosmopolitan and the Post, and the fact is the Post asked me in February if they could see the novel.[3]

Regards and in haste,

John

[1] Bennett Cerf of Random House became O'Hara's publisher in 1947 with *Hellbox* after O'Hara left Duell, Sloan and Pearce. O'Hara remained a Random House author until his death.

[2] Kenneth Littauer, *Collier's* fiction editor.

[3] No magazine was prepared to meet O'Hara's demand for payment for reading rights to *A Rage to Live*.

TO: Joseph Bryan III   TL, 1 p. PSt.
                                                   Quogue, Long Island
                                                      8 August 1948

Dear Bryan:

How long are you going to be in New Hampshire, or, to put it another way, when are you going to be back in Pennsylvania? The reason I ask is this: in September or early October I am going to take my new little automobile and penetrate old Pennsy for a week or so, as part of my researching for my novel. I have to go to Harrisburg, Lebanon, and Sunbury, and maybe to Eagles Mere, and to look at some farms. I am writing this novel mostly from memory, and not stopping for anything, but by that time I will want to go back over my MS and put things in and maybe take things out.

Well, I would like it very much if you would ride along with me. The car seats only two—Wylie crowds it when Belle is riding—and has very little luggage space, so we'll have to wear our thousand-milers and limit ourselves to a suit apiece, for visits to the fashionable hotels of the aforementioned cities. But I think it would be an agreeable jaunt. It is a pleasant drive from Lebanon to Harrisburg and up the river to Sunbury, and if you would care to see something of the coal regions we can return from Sunbury and through Schuylkill County. I'm of two minds about stopping in Pottsville, where I have three brothers, but that can be worked out later, although I would like to take you to the country club, maybe for lunch on the way home, and who [sic] you the old homestead and the farm. It would be a lazy trip because there isn't more than

50 miles between any two towns. We might spend two nights in Harrisburg.

Anyway, think it over and let me know when you've stopped thinking.

Yrs,

TO: Saxe Commins[1]　　　　　　　　TLS, 3 pp. Mrs. Commins
Summer 1948　　　　　　　　　　　　*New Yorker* letterhead

Sunday

Dear Saxe:

Thank you for the book, the Ward Greene one,[2] which arrived the very next day after you sent it, which I can tell you is remarkable down here.

I plan to come up to New York on Wednesday, for lunch with Terry Helburn,[3] and after she has paid the reckoning I will bring some product to be retyped. By that time I think I will have reached just 500 pages of the original double-spaced (I'm now 17 pages short of that figure). Where you can help me is here: I am not sure where the first retyping job ended. I think it was at the top of page 385 of the original MS, but I may be wrong. So will you please look at what you have (the triple spaced manuscript) and see what the last sentence is, and then telegraph me the wording of same. Naturally I don't want to lug the whole double-spaced MS up to NY.

You'd better get that surgical glint out of your eye, because far from my doing any ruthless cutting on the final MS, there will be ruthful additions between now and the submitting of the printers' copy. You are in for some surprises when you see the final MS; extremely minor characters as of Book I, which you may think ought to go, will be popping up all through Book II. I don't suppose any of the critics will be alert enough to notice it, but in this book I have been influenced more by Jules Romains[4] than by any other author. I am inclined to think he is the greatest novelist of our time. However, Harrisburg isn't Paris, and I am confining myself to one volume, you will be relieved to learn.

Tell Bennett I complied with his suggestion that I have my picture taken in my new car. Belle took it, and if it turns out okay I'll probably have pictures when I see you Wednesday. But if he wants to run a cut in Trade Winds[5] he is not to run a caption: "This is how Random House treats its authors." I had to write a magazine piece to enable me to pay for the car, in spite of my strong hint that RH was going to be charming and give it to me as a bonus. The title of my novel is A RAGE TO LIVE. I have tried it out on everybody from Rosemary Benet[6] to Eric Hatch's[7] mother, an enormous range, believe me. Several persons who didn't like it at first changed their minds days later. The best thing about it, or one of the best, as Rosemary pointed out, is the unusual juxtaposition of simple words. The best thing about it is how it, and the whole poem from which it comes, apply to my novel. And another best thing about it is that I like it. Actually, although my titles are usually pretty good, people don't buy books by titles as much as they do by the author's name. I know I do. I also know it's time for me to go to bed.

Hope to see you Wednesday.

Yrs,
John

title is top of page 150 in the Alexander Pope Mod. Lib.[8]

[1] Saxe Commins was O'Hara's editor at Random House for *A Rage to Live*. O'Hara could not work comfortably with him and subsequently asked for a different editor.

[2] Probably *Star Reporters and 34 of their Best Stories* (New York: Random House, 1948).

[3] Teresa Helburn of the Theatre Guild.

[4] Romains' epic, *Men of Good Will*, covering a twenty-five-year span from 1908 to 1933, was published in France in twenty-seven parts and in America in fourteen volumes commencing in 1933.

[5] Cerf's column in *The Saturday Review of Literature*.

[6] Wife of Stephen Vincent Benet.

[7] *New Yorker* writer and novelist, author of *My Man Godfrey*.

[8] "Epistle to a Lady."

TO: Joseph Bryan III   TLS, 2 pp. PSt.
September 1948   Quogue, Long Island

Dear Bryan:

I think you have the best idea: we'll leave it informal-like, and when I feel like going to Pennsylvania I'll call you up a day or so ahead of time, and you can make a trip with me if convenient, and if not convenient at that time, make it another time, or another. The distances are so short that the whole business could be covered in one day, without pushing much, but of course I want to dawdle. I could go to Doylestown some afternoon, spend the night, and next day we could drive to Lebanon, for instance, and if you had to be back that night, okay, I'd get you back, and I'd stay in a country hotel (which I want to do anyway) and next day drive to some place like Shartlesville, and then to Harrisburg, then to Sunbury, then down through Schuylkill County and Pottsville (The Best Site in the Anthracite), Allentown, Coopersburg, Doylestown, and home. I would like to catch a football game at Lafayette and drive around Lawrenceville, which I've never seen, just to get the layout.

I was interested in the Inside Information[1] because it was so frankly self-revelatory. In that respect it compares favorably with the writings of Henry Miller, Frank Harris, and Max Eastman. Someone did a beautiful re-touching job on the picture of you with the colored nurse; that is, they managed to make the nurse slightly darker than the infant Bryan, which I understand is contrary to fact, as we Latin students say. The photograph of you in uniform was naturally suppressed by you during war-time. Where did you get those German ribbons? I notice you are wearing an American Eunuch Citation on the top row, but underneath you have an Iron Cross and a Pour le Merite, which you certainly earned, but most Americans didn't wear them when they had their pictures taken.

I also was mildly fascinated by the fact or legend that seven generations of Bryans were born in the same room in the same mansion. It shows at least that the Bryans were not superstitious. In the North, for instance, we'd have taken a look at the second or third generations and planned all future accouchements accordingly; with such bad luck for two generations, we'd have said, maybe the room had something to do with it; let's have the babies in a different room. In fact, let's have them in a different house. In fact, let's not have any more babies. But I suppose the Bryans will never give up that house so long as they believe there are two pieces of silver hidden in the walls. For 28 more pieces of silver they sold Christ, a known fact that I have yet to hear you bring up in your lively recitals of the activities of your dead ancestors.

Your mention of your great-uncle John Randolph Bryan reminds me that my grandfather Mike O'Hara was Chief Burgess of Shenandoah, Pa. (Not a Virginia burgess, and not a Virginia Shenandoah, you may be sure.) I had intended never to tell you about this because of your sincere, child-like, touching admiration for your elders, but as a friend I think you ought to know that my grandfather once arrested a man in Shenandoah. Seems this man went from town to town giving balloon ascensions, which were popular in that day. Unfortunately, however, his purpose was not entirely to provide entertainment; he was accompanied by a number of cronies who, when the citizens' gaze was skyward, went around picking pockets. My grandfather arrested the ringleader of this gang, thrashed him within an inch of his life, and sent him on his way. The man's name, I distinctly recall, was Randolph Bryan, and I suppose it was your great-uncle. It was a common name, and if it was not your great-uncle but another ungrateful freedman of the same moniker, I apologize, but you must admit that the coincidence is remarkable. The Shenandoah police blotter says Randolph Bryan, 35, no home; occupation: balloonist. Did your great-uncle walk with a limp? If so, it's the same man, because he got that limp when my grandfather kicked him.

Isn't it a small world after all?

Yrs,
J O'H

---

[1] Unidentified.

TO: Harvey Batdorf[1]

TLS, 2 pp. Mr. Batdorf
Quogue, Long Island
11 September 1948

Dear Harvey:

I am contemplating a Pennsylvania jaunt with a two-fold purpose: I am writing a Pennsylvania novel, which goes 'way the hell back into the 1800's, and on which I must do some additional research (most of the research so far has been my own memory), and to pay my expenses and make a slight profit I am considering a piece for Holiday magazine[2] on the Pennsylvania colleges or maybe just Lafayette with some mention of Muhlenberg, F.&M., Dickinson, Albright, Gettysburg, et al. If you are so disposed you can help me immeasurably in two ways: I would like to do a little digging in the Lafayette library, particularly among old class-books, yearbooks, and the like, as the father of one of my principal characters is a Lafayette man around the 1870's. The other way you can help is—if I do the piece on the other Pennsylvania colleges—to provide me with letters of introduction to VIP's at each of them, so that I can give a brief history of each college, with some mention of local tradition and possibly an anecdote or two. In spite of my Pennsylvania origin and background, I don't know anybody at Lehigh or Ursinus or any other college except you at Easton.

I have a terrific new little car, an English M-G, and I will tour by motor, probably for a week. I imagine most of the colleges start the new semester about the same time, so I plan to get there after the initial excitement has died down. What would be a good time to start my trek? I would spend a day in each town and later, if the Holiday plan works out, they will send a photographer to illustrate my piece. Whether or not I do the Holiday article I plan to make the trip, and especially to visit the Lafayette library. I may have another fellow with me, a writer named Joseph Bryan III, whose articles you may have seen in the Saturday Evening Post. He lives in Doylestown, but he is a Virginian and a Princetonian and I plan to educate him Pennsylvania-wise and Lafayette-wise. Some day, when all this is over, I plan to enter Lafayette as a freshman. That would be just about the age you were when you were a freshman, wouldn't it? Put me down for the class of, say, 1958, so I'll have a degree before my daughter starts her prom-trotting. (Although she'll be 13 then, and by the look of things I won't be any too soon.)

It will be good to see you again and compare recollections. I met a Yale News lad last winter who knew your brother Larry in the CBI. Kindest regards,

Yrs,
John

[1] Harvey Batdorf was an administrator at Lafayette College.
[2] The article was not written.

TO: Robert Simonds   TLS, 2 pp. PSt.
Quogue, Long Island
13 September 1948

Dear Thurlow:

I was very sorry indeed not to have been able to come through with the five thousand last night, and I am sorry today, after discussing it with Belle, to have to report adversely on the smaller sum. The fact is that the smaller sum is not that much smaller than the five, which is another way of saying that we can't afford a fifteen hundred touch either.

I would like to re-state what I told you over the phone, so that there's no misunderstanding about the reasons. I have been working on my novel for more than a year. Started a year ago last month, was dissatisfied with what I had done, and began again in January. It has meant no outside work, with the exception of three pieces for Holiday magazine. No New Yorker work, which makes a difference of about $12,000 in my annual income. No movie work since the summer of '46. Hence my having to live on capital during a time when we have had to employ a nurse as well as the expense of raising a child, who among other things starts pre-school in two weeks. I have even been on the wagon since 1 January, which represents an important and at the same time necessary saving.

As to the future, this is a, if not the, picture. I am going to make a research trip to Pennsylvania in the near future, after which it should take me about two months to finish the novel. Through December I will be reading proofs, etc., and waiting to hear from my Hollywood agent. As I told you, I had a letter from him last week and he wanted to know whether I was interested in an assignment out there, and in spite of the fact that I have declared my intention never to go there again, the money situation is such that I told him to get me something after the first of the year. I should mention that I took a big advance in order to write the novel—advance royalty from the publisher, that is. I therefore won't be making any money out of the book until it has been selling a while, and hence the reluctant willingness to work for the movies again. I get a very large salary in Hollywood, even for Hollywood, but if you've been reading the news from that quarter you know the heat is on out there, too, but I feel fairly confident I'll get a job, and if and when I do I hope to be available for a touch. Naturally I'll know more about that after I've seen and signed a contract, which should be early in January. I don't know enough about your situation to be able to say do or don't count on me. At the moment I would say don't, because a friend of mine, a writer who has more screen credits than I, has owed me $2000 for two years—a year past the time he said he would repay the loan. Another writer owes me $500, another person $400. This is not to reveal anything more than what you already know if you are acquainted with the facts of writers' finances these days. And this is the year Belle and I had hoped to buy a house in Quogue, but it has always been that way with us: riding the plush one year, staying home and listening to the radio the next. The friend who owes me the two thousand happened to catch me after I had done some Hollywood work, and when his daughter, who is my godchild, was going away to school. If you had wanted a loan then I'd rather have made it to you.

So that's the story. It would give me pleasure to write you a cheque for the full amount and to tell you to take as long as you pleased. How about Ed Fox? I understand he is doing very well. I do not, however, recommend your going to Harry Inness Silliman.

Belle joins me in sending love to all the Simondses.

As ever,
John

TO: Charles Poore[1]   TLS, 1 p. PSt.
                                                      55 E. 86th St.,
                                                      New York City

                                                      6 November 1948
Dear Charles:
    I wonder if you will give me permission to quote from your piece this morning in a letter[2] I am preparing for publication in the Authors League Bulletin. Only this week I went to the Trib and copied Gannett's[3] thoughts on the copyright-credit nuisance, and I also am writing him for permission. My letter will be addressed to Oscar Hammerstein II, who is in an ambiguous position as president of the League and a partner in Williamson song publishers.
    For years I have been quoting song lyrics (notwithstanding the remark of the Life editorialist) but in the novel I have almost completed I

have refrained from quoting rather than give the free puff to those chiselers, the publishers, who not only steal titles of novels and use them for song lyrics, but even steal from each other. I supported ASCAP in its fight with BMI, and the only thanks I got for that was from Harold Arlen. Cerf takes a what-the-hell attitude, in spite of the way a book is cluttered up by the quotes.

It probably is too late for me to use song lyrics in my novel, which as of this morning stands at 633 pages and could have included snatches of songs back to 1899, but as a matter of principle I am going ahead with my letter and try to get some action in the League. It's a hell of a note when authors have to depend on critics to institute campaigns. Maybe you ought to start doing something for us about the Eisenhower-capital-gains-tax.

I work nights but when I don't work late I am free for lunch. How about calling me some morning, At-9-9193?

Cordially,
John O'Hara

¹ Charles Poore, book reviewer for the *New York Times*.
² Unlocated and probably unpublished.
³ Lewis Gannett, book reviewer for the *New York Herald Tribune*.

TO: Lewis Gannett

TLS, 1 p. Harvard
55 E. 86th St.,
New York City

9 November 1948

Dear Gannett:

I was at Bill White's one night about two weeks ago and they expected you to drop in. I'm sorry you didn't, because I've wanted to ask you some questions about the copyright-credit nuisance ever since you made the first and, until Charlie Poore's piece last week, only attack on it. In my stories and novels I always have had snatches of song lyrics, but I'll be damned if I'll give free puffs to those people and in spite of the fact that the novel I am working on covers a period that is rich with good and bad lyrics, I have not quoted a line.

It probably is too late now to go back and insert them, but I want to stir up some action in the Authors League and I am preparing a letter to Oscar Hammerstein II. I would like to have permission to quote your remarks, and if you have any other information would you please send it to me? I have spoken to Charlie and he has given permission to use his comments.

Faithfully,
John O'Hara

TLS, 2 pp. Columbia
55 E. 86th St.,
New York City

30 November 1948

Dear Bennett:

At this time I shall only comment on specific points raised in your letter of the 27th, paragraph by paragraph.

1. I take no delight, perverse or otherwise, in making you uncomfortable, or in making anyone uncomfortable. If you have been uncomfortable after some of my comments on some of your actions, my comments were only a stimulant to your conscience.

2. "When you suddenly need a lot of additional money for personal reasons." Are you implying that there is something naughty about needing money for "personal" reasons? Gambling debts? A mistress? What other reasons than personal reasons are there? I need the money for an income-tax payment and to run this household while I am writing a novel by which you presumably will profit personally, and what you do with *your* personal profit is properly none of my business.

3. With a single exception the advertising of HELLBOX was institutional advertising and not advertising of my book. The choice of quotes was unfortunate, in spite of the fact that I called attention to some excellent reviews that were available.

4. When you say you "had to virtually steal the manuscript to read it," you are just about stating it, and my cordiality over the telephone was an example of self-control. It was well known around your office that I did not want anyone to read the manuscript until it was finished. The construction of the novel is such that it is not fair to the author or to the reader to have the novel read in snatches, with weeks intervening. The manuscript was in your office for safe-keeping, to protect your investment and mine against damage by fire, for instance. If I had a fireproof vault or a safe I wouldn't have handed in any pages except for re-typing, and I used a Random House typist because you have a vault, or safe. The last time I saw Don Klopfer[1] he was friendly and jovial, giving no indication of frustration or disappointment, as you seem to imply. In fact, long ago he once said he was just as well pleased not to have to read the manuscript until it was finished. As to Haas,[2] I hardly know him and know nothing of what he thinks or feels. I may say that the only other time my publisher saw uncompleted manuscript was in the case of my first book, when I showed Alfred Harcourt 25,000 words (one quarter) in order to obtain a subsidy. There was no carbon copy, no re-typed job, and they set type from the original manuscript, and when Harcourt realized that it was the only manuscript he made me promise never to do that again. What should have been thoroughly understood (and I went along thinking it was) was that my novel was not officially in the office.

5. I don't understand what you are getting at in this paragraph or the two following. If you are saying, under your breath, get another publisher, please say it intelligibly and I'll set about to do exactly that. I recognize and deplore the tactics of accusing your vis-a-vis of the very thing you have done or plan to do yourself, and when you call my previous letter threatening you are employing that stratagem. My letter applying for a $10,000 additional advance contained my plan for another book after this novel.[3] No comment was made by you either in your letter that offered a quarter of what I asked for, or in the letter that offered me, as far as I can make out, the door.

Faithfully,
John O'Hara

[1] The co-founder of Random House.
[2] Robert Haas, Random House partner.
[3] *The Farmers Hotel* (1951).

TO: Joseph Bryan III

TLS, 3 pp. PSt.
55 E. 86th St.,
New York City

1 December [1948]

Dear Bryan:

I am aware, of course, that your interest in my novel is polite but perfunctory, and that what you really want to inquire about is the resumption of football relations between Fordham and Yale. Well, you came to the right man for your answer.

Bob Gannon, the president of Fordham, called me up a few months ago and asked me to have lunch with him at the Century Club,[1] where we could be alone. If you've ever had lunch at the Century you know that you can be alone even though all the chairs may be occupied. So I said to Bob, Bob what's your problem? And Bob said to me, John, I can give it to you in one word: Yale. And I said to him I thought that was Charlie Seymour's[2] problem, Bob. And he said to me it was Charlie Seymour's problem of course, but this was a different kind of problem. And I said to him, Well, perhaps I can be of help if you'll tell me what it is. So he said to me, Well, they're trying to get back on our schedule. NO! I said. He said to me, Why, John, I always thought you were fond of Yale. I thought you'd be pleased. In fact, he said, I thought maybe you had something to do with it. I understand you've had lunch with Tip Blish and see a lot of Lucius Beebe, and you even married into a Yale family. I thought you might have been swinging things. Father Gannon, I said, I also see a lot of a man named Joe Bryan but that doesn't mean I want Fordham to play Tuskegee. He said, Well, they're all steamed up about it and keep sending registered letters asking us if we won't please put them on that all-important October 1 date on our schedule. They say there is a natural though friendly rivalry between the two institutions, and that culturally the two great universities are linked by the fact that you have given your MSS to the Yale Library and you were president of your class in 1920. That is quite true, I said. The friendly rivalry between Fordham University and Yale, the Fordham of the Ivy League, dates all the way back to the historic telegraphic rifle meet of 1909, through which were formed associations which have endured to this day. But, I said, if I carry any weight I am going to make it my job to see that they don't get the all-important October 1 date on our schedule. Why? said Father Gannon. Well, I said, you remember during the presidential campaign, Father, the cock-suckers on the Yale team all signed that football for Dewey. He nodded slowly and admitted that was true. If they are trying to regain prestige by getting on our schedule, I said, they are going about it in a rather too obvious way, the cock-suckers, I said. Then the unhappy priest bowed and said he had just about committed himself, and he would give his scapular to know a way out. Well, I took out my jimmy pipe and my Persian slipper and methodically rubbed my special mixture of Gail & Ax and Royal Yacht, lit up, smiled that smile of contentment while the good priest slipped out to St. Malachy's for a fast Stations of the Cross. And when he returned I was able to meet him with, Father Gannon, I have a solution! I admonished him not to kiss my ring in front of all those Protestants in the Century Club, and told him my plan. I said, They have a fellow named Jackson[3] on the Yale team, and Gannon said yes, his father works for my great & good friend Henry Robinson Luce who mortally hates & fears Fulton J. Sheen.[4] Kindly do not interrupt me, I said, the Jackson I have in mind's father is no Luce puppet, he. His soul may be white, and that's your business Father Gannon, but his skin is black. Now it will soon be time to elect the Yale football captain, I said, and by rights Jackson ought to get it, but any bunch of cock-suckers that will sign a football for Tom-Tom Dewey won't have sense enough to vote for Levi Jackson. You can therefore say that you have under advisement the possibility of putting Yale back on the Fordham schedule, and then the day after they give Jackson the go-by you can say that Fordham, the great citadel of tolerance where a Catholic is treated like anyone else, could not possibly schedule a team that snubbed the colored boy.

Well, the rest is history. The cock-suckers crossed me and I am trying to remember how to cross myself. Does that satisfy your curiosity?

As to the novel, *Finis* is not *Farr wrong!* Do you get it? I am about ⅞ finished, but am available for lunch and/or dinner and/or both whenever a real sport comes to town loaded with flight pay. I know one whose initials are JB who was in town a fortnight ago but never called me. Not all the cock-suckers are on the Yale team. Some of them come to New York and spend their money for show, and then go home and pretend they were never in NY at all, and write letters asking if I am available for lunch/and/or/dinner, after they've spent all their money for show. I suppose the person I have in mind spent his money to try to wangle an invitation to the Payson wedding and then heard we were invited and now he wants to try to work it through us. Well, that person can go sign a Dewey football is all I can say. If Charlie and Joan had wanted him they'd have asked him is all I can say.

Yrs,

Swope[5]

I do not know whether a gorilla could or could not tear Gene Tierney apart, but any gorilla that missed a chance to pry her open a little is not a man, my son.[6] Ung gung gung gung.

[1] The Century Association, a New York men's club on 43rd St.

[2] President of Yale.

[3] Levi Jackson, a Negro, was elected captain of the Yale football team for 1949.

[4] Monsignor Sheen had converted Clare Booth Luce to Catholicism.

[5] Herbert Bayard Swope was the managing editor of the New York World in the Twenties.

[6] Former heavyweight champion Gene Tunney had claimed that a good heavyweight could beat Gargantua. O'Hara is playing on the similarity of the names of Gene Tunney and actress Gene Tierney.

TO: Charles Poore   TLS, 2 pp. PSt.
18 December 1948   55 E. 86th St.,
                                                     New York City

Saturday

Dear Charlie:

Many thanks, for the Sunday, the Thursday, and today.[1]

I noticed something—prepared for it, I guess, by your word elegiac— that was more or less common to the paragraphs you used from the History. It took me five minutes, but it came to me that where I had heard or read that style before was in the citations that are read during the conferring of honorary degrees. Have you ever gone through them? I always do. The Fordham ones indicate that the reverend Jesuit fathers have got the pipe that John J. McFetridge, Commissioner of Water Works in the city of Utica, N.Y., Papal Chamberlain, and member of the Class of '04, is right with God, having kept his hands out of the public till and off the departmental stenographers, and given six sons and two daughters to the service of God in the holy priesthood and the Sisters of St. Joseph. That's the Fordham-type citation.

But the Yale-Harvard-Princeton type seem to have been written all by the same man, whose initials are H. S. C.[2] The citations contain a nil-nisi-bonum theme, a cheerfully obscure presentation of the facts in the case, and a kind of antiseptic humor (often with a harmless little pun) that make the gentleman who is being honored sound like someone slightly human but essentially too good for this world, which, as he is handed his diploma and moves his tassel, he ought to have the grace to leave within twenty-four hours.

I have a strange relationship with Canby, whom I never have met. For years he put the knock on me in lectures at New Haven (I used to get letters from undergraduates). I in turn put the gentle knock on him when I spoke to the Elizabethan Club last year. But on the other hand I know from Phil Barry that Canby was in favor of my election to the Institute of Arts & Letters, and my candidacy at the Coffee House,[3] where I was blackballed. I believe you said Cowley[4] had written the comments you use today (I didn't save Thursday's paper), but Cowley, Canby, Schmowley, Schmanby.

The pile of blank paper in this lonely room is getting smaller. I am now at page 876, with about 200 more to go. I hope I know when to stop.

In case I don't see you—I've been at it six nights a week, and one night this week I quit at 8 a.m.—I send seasonal greetings to you and yours.

Cordially,
John

[1] Poore mentioned O'Hara on 5, 16, and 18 December in the *New York Times*. His two-part review of *The Literary History of the United States* brought this letter from O'Hara, from which Poore printed the second and third paragraphs in his 1 January 1949 column, crediting "A well-known author who will one day, we hope, write a novel called 'New York, 21, N.Y.'"

[2] Henry Seidel Canby, former editor of *The Saturday Review of Literature* and one of the editors of *The Literary History of the United States*.

[3] An eating club in New York for writers and editors.

[4] Critic Malcolm Cowley.

TO: Bennett Cerf

TLS, 1 p. Columbia
55 E. 86th St.,
New York City

26 December 1948

Dear Bennett:

I would prefer to postpone our meeting until after Mayes[1] has given me an opinion on the manuscript, and I am telephoning Saxe today to arrange for some additional retyping. I am at a loss to understand why you told Mayes you didn't see how he could make the cuts necessary for magazine publication before Mayes had seen a single word of the novel. In her letter to me, Miss Bourne specifically mentioned the possibility of printing the novel in part, and in a manuscript that is now more than 900 pages long there would be a good-sized sub-manuscript for which Mayes would be willing to pay well. But if my publisher is prejudicing the sale of my novel before a magazine editor has had a chance to read it, I naturally ask: whose side is he on? And if, as you say, you and Mayes talked about the novel for twenty minutes I am, to say the least, curious about the effect of your talk on Mayes.

I am not going to show Mayes the ending, or Book VI, unless he is willing to buy the novel on what he will have seen up to that point. As of today I have one fairly long sequence to do to complete Book V, and I expect to finish that this week. Book VI should take another week, possibly less, because I know the stuff so well and have been pointing toward it throughout the novel. Book VI is a story in itself, but it requires previous knowledge of the characters who have been introduced in the earlier parts of the novel. It is both synopsis and recapitulation and I have no doubt that I could sell it to Mayes or anyone else in the magazine field, if I would be willing to make certain revisions, but that is not the way I am doing business. It is an honest part of an honest novel, and not a digest.

Faithfully,
John

1 Herbert R. Mayes, editor of *Good Housekeeping*.

TO: Charles Poore

TLS, 1 p. PSt.
55 E. 86th St.,
New York City

1 January 1948 [1949]

Dear Charlie:

The funny thing is, during the war we lived at 27 East 79th Street, which is in the 21 Zone. Every time I wrote to some friend in the forward areas I would get back the same comment: Ha ha, always knew you would end up living in 21, or, Well, knew you liked 21 but never tho't you'd actually live there. Another funny thing (about as funny as the preceding) is that I never have had a Butterfield 8 number. I now want to get license-plate BU-8 for my little red M-G, but I suppose you personally have about as much influence in Albany as I have, so I will try some good solid GOP man.

The last time I had a low license number I was the indirect, or secondary, victim of a practical joke. A Tammany friend of mine named Paul Dezell said he would be glad to get me a low number, and went to work. But his friends thought the number was for him, so I drove around in 1935 with the Kinseyish license plate D-69. I used to come out and find strange women sitting in my car. Yrs, John

TO: Joseph Bryan III

TLS, 1 p. PSt.
New York City

20 Jan. 49

Dear Mr. Bryan:

In the holy year 1863, when those members of the Commonwealth Club[1] who were not hiding in the caves of Petersburg, which kin of mine later had the pleasure of blowing up, when, sir, the Outside Members met in Klonklave in the shack of a friendly Negro and put the torch to the Holy Bible, a copy of Magna Carta, Pilgrim's Progress, An Appeal to Reason, and other unwelcome documents, that miserable lace-handkerchief rabble killed culture forever in the South. Consequently the superfluous information that I never have been heard of in the Commonwealth Club only further revealed your ignorance of history, a revelation in itself no more unusual than the opening of your trap.

My polite note to the effect that nobody in the Chilton Club[2] ever had heard of The High School[3] was occasioned by the fact that I had been in conversation with the headmaster of Woodberry Forest,[4] who, because he is named Kelly, and incidentally was an old Grotonian and Cantabridgian, has been doing missionary work in the South. At least, at Woodberry Forest, they are trying, and consequently I passed the hat among the kindly Bostonians and with their contribution I have sent a First Reader to Episcopal High School in the desperate, Christian hope that the appearance of a book at that institution may, if only for a moment, divert the inmates' minds from the practices which we in the North find shocking but which, in the South, seem to be as common as the origin of the louts themselves.

Kindly make cheques payable to Mr. Erskine Caldwell, treasurer of the American Association for the Advancement of Culpepers.

Yrs,
O'Hara

[1] In Richmond, Va.
[2] Boston women's club.
[3] Bryan had attended Episcopal High School, a preparatory school in Alexandria, Va.
[4] A Virginia preparatory school.

TO: Helen and James Thurber   ALS, 2 pp. Ohio State
February 1949   New York City

Dear Helen and Jamie—

I enter my forty-fifth year with a burst of globe-trotting and a mixed
metaphor as I set out on an unofficial three-day visit to Reading, Pa., a
city made famous by Bobby Clark.[1] I have finished the typewriter part
of my novel and this trip is part of the pencil work. I expect to make
brief excursions to Lebanon and Sunbury (no speeches) and, with a bottle
of vanilla at my nose, the model town of Hershey.[2]

I hope I'll see you before you depart for Nassau, but if not please
give us the word on your return. We called the Algonquin and you are
not there or expected.

Many thanks for remembering me and for the beautiful brooch.

I feel no worse than I did at thirty-four, but no better than I did at
twenty-four. That about sums it up, I guess, except to add that if I
had to live it over again I don't think I could.

Love
John

[1] Musical comedy star.
[2] Home of the Hershey chocolate company.

TO: Katharine Angell White   TLS, 1 p. PSt.
                                                     New York City

                                                     2 March 1949
Dear Katharine:

With so many and such excellent stories to choose from I have had
a hard time making a selection for the 25th anniversary volume. So I ruled
out some stories in groups: no Pal Joeys or war stories and no straight
monolog pieces. I also ruled out rejections, although I think Gibbs would
include one rejection among the best I have written since 1940. I did
my selecting from two of my books, Hellbox and Pipe Night, but one
story which I have to list (I unfortunately forget the name of it) isn't
in either book. It's the story of the young man at a summer resort who
commits suicide by drowning.[1] That story, of course, has served as a
model for at least one other New Yorker writer, I happen to know.

Well, there's that story and the following others (total 5):

Doctor and Mrs. Parsons
The Decision
Walter T. Carriman

Bread Alone

The Last of Haley—

You will have to make the decision from there on.[2]

Yrs,
John

[1] "The Last of Haley," 30 August 1947. This title added below in holograph by another hand.
[2] Mrs. White selected "The Decision" for 55 Short Stories from The New Yorker.

TO: Joseph Bryan III   TLS, 1 p. PSt.

Deuxieme Bureau[1]
55 E 86

28 Ap 1949

Dear Brawn:

Apparently I didn't make myself clear, a failure on my part that I justify by considering the caliber of man I was dealing with.

I am gradually filling out the gaps all right . . . Old passport numbers, where I lived in January 1935, etc. What I was chiefly concerned with was and is the advisability, from a security point of view, of giving certain names as references as likely to arouse curiosity.[2] For social references I am giving Gibbs, Barry, and Bill Lord. For neighbors I am giving Quogue people, as I don't know anyone in this building. My other references are Lovett, Swope, Harriman, Forrestal, maybe Symington, and Ross. But if little men start going around asking Gibbs and Barry and Ross little questions, they themselves are going to ask questions too. It's all right with me if it's all right with you, but I know during the OSS check I usually knew within 24 hours that the FBI had been asking about me. I practically followed one guy around Publishers Row and Quogue. We both wore Inverness capes, I carried a dirk.

Which OSS chief do you mean? —— ——? A guy named —— something (I'll think of his name in a day or two)? A guy named —— —— (I wasn't supposed to know his name)? A guy named ——? I understand —— is no longer with us, and I would have a hell of a time getting addresses for the other guys.

Also, on the Civil Service paper, what do I put down as the job I am applying for?

I think when I get all the stuff I'll have to fly to Washington for a quick conference. That ought to be next week, if it's okay with you.

Yrs,

O

¹ French security office.
² Bryan's arrangements for O'Hara to be considered for an intelligence position in Washington did not culminate in a job offer.

TO: Katharine Angell White   TLS, 1 p. PSt.

55 East 86
(Till 2 June)

16 May 1949

Dear Katharine:

Here are the answers to the queries.¹

1. I like it my way. Softly first puts the emphasis there.

2. Telegrams can and do contain the word Signed. You can ask to have it put in, and a man like Dunning writing a telegram of such importance would do just that, for the record.

4. I was thinking of the Boston Statler, but I don't think it's cluttery.

5. I think my change is adequate. The functional rap is taken off by my change.

7.What I had in mind here was that the lady had had her plumbing removed. If Ross wants me to say that, I will, but I know the howl that would have gone up if I'd said it in the first place.

8. Absolutely no on this cut. These are people with an only child, the only one they can have. He is killed, dies under a kind of cloud. They want everybody else to forget the boy. They are not interested in keeping his memory alive among outsiders. (I'm speaking of the father's point of view.) Please reread the line: "Let's take him home and have him near us as long as *we* live." If you make the change you suggest the piece loses. This is not a boy who died a hero's death in the war or on the football field. And these are people who for the rest of their lives are going to be guarding his memory all by themselves, against the world, keeping the world out as much as they can.

I'm sorry you changed the scheduling to the fall. For minor reasons of my own I wanted it to be Spring, which is why I wrote it that way. It does seem to me that for the past year and a half the magazine has gone out of its way to antagonize me, but it may be a little early to determine the final loser.

Yrs,
J. O'H

[1] "Grief," 22 October 1949.

TO: John Steinbeck[1]

TLS, 2 pp. with holograph
postscript. Mrs. Steinbeck
Quogue, Long Island

2 or 3 June 1949

Dear John:

You have no idea what pleasure and relief I get in writing to you. Maybe I am wrong but I will go ahead in being wrong in attributing to your letter a friendliness that I sorely need. Also counted on. Let us skip a few things I want to say and let me say something I want to say.

This is the God's honest truth, John, and a great compliment: I don't think anyone ever thought that the carpets ever got so far up near your ankles that you would be tripped. I don't think anyone was badly worried about you. I think it is nice that we count on you to be the decent human being that you are. You are, too, you know. This isn't the 14th of February, but by Christ all in all you are a decent human being.

Writing. You and Ernest and Faulkner only. Me, of course. But room for all of us. You and I are the only ones who come out and get our whops. You know that the one is Faulkner, the genius. You are closer to him than Ern or I. Fitzgerald was a better just plain writer than all of us put together. Just words writing. But he dade. The working men are you and I. Faulkner, there is nobody like little Willie. Ern has become the modern syno-something for writing, and knows it. Has taken a Christ-awful beating because of a funny name. But what a good decent writer. When I think of all of you I want to crawl except when I think of what an honest writer I am. Not many, though. You name them. Not so many, and especially when you think of how many try. COULD GO ON FOR QUITE SOME TIME ON THIS SUBJECT.

Marriage. John, I am 44, 45 next Jan. I can't run the 100 in 10 or get the duke off Joe Louis, either. Now let me tell you something old Friend. I am married to the same girl. Belle, whom you know. But I was married before, which I don't think you knew, and before that I was very much in residence with somebody else. I could prove to you that I have been married in the eyes of God at least as much as you have, therefore what you told me in your letter was wrong. I always think of you as a married man, a man with a wife. Indeed I don't think of any man without a wife. Every man has a wife. The legal aspects horseshit to them. There are good writers without a wife, or woman. Tom Eliot. Henry James. But I wasn't talking about them. I don't know who yours is. Em's is (I think) Hadley. Mine is Belle. I forget the name of Bill's. Scott's most certainly was Zelda. Which one you like best I don't know. But you have one.

ON MARRIAGE & DIVORCE BY AN EXPERT. I was married in February and parted company in February, an interval of two years. My then wife, a pretty girl, a rich girl, repaired to Nevada. In due course returned to NY, whereupon we met, affectionately. You got it. What you must get now is that we very very much did not care for the individuals and the individual remarks of those who took sides. No outsider ever knows what is between husband and wife. I will say that I am sorry about your own separation, because I think you two[2] should have stayed husband and wife. But I know nothing. I know nothing.

Here. Here is my Pacific Grove. I love Quogue. Quogue is unique in that it is the only real family place-cum-Social Register on the Eastern Seabord [sic]. No throwing around of money. You don't see Quogue on the Society pages except EXCEPT!!! when a girl gets married. Well, I have my girl, Miss Wylie Delaney O'Hara (and never has there been a more mellifluous name), and her Dad won't be around for it, but by God she has to be married at the little Episcopal church.

Ah, John, you ought to see this girl.

Yes, by God, there is a forfeit. I finished my novel[3] before you did yours.[4] I forget what the amount was that night in 21. but I know it was a lot. Therefore I will settle for a silver removable belt buckle embossed B W O'H; or a little box, silver, which says to Wylie Delaney O'Hara from John Steinbeck; or an expensive cigarrete [sic] case saying From J. S. to J. O'H.[5]

There is also this: if you don't like my novel I may kill you.

                                    With affection and regard,
                                    J. O'H

No—You just like my novel, and if you don't I will be sorry.
  (Good novel though
              John

225

Good-night J O'H
Affection and respect
J O'H

¹ Steinbeck became one of O'Hara's closest literary friends. His 8 June reply to this letter is included in Steinbeck: A Life in Letters, Elaine Steinbeck and Robert Wallsten, eds. (New York: Viking, 1975).
² Steinbeck and his second wife, Gwendolyn.
³ A Rage to Live.
⁴ Probably Burning Bright (1950).
⁵ Steinbeck gave O'Hara a cigarette box engraved "The lonely mind of one man is the only creative organ in the world, and any force which interferes with its free function is the Enemy."

TO: Frank Norris[1]   TLS[2]
                                              Quogue, Long Island

                                                   July 22, 1949
Dear Frank:
   I am very pleased with your comments on A Rage To Live and—not that this has anything to do with the case—so was Belle. To get it right back on a professional basis: it has to be a disturbing book, or it might just as well be Tarkington or, on a lower level, Bromfield, or, on no level at all, Lewis.
   I have tried to do several things in this book. It may be, in the future final judgment, that I tried to do too many things. One thing I tried to do you caught right away, and you caught it specifically where I had intended it to be caught. One or two other readers at Random House caught the general idea of Anna, but did not put a finger on the spot where I wanted it to be caught, namely, of course, the turkey shoot scene. (I have a feeling this is going to be a very long letter, so light up.)
   You have to take my word for it that I never read Tolstoy, but I did see Garbo as Anna and I did hear the radio version, and I have enough of a feeling for the Russian school to know what they did, plus a scratchy knowledge. So, quite frankly, I made one effort to make Grace an example of that school, knowing that I had to do her some way besides the way she would have been done by the above authors or I'd have wasted my time.
   But being an American, and recalling an early satisfaction with the Tarkington treatment of a Caldwellian family and Fort Pennsyllian town, I also decided that I would write this novel as Tarkington might have written it if this kind of treatment could have been got away with in the time Ambersons was written, and if Tarkington had been somewhat less so totally unlike me in almost every respect. I regard myself as a

pretty good man, but I think Tarkington would have preferred to go through life completely a gentleman, not only from Indiana.

I also was strongly influenced in the constructing of this novel by a man whom I regard as the greatest novelist living today, Jules Romains. Indeed, if I thought I had the time I would go on writing about Fort Penn as Romains did about Paris. For instance, I cut out of this book a detailed picture of small-city journalism; enough of it is left to show you what I mean. Romains, you will agree, is closer to me than Tarkington is, despite his preoccupation with the politico-economic details of France. This book will be compared—not always favorably—with Lewis, but the fact is I was not even actively influenced to be contemptuous of Lewis. I might have been, say, ten years ago, but in recent years I have only regarded Lewis as passe, no matter how good he was when he wrote Babbitt.

"The idea that any social situation is likely to blow up in anyone's face at any time" is a good way to put critically what I did with Grace and Bannon. But you must also, as a critic and not merely a reviewer, bear in mind that there is nothing in Grace's background that is inconsistent with her behavior. In fact, let me put it another way: whether I succeeded or not, I did attempt constantly to prepare the reader for that business. Bannon, remember, is totally unlike Brock and Charlie Jay and Sidney and the other boys and young men Grace had known, so that when she did kick up it had to be with a Bannon, a violent fox, if you see what I mean. Some day I will tell you the model for Bannon. (You will never guess.) Aside from certain physical resemblances, I would not have known about the real-life character had I not had an affair with a girl he'd had an affair with, and she told all, in a moment of anger with *me*. Of course when I say model I do not mean, either, that Bannon is a photographic copy, but close enough to have suited my purpose. I must insist that sexually Grace had been preparing for a Bannon all her life and that it was merely circumstances that kept her from one earlier in her young womanhood, with either more disastrous results, or less. My feeling now is more disastrous results, such as happened to ——.

You must also give some thought to Bannon, independently of Grace. Then you will be less disturbed in the way you are at present. Bannon is quite a man. A hypocrite, treacherous, a lout, and all that, but not a man whose presence would be ignored, in a room or in a town.

Now what I am about to tell you you are free to use. I have considered the ethics of telling you, and decided that if playwrights can show scripts to G.J. Nathan[3] in advance, I can tell you this, but you must not let on I told you. This: I have employed a device in this novel which I doubt if any critic is going to catch on to. I have given you a complete picture of Grace, the superficial things such as a spottily good vocab-

227

ulary with a naturalistic use of grammar; her clothes, her drinks, etc. But I also have let you know how she thinks and feels AND YET AT NO TIME DO I, THE NOVELIST, ENTER HER MIND. At no time am I the omniscient, ubiquitous novelist. The God. You read that book and you *think* you have been inside her thinking moments, but the fact is there is nothing told about Grace that could not have been actually seen or actually overheard by another human being. That, my friend, is a triumph of writing. I am very proud of it, because in my own estimation it makes me really a pro.

I am glad you noticed the medical stuff. That was intentional, too. I also am waiting for anyone to pick me up on the slang of the day. I used several expressions that seem more recent than the time I used them, but I got them right out of Clare Briggs[4] in the NY Tribune. I spent many hours on Briggs alone, plus Grantland Rice.[5]

So far, of the few comments in, I am most pleased with yours. To be ingracious about it, I think Fadiman sent his in (he did it voluntarily to the publisher, not to me) to get on an early bandwagon. The sales are more than satisfactory, and the people who write the trade-press notices (PW and Virginia Kirkus) have been unequivocally all-out. The movie companies have been aloof, but I wasn't writing any God damn scenario, and if the book sells big they'll come hat in hand. Now I wish I could pay more attention to my play.[6]

Kind thoughts to you both.

John

[1] Norris reviewed *A Rage to Live* in *Newsweek* when it was published in August.

[2] Probably not mailed. This letter was shown to the editor by the late Mrs. John O'Hara and is not now locatable.

[3] Drama critic George Jean Nathan.

[4] Cartoonist.

[5] Sports reporter and columnist.

[6] Probably *The Farmers Hotel*, which O'Hara converted into a novel.

TO: Gilbert and Janet Troxell   ALS, 2 pp. Princeton
Summer 1949   Quogue, Long Island

Dear Troxells—

First of all, the name of my novel is A Rage to Live. A Rage for Living is the way Noel Coward would have taken liberties with Alexander Pope.

Second, Janet, I talk like that to Belle all the time, and in twelve years I not only have had no complaints, but she talks that way herself.

We are in Quogue, Long Island, as usual. The news with us, however, is a kind of admission, a confession: we are forsaking New York and are going to live in Princeton. Yes, Princeton. It is not that Princeton has made me a better offer, but that Yale has made no offer at all. We have leased a house and entered Wylie in a school, so the bolts are shot, and Seymour may have to stay another year. And after Dr. Canby's remark at a Book of the Month meeting that he considered my novel "vulgar" I'm far from sure that I shall entrust the MS to Yale library. It's just possible that after all these years of blind devotion, I may be wrong about Yale, or I may have been wrong about myself—secretly a Princeton admirer throughout.

Well, it was a well kept secret!

Love from us all
John

TO: Janet Troxell   TLS, 2 pp. Princeton
Summer 1949   Quogue, Long Island

Janet:

I forgive myself for seeming surly because it brought forth such a nice letter from you.

Yes, I saw the Pegler[1] piece on old Hank Canby. Tell you a little story: Grantland Rice, a friend of mine, a friend of your Pa's,[2] et al. is so well loved that Pegler once wrote that men have been known to fight bloody fights to decide who loves Grannie Rice the best. Well, Rice and Pegler have been friends for many years, and although Grannie is no New Dealer, he said to me last year, "You know, I think Peg goes too far," which for Grannie is very strong language.

We were over at the Rices last Saturday and Grannie, who is ill, and [sic] got on the subject of Peg. Grannie told us that Betty Barton, daughter of Bruce, who is a close friend of Pegler's, told Peg she couldn't read him because of his insane hatred of the Roosevelts. Pegler replied, "That's all right, I guess I'm just a phony."

The original reason behind the Princeton decision was Wylie's tendency to asthma, definitely attributable to NY City dust, for which a serum was made and used successfully. But we picked Princeton because I've always wanted to live in a university town, and we looked at Swarthmore too. Also, it is time for a change of pace; as I told someone the other day, it is time I made "21" a restaurant instead of a career. These months I spend in Quogue every year not only save my life, but have convinced me that I am happier out of NY than in it. I know too many people in NY that I don't give a damn about, and the time also has come when I owe it to myself to be more selective, to save myself for the people I do like.

If your prediction comes true and I make some money out of this book we are, as a m. of f.,[3] going to visit Ireland next year. I never have been there. If we like it we may stay a year. I do not approve of the government, but if pressed I will admit that I don't like everything they do in Washington either, lifelong Democrat though I be. Practically everything I have heard about Dublin makes it attractive to me, and not the least attractive item is the fact that if I have any relatives there, I don't know them, nor they me. Dublin, of course, will be our town. Belle likes the Dublin speech and it won't do Wylie any harm; she is normally a soft-spoken child, but is affected by the playground brats.

Is it the Garrison you are working on? Isn't that what Johnny Chamberlain[4] came to see you about? I trust the progress is satisfactory.

Love from all here,

John

[1] Columnist Westbrook Pegler.
[2] Walter Camp, legendary football coach.
[3] As a matter of fact.
[4] Book reviewer for the *New York Times*. Chamberlain interviewed Mrs. Troxell about William Graham Sumner.

TO: Fletcher Markle[1] TLS, 1 p. with holograph postscript.
Markle.
Quogue, Long Island

20 August 1949

Dear Mr. Markle:

I am very pleased that you like the book and especially interesting to me is the factor of your isolation, away from the reviews, good and bad, and the word of mouth, good and bad, which has almost got to influence people at home.

In brief, the reviews have been almost exactly 50-50. The morning Times, prissy Mr. Prescott, was rather daintily horrified, but John Hutchens wrote a long, sensible, favorable piece for the Trib (it was a lucky happenstance that Gannett went on vacation the day before publication). In the afternoons, McFee was great and said the book was, in the Sun, but in the World-Telly Sterling North was so much for and so much against that his review was practically No Opinion. The New Yorker piece, by Brendan Gill, was a bad one-joke wisecrack, but Newsweek could be quoted verbatim as an ad. Time did not review it this week, but I have reason to suspect it will be a favorable notice. Tomorrow, Sunday's Times, by A. C. Spectorsky, is almost unreadable itself, but the Sunday Trib, by Milton Rugoff, is excellent. And so it goes and will go. As to the cash register, Random House have printed (as of next Monday) 75,000 copies, without any Book Club (it is the Book Find Club choice for October, though). It is a little early for the lunatic-fringe letters, but good letters have been coming in from Frank Sullivan in Saratoga and John Steinbeck in Pacific Grove and the countrymen in between.

I was hoping you would do Appointment in Samarra on the Ford hour as I wanted a station wagon to round out my fleet of two English cars. I said as much to Miss Lemmon[2] one evening in Passy,[3] but she wasn't listening. Why don't you buy the book from Skirball and Manning[4] and produce it when you finish your play? You could shoot it in Pennsylvania . . . By PD blood do you mean Pennsylvania Dutch? Are you a Hazleton Markle? I thought you were a Canuck. I'm sure I heard that.

Well, now you know as much about the progress of A Rage to Live as I do. I wish you good luck with your play and I trust you are enjoying the Tender Is the Night country. Thanks for your letter.

Faithfully,
John O'Hara

Have you seen the Chas. Addamses? Give them our love.

J. O'H.

[1] Television and movie writer-director-producer. Markle had written O'Hara from the Riviera congratulating him on *A Rage to Live*.
[2] Lenore Lemmon was a mutual friend of O'Hara and Markle.
[3] New York restaurant.
[4] Movie producers who had an option on *Appointment in Samara*; the movie was not made.

TO: Walter S. Farquhar

TLS, 2 pp. PSt.
Quogue, Long Island

3 September 1949

Dear Walter:

I read your Musings over my new book—[1]and me. It is an excellent, heartwarming piece, and I don't know what else a man can expect. I liked particularly the way you handled what I believe used to be called the roman-a-clef aspects of novels. I am constantly telling young writers to write only what they know, and to know ten times more about the subject than they put down. It's obvious to you and me that fiction is no good unless it provides the illusion of fact; but the writer who presents only fact in the guise of fiction lacks imagination and therefore artistry, or craftsmanship, or skill, whichever you prefer. The literate public has been badly affected by the institution known as the gossip column, and thereby misses the pleasure of the storyteller's art. It used to be that a reader could lose himself in a novel, but nowadays too many readers keep asking themselves: "Who dat?"

Well, you gotta take the bad with the good, as P. L. K.[2] would say. The book is a best seller, and I certainly am not going around to the bookstores and holding up sales while I cross-question the customers. As the reviews come in from the country as a whole the score is about 70% in favor of the book, 20% against, and 10% confused. Frankly, that's a better score than I anticipated, and I am especially pleased to report on the very high caliber of reviews in such places as San Francisco, Dallas, Louisville, Kalamazoo, Milwaukee, Birmingham—to name a few. If this sounds condescending, don't forget that I have had ten books published, and too often in the past it seemed to me that either the book reviewers were society editors—or deserved to be. And you will be amused to know that the Daily Worker and the N.Y. Times made substantially the same adverse criticism.

Thank you for the understanding remarks about my own life, and I hope this finds you well and at least philosophically pleased with life. That's about as much as a man can hope for if he ever takes time out to do a little thinking.

Affectionately,
John

[1] Farquhar had discussed A Rage to Live in his "Musings" column in the Pottsville Journal.
[2] Probably Percy Knowlton, a Pottsville journalist.

TO: John Steinbeck

TLS, 2 pp. Mrs. Steinbeck
Quogue, Long Island
Monday 18 Sept 1950

Dear John:

You must not say things like that. You are the only one who knew it and saw it, and God damn it to hell, you ought not to say it. (Much as I love you for saying it.)[1]

There are only the four of us, at least that I know of, that care about every word and the sentences. It's almost a year ago that Brown[2] asked me to review the book, and Brown is a good man, because he faked not knowing what I knew and you probably did too. And Brown was on EH's side even then, so when I got the paper-bound and said I was going all out, he knew what I meant before I ever sent him a syllable. What's more, Brown is absolutely backing me up against the most letters the T Review ever got, good or bad, and most of these letters have been saying, in effect, "Lynch O'Hara." Not "Lynch EH," by the way. Wait till you see the letters the T is running.

We leave here a week from today. Belle and Wylie and nurse and cook in the station wagon, and me following in the M-G. We spend Monday night in New York and next day go to Princeton. Will you and Elaine have dinner with us Monday night (25 Sept.)? Our phone here is Quogue 305.

I wish I were in NY now, because I hate to pay money to see a prize fight, but I would like to see the Louis fight and I could get a fairly good price now that would enable me in all conscience to pay a large sum for tickets and know that the money I paid for the tickets would be taken care of by my winnings on the fight. You follow? I would, in other words, wait around the 21 bar till I heard some extravagant statement, whereupon I'd say "I'd like a hundred dollars of that, Mister." A week from today I'll be in 21, listening to the talk about Louis and the price against his winning by a knockout, but by that time the price will be much shorter than it is now. My personal price is Louis to win: 5 to 3. My big hunch is that Louis will win by a knockout before the eighth round, for which I ought to get 3 to 1.[3]

I may agree with you about the competitive spirit. I have been playing a lot of golf this summer, and the only times I make a good score are when I play against par and not against my competitor. I used to play pretty good golf, didn't play for years, started again this year, and the JO'H of 1935 would spit on the JO'H of 1950. I putt better in 1950—which probably in itself tells a lot.

You say about "the form". Do you mean the *play* form? You say you learned the hard way. Well of course you did. The hard, the easy, and the only way. Self taught. I hereby make an absolute statement about the theater: the author should direct his own play. I will not make that statement about movies. The reason I won't is that the movie director and the cinematographer usually are in cahoots and in sympathy, and the movie director invariably regards himself as a superior, nonwriting writer. I give you Jack Ford. I give you Willie Wyler. I give you, while I'm not giving anything, all of them. Huston. McCarey. Hitchcock. LaCava. I once heard one of them say "If I don't soon get a good script I'll have to write it myself." It wasn't George Stevens, but you're getting close.[4] Remember the Liberty horses?[5] That's what directors are. Goodnight all,

John

[1] O'Hara's review of *Across the River and into the Trees* appeared in the *New York Times Book Review* (10 September 1950). His statement that Hemingway was the most important writer since the death of Shakespeare attracted considerable attention and controversy. Steinbeck had written O'Hara responding to this review.

[2] Francis Brown, editor of the *New York Times Book Review*.

[3] Louis lost a fifteen-round decision to Ezzard Charles.

[4] Movie directors John Ford, William Wyler, John Huston, Leo McCarey, Alfred Hitchcock, Gregory LaCava, and George Stephens.

[5] Circus horses which performed without riders, responding to signals from their trainers.

233

TO: Donald S. Klopfer   TLS, 1 p. Random House
                                        20 College Rd. West,
                                              Princeton

                                          4 February 1951

Dear Colonel:

Thanks for the tearsheet. Now how do you ever suppose Johnny Hutchens[1] got that material? . . .

I have been studying my wafer diary and I think the dates I like for publication of my book are the 8th and the 15th of November. According to the diary, Election Day is the 6th of November, and I would like to publish after and not during the campaigns which, while there won't be a presidential one, will be like a presidential one this year. The 8th is the Thursday immediately following election day, and I pick Thursday because Charlie Poore does the Times review on Thursday, as you know, and, as you may know, he is favorably disposed toward this author.[2] Prescott is so unfavorably disposed that nothing I write can expect fair consideration, and while I have survived many bad reviews, if there is a way to avoid them it ought to be tried. Gannett is not "pro" me, but he is less "anti" than Prescott.

I have no title yet and, according to custom, probably won't have one until the MS is half finished. I will then stumble on a title, people will try to tell me it's no good, and in a month or so it will be accepted and people will even be making puns on it. That has been the way with every title, from Appointment in Samarra to A Rage to Live, even including Pal Joey.

I have had a letter from Cap Pearce about The Doctor's Son. They want to publish it as a separate volume (see correspondence with Cerf) if I will write a long foreword.[3] So I will. We'll have to work out a time arrangement on that, but there's no particular hurry.

                                              As ever,
                                              John

Who is Sonya Klopfer? I mean, I know who she is: a skater. But any kin of yours?

[1] John K. Hutchens, book reviewer for the New York Herald Tribune.
[2] Beginning with The Farmers Hotel (8 November 1951) all of O'Hara's books were published on Thursdays. With Ten North Frederick (1955) he commenced his custom of publishing on Thanksgiving Day.
[3] The volume was not published.

TO: Bennett Cerf   TLS, 2 pp. Columbia
                                                              Princeton
                                                          16 June 1951
Dear Bennett:
    I think I will be finished the novel in about another week, if it continues
to go as it has been.
    I am writing you now to warn you that my estimate to Donald about
the length (you remember he asked me at the sales meeting) is way off. It
will be much shorter than I guessed then. To be specific, I now have about
110 pages of double-spaced, which runs around 30,000 words in ordinary
MS, but this, as you will see, is mostly dialog. I don't think it will go
much more than 20 pages over what I have now. I also want to reveal to
you that this is an allegory.[1] It is not an exact allegory, but it is as simple
as or simpler than, say, Mario and the Magician. However, I am not
calling it an allegory; I am presenting it as a short novel, and if the more
alert critics and other readers spot it as an allegory (which I feel sure they
will), fine. It stands as a short novel, without the allegorical connotation.
If you, as publisher, feel you would like to pass the word that it also is an
allegory, you can use your own judgment about that, but I am not going
to make any public statement to that effect until after the second meaning
has been detected, and even then I am not going to do any interpreting.
    I believe my hunch is sound that to announce a novel as allegorical is
to create some confusion and annoyance for the book. That was not true
of The Cocktail Party, for instance, but then I am not Tom Eliot. There
always have been some secondary meanings in my apparently plain writing,
but very few people have taken the trouble to look for them because I do
write so plain. That is, I write plain and the reader reads fast. Well, that's
all right too. I may, in a way, be underestimating the sensitivity of the
readers with this book; they may Get the Idea right away. And *that's* all
right.
    I've always told you that my expectations for this book are not
sanguinary. But I also think John Steinbeck had to write The Wayward
Bus. On this cheerful note I close.

                                                                  Yrs,
                                                                  John

[1] O'Hara intended the novel as an allegory about Russian aggression, with the truck-driver Joe Rogg representing Stalin or Russia. Most readers and reviewers missed this meaning.

TO: Saxe Commins   TLS, 1 p. Mrs. Commins
                                           Quogue, Long Island
                                                    7 Sept 51
Dear Saxe:
    I am very pleased with the material you have written for the front flap
of THE FARMERS HOTEL. I especially liked the thought and phrasing:
"implications as wide as the reader's own imagination." I assume that this
in a way represents a change in policy by Bennett regarding the presentation of the allegorical aspects of the book. In that connection I will be
curious to see what Marquand[1] writes about the book. People I have
talked with are now about 50-50 on the wisdom of letting it known [sic]
that the book has a secondary meaning.
    Regarding the Purple Heart, your informant is half right, which is also
half wrong and not good enough. The Purple Heart (founded by George
Washington as a defiant answer to the Society of the Cincinnati) was not
awarded during War One, but was revived later, and wounded veterans
were given the medal by applying for it. I think that is clear in the text. I
know my medals and decorations. We are not coming to NY-Princeton
until the 17th, which please tell Bennett as we had planned to come in a
little earlier than that. Ham and Janet Cottier[2] are lovely people, among
our very best friends in Princeton.

                                                    Yrs,
                                                    John O'Hara

    [1] John P. Marquand reviewed *The Farmers Hotel* in the *Book-of-the-Month Club
News*.
    [2] Prof. Hamilton Cottier, of the Princeton English Department, and his wife.

TO: Bennett Cerf and Donald Klopfer   TLS, 1 p. (incomplete)[1]
October 1951   Princeton

    The correspondence, it might interest you, came as a result of one line in
the $3.75 copy of A RAGE TO LIVE.
    Now this part I suppose properly should be addressed to Donald, but I
go on the theory that you are partners, and on the theory that by not
answering letters you obviate the necessity for answering letters, if you take
long enough obviating. I also will point out that I will spend $45 on the
telephone before I'll shell out 45¢ in stamps. But to continue, as a No
man to a Williams man and a Columbia man, I am delighted with the
Random House product called THE FARMERS HOTEL. I was first of
all pleased that it did not turn out to be light as a feather. It is more of a
book than I had been led to believe it would be (Christopher Fadiman

236

notwithstanding, and notwithstanding is where he is with me). (John Marquand notwithstanding, and moto you, Mr. Fuck.) (Dorothy, I canfield—no great pleasure, Mrs. Fisher.)[2] In any event—except the shot put— I hefted the tome and was well pleased. Only the page-counters could keep this lovely work of art from being an enormous success prior to publication. Indeed, the more I think of it, the more I am convinced that my next time out I will write 600 pages of nothing called: AFTER LINCOLN'S DOCTOR'S DOG'S MUTINY'S TIKI.[3] It makes me throw up, but dogs get tiks on Long Island.

To resume, I am pleased with the look of the book. I can't fault it (that is horseman talk). I thought you fellows were pretty darn nice (I mean this) to line up all my accomplishments, or the published ones, on the flap. I got kind of impressed myself, and may ask for a straight 20 next time out. I have an ugly feeling that if I ask for a straight 20, it'll be my last time out—but one can dream, can't they?

Well, gentlemen—a term not usually applied by authors to publishers— we all know that there is a standing agreement relating to the sale of 100,000 copies.[4] A little arrangement for a silver cigarette box, etc. (O'Hara is pointing out, Don, that it hasn't cost us much money so far.) Well, gentlemen, I *have* a silver cigarette box. But what I aint got, and did have some oral agreement on as of HELLBOX, is parking space. You know where. So, you boys have your choice: a silver tea (for which read cocktail) service, suitably (and as nicely) engraved; or a Buick station wagon; or every Modern Library title in leather; or the same old parking space with Ava Gardner in the Buick station wagon (150,000 copies). It should be stipulated that Miss Gardner has not had anything to eat for the preceding 48 hours, and has been in the company of Mr. Sinatra all that time. I don't see how I can lose there. I don't know what I can gain, but I also know that you two and I are considering a problem which never will have to be faced.

As ever,
John

[1] Possibly not mailed. This letter was shown to the editor by the late Mrs. John O'Hara and cannot now be located.

[2] Fadiman, Marquand, and Dorothy Canfield Fisher were Book-of-the-Month Club judges. Marquand wrote a series of novels about a detective named Mr. Moto.

[3] An old publishing joke is that a book entitled "Lincoln's Doctor's Dog" would be an automatic best-seller. O'Hara added reference to Herman Wouk's *The Cain Mutiny* and Thor Heyerdahl's *Kon-Tiki*.

[4] Published 8 November 1951, *The Farmers Hotel* sold about 20,000 copies in cloth.

This is Belle's copy.
— John O'Hara

To Belle, my girl
John

No date
No place

TO: John P. Marquand　　　　　　　　ALS, 3 pp. Harvard
　　　　　　　　　　　　　　Letterhead of Nassau Club,
　　　　　　　　　　　　　　　　　　　　Princeton

19 Nov. 51

Dear John—

This is to say thank you for your BOM News piece about *The Farmers Hotel* which, as you may have noticed, also delighted the advertising people at Random House. It is always good to have the good word from another pro. Already I have had the good word from—besides yourself—John Steinbeck, Struthers Burt, Jerome Weidman and others. I cannot say I am pleased with the general critical opinions, but I keep reminding myself that the ratio of favorable to unfavorable is about the same as I usually get, beginning with *Appointment in Samarra* (which, contrary to the present-day impression, was not overwhelmingly a critical success). The lead review in *Time* the week *Appointment in Samarra* was published was of a book called *Slim*.[1] Ever read *Slim*? Know who wrote it? And I could go on, but the hell with it. This is a thank-you note.

　　　　　　　　　　　　　　　　　　　Cordially,
　　　　　　　　　　　　　　　　　　　John O'Hara

[1] By William Wister Haines.

To Helen and Jamie —

— Love —

What could be superber
Than revivals of me and
Thurber?
It may have been the
lousiest season that ever
ever was
But my friend Jim and Jim's
friend I say nuts to that
becuz
Becuz becuz becuz becuz becuz
becuz becuz.

John O'Hara

Quogue
August 1952

---

[1] The inscription refers to revivals of *Pal Joey* and *The Male Animal*.

TO: Clifford Odets[1]   TLS, 1 p. Bruccoli
                                                 Quogue, Long Island
                                                          4 July 53
Dear Cliff:
I still have three or four more days' work on the first 39 pages,[2] so I
think I'll stay in Quogue next week and, if convenient for you, will go to
New York on the 14th, Tuesday (it's impossible to get any work done on
weekends here: the social life begins Fridays, and the hangover is
Mondays).
I have had some trouble with the doctor's part in the very beginning
but it is now finished, done all over again. I also hate to take stuff away
from Charles, but I'm cutting out a good half of his reminiscences, hoping
nevertheless to retain the *quality* of his talk. As you must have guessed (we
never discussed this), in dealing with Charles I want to make people,
including the audience, wonder just how much of his recollections is true,
how much invention. Everything he says must *sound* authentic, but I
think he is more charming if a tiny doubt is created. You just wonder if so
much could happen to one man, without his being a Munchausen
character.
I hope you are having as good a spot of weather as we are having.

                                                      Best as ever,
                                                      John

   [1] Playwright Clifford Odets became a close friend of O'Hara's in Hollywood in 1936.
   [2] Revision of *The Farmers Hotel* in play form. It was produced in summer stock
and on television, but never reached Broadway.

TO: Joseph W. Outerbridge[1]   ALS, 5 pp. Outerbridge
August 1953   Letterhead of Harkness Pavilion,
                                            Columbia Presbyterian Hospital,
                                                        New York City[2]

Dear Pat—
Answering things in the order of their importance—yes, I am going to be
up there on the cart with you.[3] I will enjoy the company but it will take me
a little while to get reaccustomed to the vehicle: but the only alternative
is the glass-sided wagon with the six white horses, and where the hell can
you find six white horses nowadays?
I presume Belle has told you I ain't got cancer, my ticker is OK and so is
my liver. My chief trouble is that the belly resists booze, and if I take too
much of it I'm liable to fall over dead. As simple as that. A hell of a way
for booze to treat me after I've been so kind to it.
I get sprung here tomorrow and go to Quogue for a couple of weeks,

then a check-up, then Princeton. Do you see me in the role of a crotchety but lovable invalid? A Lionel Barrymore type? I used to watch Bill Fields put away the Martinis at Paramount and say to myself "That's what I want to be when I get big." Well, I almost made it.

I am returning your cuttings with thanks. The Pottsville, Pa. one I had seen before. It was the only mention the home town has been given in many months and the general feeling was that Mr. Heckman was a martyr to civic pride.

I have no idea why you sent me the postcard of St. Mary's church. I've always planned to be buried in Quogue.

Remember me to Sal and Patience and the boys, and I warn you that if Patience hits me in the belly, I'm gonna hit her right back.

Yrs.

John

¹ Joseph W. (Pat) Outerbridge, of Princeton, N.J., became O'Hara's closest friend.
² O'Hara was hospitalized after his ulcers hemorrhaged.
³ O'Hara stayed on the wagon for the rest of his life.

◆•◆

Belle Wylie O'Hara died of acute auricular fibrillation at forty-one on 9 January 1954. O'Hara grieved bitterly for her and was frequently despondent. In the summer he began seeing Katharine ("Sister") Barnes Bryan, and they were married on 31 January 1955. His going on the wagon and his marriage to Sister marked the inception of O'Hara's greatest productivity. Ten North Frederick was published Thanksgiving 1955, and eighteen books followed in the next fifteen years. In 1960 he resumed writing short stories and renewed his association with The New Yorker.

TO: Joseph Bryan III   ALS, 2 pp.
13 January 1955   Letterhead of Nassau Club,
                                                         Princeton

Monday 13

Dear Joe—

Thank you for your note on Sister's and my coming marriage.

Princeton, being the kind of heterogeneous community it is, is surely big enough for all of us; and the fact that Sister and I intend to spend most of our life here should offer no problems to you.

As to our own friendship, there naturally will be some early uneasiness, but time should smooth that out. We are not children. Again, thank you for your note.

Sincerely
John O'Hara

TO: Joseph W. Outerbridge

ALS, 1 p. Outerbridge
Collier's letterhead[1]

12 March 1955

Dear Pat—

As you know, I am about to go to California by airplane,[2] accompanied by my wife, whom you and I know as "Sister." In the event of my death I want to leave everything to her (Katharine B. O'Hara). In the event of the deaths of both of us, as in an airplane accident, I leave everything to my daughter, Wylie D. O'Hara. I want this to be, and it is, my last will and testament. Thank you for acting as custodian of this document.

Your friend
John O'Hara

[1] During 1954–56 O'Hara wrote the column "Appointment with O'Hara" for *Collier's*.
[2] O'Hara went to Hollywood to discuss movie work.

TO: Joseph W. Outerbridge
8 June 1955

TLS, 2 pp. Outerbridge
Twentieth Century–Fox
letterhead

Wednesday 8

Dear Pat:

It's possible, because it's a fact, that it's two weeks since we saw you, but what happened to the two weeks? What happened during them is another matter. We had a fine trip out; the Pennsy public relations department rolled out the rouge rug and on the first night we had champagne and caviar,[1] the first time in my life that there was more caviar than I could consume. In Chicago this company detailed a man and a limousine to show us the town from a rather different vantage point from the one I occupied in 1927 on my first visit to the town.

I started work on Monday and it moves.[2] In all probability I will also do the screenplay, although that is not signed and I am not buying the Mercedes. If I don't sign that'll be okay, because I can then write my novel in more leisurely fashion. We took Wylie to Romanoff's for dinner

242

our first night, and she was delighted as well as delightful. She met Gary Cooper and Darryl Zanuck and Georgie Jessel and Herbert Marshall, and saw Rocky Marciano and was entertained by Mike himself, who started things right by giving me a beautiful pair of cuff links. On Sunday we went to the dedication of the Screen Directors building and Wylie met Walter Pidgeon. Tomorrow she will meet Gable on the set. I am happy to report that when I asked her how she was liking California last night she said she still liked Princeton better; too much excitement here, she said. It turned out that too much excitement really means wearing dresses too often, instead of shorts and jeans. She is genuinely excited about the day camp she has joined, three days a week including horseback riding. Sister and I are also joining the local answer to The Country Club of Brookline: we are joining The Beach Club. I hope Sister and Wylie tell me all about it as I don't expect to see it much.

Will you tell Chas Halcomb[3] that we have rented a house. The address is 14300 Sunset Boulevard, Pacific Palisades, Calif. We move in Friday and haven't got a phone number yet, but if he will write me I will write him. I don't quite know his true address, postally speaking. The Potters are giving us a do on Friday and have invited the Bogarts, and if they come I shall brief Betty[4] on the impending visit of C.H.

It's strange, in a way, to be working on this lot again after thirteen years. A crowded thirteen years, the fullest of my life, certainly, and yet everything and many of the people are so familiar, here at 20th. So familiar that once again, today, I was introduced to Spyros Skouras,[5] and that happened the last time. One difference is that I expect to do a lot more business this time.

Would you mind dropping by and seeing if Conover put the M-G and Ford on the blocks? Because of the Memorial Day holiday they had not had a chance to do so before we took off. If they haven't, I request and authorize you to speak sharply to him.

Sister has been scurrying about looking for and finding a place for our little heads to rest. Her own daughter gets here in late June or July, then presumably goes back to Europe to get married, although the nuptial plans are not now known to us. I wish the happy couple would elope so that Sister wouldn't have to go abroad for the wedding, but I imagine there is slim chance of that. I also wish the summer were over and we were back in Princeton, but I tell myself that this visit will last just about as long as the time we spent in Princeton between Sister's and my visit here early in the Spring, and our departure for this visit. You see what I mean? I really don't like California. I like seasons, and seasoned people. I look upon California as a home-loving engineer must look upon trips to South America. Every once in a while you have to go away and build a dam, then you come home and enjoy life. I can't make myself believe my friends who have settled here and say they prefer it to the east. But then I don't believe people who say they prefer New York to out-of-New York. There is not enough money in the world to persuade me to spend the rest of my life here, whereas I don't have to be persuaded to live where I do live.

Time to work.

Best to you and Sal, and let us hear from you.

Yrs,
John

¹ Mrs. O'Hara was not joined by her husband in drinking the champagne.
² O'Hara spent summer 1955 in Hollywood at Twentieth Century–Fox writing the original treatment for *The Best Things in Life Are Free*, a movie biography of the De Sylva, Brown, and Henderson songwriting team. At the same time he was working on *Ten North Frederick*.
³ A Princeton friend of O'Hara's.
⁴ Lauren Bacall.
⁵ President of Twentieth Century–Fox.

TO: Joseph W. Outerbridge   TLS, 1 p. Outerbridge
13–14 July 1955

14,300 Sunset Boulevard (at low tide)
Pacific Palisades, Calif.

Wed 13–14

Dear Pat:

It has been generally (not unanimously, but generally) agreed that your daughter is more photogenique than mine. As it happens, it was my daughter who led this rather sheep-like, straight-(Republican)-ticket trend, and I give you one guess, but only one, as to the identity of the dissenter. This man, frequently cited for his powers of observation, notices things that the eyes of love alone may see. But I do thank you for the picture and again and just as much for sending it. It has been framed and sits on the escritoire in two positions: the first position is facing one, the second is after Wylie has been in the room. But it goes in my study when we get home, and nobody tinkers with my interior decorating there.

We are now roughly at the half way mark of our California sojourn. As I may have told you, I decided not to do the screenplay,¹ a decision which cost me the fastest $75,000 I ever came close to. But my novel comes first,² and I am not so ivory-tower that I lost sight of the possibility that by finishing the novel I stood to make more in the long run than the fast 75. If I guessed wrong, you may taunt me on alternate Thursdays, when I can't afford the buffet at the Nassau Club. I have actually turned down 75 G's before, but that was an offer for Butterfield 8 when I was in the dreamland of $250,000, and also when Wylie was not yet in existence. The current dreamland is a possible sale of A Rage to Live with the possibility of Grace Kelly playing . . . Grace![3] The deal is on the slow burner.

Straus[4] and I maintain the dignity of our sex in a household consisting at the moment of my wife, my daughter, my stepdaughter, my cook, my cleaning woman, my daughter's California playmate, and a woman who keeps calling up to get me to subscribe to the Pac Pal paper. My wife and my various daughters nip off to the Beach Club most days, which leaves me to my homework and the satisfactory knowledge that at least we're getting more out of it than we do out of fashionable Springdale. I think I should have joined Sunningdale instead of Springdale.[5] I'm sure Sunningdale has a necktie and a blazer, and I would make a big point of using it when I go to England next Spring. Also, I'm sure any good American club would accept me as a visitor if I were a member of Sunningdale, while I'm not sure Springdale members are admitted to Van Cortlandt Park,[6] not even Springdale members who are sons in law of Van Cortlandt Park Dixon Barnes.[7]

Since I have no further favors to ask, I shall close. Writing you reminds me that I haven't sent any giant postcards, so I lay that blame on you. Why didn't you keep still?

Yrs,
John

[1] The screenplay for O'Hara's treatment of *The Best Things in Life Are Free* was written by William Bowers and Phoebe Ephron.
[2] *Ten North Frederick* was delivered to Random House in time for Thanksgiving publication.
[3] The movie was made in 1965 with Suzanne Pleshette as Grace.
[4] The O'Haras' poodle.
[5] Sunningdale is a golf club in England; Springdale is a golf club in Princeton.
[6] Public park in the Bronx.
[7] Sister O'Hara was the daughter of Courtland Dixon Barnes.

TO: Joseph W. Outerbridge   TLS, 1 p. Outerbridge
21 July 1955   14,300 Sunset Blvd.,
                                             Pacific Palisades

Thursday

Dear Pat:

I trust you have had a long look at Pages 80 and 81 in the current Time, for corroboration and confirmation of methods you have already spoken of.[1] Scary.

I have a favor to ask, naturally. I am going to send a boy to St. Paul's School. The boy is, of course, a character in my novel,[2] and it suits my purposes to have him go to SPS for the last three years of his prep education, before going to Yale. The time of his entering SPS is exactly four years after you were there; he would be in the Class of '29.

What I would like from you as an authority with a good memory is some strictly local color, peculiar to your peculiar alma mater at Concord. I hope to start you off on reminiscenes [*sic*] that will fill a page by asking you what they called the can at SPS. I can't remember what it was called at Niagara Prep Sch but at Fordham it was The Jakes. In addition to that skatological information, this is the kind of dope I would like:

Any and all special slang.

Customs for indoctrinating new boys, pleasant and unpleasant.

Special treats. Special clothing regulations. Special quarters. Disciplinary measures by faculty and students. Songs, clean or not. Concord hangouts, approved or otherwise. Special games (such as Sniff, or The Wall Game). Names for girls (in Pottsville, Pa., they were called spivots, a name I never heard anywhere else). I guess you get the idea.

Would you describe for me a boy's first day? I assume he would arrive in Boston, take the . . . train on the B.&M., and get off at Concord with a lot of other new boys, check in at the asst head's office (is he called The Head at SPS) and be assigned his room and roommate(s). Are there any ceremonies or anything like that that I ought to know about to make the thing credible, or keep it from being incredible? I also want to have him in the infirmary for a time so that he falls behind in his classes but makes it up. If I remember old photographs correctly, SPS used to be all one big building. Was that changed by the fall of '26? I know you didn't play interscholastic football, so what about letters?

This should give you a chance for such nostalgia as can only be found in a bottle of whiskey. In return I promise to mention your name again to Grace Kelly, if I see her.

Assurances of my highest.

John

---

[1] "The Raiders," an article on company raiding in the 25 July 1955 issue of *Time*.

[2] Joby Chapin in *Ten North Frederick* attends St. Paul's, but the novel has no scenes at the school.

TO: Katharine Barnes O'Hara

Inscription in *Ten North Frederick*. PSt. Princeton

To K. B. O'H.

with love
J, H. O'H.

28 October 1955

TO: Lewis Gannett

ALS, 1 p. Harvard
20 College Rd. West,
Princeton

24 Nov. '55

Dear Mr Gannett—

I do not as a rule write to reviewers—win, lose, or draw—but I must thank you for today's piece on my novel.[1] All I ever want is a considered, respectful comment, and when there is more, I am delighted.

Cordially
John O'Hara

[1] *Ten North Frederick.*

TO: John Steinbeck   ALS, 1 p. Mrs. Steinbeck
                                            20 College Rd. West,
                                            Princeton
                                            6 April 56
Dear John—
    The Dictionary of Early English has arrived and I have been—as you
will note in a future Collier's—dipping into it. I've already found four or
five words I never knew that Chaucer knew. (Take that either way.) Many
thanks. Are you hard at it? I'm hard at it.
    Love to Elaine

                                            As Always
                                            John

TO: David Brown[1]   TL (copy). Twentieth Century–Fox
Received 23 July 1956   Quogue, Long Island

Dear Dave:
    I have finished reading THE BRAVADOS by Frank O'Rourke and as
a starting point for a screenplay I like it, but first I would like to find out
a few things.[2]
    It is policy at TCF, I believe, for the story department to consult with
an individual producer before buying a property, and I therefore would
like to know what Swope[3] particularly admired in THE BRAVADOS
that urged him to encourage the sale. The reason I ask is simple and profound: if he mentally committed himself to some features of the story
that he would not want changed and that I *would* want changed, I would
prefer to pass on to another story. If on the other hand he also sees it as a
basis for a straightforward screenplay, and only a basis, then I am actively
interested.
    As you know, I am very careful about criticizing other writers' work
especially when pictures sales, past and future, may be involved. But I
violate no principle of my own when I say that this story as it is now
would be pretty boring if followed faithfully in screenplay. It is an extended
chase with no character fully developed. And yet it has possibilities in all
departments, and that's what interests me. I have always wanted to do a
good western, and this could be it. But as it is, it is more a point of departure than a framework, in spite of the fact that O'Rourke obviously
knows his way around an arroyo.
    So the important question now is, will Swope hold still for all the
changes I might like to make? I would not waste my time whimsically
making changes for the sake of making them. I would not, however, put
my name on a story which didn't have solider people than are there now.

There is another factor. I do not want to assume the blazer of a producer, but I would like to do this picture as a sneaker, low-budget, and
non-star. That's how I'd like it to get done, although I have my doubts
that I will get my wish. This is why: I don't want to tailor it to a Gable
or a Cooper. I'd rather have a Bruce Bennett or someone like that in the
Douglas role so that it wouldn't get to be known as the latest Cooper or
Gable. Then if the writing is as good as I want it to be, the *picture* will
sell, and not just the star name. I am not knocking the star system. I
believe there should be top stars in TEN NORTH FREDERICK, for
instance. But if the studio makes a million dollars profit on a million-
dollar budget picture, that's better than a $700,000 profit on a $4,500,000
budget picture. And naturally I am making it my picture rather than
Gable's. No matter how good a story is, if it's successful picture [*sic*], the
star gets the kudos. If it turns out to be a dog, the script is blamed. Always.
Even in the case of the few stars who have absolute script approval. How
do you and Swope feel about all this? Isn't it worth considering?

Next question. Is there any chance that Swope might be coming East
so that we could have our first conferences here instead of my going to the
west coast? Ideally, from my selfish point of view, we could have our talks
here and I could get to work right away. Then when I have completed the
script, I would go west for the final conferences. Under our contract I have,
I believe, 20 weeks in which to do the script, which, if we started in
September, would carry me into February, a very nice bit of timing for
taking Sister to Palm Springs, for instance. I would hope to have all the
script completed weeks before the time allotted, but we all always say that.
The hardest parts of scenarizing THE B'S is to get the beginning right,
which it isn't now, and then to cut in and out with those episodic pieces
of the chase without losing tension. The characterizations would involve
completely or almost completely creative writing, but I can handle that all
right. I am all in favor of the episodic treatment, by the way. I can't think
of a better way to do it. There is no better way, since I am sure we would
plan to tell why each of the guys is in jail as a way of characterizing him.
Well, never mind that for the time being.

We have been doing nothing, absolutely nothing, all summer. Except
golf which we have been playing frequently, if not beautifully. It has been
the longest Spring in history and real summer probably will arrive as we
have to take Wylie back to school. But it has been a good loaf, which I
think I have earned. I have no professional news for you. I have received
my first copy of A FAMILY PARTY and there is a big deal (not movie)
in the conversational stage about it. Oh, yes. Cerf told me Irving Lazar[4]
has some ideas on APPOINTMENT IN SAMARRA he wants to talk
about, but I wouldn't let Cerf give Irving my phone number. Let him
write a letter. Several letters. I trust you and Wayne have been more
industrious than we. After all, you California folk have summer always, so

you are much more accustomed to working through it than we are. And how was the smog this morning?

Always the best,
John O'Hara

[1] Producer at Twentieth Century–Fox.
[2] O'Hara's screenplay for *The Bravados* was not used.
[3] Herbert Bayard Swope, Jr., produced *The Bravados*.
[4] Agent.

TO: David Brown

TL, 1 p. (copy). Twentieth
Century–Fox
Collier's letterhead

30 July 1956

Dear Dave:

Thank you for your letter, what it said and the way it said it.

I have said nothing to my corps of agents except that I was at the discussion stage. My thought after your letter is that there is nothing more to discuss except one detail: I don't want to end my vacation prematurely, since it's the first real one I've had in three years. Therefore, I propose to go to the coast along about the middle of September, which is when school reopens and we close this house. That would be somewhere along about the 14th. I can leave the actual closing of the house to Sister and the maid, and go from here to the airport without returning to Princeton. I infer that that would be okay with you fellows.

I have as yet no true story line and I'm not at all certain I'll have one when I come out. I am chiefly concerned now with developing the characters. Two of them, as you probably noticed, kind of get mixed up with each other, which may mean the elimination of one of them. Since reading the script I have been boning up on westerns via the TV, and going to see The Searchers, which is a much better picture than the notices and also not as good. Ford got so carried away doing a cinema that at least to two members of the audience he did not straighten out several story points. But it is a thriller and beautiful. Do you think you could get me a shooting script of Bad Day at Black Rock? That was one of the best ever and I would like to check it against my memory of the picture.

This job gives me a chance to demonstrate several notions I have about the people of the West. The old Romans and Greeks always seemed to me to be pure white as to hair and complexion, and blind, because the only likenesses we have of them have been in statuary. The westerners were not *all* crack shots, etc. Even crack shots miss. And they don't all wear chaps, etc. I have lived in tough towns, where there would be a fatal stabbing or shooting every payday, and I think that kind of controlled violence was closer to the real west than the more obviously exciting stuff we have seen and read, in which somebody is always saying "Reach!" I will go into all this later. When I hear from you about the time for my departure I'll notify Freedman[1] and we will be in business.

All the best always,

John O'Hara

[1] Harold Freedman of Brandt & Brandt, the agent for O'Hara's plays.

TO: Charles Poore   TLS, 2 pp. PSt.
16 August 1956   Quogue, Long Island
                                            Thursday 16

Dear Chas.:

Once again the cheery task of trying to say thank you for words of yours about a book of mine.[1]

I wonder if you realize how important it is for me (and I suppose all the others) to be able to feel during the writing of a novel—or a novella—that when the work is finished there will be one man who will treat it and me with respect for the work and the worker, and who will additionally have the subtlety to look for and catch the non-obvious pieces of writing and the grand plan as well. As you have heard me say, I used to write in the hope of appreciation by F.P.A., Dorothy Parker, Scott Fitzgerald, Sinclair Lewis. I would still hope for their approval if they were functioning now. But they're not, and I can tell by the number of times I say to myself, "Charley Poore will like this, Charley Poore will get this," that you have become—I almost said my literary conscience, but that would have been wrong. My professional conscience is no one but me. Instead of calling you my literary or professional conscience I'll put it another way: you, by which I mean your work as a critic, represent the difference between working and working-without-reward. I know how good I am. I know what I can do that no one else can do, because I see them try and I see them when they're not trying. But I cannot honestly accept the artistic article of faith that one writes for oneself alone. It's true to the extent that while writing it I write it my way, but when it's finished it is presented to be read, and that's where you come in. As you know, I distrust figures of speech, but this is a private letter and not my public self, so I permit myself a simile: it is like a horse breeder offering a horse for sale. I know that there will be some people who will not like it at all; others who will say "What a pretty horse"; and finally the man who knows horses, conformations, coat, manners, blood lines, and who will buy my horse, not merely because it's a pretty horse, but because he, the buyer, is a good judge of horseflesh. And I, the seller, am pleased that my horse is approved by the man who knows. It's an imperfect analogy, as they all are, but it's a pretty good one. I have heard horsemen say things like "If you run into Charley Poore you tell him I got a colt I'm gonna let him have a look at when he's ready." The final judgment isn't made until the colt or the book is ready, but the breeder or the author is sustained by the confident knowledge that at least one man is qualified to pass judgment.

I hope to see you at the 43rd Street Tomb[2] in a few weeks when I shall ask you to explain a line in a piece of yours: you said you had been to all those places by rail and by motor. Did you avail yourself of the railroads' piggy-back service? Put the station-wagon on a flat car for those tough climbs over the Rockies?

Our good wishes to Mary and to you.

As ever
John

[1] *A Family Party.* When one of his books was published in the summer, O'Hara preferred 16 August as publication date because it was the anniversary of *Appointment in Samarra.*
[2] The Century Association.

TO: Frank Sullivan   TL, 3 pp. Cornell
Summer 1956   *Collier's* letterhead

Sunday
Dear Sol:

I'm sorry we missed you at the Crouse party. We'd have been there but for that one small oversight on the Crouses' part: they don't know we know you. It's funny how that can happen in New York. I have been trying for years to get Crouse and a fellow named Howard Lindsay together. But do you think it ever works out that way? Something always comes up at the last minute and either Crouse can't make it or Lindsay can't, so I've just about given up trying.[1]

Thank you for sending me the Punch review. I might not have seen it otherwise, since the Quogue Field Club doesn't subscribe. I am now a member of the Century Association, feeling as I do that The Time Has Come, and I see Punch there and at the Nassau Club in Princeton, but I am so dug in here for the summer and have been since mid June that I am not up on my British magazines. Also, my English publishers are not the aggressive type. For years I was published by Faber & Faber. There is only one Faber, a fellow named Geoffrey, but he was so modest that he made the firm name the way it is. Denis Cohen, of Cresset Press, is a Jewish Geoffrey Faber. A quiet, nice guy but not one to bombard his authors with press cuttings. Nor one to go broke advertising his authors' books either.

I too am taking a real holiday. I have a play for production late fall,[2] but I spent some time working with Herman Shumlin[3] this spring and I'm afraid I'm not much of a collaborator, so I am stalling and vacationing. We play a lot of golf and yesterday I was put out of a tournament by a man named Malcolm McLean, which seems only fair. But you will be happy to know that he only won 1 up, 19 holes. When I say we play a lot of golf I mean we play 9 holes at a time. I was really bushed after 19 yesterday, but then I have already told you I am a member of the Century. I can remember Sundays back at the Schuylkill Country Club when we would play tennis from 2 to 4, then play golf until dark, go back to town for a date, drink and neck until 2 a.m. and then get up for work, manual labor, at 6.30. We all or most of us had summer jobs that involved muscle work. Can't do that any more. It'll be three years next month since I've had a drink and 11 years since I've played tennis, although my doc amazed me by saying that as far as my heart's concerned, I could play tennis this summer. But as Alva Johnston said when he gave up newspaper reporting, the legs aren't what they used to be.

Austin O'Malley was a crime reporter, best known in Chicago but also a frequent jobholder on the Mirror and the other Hearstpapers. There was also an Austin O'Malley who was a prof of philos at Notre Dame. Not him.

I detect a struggle about liberalism in your letter, or think I do. I believe you are a liberal, but I don't think the people in the so-called liberal movement are any longer liberal. You are not going to sit there in the New Worden and tell me you think Mrs. Roosevelt is a liberal. Herbert Lehman a liberal? In a pig's ass. They are bigots. I'm not going to vote for Stevenson or Harriman or anyone else who is likely to get the Dem nomination. I would vote for Warren, my first non-Dem straight ticket vote. I don't think I could pull the lever for Eisenhower-Nixon. So the way it looks right now, I'm not going to vote. I didn't like Stevenson or Eisenhower in '52, so I didn't vote. Belle voted for Stevenson at the last minute, having been for Eisenhower. Sister voted for Eisenhower and I imagine she will again.

This is an interesting campaign. Stevenson is letting Harriman shoot off his face for a New Deal campaign that is supposed to catch organized labor money and votes while Adlai momentarily lies doggo and somehow gets to be known as a moderate which he isn't, but a lot of people who are honestly concerned about a dying man may accept Stevenson as a liberal moderate. I mean people who would like to vote for Eisenhower again if he were the '52 version. If I were a Republican power I'd be working my ass off for an Eisenhower-Adams ticket, sub rosa, and ditch Nixon at the convention. If I were a Dem power I'd go all out for Stevenson and Kennedy. Joe Alsop[4] told someone, I think it was some friend of Sister's, that Ike would be elected and dead in five months. That was before the ileitis. I give him a year, elected or not.

Well, I said Nashua would beat Swaps last year.

Love from all here

[1] Russell Crouse and Howard Lindsay had collaborated on several successful plays.

[2] The play was not produced; possibly "The Sisters," which O'Hara rewrote as the novel *Elizabeth Appleton*.

[3] Play producer and director.

[4] Washington columnist.

TO: J. Donald Adams[1]
28 September 1956

TLS, 1 p. University of Texas
20 College Rd. West,
Princeton

Friday 28

Dear Mr. Adams:

I've never voted anything but the straight Democratic ticket, but at the moment I honestly have not made up my mind. I lean towards Eisenhower —or away from Stevenson—but my final decision has not yet been made. I supported Roosevelt right down the line, including the court-packing plan about which I now have serious misgivings. My concern now is that if Stevenson gets in, the people behind him are going to give us a government that will make the New Deal look like McKinleyism, and I subscribe to the Jeffersonian doctrine that the least governed is the best governed. Nevertheless I am not at this time prepared to join any committee.

Let us by all means have lunch at The Century one of these days. I get to New York about once a week. I'll telephone you.

Faithfully,
John O'Hara

[1] Columnist for the *New York Times Book Review*.

TLS, 2 pp. Swope
                                                              20 College Rd. West,
                                                                         Princeton

                                                                       31 Oct 56
Dear Ottie:

This is to let you know that I have completed the first-draft screenplay of The Bravados and have delivered same into the hands of Harry Klinger in New York for retyping. He thinks the retyping will be finished by Monday next and he will be sending you a copy.

I have worked intensively on this job because I wanted to have the story in screenplay form, complete, rather than to do it the other way, which is to pick away at it, scene-conference-contemplation-rewritten scene, etc., which is a good way to stall and a hell of a way to waste time. With a complete screenplay we are not dealing in dreams.

I have not even re-read what I have written. But I know two major re-working jobs I want to do. I have an idea for adding something to the very beginning, and I want to do something else with one of my characters, something more, rather than very different from what I have done. I have just about eliminated the long chase sequence, if sequence is not too inadequate a word. Instead I have done that part episodically. The reason for that, and I hope you all agree, is that a chase as long as that one is very hard to follow. If you could set a camera on top of a mountain and do the whole thing in a series of long shots, that would be one way. But when you try to do it scene by scene and all part of a physical development that you cannot actually see, you get tedium. I'm afraid the long chase in the original was tedious, and I am equally convinced that my way of doing it is an improvement. Each incident stands pretty much on its own, *dramatically*, while at the same time advancing the whole story. This is a good motion picture and will shortly be a very good screenplay. I am terribly pleased with the final sequences, especially the use of Josefa's father and of Emma and Gus—all my invention, but dramatically or dramaturgically logical.

I am hoping you really can get to New York soon. I think it would be foolish to do any more until you have read what I have written. Then I will tell you about the two things I spoke of earlier in this letter. They do not drastically change what there is. In fact, they do not actually do any changing, but rather they provide extra development. So please don't read the script tentatively, in spite of what I tell you about projected additions. (It would be interesting if you came to the same conclusions independently of my own.)

I trust you are not thinking of Elvis Presley to play Douglass. Too young.

                                                                  All the best,
                                                                  John O'Hara

TO: Edgar Scott[1]   TLS, 1 p. Scott
Fall 1956   20 College Rd. West,
                                                        Princeton

                                                          Tuesday
Dear Edgar:
   Two items, an invitation and a favor. You and Hope might not be
hunting on the day of the Harvard-Princeton game. If not, please come to
our party after the game.
   The favor: do you still belong to the Philadelphia Racquet Club? If you
do, would you consider putting me up for non-resident membership?[2] I
now belong to The Century, The Leash, the Coffee House, the Nassau
Club, the Quogue Field Club, the Shinnecock Yacht Club, the National
Press Club and The Beach Club of Santa Monica, which makes me the
William Rhinelander Stewart[3] of Pottsville, Pa. I have an old P.R.C.
roster and I know quite a few members, but I don't think any of them
would carry as much weight as you. Certainly none I'd rather have go to
bat for me.
   Sister and I plan to go to the Orchestra this season, so I hope we'll be
seeing you and Madam. In any event, love to all there from all here.

                                                         As ever,
                                                         John

   [1] Edgar Scott of Philadelphia was an old friend of O'Hara's.
   [2] O'Hara became a member of this club.
   [3] Prominent New York clubman.

TO: Herbert Bayard Swope, Jr.   TLS, 2 pp. Swope
                                                 20 College Rd. West,
                                                        Princeton

                                                    11 October 1956
Dear Ottie:
   This is a sort of lunch chat, the kind of talk we would have if I were in
California instead of the delightful place where I am.
   First, I have finished the first third of the first draft, and it is so much
better than it was that you may wonder what ever happened to the original.
I am really enjoying this, which means I am pleased. I now have, for
instance, a genuine reason for Emma's being kidnapped, which grows as
much out of her character as out of manufactured plot. I have an easier
reason for Douglass' being in prison, and one that is not some business
about a distant transaction. The men in prison now consist of Taylor,
Zachary, Lujan, Mirabel, and Douglass, and that's all. I have made a real
character of Lujan. I have also done good things with Gus and Emma and

their relationship, and I have created a Velarde, Josefa's father. I have even created a poetically just reason for Douglass's getting in on the pursuit of the prisoners: he would not be in prison if it hadn't been for Emma, and she would not be in a jam if it hadn't been for him. And boy was I right about not starting the picture in the cellblock! The murder of Primo is now accomplished after a period of suspense, instead of throwing it away at the outset. There is a reason (shown) for an animosity between Mirabel and Taylor, which will come in handy later, and I have not forced a mutual attraction between Josefa and Douglass.

Douglass is no longer quite the chump he was, and he is not just a nothing. As you know from Dave, I have made him a surveyor, an Easterner, with a cloud hanging over him in the East and therefore a somewhat more interesting reason for his being in Arriba. In those days a "civil engineer" was not necessarily a college man, and Douglass is not a college man. In those days you could get to be a civil engineer by working your way up through the grades of a surveying party, and learning the math from what was always called the Chief of Party. He is a drinker, and he obviously goes for the girls. As you know, I have had a mental picture of Holden in the part, but I can't help noticing that Duke Wayne owes the lot a picture and this story could also be for him. (Although Duke Wayne, of course, is a graduate of that sterling educational institution, the U.S.C.)

The—for me—hard part of the screenplay is now beginning. I mean the details of the pursuit and capture. So if you notice a long silence, that will be the reason. It will also explain to my neighbors why my light is still on at 6.30 a.m., but they should be used to that.

I called Harry Klinger at the 20th New York office to find out about a girl who has had script-typing experience. There is no immediate need, but in a few weeks I am going to have to have that kind of help. I would like to get this work finished—meaning the completed first draft—sometime between Thanksgiving and Christmas, have it typed and sent to you. When I speak of first draft I do not want you to think it is a tentative draft. I never write that way. When I put it down I put it down for keeps, and I must ask you not to judge what you see as tentative. For instance, I know you could shoot what I have now. I am not, in other words, a re-writer or a carpenter. One reason why pictures are not better, or that there are not more good pictures, is the business of rewriting, which is partly the fault of the producers and partly the fault of the writers, both of whom too often take the attitude that "we'll fix that later". What that does, at least with a good writer, is to disturb the even, if ragged, flow of his story-telling. If a good writer is allowed to make his own mistakes, the story achieves a personality of the more or less anonymous story-teller. The story will have its ups and downs, not all in the right places, but you will have felt at the end that you were in the presence of a story-teller telling a story, and not just examining an assembly-line product, much like any other example of the assembly-line. Unfortunately The Director is King in Hollywood. There is not a director in the business who is not a frustrated writer, who does not think he is better than a writer, and who knows damn well he can't write. But The Director is King, and the result is that it is the directors who are permitted to stamp their personalities on motion pictures, when it should be the writers—and never has been. It is to some extent, but not the same extent, true in the theater. I have too many things I want to write—novels, plays, short stories—so I haven't got the time, but if I did have the time I would like to write a picture, then get together with a guy like Shammy,[1] a first-rate camera man, and direct the picture myself. But I already know the novel I want to publish in the fall of '58 and the musical I want to have on Broadway in '59.[2] I have given this little sales talk to every producer I have ever worked with, and it has done no good, but I keep trying, because after I have had a look at the completed picture I am convinced I was right and the picture would have been better, or not as bad, if I, who created the people, had been allowed to prevail. Last year I kept hearing that they were trying to "put O'Hara back" in The Best Things in Life. Why did they take him out in the first place? I want to do a Western that the average guy will look at and say to himself, "I don't know why, but I liked this one a little better than most Westerns." I don't want him to know why, any more than I want him to come out saying Al Newman[3] did a splendid job.

This letter is written in daylight, on my own time.

Hello, Dave. Hello, Buddy. So long, Ottie.

Yrs,
John

[1] Leon Shamroy.
[2] Nothing is known about this project.
[3] Alfred Newman, Twentieth Century–Fox music director and composer-conductor.

TO: Edgar Scott   TLS, 3 pp. Scott
                                                  20 College Rd. West,
                                                          Princeton

                                          Thursday 15 Nov 1956

Dear Edgar:

I hope you are encountering no great resistance to your efforts in my social behalf. I was once blackballed from a club by a man I'd never met, whom you may have run across. Fellow named Harrie T. Lindeberg, an architect. Harrie, which is how he spells his name, was a member of The Players club and so was I, but he was not a frequent visitor to same, so when he dropped in late one afternoon and had the rare good fortune to hear me making a speech while standing on top of the bar, he fled the place but with an indelible memory of me. Little did he realize that because my middle name is Henry, I have frequently, under certain bygone circumstances, felt I had something in common with Henry Clay. Well, I was put up for the Coffee House and my name was scracely up before Harrie T. (do you suppose his mother's name was Harriet?) shot so many cough drops at it that it took me weeks to recover. Later on I got a succinct note from Page Cross, inviting me to join the C.H., and I did so. I don't go there much because the few times I've been there Harrie T. was not, and I really joined only so that some day I might be able to stick my tongue out at him.

I was once a member of the New York Athletic Club, which, as you know, is the Irish Racquet Club. During the War they had Sunday night suppers and they always served roast beef an inch thick, plenty of butter in the baked potato, and deep-dish apple pie. Belle was a great admirer of roast beef. She used to say she could eat it three times a day. So as a good provider I took her there almost every Sunday night. You may be sure she never saw anyone she knew there, and even I didn't run into many of my Fordham Prep–Tammany friends. Then one Sunday night she said, "This place is getting awfully chic."

"Yeah," I said. "Frank Erickson (the big bookmaker) lives here."

"I mean really chic. Look at that table over near the window."

I did, and at a large table, in among all the Irish politicians and lawyers and ex-bootleggers and bookmakers and weight throwers, were Maury Paul[1] and Clifton Webb[2] and six of their intimate friends, just as gay as could be, my dear.

They were there every Sunday night. Not always Clifton and dere Mabel, but other members of that set. Hebdomadally my feeling for the N.Y.-A.C. underwent a change. It was as though I had encountered Max Boo-Boo Hoff[3] at a Sunday at The Rabbit,[4] or Magistrate McDevitt[5] at a dinner of the City Troop.[6] So I resigned from the NYAC, although I kept my hatband. If the word seeps back to you that I am not going to make it at the Philadelphia R.C., I am going to ask you another favor of more or less the same kind. Do you think you could get me in the Klein Klub?[7] I know it is too late for this year, as I understand the boys start working on their costumes in July or August. But I think Sister and Wylie would be awfully proud to know that Daddy was marching on New Year's Day 1958. When I was a boy in Pottsville there was a group called Ted Bushar's Sour Kraut Band that always marched in the Mummers Parade and always took a prize. Ted and most of the members of his band are now marching on That Big Broad Street Way Up Yonder, thanks to the passing of time and the fact that they trained all year on 85 cent whiskey. But it would be nice to have another Pottsville boy carrying on the old tradition with the Kleins.

So if I don't make the Racquet, can you fix me up with the others? I am nothing if not adaptable.

We are looking forward to our visit chez vous as well as to dinner at the Dils'.[8] I don't think I've ever met the Scaifes, but I know the name. It always makes me think of what happens when I bump my boot against a concrete mounting-block. An experience which, as you know, happens to me all the time.

Love from all to all.

John

One more Club Life anecdote. Sister and I were in a southbound taxi on Broad Street a couple of weeks ago and I chanced to see Dicky waiting for a light. I said to the cab driver: "I just saw your mayor back there." "Not in front of the Union League, I hope," said the driver.

[1] Gossip columnist "Cholly Knickerbocker."
[2] Dancer and actor.
[3] Philadelphia racketeer during Prohibition.
[4] Exclusive Main Line eating club.
[5] Judge Harry S. McDevitt, a powerful and controversial figure in Philadelphia politics.
[6] First Troop, Philadelphia City Cavalry—a volunteer cavalry corps with strong social connections.
[7] One of Philadelphia's Mummers clubs.
[8] Philadelphia Mayor Richardson Dilworth.

TO: Louise Bogan[1]   TLS, 1 p. National Institute of Arts and Letters
20 College Rd. West,
Princeton

23 January 1957

Dear Miss Bogan:

Thank you for the notification of my election to the National Institute of Arts and Letters, which I accept. As to the two glossy prints, I have none. However, you might try Bennett Cerf at Random House. I am not photogenic, so it doesn't much matter.

Faithfully,
John O'Hara

[1] Poet Louise Bogan was secretary of the National Institute of Arts and Letters.

TO: Deems Taylor   TLS, 1 p. National Institute of Arts and Letters
20 College Rd. West,
Princeton

23 January 1957

Dear Smeed:

I am not likely to get haughty about the Institute when I consider with pride and pleasure—all right, and prejudice—the men, beginning with J. D. Taylor, who have been going to bat for me all these years. You, Phil Barry, C. B. Tinker, Untermeyer—so many of you and so good. Even Struthers Burt, whom I didn't know very well, was indignant when I referred to the elections as My Annual Snub; he thought I had been a member all along.

Well, I got the notification in the same mail that your note came in and I plan to spend the afternoon with a razor blade, slitting the stitching in my lapel buttonholes to make way for the rosette. (Ready-made clothes, you know.)

In the same mail also came (a) a note from Max Gordon,[1] who says he has an idea for a musical he wants to discuss with me. That should have made my day all by itself, as Max was personally outraged by Pal Joey, the dirtiest show he ever saw; and (b) an anonymous letter from a Detroit citizen, who suspects my real name is not O'Hara and that I am not a product of the Isle of Saints and Scholars.

I am so glad I gave you that Psi U badge, although I shudder to think whose garter it ended up on.

As always,
John

[1] Broadway producer.

TO: David Brown   TL, 2 pp. Wyoming
20 College Rd. West,
Princeton

6 Feb 57

Dear Dave:

You have made an extremely interesting and valuable point, and you are the first ever to make it. I *do* tend to overburden my dialog with matters that rightly belong in the unspoken part of a script. Sidney Howard[1] once said that movie dialog should be written in the sparse manner of a telegram, which was an overstatement, but had thought behind it. One of my troubles may be that I *like* to write dialog; I like to hear my people talk, especially because almost everything everybody says contributes to a fuller knowledge, and therefore, better understanding of character. At the same time I *hate* to write what will not be heard or read, in play or movie script. I have no doubt that if you go a bit deep you will discover that the reason is that what I write, the unhearable and unreadable, is by its very nature not mine, in the sense that the non-reader and the non-hearer has no communication with me, the author, or I with him. In the case of THE BRAVADOS I tried to get away from the rigid form of the Western, which is as restricted in its way as the Pierrot-Pierrette-Columbine classical form. If I have failed in performance it is because I stubbornly believe that plot is diminishingly important and that a little bit of action goes a long way, but the one thing that makes you remember a picture or a book or a play is the people. What do you remember about the ten best pictures you ever saw? You remember the people and maybe two scenes. As I think I once told you, years ago I wrote a long memo to Zanuck (1939, it was) on this same subject, and I like to think my memo was partly responsible for Zanuck's then new approach to movie stories. I was the one who at Metro in 1945 wrote profiles of my characters before actually getting into script. When Sam Katz[2] saw them he was at first annoyed, but when he had time to think he realized that it was a procedure that would save the studio money. The reason I did it was that I was working on a very bad Sinclair Lewis novel,[3] and by the time I was called in old Room Temperature Hornblow[4] was all confusion about the characters and was passing on his confusion to Sonya Levien[5] and me, and somebody had to start somewhere. Your letter, which arrived only an hour ago, got me rolling more than I had expected, but when you touch on writing you take that risk, for that's all that I am and what I care about most.

If I hadn't got rolling I'd have told you on the preceding page that I have taken the plunge. I am now actually writing my big novel.[6] Not researching, not blocking out, but writing. I have told Random House it is for 1960 fall publication. I am giving myself that much time at a time when time becomes more precious because I want at the start to eliminate the element of pressure. This is the father-and-son novel, which begins in Pennsylvania and ends in California. If I suddenly need money along the way I will ask you to give me a job, but I'd rather make a deal with you on the novel, one that would enable me to complete it without interruption. If I ever make any deal on the novel you, Dave Brown, will have the opportunity to speak before I commit myself. In my entire professional career— magazines, books, theater, pictures—I've never known anyone whom I'd rather do business with, from the standpoint of understanding, sympathy, taste and integrity. I think we go through life leaving too many things unsaid because of manly reticence, then one day you end up like Bogie, stunned by the fact that a lot of people really liked him. Even Benchley, a *popular* man, failed to comprehend the effect he had on his friends. He used to worry because Lionel Atwell[7] didn't like him! Well, I didn't mean to, as we used to say, rush St. Valentine's Day.

As ever,
John O'Hara

[1] Playwright and screenwriter.
[2] MGM vice-president.
[3] *Cass Timberlane.*
[4] Arthur Hornblow, Jr., an MGM producer.
[5] Screenwriter.
[6] *From the Terrace* was published in 1958.
[7] Lionel Atwill, character actor.

TO: Charles Poore   TLS, 4 pp. PSt.
12 August 1957   Quogue, Long Island

Saturday

Dear Chas.:

It isn't often I get a chance like this, and, knowing me, you will not be surprised to note how fast I get to the typewriter.

Honestly, Charles, playwrights and novelists did not "invent" the swaggering yellow-slickered reporter.[1] The playwrights and novelists only reported him. In 1928, when I first went to New York as a breath of new life in metropolitan journalism, there was not a paper that didn't have from one (the Mirror) to 25 (the Times or the Trib) reporters of the type you mean. To begin with, we all carried canes. Ask any Silurian[2] of the present day, who was working in the late Twenties, not whether he carried a cane, but what kind of cane he carried. I must have had a dozen, not one of which I bought except for one I bought for a penny from Helen Hahn Haven Asbury. Let me rattle off a few names. Joel Sayre used to wear a blue blazer and a bowler hat. Gordon Kahn, a tiny little guy on the Mirror . . .[3] actually wore a monocle. Red Dolan never wore a hat but he always, in those days, toted a malacca, which, by the way, was the most popular stick wood. Russ Porter was a cane man. I don't think Alva Johnston was, but he was unique in other ways: he was the best, for one thing, and for another, he was the only one who took his notes in short-hand and wrote them in flip-over notebooks, the kind stenographers use. But he had a slight eccentricity: he always wore the same suit, copied over and over again, and it made him look deceptively like a Methodist clergyman. (Light gray, single-breasted; plain necktie.)

If you went to Bleeck's in non-overcoat weather you would see the canes hanging by their crooks from the old, backroom bar, and they would belong to Clare Briggs, Bill McGeehan, or the fresh kid from Pottsville, Pa. And, I believe, as a result of our taking up that fashion, it was also adopted by the town blades. I know that the Racquet Club types at Dan Moriarty's[5] took it up after we had established it.

I dwell on canes? For a reason. We did not carry golden-knobbed canes like Mr. Morgan's. Mostly, as I said, malaccas. Mike Romanoff had one with a leather thong for his wrist. The thing about our canes was that they were part of the dash and the swagger. Ed Hill, it is true, rented a cutaway and diplomatted his way into an interview with, I think, Ramsay Macdonald, but that was part of the swagger. Red Dolan was not carrying a cane when he swam out to Lindbergh's yacht for a (refused) interview, and there were plenty of assignments where a cane got in the way. But we did have the swagger and the slicker. I even had a coonskin coat, in and out of hock, but I had it, and I am the guy who wore out one coonskin coat and got another.

Now let me examine the Mercury legend. Did you ever see the magazine man, who peddled magazines in the editorial rooms of the Times and the Trib? I'm quite sure he sold more Mercurys than any other. At that time The New Yorker was not respected very much. It was kind of sissy, in the opinion of most working press, just as Time was kind of half-assed and laughed at as a journalistic hyena (which it was). But the Mercury printed Americana and the other short stuff as well as the longer stuff, and Mencken (but not Nathan) was considered to be a working newspaper man and closer to us, and his combination of erudition and beer and farting and sarcasm had a great appeal below the managerial level. Ross, of course, was nearer to the newspaper man's idea of a newspaper man than Mencken was in actuality, but remember very few people at that time had laid eyes on Ross or even knew much about him. In 1928 I arrived in NY and almost immediately made both Time and The NYer, and never did make the Mercury, but I'm giving you what the average NY newspaper man thought and not what I thought. The New Yorker was Peter Arno and Lois Long; the Mercury was Herbert Asbury and Mencken. You see the big difference from a working newspaper man's point of view? And the magazine did fit in a topcoat pocket. And it was more alive than the old Quality Group of the Atlantic, Harpers, and Scribner's, while still high-brow enough to suit the tastes of the men who voted for Norman Thomas because Al Smith was a Catholic (that's a big statement: most reporters came from good, solid Protestant families; they were intellectuals in college, etc., but they could not finally vote for a Catholic king).

What I object to in your saying that novelists and playwrights invented the type is that it ignores the reality. When Winchell began to get power he pretended that the other type was rare, then he pretended that it did not exist, and finally he claimed to be (since he was not the other and never could be) the beau ideal of newspaperdom. The other type, in general, came of a good, middle-class family; Winchell was a Broadway sharpie. He began calling the real thing a scenario-writers' creation, and he was joined and assisted by Louella Parsons, so that when there was an occasional reporter who looked and acted like one, Louella and Winchell denied his authenticity.

I am not claiming much for the type. He was often a sour, jealous, name-dropping frustrate, who got as far as he could with what he had and hated whoever and whatever was beyond his own achievement. And he *was* a type, but he was more interesting to read about or to see than his fraternity brother who became a customer's man, and he got written about and seen. But he had existed and been seen before he was written about by the novelists and playwrights. And may I remind you that he exists today in great profusion in Fleet Street? The English always copy the wrong things about us, and not very well. (Ever hear an Englishman try to speak Runyonese?)

In about four or five months I will be coming to a point in my novel where I could legitimately develop some of these thoughts and maybe I will, if it flows right. Then a year or so later you will come upon some of this letter in quite another form, but remember, you saw it here first!

Our best to Mary and to you. If what you really want to know is how my golf is, one day I played 9 holes, got three birdies, and still had a 45. I just can't win. I have been playing golf for 38 years and I've never broken 80.

As ever,
John

[1] In his 10 August 1957 "Books of the Times" column Poore referred to "the days when playwrights and novelists invented the type as a swaggering fellow wearing a yellow slicker with a green copy of The American Mercury sticking out of his pocket."
[2] Organization of veteran newspapermen.
[3] Four words omitted by the editor.
[4] Speakeasy next to the *Herald Tribune* favored by reporters.
[5] Midtown speakeasy.

TO: David Brown   TLS, 2 pp. Wyoming
                                               Quogue, Long Island

12 August 57
Dear Dave:

My first impulse on reading a mention of TENDER IS THE NIGHT in Hedda Hopper's[1] column was to dismiss it, especially since in the same column she refers to something called NUMBER TEN FREDERICK STREET. Hedda and Leonard Lyons[2] may not vote alike, but they have identical attitudes toward accuracy.

I am acting on my second impulse, which was Write to Dave and find out all about it. What (all) about it, Dave? Is the studio doing TITN? Who is producing? Who, besides the dubious choice of Jennifer Jones, is set for it? Who directing? And, above all, who writing? I seem to recall several years ago one of those shotgun announcements that David Selznick had the novel tied up, and if he is still to be producer, my enthusiasm goes limp as quickly as it rose. David can't write, but he writes; he can't direct, but he directs. But if he is not, as we say, in the picture, I would like very much to have a talk with you on the subject of the screen play of TENDER IS THE NIGHT.[3]

I may have told you this before, but if not, I tell you now that as a personal favor to Fitzgerald, I read page proofs and galley proofs on that book. At the time of publication, just before and just after, I was quite possibly the only writer who *loved* the book. Dottie Parker also had proofs and I telephoned her late the first night and told her how much I liked it; she said she had been unable to stay with it, and I urged her to go beyond the very early spot where she had given up. As a result she telephoned me to thank me. Dottie's first judgment was typical, not so much of her as of the professional and non-professional judgment. The book came out at precisely the wrong time in the national history. No matter how good it was, it was about the Bad People, the well fed, well housed, well educated, well born—the villains of the depression. It was a time for Odets and the imitators of Odets, and of Steinbeck and the imitators of Steinbeck. I am, as you know, an Odets man and a Steinbeck man, but I did not feel compelled to hang Fitzgerald and Phil Barry as counter-revolutionists, and I am proud to say I did not go along with the gutless thinking that all but destroyed TENDER IS THE NIGHT and without a doubt broke Fitzgerald's heart. One group, which I shall disguise under the heading of Hammett-Hellman-Perelman-Kober[4] group, had no time for Fitzgerald (or, later, me), and I note with some sardonic pleasure that they are now having trouble convincing the people that Pep West[5] was better than Fitzgerald *and* Jonathan Swift. He *was* better than Cornell Woolrich,[6] but that's as far as I'll go.

I shall abruptly terminate this high-level literary essay. We are on company time. If Selznick is producing, I am out. But if he is not, I would like you to consider me in the writing plans for TITN. I expect to be another year on FROM THE TERRACE, my own novel, and that may seem a long way off, but as we both know, a year zips by in the pre-production stages of a motion picture, and TENDER IS THE NIGHT has been around even longer than PAL JOEY. (Even longer than APPOINTMENT IN SAMARRA!) If you have not assigned the book to another writer, and you are not in too much of a hurry, I may be your man.

When are you coming East? I have another project I would like to discuss with you, which I was going to write about before I read the morning papers. This project is timeless and untopical and does not even exist until we have had our talk.

We are having a good summer, by and large. I am still able to defeat my wife at golf, although this may be the last year I do so as she is getting better and steadier. Wylie was away for a month but is home again, and Sister had to go to Paris for a quick trip when her daughter got a concussion in a motor accident, but she is back, with daughter, who is resting here. I hope your own summer has been a good one.

Give my regards to Buddy.[7] From what I read, you two are almost the only guys who can still go to Romanoff's[8] without fear of subpoenas under the menu. As to that I can only say I'm glad there was no Confidential[9] twenty years ago when I was doing my research. I was a very diligent scholar.

As always,
John

[1] Syndicated Hollywood columnist.
[2] *New York Post* columnist.
[3] Selznick sold the rights to *Tender Is the Night* to Twentieth Century–Fox, but retained approval rights. The screenplay was written by Ivan Moffat.
[4] Dashiell Hammett, Lillian Hellman, S. J. Perelman, Arthur Kober.
[5] Nathanael West.
[6] Mystery writer.
[7] Buddy Adler, Executive in Charge of Production at Twentieth Century–Fox.
[8] Hollywood restaurant.
[9] Scandal magazine.

TO: Bennett Cerf   TLS, 1 p. Columbia
22 September 1957   Quogue, Long Island

Sunday 22

Dear Bennett:
I assume, or let us say I hope, that when you go to the office tomorrow you will raise some hell about the item in today's Times.[1] Du Bois wrote in the friendliest spirit, and I have thanked him; but only a week ago you got a letter from me about the premature and inaccurate announcement of the time when FROM THE TERRACE will be ready for publication. You have made no reply to that complaint. You have ignored that complaint, and today there is a more elaborate repetition of the error.

Whoever is responsible should be told off, and good. If it is in any way an attempt to make me hurry with the novel it is bound to be unsuccessful, and it may also be the biggest mistake ever made in my relations with Random House. Hereafter I want all publicity cleared with me, and I will know exactly what information was given by me to Random House.

Yrs,
John

[1] William Du Bois announced in the *New York Times Book Review* that O'Hara's novel tentatively titled *On the Terrace* would be published in 1958.

TO: Malcolm Cowley[1]   ALS, 2 pp. (copy) National Institute of Arts
                                                              and Letters
                                                 Century Association letterhead

17 Dec. '57

Dear Malcolm:

I have been informed by counsel that my presence in New York makes
me liable to service of papers compelling my appearance in Albany to
answer charges of obscenity made against my novel, *Ten North Frederick*.
I have been indicted on this charge, can be arrested, and held in prison
until bail is found.[2]

I had intended to go to tonight's dinner,[3] and came to New York for
that purpose. But I have been informed that the longer I stay in New York,
the greater the risk, and I am therefore returning to Princeton and missing
the dinner.

I am hopeful that I can count on the moral support of the members of
the Academy and the Institute. This is a dangerous action affecting not
me alone.

Cordially,
JOHN O'HARA

[1] Malcolm Cowley was president of the National Institute of Arts and Letters.
[2] O'Hara did not appear at the Albany obscenity trial; the charges were dropped on
a technicality.
[3] Of the National Institute of Arts and Letters

———◆◆———

*In 1957 the O'Haras built a house five miles outside of Princeton. Since
it was near the intersection of Pretty Brook and Province Line roads,
O'Hara named the house "Linebrook." He designed an emblematic letterhead with straight and wavy lines.*

TO: Louise[1]   TL, 2 pp. (not mailed). PSt.
                                                                  Princeton

22 January 1958

Dear Louise:

It is almost four years since you kindly left this book[2] for me to learn
from, but my ignorance has been obstinate, and I am surrendering the
book with all sorts of apologies.

There are two reasons for my resistance to M. Maritain, and only one

268

of them is real obstinacy. The first, non-obstinate reason is that a book of this kind demands a classical erudition that I simply do not possess. A great deal of a book like this is practically in code which I can't break, and the references and allusions are to works that I skipped while absorbing other information. The other reason for my resistance—and this, I'm afraid, is obstinacy—is my novelist's petulance when I come across something like this: "Great novelists are poets. They are few. In order for a novel to be poetry . . ." Great novelists are probably few, all right, but I do not believe that when a novelist does achieve greatness as a novelist, he has one more step to go, one higher rank to achieve, namely that of poet. I believe that it is if anything quite the other way. I have seen a great deal—for me—of two poets in the past year, and the petulance of poets when they speak of "you novelists and your best sellers" is childish in the less charming meaning of the word. A great many poets and a good deal of poetry have no other claim on artistic status than their failure to be read. Two years ago, when we both were getting the National Book Awards, Mr. Auden got up before an audience of a thousand people and spoke contemptuously of me as "a good property" for Random House. Is that all I am? Does the poet easily convince himself that that is all I am? What about the 408-page novel that won the award? Was that something I dashed off to make Random House happy? If so, the little poems of Mr. Auden must be judged by the same standards, since we were getting the same awards from the same jury, and Mr. Auden, who is not a good property in those terms, was inadvertently announcing his failure.

The failure of the poets to communicate with the people is always a sore point with them, but poets used to communicate with the people. Why do they not now? Why do not poets communicate with the people at a time when music, for instance, or painting, is communicating with the people more universally than ever before in the world's history? I think I have one answer: poets' obscurity, which comes out of snobbery and jealousy. "In order for a novel to be poetry . . ." says M. Maritain. Who the hell wants it to be poetry? I don't. Unlike Moliere's man, I've known all along that I've been speaking prose, and I have been amused rather than complimented on the occasions when a reviewer commented on the poetry in my prose. The poetry, I assure you, is entirely accidental; the good prose is not.

I have examined the prose of many poets, and they have a lot to learn. When they free themselves of the restrictions of the poetic forms they spend their words not like drunken sailors and money, but like miserable absconding bank clerks. M. Maritain quotes M. Mauriac: "the aim of the novel is knowledge of the human heart." That's a considerably more laudable aim than the compressing of a poet's observations to comply with poetic restrictions. I therefore deny that when a novelist is called a poet, or his work poetry, he is being promoted.

This was not intended to be what it turned out to be, an early-morning essay. I just want to apologize for keeping the book so long.

Affectionate regards to you and Mars,

As always,

¹ Unidentified.

² The letter was laid in a copy of Jacques Maritain's *Creative Intuition in the Arts and Poetry* (1953) in O'Hara's study at "Linebrook."

TO: David Brown   TLS, 3 pp. Wyoming
                                                                        Princeton

24 April 58

Dear Dave:

We went to see TEN NORTH FREDERICK last night, and the word for which you've all been breathlessly waiting is that I liked it. I was very deeply moved, and I was pleased with the production. Most important to me was the fact that there has been a minimum of tampering with the characters I created, and there we get from the specific to the general: if your characters are good to begin with, there is a kind of artistic logic about their behavior, a consistency that either prevents them from doing artistically foolish things or, if the adapter tries to make them do artistically foolish things, the literary creations rebel and will not function for you but against you. In that respect I think Phil Dunne¹ has done a sound job and I was seriously annoyed only once: in the scene at the amusement park. I think that whole scene is bad, but I won't dwell on that now.

That's a large projection room, almost as large as some theaters the picture will play in, and those are tough audiences. Who *are* those people? They look like faces from the legal department and accounting and real estate. The men and the women are wise-guys, and they are like benefit audiences in the theater. But they were attentive last night, and at the end there was applause. I'm sorry this picture is not playing Radio City. But I'll tell you one thing about this picture that I learned last night: men are going to like it. Men *do* like it, and if the campaign is not all set and locked up, this fact should be borne in mind in the advertising. You damn seldom get a picture men will like that is not a head-them-off-at-the-pass opera.

Sister and Wylie and I had guests. We fed them at 21 first. They were Sister's brother and sister-in-law, Mr. and Mrs. Courtlandt Barnes, Mr. and Mrs. Charles Poore (NY Times Books), Mr. and Mrs. Pat Outerbridge (one of my best friends and a Harvard classmate of P. Dunne), Deems Taylor, who is an old friend of mine, and William Lord, another old friend who is one of the Lords of Galey & Lord, textiles. Deems and

Outerbridge wept and said so. There were the routine compliments, and the closest to a knock was Courty Barnes's remark that it's a good picture but the book was better, or Lord's that he had not remembered there was "so much East Lynne in the book". One universal and spontaneous comment from our group: it is the greatest performance Gary[2] has ever given, in which I may say I concur. Charley Poore said he wished there had been some of the stuff at the farm and the farm itself, but I can see why that would have to be sacrificed.

I thought the sets were fine, and the interior of Number 10 was perfect. (I noticed that the house didn't have a busybody, but I guess Brackett[3] gave up on that.) And the musical scoring was right, sympathetic but unobtrusive. (I wish I'd thought to buy the copyright of Sweet & Lovely.)

The acting was excellent, beginning with Gary and through even to John Emery, who gave his eyebrows a rest. The women, beginning with my wife and my daughter, loathed Edith and could not believe Geraldine[4] could look so horrible. My one objection is to the young man who played Bongiorno,[5] and it is the one character Phil loused up. He made him meatballish, which he wasn't in the book, and as a consequence the love-making in the car was rock-and-roll and rape. A small but annoying detail was the way the young man handled the trumpet. But a detail that annoyed the hell out of me was the dialog when Bongiorno and Ann are getting in the car and immediately thereafter. Bongiorno is made to say, "Be my guest," an expression that came into the language about 1953, and "for kicks" which is strictly rock-and-roll switchblade talk. I am a student of the language, but the non-students among our group were also thrown by those anachronisms. I might point out here that there is wisdom as well as courtesy in sending the original author a shooting script. I would have flagged those errors. But of course I never saw a script, and so you have 1930 people talking 1957 slang.

When I was with Collier's I wrote about wardrobe and costume people. They will spend a week trying to find out how wide the braid is on a sub-leftenant's sleeve in the War of 1812, but they won't try to dress people in clothes appropriate to the changing periods of modern times. The young man who ditches Ann in the amusement park scene is a case in point. He was supposed to be Ivy League, but he had only a button-down collar (wrong kind) and striped tie to prove it. He had one of those cascade hair-dos like Pat Boone's[6] which were not worn by anyone in those days and never have caught on in the Ivy League. If you think that's unimportant, let me point out that the boy looked as though he *belonged* in that amusement park and therefore wasn't so very different from Bongiorno. That's why I sweat so much over detail in my novels. You louse up one scene and one character in that scene, and you got a rotten apple: later (in time and in sequence) you do not feel that Ann lost anything by losing Bongiorno, and you *need* to feel that. Instead you feel she was well rid of him and that she is a rather ornery little bitch to complain. No sadness, no sympathy. The result was an awkward scene when Bongiorno is offered the bribe.

On policy I think a great mistake was made in taking the story out of Pennsylvania. There are so many obvious reasons for my thinking so, but there is another that certainly did not occur to you personally: if you ever buy APPOINTMENT IN SAMARRA or FROM THE TERRACE or any other Pennsylvania stuff, you now have no link with TNF. Literally millions of people know that Gibbsville is in Pennsylvania, but it seems to me Phil and Brackett or whoever (legal department, to be sure) went out of their way to throw that away. I invented a town. Gibbsville. The legal department forgets that in hundreds of movies Chicago is identified by name, and no d.a. or police official ever sued because of a crooked d.a. or cop in a Chicago picture.

On the way back to Princeton I asked Wylie, who is a very wise little girl, how she thought the picture would go in her group. She said she thought Barbara Scheide (classmate and the best writer in the class) would like it but not many of the others. Well, that delighted me. Wylie has a pretty good score on picking hit movies, by which I mean that the pictures she likes are usually the smashers, and she is not influenced by reviews or ads. She likes TNF. She did not go overboard on PAL JOEY, and she was yes-no on THE BEST THINGS IN LIFE. My lovely daughter.

And so back to work. In a few days you will read an announcement that I have authorized: FROM THE TERRACE is to be published on Thanksgiving Day, this year. I will have finished the writing by the first of August, Deo volente. You are first in line. Is there any chance you will be coming to NY in the next three months? Bennett Cerf is a director of Metro. And my lawyer is Louis Nizer of Phillips, Nizer, *Benjamin* & *Krim*, if you see what I mean. I shouldn't think there'll be galleys before the third week in August.

Well, we've got a first-rate picture going for us, and as far as I'm concerned, where you are, that's where I want my novels to go. As always, warm regards,

John

---

[1] Philip Dunne wrote the screenplay and directed *Ten North Frederick*.
[2] Gary Cooper played Joseph Chapin.
[3] Charles Brackett produced *Ten North Frederick*.
[4] Geraldine Fitzgerald played Edith Chapin.
[5] Stuart Whitman.
[6] Singer and actor.

Chas.:

Oooh, what you said! Pottstown when you meant Pottsville.

As a matter of fact, you are prescient, all unawares, and to cover your embarrassment I will tell you a secret. FROM THE TERRACE *is* more Pottstown than Pottsville, although I will be the first to deny it if you mention it. Pottstown, of course, is the seat of The Hill, sometimes called the Hill School, usually regarded as a prep for Penn and Yale in my younger days, and an arch-rival of Hotchkiss, Lawrenceville, and Mercersburg. The other industry was the McClintock-Marshall steel mill, which is why I will deny any resemblance to the town in FROM THE TERRACE.

Our country club, the Schuylkill Country Club, was about seven miles from Pottsville. Whenever we blades or our girl friends had visitors from out-of-town we of course took them to the Club for tea, tennis, dances, tea dances, and the view. On the way from Pottsville we would always point out, on the left, a beautiful installation of dormitory-type buildings, smaller residences, barns, etc., and remark, "You've heard of the Hill School? There it is." Sometimes there would be a puzzled look on the visitor's face, which we knew was caused by some vague recollection that The Hill was in Potts*town*, but they all went away thinking they had seen The Hill, and we used to wonder how many bets were made, and lost, by the victims of our hospitality as to the location of The Hill School.

What they had seen, of course, was the campus of the Schuylkill County Almshouse & Hospital for the Insane.

Further to complicate matters and to cautiously avoid splitting an infinitive, there was a private day school in Pottsville, the successor to Mrs. Thurlow's. (The O'Hara children did not go to Mrs. Thurlow's; we had gone to Miss Katie's, conducted by Miss Katie Carpenter,[1] but Mrs. Thurlow did not take Catholics, even though they had been to Miss Katie's, a *much* sweller school.) When Mrs. Thurlow retired, the school was taken over by Miss Mary Hill, and it became known as the Hill School. Quite a few boys went from the Hill School to The Hill, 59 miles away. But then two of my nephews went to Harvard and then to Yale College and to Hotchkiss, respectively. Those would be my Potter nephews, who had attended Harvard Military Academy in the San Fernando Valley.

I am getting to be the kind of man who, when you ask him how he feels, tells you.

Sister and I had a lovely evening with you and Mary, and we caught a train that the Pennsy doesn't even schedule. Sometime let me tell you about the night I personally tied up the whole Sunbury Division, which was the biggest coal-hauling operation in the anthracite region.[2]

As ever
John

[1] O'Hara dedicated *From the Terrace* to Miss Katie Carpenter.
[2] O'Hara was working as a callboy and failed to wake the train crews.

TO: Joseph W. Outerbridge   TLS, 1 p. Outerbridge
Late August 1958   Quogue, Long Island

Sunday
Dear Pat:

Thank you for the words about Gibbs.[1] I had hoped, without much hope, that he might last out this phase and be one of my old-age cronies as he had been of my youth, but the whole business of life was stacked against Gibbs. I know of no one who had better reasons for being soured, and he is all the proof you need that things do not even up in the end. They never evened up for him.

I am now reading galley proofs of my novel[2] and it is a chore. They are sending me a batch every day because it all has to be in by 17 September, which means you probably won't get to see the last part until they have bound galleys or paperback books. I am staying down here until mid-September and it'd be nice to have you here any time you felt like it. Joan Bryan Gates[3] and husband and child are going to be in Princeton next week for an indeterminate stay.

We have decided to buy a Renault, not a Dauphine but the CV-4, I think it's called. It is, I believe, sold by Lahiere's.[4] I am told it will run on olive oil, vinegar and a touch of salt.

As ever
J. O'Ha

[1] Wolcott Gibbs died on 16 August 1958, the twenty-fourth anniversary of the publication of *Appointment in Samarra*, the first Gibbsville novel.
[2] *From the Terrace*.
[3] Sister O'Hara's daughter by her first marriage.
[4] French restaurant in Princeton.

TO: Red Smith,[1] *New York Herald Tribune* (31 August 1958), III, 1

Ever since I got a medal for being Literary Father of the Year (1956) I have taken parental responsibility awfully seriously. Not that I hadn't before; I remember writing a column for you so that you could have a day off to attend your daughter's graduation. But you didn't give me a medal, not even an old, out-of-date Turf Writer's badge, and I can't claim to have buckled down until two years ago.

A medal does something for a man; at the same ceremonies they decorated Walter Alston,[2] who was actually a grandfather, and look where he is today. But I must quickly forget about him because I have a few words to say about horse racing, and everyone knows that horse racing and baseball are furlongs apart.

I am, of course, about to comment on some aspects of the New York Racing Association's decisions regarding adult minors at the tracks. In a column on the subject you quoted your friend Al Vanderbilt, and that's funny because as soon as I heard the news, I right away thought of Al Vanderbilt.

In my mental files I carry a note on Mr. Vanderbilt that proves that, rich or poor, kids have it tough. It seems, if my recollection is accurate, that when the boy Vanderbilt was at St. Paul's School, Concord, N.H., he received every day, in a plain wrapper, a copy of "Racing Form," which he infinitely preferred to the "Christian Science Monitor" and "The American Scholar." Beloved old S.P.S., however, did not feel the same way about it, hence the plain wrapper. The young Vanderbilt obviously cared more about Mr. Campbell on weight assignments than he did about Bennett (or whoever) on the ablative absolute and the passive periphrastic.

Now I have the highest admiration for Mrs. Emerson, Mr. Vanderbilt's mother, but it does seem to me, from this vantage point of thirty years, that by packing her son off to New Hampshire she was refusing to bow to the inevitable. If she had to send her boy to a St. Pauls, she could have chosen the one at Garden City, L.I., and made it that much easier for him to sneak out in time for the first race.

Horse racing, they say, is in the blood. My grandfather had a quarter-mile track on his farm, complete with judges' stand and bell. I never saw a race there; that particular Michael O'Hara died before I was born. But my father used to take me to such fashionable meetings as Cressona, Gratz, Reading, Allentown, Lebanon and Kutztown.

At most of these gatherings of the elite, the horses pulled sulkies (and the drivers pulled the horses). Sometimes there were saddle races on the grass. But grass or shale, the races were part of my education.

My father was a surgeon who also knew a great deal about horse anatomy, and we would bet dimes and quarters against each other. I almost never lost, although I didn't know a cannon bone from a stifle joint, and thus learned early that an expert is the man who has just won the previous race.

It took many years, and something more than dimes and quarters, for me to learn that whether or not horse racing is in the blood, the best equipment a man can have when he goes to the track is an ancestor who owned the New York Central.

That's the most valuable information I can hand down to my own off-spring, who is now eligible to send her first messenger to the two-dollar window.

¹ Sports columnist.
² Manager of the Los Angeles Dodgers.

TO: Joseph W. Outerbridge
TLS, 2 pp. Outerbridge
Quogue, Long Island
11 Sept. 58

Dear Pat:

The information I would like to get from you I could just as well get from a high-priced lawyer, but first I want your advice on whether or not I should get a lawyer.

In the process of unwinding after completing my novel I naturally began to wonder what to do next. Write, obviously; but too obviously, and I wanted to, and did, think along other lines. I finally decided to become a publisher. I have decided to establish The Linebrook Press.¹ The Line-brook Press is going to start as modestly as possible: I am going to get a one-room office in Princeton, furnish it, have stationery printed (like the Kew-Teddington project,² this is, somewhat), a telephone put in, an umbrella stand laid on, a key to the washroom secured. Then I plan to go to the office several times a week and sit, to keep from sitting in my study at home and never budging out of there, which is a too-strong temptation. As I sit I will think up ideas for the Linebrook Press, and I may be in business a year before I get a feasible idea.

In a vague, general way, I plan to publish books and pamphlets that are not likely to be published by the regular publishers. I may publish one pamphlet a year, or I may publish two books. I do not expect to make money on this project; if I break even that will be gravy. This is something to do that is not writing but for which I am qualified by experience and reputation, and although I sound casual enough, it is essentially a serious, long-range project in that I will let it be known that I am the Linebrook Press and will, in actuality and effect, give the imprimatur of the Linebrook Press and, inferentially, my name, to The Product. The Product may be a scholarly work by a Princeton professor, it may be a pamphlet I write, it could be a slim volume on Jazz by W. Hobson,³ etc., etc. I am going to take some "card" ads in the book sections, which simply say: The Line-brook Press, 345 Nassau Street, Princeton, New Jersey.

As to the physical part, I will arrange for printing and binding and distribution when I have something to publish, and there are two houses in Princeton that I am sure would be delighted to get that work. I will be a variant of the so-called vanity publishers, who as you know publish books and charge the author for publication. I won't work that way; I don't expect to make a profit on the author himself, although in the even [sic] of a lucky accident I will not refuse to take a profit on his work, which I shall then plow back into The Linebrook Press. But I am not at all hopeful of making any profit at all.

Now you have had experience along these lines and my first question is, as a private, one-man operation, do I have to incorporate and get a charter from the State, and/or a license to do business in Princeton? I am thinking now particularly of the tax situation, since I hope to deduct my expenses in this venture. In order to qualify do I have to incorporate, or can I just announce that I am a publisher and begin to charge off my losses? From such modest beginnings it is quite possible that I might turn into a profitable enterprise several years hence, and I wonder if I might not be better off incorporated from the beginning, since this somewhat whimsical venture could just possibly become an asset. I know a rich man who has a private press, completely equipped, and as far as I know his principal object was to print pornography, which is not my object at all. My object is to give me something to do that is not writing but that will interest and entertain me while possibly making a contribution to the world of belles-lettres. In my modest opinion a slim volume published by me (written, say, by a Lawrenceville instructor) will be more respectfully received than if it were published by one of the many vanity publishers. I would perform somewhat the same function as the various university presses, but on a much more modest scale in every way while at the same time giving the publications whatever prestige my personal connection would entail. There we get into the value of my presence in the picture, since I will not publish anything I don't like but will, on the other hand, get behind what I do, and potentially we proceed from there to my worth as consultant, etc., and a lawyer will be needed in shaping up contracts. But what do I have to do to get started? What would it be wise for me to do? Incorporate, or not? Get a State charter? A mercantile license? Or am I better off just taking an office and doing no more than call myself The Linebrook Press and let it go at that? As the founder and editor I will be doing a negative thing by rejecting manuscripts, which is expert opinion and therefore of indeterminable value.

I am going to the coast next Monday for a week and I'll see you when I get back and we can have a chin on the subject. I should add that I do not want to announce this as a non-profit enterprise, since that smacks of amateurism and this will not be that. It will be professional even if it doesn't make money, and I hope that in five years from now the name The Linebrook Press will mean something in the trade.

As ever
John

[1] This publishing project never materialized.
[2] The Kew-Teddington Observatory Society was a "toy society" created by Outerbridge, in which he awarded membership to his friends.
[3] Wilder Hobson, magazine writer and editor who was a jazz buff.

TO: Charles Poore   TLS, 2 pp. PSt.
                                                    Princeton

                                                    23 Oct 58
Dear Chas.:

Where are you? Curled up, I hope, with a good book called I don't have to tell you,[1] and curled up is the phrase if they sent you galleys. There were, I think, 340 of them.

No matter what Millstein or Mitgang[2] may say about this novel, I don't want them to review it, and no matter what you say about it, I do want you to review it. There are too many things in it that they will miss, and that is quite candidly a snob remark. The state of reviewing is such that if you and John Hutchens don't say the right things about FROM THE TERRACE, there is not much chance that they'll get said. If they get said elsewhere it will be more luck than I have a right to count on.

I am very much interested in my own feelings about it. I have always worried about a new book, but if I am worried about this one my worrying is secondary to a kind of fatalistic joy that I was able to live long enough to finish it. Random are printing *and binding* 100,000 for a starter, and yet I feel that if only 100 copies existed, my place in American literature would be established. I like to write, but I have never known such pleasure as I have had with this novel; brutally hard work, sure, but work with a pleasure and a purpose, the pleasure of mastery of my characters and of technique. I swore after TEN NORTH FREDERICK that I would never work so hard again, but I did. The difference now is that if I were told that this had to be my last, I could say, "Well, all right." I told a literate friend of mine in the movie business that for 24 years everything I did was, for comparison's sake, judged from APPOINTMENT IN SAMARRA onward. Now, I think, they will go back from FROM THE TERRACE.

Poor Scott was, I sometimes believed, suspicious of me when I told him how good TENDER IS THE NIGHT was. As you know, I read proof for him when he could no longer look at the words and lines and pages. I believe he died without ever knowing how good it was. The atmosphere was hostile when that book was published. It was the time for Odets and Steinbeck and, to some extent, me, although I came in for some of the same kind of hostility toward the kind of people Scott and Phil Barry were writing about. The Theatre Guild became the Group Theater, and I declare Ina Claire became almost a public enemy. The people who bought books and went to plays, and who wrote about the books and plays, developed a mass bad conscience that was a miniature social revolution but like many revolutions, came from unworthy origins for unpraiseworthy reasons. The handy victims were Vanity Fair, the Pierce-Arrow, the Hangar Club, and F. Scott Fitzgerald. Scott should have been killed in a Bugatti in the south of France, and not to have died of neglect in Hollywood, a prematurely old little man haunting bookstores unrecognized (as he was the last-but-one time I saw him). I am immodest enough to believe those who have told me that my preface to the Viking Portable Fitzgerald started the revival that would have started anyway, later or much later.[3] I therefore feel involved in the revival as I always felt involved with the living man, even before I ever laid eyes on him. And feeling that way I sometimes go back to a thought that used to bother me, oh, say, fifteen years ago. I would compare Scott's career with mine: off to a good start with a first novel, then a pasting for the second novel. Then I would think about my next big one and worry about it for fear it would have the same fate as TENDER IS THE NIGHT. But my next big one turned out to be A RAGE TO LIVE and I realized then that I had been forcing the comparison, although the resemblance came to mind again when I published THE FARMERS HOTEL, with the rather major difference that THE GREAT GATSBY was an instantaneous and enduring success, while THE F H had only a mild success and is only lately getting asked about again. I suppose that I forced the comparisons between Scott's career and mine because I was so full of admiration of his work that I tried to see resemblances in the two lives, resemblances that did not really exist. I go on at such length now because I can see my life and my career as mine and not for their similarities to anyone else's. From that you will infer that I have attained a retroactive self-confidence, and you will be right. And it is largely because of what I did and learned and learned about myself in this middle-aged novel.

I suppose that I have had periods of unhappiness as painful as any man ever had, but I don't think they have been as damaging to me as they were to Scott and to Wolcott Gibbs (who actually were much more alike than Scott and I, or Gibbs and I). This leads me to wonder if my ability to bounce back hasn't something to do with the fact that in spite of the abuse I have given my body, I was always stronger than Scott and Gibbs. There was always something a little desperate about the humor of Scott and Gibbs; delicate, bitter, fragile, sharp are the words that come to mind. I could be subtle in ways that escaped them both, but here subtlety means restrained power, or strength, strength which I demonstrated to myself in my three big novels of the past ten years. Gibbs had all the equipment to become a first-rate novelist except strength, or endurance, if you prefer that word. A big book was beyond Gibbs (which is a real tragedy for Amer. Lit.), and a big book may have killed Scott.

What am I saying? Well, among other things I am saying that your frequently repeated injunction to me—"write more novels"—and McKelway's opening remarks in his review of TEN NORTH FREDERICK, and the words of an anonymous reviewer on Time, of all places—"you know that you are in the presence of a real writer"—have been decisively important to me.

. . . I just found out a little, but not all, about your family troubles in Saudi Arabia. It makes this letter seem pretty silly, but I'll send it anyway with Sister's and my affectionate good wishes to you and Mary. Let us hear from you when you get back.

As always,
John

[1] *From the Terrace* was published 27 November 1958.
[2] Gilbert Millstein and Herbert Mitgang, *New York Times* book reviewers.
[3] O'Hara's introduction to *The Portable F. Scott Fitzgerald* had appeared in 1945.

TO: Felicia Geffen[1]　　　　　TLS, 1 p. National Institute of Arts and Letters
Princeton
14 November 58

Dear Miss Geffen:

I have your letter dated November 14, which arrived here in the morning mail and was postmarked November 13. Although I do not like the censorious tone of your letter, and do not intend to engage in a correspondence regarding my indictment, I shall comment on some of the statements contained in your letter, merely for the record.[2]

The minutes of the January 22 meeting create one false impression and contain one error. The false impression is caused by the words, "Mr. O'Hara would appreciate some action," which would seem to say that I was seeking some action and requesting it. The action should have been spontaneous on December 17, when I sent the note to Mr. Cowley (who I later learned was abroad). I never thereafter sought action by the Institute.

The error is in the words, "he was to appear in Albany the following Friday." It never was my intention to appear in Albany, I never said I intended to appear in Albany, and indeed I stayed out of New York State in order to evade arrest and an appearance in Albany. I did not even retain counsel to defend my case, since I felt then and I feel now that the Institute, along with the Authors Guild and the Civil Liberties Union, should have taken action without my uttering a syllable. My case was of far greater significance to American artists than the Pasternak case[3] and it is 4,000 miles nearer home. Mr. Ciardi[4] will tell you and any interested parties that I did not encourage him to make cause celebre of my case in the Saturday Review, and I would like it on the record that in my conversations with Mr. Ciardi he was speaking as a writer for the Saturday Review and not as a member of the Institute.

I beg leave to state that since you wrote me on Institute stationery, in my opinion you took upon yourself, by your censorious tone, a privilege that belongs to elected members of the Institute. If your letter does represent an Institute opinion, I would like to see it signed by an officer of the Institute and I shall then proceed accordingly.

Very truly yours,
John O'Hara

[1] Assistant Secretary of the National Institute of Arts and Letters.
[2] Miss Geffen wrote O'Hara on 14 November 1958 responding to an interview in the 3 November 1958 issue of *Publishers Weekly,* in which he commented on the Institute's failure to act on the Albany obscenity charges against *Ten North Frederick.*
[3] Sanctions had been taken against author Boris Pasternak in Russia after publication of *Dr. Zhivago.*
[4] Poet John Ciardi, a member of the Institute's Council.

TO: Charles Poore   TLS, 1 p. PSt.
25 November 1958   Princeton

Tuesday 25

Dear Chas.:

In 1928 Harry Luce and I agreed (since I was hardly in a position to disagree) that a certain writer on the magazine had to go. Why? Because damn near every piece she wrote used the banquet metaphor. She was a critic, oh, hell, let's come right out and say it, she was a music critic, and every God damn symphony became a 7-course meal. In fact not only every symphony, but every program. So ever since then I have avoided the prandial figure. However, I make a seasonal exception now: you loaded my board with delicious viands, from succulent bivalve to sharp peppermint, with a generous helping of Maryland Tom. Have a cigar.[1]

There is one thing the thoughtful review does that I think is generally overlooked by authors and never even suspected by non-authors, and that is, it can make a man who has worked hard on a book to the point of semi-exhaustion feel his interest revived by a comment or comments written by the thoughtful reviewer. I have known since last winter that I was in the midst of something big (and not only large), and in a more or less routine way this knowledge goosed me from time to time when I needed it. Then when I finished the writing I spun down, and when Cerf telephoned me last week and told me about Mizener's review[2] and cautioned me not to read it (which I haven't, but maybe more of that later), I hit bottom for the past three years. The only review I had seen was an anonymous one in The Bookseller. Cerf sent me the Sunday section and Sister read it and also cautioned me not to read it, and I didn't, but for most of last week I lived with the only certain knowledge that I and my book had been smeared and blasted. I then read Rugoff in the Trib, and that was good and good for me, and I was breathing again. But today in your second paragraph I got what I wanted: "A man needs every bit of the space he can get when he wants to write his own 'Moby Dick', his own 'War and Peace,' his own requiem, if you will, for a time when the only change we can confidently expect is change itself." That was what I wanted someone to say, and the only ones I could *count on* to say it were you and John Hutchens. I will borrow your Protestant, and therefore misguided, missal and I will scratch out "requiescat in pace" and otherwise accept the metaphor. Among other things I did say a Mass over those times and customs, and it's quite possible that one of the reasons I pressured myself is that I wanted to get it down in print before we all go up in smoke. (That sounds as though I were under the influence of Louis Kronenberger's Time reviews. Quite accidental, I assure you—and assure is the word I want.)

I shall not detain you any longer at this time, but on other times frequently. Thank you for, among other things, comparing me to Chaucer. But if I had a son I wouldn't call him Geoffrey. There already is a Geoffrey O'Hara. He wrote "K-K-K-Katy."

A lot of warmth from this house to yours, and good wishes.

Ever,
John

[1] Poore's receptive review of *From the Terrace* appeared in the *New York Times* on 25 November.
[2] Arthur Mizener's unfavorable review appeared in the *New York Times Book Review* on 23 November.

TO: Robert Kirsch,[1] *Los Angeles Times* (28 December 1958), V, 1

First I heard about and now I have read your magnificent review of FROM THE TERRACE. You have said what I have been hoping some-one would say, not only about this novel but about my work as a whole: ". . . From the very beginning O'Hara has resisted the fads and fashions of the novel. He has matured and developed in his craft, writing on the basic assumption that his readers are intelligent enough to understand without facile interpretation or special psychiatric theory. The result is that more than any other American novelist he has both reflected his times and captured the universal, the unique individual for the generations to come." It is important to me to be able to read those words because finally one man, and a man I've never met, has shown that he has known what I have been doing. I have been consciously, deliberately doing it since 1947, when I was getting ready to sit down and write A RAGE TO LIVE. Before that I wrote largely by instinct and from inside myself and my own experience, but in 1947, or maybe 1946, or maybe even 1944—who knows when those things begin?—I consciously brooded about the novel, the construction, technique, etc. As you know, I had a somewhat less than universal success. Eleven years passed between the publication of HOH and ARTL, and the success of the stage show PAL JOEY, which was in that period, almost diverted me into the theater. But I am a novelist and not a dramatist. There is fun and excitement in the theater, but there are too many carpenters and nurses and other helpers, and my conscience kept nudging me. So I returned to the novel, where I belong, and where I shall stay.

This is really an amazing experience. As I read your review I kept saying, "Yes, yes. Attaboy, Kirsch. Oh, you noticed that, too?" And when I came to the last paragraph I said, "He even sensed that." For since 1947 I have not written a line that was not only a line in the novel at hand but also a part of my work as a whole. I want the Nobel prize, as Joe DiMaggio said in quite another connection, so bad I can taste it. And as long as I live and can be wheeled up to the typewriter, I'll try; by God, I'll try.

JOHN O'HARA

1 Book reviewer for the *Los Angeles Times*.

TO: Malcolm Cowley   TLS (copy). National Institute of Arts and Letters
Princeton

1 Dec 58

Dear Malcolm:

Many thanks for your good letter. I believe that the Institute should not take a stand in political matters. Until the first Eisenhower campaign I was a lifelong, straight-ticket Democrat, and I am now a straight Republican voter, and I could therefore have found myself twice at variance with the Institute political stand in a relatively short time. The real strength of the Institute, I believe, is in the prestige of its membership as the elite of arts and letters. But all the more reason why it should speak up when one of its members is threatened.

Election to membership in the Institute is evidence that an artist is a recognized practitioner. I, for one, waited twenty-two years before I finally got in. But once a man (or woman) gets in, he should be able to count on the Institute prestige when, as in my case, he is threatened by police action in a matter involving artistic liberty. A two-thirds' vote to support him is extremely difficult to obtain, and it should not be made that difficult for a person who has already qualified by virtue of election. Machinery should be available whereby in an emergency such as mine, with prison a very real threat, the Institute can state its support of the artist. Either a separate committee should be established for just such purposes, or the trustees should be empowered to speak for the organization after having been polled by telephone.

I never intended to go to Albany, I did not retain counsel. The case, I strongly felt, was for the Guild, the Civil Liberties Union, and, if possible, the Institute to fight immediately, spontaneously and thoroughly. When the charges were brought against me it became, I felt, a much bigger thing than an attack on a single author. Whatever the reasons for the aloofness of the three organizations, the big fact on the record is that they did nothing. It may turn out to be a very unwise decision for American literature, and as though Pearl Harbor had been allowed to pass unnoticed. For the disposal of the case in Albany, although the indictment against me was not pressed, is very unsatisfactory. I was freed on a legal technicality: the grand jury had not read the whole of TEN NORTH FREDERICK but had indicted on isolated passages, and that is contrary to the state law. So no real victory was won; the same situation can be created again in any county in New York State (and many other places), and this time, this next time, if there is one, the local district attorney will prepare his case more thoroughly. The crank letters have started to come in on FROM THE TERRACE, and if there is action again, I again am not going to defend unless and until the Guild, the CLU and the Institute forthrightly announce their support of my case. I would be much better off, I think, if the Institute alone backed me; the Guild is ineffectual, the CLU is hardly less so. There is not the slightest doubt in my mind that one reason the Guild and the CLU dragged their feet was their knowledge that I personally have changed my politics, and what price liberalism there?

It is on the record, Malcolm, that I was once indicted. Any moderately intelligent district attorney will see that the trial judge and/or jury is reminded of that fact, in spite of a defense attorney's efforts to have the reminder stricken out. My co-defendants in the Albany case were 35 dealers in smut magazines, and I was the *only* author of standing to be proceeded against. Instead of staying out of these things the Institute should be the first to come to the defense of *a member*. The Institute need not commit itself to the automatic defense of every author and artist in the country, but having elected a man, it should support him vigorously, if only to say to the world that membership carries distinction.

Congratulations on your own election to the Century, which in your case was almost automatic. Maybe we can arrange our visits to New York to coincide at a lunch table? I get in about once a month, but I can always make it twice. I am going in this week to turn over the manuscript, galleys, etc.,[1] to guess what? The Harvard College Library. If Larry Lowell[2] is burping in his crypt, at least Benchley will be pleased.

Cordially,
John

[1] For *From the Terrace*.
[2] A. Lawrence Lowell, President of Harvard University.

TO: David Brown

TLS, 2 pp. with holograph
postscript. Wyoming
Princeton

14 Feb 59

Dear Dave:

I wish we were having the pleasure of your company at THE PLEASURE OF HIS COMPANY[1]—a remark which ought to put me up there with Arthur Murray[2] and Harry Kurnitz[3] as one of the wits of my time.

The only news I have to report from my mountain fastness is the appearance of my annual head-and-chest cold, and the fact that I am ⅔ finished my new novel and have a title for it. I am calling it OURSELVES TO KNOW, which you will instantly recognize from the last line of Pope's An Essay on Man. Pope is full of titles; I got from him A RAGE TO LIVE. The new novel is now on P. 262 of double-spaced yellow second sheets, so you can figure out its eventual length. I don't think there will be much action on it for a picture sale, but I would not be surprised if there were efforts to make it into a legit play, say five years from now. I think I'll bring it out next year, what publishers call the Spring of 1960, meaning January or February. It is not going to be, is not now, a lovable book, but I have been held by it. I shall finish it in about two months, then put it away until July or August and reread it. It is intricately constructed and unlike anything I've ever written. I have not even told Random House the title (which I just arrived at last week) and I am not committed to them as publishers.

OURSELVES TO KNOW (I am trying out that title, although it is to be permanent) is experimental in several ways: as a novel, as a novel by me, and for its construction. I have been spending a lot of time with the old masters, beginning with Fielding himself, and this novel will reflect my research in techniques. But it also represents a policy decision on my part. In the old days novelists were good for a novel every year or so. Think of the volume of work put out by men like Howells—and good work. But in the present situation a novel every three or four years is about par. That is partly due to laziness, partly to the merchandising techniques of publishers, greatly due to the tax situation, and partly to the well founded belief that the critics get tired of authors. But taking that last item first, I get so many hostile reviews that critical reception does not really affect the general reception of my books. As to taxes, I have already put myself in disgustingly high brackets, so it doesn't make much difference. As to the Annual Model vs the Triennial Model that the publishers seem to prefer, I really don't think publishers know very much about publishing. As to laziness, I am lazy except where writing is concerned. And so I am going to bring out a standard size novel within fourteen or fifteen months of a giant and take all the risks of wearing out my welcome. It is now pretty well known that I write fast and do not rewrite, so why pretend? If you look at your correspondence you can easily figure out that FROM THE TERRACE took me less than two years to write, and during those two years I took out about four months. The over-all time was from February 1957 to August 1958; the actual writing time was considerably less. What this proves is that I am capable of writing first-class novels as fast as my 19th Century predecessors did. It is really shocking to hear, as I have heard, that Hemingway has a novel all finished but is sitting on it because of the economic-tax-merchandising situation. Not that I blame him a bit; but artistically he ought to publish oftener. I am hard to convince that an author owes a damn thing to the public as such, but in his case there may be some truth in the notion. He ought to be at work 75% of the time, and so ought Steinbeck. But they waste their time and their lives, and for that I do blame them; if Hemingway has not one but several novels he is sitting on, then he has an excuse for seeming to waste his time, but I doubt that he has more than the one and therefore he is guilty of time-wasting.

This all seems to be self-justification and it may well be. I am certainly doing it the hard way, by going against present-day policy of prominent authors, and I may have to suffer the consequences. But who is going to care 25 years from now whether I allow only one instead of three years to elapse between publications? And if I don't care about 25 years-from-now's opinion, why should I care about now's. So I am changing my policy: I am going to write novel after novel while I am able to do so, and if they result in my being published annually, I'll at least be demonstrating that I'm alive. That won't always be the case.

I am 50% sorry that TCF[4] didn't grab off A RAGE TO LIVE. It would be nice to think that at any given moment in the next five or six years I would have something in preparation or production or distribution on the lot. It might entitle me to a parking place with my name on it, which has always been one of my unfulfilled ambitions. For years I wanted to have my name on newspaper delivery trucks, and when I made it I made it in New York and London simultaneously: the Post[5] was running some stories of mine at the same time the London Beaverbrook[6] was running the Joey stories. I have had marquee billing on legit and movie theaters, but a personal parking space at Pico[7] or Belmont. . . . Still, it is psychologically a good thing all around to have had ARTL and BUTTERFIELD 8 taken by other studios, although I regard the other auspices as less secure. The worst that can happen to TCF is that it might have to take over Hillcrest[8] and run it as a driving range. But now nobody can accuse you of wanting to have an O'Hara festival in perpetuity, and knowing something of the motion picture mind, ARTL and BUTTERFIELD 8 have increased in envy value at my home lot, if I'm not mistaken. Meanwhile there is always APPOINTMENT IN SAMARRA and maybe there always will be. Double meanwhile: do you know *anyone* who has read EXODUS?[9]

I shall toast you in coffee next Wednesday evening. Sister joins me in thanks for your second time as our host this season, and in my usual message of warm regard.

As always,
John

Just for the hell of it I wrote a short story for the S. E. Post. It will appear in November.[10]

J.

1 Play by Cornelia Otis Skinner and Samuel Taylor.
2 Dancing teacher.
3 Playwright and screenwriter.
4 Twentieth Century–Fox.
5 The *New York Post*.
6 Lord Beaverbrook was publisher of the *London Daily Express*.
7 The main entrance to the Twentieth Century–Fox lot was on Pico Blvd.
8 Country club across from Twentieth Century–Fox.
9 By Leon Uris.
10 "That First Husband," 21 November 1959.

TO: Mark Schorer[1]   TLS, 3 pp. Berkeley
                                                    Princeton

17 Feb 59

Dear Mr. Schorer:
    In reply to your letter, I am perfectly willing to say what I thought of Sinclair Lewis "as a writer in those years when he was at the crest of his

wave." As to the Algonquin incident, we might as well get that straight, too, although it hardly seems worth the necessary wordage: In 1934–35 Lewis, whom I had never met, wrote a review of a Henry Seidel Canby book for the Saturday Review of Literature, which was not so much a review of Canby as an attack on me and APPOINTMENT IN SAMARRA. It was quite a blast from a man of Lewis's standing, and considering my admiration for most of (but not all of) Lewis's writing, quite a blow for a first novelist. It was probably good training for me, although it hurt at the time. The obvious explanation was that Lewis was jealous, and that explanation was made; but a less obvious one concerned his relations with Harcourt, Brace. As you must know, Alfred Harcourt, Donald Brace and Lewis really started Harcourt, Brace, and Alfred Harcourt and Lewis were close friends. But when Lewis left H-B for Doubleday, and Nelson Doubleday, at Lewis's urging, tried to buy up all reprint, etc., rights to Lewis's books, Alfred let them go for, I think, $25,000. It made Lewis sore as hell that Alfred didn't demand a bigger price. So there was more to the denunciation of me than met the eye; it was not *purely* outraged decency. Four or five years later, still never having met Lewis, I was taking a leak at 21 one night and noticed that the man standing next to me was Lewis. "Well, Red," I said. "I've always wanted to tell you off, and this seems the right place for it. I'm John O'Hara." "I know you are," he said. He finished his leak before I did and scampered out, so I didn't get much chance to tell him off, and I was, I may say, highly amused—and so, too, was Lewis, I later learned. By that time Lewis had become something of a nuisance drunk, and if you look in BUTTERFIELD 8 you will find some reference to the system for getting rid of drunks at 21. At least I think you will: I know that I wrote that Harry S. Lewis, a novelist, was getting the drunk treatment.[2] Harcourt asked me to kill the line and maybe I did. I was a great admirer of Alfred Harcourt.

More years pass and I took a literary wallop at Lewis and one of the gossip columnists asked him if he had read my crack and Lewis said he hadn't because maybe I was right. That amused me, and one night when I saw him in the Algonquin after I had failed to make a successful adaptation of CASS TIMBERLANE, I sent him a note which apparently he treasured. I don't know what I said in the note; I was quite tight. Lewis did not join me; instead he ducked out. I don't think I ever saw him again. But I never met him and except for the few words at 21, in the can, never spoke to him. So much, too much, for that.

Lewis was a great American novelist and long before the Nobel people got around to giving him the prize, I said I thought he deserved it. BABBITT is a great novel, and no one else could have written it. The fact is that no one else did. The only other man who could have come close was Newton Booth Tarkington, but Bar Harbor, Princeton, and a certain gentleness got in the way. Lewis was as fascinated by his country as I am, and that's saying a great deal. He observed well, he retained, he had a good sardonic sense of humor, and he also had a sense of history, by which I mean the luck and intuition to be aware of the big and little things that were going on and that are forever lost if there is no journalist-chronicler type of author to put them down at the time. I have always thought that Lewis was much too impressed by university type erudition and I think I know why: I think he wanted to impress Chauncey Brewster Tinker, a great scholar and a man I dearly love. He did not impress C. B. Tinker, who would not be deceived by classical allusions that Lewis was so fond of dabbing into his topical novels. It could be argued that Lewis never should have gone to Yale—and I'll argue either side. Another weakness in Lewis was his women, in and out of his novels. He wanted to be a Lothario, but he was not very good at it, and in that enterprise anything short of complete success is total failure. He never wrote a credible woman, but he kept on trying and got worse. His third major weakness was in his dialog; he had a tin ear. The critics and scholars who talk about his mastery of "American speech" have no better knowledge of American speech than Lewis had. Dialog is not written around a peculiarity, but Lewis thought it was and the critics and scholars (most of them) gave him high marks in Speech when he had only earned them in Observation. Wolcott Gibbs had something to say about that in his preface to PIPE NIGHT. But all authors have their weaknesses that are not too hard to find if it's weaknesses you're looking for. The strength of Lewis at his best may be harder to find. There was his capacity for work, which in itself is too often underrated. It is too often dismissed by people who are themselves plodders or by the aesthetes who are looking for that one perfect rose. Lewis was only at his best when he was working, and I say that in spite of his reputation as a parlor entertainer at the Van Dorens'[3] etc. The cliche is that writing is lonely work, but unlike so many cliches, it happens to be an incomplete truth; when you are working well you are not lonely. How could you be? The time-wasters, exterior and of your own invention, are always available, but art is not. It was time-wasting that destroyed Lewis, not work. And don't forget that time-wasting is often justified under the heading of work, which happened to Lewis and is happening to other authors that I admire. Except for Ernest Hemingway, who is unique, I do not believe that American authors should waste their time in writing novels about foreigners in foreign lands. I do not believe that any American (Hemingway included) is ever anything but a foreigner; it is impossible for anyone to master a foreign language even in speaking, and I am now referring to linguists, not to authors. It is therefore impossible for a much less accomplished linguist, an author, to appear before a Frenchman or an Italian as anything but a foreigner. Likewise an American who attempts to steep himself in a foreign culture is forcing it, and that will tell. This all has to do with Lewis because it illustrates the most obvious point in the world: write what you know about. Lewis did know this country, its history and geography and social usages and car-loadings and bad jokes, and he knew it big and he knew it better and he knew it first. Howells knew it too, but nobody compares Delaware with Texas. Lewis was born to write Babbitt's story.

That was enough. It wasn't all, but it was enough. One man out of many thousands of authors and journalists and poets and playwrights was properly equipped in all or nearly all the essential ways, and by the accidental timing of his birth, to be present and able to observe, reject, and finally to create George F. Babbitt. All the commonplaces about the similarities between Babbitt and Lewis himself ignore the factor that made Lewis and Babbitt totally dissimilar: Lewis, and only Lewis, saw Babbitt. All the other novelists and journalists and Babbitt himself were equally blind to Babbitt and Zenith and the United States of America until 1922. Do you know of anyone since Fielding who made such an important discovery-creation, and without a war for a backdrop?

Faithfully,
John O'Hara

[1] Mark Schorer, Professor of English at Berkeley, wrote *Sinclair Lewis: An American Life* (1961).
[2] The novelist's name in *Butterfield 8* is Henry White.
[3] Carl Van Doren, critic and historian, and his brother Mark, critic and poet.

TO: David Brown   TLS, 3 pp. Wyoming
                                                        Princeton

                                                        6 April 59

Dear Dave:

Having made a clean sweep of the Academy awards—not even a set dressing nomination[1]—I can give an objective opinion of the ceremonies, and I would say that except for Jerry Lewis and Mort Sahl, it was the dullest exhibition I've ever seen in person or on TV. Luckily, however, Jerry Lewis and Mort Sahl were there to remind everybody that no matter how good the pictures may be, Hollywood can always be depended upon to make a horse's ass of itself. The great tradition of cheapness and vulgarity will be maintained, even if only by a few stalwarts like Lewis and Sahl. The selection of those two snipes was an inspired one, and if they can't be signed up for next year, the Academy ought to start right away to make a deal with Mickey Cohen[2] and Oscar Levant, the only two names that come to mind as I consider the field of worthy successors.

My personal interest in the proceedings began with Bergman, and I yield to your earlier judgment: for FROM THE TERRACE she won't do. But I also yield to you as the picker of Rock Hudson. He might do.[3] I know I have seen him in pictures, when I was writing the Collier's column, but I honestly don't remember him. However, he looked all right tonight. With sadness in my heart (for she was lovely in her day) I confess to the thought that in not too many years Bergman will be able to do the Life of Eleanor Roosevelt very convincingly (we explain the accent by planting early that she had a Swedish governess) but not all the skill of Shamroy, Ruttenberg, Barnes, Daniels[4] and Thomas A. Edison will make her a convincing Natalie. The only technician who could help her is Paul Weatherwax, who, as you know, is a cutter; unless we resurrect Joe von Sternberg,[5] who, long before you got in the business was famous for shooting through tennis racquets. But if we're going to shoot through tennis racquets we might as well sign Althea Gibson[6] and get a little action for our money. I can also see that signing Althea might have other advantages, such as presenting the American way of life favorably to the foreign market, which would make us real big at the Cannes Film Festival, the club theaters in London, and Loew's Nairobi. Let us think about it. She is probably handled by Doc Shurr,[7] who always liked tall ones.

My other personal interest tonight was in Susan Hayward, who may or may not do A RAGE TO LIVE. I couldn't tell much, because she appeared to be loaded with a tranquilizer. Nobody has *that* much dignity, unassisted. If she has, she'd certainly be perfect for Grace, since the one way to ruin Grace on screen will be to show her without dignity.

Elizabeth Taylor has been spoken of as the lead in BUTTERFIELD 8 but since then she has announced she is quitting pictures, and strangely enough I believe her. A long time ago I used to hear that she hated pictures and was forced to work by her ever-lovin' family. By the look of Mr. Fisher[8] tonight she is still going to have to work, but I don't think all the returns are in yet on Miss Taylor. For years I have had a morbid hunch about that girl, and when Todd[9] was killed, you remember that the first reports had her on the plane. The Irish, of which I am one, do have these morbid hunches about certain people. True, we may have them so often that we kind of copper our bets, but when I've had them strongly, they often come true. Too often. If I were a serious young novelist I would make myself an authority on Elizabeth Taylor, because she has such stuff as great novels are made on. Thus, when I read that she was going to do BUTTERFIELD 8 my immediate reaction was that Larry Weingarten and Pan Berman[10] had much more sense than I ever gave them credit for; and my secondary reaction was that if she ever read the book she would shy away from it because I invented her in the same sense that I invented Frank Sinatra. (When I invented Joey, Sinatra was about 18; when I created Gloria Wandrous, Elizabeth Taylor was 2.) But the big difference between Elizabeth Taylor and Gloria Wandrous is the difference between a local novel at a very specific time, and a novel about a world symbol in what many people (not I) think are the Final Fifties, which are anything but specific. It may be too big a theme for a novel, although Cleopatra and Catherine the Great have been cut down to size, centuries later.

In moments of humility and disappointment I sometimes think of my own contributions to literature *qua* history, and I feel better. Julian English. Gloria Wandrous (and Weston Liggett). Jimmy Malloy. Joey Evans. Grace Caldwell Tate. Joe Chapin. Alfred Eaton. It's quite a roster, but nobody's going to know it in our lifetime.

My new novel is coming into the stretch, a figure I use because it finishes in a gallop, not because I am racing against anything except, possibly, time. But then I can't seem to help that. I predict that it will sell about 40,000 copies in the trade edition, and that it is going to throw a lot of people. I will lose some admirers, but that figures anyway. I got some new ones with FROM THE TERRACE; I can tell that from the letters; especially many who had never read me before. That is a book that people take personally, men and women, more than any of my books except APPOINTMENT IN SAMARRA. But I don't figure to gain substantially from now on, in circulation; and critically I can only expect what might be called a consolidation of respect while at the same time losing some of those who have gone along with me so far. With that knowledge I have written this novel under less tension than my last two big ones (this one will be about the size of TNF, or less). I foresee no picture sale, by the way, so you will have to read it on your own time, as a friend. There is a possible play in it, but I don't know who could dramatize it. Tennessee Williams has already redramatized Pal Joey under the title Sweet Bird of Youth, or I might have suggested him. But I guess this is one of those novels that should stay in its original form. When I've finished I am going to think up something that will make a good picture, specifically for the medium.

Come and see us soon. Sister joins me in affectionate regards,

John

p.t.o.

1 For *Ten North Frederick*.
2 Los Angeles gangster.
3 *From the Terrace* starred Paul Newman and Joanne Woodward.
4 Cameramen.
5 Director Joseph von Sternberg.
6 Negro tennis player.
7 Louis Shurr, talent agent.
8 Eddie Fisher, Elizabeth Taylor's fourth husband.
9 Mike Todd, Miss Taylor's third husband.
10 Laurence Weingarten and Pandro S. Berman, MGM producers.
11 Vice-President in Charge of Production, Warner Brothers. The Irving G. Thalberg Memorial Award is given by the Academy of Motion Picture Arts and Sciences for "production achievement by an individual producer."

Any Californian who survives a motor accident is entitled to some recognition, but does that justify giving Jack Warner the Thalberg award?[11]

J.

TO: Charles Poore   TLS, 2 pp. PSt.
                                                              Princeton
                                                            21 April 59
Dear Chas.:

I read into the last sentence of your last paragraph today a kind of dour prediction that exactly matches my own misgivings and apprehensions. In plainer language, weren't you telling them to give me the Pulitzer prize and not be afraid to?[1]

My guess is that THE UGLY AMERICAN[2] has got them off the hook. I have no idea who have the say this year, but on past performance they would have had the choice (which they would create) of giving it to me or not giving it at all. In January I predicted, in a sealed envelope and to John Hutchens, that I would get the National Book Award and that THE UGLY AMERICAN would get the Pulitzer.[3] But that was before I knew that Kazin and Hansen[4] and Harvey Breit's ex-wife[5] were on the N.B.A. jury. As soon as I saw their names I told Cerf to forget about the N.B.A. Cerf, with his highly developed instinct for misjudging people, said that I might have to eat my words if Kazin turned out to favor my cause. Well, of course no author finds his own words unpalatable, but even so I had to eat dirt (native grounds).[6]

The arguments in favor of THE UGLY AMERICAN are that it is *about* something, a very important argument nowadays when novels are more likely to be about somethings than about someones. Gradually people will disappear from novels entirely, and the Columbia-Kenyon boys will have their wish. In the case of THE UGLY AMERICAN, then, we have a novel about something; it is on the side of the angels; it is, I suppose, clean (I haven't read it); it was, if I remember correctly, serialized in the Satevepost; it is a best seller; and nobody is sore at it.

When you talk to people about the Pulitzer prize, meaning for the novel or the play, they say it is discredited. I go back to the storm of ennui created by the award to ALISON'S HOUSE,[7] which was even before APPOINTMENT IN SAMARRA was ignored. The novel and play category (I lump them for my present purpose) was given new standing with the award to OF THEE I SING,[8] but I beg leave to point out that that was about something and the only someone was Alexander Throttlebottom. The attempt to revive it a few years ago showed that it didn't have much but the Gershwin-Gershwin score. Kaufman and Ryskind really got a free ride on Ira Gershwin's satire. But let's concede that the committee deserve full marks for honoring an innovation; they crawled back into their shells until PAL JOEY was safely past. The awards are generally gutless, and the criticism that they are discredited is all right, as far as it goes. But the term Pulitzer Prize has a prestige that the N.B.A. has never had and never will (especially with a few more awards of the kind they've given as the N.B.A.). Pulitzer Prize, including the common mispronunciation of old Joe's name, is in the language, like Beech-Nut and Chevrolet and New York Yankees. It is a brand name, and the name of a brand, if you will. Consequently it is an honor that you have and put away, as most men put away their Phi Bete keys. The man who averaged 84 instead of 85 can't knock the Phi Bete key, because to do so would be ungracious near-missing. The only people who can knock Phi Bete or the P.P. are those who got them or were never, never in the running. Meanwhile, to the ineligible public Phi Beta Kappa and Pulitzer each uniquely represents rewarded accomplishment.

This, I feel sure, is my last chance to get it. The novel I am bringing out next year[9] will not get it or anything else. It is transitional and will be baffling to most people and will make too many angry. It is not as good as FROM THE TERRACE, which is a hell of a thing to say to a man who will probably have to pass public judgment on it, but as I say, it is transitional and evolutionary. Growing pains at 54! I shall go on trying to earn the Nobel, and maybe I'll be one of those horses that win the Derby and the Belmont, but lose the Preakness.

I phoned you yesterday but your line was busy. I wanted to chin about a publishing rumor I've heard and quite frankly to ask for information that might serve as advice. I will try you again.

Our warm greetings to Mary and my kindest to you. Sister's kindest to you, too, and my warmest to you and my kindest to Mary. Love is everywhere.

John

---

[1] "Meantime, let us have none of those discretion-is-the-better part-of-valor 'no award' categories this year when the laurels of Morningside bloom in May." O'Hara never received the Pulitzer Prize.

[2] By William J. Lederer and Eugene Burdick.

[3] In 1959 the Pulitzer Prize for fiction went to Robert Lewis Taylor's *The Travels of Jamie McPheeters*; the National Book Award, to Bernard Malamud's *The Magic Barrel*.

[4] Book reviewer Harry Hansen.

[5] Alice Morris.

[6] Reference to Alfred Kazin's *On Native Grounds*.

[7] By Susan Glaspell; Pulitzer Prize for drama, 1931.

[8] By George S. Kaufman and Morrie Ryskind, with songs by George and Ira Gershwin; first musical to receive the Pulitzer Prize.

[9] *Ourselves to Know*.

                                                           23 May 59
Dear Dave:

Thank you for your note, which contained two thought-provokers of a professional nature. In reverse order, I am glad that FROM THE TERRACE is shaping up well. Frankly, added to my other worries was one that FTT was causing trouble in script preparation, and that Lehman[1] was too proud to ask for help. Since I do not know Mark Robson[2] I do not know how he would handle such a situation. It is all too easy to sit here, 3000 miles away, and imagine the difficulties a writer can encounter in preparing a 900-page novel for the screen. The novel *should* be one of your best; the stuff is there in abundance; the people and situations are there, and the pictorial values are there.

The other topic is the Great Lakes story.[3] I assume that you have read the "beginnings" of the story you have in your files, and I wonder if, knowing me, you think it would be wise for me to read what you have or to pretend it doesn't exist. I myself am inclined to favor ignoring the material you have, at least until I have created the principal characters and story line. I wish you didn't have anything, for selfishly I want this to be my baby entirely. I don't know of any novel or play that dealt with the Great Lakes, although there must be some. Of course there was Anna Christie,[4] but the Great Lakes was, as I recall it, not of special interest in the O'Neill play or the movie, and therefore I am not terribly concerned with the casual references to that area, since O'Neill himself was not disposed to make that region a character in his play as, for instance, the house at No. 10 North Frederick Street was a character in my novel.

Speaking of O'Neill, I can easily segue into a discussion of the Post (N.Y.) series about me.[5] I have read all but the last instalment, which comes out today and which I do not see until tomorrow. When I first heard about the series I figured they would be doing a Fitzgerald on me while I am still alive, but as I read it I also felt that they were trying to do an O'Neill as well, a thought which naturally occurred as the two books about O'Neill were reviewed. (The Max Wylie and Croswell Bowen books.) The Post series must have been very tiresome reading to anyone not closely associated with me. For about 40 years it has been no secret that I wanted to go to Yale or to have gone there, that I was a drinking man, that sometimes I was happy and sometimes I was blue-hoo. But the constant repetition of that theme in the series would make any reader who stuck with the series wonder when I got time to do all that work. The errors in available, ascertainable fact average about one to a paragraph, and they're short paragraphs. They range from calendar errors—two, three, four years away from the actual time I held a job or wrote something—to what kind of cars I own (I haven't owned a Mercury since 1942, but the dame who wrote the series has me owning one now), to things that never happened and sayings that were never said. I am almost, but not quite, tempted to sue the paper not on grounds of defamation or libel. . . .[6] The other biggest source of quotes was a piece that Gibbs had in the Saturday Review in 1938! What delighted me was the way so many people, you for instance, brushed her off. In Pottsville, for another instance, she has made errors of time, spelling, location, etc., that indicate her sources there were protective of me or never knew me. Nevertheless I was not made to look good to the Post's Porto Rican circulation or to the alumni of CCNY. There is an old saying that is, I believe, of Italian origin: "The little dogs bark, the circus passes." As I grow older I find that the people I don't want to like me, don't embarrass me by doing so; the people I want to like me, do. I do my work, the best I know how, and those whose approval would bother me turn out to be violently antipathetic toward it and me. And in many cases they are fanatically fond of people and things that I abhor. So it works out quite nicely.

Wylie leaves for a ranch in Colorado at the end of June, and Sister and I go to Quogue immediately thereafter. I hope you will come see us here or there—more comfortably there, since June in Princeton is awfully hot and sticky, and we are slowly getting to be the last family without a swimming pool. Also, I will, I think, have made up for lost time in my new novel, which I would like you to read. You can justify your trip at studio expense by coming to Quogue for the first reading—and turn-down. On the positive side you may want to take an option on it for a dramatization, but that's a very remote possibility. As a novel it is not going to be the big seller that some of my others have been, and studio interest will be moderate to cool. But it will be talked about, argued about, and, as I believe I told you before, will sell about 40,000 in the trade edition.

By the time you get East I should have a better idea of the extent of my personal mobility. I am tightly corseted and I carry a cane and I am learning to rise, walk, sit, etc., to avoid sudden twists. In six weeks I am to start taking physical therapy and I am hoping to be able to play golf and drive a car, activities that seem unlikely at this moment. All this, of course, will affect my plans to go to Duluth and other Great Lakes towns and make the trips I want to make. I would not think of driving a car until I get the doctor's okay: if I were driving alone and got another seizure I'd be as helpless as a man with a heart attack—and as dangerous. However, physical therapy may correct that and remove that apprehension. My brother-in-law (who did the operation on Arthur Godfrey) says he expects to play a lot of golf with me this summer, and I only hope he has some inside information. I shall have to learn some new work habits, too. Principally, I suppose, cultivating the habit of shorter hours at the typewriter. This is a hell of a note at a time when I am potentially more productive than ever before in my career.

But we can always talk. So come see us.

All warmest regards,

John

[1] Ernest Lehman wrote the screenplay for *From the Terrace*.
[2] Mark Robson directed and produced *From the Terrace*.
[3] On 17 May O'Hara wrote Brown that he was interested in writing an original screenplay for Ingrid Bergman about the "fascinating life of the ore and wheat boats on the Great Lakes." This project did not develop.
[4] *Anna Christie* was set in New York.
[5] Beverly Gary published a six-part "Post Portrait" on O'Hara in May 1959.
[6] Fifteen words omitted by the editor.

TO: David Brown
TLS, 2 pp. Wyoming
Princeton

23 June 59

Dear Dave:

I completed my novel at 0455 yesterday morning and I am, to my surprise delighted with it. Who else will be is another matter, but on the very last night I worked out a problem that had been bothering me from the first page. It might be said to have worked itself out. I always knew how it was going to end, but I was worried about how I would achieve the writing of how it was to end. Now I am satisfied. OURSELVES TO KNOW is a good novel; I think it will be more successful than I felt it would be as recently as your visit, and Sister wants me to take a long rest. But my rest will not be loafing. I doubt if I'll be allowed to play golf, and instead of resting through idleness I will rest through change. And that is where you come in.

You asked me when you were here to tell you briefly what I had in mind for a screen original when I got an idea for one. I have the idea, and I now present it to you (I have not yet seen Swanie[1]) in embryo.[2]

The scene is an imaginary island in the Mediterranean. Imaginary, but not unreal. We open with an attractive American girl named Mary, who has just met and likes an attractive young American named John. The time is approximately the present. John and Mary are tourists, at the moment in a town in the south of France. John charters a small auxiliary yawl, and they set out to visit this small island that can be seen from the mainland. When they reach the island and go ashore and wander through the tiny fishing village John notices that Mary is strangely reticent and at the same time he notices that the older people among the natives do double takes when they look at Mary, although she speaks to none of them and John, though beginning to be mystified, has no reason to believe that Mary is recognizing any of the natives. Recognition is all on their side, and yet there is no denying the strangeness in her behavior. The natives' apparent recognition is multiplied, they talk among themselves and stare at her until there are so many of them staring at her that a situation develops that is embarrassing to Mary, and she persuades John to take her back to the yawl.

He agrees to take her back, and as they are returning to the mainland he asks her to tell him why the natives had behaved so oddly and why she herself seemed to know the reason for their behavior. After some hesitation she tells him: "I was born there."

She is obviously not Italian or French or Spanish—blonde, blue-eyed, American-looking.

And then the story begins to unfold. The island was at one time owned by her grandfather, Michael Brady,[3] a crooked tycoon who fled the U.S. to escape prison. And the rest is not yet ready to be written down, although you may be sure my imagination is at work. But that is as much as I want to write about it now. Is Hitchcock going to be available in 1960?

Incidentally, or not at all incidentally, I know how this one comes out too.

Warm regards,

As always,
John

[1] H. N. Swanson, O'Hara's Hollywood agent.
[2] O'Hara developed this idea into an original treatment, "The Man Who Could Not Lose," which Twentieth Century–Fox bought for a reported $75,000 but did not produce.
[3] The character is named Martin K. Ziegler in O'Hara's treatment.

TO: Wylie O'Hara   TLS, 2 pp. Mrs. Doughty
Postmarked 12 August 1959   Quogue, Long Island

Wednesday

My dear:

Sister is in Princeton, checking up on the new tool shed and the relaying of the stones on the terrace. Misty[1] is in our bedroom, sitting on a rafter above my bed and misbehaving. Pat[2] is out on the dune, rolling in the sand. I have just returned from a trip to Southhampton. I took Uncle Bob with me to the Ram Island Club to order our dinner for Saturday night.

I guess you don't know about that. Sunday, the 16th, will be the

25th anniversary of the publication of APPOINTMENT IN SAMARRA, and we are having the Bob Wylies, Mr. and Mrs. Lord, and Bill Marvel to dinner in a mild celebration. Twenty-five years! I remember that night in 1934. Friends of mine, Mr. and Mrs. Herbert Asbury, had a big party to celebrate my first novel. It was at their house in Beverly Hills. At about ten o'clock that night they sent the butler down to Wilshire Boulevard and he bought 50 copies of the Los Angeles Examiner, which had a good review (I have it here, in the bedroom) and distributed them to the guests, most of whom were friends of mine from the East who were working in the movies. By that time some of them couldn't read—I was on the wagon—but it was a wonderful party.

Today, speaking weatherly, is the best day of the summer. This whole area looks like a Saturday Evening Post cover; people in cars, boats, walking, in bathing suits, etc. And the Yankees have won 6 straight! Yogi hit his 300th major league home run the other night, making it possible for the Yanks to go on and win, and I was so delighted that I sent him a copy of A FAMILY PARTY, inscribed as follows: "To Lawrence 'Yogi' Berra—on all occasions, but specifically on the occasion of his 300th home run—in admiration."

Oh—if you receive a letter from the Tribune Fresh Air Fund, this is the explanation: I have occasionally given them a contribution because I think it's one of the best charities. This time I sent a cheque for $10 in your name. As you may know, the Fresh Air Fund sends underprivileged kids to camps every year and has been doing so for many years. I thought I would start you out as a contributor, and in the future you can send them whatever you like, if you decide you would like to continue to be a contributor. A small contribution does more there than in some of the big charities.

Soon you will be home, and that will be fine.

Love
Dad

[1] A parakeet.
[2] The O'Haras' golden retriever.

TO: Robert Moses[1]   *Park East* (10 January 1974), 5.
August 1959   Quogue, Long Island

Tuesday

Dear Bob:

Thank you for sending me your Yale remarks.[2] The sad thing about your comment is that Yale has no one, and since Red Lewis[3] has had no one, who went to Yale and from there to the typewriter to comment on 20th Century America and 20th Century Yale. For that combination you have to come to me, Niagara Prep '24.

I could take up a great deal of your valuable time, and my own, to explain why Yale has not produced a novelist like Fitzgerald. Cyril Hume, with *The Wife of the Centaur*, and Steve Benét, with *The Beginning of Wisdom*, started out on the path for which Fitzgerald had been the brush-cutter. You know what happened to them. You also know what happened to Phil Barry. But *why* it happened and has been happening in the forty years since those men were Yale men is something I shall be happy to go into when Yale gives me a Litt.D. And you should live so long. But I'll give you a hint: Yale men who want to write usually fall comfortably into the hands of Harry Luce. Poor little lambs that have lost their way—in a Borden's bottling plant.

Cordially,
John O'Hara

[1] A New York public works official, Moses wrote a column, "Bits and Pieces," for *Park East*.

[2] At the 50th Reunion of the Yale Class of 1909.

[3] Sinclair Lewis.

TO: Wylie O'Hara

TLS, 2 pp. Mrs. Doughty
Princeton

22 Sept. 59

My dear:

Welcome to St. Tim's![1] I am writing this on Tuesday afternoon. You are upstairs, I am in my study, unable to leave because I am expecting two telephone calls. Hot out, isn't it?

By the time you read this you will have spent your first night in your new room, or so I imagine, and I am also imagining what your first day will be like. You will be doing and seeing so many new things and meeting so many new faces that you will wonder how so much could be crowded into one day, and you won't have a chance to think about it until you go to bed, the second night. That's the way it will be for a week—you must have had much the same experience at Interlaken and Ralston Creek. Then, almost without realizing it, you will find yourself a member of a new community.

And that's something I would like to talk about. Just as I am going on a voyage,[2] so are you embarking on a journey that is much more important than my quick trip. Mine will be over in a month, and the real purpose of my trip is to get away from my typewriter and my habits of work in order to get a new perspective and come back, I hope, the better for my holiday. But your journey is more important because you are entering into a new phase of your life. Beginning with the day you read this you cease to be a child. Your memories, naturally, will all be memories of childhood, the life you have led so far. But each day will be part of the future that you have been looking forward to all your childhood days. You will be assuming new responsibilities but you will also find that responsibility does not necessarily mean something irksome. Responsibility, and responsibilities, can be a pleasure. The greatest pleasure I have in life is the responsibility of being your father. It is a greater pleasure than my work, which is saying a lot because I love my work. But a man is not born with a love of his work, and he *is* born with the nucleus of a love for his children, and his responsibility toward them, or toward her, in my case, is only the practical side of that love.

In the Catholic Church you are taught to start each day by dedicating everything you do that day toward the greater honor and glory of God. Most Catholics forget that, and none of them remembers it every day, throughout the day. We are all human. But it is possible to copy something from the Catholics that is helpful: as I wrote you two years ago, "to thine own self be true," and if you do that every day you'll be all right. When I stopped drinking I did not say to myself "Quit for a year." I did it a day at a time; get through one day, then repeat it the next. Well, that's more than six years ago. And quite frankly, I still do it day by day. I take those damned exercises every day, not with the thought that I will be taking them for the rest of my life, but with the thought that I will do them today—and let tomorrow's temptation to skip them take care of itself tomorrow.

I hope you will write me while I am abroad. The address is at the bottom of this page so you can tear it off. After the 15th of October write me at home, as letters sent abroad will not reach me after that date.

I wish you happiness in this new phase of your life. You have come through childhood as a fine person, with wonderful prospects for a wonderful future. You have made Sister love you as though you were her own. And I was born loving you.

Dad

Care of Cresset Press,
11, Fitzroy Square—London, W.1, England

1 Wylie had just entered St. Timothy's School in Maryland, which her mother had attended.
2 O'Hara sailed alone to England; Sister, who had flown ahead to Germany, met him in London.

TO: Wylie O'Hara
29 September 1959

TLS, 2 pp. Mrs. Doughty
Princeton

Tuesday p.m.

My dear:

The Outerbridges very thoughtfully, very kindly had me to dinner tonight, otherwise I'd have been alone at home. They also invited Mr. and Mrs. Bramwell.[1] We watched the Braves lose to the Dodgers until five minutes of nine, when I excused myself to telephone you. I wanted to speak to you again after you and Patience[2] had your chat, but I guess she misunderstood me and the connection was broken. So I am writing you to finish up what I wanted to say—and probably will say it a little better here than on the phone.

You and I are really very close, I think. I think we understand each other because we are both sensitive people. I'm sure, for instance, that you understand what I mean when I say that I have misgivings about my trip, somewhat the way you felt when you were getting ready to go to the ranch last June. We are both shy people, and yet are fond of other people. For instance I had a good time with Mr. and Mrs. Outerbridge and Mr. and Mrs. Bramwell tonight because I know them and am relaxed with them. When I get on the ship tomorrow I will not know a soul, and even though there is quite a good chance that I will run into people I know, I am prepared to spend the entire time alone. The Cunard Line has put a typewriter in my room, and I have a book I want to read (The Education of Henry Adams) and a double-crostic to do, so I will be able to occupy myself until I meet Sister in London.

It would have been a lot easier for me just to stay home and not to take this trip. But because it would have been easier is precisely the reason I am going. I love my work, I am happy when I have work to do, but if I sit here in my study in Princeton I am really pampering myself, even though I may justify it by saying I am working. It is a dangerous thing for a writer to do, to bury himself in his work and never stir away from it. I know that is true, because I will confess to you that I am *afraid* to be alone in England, etc. I would not make the trip if I were not going to meet Sister. Now that is proof of the danger of sitting here and burying myself in my work. My life has become you and Sister, and even my friends don't count as much as they should. What remains is my work, with which, as I say, I pamper myself and make excuses for not participating in life.

What I am leading up to is that life is or should be full of doing things you would prefer not to do. The best recent example of that was the ranch experience, which you didn't want to do, but ended up being glad you did it. Believe me, it is easier to learn self-discipline when you are young than when you are older. By self-discipline I mean obeying your parents and your teachers. Yes, that may seem contradictory. You may think of it only as discipline and not self-discipline, but it is *self*-discipline if you follow advice in the proper spirit. It is discipline when you obey because you have no other choice.

Life is tough, Wylie. But you don't have to be tough to enjoy it. However, you do need some toughening, and the best toughening is that which you give yourself. In fact it may be the only kind that has lasting value. It becomes part of you and not something that originated with someone else.

You have only to look at the faces of men and women who have not learned to discipline themselves. Then look at those who have. Whom do you trust? Whom would you count on? Your Grandmother O'Hara is a case in point. She was very strictly brought up in a family who were in comfortable circumstances, able to send her away to boarding school. Soon after that she married my father and she began to have children, eight of them, with all the problems of a large family. Then when my father died and there was practically no money and none of us old enough to make a decent living, she had to struggle somehow to keep a family going, giving up things she had been accustomed to, unable to provide what she wanted to provide. But I never heard her complain, and neither did anyone else. Sometimes I would come home and find her doing household arithmetic, trying to figure out how to pay taxes, grocery bills, etc., but there would be no complaints, although God knows she must have stayed awake many nights wondering and worrying. Now she is over 80, as enthusiastic and loving about you as though you were her first-born, and if you study her face you will see that it is remarkably unlined. There are women, and men, many years younger, who do not have her serenity, and the reason is that they do not have her character. And the character was something she acquired through self-discipline.

Already you have shown me that you have some of the same qualities. Honesty. Kindness. Sweetness. Courage. Understanding. You have all of these to a degree that is extraordinary in a girl your age. There are unlucky girls who grow into womanhood without any of them. You have something else: humility. And it is your humility that keeps you from realizing that you have the other qualities. Humility is a quality that the possessor of it does not enjoy, but that makes her or him easier to live with. Sometimes it is seen as shyness and sometimes as sensitivity. Whatever it appears to be, it is a gracious quality, a warm quality that is particularly attractive when it is accompanied by the five other qualities I mentioned. I'm very glad you have it now, because you are also going to become a handsome woman, and it is as a handsome woman that you will live the greater part of your life, not merely as a pretty teen-ager.

Please do me a favor. Save this letter and read it when you have time to give it some thought. There are things in it that will guide you and that you may overlook in a quick, first reading.

As I told you, we'll be on our way home before you will get my later communications. We sail from England a month from today and will be home on the 3d of November, and I will make plans to go see you. Do write me, all that you want to tell me. Once again the address: Care of Cresset Press; 11 Fitzroy Square; London, W.1; England. But letters mailed after about the middle of October will probably not reach me.

All my love
Dad

¹ Gerald and Kate Bramwell of Princeton. Mrs. Bramwell had been Belle O'Hara's closest friend.
² Daughter of Pat and Sal Outerbridge.

TO: Wylie O'Hara   TLS, 4 pp. Mrs. Doughty
30 September–4 October 1959   Aboard the *Queen Mary*

FIVE LETTERS! Take Your Time.¹

My sweet:

This is going to be an odd letter. Not one, but several. This is my first night aboard the Queen Mary, and I have decided that instead of writing you separate letters, I'll write you something every day while I am on shipboard.

WEDNESDAY. I had no one to see me off unless you count a reporter and a photographer. Blackie drove me up from Princeton, so I didn't have to say a word except "Oh, really? Is that so? My goodness." I don't think Blackie approves of St. Tim's, but his reason is his own: he approves of Quogue, for instance, and Pittsburgh, Pa., because he has driven people there. In 48 miles I am brought up to date on Blackie's family and financial affairs, the latest dope on his tires, the cars that make good taxies, and little bits of gossip about Princeton residents.

The ship sailed at 5 on the dot (scheduled departure, 4.30) but it was a beautiful day and a beautiful sight, Manhattan Island from the Hudson River. I found quite a bit of loot in my stateroom: a handsome book about the Irish from Tracy and Janet; flowers from Mr. and Mrs. Grant; books from Mr. Cerf; hard candy from 21; books and a leather notepad and scrabble set from Sister; telegrams from Mr. Outerbridge and Mr. Freedman. I was very touched. Then when I went to the promenade deck to reserve my deck chair the asst chief steward said, "You'll be having yours on the terrace?" I honestly didn't know what he meant until I saw the twinkle in his eye. I thanked him for his little joke and apologized for my own obtuseness. So I felt a lot better.

There is no one on the ship that I know. I saw a Southampton man

304

and a jerk I used to know slightly when I belonged to the Players Club, but they must have got off before sailing. Or maybe they are in the smaller diningroom or the bar. I hope they stay there. Many Hindus on board. Also a bunch of Catholic bishops. The man who assigned me my table also asked me if I could be the author. My bedroom steward, Mr. Hunt, has exactly one front upper tooth and one front lower one. He is a good steward, though. My room has two portholes, now both open to bring in the breeze although we must be about 350 miles from NY. Hurricane Gracie seems to have missed us; I hope it missed you; the morning weather report had it headed in your direction. But a ship as big as this can ride out any hurricane. They get a worse beating in late winter on the North Atlantic. I am the second of the O'Hara Bros. to sail in this ship. My brother Jimmy got a free ride on it in 1943, when he was in the army. I understand they used to carry 30,000 soldiers on this ship during the war. A little too close for comfort.

I wonder how many different typewriters I have used in 35 years of punching them to make a living. But you want to know something? I have only owned four! And I still have three of the four.

I hope that when you take your first trip to Europe you will go by ship. I have flown across the Pacific but never the Atlantic, and this is the way to go the first time, at least. Only one girl your age that I've seen. She is traveling with her mother, an attractive woman, and I'll bet anything Ma is taking daughter to school in Paris or Switzerland or Florence. Two or three sexpots in their twenties on board. One is French, traveling with husband, and my guess if [sic] they are returning from their wedding trip. The others? They are taking sexpotluck. Enough for tonight. Goodnight, my love.

THURSDAY. You will be glad to hear that Mr. and Mrs. Cow are aboard. That's what it says on the passenger list:

MR. NOEL COW
MRS. COW

I guess that's what the steward meant last night when he said I could have fresh milk all the way over.

One thing about an ulcer: it provides conversation. I now know that the head waiter, or steward, was captured by the Germans in one of the African campaigns and was nearly starved, then when he was liberated he developed an ulcer. People tell me everything, and a lot of it is dull but a lot of it is interesting. You would never guess that a mousy little man like him had gone through so much.

FRIDAY. Today a whale! When I got up this morning I looked out my porthole and about half a mile off the starboard beam a whale was spouting. It is always a little surprising to realize that they really do squirt water up in the air as they do in pictures. It's a lot colder today, and we are definitely in the North Atlantic. One month from tomorrow we'll be back in Princeton. One month ago we were still playing golf in Quogue. The time moves so fast. Today before lunch I went to the purser's cocktail party. He has to give it, and it is rude not to go, so I went and first sat next to a bishop, then was moved and placed next to a bright little old lady, a Mrs. Roebling from Bernardsville. Knows the Archie Alexanders, lives next door to them. Had read Ten North Frederick. Taking her granddaughter to school abroad. I did not get to talk to the girl but Mrs. R. invited me to dine with them Sunday night. Mostly English people at the party, and all very friendly after their first cocktail. Last night I saw North by Northwest. Did you see it? Tonight the movie is The Devil's Disciple. I like N by N but it was overlong. It was written by the man who has written the movie of From the Terrace.[2] I know why this trip seems strange: it is the first time I've been on a ship and on the wagon at the same time. As a passenger, that is. My first trip to Europe, 32 years ago, was not as a passenger. I was a steward, working like hell. I was not seasick but I was afraid I would be, which is almost as bad, especially when we ran into some heavy weather and most of the passengers were unable to look at food. It took us 13 days to get to Germany. In the Queen Mary we leave Wed. afternoon and arrive in Southampton Monday night. Early Tuesday morning we go through customs, then take the train to London and are there at ten-thirty that morning. I imagine you will get this letter in the middle of next week, air mail from England.

I'm sure you will be proud to know that two ladies have flirted quite frankly with your old man. One of them is the French dame; the other, I believe, is English. But the day when I flirt back has long since passed. However, I admit quite frankly that I am pleased when it happens to me. At 54 you better be pleased!

SATURDAY. We're getting there. Tonight is Gala Dinner night. Prizes for funny hats, etc. Tomorrow is the last night for people who leave the ship at Cherbourg. From Cherbourg we go to Southampton. On the way home we make Cherbourg our last stop. I worked yesterday afternoon, did half of a short story, then last night I was so bored with The Devil's Disciple that I went to my stateroom and finished the story, which I will send to the Sat Eve Post. It is a story about a man, his wife, and a younger man, on shipboard.[3] It was fun to write. It was all invention, and all new yesterday. Not bad, either. I still think you might be a writer. You won't really know for a couple of years whether you want to make it a career, but you have thoughts, you observe well, and you express yourself well, in conversation and on paper. In other words, you already have some of the equipment a writer must have. What you lack now is the desire to write, and nothing anybody says can make you write, any more than anything anybody says can make you stop if you have the desire. The most fascinating thing about writing as a career is that you never stop learning. At 54 I am still learning; at 74 I'll still be learning; at 94 I'll still be learning. If I'm writing, that is. The first thing you do is learn the basic rules, then as you get more confidence you decide which rules you want to break. In that respect, of course, it is like a lot of other things. Golf. Tennis. Surgery. Music. Even our old friend Math. You learn the essentials, then you make your own, personal contribution. Hogan in golf, Tilden in tennis, your Uncle Bobby in surgery, Stravinsky in music, Einstein in math, and every important writer right down to your old man. Every time your Uncle Bobby performs one of those marvelous operations on the heart, he brings to it the skill he acquired as a medical student, as a young doctor, and as a mature surgeon—and then because he is a genius (and he is), he can ignore some rules and create his own. Your Grandfather O'Hara was a *great* surgeon, make no mistake about that. There are people alive today who would not be alive had it not been for his skill, and his name is still respected and even revered by those who knew what he did. But he did his work a generation before Bobby, and there are hundreds of techniques they know now that they didn't know then. Every surgeon, every composer, every author adds to the knowledge and techniques of his own profession. Next February, when my new novel[4] comes out, there will be reviews that will comment on how different this book is from all my earlier ones. (Mr. Cerf already likes it better than anything I've ever done.) There will, of course, be the usual panning, but practically nothing that was an innovation in writing, music, or art was accepted right away. Even Debussy, whom we take for granted now, was considered daring and unmusical. One time your Grandfather O'Hara was about to operate on an appendix. When he made the incision on the *left* side the nurses and assistants thought he had lost his mind. But when he completed the incision, that's where the appendix was, and *not* on the right side. What's more, the patient had a sister who also had her appendix on the left side, and my father operated on her the same way! Nobody gave Arthur Godfrey a chance to survive, but after your Uncle Bobby operated on him Godfrey was able to leave the hospital in three weeks, and walking, at that. The next day he was flying an airplane. You see, you have the stuff, on both sides of the family. Don't ever forget that, at St. Tim's or anywhere else. You *are* as good as they come, and you *will be* as good as you make yourself, whether you decide to be a writer or a nurse or an actress or the mother of triplets.

LATER. I won! I won $50 in the Hat Pool. No skill, all luck. Last night I paid $5 to enter the Hat Pool, which I shall explain to you. Every day the captain sends down word on how many miles we did in the previous 24 hours, such as 651, 662, 663, or whatever. You pay $5 and that entitles you to a number from 1 to o (10). Numbers 1 2 3 4 5 6 7 8 9 o are placed in a hat and you are given a number. Mine was 8, and the ship then traveled 658 miles, so I won the pool. Naturally I entered again for tomorrow. The $50 will cover my tips to my bedroom and diningroom stewards, in addition to the $5 you're expected to give the smoking-room steward when you win the pool. Pure, unadulterated luck, and the first time in my life. I've won at horse racing, bridge, crap-shooting, 21, poker, backgammon and on prize fights and elections, but never anything that I bought a chance for.

SUNDAY. The last full day at sea. We stop at Cherbourg at noon tomorrow, and tomorrow midnight, Southampton. Helter-skelter has begun for the people who are going to France. Final packing, etc. Tips to the stewards. Preparations to go ashore. It is always strange to be considered an alien, a foreigner. I have gone to Europe in French, Italian, and English ships (and American) and it always gives me a slight jolt to be reminded that I have to go through immigration inspectors. Of course all that it consists of is filling out cards and showing your passport, but there it is. Today I start using English money. We are actually on London time now (Sister, in Germany, is an hour ahead.). Tomorrow, in Cherbourg, the people getting off will be on Continental time, while we remain on London time. I have been studying the map of London to reacquaint myself with the streets and other locations, and I've been studying how much pounds and shillings are worth in our money.

Tomorrow I fill out a customs declaration for the British customs. That will be easy: I just write "nothing to declare" and sign my name. Of course I am going to have to explain one piece of luggage that is filled with feminine attire. It belongs to Sister. Parenthetically, I wonder if Mrs. Bramwell retrieved Sister's (really Joan's) fur coat from the Pennsylvania Railroad.

At Southampton there will be a special train to London for Queen Mary passengers. It arrives at Waterloo Station, then I take a taxi to the Savoy Hotel. I have a bunch of small things to do, then Sister arrives the next day, Wednesday, by air. By that time I will have transacted my business. For the next few days it will be shopping, seeing people, going to the theater. I know one thing I want to get you, which I will order on Tuesday so it will be ready before we come back to London. It is something I was often tempted to buy you in NY but I was determined to wait till I visited London. I have no idea what to get anyone else except Mr. Outerbridge, who told me what he wanted and offered to pay for it, or them: an Ocean Cruising Club tie, and a Royal Ocean Racing Club tie.

What else do I want to do in London? Go to Scotland Yard, attend a court of law, take a couple of bus rides, see some racing and football (wholly unlike ours). I am probably going on TV, but not till I return to London from Dublin, and my publisher is having a dinner party sometime, although the last two are not, strictly speaking, among the things I *want* to do. I have been reading a book on Ireland, and I am looking forward to some sightseeing there, and racing, and the theater, and a game called hurling, which is Irish and very rough, sort of like lacrosse. No, I am not going to play it, just watch it.

I'm afraid this adds up to a pretty dull letter. I've enjoyed writing it because it is vaguely like chatting with you, although only a substitute. I am going to close now so that this gets into the U.S. air mail sack and will be put ashore when we land. It has been an extremely quiet, restful trip, with no excitement except my winning the Hat Pool. I hope you realize by this time that there are other girls at St. Tim's who felt exactly as you did, but I couldn't tell you that on Tuesday night. It is something you have to find out for yourself. I went through it, your mother went through it. Frankly, if you had fallen in love with boarding school in your first week (and some do) it would have meant that you were too glad to be away from home. I will come and see you, if you still want me to, the first week I am home. Meanwhile, bear this in mind: you are smarter about people than most girls your age. If you put that gift to some use, along with your gift for friendship, the world is yours.

All my love,
Dad

¹ Holograph note.
² Ernest Lehman.
³ Possibly "Our Friend the Sea," which did not appear in the *Post* until August 1963.
⁴ *Ourselves to Know.*

TO: Wylie O'Hara   ALS, 6 pp. Mrs. Doughty
                                    Letterhead of North British
                                    Hotel, Edinburgh

Saturday 10 Oct. [1959]

My dear—

The train was called "the Queen of Scots" and it departed from Kings Cross station, so there was no doubt about it: I was traveling abroad.

Whenever I do, on a train, I can't help thinking that the stations are part of a movie set and that all the people are really actors. I also think the freight trains, which are known in Britain as "goods" trains, are toys. They are much smaller than our freight cars, possibly because British and European tracks are not made of as heavy iron as ours, and partly because their railroads are often very curvy and cannot accommodate long cars. Another reason they seem toy-like is that when I was a boy, most trains, toy trains, were imported from England and Germany, and they naturally copied English and European trains, not American. Even when "Union Pacific" was painted on them!

Sister and I had seats in the Pullman "Penelope,": the next was "Cynthia." Big chairs, one on each side of a table, on which our lunch and tea were served. The decor was old-fashioned, beautiful wood paneling. The overhead lights looked like that torch cigarette lighter on the backgammon table at home. The food—not so good.

We now switch to ball-point. London was very pleasant. We saw three plays; one a musical, one a comedy, the other a very serious one which did not come off. I renewed acquaintance with my old friend John Hayward, who is helplessly and hopelessly crippled but a lovely man, with great humor and friendliness as well as a high literary reputation. We had lunch with him and my London publisher, Dennis Cohen, and are seeing him again when we go back to London. We went to a party on Thursday night, which was Election Night in Britain, a very exciting election and important to Americans because MacMillan, the Conservative, is pro-American (his mother was born in Indiana), and the Labor Party includes a lot of men who are anti-American. MacMillan won decisively, more so than had been hoped. Going from place to place in a taxi was like New Year's Eve, especially in Trafalgar Square, with thousands of people, and the lights making it as bright as day.

I had a press conference on Wednesday. I hate them, but except for one jerk it was not too bad. Tomorrow the London papers will review From the Terrace . . . I shall be safely remote here in E., 400 miles from it all. Your old man is pretty well known over here and those who are on my side are very much so. The advance sale of F. the T. is 50% greater than any book I've published here, but I know nothing about the critical reception. Neither do my publishers.

Spoke to John Wylie[1] on the telephone. He is coming to London two weeks from tomorrow to spend the day with us. I have a letter to the head of Scotland Yard, and that seems like a good way to entertain him. He didn't say very much about school, but I'll know more later. We go to Dublin next Thursday or Friday, spend a week there; back to London, then embark for home. I can't tell you anything about Edinburgh, since we arrived only two hours ago, in the dark. Actually I haven't told you much about London, but I will from time to time. Probably talking about it for the next five years, if anyone will listen. For instance, as we left London today it began to rain heavily for the first time since May. The worst dry spell in 200 years, and you could see the effects from the train. But the people generally are prosperous and happy. It's a damned sight better than the shower of bombs of 15 years ago.

All my love
Dad

[1] O'Hara's nephew.

18 Oct. [1959]
Sunday a.m.

Wylio—

A very pleasant evening at Geraldine Fitzgerald's. Her mother was there; her sister, who saw you when you were a baby, at 86th Street; her son Michael Lindsay-Hogg (by her first marriage); her friends, who included a Mr. Hilton Edwards, a Dublin theatrical producer; a couple named Birkin, who are having us to tea tomorrow; a Mrs. Guinness, who is a painter; Sir Robert and Lady Leacock; and two others whose names I did not get.

I talked to Lady Leacock partly about writing, partly about Roosevelt and other politicians. Her husband, Sir Robert, was head of the Commandoes during War II. Very nice man. Most interesting to you would be Michael, who is now about 19 or 20 and remembers Caesar, the wirehair. He is quite handsome, fierce-looking but not fierce. He was at Oxford last year but got behind in Latin and Anglo-Saxon, so is now cramming to get back in. He wants to be a writer *or* to get into the TV production, so I don't think he will be a writer. Michael's father, The Hon. Eddie Lindsay-Hogg, is married again and lives here, so I hope to see him. We were friends years ago. He is the son of an earl, a former gentleman jockey, one of the Englishmen who came to Ireland for a visit, married, and made Ireland their home.

We took a drive in the rain yesterday, along the seacoast, then inland to a place called Powerscourt, a vast estate with a big stone manor house, which was used as the scene of one of Laurence Olivier's movies. We got up in the Wicklow mountains for the view, which was magnificent even in the rain. Today, as I write, I can see some of those mountains. This afternoon we are calling on some Irish friends of Geraldine's whose names I don't know but whom she chose because they are Irish and have a house she wants us to see.

Later—same day

Their name was Lord and Lady Glenavy, their place is called Rockbrook, and they have a wonderful old house with a view of Dublin and Dublin Bay and the Irish Sea. The house is full of nicknacks and souveniers and Lady Glenavy's own paintings. Lord Glenavy started out by saying he had never heard of me, much to the embarrassment of his wife and Geraldine; but for some reason his rudeness did not bother me and he ended by telling me about his daughter, who was killed in London during an air raid. . . .[1] Lady Glenavy (GLENAVY) was charming, well read, good talker, wanted to go on talking. They were a perfect picture of the fading aristocracy, with the good and the bad, the sad and the pleasant in proper mixture. Their kind is dying out, but what is to take its place? Your generation will decide.

Love
Dad

¹ Thirty-six words omitted by the editor.

TO: Wylie O'Hara

ALS, 4 pp. Mrs. Doughty
Letterhead of Shelbourne
Hotel, Dublin

Friday 23 Oct. [1959]

Wylie-o—

In Edinburgh the men are generally better looking than the girls. In Dublin there are more pretty girls than handsome men. I have seen several girls who looked for a moment like you, which is perfectly natural, considering that you are about 50% Irish (not quite 50%; on my side there is some Dutch and English). In Dublin the men have more style —dash—whatever you want to call it—than the men in Scotland. Here the men dress more carefully; slacks and tweed jackets. In Edinburgh, of course, you see men in kilts, and I have not seen one here, although in some parts of Ireland they do wear them. The Irish girls have good coloring; some like yours, dark hair and very white skin. Your Aunt Kathleen would be taken for a native here, as she has the same coloring as you. But you also see a great many fiery red heads of both sexes, which are not so common in Scotland.

This is more a country of individuals. The grooms at the Aly Khan's farm; the men driving the big brewery wagons of the Guinness brewery; the very poor in the Dublin slums—they all, and people in their class, give the impression that they are not really working steady, but are only helping out temporarily. They wear tweed caps at a jaunty angle, cigarettes dangle from their lips, and they gaze about as if they were more concerned with other things than with this silly task, whatever it is. The Scots are not that way, and neither are the English—which may explain why so many Irish families stay poor for generation after generation . . .

A farewell party for us this afternoon, with some new faces. A youngish couple named Lord and Lady de Frehn (DE FREHN; I know how to spell it because it is also an old Pottsville name). I told her where you were in school and she said, "Oh do they allow her to hunt? Is she keen for horses? That's hunting country, Maryland." Tomorrow—actually, today as it is past midnight, we leave Ireland and will be back again in London.

Love
Dad

TO: Wylie O'Hara

ALS, 4 pp. Mrs. Doughty
Letterhead of Savoy Hotel,
London

Saturday—24 Oct. [1959]

Dearest Wylie—

I would like this hotel if only for two reasons: when I arrived here the first time, and when I arrived here today, each time there was a wonderful letter from you. I can't begin to tell you how pleased I am with you, and maybe I'd better not try. But I wonder if you, with your keen perception, might not have guessed that coming over on the Queen Mary it was a question of who was homesicker, you or I. The letter that greeted me here then was reassuring: the letter today was that and more. I like the motto of St. Tim's: "Truth without fear" seems to me to apply to you and is another way of saying what I have so often said to you: "To thine own self be true." It also goes well with the single word for the O'Hara coat of arms: "Try." You are now on your way, and I repeat: the world is yours, the world you want to live in, whatever it may be. I shall now step down from the pulpit, but with an admiring glance at my daughter of whom I am so proud.

I enclose a contract for an ad in *The Steward*.[1] The Linebrook Press is the name of the tiny publishing venture I have been contemplating. I am going to take some of the money from the movie sales of Butterfield 8, A Rage to Live, and From the Terrace, and use it to establish a publishing firm which will publish books that ought to be published but that have little or no chance of commercial success. I have already conferred with Mr. Cottier and when I get home will do so with Mr. Lee, to ask them to be on the lookout for authors whom I will publish. Mr. Lee is one of the world's great art historians, and Mr. Cottier of course has the inside among university people. So "The Steward" will print my first ad. I expect to lose money on this venture, but I may do some good.

I am glad you like Nancy Ryerson. An uncle or maybe a cousin of hers lived in Princeton, now lives in Boston. He and his wife used to have dinner with your mother and me and the Outerbridges and the Holcombs when we used to go to the Nassau Club on Thursday nights, long ago. Confidentially I liked Joe Ryerson, but I didn't go overboard for his wife.

Sorry your trip to Gettysburg wasn't much. Your great-grandfather's name is on the Pennsylvania monument. He was Michael O'Hara, of the Union cavalry, and from all accounts quite a man, a la the late Errol Flynn (a friend of mine, by the way). I must get this off so you can give the contract to Miss Johannsen. Twelve letters in one day! Jesus!

Love
Dad

¹ St. Timothy's School yearbook.

TO: Wylie O'Hara

TLS, 2 pp. with holograph postscript. Mrs. Doughty Princeton

Tuesday 17 Nov [1959]

My dear:

I have not yet received your report from St. Tim's, so I am unable to comment on it; but your own report on yourself prepares me for a bad one from school.

There are two things that I want to comment on. In your letter you say, speaking about the loss of your retainer, that you hoped that we wouldn't notice you did not have it. Never do that again. We have a pretty frank, pretty candid relationship. Don't spoil it. Don't "hope" that we won't notice things. We won't notice things. We rely on you. I want you to feel and go on feeling that when you lose something, or have bad marks, or have any unpleasant news, you can tell us. If you don't tell us, if you keep it to yourself, you only make it worse for yourself when it has to come out. Meanwhile you have been worrying about it in secret. You worry not only about the thing itself, but also about how we are going to take it.

Now in this case if you had told us about the retainer when we were there, we could have made immediate plans for its replacement, instead of losing two weeks or more. You know this yourself.

The other thing concerns how you feel about —— ——. There will always be a villain. We always have villains, in school life, social life, business life. I have them; in my life the villains are the hostile critics, those who are against what I write even before I write it. There is nothing I can do about them. I can't shoot them. If I shoot one, there'll be another. The only thing I can do about them is to try to minimize their effect on me, which I do by thinking of the good critics who respect and admire my writing, and try to forget what the others say. I would

314

have quit twenty-five years ago if I had believed some of the critics; but the amusing thing is that as the years go by, some of those same critics now like to think that they admired APPOINTMENT IN SAMARRA when it came out. You have no idea what a beating I took from Atkinson of the Times when PAL JOEY first appeared. But when it was revived 11 years later he voted for it for the Critics Circle Award as the best musical of the year. In other words, the villain changed; Pal Joey didn't; it was the same show.

But the danger a villain can be, the harm he can do, is the harm that we do ourselves by brooding over his attacks. You get so that you blame the villain when your own work is at fault. In your case, you must concentrate on the people whom you like and who like you. Furthermore, you must remember that in your studies it is a matter of the subject and you. It is you and Math, it is you and History, it is you and Current Events. Forget the personality of the teacher, put the teacher out of your mind. I realize that that is asking the impossible, but I suggest you try it.

I also urge you to work harder on the things that you like and the things you do well. I have never known it to fail that when you are excelling in one or two things, the hard things are made less difficult. Success begets success. I have a short story in this week's Saturday Evening Post.[1] You may remember when I wrote it, last spring. I was then working on my new novel[2] and it was going well. Because it was going well, I was able to write the short story in a few hours, although the novel and the short story were, you might say, two different subjects.

You are in school to learn, this is the learning period of your life, and learning is never all easy. If it were, it would not really be learning, would it? But some things are easier to learn than others, and if you work harder on the easy things *than you have to*, I repeat, the difficult things will be less difficult.

Sister is in New York, saying goodbye to her brother Courty, who leaves for Europe this week, so I don't know what the procedure is about your retainer.

I saw The Doll's House too. (A Doll's House, actually.) Ibsen wrote that play in 1879, eighty years ago! And it's just as true to life now as it was when it first appeared. The woman who would not grow up, and who thereby got herself and others into trouble. That's why you found her unattractive when she was being coy with her husband. As you grow older you will find that there are quite a few girls who resemble Nora, who won't grow up, who won't face facts, who try to get by on tricks. And she got a husband who was just as bad.

Love
Dad

I'm glad you spoke frankly to your Math teacher. When you don't understand, say so. They will know you're trying.

D.

[1] "That First Husband," 21 November 1959.
[2] *Ourselves to Know* (1960).

TO: *Holiday*, XXVI (December 1959), 4

The true story about my shillelagh in *Costello's: The Wayward Saloon* (October HOLIDAY) is this: on a St. Patrick's night years ago I went to Costello's alone, carrying my walking stick. Presently out of the back room came Ernest Hemingway, John Steinbeck and John Hersey, and Mrs. Steinbeck and Mrs. Hersey, if I remember correctly. They stopped to say hello to me and Hemingway commented that my walking stick was not a real blackthorn. He bet me fifty dollars he could break it over his head. I didn't want him to try it, because I understand Ernest has a silver plate in his skull, but he went ahead and broke it.[1] When I went home that night I sent him a check for fifty dollars, which he promptly returned. But I again sent it to him. I pay my bets. This time he kept the check but said he would buy me a real blackthorn and send it to me. That was in 1946, I believe, and I have yet to receive Hemingway's blackthorn. However, John Steinbeck brought one back from Ireland and gave it to me on my birthday, January 31, to make up for Hemingway's forgetfulness. That was in 1956, or ten years after the main incident, but I consider that Steinbeck got Hemingway off the hook.

JOHN O'HARA
Princeton, N.J.

[1] Hemingway had no such silver plate.

TO: Wylie O'Hara   TLS, 2 pp. Mrs. Doughty
3 December 1959   Princeton

Thursday

My idiosyncratic dear:

I am the secretary of the O'Hara treasury, so it devolves upon me to handle the matter of your finances, although naturally Sister and I discuss the matter.

At home your allowance was $12 a month, which is lessened by $4 a month at St. Tim's. We feel, however, that you are entitled to the difference. That is, we believe that you should live within the $2 a week allowance at St. Tim's, because that is the democratic thing to do. There are plenty of girls at St. Tim's whose families have much, much more money than I have, and there are some whose families have a great deal less. It is therefore just and fair to have a uniform allowance for all the girls, and I'm sure you really believe that. On the other hand, as I said before, you are entitled to the allowance you would have got here. The question is, when to give it to you?

Well, Christmas is the logical time, because it is Christmas, and because it does not interfere with the program that St. Tim's has decided for all the girls. I naturally plan to stake you to things at Christmas that would not be charged against your allowance. I also plan to give you money as one of your Christmas presents.

Neither Sister nor I is exactly famous for stinginess. If I were to tell you how much money I have earned, and spent, in the past 25 years, you would be astounded (so am I, when I think about it). But I have to restrain Sister and myself from casual spending. It is much easier to spend than to save; it is more fun, and for us it is the natural thing to do. But if someone doesn't take a firm stand, no one will, so I elect myself to be the one who takes the firm stand, because that is traditionally the father's duty.

So I am sending you herewith $7 which is what I happen to have in my money clip, and some stamps I happen to have on my desk. You did not say how much you have borrowed or how much you need, so I am sending what is in my pocket in the hope that it will get you off the hook at least temporarily. (It also means I owe you some money from the money that I withhold from your regular allowance.) When you get home we will have to have a conference about money. But I'm sure you realize that I am not going to oppose the school rule of $2 a week. The basis of our discussion will be to decide what should be done about the $4 a month difference between your regular $12 a month and the $8 at St. Tim's. Sister has a good idea, which is to start a Christmas fund for you, so that every year you will have that waiting for you when you come home for the holidays. A dollar a week, for instance, means that your Christmas fund will have $50 in it when you come home, which is quite a sum for a 15-year-old girl, which you will be next Christmas, and also, considering that I pay your clothes and other such bills. Incidentally, you already get a lot more than I got in my last year in prep school—one buck a week. If I hadn't been a pretty good bridge player I couldn't have paid for cigarettes, movies, etc. And when I *lost* at bridge. . . . . . . !

My trip to Saratoga was very pleasant.[1] At least my stay there was. Saratoga is not far from Altamont, so when I tell you that my train took seven hours to get to NY, you will understand that we had quite

317

a delay. Engine trouble. But the dinner was a great success. Frank Sullivan has always written nicely about his home town, and the towns-folk used his new book, A Moose in the Hoose, as the excuse for giving him a dinner. It started out to be a luncheon for 25 people; it ended up as a dinner with 260 present and many turned away for lack of room. Very sentimental occasion, and Frank was nervous, but they really gave him a good time. His high school class, class of 1910, were present; 35 out of 50 are still living, and an unusual thing: seven of his high school classmates are doctors. The women among his classmates looked nice, solid, small-town American. Frank himself reminded me that it was like my little Book, A Family Party, which actually I never thought of. The other "famous celebrity" present besides your old man was Russel Crouse, co-author of A Sound of Music, Life with Father, etc., and he made a nice speech. Mine was brief, humorous, slightly senti-mental, and painless. The best thing about the trip for me was Frank's being touched by my making the trip. Well, he is a dear, lovable friend. Asked all about you, hasn't seen you since you were four years old, but one year he put you in his annual Christmas greeting in The New Yorker, a copy of which I still have somewhere. It was your second appearance in print; your first was in Time, Milestones, when you were born.

Had my check-up with Dr. Bailey, and you will be glad to know I am in pretty good shape physically. Bought Sister her Christmas present, had lunch at 21, and was awfully glad to get home after two nights away.

Frank reminded me that you were almost a resident of Saratoga. When you were two years old we started looking for a place to live, away from NY, and went up to Saratoga for a look. Then we learned that Saratoga is not a good place for people with asthma, so we gave it up, finally settling for Princeton, and I am glad we did, and I imagine you are too.

Love,
Dad

¹ O'Hara spoke at a dinner honoring Frank Sullivan on 1 December.

TO: Wylie O'Hara   TLS, 2 pp. Mrs. Doughty
Winter 1959–60   Princeton

Saturday

My Dear:

I am so *pleased* with your letter to me that I am replying right away. It is one of the best I ever got from you (or anyone else).

My suggestion that you, and maybe Nancy too, might call an informal meeting of your class was of course subject to your decision, based on your knowledge of your position. In such matters I would always defer to your judgment, which is sound because it is honest.

Your estimate of yourself is awfully good and awfully mature—and modest. But I would like to add one observation of my own: you say you are regarded in some cases as a comic; never underestimate the power of a comic! People do not laugh with someone they dislike. When I was a young man (and not too young, too) I learned that girls liked two things about me: one, I was a good dancer; two, I made them laugh. There were boys who were richer than I, and better looking than I. But I would walk away with their girls. I have actually been written up in columns as "the best dancer among the literati". But what was not written up was the fact that I could make a girl laugh. Ask Sister. Before we were married she once said to me, "I never knew you had this mad sense of humor," although I had known her for 25 years. Anyway, I repeat: don't underestimate humor, on any level. For instance, Churchill is a humorous man, and Hitler and Stalin were completely devoid of it.

As to your hope that I am not disappointed in you, I know the human race. It is divided into two major classes: people of good will, and people lacking in good will, People of good will do not always do the right thing, because they are human, and not divine. But people of good will have a better score than the others. They do more good things than bad things. I may disapprove of an action of yours, but your over-all score is good.

Now we come to something that pleased me enormously, something you achieved unintentionally, or not deliberately. I refer to the *writing* in your letter. Wylie O'Hara, you are a much better writer at 14½ than I was at your age. You express yourself lucidly, simply, and at the same time maturely. When you sit down to write, you know what you want to say, and you say it in plain, adult language. In the same mail with your letter I got a letter from a man in—believe it or not—Baltimore, who wants to be my "protege". He is 35 years old, told me all about himself—and told me a great deal more than he intended to. He says he has written two unpublished novels. I thought as I read his letter, "My daughter writes better than you do and she is less than half your age." And it's true. You have the instinct, the writing instinct. It remains for you to decide whether you want to make writing your avocation or your career, and it is a decision you won't have to make for another five years. But you have the basic equipment: the talent, and the honesty. (The man who wants to be my "protege" isn't even honest with himself; I could read that between the lines.) And even though you may not decide to become a writer, the ability to express yourself clearly and concisely is a gift of the gods that you can put to other uses.

I am delighted with the inside info on the Math exam. All in all, you have given me a hell of a good weekend. Thank you.

Love
Dad

TO: John K. Hutchens   TL, 2 pp. (not mailed). PSt.
                                                              Princeton

                                                              12 Jan 60

Dear John:

I am glad, but not a bit surprised, that you gave Errol Flynn a break.[1] I knew Flynn pretty well. He was the kind of guy who would see me in 21 and get up from his table to come over and shake hands with me. That, I need not tell you, is not Hollywood protocol, and only one other big star also always did it—Humphrey Bogart. Wrong. Spencer Tracy and Gary Cooper do, too.

Flynn introduced himself to me in 1936, at a tennis club of which he and I were members, and where, incidentally, he took on people like Frank Shields and Sidney Wood and Gilbert Roland and Aidan Roark, sometimes beat them, sometimes lost, but always gave them a game. I was in the bar and he came over and said, "I'm Errol Flynn, and I want to tell you how much I admire your stuff." Then he said he didn't think I'd approve of him, because he knew I was not on the Franco side in the Spanish troubles, but he hoped we would be friends in spite of political differences. Well, we were.

When FROM THE TERRACE was bought by 20th Century–Fox I wrote them and told them I would like them to give Flynn a test for the Alfred Eaton part. They amazed me by saying it was a good idea. But nothing came of it; I don't know how hard Fox tried to get him, but he was hard to find, dodging processes and popping up all over the place, and very much on the sauce. I wish they had got him. It might have made a difference in his life, and entre nous, he would have been a happier choice than the man they finally settled for.[2]

The New York Post kind of hardbrain that scorns Flynn is not for me. Let me put it another way: I despise them. No one, least of all Flynn himself, tries to make a Schweitzer image of Flynn. The thing that baffles and infuriates the hardbrain is charm, which they hate and fear because among them it is non-existent and because it eludes their analyses. The hardbrain's answer to charm is the sicknik, the Oscar Levant, Mort Sahl et al. kind of non-conformism that is conformism at its worst. I remember watching Flynn on the Paar show after he had been with Castro. He came in carrying a considerable load, no tie, old clothes, and was introduced to Genevieve. He bowed just right, tossed her a few words in French, and for three minutes the Paar show was a drawing-room, made so by one man's charm. A hundred generations of Levants and Sahls and Bermans[3] couldn't achieve that, and it's what they finally envy the most. The unattainable. Don't think I am unaware that the hardbrain applies the same standards of judgment to characters in my novels. And by the way, I'm sure the hardbrain would not approve of your remarks about Elizabeth Bowen. I will match you in courage: I think women just can't write. I reread A Lost Lady last year, and now I am almost afraid to reread Edith Wharton.

I am tempted to hold this letter for a while, since you will shortly be getting my new novel,[4] but what the hell? I don't know what you won't like about it, but I am pretty sure I know what you *will* like.

[1] Hutchens reviewed Errol Flynn's autobiography, *My Wicked, Wicked Ways,* on 12 January.
[2] Gary Cooper.
[3] Comedian Shelley Berman.
[4] Hutchens did not review *Ourselves to Know,* which was published 27 February 1960.

TO: Charles Poore   TLS, 2 pp. PSt.
                                                     Princeton

                                                     28 Jan 60
Dear Hamlet:
    While you have been sitting in the hospital, contemplating your spleen, Mr. J. J. DuBois, administrative assistant, and other fans of Oswald Brian Donn Byrne[1] have been busy busy busy, as the enclosed literature proves. Unfortunately I did not save the first invitation, which showed that Lowell Thomas, Senior *and* Junior; O. Roy Chalk, who is going to buy the subway or the bus system or maybe the roller coaster at Coney Island; Sam Pryor, who has already bought Gene Tunney; Jim Farley, who sold Tunney to Pryor; the Mr. Crown who owns the Empire State Building, and Herbert Hoover, who can stick his tongue out at the Empire State Building from his suite in the Waldorf Towers—had got together with some other esoteric executives and formed the Marco Polo Club. Almost the first thing they did was to invite me to join, or at least so I was assured. I trembled with excitement at the thought of getting together with all these fellows and joining them in a hymn of hate to The Links, the Union Club, the Racquet Club and the modest but offensive little Brook.[2] But today the grunt arrived, and I'm afraid I have no way of deducting the $250 initiation fee, or even the $125 for nonresidents, or the $50 annual bite for Internationals. My knowledge of mythology is so sketchy that I do not recognize the Club symbol, a sort of leonine Monty Woolley,[3] but I'll bet the Countess Mara[4] whips

up a keen $15 necktie, and I'll be sorry I didn't scrape together the initia-
tion fee. And I'll never be able to say, when somebody asks for my
credentials: "Sir, I'm a 10-goal man at the Marco Polo Club." Still, there
is going to be some confusion: Winston Guest owns the Westbury, which
has a Polo Bar . . . Chaos in Manhattan!

You may keep the literature. I suggest you file it with your copy of
Mr. Cleveland Amory's[5] Celebrity Social Register, or whatever the damn
thing is called.[6] See you soon.

John

[1] Author of *Messer Marco Polo* (1921).
[2] Exclusive New York men's club.
[3] Bearded Hollywood actor.
[4] New York haberdasher.
[5] Writer and social commentator.
[6] *Celebrity Register;* later *International Celebrity Register.*

TO: Charles Poore   TLS, 1 p. PSt.
February 1960   "Linebrook" letterhead

Saturday

Dear Chas.:

I am trying to let you alone during this getting-to-be-annual, delicate,
critic-author period, when you are considering or are about to consider
one of my books. But I must really protest your giving me credit for a
bon mot that I *wish* I'd said originally but can only repeat—with credit
where it's due.

You remember Mr. Benchley's "out of these wet clothes and into a
dry Martini"? I once told him it was an inspired, beautifully funny
remark. "Yes," he said, "and I didn't say it. I wish I had, and I don't
even know who did."

Hippic epic is a classic, is classical, and has class, and it is yours. Please
don't tempt me to steal it. If you leave your neckties in my drawer,
sooner or later I'll wear them.

Changing the subject, have you been reading Behrman's pieces on
Beerbohm?[1] I have been writing you a long letter about them, but I
have put off mailing it. My theme is that Behrman literally bored Beerbohm to death. More later.

Four, the right four, is the right number for a successful dinner party.[2]

As ever
John

[1] S. N. Behrman's profile of Max Beerbohm appeared in *The New Yorker* (February–
March 1960).
[2] Last four words in holograph.

TL, 2 pp. (not mailed). PSt.
                                                      Princeton
                                                    27 Feb 60
Dear Chas.:

I have just read your review of OURSELVES TO KNOW and it started me trying to remember a drama critic—I seem to recall it was John Anderson, but I'm far from sure—who was annoyed at the Shuberts[1] or somebody, and wanted to write a review of a play he liked without giving the Shuberts anything to quote. I must say you have made it tough for the advertising department of Random House, but then so do I, so I cannot chide you for that, when I didn't even have a new picture taken for this book.

I am, of course, disappointed in your review, because there are things about OURSELVES TO KNOW that I expected as well as hoped yourself to know. You came close to discussing one of the things when you spoke of "the novelist's right to omniscience." It is a right, no doubt, but it is an option I don't pick up without justifying my action. The device I use in OTK, which bothers so many critics, is the best way I knew to tell a lot of things that happened before my time. If you ever read this book again you will realize that I played entirely fair, that things that happened a hundred and more years ago could have been passed down in conversations between Moses and Robert and then to Gerald. In relating them I did not exercise my right to omniscience but only my ability to present them without merely stating them. I was acquainted with two men who served in the Mexican War; I go back that far in human contacts, even though I didn't talk with them about that war. I had a dear friend named Bill Irving, who lived in Lykens, Pa., my mother's home town, who was a Civil War veteran. In spite of the great disparity in our ages, whenever he came to Pottsville for the annual G.A.R. Encampment, he would call me up. And I spent many hours sitting on a bench with him—he smelled very strong of whiskey and cigars —watching the Lykens people go by and laughing and talking. I loved that old guy, and I loved that little old town, and as I got older it was not hard for me to unpeel the crusts of the decades going back to 1863. It is not the same thing as trying to reconstruct the Continentals in their ragged regimentals, although that would be one of the rights of the novelist. But the unorthodox construction I employ in OTK had not only to justify recollections of an ancient time, but also to justify the kind of probing into Millhouser's mind that was essential to the presentation of this character. Nothing annoys you more than passages in which thoughts and conversations are stated that the author could not possibly have known about, but in this case the narrator, Higgins, had every reason to know and was encouraged to inquire. I have noticed in the past year that you frequently object to the use of the flashback, but unless an author tells his story straightforwardly from very beginning to very ending, the flashback is unavoidable for exposition, among other things. And some stories should not be told as "John was born . . . John died," with a whole novel in between.

As to detail, you qualify your beef by bringing up its effectiveness, which almost but not quite makes it impossible for the author to rebut. You say, "It wasn't effective," and the author is supposed to shut up. Well, I won't. Detail and dialog furnish or should furnish the critic with the handiest clues as to the author's study and understanding of his characters. To me one of the most irritating elements in novels and plays is the sore-thumb anachronism, the Norfolk suit in 1928, the soldier-boy of 1918 saying "You can say *that* again." How many readers know that those things are wrong? Not many; but they make me distrust everything else about the play or the novel. You may say that I fail to answer the charge of excessiveness, but I will let you in on a novelist's secret: a big block of type which contains a lot of detail is restful. The reader who is not going to have to write about the thing he is reading sees a lot of nouns and relaxes, but he remembers. I have had two laymen's comments—a man and a woman—on the same detail, a crate of pigeons, and these readers said substantially the same thing, that the crate of pigeons gives you the whole picture. Well, it doesn't; but at the end of a block of detail it has that effect. A novelist who works as hard as I do to make the work look easy must play a lot of legitimate tricks on the unknown reader. One of the reasons I get such casual critical consideration is that I do make it look easy. Fadiman, for one, usually speaks of my "readability" as if it were something I should unlearn. The curious thing so far (the book has really been out about a month; the booksellers jumped the deadline by that much) is that not one, not one layman has complained of the technique I used in OTK.

By a coincidence, you and Johnny Chamberlain (tomorrow's Trib) are somehow reminded of Dostoevski, which is complimentary and intended to be. But this is not the first time, and I wonder what would happen to D. if he were to come out now as a brand-new novelist. I think I know my place in Am. Lit., as of five or ten years after I cool, but I would love to be able to enjoy some of it now, while I am alive. Now, especially, the author who writes for posterity is taking an awfully big chance. He always did.

FROM THE TERRACE is a better novel than OURSELVES TO KNOW, but it is more obviously so and easier to say so. But OTK is a part of what FTT is a part of, that APPOINTMENT IN SAMARRA was a part of and all the rest of my Pennsylvania protectorate.

Oh, what the hell? I wanted you to like this book more than you did, and in saying so I have given you a letter which you can enter in evidence on the charge of prolixity.

As ever

¹ Producers and theater owners.

TO: William Hogan¹   TLS, 2 pp. Hogan
                                             Princeton

                                             10 March 60

Dear Mr. Hogan:

Bennett Cerf telephoned me this morning to read your review of OURSELVES TO KNOW, and then an hour later from one of your readers came a clipping. Thank you for your personal nomination for the Pulitzer prize, but that's as far as it will get: I accept *your* nomination, and I won't get the committee's. I have been up for it four times. Your guess is as good as mine why I didn't get it. The nominations were for A RAGE TO LIVE, THE FARMERS HOTEL, TEN NORTH FREDERICK, and FROM THE TERRACE. APPOINTMENT IN SAMARRA was not considered. The committee gave itself an out in the case of THE FARMERS HOTEL because the word fuck was in the book. No kidding. I just found out about three months ago that the member of the committee who held out against FROM THE TERRACE was the person who reviewed the book for the Sunday N.Y. Times.²

As Cerf said this morning, "You won't get it, because there are people who just can't stand you."

I would like to get it, and I would accept it, because I really don't feel free to make certain comments on the Pulitzer Prize until I have been given it. I never got the O. Henry prize for a short story, either, and that failure restricts my comments on it. I am all for prizes, but what I have to say about them has less force than if I'd garnered them all. Did you know that Nabokov turned down membership in the National Institute of Arts and Letters? I voted for him, and I think he should have accepted membership, however late, in the same spirit that I accepted it after having been up for more than twenty years. When I was finally elected, I had more members seconding me than any other candidate in the history of the Institute. I know that, because I saw the list, which incidentally was fascinating for those who seconded me and those who did not. A friend of mine in the Academy gave me the list of members of the Academy and the Institute who had seconded me, and in effect said I couldn't be discourteous to people who had won out after all those years. As you know, Hemingway turned down membership some years ago, but then he accepted the Gold Medal later on. The way I figure, election to the Institute makes you eligible to the highest distinction your fellow-authors can give you, which is membership in the Academy. You do not snoot the best people in your profession, especially in view of the fact that in some cases their honoring you has meant for them a reconsideration of their earlier opinions of your work.

I don't think any first-rate author works for honors, any more than he works for money, or for good reviews. I don't know how old you are, but your favorable mention of BUTTERFIELD 8 reminds me once again that if bad reviews could demolish an author, I'd have been flattened out in 1935. It has been 25 years of mixed reviews for me (read some of the notices for APPOINTMENT IN SAMARRA). No book of mine has been anywhere near unanimously praised, and no book ever will. I now skip the lunatic pannings; I read the ying-yang reviews quickly; and I linger over, and reread, those reviews that are sensible, sensitive, and generally favorable.

Obviously this letter is not for publication and is much too long, but your review got me off on a subject I don't often discuss. Thank you for the boost, and when May comes and the prize goes to ADVISE AND CONSENT,[3] we can share a snarl. (My guess for the National Book Award: THE DEVIL'S ADVOCATE. I saw the names of the committee.[4])

Faithfully,
John O'Hara

[1] William Hogan, book review editor of the *San Francisco Chronicle*, was a consistent admirer of O'Hara's work.
[2] Arthur Mizener was not one of the fiction judges: "The jury of John K. Hutchens and Professor Carlos Baker of Princeton had urgently recommended a Pulitzer Prize for John O'Hara. . . . There was no argument within the Board on O'Hara's merit; the doubt attended only to the book that was recommended, *From the Terrace*. In the end the doubts prevailed, O'Hara's lost the prize, and Taylor won" (John Hohenberg, *The Pulitzer Prize* [New York: Columbia University Press, 1974]).
[3] By Allen Drury. O'Hara's prediction was correct.
[4] The award went to Philip Roth's *Goodbye, Columbus*.

TO: John Hayward

TLS, 2 pp. King's College
Library, Cambridge
Princeton

22 March 60

Dear John:

I have just sent off a sharp letter to the Covent Garden branch of Barclays Bank, upbraiding them for sending me some cancelled cheques belonging to a Miss Juliet ——. From the size of one of her cheques to a wine society I can only conclude that Miss —— likes her booze, but that should be her secret. There was a time in my life, believe me, when I would not have been happy to hear that a total stranger was pawing over my cancelled cheques. My good friend Robert Benchley made me acquainted with a lady whom I shall designate as a therapist. She was actually known, in a spirit of fun, as Dr. C., although her first name was ——. I was sitting around one night with Benchley and he suddenly said: "Let's have Dr. C over?"

"Who is Dr. C?" I said.

"You mean you don't know —— C?" said Mr. B. "We're [sic] got to fix that right away."

The doctor arrived, carrying her little kit, and presently a whole new world was opened to me. I thought I was a pretty sophisticated fellow, but as Benchley had said, "you haven't lived until Dr. C gives you a treatment.

In succeeding weeks I made frequent use of the doctor's services, which came pretty high as she always brought along an assistant—never the same assistant twice, by the way, and one of them looked so much like a young movie starlet of that day that I have never been sure it was not she. I didn't keep much cash in the house, so I would pay the doctor by cheque, which is what got me off on this reminiscence. But since I have started it I must add one detail, which I have always kept in mind when I began to doubt that California was the place where anything could happen.

Dr. C was available any hour of day or night. But if you required her services on *Saturday* night you had to do so before two a.m. Her explanation, which I have never doubted, was that she belonged to a religious cult that congregated early Sunday morning. And guess what she did in church? She played the organ.

Well, having bawled out Mr. Lee of Barclays Bank, I was smitten with a bad conscience toward Britain and I thought I might make amends by writing to you. At the moment Sister and my daughter Wylie are off on a fortnight's visit to Spain, where Sister's daughter, son-in-law, and two grandchildren are enjoying Peter's release from the army. I hate to fly and I have no interest in Spain, so I stayed home to work. Work is plentiful. I finished a novella last night,[1] and I am about to resume work on the final quarter of a full-length novel that I am calling ELIZABETH APPLETON, and which I will publish in 1961.[2] I have written a play called THE CHAMPAGNE POOL. I wrote it in 17 days, to occupy my mind while the reviews of OURSELVES TO KNOW were coming in. Most of them are in, and rather to my surprise they shape up at about 50-50, for and against. I had predicted that the book would get mostly bad reviews, especially out of town, but it has worked the other way. In Boston, Chicago, and San Francisco I got three solid raves. I also got my share of blasts, but I don't read them any more; they give themselves away in the first and last paragraphs, or sometimes in the headlines. The book is high on the best-seller lists; not Number 1 so far, but it may make it. I would say that nationally it is No. 3, with the biggest sales in Philadelphia, Chicago, Los Angeles and San Francisco. My play is a comedy; it has some attractive characters, some wit, some warmth, good dialog, and instead of a plot it has a legitimate third-act gimmick. I have a feeling it would go well in London because London playgoers like good conversation.[3] It is an intra-mural play about theater people. If it gets produced in London I'll see to it that Queen Elizabeth the Queen Mother and you have comfortable seats, and then when I get the O.B.E. I'll shout "Hurray, hurray, we've won the day!"[4] And, sotto voce, "Fuck you, Fairbanks."[5]

Have you been reading Sam Berhman's pieces on Max Beerbohm in The New Yorker? They prove conclusively, to me, that Behrman killed Beerbohm with obsequious boredom. The Beerbohm project originated with Wolcott Gibbs, who was one of my closest friends, and who monkeyed around for years in attempts to dramatize Zuleika. Gibbs drank himself to death, as you may know, but at one time he was going to substitute a Profile of Beerbohm for his efforts to make a play of Zuleika Dobson. (The real inside gossip, entre nous, is that Gibbs's wife was once Behrman's mistress. I know, because I introduced Gibbs to the lady, way the hell back in 1933.) Behrman, who looks like a quietly successful haberdasher, also had an affair with. . . .[6] He is a really dull man, but come to think of it I'll bet —— is too. As to his pieces on Beerbohm, I have never read anything—except the Pal Joey letters, which I wrote—in which a man who is writing about himself so completely reveals his worst side. Behrman comes through in line after line as a pushy, sycophantic, relentless pest, with the hide of an ox and the sensitivity of an embalmer. I never knew Behry, as he is called, very well, but what I always took for shyness I now recognize as smug conceit. The pieces are to appear in book form, published by Random House, and it will sell a million. I don't suppose a half a dozen reviewers in the world will feel as I do; most critics will be reviewing the Beerbohm legend, which is one of those things like the Lincoln legend, the Thurber legend, that you do not question, under penalty of losing your Egghead badge.

I just go on, in these lucky years of contentment, trying to avoid the slings and arrows by ducking behind my work, loving my wife and child and a few friends, hoping that some day I'll win the Nobel, and now and then pausing to wonder at the whole business, but quite sure that it would be a waste of time to search for the answer.

Affectionate regards,

As ever
John

[1] Possibly "Imagine Kissing Pete."
[2] Published 1963.
[3] The play was never produced; it was published in *Five Plays* (1961).
[4] Reference to comment by Queen Mother Elizabeth after she obtained permission for Hayward's wheelchair to be placed in a theater aisle.
[5] Actor Douglas Fairbanks, Jr., was made Knight Commander of the British Empire in 1949.
[6] Twenty-four words deleted by the editor.

TO: Hoke Norris,[1] *Chicago Sun-Times* (3 April 1960), III, 1, 5

You say I am not "ambiguous or obscure enough" to catch on with the critics. . . . Okay, who are the critics? . . . The hidden-meaning people, the searchers for the obscure and the applauders thereof . . . the Droppers of the Name of Dylan Thomas—. . . And I will not play their game. They are the anti-conformism conformists and they are death on art, but death to it. . . .

Fitzgerald, like Phil Barry, was a casualty of the Depression. Admirers of both men deserted them for Odets and Steinbeck, because the people I have in mind are the people you have in mind. I could, did and do admire Fitzgerald, Barry, Odets and Steinbeck, but these people can't. The faddists can't afford to. The fad in 1934 was the New Conscience in Social Consciousness, so Fitzgerald and Barry had to go. It took these people 10 years or more to realize that Fitzgerald was something more than a frivolous, readable author, and I am beginning to see some signs of a Barry revival, as evidenced by appearance of his plays and movies on TV. They jackalled Fitzgerald and now he is dying again, but painlessly this time. They can't kill him twice.

Hemingway is a separate phenomenon, the brand name of our time, and not successfully assailable. They blasted "Across the River" and blasted me worse for counterattacking in his defense; then they over-praised The "Old Man and the Sea" because they were afraid that Hemingway was still good, and they didn't want to be caught on the wrong side of the Nobel Prize. Very little of what Hemingway says for publication carries any weight with me; but everything he writes is important to me and to everyone who reads, because in his writing he is alone with his professional conscience and his art, and when he talks to an interviewer he is just showing off, peevish, and bitchy. They are not going to hurt Hemingway the artist; and they can't hurt Hemingway the person as much as his petulant arrogance hurts himself. So he is the one writing man in our day who is impervious to the changing fashions, and the followers of fashions might just as well give up on him. Artistically he is invulnerable.

And where am I? Well, the only thing I'm afraid of is death, which I came close to 6½ years ago. I am afraid I will die before I finish all the things I want to do. I have a novel ¾ completed, I am working on a play that I have been writing for the past two weeks and that I will finish next week and then return to the ¾ completed novel. The novel is called Elizabeth Appleton, for the record. But all the time I am writing these things I am thinking out a big novel, which will be big in size because it is big in scope—an expression I have never used before. If I finish it by the time I'm 60, I'll be happy. I don't say I'll quit then; I'll never quit voluntarily; but I will have said all I now want to say.

¹ Book reviewer. O'Hara wrote this letter in response to a review by Norris of *Ourselves to Know*. Norris' introduction notes: "With his permission I'm quoting it here, in part, with paraphrases of some portions perhaps best not exposed to public view until his biographers get to work, as they surely will some day." Ellipses represent those parts of the review which do not quote directly from O'Hara. The original letter cannot be located.

TO: The *New York Herald Tribune* (5 April 1960), 18

I have read and listened to the obituaries and panegyrics of F.P.A., and most of them were pretty routine stuff. But W. L. Werner, retired professor of English at Penn State, who writes a column for "The Centre Daily Times," State College, Pa., has made one point that all the others overlooked. "All over the country," writes Professor Werner, "lonely persons in little towns looked to his humor as an escape from Main Street and Winesburg and Spoon River; in country newspaper offices he was a god."

Part of my job when I first started in this business thirty-six years ago was to talk on the telephone with newspapers in neighboring towns. I, representing "The Pottsville Journal" (olav hasholem, as F.P.A. would say), would exchange information with Russell Green, of "The Mahanoy City Record-American" and Bob Meredith of "The Tamaqua Courier." The information usually consisted of the box scores of high school basketball games and lists of pallbearers at reasonably important funerals, with an occasional payday stabbing or mining fatality that might be worth a 30-point Condensed Gothic head. But no matter how dull the news, we would nearly always profit by the cultural exchange, which consisted of comments on that morning's Conning Tower.

In my town there were probably a dozen F.P.A. fans: the staff of our paper, and a few other literates including a former trooper of Troop C, Pennsylvania State Constabulary. (His name was Hobart Uhl, and I naturally called him The Uhlan.) There were a dozen disappointed faces at the newsstand on mornings when "The World" had not made the train.

F.P.A. got me my first job in New York—on the Herald Tribune. Six years later I was able to say thank you: I dedicated "Appointment in Samarra" to him.

Princeton, N.J.   JOHN O'HARA.

TO: Bennett Cerf   TLS, 1 p. Columbia
                                                            Princeton

                                                        7 April '60
Dear Bennett:

I have written an 85-page novella, as yet untitled, which is to be one of three that I would like to publish under the all-embracing title SERMONS AND SODA-WATER, a quotation from Byron that is very apt. (See Bartlett.) All three novellae will have to do with the Twenties and Thirties.

I would like them to be published as a three-separate-volume item in a single container, to be sold all three together, but removable for separate reading. I can hear you scream already about manufacturing costs, but if you publish the trio in time for the Christmas trade, next November (1960), you might break even.[1]

I have a long-range purpose in this project, a dual purpose. Before I come out again with a biggish novel, I want to come out with some examples of my work in the shorter form (and no cracks about income tax short forms). A FAMILY PARTY got some bad reviews, but most of the reviews were good, and I want to hold on to those readers who like my shorter items. Strategically it is also a good idea, I think, to display some versatility, especially if in so doing I may recapture some readers, and at the same time give those who like my longer books, the newer readers, something to think about.

I am in a peculiar position. I am working harder and more successfully than ever before. I have just finished a full-length novel called ELIZA-BETH APPLETON. I wrote a play in 17 days that is now in the hands of Harold Freedman. It is a comedy called THE CHAMPAGNE POOL. What happens to the play has no effect on my standing as a novelist, which is what I am first and foremost. But I know perfectly well that if I had delayed publication of OURSELVES TO KNOW for another year, it would have got a better reception. Most novelists are such plodders that they take longer to write one novel than I do to write two. That's partly because they stall and partly because they don't know their business. (I just read a chapter of ADVISE AND CONSENT in today's paper; the man is one of the worst *writers* in the business. Really shocking.) But I will be dead a long time and I want to publish while I'm alive. However, I don't want to come out with another full-length novel too soon after OURSELVES TO KNOW, and yet I do want to publish. So the answer is SERMONS AND SODA-WATER, a good book, but not a full-length novel that will suffer from what you TV people call over-exposure. If I publish again early in 1962—a full-length novel—it will have been two years since OURSELVES TO KNOW, an illusion I am anxious to create.

So you can put me down for next winter's list, but don't announce it before September. Actually, this three-volume item, trilogy, if you wish to call it that, might very well be a sneaker. I am working on the second volume now; the first is nothing to be ashamed of.

Yrs,
John

¹ O'Hara's format suggestion was accepted.

TO: Albert Erskine¹   TLS, 1 p. Erskine

"Linebrook" letterhead

21 April 60

Dear Albert:

Welcome to the Society of Fathers of Only Daughters—in your case, probably a temporary membership. Thurber, Faulkner, Truman and I come most quickly to mind, but there undoubtedly are others. Those I mention are not likely to become ineligible, but you may have to resign in a year or two.

One of the nice things about having an only daughter is that you can make a public slob of yourself in ways that are not permissible if you have a son. It doesn't much matter what happens to a boy; everything matters if you have a girl. Also, you realize early that you are only the custodian of a girl, until she falls in love and then you recede and she becomes independent (of Daddy, that is; not of Mum). So you enjoy your fatherhood while you can, and that is an injunction.

Congratulations to you and to the lady who brought it off.

Yrs,
John

[1] Albert Erskine became O'Hara's Random House editor in 1955 with *Ten North Frederick*. Their working relationship was peaceful for the fifteen years Erskine edited O'Hara.

TO: Wylie O'Hara   TLS, 1 p. Mrs. Doughty
Spring 1960   "Linebrook" letterhead

Wednesday

My dear:

As you surely know, the high point of the last three weeks was, for me, our lunch at 21 and the matinee of Sound of Music. Thank you for inviting me, which you didn't have to do. I really meant it when I said you could take anyone you wished, and that was all I had in mind when I ordered the tickets.

I was also pleased to notice at the station that your friends were glad to see you and you were glad to see them when you got on the train. You are making a life for yourself that you will remember always. You have a positive personality, a good mind, and basic good looks. You are off to a good start at St. Tim's. If you follow the program suggested by Dr. Moore you will see and feel the results when you are ready to take off for California in June. Neither Sister nor I is capable of a mean thought concerning you, and in your heart you know that. I may appear to be the villain when I seem to oppose your wishes, but I get no pleasure out of opposing them. The easy way is to say yes to everything—and it is the cowardly way and in the end you would not thank me, because I would have left you unprepared for your future. Your future? The world is yours.

Love
Dad

TO: Bennett Cerf   TLS, 1 p. Columbia
                                    Princeton

23 April 60

Dear Bennett:

Sister and I had a very enjoyable evening with you and Phyllis.[1] I liked the play[2] better than you did, so I had a good time all around. I was particularly impressed by Mary Ure's performance, which in my opinion was underpraised—the old story of critics reviewing the character instead of the performance, which I may say they also do in novels. When I was young I used to cover three football games a weekend sometimes, and always two, and not until I gave up being football editor of The New Yorker did I really begin to relax at games. Same thing is true of my theatergoing. When I go as a non-critic I have a better time.

As to SERMONS AND SODA-WATER: I would like the spine of each book to be in a varnished blue or black, and the flat cover in any good contrasting color such as light blue or yellow. I think uniform binding is desirable so that, in effect, each individual volume will advertise the others when they are taken out of the box and one is lying on a coffee table, one on an end table, one on a night table. The color selections should, of course, be governed by the content of the books, which will be, in this trio, fast-moving, bright, and of their time. I like the rather episcopal idea of a blue or black spine and the yellow, non-episcopal flat sides —an aproned clergyman in tennis shoes.

I have finished Novella II. Novella III should be finished by the middle of June or early July. I have not decided which of several ideas to use for the third novella. You will have the MSS of all three by Labor Day, and I would like the official publication date to be Thanksgiving, 24 November. You and the booksellers will ignore that, of course. You will deliver the books in October and they will start selling right away; but if the reviews are concentrated over the Thanksgiving weekend you will get the benefit of the publicity in one big blast at the right psychological moment, as with FROM THE TERRACE.

For the catalog: I am going to write a foreword for the three books in which I will say that there are three stories of men and women who were a bit too young to have been disillusioned by World War One. Everybody can understand a war. But it is not so easy to understand an economic revolution; even the experts continue to be baffled by it; and the people of my time never knew what hit them or why. When some semblance of order was restored to the domestic economy, we looked about us and the world was already in cataclysm, not much easier to understand than the economic bafflement and over-simplified by the twin villains, Hitler and Mussolini, somewhat complicated by our convenient courtesy to the third villain, Stalin.[3] It is not my intent and not my job to analyze these factors in SERMONS AND SODA-WATER but only to look at some of the people who were affected by them, in the Twenties, Thirties and Forties. The stories take us to New York and Pennsylvania and California; Wall Street, Broadway, Hollywood; speakeasies, fashionable hotels, country clubs, war plants, and the homes of men and women up and down the economic scale. The set will sell 101,000 copies, provided the publisher does not send too many to his friends for Christmas.[4] The foreword will appear in the first novella. They will be numbered 1, 2, 3, and each will have a separate title under the all-inclusive SERMONS AND SODA-WATER (which, by the way, *everyone* likes). By the way, how is OURSELVES TO KNOW coming?

As ever,
John

[1] Mrs. Cerf.
[2] *Duel of Angels* by Jean Giraudoux.
[3] The published foreword did not address itself to these ideas.
[4] *Sermons and Soda-Water* sold about 44,000 copies.

TO: David Brown

TLS, 2 pp. Wyoming
Princeton

9 May 60

Dear Dave:

This was TCF day chez moi. Einfeld[1] telephoned this morning while I was yet abed, to say there would be a screening of FROM THE TERRACE at 6, but I could not make it on such short notice. Then your letter with the cheerful reports from the two Sans, Diego and Francisco. Once again I express the hope that this will confirm your confidence in my works to your own satisfaction and to the consternation of Others.

I have finished all three novellas of SERMONS AND SODA-WATER, and I am well pleased with them. The publication date is next Thanksgiving, 24 Nov. 60, and I have a hunch this threesome-in-a-box will sell extremely well here and abroad. Each of the items could have been made into a full-length novel, but I discuss that in my Foreword. The separate titles are: THE GIRL ON THE BAGGAGE TRUCK, IMAGINE KISSING PETE, and WE'RE FRIENDS AGAIN. The stories are cross-integrated but each stands up alone.

My play, THE CHAMPAGNE POOL, has been turned down by David Merrick, Saint Subber, Fred Brisson, Alfred de Liagre and a man named Cantor.[2] Nobody likes the third act, which is where the heart is, and without which the play lacks the warmth that a comedy must have. Freedman has taken it to London to show it around there. I think it might have a modest success there if Beaumont or Sharek[3] would do it.

As soon as I finished WE'RE FRIENDS AGAIN I went right to work on my big novel.[4] This is the one I am planning for 1965, and I had had no intention of starting so soon, but the opening scenes came to me and there I was, with a typewriter and the time, so I am in business, with the first sequence completed. It is interesting work because once again I have set myself problems of technique and construction that no layman (and damn few critics) will ever recognize. But one reason I have so many readers is that I write a new novel every time. If the readers don't know *why* the novels are new, that's all right with me. They have, in a sense, been tricked by technique. I learned a few things in writing the stories in SERMONS AND SODA-WATER that I am already using in NOVEL XYZ. The writing of any lengthy work could be a chore if I did not give myself problems. I start by conceding myself full knowledge and understanding of my characters and certain other abilities such as attention to detail and dialog. In plain, unmodest words, I concede myself the equipment of the competent novelist, which is my business. But I would lose interest and consequently readers if I did not also have the stimulation of evolving new techniques. I would become a hack. When I wrote THE MAN WHO COULD NOT LOSE, *even* when I was writing something that was written for the eyes of a small and special group who are themselves technicians, I was determined to get away from the Hollywood practice of writing a screen original so that even Jack Warner would understand it. I get so bored with writers who hate to write. They have a very good reason for hating to write; they're in the wrong business.

I should think you would have little difficulty in getting a producer and actors for THE MAN WHO —— if you make the picture on location. I might even get into the act myself as a consultant on old cars and fiacres. And of course my wife, who speaks French, Italian and Spanish, and is fluent in English, could render invaluable service as a coordinator. The time to be in production is Summer 1961, when my wife and I and Wylie expect to be in Europe.

The last figure on OURSELVES TO KNOW, two weeks ago, was 58,000 sold. It jumps around on the best-seller lists, sixth here, third there, and it has never been Number 1 anywhere, but I'd much rather have written OURSELVES TO KNOW than ADVISE AND CONSENT, the Pulitzer prize winner, or that other book, title and author forgotten, that got the National Book Award. In fact, I did. I do not want to be the winner of a $1500 claiming race and miss out on the Swedish Derby.

Kind thoughts and affectionate greetings to you both,

As always,
John

[1] Charles Einfeld, publicity director for Twentieth Century–Fox.
[2] Broadway producers.
[3] London producers.
[4] *The Lockwood Concern* (1965).

                                                                         3 June 60
Dear Kyle:

You obviously haven't been reading the Sunday Times Book Reviews
of my books in recent years, or you'd know what a powerful influence I
don't pack there. Francis Brown said to Cerf, when Cerf complained about
the review of FROM THE TERRACE: "What the hell? It'll be a best
seller, so what you are squawking about?" As to the Trib, I honestly
don't know who really edits their book section.

My experience over 26 years of publishing books is it's best to leave
critics and editors alone. When I get a thoughtful, complimentary review,
I sometimes drop a note of thanks to the reviewer, but I *know* an author
is better off in the long run if he stays away from critics and editors—
unless you happen to belong to a clique, like the Kronenberger–MacLeish–
Mason Brown—Lillian Hellman pack, a mutual assistance group that are
very influential but who bore me to death. They get together and all
try to say the same thing first and regard it as intellectual conversation,
and freeze if there is the slightest deviation from their line. Well, you
ought to know. You did it yourself long enough.

I would consider, but I would have to consider, volunteering to review
your book[1] for the Sunday Trib, but not for the Times. If I didn't like
the book, you know damn well I'd say so, and I don't want to say so; partly
out of old friendship, partly out of my feeling that unless a guy is a
complete shit, I don't want to pan his book under my byline. I think it
does me no good to pan a book like yours. I would not hesitate to pan
certain authors and certain books, but they would have to be best-seller
writers or 33d degree eggheads.

As to practical advice: it has been my experience that the book editors
will hold still for a pressure job (done gracefully) once a year, provided
that the pressure is done by the publisher and is done only for that book.
In other words, if Doubleday will get behind your book big, they can put
it across; but then they'll have to lie doggo for the rest of the year and
the rest of their list.

If your book is good, you are not going to feel any better about it
if you do personal plugging of it. And if your plugging is not successful,
you are going to feel ashamed.

For some mysterious reason, the only guarantee I know of for Page One
consideration is Book of the Month selection, which still influences those
editors. If the BOM poops have not taken your book, then it's up to
Doubleday. I wish you luck, and if I don't like what you've said about

me I will kick you right in the balls. I would give you the knee, but the center jump isn't used as much any more.

As ever,
John

¹ *Total Recoil* (N.Y.: Doubleday, 1960). O'Hara did not review Crichton's book of recollections.

TO: William Maxwell   TLS, 1 p. PSt.
                                                Quogue, Long Island

                                                    22 June 60
Dear Bill:
There is only one ms of each of my three novellas, no copies at all. If you would like to come down to Quogue and read them, you are welcome to do so. The train service is not good, and if you depend on it you would also have to count on spending the night here. It would probably be a great deal less exhausting if you spent the night even if you came by motor, and you could also bring your wife.
I would confine our discussions to the basic ones: do you want to buy the story or stories,¹ and such things as scheduling. If you wanted to buy, then there would be fiscal matters to take up with Shawn.² If you don't want to buy, that would be that, and no discussion with Shawn would be necessary.

Yrs,
John

There are three stories in the collection; the fourth is not finished and will be published in a later collection, probably next year.³ The 1960 item is three separate books under the overall title SERMONS AND SODA-WATER.

¹ Maxwell took "Imagine Kissing Pete," which marked O'Hara's return to *The New Yorker* after eleven years.
² William Shawn had succeeded Harold Ross as editor of *The New Yorker*.
³ Unidentified, possibly "Mrs. Stratton of Oak Knoll," published in *Assembly*.

TO: William Maxwell   TLS, 1 p. PSt.
24 June 1960   Quogue, Long Island

                                                    Friday 24
Dear Bill:
It may be, as you say, that one editor's reading does not clinch the acceptance, but I could tell from your opinions whether I wanted to have

the stories further processed. In other words, it would be the degree of your enthusiasm for the story or stories that would indicate my next step. These stories are totally unlike anything that The NYer has ever printed, and I am not going to have them pawed over by a committee unless I know that one editor, you, will go to bat for them.

As to your seeing galleys, I have told Cerf I will not let him see the stories until August. OURSELVES TO KNOW was on the best-seller list *two weeks* before publication day, and I don't want SERMONS AND SODA-WATER to be available too soon, or over a long period of time. Galleys therefore will not be ready much before Labor Day, and we are planning to go abroad as soon as my daughter goes off to school, so time will be a factor then. And so will money, which I won't go into now.

So I think we ought to have a summit meeting of you, me, and the manuscript.

Yrs,
John

TO: David Brown   TLS, 3 pp. Wyoming
                                                         Quogue, Long Island

26 July 60

Dear Dave:

Many thanks for your letter and the clippings. As you must have read, between the lines of my letter, not a little of the irritation I expressed was traceable to my bafflement over the choice of a successor to Buddy.[1] Studio politics is as fascinating to me as governmental or medical or any other kind. Politics, after all, is just human maneuvering for power of some sort or other, and a hostess is being a politician when she arranges the seating of a dinner party, as much as a prime minister is when he makes his larger decisions. The study of politics is the acquiring of all possible information pertaining to the persons involved and the possible moves and the advantages and disadvantages. Since my information is limited, I could only *hope* that you would be chosen, without accurately appraising your chances. I would say, however, that one reason you were not chosen is that you are not enough of a son of a bitch. The son of a bitch in a man appeals to those who are in a position to intrust him with power, who themselves already have power, and as sons of bitches can recognize the quality in other men. I suppose it is possible to have power and not be a son of a bitch, but it is much simpler for the powerful to deal with other sons of bitches, so it is hard to find cases of men who have been given power without qualifying as sons of bitches. I am inclined to regard General Marshall as a non–son of a bitch who was given power by sons of bitches; but he got a screwing before it was over. He got his screwing the day Eisenhower shook hands with McCarthy after McCarthy called Marshall a traitor, and there, of course, politics was the motivating force. So we come full circle there.

In picture business it is almost desirable to have a qualified son of a bitch as the power figure. The head of a studio is a terribly powerful man by virtue of his position; and since there are so many sons of bitches in the industry—producers, directors, actors, writers, set dressers (who are also bitches as well as sons of bitches)—the man who is elevated to head of a studio is more acceptable if he is a son of a bitch, too. If he isn't a son of a bitch, the other ones are going to take advantage of him until he qualifies. And another thing that militated against you is that you are too much of a gentleman, and they know it. In picture business a gentleman can't be trusted, not, at least, with supreme power. A gentleman gives his word, and he keeps it. Now how could a man like that deal with Jack Warner, Louis B. Mayer, Harry Cohn, Sam Goldwyn? Part of the protocol of the industry is the confident knowledge that the other guy is going to give his word, and break it. Therefore, a man who gives his word and keeps it is undependable. He is unreliable in inter-studio dealings, and he is not playing the game to the advantage of his own studio. I wanted you to have the kudos of head of production, but I did not want it for *you*. I would like to see you head your own production enterprise, which is a very different matter from being head of TCF production. I would go in with you for $1 and your count of what might be coming to me on percentages, and you know that. Until that comes to pass, you probably are just as well off in your present situation. The power you now have is not going to hurt you, and the money you get must be satisfactory.

Money, oddly enough, is no longer power to the extent that it used to be. The extremely rich are still powerful; but the man with 5 million is only comfortable. He has nothing that is not available to a dozen heads of labor unions. Indeed, the labor boss is better off, since he has not only the luxuries, etc., but also controls votes, which the 5-millionaire does not. As I look about this country, I would say that the only people who turn their money into power are the gangsters. A gangster can still buy another man's life; he can have an enemy murdered for $10,000, and what is that compared to the labor leader's controls over the grocery purchases of the members of his union, who may number in the tens of thousands? You and I will never have the big money, and it is just as unlikely that we will get the big powers. So what is left for us is the satisfaction of accomplishment, achieved in the most comfortable circumstances possible in 1960, and with our personal integrity intact. Not bad; and in one respect you are better off than I am: you can have a Martini if you feel like it. (For some strange reason, as I end my seventh year on the wagon, I have been developing a thirst for beer and whiskey, but I know what one glass of beer will do to me and those I love. I promise myself that when I am 60 I will be stronger.)

4 Aug

At this point I change the ribbon on my typewriter in celebration of the announcement I spoke of in my previous note. It is confidential and must remain so for the time being, but I think you will be pleased to learn that I have made my peace with The New Yorker. Beginning some time in October I resume contributing, after an absence from those pages of 11 years. My first contribution will be a 23,000-word novella called IMAGINE KISSING PETE, which is one of the three novellas that I am publishing on 24 Nov. under the general title SERMONS AND SODA-WATER. The novella will appear complete in one issue, and I think, in all modesty, that the combination of my reappearance in The New Yorker and the publication of SERMONS AND SODA-WATER may well turn out to be the publishing sensation of the season. Only a very few people know about this; you and Cerf are the only ones except for the New Yorker top editors and Sister and me. I am hopeful that the secret will be kept at least until after Labor Day, and then I don't care much. I think that if nothing is said until the middle of September, this whole development should create a big stir, with happy results for all concerned, that would last through December anyway. I have *not* told Swanie. I have not thought too much about it, but I rather incline to the guess that when I have thought it over, I am going to insist on keeping *SERMONS AND SODA-WATER* intact for picture sale. In other words, not sell the stories separately, although each novella does stand on its own. I am in no hurry to sell in any case, but I am giving you personally the first information for your guidance. They are pretty high on the stories at Random House, and I am too. I was before this New Yorker factor, and now I am doubly so. The odd thing is that without knowing anything about the New Yorker deal, Cerf stated a preference for the other two stories and liked IMAGINE KISSING PETE the least of the three. The story of my literary career, *in parvo*. As to the negotiations, etc., leading up to my return to The New Yorker, I will tell you all about that at some other time. Meanwhile I have also written another novella and eight shorter stories, which will be in a book I will publish late next Spring, conditional on how many of the stories The New Yorker buys and the scheduling of them in the magazine.

One of the things I like about this whole situation is the anticipation of the bafflement of the critics and the trade press. There will be a great deal of misinformation and guesswork, and I shall contribute to it because I am going to refer all questions to Shawn as editor of The New Yorker. But more important than that is the critical reception; the boys and girls are going to be so divided that they won't know where they're at after reading each other. The stories are an odd length, each about 23,000 words long, each standing on its own but interrelated. Incidentally, I almost shudder to think of the reprint sales. But long before that arangement comes to pass I'll be back at work on my next big novel.

In all likelihood Sister and I will be going abroad in late September, for a trip like the one we took last year, except that this time I am going to have my first look at Paris since 1938. We will be back in time to vote and see the major football games at Princeton, and if I don't see you before then, you must plan to bring Helen east to study the play situation. Meanwhile, kind thoughts as always,

John

[1] Robert Goldstein succeeded Buddy Adler as Executive in Charge of Production at Twentieth Century–Fox.

TO: William Maxwell   TLS, 1 p. PSt.
12 August 1960   Quogue, Long Island

Friday 12
Dear Bill:

On returning from your holiday you will find that the work has piled up on you—and I have been adding to the pile. I have finished ten short stories and a novella, some of the best writing I've ever done and a great pleasure to do.

At a signal from you I will submit the whole lot. You pick out the ones you want to buy, and on your selection and scheduling of the stories will depend the date of publication of this collection, which would not be before May 1961 in any case. Just guessing, of course, I would say you might pick five, not including the novella (meaning, you will reject the novella). That would mean about one story a month after Christmas that you would publish, bringing me up to the approximate publication date of the collection. In the astronomically unlikely event that you would buy the lot, or as many as ten, I will postpone the book until autumn 1961,[1] but I am not too eager to do that.

We go back to Princeton immediately after Labor Day and I return to work on a big novel, which I don't want to interrupt for short stories. I am putting off final decision about our trip abroad, pending developments over which I have no control.

As ever,
John

[1] *Assembly*, published November 1961, included ten stories from *The New Yorker*.

TO: William Maxwell   TLS, 1 p. PSt.
28 August 1960   Quogue, Long Island
                                                            Sunday 28
Dear Bill:

Herewith the IMAGINE KISSING PETE proof. You need not return the MS; this is a typed copy of the original, the original being at Random House, but this typed copy was made for The NYer, which fact should satisfy the legal department, since it was the only one submitted to you.

As to the other stories and MSS, we can work that out later. I have not yet decided what college library to give the originals to. As you know, the custom now is to get an appraisal and thereby qualify for a tax deduction.

I was very moved by the ending of IKP. In fact, the sudden impact made me weep. I am very glad this story will reach a larger audience than the limited one that reads collections, although SERMONS AND SODA-WATER is not actually a collection; but it isn't going to sell as many copies as there are readers of The NYer.

I hope you will go to bat on the word nooky. It hasn't been a naughty word in our lifetime, except to people who won't spell out d—n. In that connection, Jim Tully, in Circus Parade (circa 1928), had a character called Goosey, who was goosey and who was goosed. I think the story first appeared in Vanity Fair. Maybe the Mercury. I have heard the word used on TV, and if Fadiman can use the word fellatio in Holiday, I really think The NYer can be brave enough to say goose.

                                                                  Yrs,
                                                                  John

TO: Albert Erskine   Note typed at bottom of
                                             Erskine's 29 August 1960 letter.
                                                            Random House
                                                       Quogue, Long Island

Cloud 90.[1] And don't cite dictionaries to me, on dialog or the vernacular. Dictionary people consult me, not I them.

                                                                  O.

---

[1] Erskine had queried O'Hara's use of "Cloud 90" in *Sermons and Soda-Water*.

TLS 2 pp. with holograph postscript.
                                                              Wyoming
                                                      Quogue, Long Island

                                                    Last Day in Quogue
                                                              6 Sept 60

Dear Dave:

My feeling about APPOINTMENT IN SAMARRA in a film is that it must be done in the period, and with the suicide ending; and for a change this is not just another case of an author's maintaining the integrity of his work. In this case we have had the benefit of an out-of-town tryout, so to speak, and to do the film in any other way would be disastrous, to the book, to me, and to you as producer.

Bob Montgomery, who wanted to do the novel when it first came out in 1934, finally did it on his TV show, playing Julian English. The script was written by a man named Irving Gaynor Neiman, or something close to it. I went through the script for gaffes, found plenty, but Montgomery followed my suggestions for changes, and a good job was done.

I will tell you a story in a small aside. Belle and I went to see the (live) broadcast and were in the sponsors' booth. When it came time for the commercial I heard a voice saying angrily: "They shouldn't interrupt this story for a commercial." The speaker, whom I met later, was the sponsor's wife. That gives you a hint of the impact. We were all weeping at the end: the small group of us in the booth, the actors, the juicers. I went down on the multi-scene set and there was a quiet that I have never seen on any sound stage, movie or TV. People came up and shook hands with me without saying a word, just looking at me.

NBC Continuity Control had said to Montgomery, a week before the broadcast, that the suicide ending was out, absolutely out. They thought they would leave him so little time to argue that their wishes would prevail. But Montgomery had guts. He said, "Speaking for myself, and I know for O'Hara, the suicide ending stays or we don't do the story." There were no squawks, not even from the Church, and Neiman got the Sylvania Award for the script.

I tell you this—which I may have told you before—because this novel is a work of art and cannot be tinkered with. There is no other ending for this story. There is not even another form of suicide, such as poison or shooting. This man has got to die by motor car, by Cadillac motor car. It is equally true that this whole thing must take place in 1930. I would sooner update WUTHERING HEIGHTS than APPOINTMENT IN SAMARRA. Both are firmly fixed in their periods. Remember that in 1930 there was not yet an FDR to revive hope; the nation was stunned by the first blows of the depression, with other blows yet to come. In Pegler's great phrase, the Era of Wonderful Nonsense was at an end, but the only hope people had was that the Era was not over; the hope was not for a bright future; the hope was for the resumption of the immediate past. GATSBY is a great book, but GATSBY is satirical. APPOINTMENT IN SAMARRA is not satirical; it is, literally, deadly serious. It is not a sarcastic comment on the time; it is *of* the time—and should be done as a motion picture, with every last detail correct.

The universality of the character Julian English is largely responsible for the wide and enduring acceptance of the novel. But if he were a 1960 character he would not commit suicide. He would be Alfred Eaton as I wrote him in FROM THE TERRACE. A present-day Julian does not commit suicide; he just drifts. It is nobler to commit suicide if you have to. But we are at the stage of the development of the welfare state when we are not even allowed despair. The decline of love is another example of what is happening to us, but Julian English lived and died too soon to be affected by the decline of love. We are having honest fear and despair and love processed out of us, and the big imminent tragedy now is that we don't know it.

I know you will be reading IMAGINE KISSING PETE, my novella which comes out in The New Yorker in the 17 Sept. issue. In it please note a contemporary comment on the suicide of Julian English.

But to return to the business at hand which, as Mr. Coolidge said, is business. It would be false to present APPOINTMENT IN SAMARRA in the present or with any other ending, and a false, synthetic film version would make us all the targets of world-wide abuse, with resultant effects on the boxoffice. On the other hand, an honest, faithful job would immediately establish you as a producer, the man who did what no one else could do. You would get an overnight reputation for independence, guts, and taste, and in so doing you would make money for everybody. The world market for APPOINTMENT IN SAMARRA will astound you, and if the story is done right the whole film industry will benefit. It is not here a question of "licking" the story. It is a matter of resisting the temptation to depart from the story and make it something else, thereby throwing money away as surely as leaving Marilyn Monroe on the cutting-room floor, while playing up Jack Lemmon. I have a price of a million dollars on APPOINTMENT IN SAMARRA, which keeps out the grocery clerks. If you will do the picture my way, which is the way the book reads and was proven successful with an audience of millions on TV, we will have no trouble about money.

I keep seeing news items that there is to be a sequel to FROM THE TERRACE.[1] The husband, as they say, is always the last to know. Incidentally, I never got an answer to my letter to Skouras. If I am to go on considering Fox as my home lot, an answer is indicated. I may have something he wants some day, and I can get very remote all of a sudden.

We are going back to Princeton tomorrow and will be there until sailing time, the 28th, I think it is, in the Queen Mary. In London we will be stopping at Claridge's for about ten days, then to Paris, where we will be at the Prince de Galles, returning in the Queen Elizabeth from Cherbourg, 27 October, in time to vote against Reuther and Quill.[2] Then I resume work on my big novel. I have sold five short stories to The New Yorker, which will be coming out at a rate of one a month after the first of the year until publication time for a short-story collection next June. These stories are in addition to IMAGINE KISSING PETE, which is one of the three novellas in SERMONS AND SODA-WATER, due on Thanksgiving Day. I will miss the opening of BUTTERFIELD 8, which I am told is a real smasher, but they may have a print on one of the ships. By the way, I saw Bob Gillham[3] at lunch Saturday and he was very curious to know about what editions APPOINTMENT IN SAMARRA had gone into, etc. His interest, I feel, was not purely literary.

All kind thoughts to you and Helen.

As ever

John

Make that *six* stories to the NYer; just sold another.

J.

[1] No sequel was produced.
[2] Walter Reuther of the United Auto Workers and Michael Quill of the New York City municipal employees' union. O'Hara is referring to the 1960 Presidential election, in which he voted Republican.
[3] Executive for Paramount Pictures in New York.

TO: William Maxwell   TLS, 1 p. PSt.
                                       "Linebrook" letterhead

                                              17 Sept 60
Dear Bill

Regarding payment for the stories that the New Yorker has accepted, I am willing to grant permission to The New Yorker to publish the stories while we are still negotiating as to price, provided that favorable adjustments will be made retroactively. In other words, when we agree on terms, The New Yorker will pay the same money for already printed stories that it agrees to pay for stories after the negotiations are completed.

Inasmuch as we are going abroad next week and will be out of the country until November, I shall have to postpone actual negotiations until my return. When I get back I hope you will be able to come to

Princeton for discussions in December, if not before. I have no doubt we can come to terms that will be mutually satisfactory.

Yrs,
John

TO: John Hayward   TLS, 1 p. King's College,
                                                          Cambridge
                                                          Princeton

                                                          19 Sept 60

Dear John:

You came to the right man, if what you're looking for is the history of "What ho?" It happens that I have just spent four years in the Library of Congress, the Sterling Library at Yale, and the Edwin D. Humperdink Memorial Library at Sioux Falls State Teachers College, Sioux Falls, South Dakota, researching, as we say, the etymology of "What ho" with a team of philologists from the Ford Foundation.

I think we all know what "what" means, so let us on to the "ho" part.

Van Blunk, writing in The American Scholar, pp. 124–366, Vol. XXIII, 2 June 1906, advances the interesting theory that the expletive "What ho!" was first uttered by a self-taught Yorkshire gamekeeper, who, upon first seeing an early Franz Hals exclaimed: "Watteau!" The squire, a kindly man, did not wish to correct the poor fellow, but "Watteau" became, in the squire's set, a sort of verbal symbol for pretentious ignorance, and was used on many occasions. When the squire went up to London for the season, his town servants, who spoke in the accent of Bow Bells, picked up the expression, but pronounced it watt-heau.

Van Blunk's theory was given wide credence until Jinsford-Wyx savagely attacked it in 1912, causing a scene at the Reform Club that led to the resignations of four members. The entire membership quickly closed ranks, and I have never fully ascertained the remarks that touched off the scene, but London shook with the reverberations. Winsford-Jyx had his own theory, of course, which was that an Elizabethan chiropodist, treating Her Majesty for an ingrown nail, pretended to see nothing wrong with the royal pedal appendages, and inquired: "What toe, ma'am?" Raleigh spread the story, and for a while "What toe?" took its place alongside the legend of the naked king and his sycophantic couriers.

Concurrent but independent research on the part of Saltonstall-Hallowell at Harvard resulted in findings similar to the preceding, but in this case the originator of the remark was a Yankee farmer, who, faced with a collection of agricultural implements, said: "What hoe?" Later, however, certain scholars at Birmingham University cast doubt on both theories, on the

347

ground that the royal chiropodist and the Yankee farmer would have been more likely to say "Which toe?" and "Which hoe?" There the matter rested until 1937, when the French lexicographer Morand discovered an old Breton patois, a dialect similar to Papiamento, in which the expression "What haut?" meaning "How high?" was frequently used. I go along with Morand.

Yrs,
John

TO: William Maxwell

TLS, 2 pp. PSt.
New Yorker letterhead

Friday 23 Sept [1960]

Dear Bill:

Tom Gorman sent me a supply of this years ago and it has been sitting here. No envelopes, but I had to answer a fan letter day before yesterday and since the letter was about IMAGINE KISSING PETE, this stationery seemed appropriate.

I would like to continue our discussion of Hemingway, and maybe the best way is to start anew.

We have in Hemingway the most important writer of our time and the most important writer since Shakespeare. That is the statement I made in the famous Sunday Times review of ACROSS THE RIVER AND INTO THE TREES. The various circumstances that have made him the most important are not all of a purely literary nature. Some are anything but. We start with a first-rate, original, conscientious artist, who caught on because of his excellence. The literary and then the general public very quickly realized that a great artist was functioning in our midst. Publicity grew and grew, and Hemingway helped it to grow, not always deliberately but sometimes deliberately. He had an unusual, almost comical name; he was a big, strong, highly personable man. He associated himself, through his work, with big things: Africa, Italy, Spain, war, hunting, fishing, bull-fighting, The Novel, Style, death, violence, castration, and a teasing remoteness from his homeland and from the lit'ry life. All these things make you think of Hemingway, and each and all of them add to his importance, that carries over from one writing job to another. I have a theory that there has not been a single issue of the Sunday Times book section in the past twenty years that has failed to mention Hemingway; his name is a synonym for writer with millions of people who have never read any work of fiction. Etc., etc. He is the father image of writing as FDR was of politics.

Now this has not all been good for Hemingway, and Lord Acton's remark

348

about power can be applied here, substituting acclaim for power.[1] It is not good for any artist if he does not keep on working as, for example, Picasso has kept on working. The test of the man, and possibly of the artist, is what he does after he gets the Nobel prize. Hemingway, I'm afraid, has not done well in that test. It is not only that he has rested on his laureate; he might have done better to have rested. I am told, but I do not quite believe it, that he has several novels in a bank vault. I believed it for a while—until I saw the Life pieces.[2] I now believe that he has been wasting his time, which would be okay if he had decided to quit, to decide that he wanted to write no more, and stuck to that decision. But there is a cheapness about Hemingway that I deplore. He likes to get a favorable mention in Leonard Lyons's column, which is cheapness at its cheapest, and extremely costly to the man who is willing to settle for it. Hemingway can't stand the quiet of retirement, and he can't stand the company of the ass-kissers with whom he deliberately surrounds himself. They don't realize that you can't win with Hemingway. He will give you an argument on anything, and he hates you just as much for arguing with him as he does for agreeing with him; and yet he can't reject the toadies. He comes to New York, makes an ass of himself with Earl Wilson[3] and Toots Shor, then hurries away to what? To watch bullfighting and, later, to write about what is to me the most disgusting spectacle in modern Western sports-entertainment. But the worst spectacle in the Life pieces was not the bull-fighting itself but the collapse of Ernest Hemingway, artist and man.

I do not permit myself to believe that there may never have been any more there than appears in the Life pieces. As a writer I know better. There was always great art in Hemingway, often when he was at his mumbling worst. But in the Life pieces we see our ranking artist concerned with a disgusting spectacle, adopting a son-hero and wishing him dead in conflict with a former son-hero, Dominguin, whom he also wishes dead. He wants to see them die, to be there when they die, and I got the feeling that he particularly wanted Dominguin to die because Dominguin had not been as easy to adopt as Ordonez. Hemingway is *afraid* to lose Dominguin in life, and rather than lose him in life he wishes him dead. The competition between the two bullfighters, as presented by Hemingway, actually gets us away from the bull ring and could just as well have been a fight with knives between the two son-heroes. It is a terrible thing to get old that way, as Hemingway has done; to feel so strongly about two young men that you want them to kill each other, to play the one you like less against the one you like more—Ordonez against Dominguin. And all the while there is this cheap, vulgar thing I spoke of: the heartiness, the rough play, the feats of strength, the explicit hints of sex orgies, the boy-did-we-raise-hell stuff, did-we-give-it-to-that-cunt, that reminds me of John Ford and John Wayne and Ward Bond on location, and Lucius Beebe's accounts of drinking bouts. There is very little to choose between going out that way and Mr. Eliot's whimper. It's a good thing Gibbs isn't around to write the parody; that would really destroy Hemingway.

As ever,
John

[1] "Power tends to corrupt and absolute power tends to corrupt absolutely."
[2] "The Dangerous Summer," a series on bullfighting, appeared in *Life* (5, 12, 19 September 1960).
[3] Broadway columnist.

TO: William Maxwell
29 October 1960

TLS, 1 p. PSt.
Letterhead of Hotel Prince
de Galles, Paris

Sundqy

Dear Bill:

On this borrowed Hermes the letters are rearrqnged: The q is where the a should be, the z is zhere the w should be, etc. You hqve to shift to nqke q full stop.

The title of this trip could well be With Aspirin qnd Kleenex at Claridge's and the Prince de Galles. We have been Cqmilleing it all over the place, and in Londres I becane violently allergic to one of the wonder drugs. I would have felt really awful if I had not been joined in my hacking by my sympathetic wife. Babylon Revisited[1] indeed. I did not recognize George of the Ritz,[2] qnd he did not recognize me. We have since been trying to make up for the lapses caused by 22 years, but the brutal truth is that we catch eqch other sneaking a look and thinking "It can't be, it can't be." It can, though.

I have fixed this piece,[3] not, I fear, with very good grace, since the naughty part was really so innocent that the objection seems foolish. I have been reqding the testimony in the London Times report of the Lady Chatterley case, and really The NYer ought to tear some sheets off the calendar.

I have q lot of things to say about Paris and the French qnd London and the English, but they will have to wait for a typewriter thqt does not throw q's at me when I am meast suspecting it.

See you in two zeeks; possibly to wave to from my oxygen tent.

Yrs,
John

[1] Reference to F. Scott Fitzgerald's short story about Paris.
[2] The head barman.
[3] Unidentified; possibly "It's Mental Work," 26 November 1960.

TO: Bennett Cerf   TLS, 1 p. Columbia
                                                           Princeton

                                                           5 Nov 60
Dear Bennett:
    Referring to your letter of 3 November, as to item (1), I am writing to
London this morning for a photostat of the letter sent to Random House
regarding the printing difficulty that postponed publication of OUR-
SELVES TO KNOW. As to item (2), the special instructions as to payment from the French Readers Digest were in a telephone conversation
between you and me. To quote you, the blame for this failure can be
placed squarely on you. I told you what I wanted done, and you simply
paid no attention.
    The time has come for me to take the stand I took once before but did
not maintain. Hereafter, if you or Donald or Erskine or anyone else has
occasion to speak to me on the telephone, you will have to do what I do,
which is to make the call without the assistance of secretaries or operators.
No more of this "Get O'Hara on the phone," and then keep O'Hara waiting while Big Shot picks up the phone. When Shawn and Maxwell want
to speak to me, they are on the phone when I answer it. When Bob
Lovett and Jim Forrestal were Secretary of Defense, they did me the
courtesy of being on the phone when they wanted to speak to me. Buddy
Adler and Dave Brown did not have their secretaries keep me waiting.
    The worst offender is you. Time and again I have answered the phone,
the secretary or operator says, "Mr. Cerf calling," then a minute or two or
three later you get on the phone and say "Who's this? . . . Oh, O'Hara."
Well, since you don't seem to pay much attention to what I say on the
phone, anyway, there is not much point in my submitting to this dis-
courtesy. So be informed that I am not going to answer the phone for
your or Donald's or Albert's secretary or for the Random House operator.
Just make the call the way I do; and try to bear in mind that aside from
considerations of courtesy, I regard my time as important as you do yours.

                                                           Yrs,
                                                           John

TO: William Maxwell   TLS, 1 p. PSt.
9 November 1960   New Yorker letterhead

                                                    K-Day Plus One
                                                    (I voted for N)[1]

Dear Bill:
    As you see, my method of disposing of tinkering with dialog is to stet it
the way I wrote it. Ross had to learn, too. On matters of office style, I

will nearly always yield, but it seems to me the NYer style used to call for a colon before a bit of dialog.

I am pleased with the response to IMAGINE KISSING PETE, here and abroad. I got a fan letter from the mayor of Philadelphia,[2] who is a friend of mine, and he said something about a statement given out by Katharine White on my return to the magazine. Do you know anything about it? He just remembers that it was a quote in "one of the columns". Must have been while I was away. We are dining at the Meyners'[3] tonight, and I guess that's the only Democratic politician's household where the gloating will be restrained. Actually I think this election may be a good thing. It should lay that Catholic ghost forever and let us get on to more serious matters; and it should in time make the Catholics themselves more bearable, although you mustn't expect miracles.

Yrs
John

[1] The Kennedy-Nixon election.
[2] Richardson Dilworth.
[3] Robert Meyner, Governor of New Jersey.

TO: William Hogan   TLS, 2 pp. Hogan
                                                                    Princeton

29 Nov 60

Dear Mr. Hogan:

I enjoyed your review of SERMONS AND SODA-WATER, and also the advance piece, both of which were sent me not by Random House, as you might suppose, but by a mutual fan of yours and mine named Dawson, in Carmel. Random House is always late, since the advertising boys have to pore over reviews.

It is quite true, as you quoted from the PW, that I set a price of $750,000 for the three novellas. It is also quite true, in my opinion, that they are worth that, in the present market. But it will also be quite true, I predict, that I will get no such price, if I get any at all.[1] (This information, by the way, is confidential.) I set such a big price well in advance of publication because (A) I wanted to keep out the grocery clerks, the if-money producers and (B) I told my Hollywood agent that I did not want to be bothered by movie companies' offering to buy the stories separately. There was action as soon as IMAGINE KISSING PETE appeared in The NYer, and I simply said I was not interested in separate sales. These novellas are, in effect, insurance for when, as is inevitable, I cannot produce as much as I now do. I'll be 56 next month (or January, actually) and Things Happen.

I hope you realize that regardless of the vast sums of money I have made in the past, say, six or seven years, it is impossible for me to lay up any capital. This, of course, is true of all other authors in the same or even better position. My *earned* income is higher than that of a millionaire, but I will never *be* a millionaire, or anywhere near it.[2] Marquand was a millionaire, Tarkington, and others who made it big before the modern confiscatory taxes, but when you think of the dough Tennessee Williams, for instance, has made, and what he has left after taxes, the picture of the opulent author changes. Moss Hart has an income of about $8,000 a week from MY FAIR LADY. His net is $700. You don't get much sympathy if you are making $35,000 a year, but the fact is that you *have earned* that $8,000; that is your earning capacity, in a highly competitive and hazardous occupation; and in effect you are punished for being good at your job. That is the way Mrs. Roosevelt wanted it—and she said so, years ago: nobody should have an income of more than $25,000 a year, she said, speaking for herself and for the New Dealers, of whom, God help me, I was one.

I am writing you at such length about this because the casual reader of your last paragraph—or anyone who reads about how much I *earn*—does not stop to think how much of $750,000 I would hold on to, even if the movies met that price. The fact is that in spite of the simple way we live, at least once in the last seven years I had to borrow money to pay my income tax. I had to borrow $5,000, so you see how close I play it? In other words, that year I was not able to save a God damn nickel. And that's how it looks for 1960, too. One more fact: I gave the original typescript of FROM THE TERRACE to the Harvard Library, after it had been appraised by Duschnes at $3,000. The tax boys got their own appraisal, cut down the value to $1900, and I therefore have to pay an *extra* $930 this year on my 1959 tax. That extra $930 represents about $6000 *net* income.

If this be proselytizing—please do make the most of it.

Kind regards,

Yrs,
John O'Hara

So that this won't be a total loss for you, here is some news that has not been printed: In addition to IMAGINE KISSING PETE and the story in the current issue, The New Yorker has bought nine other stories from me. They will be appearing once a month till next fall, then will be in a collection that I am calling ASSEMBLY.

J. O'H

---

[1] *Sermons and Soda-Water* was not bought for the movies.
[2] O'Hara was a millionaire at the time of his death.

TO: William Maxwell   TLS, 1 p. PSt.
Late 1960   *New Yorker* letterhead

Bill:

Tired of westerns on TV? Fed up with violence and sex and all like that?
Do you think John Crosby[1] is the coming Lewis Mumford?[2] Did Nixon
really win Alaska?

Read REASSURANCE,[3] the enclosed long short story by Gabe
d'Annunzio, the man of the people, and remember: save your money, or
sleep in the park.

                                                            Yrs,
                                                            John

[1] Television columnist.
[2] Culture critic.
[3] Declined by *The New Yorker*; published in *Assembly* (1961).

TO: Ernest Hemingway   Wire. Kennedy
11 January 1961   Princeton

WHATEVER IT IS YOU CAN LICK IT GOOD LUCK=[1]
O'HARA.

[1] Hemingway was being treated at the Mayo Clinic for depression and high blood
pressure. His presence there was kept secret until 11 January 1961.

TO: William Maxwell   TLS, 1 p. PSt.
                                               New Yorker letterhead

                                                        26 Jan. 61
Dear Bill:

I saw, in my mind's eye, these two people sitting together, and for two
weeks or more they have been sitting there, practically accusing me of
fear of them, daring me to put them down on paper.[1]

Well, I fixed them.

While I have your attention: will you ask the bookkeeping department
how much The New Yorker owes me? You can send the cheques any time
you care to, but I would like to have an estimate of 1961 to give my tax
man. I am now, at this moment, at the all-time peak of my riches, the
perfect moment to flee the country forever. I could now put a dollar value

354

on how much I like to live in the USA. It is, for me, staggering. I wish I had it.

Yrs,
John

1 Unidentified; probably "Call Me, Call Me," 7 October 1961.

TO: William Shawn   TL, 1 p. (copy). PSt.
                                                      Princeton

27 Jan 61

Dear Bill:

Thank you for the cheques. It is a dubious pleasure to be no more than temporary custodian of the money on its way to the federal treasury, but then as the Irish say, it's better than a poke in the eye with a sharp stick.

More satisfactory is the pleasure of writing short stories once again and the comfort of seeing them in the magazine. Of course you make a mistake now and then; I think you should have bought two stories that you didn't buy; but it's your magazine, not mine, and publication in my book next fall is the next best thing to publication in The New Yorker.

Cordially,
John O'Hara

TO: Wylie O'Hara   TLS, 2 pp. Mrs. Doughty
Early 1961   *New Yorker* letterhead

Saturday

My dear:

I am very pleased with your B- and 1 for effort in English. Your report came today and I have been studying it. I note with pleasure, too, that you hit the mid-year French exam for a B-plus. You, of course, notice that your best mark, the B- in English, is also accompanied by your best rating for Effort. I am glad, too, that Miss Watkins[1] was pleased with your examinations in French and Geometry. All these are healthy, optimistic signs, that confirm what we have felt all along: namely, that your intelligence is good, your capacity to do good work is there whenever you call upon it.

It is interesting to me that by a coincidence, as I told you, I was thinking a couple of nights ago that in a few months half your time at St. Tim's will be over, half your prep schooling will be finished, and you will be sixteen years old. Perhaps I arrived at that thought as a result of my conversation with Townsend Kemp. I had told her that I understood that the best colleges nowadays go through a student's entire prep school record before deciding to admit her, or him. Then, as you know, Townsend told me that in her first two years at Westover her marks were not good, but that they got better in her last two years, and when she took the aptitude tests, Bryn Mawr, to which she had not applied, invited her to make an application and she was accepted.

All these facts gave me the hope that your marks would begin to get better—and they have. And it certainly is a greater pleasure for me, as it must be to you, to be able to discuss your reports on the positive side rather than the negative.

You will soon be sixteen and in many ways you are a wiser and older girl than sixteen. Not in all ways, thank God, but in some good ways. Your observation is pretty keen, and if that, plus your intelligence, can be directed right, you will enter young womanhood with confidence and you will get the most out of your life.

The thing to bear in mind now is that in this changing world you are probably going to have to get a job as soon as you get out of college. Nearly all girls get a job before they marry, and some hold on to their jobs after they marry. You will have financial security, but you will not be rich, even after I die. The government will see to that through taxes. You will have the modest income that will make the difference between having to take the first job that is open—a clerk in the dime store, a waitress in a drive-in—and taking a job that offers a better future and a more interesting present.

I believe that too many people go to college who are not qualified, but that's the way things are going. A college education nowadays is as available as a high school education was when I was young. Therefore you are going to have to plan your life *now* with the idea of going to college, because a college degree is going to be a minimal requirement for the interesting jobs. I would prefer that you go to Bryn Mawr, Radcliffe, Smith, Wellesley, Vassar—one of the those. But I will settle for one of the big coeducational universities as a second choice. Or I will pay for your college education abroad. You are a lady, and I have sent you to the kind of school a lady ought to go to and that you will be proud to have gone to all the rest of your life. But college, even those colleges I prefer, is not going to be made up of girls who are ladies or boys who are gentlemen. College will be your first experience with the new world, meeting all sorts of people whose standards are not going to be as high as yours. Since that is the way the world is and is going to be, I believe in preparing you for that world. I am facing facts that are not all pleasant, but it is going to be your generation's world, not mine. St. Timothy's is for what you *are*; college is for what your world will be.

So the rest of this year and the next two years will determine what kind of college you get into. That is what I meant by "something to think about"; at nearly sixteen you should begin to think about the kind of college you want to go to, and then later, in college, you will be able to think about what kind of job you want to look for.

I congratulate you on your improvement, and I shall say nothing now about the lower marks. No one knows better than you do that the lower marks can be raised. You have proved that to us and to yourself.

Love
Dad

[1] Headmistress of St. Timothy's School.

TO: William Maxwell   TLS, 2 pp. PSt.
                                                New Yorker letterhead
                                                         9 Feb 61

Dear Bill:

Yes, I am concerned and always have been, with "the whole thing from the cradle to the grave." Friends have kidded me and non-friends have assailed me for my awareness of death, not realizing that in my boyhood death was a commonplace. Every time the telephone rang there was a chance that death would be in on the call, especially late at night. "He died on the table," was a sentence I heard a hundred times—at the dinner table. Also, I saw the dying in hospitals, and once I held a brakeman's hand as he died after my father had amputated both his legs. I did not grow up in the Schuylkill Country Club—or the Stork Club. I grew up one Christmas day, stopping to pick up the priest in my governess cart so that he could take Holy Viaticum to Stink Schweikert's father, who was lying on a railway track with a leg mashed off. I grew up when I had to take something, I don't remember what, to a Mrs. —— house, a widow with one daughter a few years older than I, and I had to stand there and mutter to the girl, alone with her, and then a year or so later I heard that the girl had become a whore, but that day I was alone with the girl and her dead mother and I did not know what I was feeling till I got the same feeling reading DUBLINERS. Did you ever see a beheading? When I was a movie press agent I saw a great many newsreels that were not issued to the theaters, and one I will never forget was the beheading of a group of Chinese bandits. There was something funny about an officer with a Luger giving the coup de grace to the headless torsoes. I also saw some Signal Corps movies of hand-to-hand combat in WW 1, taken from a dugout. Bayonet stuff, and men kicking each other in the nuts. I will never forget being the first to discover a Negro lying dead from knife wounds in the chest and then having to notify the state police that I had found him.[1] Or being in a railway wreck when I was about four years old. Etc., etc. Not to mention some things I saw in the war, like a shot-up plane landing on the deck of our carrier, then going over the side before anyone could get out of it. Etc., etc.

I have to force myself to remember these things as separate incidents, as details. I do not not go around thinking of them. They are like listing the girls I have slept with. Once I did that and I accidentally left out two: a girl I had lived with, and my first wife. That, I daresay, is the extreme opposite of the death catalog. In between I have, I confidently believe, struck some sort of balance. They all, along with many other lived and vicarious experiences, make me what I am, and what I am makes me an author. It has been a very full life, full, naturally, of the kinds of things I write about, which I attract or have been attracted to, often against my will. But I so well understand what Tennessee Williams means when he calls himself a compulsive writer. He is committed to homosexuality and is in my opinion therefore a cripple, willingly rejecting the whole experience of living with a woman; but from what Gibbs told me about Williams I gather that he lives his crippled life fully, in spite of having to miss out on the unimaginable experience of loving a woman and being a father. Whatever you live, if you live it big enough, and you are also a writer, I do not see how you can fail to be a compulsive writer—if you look at the calendar.

In a way, of course, the compulsion to write could be said to be a resistance against the inevitable, and by the same token an author who stops writing has given in. The only time in my life when I could not write was during the war. I could write pieces, but pieces are only what they are called—pieces. Even when they are Art. Did anyone ever say that Sinclair Lewis was an artist? William Dean Howells? I don't think so. But Howells was very nearly an artist, and BABBITT was a work of art. I could not produce anything but pieces while the war was on, because the war was too big a distraction, an overabundance of material, a matter, you might say, of life and death, of hotel reservations and gas rationing, of mice and men, of me in all that confusion. Well, now I have got rid of most of the confusion and distractions, no longer feel that my participation will restore order to the world, and ask for nothing much more than time to do my work and once in a while a little pat on the back, the same as you'd give a horse. Or even a mule.

Yrs,
John

[1] When O'Hara was a reporter on the *Pottsville Journal*.

TO: Bennett Cerf   TLS, 1 p. Columbia
                                                            Princeton

                                                       25 Feb 61
Dear Bennett:

As you know, I have a full-length novel in my drawer;[1] I have enough stories and more for the collection I plan to bring out next Thanksgiving;[2] and I am well along the way in a large novel; now past 300 pages.[3]

As you do not know, my mother, who has been in the hospital for three weeks, underwent surgery yesterday. She is 81, and if she recovers it will still be a heavy drain on my finances. It already has been.

I now serve notice on you that the 50-50 reprint deal is a thing of the past, and if you are going to repeat all the answers you had three years ago, don't bother to answer this letter. I know all those answers. You and Donald and whoever else is involved are going to have to come up with a new deal, more favorable to me, and I suggest you use as a working basis the plan outlined in the current Authors Guild Bulletin.

As matters now stand, Random House is getting rich on my money, and I am *not* getting rich on my money. Your wife and sons will get and are getting the benefit of my work, but my wife and my daughter are not. Your wife and sons are in Random House, I am not; I contribute to the financial well being of Random House; your wife and sons do not. You offered to *sell* me stock in Random House!

So I want you and Donald et al to sit down, as you refused to do three years ago, and draft a complete new plan that will be to my financial benefit and that of my wife and daughter. Louis Nizer is not in on this; I no longer am a client of Louis Nizer's, because of the way he handled the negotiations three years ago. What you do is submit a plan, then I will show it to a lawyer and tax man, and we can negotiate from there.

If you do not wish to submit a plan, I of course can only take your refusal for its obvious implication.

                                                            Yrs,
                                                            John

[1] *Elizabeth Appleton* (1963).
[2] *Assembly* (1961).
[3] Probably *The Lockwood Concern* (1965).

TO: Bennett Cerf   TLS, 1 p. Columbia
                                                      "Linebrook" letterhead

                                                      7 March 61
Dear Bennett:
   Two weeks is long enough for Random House to come up with a pro-
posal for the renegotiation of reprint rights to my books. Actually, of
course, 24 hours is long enough for you to have replied that you received
my letter and that you and Donald were working on a proposal.
   Accordingly, after next Monday, the 13th, I shall feel free to begin
serious discussions with other publishers, as I intend to bring out
ASSEMBLY, my short story collection, in the fall.
   In answer to no question from you, my mother is doing well.

                                                      Yrs,
                                                      John O'Hara

TO: Bennett Cerf   TLS, 1 p. Columbia
                                                      "Linebrook" letterhead

                                                      9 March 61
Dear Bennett:
   Very simple formula. I want two-thirds of all paperback rights as we
know them now, with the exception of SERMONS AND SODA-WATER.
As you know, I have not yet signed the SERMONS AND SODA-WATER
CONTRACT between Random House and me, but I am an honorable
man and although the book was published without a contract, I had not
agitated for an increase in my cut of paperbacks; therefore, I will sign that
contract on the old basis. This renegotiation also means that I want two-
thirds of Modern Library paperbacks; as to the regular Modern Library
editions, so long as they remain in their present form and format, the
present agreement still stands. I am prepared to sign a contract for
ASSEMBLY, my collection of short stories, on the day you agree to the
new terms. This also goes for the SERMONS AND SODA-WATER
contract.

                                                      Yrs,
                                                      John

TO: Bennett Cerf   TLS, 1 p. Columbia
                                                    "Linebrook" letterhead

                                                    30 March 61
Dear Bennett:
   Herewith the contracts, witnessed and signed.
   I was naturally interested in the reprint figures, especially pleased about
TEN NORTH FREDERICK (and you might remind Dystel that he
owes me a cigarette box for that one).[1] I would also like to know about
A RAGE TO LIVE, since that is one of my movie propositions. Also, I
wish you would obtain figures on foreign editions, including English.
   I was infuriated by that piece by Nichols[2] last Sunday about fiction not
selling, including the quote from that jerk at Knopf's. You can shut *him*
up, I should think. I will bet that SERMONS AND SODA-WATER sells
a million within one year of paperback publication. At the moment I am
probably the country's most formidable competition to television, and
should remain so for at least three years, but there is no gratitude among
the booksy folk, only envy.

                                                    Yrs,
                                                    John

   [1] Oscar Dystel of Bantam Books. It was the custom for Bantam to give O'Hara a
cigarette box when one of his books sold a million copies.
   [2] Lewis Nichols of the *New York Times Book Review*.

TO: Martin O'Hara[1]   TLS, 1 p. O'Hara
March 1961   Princeton

                                                    Monday
Dear Mart:
   Thank you for the Gettsyburg books, which just arrived. And keep up
the good work.
   Perhaps M. J. O'Hara was in the South at the time of Gettysburg. If he
was with General Terry, he was in the South, at least the Terry that I have
discovered.
   But more convincing than that is a legend that was told me years ago.
Our grandfather, participating in Sherman's March to the Sea, and in
command of a troop of cavalry, came to a plantation that he knew was
owned by a cousin. He ordered his men not to loot or destroy or otherwise
harm anything or anyone on the plantation. Then he went up to the house,
the door was opened by a young woman, and he introduced himself. "I
am your cousin, Captain (as it was told me, Major) O'Hara." "I know you
are," the young woman said, and spat in his face. I do not know what

                                                    361

happened next, but it would have been in character for him to lift the previous order. At the same time, it would also have been in character for him to make the order stick. He was a wild man, but he had other qualities too.

Now the point of that anecdote is that the March to the Sea took place in 1864. He therefore had to be in the South in 1864, the late summer, fall, and early winter. He was married on July 5, 1864, but that could still have given him time to rejoin the army with Sherman. I'm not sure, but I think I got that anecdote, along with some others, from an old man named McFarland, whose son owned the Pottsville Foundry on Coal Street or maybe George Street. I forget. Anyway, McFarland was a wonderful old guy that I used to have lunch with at the Alco, and he knew M. J. O'Hara in Shenandoah. He had a lot of stories, including one about how our grandfather stood up to the Mollies and told them to go to hell, for which there was a plan to assassinate him on the Broad Mountain. Too long to tell now. McFarland was close to 70 when I knew him, 35 years ago, and he is no longer with us.

There is a book called the History of Pennsylvania, in the Library. The old man is in it, with pictures and coat of arms. It was what is known as a puff book; you write your own facts, etc., but it should have stuff about the old man's parents, etc., including M. J. O'H's war record. If you want to dig, you will discover that we had a great uncle who lived in, I think, Elmira, N.Y. and worked for the NY Central. He practically invented the Westinghouse air brake, but his wife swiped the drawings when she left him, and gave them to I don't-know-who. You also know about Sister Lucy, head of the Little Sisters of the Poor at Pawtucket, R.I., who was expelled from France. You might even remember Great-uncle Jim O'Hara, a handsome old giant of a man, and a bum, just like plain Uncle Jim, but more attractive. I have a theory that Grandfather O'Hara was preceded in this country by older brothers. One such helped to settle Putnam County. At any rate, an O'Hara did; and the town of Aspinwall in Allegheny County was originally called O'Hara. Those O'Haras were very social in Pittsburgh. And very rich. But they have died out. In 1933 when I worked there they were only two old maids in the Social Register.

Yrs,
John

---

[1] This letter was printed in Walter S. Farquhar's "Editorial Musings" column in the *Pottsville Republican* (5 April 1961).

TO: Richardson Dilworth

TLS, 1 p. PSt.
New Yorker letterhead

13 April 16

Dear Dick:

I quote from your letter dated April 6 (which arrived here today): "I was fascinated by the fact that once you settle down to the final typing, you have so few corrections to make."

It may fascinate you even more to learn that what you saw at Penn State[1] is the *original* typing. It also happens to be the *only* typing.

I work directly on the typewriter, making no carbons. In the case of longer work, such as novels, I engaged a typist to copy what I have typed; but what you saw at Penn State is the way it came out of my brain.

I am telling you this because it makes the MSS more valuable to scholars and collectors. I never have written anything in longhand, for publication, that is.

There is only one copy of APPOINTMENT IN SAMARRA, not even a typist's copy, and there are no carbons. They set type from the original typescript as I gave it to the publisher. That MS I gave, in a leather case, to Adele Lovett 25 years ago, and I later asked her to give it, will it, to Yale. But Yale has never done anything for me, so I am considering asking Adele to change her will and leave it to another institution.[2] Yale already has the original of BUTTERFIELD 8 plus various other items that Thornton Wilder and C. B. Tinker persuaded me to donate to the Yale Library years ago. But all Yale ever did was ask me to give them some more, and make me a Friend of the Yale Library. Meanwhile they gave honorary degrees to E. B. White, a Cornell man, and James Thurber, an Ohio State man. Your alma mater, guided I suppose by Archie MacLeish and Lefty Lewis,[3] seems to think it was a great honor for me to be allowed to donate my MSS to it. I don't look at it that way.

Your round-the-world trip sounds like fun, and I hope it will be. Just stay out of Italian ships and steer clear of Swedish ones.[4] Bon bon voyage to Ann and to you,

As ever
John

---

[1] O'Hara presented the typescript of *Sermons and Soda-Water* to Pennsylvania State University in honor of Mayor Dilworth.

[2] Mrs. Lovett gave the typescript to Pennsylvania State University after O'Hara's death.

[3] Wilmarth S. Lewis, Walpole scholar active in Yale Library affairs.

[4] Reference to the collision between the *Andrea Doria* and the *Stockholm*.

Wednesday

My dear:

I trust that by now you have received my note and the 25 stamps enclosed. The mails have been most irregular, my dear.

I feel quite entitled to write on New Yorker stationery today. Last week I wrote two short stories—one of them for next Christmas—and sent them in, with some apprehension, because I had not sold the previous two I sent them. Today, however, William Maxwell telephoned to tell me that they are buying both stories. I don't know what I'd have done if they had rejected the one that is not about Christmas. It is called THE FATHER[1] and if I do say so, it is a work of art. I do say so.

Today I also received two new silver cigarette boxes, the small rectangular ones that I get for selling a million copies of a novel. These are for A RAGE TO LIVE and TEN NORTH FREDERICK, both of which have passed the million mark, and that makes four so far. They expect the SERMONS AND SODA-WATER trilogy to do that next year, and they are optimistic about OURSELVES TO KNOW. I am less optimistic about OURSELVES TO KNOW, but we shall see. My books and for that matter my other work too have a way of catching on late. It is true that APPOINTMENT IN SAMARRA and BUTTERFIELD 8 were bestsellers when they first came out in 1934 and 1935, but BUTTERFIELD 8 lay quiet for many years (except in England, where it continued to have a moderate sale), then when the movie came out it came alive again and sold over a million paperbacks in less than a year! I trust you were as amused as I was that Miss Taylor got her Oscar, and accepted it, in spite of her original reluctance to play the part. That, by the way, is a good illustration of what I was saying in my little lecture when you were home: you sit at the typewriter with a stack of blank yellow paper, you go to work, write your novel, publish it—and 25 years later the hairdressers in Hollywood are busy as bees, getting the girls ready for the Academy awards of which the high point was the award to Miss Elizabeth Taylor in a part that I created in 1935. Of course my name was not mentioned, but I guess most people are aware that it was not William Faulkner, but your old man, who wrote BUTTERFIELD 8.

I had a session with Dr. Pickering today and at the end he told me he did not have to see me again till September. On the way out I was thinking of all that will happen before I see him next. You will have made your second trip to Europe (I was 22 when I made my first) and seen places I have yet to see. Your life is full of the future, but remember that it is what you do in the present, this very day, that will largely determine what that future will be.

Love
Dad

[1] 28 October 1961; the other story was "Two Turtledoves," 23 December 1961.

TO: Wylie O'Hara   TLS, 1 p. Mrs. Doughty
23 April 1961   Princeton

Sunday

My dear:

If one lone teacher said that you were capable of doing better, I would be inclined to think that that teacher liked you and was making excuses for you. But all your teachers say that, and they have always said it. And they are right. The fact is, you have improved in this report over your previous one. I was particularly interested in what your French teacher said: "In spite of these things, she does fairly well *compared to the class but not well enough for her.*" That is one of the highest compliments you ever got. It expresses both admiration and hope.

Last year you finished strong, as they say in horse-racing, and I hope you will again this year. Your English teacher says, "I hope her work will continue (note that word) to improve during the remainder of the year."

I have been with you, in a way, this afternoon and yesterday—the Yankees are in Baltimore, not doing too well, I regret to say. But it gave me an odd feeling to watch the games coming from a field so close to where you are.

Last night your Uncle Eugene phoned from Pottsville, and when I said "What's on your mind?" (for I knew something was), he said, "Well, they're having a dinner on May 6th, to celebrate the 40th anniversary of the country club, and a lot of your old crowd want me to ask you if you'll come." So I thought it over and I tentatively accepted.[1] I think it will be fun, in a quiet way, to go back. Most of my friends now have married children and are grandparents, and it will not be the rowdy-dow party it would have been in previous years, but that's all right. My rowdy-dow days are over anyway.

Next weekend, as you know, we are going to be at Jock and Betsey Whitney's, at Greentree, which you have seen. Coincidence department: Betsey Whitney, as Betsey Cushing, went to Westover with a girl called Augusta Yuengling, who will be at the Schuylkill Country Club anniversary dinner. Augusta was my first sweetheart, when I was even younger than you are now. She is still very pretty.

I didn't tell you about the dinner in Newark, where I was made an honorary member of Pi Delta Epsilon, the college journalism fraternity. It was quite pleasant. For instance, I was agreeably surprised by the students, who, although they are all studying engineering, are equally interested in cultural matters, expressed themselves well, and were uniformly well mannered. The president of the college, in his introductory remarks, said: "I have something very much in common with one of our distinguished guests," and I called out, "I know what it is," and he laughed. He and I were both born on Jan. 31, 1905. He and I had looked each other up in Who's Who.

Hang in there, pal.

Love
Dad

[1] The O'Haras did not attend.

TO: William Maxwell
Spring 1961

TLS, 1 p. with
holograph footnote. PSt.
"Linebrook" letterhead

Tuesday

Dear Bill:

I felt that you were depressed by the rejection of that story.[1]

In about three weeks* ask Shawn if he has wondered about that young man and his wife waiting in the kitchen. If he has, I'll send the story back to you. I would like to see it in The NYer because I know how good it is. Shawn will remember those people long after he has forgotten many other things, and *then* he will realize what I was saving up for. The almost casual reference to the early suicide, the underplaying of the young man's time in prison, and most of all, his actual pride in his control of his nerves, which enables him to sit and wait for a man he is going to blow to bits. This story may be well received when it comes out in my book.

Yrs,
John

*Or even three months.

[1] "The Free," *Assembly.*

17 May 61

Dear Bill:

It was a very distressing conversation, but I am tougher than you, having been toughened, and I should not have let it go on.[1]

You apparently are not aware of what the publication of a book can do to you. It is really foolish to try to pretend that it has not happened. You got uniformly good reviews, as far as I have seen, and you should let yourself enjoy them; and if you run across any bad ones, you might just as well suffer through them. It is all part of the postpartum part of the creative process. I have come out 17 times, you have come out three, and at longer intervals; and I know what to expect. I no longer read all my reviews; the really bad ones are screened by Sister and Bennett Cerf, and certain reviewers and certain publications are predictable. But for my first ten books I read everything, everywhere, and the only thing worse than reading some of those reviews would have been not to read them.

When you publish as infrequently as you do, the whole process, from basic idea on, lasts that much longer, and you cannot convince yourself that it is concluded when you have okayed the final page proofs, or given the first copy to Emmy.[2] Whether you actually read the reviews or not, you know they are there, and anyone as sensitive as you is going to be affected. This is especially true now, with THE CHATEAU a popular success.

What I do nowadays, when I come across a serious, respectful review, I write a note to the reviewer. These notes all say just about the same thing: that as a serious author I am entitled to serious, respectful consideration, and thank you for such consideration. The others I ignore, except for a review in Harpers of OURSELVES TO KNOW, in which a man named Pickerel, writing an unfavorable review, quite obviously skipped a lot and said that Higgins, who "of course, went to Princeton." Well, he had gone to Lafayette, and quite a bit of space was taken up about Lafayette. He had gone to Princeton for his M.A., and you could see where Pickerel had skipped. He also had other errors of that kind. But that is the last letter of protest I wrote, and it is a waste of time, even when you have the critic dead to rights. The reason I am telling you this is to show you how I try to handle the post-publication throes. It keeps me busy, keeps me feeling I am participating and not just ignoring what I cannot ignore, the publication of a novel that I have worked hard on. The other thing I do is write a play. The plays get nowhere, but I wrote one play under such conditions, then started all over again and wrote it as a novel,[3] which now sits in my desk awaiting publication—and the chance to write another play, I suppose.

Another reason for being tired is that you are 52. There are no ways out of that. I am doing more work than ever before in my life, and I am enjoying it, but I no longer can do eight-hour stretches of work. The most I can do now is four hours, although three years ago I could still do eight.

I am going to stop writing short stories at least until I finish my long novel. I have proved my point, to myself and to the readers of The NYer, and my artistic conscience is frowning and pointing to the hourglass.

Yrs,
John

[1] O'Hara and Maxwell had discussed the critical reception of Maxwell's recently published novel, *The Chateau.*
[2] Mrs. Maxwell.
[3] *Elizabeth Appleton* (1963).

TO: David Brown   TLS, 1 p. Wyoming
                                                        Quogue, Long Island

                                                              13 July 61

Dear Dave:

I wonder if you would have Research do a bit of local research for me? I would like to know the name of the telephone exchange for phones in Malibu in 1930; and the name of the exchange for Santa Monica phones at the same period.

As you will immediately infer, I am working on something that has to do with the movie industry around that time.[1] I put aside my long novel for the summer, to take it up again in the fall, when we return to Princeton. I started work on a project that I intended to keep within novella length, but it has got away from me, or, to put it more accurately, I got too interested to stop at 75 or a hundred pages. I have already passed the latter point.

It was a good thing I had this work—which I expect will be a short novel—these past two weeks. I cannot say I was surprised by Hemingway's suicide (and I refuse to call it anything else; give the man that last honor). When I read those pieces in Life last year I was sure he'd had it. His thinking, his behavior, and his giving permission to print the pieces. Then in London last fall I talked with an old friend of mine, Dick Pollard, who is a Lifephotographer and who was with Hemingway on the Life assignment. Pollard said Hemingway's descriptions of his behavior were not exaggerated. Four days before Ernest shot himself I wrote to my doctor to see if he could find out through medical channels whether Ernest had had a vagotomy[2] at the Mayo clinic. My doctor has not yet learned, one way or the other, about a vagotomy. But having this novel in work has been a good thing to fight the depression that came over me when what I was sure would happen, happened.

I made one brief statement to the press, and that is all I am going to say publicly.[3] Predictably, more crap has been written by people who had no understanding of the man than—well, since the death of FDR, possibly. Some day, years hence, I may write a piece about him, but not now. And I may not write anything ever.

I am a bachelor; Sister and Wylie went abroad Sunday, to be gone a month. I am playing a lot of golf, and writing every night.

I keep reading dispatches concerning TCF and Levathes[4] (whose name I am not able to pronounce with confidence), all very bewildering at this end. But what, in this strange world, is not?

I trust all goes well with the Browns of Pacific Palisades.

As ever
John

[1] *The Big Laugh* (1962).
[2] Surgical division of the vergus cranial nerve.
[3] "As an artist he was unique and irreplaceable. I can't think of any other author in history who directly influenced so many writers. On the personal side, he inspired enduring affection."
[4] Peter G. Levathes, Executive Vice-President in Charge of Production, Twentieth Century—Fox.

TO: William Hogan   TLS, 2 pp. Hogan
                  Quogue, Long Island

2 Aug. 61

Dear Mr. Hogan:

I am glad you enjoyed the foreword to my Five Plays. I don't expect that the book will—as they say on Madison Avenue—do much, but now I've had my little say on some things and I can proceed with the work I do best. I put aside the big novel I am writing because here there are not the facilities for quick research that are available at home in Princeton. But I did not stop writing: I got started on a novella, which took off and is already more than 200 pages long and will reach 300. I have a title for it: THE BIG LAUGH, and I will publish it next Spring. The longer novel will not be ready then. The title of the long novel is THE LOCKWOOD CONCERN and covers 100 years of a Pennsylvania family; THE BIG LAUGH is a Hollywood success story. You will also be called upon to pass judgment on ASSEMBLY, a collection of long and short stories which comes out this Fall, and that I am optimistic about.

You are the first person ever to suggest that I write an autobiography, and I am complimented. Having been born with at least the normal supply of egotism, I have thought about an autobiography. But I would not be able to do one unless I leveled all the way, with myself and with the great and non-great whom I have encountered and, in some cases, known extremely well. For instance, I know the President of the U.S., but I have known his father for many years and consider him a friend of mine, as I do Mike Romanoff and Robert Lovett and Sol Joulwan. Sol Joulwan is a gambler whose son was Most Valuable Player on the West Point football team last Fall, and I went to St. Patrick's School with Sol, whose father was King of the Syrian colony in Pottsville, Pa. Big Mike, the strongest man in the steel mill.[1] You see what the word autobiography does to me? You also see why I will never run out of material. And that in a way presents a problem.

I have so much I want to write in the freedom of fiction, and that I want to see published while I am alive. An autobiography would have to be published posthumously, and posthumously to the death of many of the people mentioned in it. I hope my desire, my compulsion to write fiction will continue, but if it does, an autobiography keeps being postponed. For instance, if my doctor said to me, "John, you have five years to live," I could not start my autobiography, because I have five years' fiction to write. If he said, "John, you have ten years to live," I might decide to use five of those years for fiction and the last five for an autobiography. But the latter would be an enormous book; two volumes, preferably illustrated with photographs—and I would never see it! And I write for publication in the immediate and literal sense. I rarely believe writers who say they have been or are working, working, working, and then at the end of five years come out with one thin novel. I think those writers are trying to impress the critics with their painstaking dedication, and there's no doubt that the propaganda often works. But those writers inadvertently expose their incompetence when they have so little to show for all that polishing and rewriting, etc. But that's another matter, and maybe I'd better save it for my autobiography.

Many thanks and kind regards,

John O'Hara

[1] Mike Joulwan was a Pottsville merchant. Sol Joulwan's son did not play for West Point, but the son of his cousin Alfred did.

TO: Charles Poore

TLS, 1 p. PSt.
Quogue, Long Island

15 Aug 61

Dear Chas.:

Many thanks for giving FIVE PLAYS BY a boost. I have not been too optimistic about the book. The principal reason for bringing it out was to establish a copyright on the plays so that Sister and Wylie would have that protection in the future.[1] Of course I had a good time writing the fore-word, too.

You know my ultimate ambition, and I shall continue to publish at brief intervals regardless of the overexposure hazard. In the fall, a collection of short stories and novelle; and in the spring, a novel; and in the fall of '62 a very long novel, and so on. I am amazed at the paperback sales of my books, here and abroad, but what pleases me most about them is that an entirely new public has begun to read me. Me, among others, of course. If I were Paley and Sarnoff[2]—we call that the Paley par lay—I would be a little worried. Books have started to strike back at the black box. I tell my family to pray every night that TV put on more and more hippic epics.

Our best to you and to Mary,

As ever
John

[1] O'Hara was in error: unpublished dramatic works could be copyrighted.
[2] William S. Paley, Chairman of the Board of CBS; David Sarnoff, Chairman of the Board of RCA.

TO: Charles Poore   TLS, 1 p. PSt.
                                    Quogue, Long Island

                                        19 Aug [1961]
Dear Chas.:

I seem to recall your telling me that you don't read the NY Post, which means you don't see Leonard Lyons's column. I *do* read Lyons, not carefully, mind you, but down the middle. And once in a while I am rewarded.

For instance, the other day he had a paragraph about Garson Kanin and Gertrude Stein. The anecdote matters so little that I promptly forgot it, but I have not been able to forget this one line: "Garson Kanin, whose writing was influenced by Gertrude Stein . . ."[1]

There it was, just casually tossed away in a more or less routine paragraph; the answer to the question that has been bothering the literati since dear knows when: who influenced Garson Kanin? People have sat up half the night arguing the question. During the War, on troopships and foxholes, our GI's would while away the lonely hours with thoughts of the peanut butter the folks back home were enjoying, and with discussions of who influenced Garson Kanin. I wonder how many times a mischievous undergraduate has dropped in at the Lizzie Club[2] and, over the tea and cookies, dropped that hot potato into the serenity of literary conversations about Walpole and Lefty Lewis. You could nearly always, by picking your man, relieve the tedium of a long train ride by saying, "I beg your pardon, but I happened to notice that you're reading a book, and I wondered how you stood on the question of who influenced Garson Kanin." Once in a while, of course, you would run into some stuffy fellow who would bristle and say, "Nobody influenced Garson Kanin, sir. He is sui generis," and hide himself behind the New Statesman. I understand that there was a dreadful scene at the Saturday Club[3] between Archie MacLeish and M. A. DeW. Howe[4] that all started over this controversial question. Some pundits have held out for Moliere, some for Sheridan. Racine has been mentioned. Walter Pater. Corneille, of course. But nobody had thought of Gertrude Stein! Nobody, that is, except Leonard Lyons, who must have known it all along. Now at least I go to my grave with that problem solved.

Yrs,
John

[1] 16 August 1961. Lyons wrote that playright/director Garson Kanin "was influenced by the writings of the late Gertrude Stein. . . ."
[2] The Elizabethan Club at Yale.
[3] A Boston literary club.
[4] Assistant editor of *The Atlantic Monthly*.

TO: Katharine Barnes O'Hara

Inscription in
Sermons and Soda Water
(London: Cressett, 1961).
PSt.

*This edition printed on
mould made paper and signed
by the author is limited to
525 copies*

**THE NUMBER OF THIS COPY
IS 1**

John O'Hara
to
Sister, who is also
Number 1, et ad infinitum
— John
29 Sept. '61

                                                        4 Oct '61

Dear Bill:

Let me give you and Shawn a little lecture.[1]

The change Shawn suggests ("Two hours ago he had made love to
her and that was all right," instead of ". . . and it was all right") is not
all right here, in this story, for this woman, at this time on this Sunday
morning. If this woman were still enjoying the happy glow from the love-
making, there would be no story. The happy glow has vanished quickly
in the routines and chores, etc., of the Sunday morning, which are com-
pounded by the weather. Ross used to complain: "God, what would our
authors do without the weather?" (He had a certain author in mind;
not me. A lady author.)

It is Sunday morning—to go on—drizzly and cold. The lovemaking
glow is over, a deep-seated discontent has taken over once again after
the satisfaction of a routine piece of tail. The young woman already
has had time to let the piece of tail fall into the category of routine,
and she therefore thinks "it had been all right." She is not, in other
words, to be gotten out of her sour mood by reflecting on the pleasure
of two hours ago. This, I believe, is characteristic of this kind of woman
at this time, and it is no more masculine than feminine. Don't forget
that this woman has been married 12 years and has had two children,
and remember, too, that later in the story she is very nearly receptive
to the play made for her by a man she doesn't like.

The story loses a lot by Shawn's change: it loses the point—an important
one—that Sex is not all-powerful at this stage of this kind of marriage.
If this woman were much younger, or if her husband had been away
in the Army for several months, her sexual need would prevail, but that
would be quite another story. Here Sex is pleasant, but in two hours
can become and has become an episode in the routine.

I haven't got a carbon of the story, and I have been unable to rewrite
the passage you quoted in your letter, without sacrificing my point about
the relative unimportance of the two-hours-ago lovemaking. I doubt, by
the way, that if you showed the story cold to a woman, she would
volunteer the objection Shawn has made. This is the kind of story women
write me letters about, and they have been known to include snapshots
of themselves in bathing attire. It is a story of vague discontent; from
here on the marriage could go anywhere, but it *has* reached *this* stage.
She does not hate her husband, they have had no quarrel, they are
not dramatically incompatible. That's why I used that word universality.

Finally, I have given this attractive girl no record of infidelity; if she had slept around this would again be a different story.

Next week we will take up Hedda Gabler.

Yrs,
John

[1] "Sunday Morning," 13 January 1962.

TO: Matthew J. Bruccoli

TLS, 1 p. Bruccoli
New Yorker letterhead

1 Nov 61

Dear Mr. Bruccoli:

With some reluctance I give you permission to quote, from MRS. STRATTON OF OAK KNOLL, the dialog on pages 18 and 19[1] in my short story collection, ASSEMBLY.

My reluctance is because I am already on record as having opposed the continuation of the Fitzgerald revival. I say let him rest. It seems to me that the posthumous interest in his writings has reached the stage where it does his reputation no good. There was only just so much written by Fitzgerald, and some of it was uneven as every writer's work is uneven. But in recent years anything and everything that bore his name has been revived, or re-presented, and I know damn well he would protest if he could.

Five or six years ago I adopted a personal policy of giving no more interviews to people who wanted to ask me about Fitzgerald. The would-be interviewers wanted to ask the wrong questions, and most of them had no understanding of the man or his work.

The only car I associate with Fitzgerald was a Nash touring car. Somewhere there is a photograph of him in a Norfolk suit standing beside a Nash.[2] There is some reference, I recall, to a Locomobile in THIS SIDE OF PARADISE; but I would guess that Fitzgerald's preference would have been for a Mercer, either a Raceabout or a Touring Car. The Mercer was built in Trenton and was a popular Princeton car.

This is a private letter and I do not wish to be quoted. I gave out one statement when Hemingway died, and that ends that, although there again I have been asked to talk on TV and the radio, etc., about Hemingway. Some distant future day I may write about both men and their work, but that is a long way off.

Faithfully,
John O'Hara

[1] Conversation about F. Scott Fitzgerald's heroines.
[2] In the illustrations for Fitzgerald's "The Cruise of the Rolling Junk," 1923.

TO: Glenway Wescott[1]   TLS, 1 p. National Institute of Arts and Letters
                                                    "Linebrook" letterhead

7 November 1961

Dear Glenway:

I hereby tender my resignation from the National Institute of Arts and Letters, this resignation to take effect immediately.[2]

Faithfully,
John O'Hara

[1] Novelist; president of the National Institute of Arts and Letters.
[2] O'Hara resigned after he was not nominated for the Institute's Gold Medal for Fiction. The nominees were William Faulkner, John Steinbeck, Katherine Anne Porter, and Kay Boyle.

TO: Glenway Wescott   TLS, 1 p. Wescott
                                                    New Yorker letterhead

13 November 61

Dear Glenway:

A man as sensitive as you will understand what is behind my decision, and I write you this personal letter in reply to the letter of a sensitive man.

My decision stands, and what I say here is in confidence. Twice in the past six years I have been passed over for the Nobel prize—twice that I know of, and I don't know how many other times. But the Nobel people take in the world; the Institute-Academy people take in the work of U.S. citizens only. Not even to be nominated for the fiction prize is a judgment that, considering my work since 1948, I cannot accept with any grace. So I have to separate myself from the organizations that passed that judgment.

I intend not to make any public statement about my resignation at this time, either in criticism of the Institute or in defense or explanation of my own position. But I owed you this letter in appreciation of yours to me.

Faithfully,
John

TO: Joseph O'Hara   TLS, 1 p. O'Hara
                                                          Princeton
                                                       27 Nov. '61

To Joe, Mart, Tom, Jim, Gene and Kathleen:[1]

I have decided to give each of your children $1,000. This comes to an
overall gift of $19,000, and I have already begun arrangements for the
sale of securities that will enable me to raise the cash. The money will
be distributed within the next few weeks.

This money will be turned over to the various fathers, in trust for
the various children, except for Patricia O'Hara, who is over 21. I have
not worked out the details with my lawyer, but that is essentially what
I plan to do.

There are strings attached to these gifts: the money is to be used only
for education or health. That is, to be paid either to an educational
institution for actual board and tuition; or to a doctor or a hospital. It
is not to be used for clothes, travel, cars, or any luxury. If any of you
have any objection to these restrictions, say so now, and I will remove
your name from the list.

I suggest, but do not insist, that the money be placed in savings
accounts, to draw interest over a period of years, and to provide an
emergency fund for each child. I have made no distinction as to the
various parents' financial status, and I rely on the parents to see that
the conditions of those gifts are carried out.

Finally, for your information, under present tax rules this sum of
$19,000 represents, for me, about $80,000 earned income, at the very
least. And the gift is not deductible.

                                                          John

[1] O'Hara's brothers and sister with children.

TO: Robert Moses, *Park East* (17 January 1974), 5   *New Yorker* letterhead
                                                        4 Dec '61

Dear Bob:

I had a hell of a hard time finding the Niagara campus in the aerial
photographs in the Frontier progress report. This is somehow appropriate
since Niagara, the educational institution, would have a hell of a hard
time finding me.

I went there for my last year in prep school (my father also had gone there before entering the University of Pennsylvania to study medicine). I was valedictorian of the class of 1924, Niagara University Preparatory School, but then I was retroactively expelled for getting drunk on commencement night. Before going to Niagara I had been kicked out of two other schools and had spent one year working for J. G. White, and I felt I was about 55 years older than everyone else in the school. It is a sorry record, and my quick entrance into the newspaper business was inevitable after that. Incidentally, it was the last year of the existence of Niagara Prep; it has been defunct ever since I made my presence felt as honors student and rakehell.

But I had a good year there. Nearly every afternoon I went for a walk to Lewiston, all by myself except for a book and a pipe, and I always used to pause for the view from the Niagara Falls Country Club and watch the Toronto boat come in from the Lake. Some days I would walk all the way to Fort Niagara, where a former chauffeur of my father's was a regular army sergeant. When he was in the AEF in France I used to write to him and he brought back a handsome German belt for me and an Iron Cross. He was a wild Irishman called Foxie Cole, and at Fort Niagara he would lecture me on drinking and smoking, to both of which my father was fanatically opposed, but he and I would then light up a couple of Piedmonts and he would take me to the canteen and treat me to a bottle of pop. I loved the village of Lewiston, and I hope you have kept it the way it used to be, but I would guess that the realtors and improvers got there before you did.

Some time when you are making a speech you might mention that the road from Niagara Falls to Rochester was once known as the Million-Dollar Highway. What would it cost today? I note a Porter Road near the country club. Was it built of shredded wheat?[1] I would match shredded wheat against Ed Flynn's[2] Belgian paving blocks any day.

As ever,
John O'Hara

[1] Alexander J. Porter, President of the Natural Food Company, which manufactured shredded wheat in Niagara Falls.
[2] Edward F. Flynn, New York City politician and Chairman of the Democratic National Committee. In 1942 he was accused of using city employees and material in making a courtyard for his summer home

Dear Dave:

Thank you for sending me Kirsch's review,[1] which, of course, delighted
me. I had not seen it, as the Random House publicity department is run
by a woman who must run a candy store in Hackensack, N.J., and has
an assistant who is taking "diction" at Cooper Union. Last week I got
a batch of reviews of my FIVE PLAYS book, which was published in
August. Peak efficiency.

I wrote to Cerf and urged him to reprint Kirsch's review in a photo-
static layout, because Kirsch said, and said angrily and well, so many
things that ought to be said out loud in the East. Kirsch, Boroff[2] in the
Sunday Times, and John Hutchens in the daily Trib have written what
I consider the soundest reviews of this book, and I like Kirsch's best
because it is vital. He missed none of the points I hoped to make by
this book: for instance, the range of topics. There isn't anyone else today
—and I don't know when there has been anyone else—who takes this
whole country and all social strata to work with. It amuses me to read a
Time review that calls me an outsider giving an outsider's view of the upper
crust. It happens that I am not quite so far outside as those people would
like to think, but that isn't what's important. What *is* important is that
those very same people accept as gospel whatever Margaret Mead writes
about the savages in the South Seas, to give one example. But I have spent
far more time among the American natives, I know their language and
their customs, and I move about among them freely and inconspicuously
because I happen to be one of them. The inverted snobs who want to
believe that I am an outsider so they can attack me on that basis are
revealing only that they want to have some basis for attack. I never see
them at the weddings and funerals and parties I go to or at the clubs
I belong to, and I never will, but when they cast doubt on my credentials
they inadvertently admit that they have never been admitted. But as I
say, it goes deeper than that. I get no complaints of inaccuracy from
the socially secure, believe me. So it would certainly appear that the complaints that come from the social nobodies, the hack reviewers, indicate
that they are over-impressed by a life they pretend to despise. That being
the case—and it is—how trustworthy are their judgments of work that
does not deal with the upper crust? And if they can be so wrong about
me and my lifelong meanderings among the upper crust, which are simple
verifiable facts, how right can they be in their literary judgments?

The quote from Joseph Conrad that I used as an epigraph for
ASSEMBLY was a wonderful piece of luck for me.[3] It didn't have to
be me stating the case; it was Conrad, who has nearly always been an
egghead favorite. It should have been a warning to some of the critics,

but it hasn't seemed to affect those who could profit by a warning. They still dismiss my eye and my ear, but everybody has eyes and ears. These people go right on as though a good eye and a good ear (which are not standard equipment, although we all have eyes and ears) function independently or in the absence of a good mind and craftsmanship and what is poetically called a heart.

And what is the other thing they attack me on? That I am a copy of Hemingway and Fitzgerald. Well, when I wrote APPOINTMENT IN SAMARRA I had read THE KILLERS and A FAREWELL TO ARMS, but a critic would have a hell of a time proving a Hemingway influence there, and after that I was on my own. As to Fitzgerald's influence, it was largely in choice of material rather than in viewpoint or literary presentation. Fitzgerald really didn't like APPOINTMENT IN SAMARRA or BUTTERFIELD 8, because he was basically a prude. I wish I had saved a letter he wrote me about BUTTERFIELD 8, in which he said something to the effect that sex should be used sparingly, and refused to give Harcourt, Brace a quote for an ad. Much as I admired Hemingway and Fitzgerald's work, my considered opinion is that I was more strongly influenced by Tarkington, Galsworthy, and Lewis than by the younger men. If Tarkington had lived a little later and had not been influenced by Bar Harbor,[4] he would have been the best of us all. Now I think I am. At 57-less-one-month there is no time for spurious modesty, and I think I am the best. Mind you, I think there could be better; I know my shortcomings; but no one else has done what I have done with this country in our time, no one else has worked so hard and with such purpose or with a grand scheme. Beginning with A RAGE TO LIVE, I knew I had a grand scheme, of which the individual works were each a part. My best is FROM THE TERRACE; but the one where the serious critics missed the boat is OURSELVES TO KNOW. Some day critics now unborn and removed from contemporary influences may argue that it is my best. If Kirsch gets his (and my) wish, the Nobel, neither he nor I will have to be ashamed of the honor. Kirsch won't have to make excuses for supporting me, and I won't have to be any more modest than I am now in accepting the prize. The choices among Americans have been, with the exception of Pearl Buck, good. It would be such fun for me and my family and my friends. Do you like aquavit?

I shouldn't think Cukor would have much difficulty with MM.[5] I've met him only briefly once or twice, with no memorable conversation, but I'll bet he had more trouble with Kate Hepburn and Norma Shearer than he had with Garbo. And with Arthur Miller (who I think is a prime horse's ass) out of the way, MM should be more tractable.[6] Cukor worked with Jeanne Eagels, who was a junkie, and he is now 61 years old, and the only thing Hollywood has to offer a man with his record is the opportunity to make a good picture. That's a very good spot to be in, for you as well as for him.

This afternoon I put a stamp on a Christmas card to you and Helen, so at the risk of redundancy, I repeat the greeting from us both.

As ever
John

[1] Robert Kirsch's review of *Assembly* in the *Los Angeles Times*.
[2] David Boroff.
[3] "My task, which I am trying to achieve, is, by the power of the written word, to make you feel—it is, before all, to make you see. That—and no more. And it is everything."
[4] A fashionable resort in Maine where Tarkington lived during the latter part of his life.
[5] George Cukor was directing Marilyn Monroe in "Something's Got to Give," which was not completed.
[6] Marilyn Monroe had been married to playwright and novelist Arthur Miller.

TO: Bennett Cerf

TLS, 1 p. Columbia
"Linebrook" letterhead

18 Dec 61

Dear Bennett:

I think the Kirsch review ad looks fine, and I think it will be effective. In our conversations on it I did not have a chance to point out the hard-sell in the last two paragraphs, especially the very last, which make ASSEMBLY just the book to give Junior to help him in his creative writing course.

An odd thing about this book: it has not appeared on the best-seller lists, but it has been on the Times recommended list for two straight Sundays, on the Time list for two weeks, and did you see the page-wide box in yesterday's Trib? I think it will go to 25,000,[1] which is all I ever hoped for it.

You have been a good boy, so I am going to give you a best-seller for May: it is THE BIG LAUGH, a novel about an actor and the Hollywood that is no more. It is not like any Hollywood novel you ever read, and not very much like any anywhere-novel. No one else could have written it. No one.

Yrs
John

[1] *Assembly* sold 24,000 copies in cloth.

26 Dec 61

Dear Bill:

I am very disappointed that you are not buying the story about the advertising woman.[1] The previous story that you also rejected was,[2] as I told Maxwell, a *multum in parvo* kind of story that would have been better if expanded to twice the length. Some stories that try to compress in two or three thousand words what should be told in ten thousand do not come off, but that was not the case with the advertising woman, and I think this rejection is a mistake.

It sometimes seems to me that you turn down pieces before you have given them a chance to take effect. This is especially true when the stories are concerned with people who might be called the affluent. That has been my experience; most of your rejections, nearly all, have been of stories about the well fixed. Such stories appear to have one strike on them at the very start.

All I can do is protest, in the hope that in so doing I can persuade you that it is I, rather than The NYer, that will take the rap for stories that do not come off, or that you are inclined to think do not come off. Most of the reviews of ASSEMBLY are now in, and they are interesting for this among other reasons: the one story that was almost unanimously well received, MRS. STRATTON OF OAK KNOLL, was a New Yorker rejection, and a fast one. Next in favor was THE GIRL FROM CALIFORNIA, the story about the young movie stars that did appear in the magazine (and was chosen for the O. Henry collection, although I refused permission to reprint). MRS. STRATTON etc was about the affluent; the California girl was really not, although movie stars were involved.

It has been my experience, through several books of short stories, that every story in the book, each story, will turn out to be the favorite of some reviewer. Predictably. I remember a story called WHERE'S THE GAME?, about a small time hangeron in mob circles in the Bronx.[3] It was extremely successful as to reviews and anthologies here and abroad. Gibbs said, "Why didn't you show us that story?" And I said, "I did. You rejected it." That was some time before you became editor, but it illustrates my point. Another story that always got good reviews was called A PHASE OF LIFE.[4] Gibbs tried to get the magazine to buy that one, but failed because it was about a whorehouse in Harlem and purity prevailed on 43rd Street. It is a pretty tame piece in 1961. But I like to be a little ahead of my contemporaries. There is no one around at The NYer now who can testify to my early struggles to get past obtuseness and purity in the exalted echelons. Ross's wisecrack—"Be damned if I buy another O'Hara story that I don't understand"—may have been funny enough at lunch at the Algonquin, but there is no doubt that it influenced policy. That, and Mosher's favorite word, elliptical. Do you know what finally broke the ice for me? The fact that in 1931 Scribner's, then a good magazine, bought a story I had not even bothered to submit to The NYer and ran my name on the cover.[5] Had it not been for that bit of luck I'd still be writing those dreadful little potboilers in the back of the book. And yet as late as 1938 Ross wanted me to make a career of the Pal Joey pieces. (In 1942 he thought it would be a swell idea to have Joey join the Navy and write a modern version of Dere Mabel. At the same time he quite angrily rejected a story called PATRIOTISM[6] because it would be destructive to morale.)

We both know that if I want to see my stories published they have to be in The NYer or nowhere else except when I bring out a collection. This, therefore, is a protest without any force, and with the advantages all on your side. Your argument, of course, is that you run the magazine, and I can take it or leave it. But I don't really write that many bad stories. I have never submitted one that you or I would have to apologize for.

Yrs,
John O'Hara

[1] "The Nothing Machine," *The Cape Cod Lighter* (1962).
[2] Unidentified.
[3] *Pipe Night* (1945).
[4] *Hellbox* (1947).
[5] "Alone," *Scribner's* (December 1931).
[6] *Pipe Night*.

TO: Wylie O'Hara   TLS, 1 p. Mrs. Doughty
c. 1961   "Linebrook" letterhead

My dear:
    Your nephews, Payter and Courtie[1] (and they are now, you know, Aunt Wylie[2]) are here with your Sister Joan, and they are very cute. They love my study, with all the knickknacks, especially scissors and letter-openers and anything else that's sharp or lethal. I look at them and wonder if I will be around to see children of yours. I never saw my Grandfather O'Hara, and my father never saw any of his grandchildren. If you think I spoil you, it's nothing to what he would have done. You'd have had a horse and probably a mink coat, and certainly nothing so modest as a charm bracelet with its annual additions. Your Greatgrandfather Delaney would have been the same way.

You were at your relaxed and friendly best over the weekend, and I want to tell you again how much pleasure you gave us both.

Love
Dad

¹ The children of Sister's daughter, Joan Bryan Gates.
² Wylie had been adopted by Sister O'Hara.

TO: Wylie O'Hara   TLS, 2 pp. Mrs. Doughty
7? January 1962   Princeton

Sunday

My dear:

I have been thinking about our conversation of last night, and I hope you have too.

1962, in some ways, is Wylie O'Hara's Year of Decision. Some of the decisions you make this year will have an important bearing on decisions you may want to make several years hence.

For example: suppose that when you are 20 or 21 you should discover that you want to participate in one of the many activities that will be open to young people in the federal or state government. The first thing they will want to know is what education and/or training you have had. Nowadays the minimum, absolute minimum requirement for hundreds of jobs is two years' college, either at a four-year-college or at a junior college.

For another example: you have said that you don't expect to marry before you are 23. Well, that is something you can't be sure of, but suppose you do wait till you're 23. Suppose your fiance-husband is a young man who is taking graduate work at some university—law, medicine, the sciences, government work, etc.—and you and he are living in the vicinity of his graduate school. You may want to do work on the college or the graduate school level yourself, but I assure you you will not be very enthusiastic about it if you have to start as a freshman of 23.

Now I could go on at some length, but the point I am aiming at is this: I want you to think very, very seriously about what you are going to do after St. Tim's. You are not Miss Richbitch. You are not going to be Miss Churchmouse, either, but you must think in terms of being able to earn at least part of your own living. I don't think you are going to fall in love with a dumbhead. I think a dumbhead, rich or not, would bore the hell out of you. Therefore it is extremely likely that the kind of boy you will like and fall in love with is going to be one who uses his brains to earn his living. That almost automatically means that he will be taking either graduate work or special post-college training of some sort. And even if you have children right away, you will want to keep up with him intellectually.

I can tell you from my own experience how important it is to have a wife with whom to discuss one's work. My first wife was a Wellesley B.A. and a Columbia M.A. and a diplomate, I think they are called, at the Sorbonne. Your mother did not go to college, but she could have. Sister and your mother both graduated from good schools and took courses at Columbia and your mother even attended lectures at Oxford without having to enroll there. Both your mother and Sister loved to read and read a great deal, and Sister is multilingual. Both your mother and Sister disliked women's colleges, but they did not dislike higher learning. They formed their dislike of college-girl types thirty years ago. The type has almost vanished, because the kind of girl your mother and Sister were then would be applying for college today. Everybody goes to college.

Now this is what's on my mind: the tentative program you have outlined for yourself does not seem to me very "realistic" in 1962 and 1963 and so on. I am hopeful that you will redirect yourself toward a good college so that you will get those two minimum-requirement years on your record and then be able, three years from now, to qualify for jobs or continue working for a degree. You will not regret having those two years on your record, whereas you might easily regret *not* having them. As your father I have a duty to point these things out to you. But once I have done that I have to leave the real decision up to you.

I had a wonderful experience at Trenton. I waited on the platform, in case you did not take that train. Right in front of me there was a Pullman car, and I happened to notice that an austere woman was reading SERMONS AND SODA-WATER (the three-volume edition). I knocked on the window, and she was understandably confused until I pantomimed "book" with my hands and pointed to myself. She got it, got all excited, and spoke to her husband in the chair adjoining hers. He was delighted, recognized me right away, and so did a woman who was in the other neighboring chair. Then the people in the other chairs, overhearing the excitement, all laughed and waved to me. So I clasped my hands like a prizefighter, and took off my hat and bowed. I'm sure I'll get a letter from my reader on the other side of the Pullman windows. It was fun.

Love,
Dad

TLS, 1 p. Mrs. Doughty
Princeton

Friday

My dear:

I am so glad they found your suitcase. I personally am pleased because I was saddened to think you had lost your charm bracelet. I telephoned Mr. Sturhahn and told him to call off the search.

It embarrasses me to have to report that *I* flunked a test today. I wrote a story[2] for the Saturday Evening Post, and they rejected it. However, I sold a longer story[3] to The New Yorker yesterday, so we take the bad with the good. I suggest that you substitute a private, secret nickname for History. Call it something like Gossip of the Past, which in a sense it really is. As I said on the telephone, don't think of those people as bloodless, cold hunks of marble. The Stuart portraits of George Washington don't indicate that he was a very human being, who had false teeth (made of wood), who swore like a trooper, liked his booze, and had money troubles. Lincoln loved to tell dirty stories, and he sometimes went a week without going to the bathroom. Andrew Jackson killed several men in duels and had a mistress publicly. Jefferson is said to have had a love affair with the wife of his best friend; he loved to play the violin and he was a damned good carpenter and poet. Alexander Hamilton was a bastard, an illegitimate child. (So was Ramsay MacDonald.) And so on and so on. You won't find these things in prep school history books, but they are true, and if you will only remind yourself that *all* the people in the history books were first of all people, you will begin to view the subject as a human interest story. And that's what it is. Behind every great army is always some general, who may be a genius or a coward, but is also hungry and homesick or a little cracked or all these things. Franklin D. Roosevelt died while his girl friend was reading to him, so I'm told. So you see, you have to use a little imagination in studying history. You wouldn't want to entertain those kings of England. They never bathed. Neither did good Queen Bess, for that matter.

Love
Dad

---

[1] Wylie read this letter at the memorial service for her father at Random House, 13 May 1970. At the top of the original she had written: "HERE'S HOW MY FATHER USED HIS TALENT TO MAKE PEOPLE COME ALIVE   TO HELP HIS DAUGHTER WHO WAS FAILING HISTORY."

[2] Unidentified.

[3] Unidentified.

TO: Wylie O'Hara   TLS, 1 p. Mrs. Doughty
28 January 1962   New York City?

                   Sunday

Dearie:

Everything fine today.

I was with Sister from lunch to dinner. I could not believe how well she looked when I saw her today. After all, only a little more than 24 hours had passed since her operation, but she looked better today than she did on Friday, the day before she was operated on. I talked with Dr. Damon and also with Dr. Bailey, and they are as pleased as I am. She had no nausea today, and only a little pain sometimes. She even talked about going home, but I told her that my scout training did not include learning how to remove stitches, so she would have to stay at Harkness till a week from tomorrow. She was out of bed, walking a few steps this morning, and tomorrow will be out twice.

I had the first real night's sleep in six months last night. Phoned Courty at 9.30, then went to sleep and did not get up till 11 this morning. I have been worried a long time, even before Sister had the polyp removed. Don't ask me why; I don't know why. Maybe I'm just a chronic worrier. But I slept last night.

Your Uncle Bob called on Sister before I was there, so I didn't see him today, but yesterday when I saw him he asked me if you were going to go to Stowe with them. I said I didn't know. But he said he had heard you liked your first experience skiing and he hoped you would be with them. I hope so too. You are a member of a family, you like most of them, and they like you. They more than like you, and I think they were a little hurt when you didn't go with them last year.

Well, bedtime for Daddy-o.

                   Love
                   Dad

TO: Wylie O'Hara   ALS, 3 pp. Mrs. Doughty
30 January 1962   Letterhead of The Lowell,
                 New York City

                 Tuesday

Deario—

Sister loved your letter. She called me up as soon as she got it. Said it was so nice it made her want to cry. (I wouldn't be surprised if she

387

did.) I—we—were delighted with your examination scores. Two subjects in the "B" class shows that you are really in there trying, not just at exam time, but day by day. That, of course, is what exams prove, and that is what exams are for. You also staged a good comeback in your old pal, History. I think part of your success in the History exam is due to a more relaxed attitude. I repeat: except for the problem of memorizing dates, History should be your easiest subject, since you care about *people*.

The word is that Sister is to go home one week from today, Tuesday, and that is definite, according to Dr. Damon. You can plan to come home any weekend after that. Sister will be convalescing, of course, but I will do the chauffeuring.

Tomorrow night Mr. Outerbridge is giving me a birthday dinner for two at the Harvard Club. Your old man will be 57, and that's old, kid, that's old.

I gave Sister an anniversary present. A gold square with seven tiny diamonds for our seven years. She can wear it as a charm on her bracelet, or around her neck. On the back is

31 JAN. 1955
31 JAN. 1962

and her initials.

Love
Dad

TO: Glenway Wescott   TLS, 1 p. Wescott
                                   "Linebrook" letterhead

6 Feb. '62

Dear Glenway:

Thank you for your good letter. I am glad that the problem of my resignation has passed from you to Malcolm.[1] I am touched, too, by the fact that it has been a problem, and honored by your concern.

I assure you that if Malcolm puts this and that together and concludes that the Gold Medal had something to do with my resignation, it will not, would not have crossed my mind that you had broken a confidence. I may not know you very well, but I know you that well.

I don't belong in the Institute. They took so long in getting around

388

to electing me that they would have to give a special medal for longevity before I got anything else—and I'll never be eligible for that.

With kind regards,

Yrs
John

¹ Malcolm Cowley.

TO: Malcolm Cowley
TLS, 1 p. Newberry
Princeton

9 Feb. '62

Dear Malcolm:

When I was finally elected to the Institute, *in* 1957, there was just about no one left on the outside. The Institute had already taken in ahead of me a considerable number of men and women whose work, in my opinion, did not qualify them. But I said to myself, Better late than never—and became a member, with a secret mental reservation: that I would wait three years for election to the Academy,¹ and if at the end of three years I wasn't in the Academy, I would get out of the Institute.

Well, I forgot about my mental reservation, or rather I forgot to look at the calendar. The Howells medal was awarded, but not to me; and then, last Fall, came the ballot with the four names of authors who were to be voted on for the Gold Medal. Then I looked at the calendar and said to myself, What the hell? You have been passed over by the Academy, you have been passed over for the Howells medal, and you have been passed over for the Gold Medal. Time to get out.

So I wrote to Glenway Wescott, then president, and formally resigned. Glenway was quite upset, asked me to reconsider, and was kindness itself. But I pointed out to him that by staying in the Institute I was, in effect, concurring in decisions that I did not believe in. I also told him that I was not going to make any public statement regarding my resignation at that time. I repeat that to you: I am not going to make any public statement now, but will probably put my case in a Foreword to a collection of short stories I expect to publish in late 1963.²

My work—my "body of work"—can speak for itself, and I have no desire to kick up a fuss. I will make my statement where I think it belongs—in a book, the 1963 collection—and for the record, and there the matter will end. I am, and hope to continue to be, too busy with my work to engage in literary controversy. I happen to know that as of three years ago I had been up twice for the Nobel Prize. I don't know what has happened there since then as my source has not volunteered any additional information. (My source, I may say, is not an American.) When

I tell you that I have two novels completed (one to be published in May 1962) and a third about two-thirds completed (the third a very long book) you will understand why I cannot afford the time and energy on non-creative activity.

Meanwhile, my resignation stands, as of the date I wrote to Glenway. With kind personal regards,

Faithfully,
John O'Hara

[1] The American Academy of Arts and Letters elected its members from the National Institute of Arts and Letters; the Academy's membership was smaller than that of the Institute.
[2] O'Hara did not include this statement in the Foreword to *The Hat on the Bed*.

TO: William Maxwell   TLS, 1 p. PSt.
                                                              Princeton

                                                          23 Feb '62
Bill:

My brother sent me this clipping from the Pottsville Republican, and it has been lying on my desk, staring up at me, for a week. Nothing I can think of recently has made me more conscious of the passage of time.

Bobby Snyder was the freshest punk kid in our crowd, and I have not seen him since 1930. He appears in one of my books as a minor character at a dance, right out of life, because at 18 he came to the Assembly wearing his late father's tails when all the rest of us younger ones were grateful to have a Tuck. He was quite good-looking in a neat, regular-featured way, but I hated him. He talked dirty all the time, and he used to put his hand up girls' dresses and whistle through his teeth. He was really in my sister's crowd, and I moved more in an older crowd, but Bobby was "adorable" and "fun" in the stupid opinion of all girls. I loathed him, and he would not fight me.

His mother was a widow, not too well off financially, but a snob. Bobby had an older brother, Baird Snyder IV, who was about as much older than I as I was older than Bobby. Bobby "imitated" Baird, who put his hand up girls' dresses and whistled, and told dirty stories in mixed company. Bairdie was authentic Fitzgerald-plus. He went to Kent, then, incredibly, to Yale, Cornell, and M.I.T., finally getting a degree at M.I.T.

Our club, the predecessor of the country club, was called the Outdoor Club, and there was a dance every week in the summer. The orchestra was called the Tasmanian Tinsmiths. Van Dusen Rickert, Princeton, on the tenor sax; Pete Williams (West Point *and* Colgate) on the piano; Dooley Womer, Pottsville High School, on violin; Carleton Simonds,

Dartmouth, on banjo, and Bairdie Snyder on drums. Bairdie had a big suitcase to carry his traps—cowbells, wood blocks, ratchet, etc.—and as soon as his mother went home, around eleven, Bairdie would open the suitcase and trot out the liquor. Bairdie married a very attractive girl from New Jersey named Lydia Collins, had two kids, and then they were divorced. I don't think I ever saw Bairdie after 1927, although I did see Lydia in NY a couple of times. Bairdie, along the way, had picked up TB, and I had some notion he had died in Arizona. But in 1936, when I was in Hollywood, a Guild official said there was a man from Washington, D.C., in town who was asking for me. Next day I saw in the paper that the man was Baird Snyder IV, special assistant to Harold Ickes[1] and Coordinator of some arcane New Deal enterprise. Of all the unlikely people to be mixed up in the New Deal, Bairdie Snyder topped my list, and that goes for FDR and Averell Harriman. I telephoned his hotel, but he had gone to San Francisco, and I never did see him.

I can't believe that Bobby ever got to be 54-less-two-weeks. I'm sure my sister shed a tear for him, and I feel frustrated because I never gave him a crack in the mouth. A girl once said to me, "You're worse than Bobby Snyder," and I wanted to throw her out of the car.

John

[1] Secretary of the Interior in Roosevelt's Cabinet.

TO: Wylie O'Hara   TLS, 1 p. Mrs. Doughty
                                                      Princeton
                                                    28 Feb '62

My dear:
I am terribly sorry to hear, from Miss Watkins in today's mail, that Kassie Wilson died. I know how it must sadden you and Patience and the other girls in your class.

When I was about 14 or 15 the phone rang at our house one day. It was the priest who was assistant pastor of St. Patrick's Church, my church, to tell me that a girl named Beulah Keiter had died and that the family wanted me to be a pall bearer. It was all very strange, because Beulah had lived in Pottsville only a few years and had moved back to Williamsport. I can't remember why they were holding the funeral in Pottsville. But this much I do remember: Beulah was one of the first girls I ever kissed. She was a quiet, sexy girl, my age, who wore high heels before other girls did. I was in love with her for a month or so, before she decided she was more in love with a boy named Pat Little, and I decided I was more in love with Catherine McGinley.

I could not understand why the priest picked me as a pall bearer, until I learned that many years earlier the Keiter family had been friends of the O'Hara family, my father's people, in Shenandoah, Pa., and that the Keiters wanted me because of that old friendship.

All I had to do was meet at the church with five other boys and walk up the aisle as they pushed the casket to the altar rail. As an altar boy I had often served Mass at funerals of people I did not know, but I had only been to two funerals that affected me personally: my favorite Uncle Eugene Delaney's, and my favorite Grandfather Delaney's. But they were family. I cried all through Beulah's funeral, because no one my age had died before and because I had once been in love with her.

In later years I had a couple of dates with Beulah's older sister, and we made out, as your generation says, but she did not seem to have any connection with Beulah. Beulah was separate and distinct, and always has been, all my life. She was my first sadness of that kind.

Why am I telling you this? Because if it's any comfort to you (and Patience and the other girls), Kassie is someone you will always remember with sweet sadness. You will remember her after you have ceased to remember some of your friends who live on. And it is a nice thing to be remembered.

I had a friend years ago who had to drop out of Yale and graduate with a later class because he had encephalitis. It is a form of sleeping sickness. My friend is still alive, was one of the early editors of Time, good tennis player, etc. They know so little about it, and I have a theory that it isn't one disease but several, like polio.

Sadness is a part of growing up, of maturing, of learning to live.

Love
Dad

TO: William Hogan
TLS, 1 p. Hogan
Princeton

13 April '62

Dear Mr. Hogan:

Delighted to get your note about my piece in last Sunday's Trib.[1] The piece was long overdue, but when Kazin's book[2] and my retired-professor friend's[3] letter arrived here almost together, I took down the scatter gun and let go. The response has been good. Old friends of my Mother's are pleased; old Pottsville friends of mine are pleased; and the Irish are pleased. As a general rule the Irish are as sensitive as the Jews, and particularly when one Irishman presumes to get out from under the stereotype. The non-Irish, especially the eggheads, prefer their Irish to conform to the James T. Farrell description; but in San Francisco that isn't easy, and now, with the U.S.A. turning into the Dominion of Kennedy, it's finally getting through the eggheads' eggheads that it's time for an agonizing reappraisal.

Seventy years ago my old man graduated from an Ivy League university, when the Ivy League was known as the Big Four; somewhat less than that my Mother graduated from a Sacred Heart school. (There aren't many eggheads who dare go back that far in their own backgrounds.) And they weren't poor folks then . . .

I hope you like THE BIG LAUGH. It is, in its modest way, the only picture I know of of a phase of Hollywood-cum-theater life that was important for its influence on the nation and the world at large. I don't write about influences as such, but I get the idea across through my characters.

The Random House secret service never sent me your review of ASSEMBLY—if any. Do you suppose you could dig one up and send it to me?

Cordially,
John O'Hara

¹ "Don't Say It Never Happened," an article in which O'Hara refuted the assertions about his deprived childhood, was published in the *Herald Tribune* book review section (8 April 1962).
² Alfred Kazin's *Contemporaries* (1962) referred to O'Hara as "a social sorehead from the wrong side of the tracks."
³ Prof. W. L. Werner of Pennsylvania State University.

TO: William Maxwell
TLS, 1 p. PSt.
"Linebrook" letterhead
18 April '62

Dear Bill:

Thank you for your note. By "letter" I hope you meant my piece in the Sunday Trib.

I have not been able to get back to writing my big novel,¹ so I wrote a play and some stories. I plan to publish a book in the fall to be called THIRD CLASS CITY,² which will be several long stories about guess where? I don't know how marketable they will be at The NYer, but you can see them if you like. The publication date is Thanksgiving. All the stories are not yet finished. I think I have finished two and am finishing a third. Very confusing to keep track of so much work, and I have had many distractions lately.

Yrs
John

¹ *The Lockwood Concern*. O'Hara interrupted work on this novel and published it in 1965 as a 400-page book.

² "Third Class City" was never published. The Thanksgiving 1962 O'Hara book was *The Cape Cod Lighter*.

TO: Katharine Delaney O'Hara

Inscription
in *The Big Laugh*.
PSt.

To Ma
this should
clear your sinuses
Love
John
20 April 1962

TO: The *New York Herald Tribune* (29 April 1962), II, 3

Down in Jungletown, where I now live, I am sometimes regarded as a Yale spy because it seems to have got around that in my youth I wanted to go to Yale. And didn't. So when Yale thinks out loud about admitting women as students, I am expected to comment. All right, I'll comment: I have absolutely no connection with Yale, and yet in my small way I may have been responsible for breaking down the misogynistic barriers at New Haven. I had nothing whatever to do with getting girls into Yale, but I had a lot to do with getting a girl into the bar of the Yale Club.

The time was 1929, and I was an almost daily and nightly visitor to the Yale Club, usually with a friend whom I shall call Willard Newton (names changed to protect the innocent, if any). Newton and I had a friend, a very pretty girl whom I call Jean Acheson, who like so many girls in 1929 had tried in vain to gain entrance to Dan Moriarty's all-male speakeasy on East 58th Street. Failing Moriarty's, this screwball decided she would like to crash the bar of the Yale Club, and it seemed like a sensible idea. So Jean, who was a model and fairly tall, put on a suit and shirt and shoes of mine, and a Borsalino hat that I had swiped from the Princeton Club, and she and Newton, during the 10 p.m. lull, entered the Yale Club, went upstairs to the bar, had a couple of silver fizzes, and were having a quiet chuckle in the lounge when one of the staff got suspicious. Jean's laugh did it, I suppose, although it may also have occurred to the staff that they had never seen a Yale man so pretty. In any event, Newton and Jean were given the heave-ho.

I was then a rewrite man for the Daily Mirror, and I ghost-wrote "How I Crashed the Yale Club Bar, by Jean Acheson."[1] Jean was paid $50, and she paid me $25 she owed me. Our friend Newton was suspended from the Yale Club, which was not much of a hardship as he was moving to St. Louis. And history was made. The Yale Club bar has never been the same since, and what is happening at New Haven now is no more than a logical sequence of events. You know, like Bleriot to Glenn.

JOHN O'HARA

Princeton, N.J.

[1] Jeanne Atherton, "Girl Invades Yale Club Bar, Only for Men," *New York Daily Mirror* (29 July 1929).

TO: William Maxwell   TLS, 1 p. PSt.
May 1962   *New Yorker* letterhead

Dear Bill:

Own up. After Sunday dinner didn't your father and your uncles Talk Business while the women discussed the new-Axminster-in-the-upstairs-hall? So it really isn't so strange that we have got around to tax advantages and preferred stocks. I can hear your grandfather saying to your uncle, "Alec, look into that piece of property for sale, out by the C.&.A. siding." And your uncle saying, "They'll want too much for it, those Pagenstechers. But I'll ask around tomorrow, next day."

My mother is in the hospital, it's very doubtful that she will come out alive,[1] so I have been making conversation with some of my brothers, of whom I have five, and sisters, two. Yesterday my youngest brother, 43, gave me a complete report on how he and another boy shot a prize-winning hog while gunning for rabbit. It cost my mother $12, thirty years ago. You might have thought he was talking about something that happened last week. Every detail. The size of the lumber used in the hog pen. The roundabout way they took getting home. Four boys' parents had to shell out twelve bucks apiece. At the conclusion of the story I said, "Were you allowed to keep the meat?" No, they weren't, but they weren't prosecuted for having shotguns at that age or trespassing. And so on. But I know the most wonderful story about this same brother that he didn't tell me.

The family had no money left. One night when he was about 13 or 14 he came home very late, 11 o'clock, and woke up my mother and gave her $2. All he would say was that he had got it honestly. Later my mother found out how he got it. He went to the weekly prize fights, entered the amateur fight for that night, and got paid the two bucks. I'll never forget his nom de boxe: Young Pat Igoe.

Yrs,
John

[1] Katharine Delaney O'Hara died 13 May 1962.

TO: Wylie O'Hara

TLS, 1 p. with holograph footnote. Mrs. Doughty "Linebrook" letterhead

27 May '62

My dear:

This is a day on which I am very proud of my lovely daughter. I am especially pleased because this honor is a gift of the people who live, play, work with you and probably know you better than I do, in many ways. They are likely to be more severe in their judgments, therefore their opinion, when it is favorable, is valuable.

But it isn't only today I am proud of you. I am retroactively pleased for the day after day week after week, undramatic times when you were revealing yourself for what you are: a kind, generous, humorous, honorable girl who is growing into a fine woman. That is what your classmates were telling you today. And don't forget this: they would not have elected you their senior class president if they had not admired and respected you for your job as first semester president this year.

Bulletin: just got a nice telegram from Miss Watkins, announcing
the good news.*

Love
Dad

*—But I'm glad I heard it from you first!

D.

TO: Charles Poore

TLS, 1 p. PSt.
"Linebrook" letterhead

11 May 62

Dear Chas.:

Like recording a bet at White's Club, I want to register with you my
selection for the egghead word that stands the best chance of equaling
the popularity of valid-validity. My candidate is accommodate-accommodation.

This word has already shown early foot, and so did valid. Denigrate
and dichotomy were slow starters, did well in the back stretch, but had to
drop out for lack of staying powers. Valid romped home to win the
Triple Crown: first in the political world, the entertainment world,
and with the public.

Accommodate-accommodation may well be the Kennedy administration's answer to Truman's valid. Eisenhower's ghostwriters took up valid,
and Kennedy went along with it, but now he has his own word. Of
course it may also turn out to be as embarrassing to him as appeasement
was to N. Chamberlain.

To me, an old railroader, accommodation means a train that stops
wherever the engineman sees two milk cans.

Regards,

John

TO: The *New York Herald Tribune* (5 June 1962), 20

If the President is not going to read anything I say in the Herald
Tribune, or that the Herald Tribune says about me, I don't know how
I am going to get across to him.[1] Possibly through a series of oversights,
I have not been invited to any of the cultural evenings at the White
House, so I have missed out on that opportunity to give him the benefit
of my experience in international and domestic affairs.

I would be the last man in the U.S.A. to wish to trade on my slight acquaintance with the President, but the layman must realize that the Presidential imprimatur is of inestimable value in literary circles. It was Woodrow Wilson, I believe, who first respectabilized the mystery story, but it remained for Mr. Kennedy to be the first President to single out a whodunit author. I am a little sorry that the author had to be an Englishman and not Mickey Spillane. (As it happens, I have not read Ian Fleming or Mickey Spillane, but I like Mickey Spillane just from hearing him on the radio and seeing him on TV, and I don't think I would like Fleming.) However, we have to take those things as they come, and Spillane and I may get our turns in a later Administration.

For a few minutes after I heard that the Herald Tribune had been banished from the White House breakfast tray, I entertained the immodest thought that Mr. Kennedy was sore at the stupid review my latest book was given in the Sunday Trib. But then I remembered that I had not been invited to the cultural evenings, and I had to consider the possibility that Mr. Kennedy was sore at the favorable review my book was given in the daily Trib. These Kennedy boys are inscrutable—a word that has Oriental associations. Indeed, now I think of it, Jack reminds me more and more of Nehru, and Bobby of Krishna Menon.

A good thing they stopped reading the Trib, or I certainly would have blown my chances with that crack. If it ever gets back to the White House, I'm really cooked. Alsop, Lippmann,[2] you just keep that in the family, do you hear?

JOHN O'HARA

Princeton, N.J.

---

[1] It had been announced that Pres. Kennedy had stopped reading the *Herald Tribune*.
[2] Joseph Alsop and Walter Lippmann, political columnists.

TO: W. L. Werner   TL, 1 p. (probably incomplete).
                                                    Mrs. Werner
                                          Quogue, Long Island

                                                    20 June 62

Dear Bill:

In the near future I will arrange for an appraisal of THE BIG LAUGH manuscript, etc., and then give it to the Penn State Library. As you know, the University of Texas is shelling out big money for such items, and their consultant is a friend of mine (John Hayward, of London), but I really think Penn State, rather than Texas, ought to have my stuff, and that I ought to give it to them.

I would have accepted an honorary degree from State,[1] for the same chauvinistic reasons (I really hate that word chauvinistic). Candor compels me to reveal that I have had only one opportunity to get an honorary degree, and I turned it down.[2] I would accept a degree from Yale, Harvard, Princeton, or State—or Oxford—but I would almost as soon be given an honorary membership in Phi Beta Kappa, which did start life as a literary society and is somehow more appropriate recognition for an author. (Elia Kazan[3] just got a key from Williams, his alma mater, and no writer he.) You tell Kit[4] I want her to have me for a fraternity brother, and for her to be my sponsor in the fratres in urbe at State, not Mount Holyoke.

The Herald Trib piece raised hell, as I intended it to. I grow weary of the efforts of people like Kazin to squeeze all Irish-named people into a Studs Lonigan mold. On the Delaney side I go back to pre-Revolutionary times, straight line, and even my O'Hara grandfather was an officer in the Civil War. In Ireland O'Hara is one of the four or five names that go back to the 10th Century. An O'Hara took Cornwallis' sword to Washington at Yorktown. When you know these things you do not forever sit silent.

[1] Pennsylvania State University does not grant honorary degrees.
[2] The institution that offered O'Hara an honorary degree has not been identified.
[3] Broadway and Hollywood director.
[4] Prof. Werner married Kit Bowman, who had worked with O'Hara on the *Pottsville Journal*.

TO: Charles Poore

TLS, 1 p. PSt.
Quogue, Long Island

3 July 62

Dear Chas.:

Ah, but I do write like Kafka. Somewhere in one of those 14 volumes of scrapbooks that Sister has collected since we were married 7½ years ago there is a high-tone think piece that groups me with Kafka, Kierkegaard, Camus and Sartre. Somewhere else, of course, I am in the company of Cain, Chandler, Hammett and Spillane. And, somewhere else, Edith Wharton and Henry James. And somewhere else, Zola and Sinclair Lewis. I am a sort of utility outsider, an all-purpose for-instancer. And I think I know why.

The same man wrote OURSELVES TO KNOW, the three novellas in SERMONS AND SODA-WATER, FIVE PLAYS, ASSEMBLY, THE BIG LAUGH and—for November publication and October availability—the stories in THE CAPE COD LIGHTER. Bang, bang, bang, etc. I have a story coming out in The New Yorker this summer called THE BUCKET OF BLOOD. If it didn't have my name on it it would not be recognizable as the work of the author of THE WOMEN OF MADI-SON AVENUE. But it *is*, and it does have my name on it. And the next story after that is WINTER DANCE (I think), which would further confuse the authorship identification. Knuckle ball, slider, high hard one, letup ball, etc. I do it that way because I love to do it that way, to sustain my own interest, and only incidentally to confuse the people who put me in lists that prove with eternal finality that I am not as good as Louis Auchincloss, or Ring Lardner, or Philip Roth, or Saul Bellow, depending on which list they are making.

One thing I needn't worry about: that a year from my death a Geismar[1] will solemnly announce that maybe I wasn't so good after all. A year from now the geismars and kazins ought to have Hemingway bracketed with John Updike and William March.[2] And ten years from now *they* will be bracketed with J. Donald Adams. Yo-ho-ho.

John

[1] Critic Maxwell Geismar.
[2] Author of *Company K* and *The Bad Seed*.

TO: William Maxwell   TLS, 1 p. PSt.
                                                      Quogue, Long Island
                                                          23 July '62
Dear Bill:
Sorry I missed you, telephonically, on Friday. I then talked to Shawn and he reported that THE BUCKET OF BLOOD has not been scheduled, but that he would ask you to notify me when a date is set.[1] I am looking forward to seeing it in print.

I finally traded in my Mercedes-Benz on a 3.8 Jaguar. I lost money on the deal, but the cash consideration came out of my Sterling account in London. In some ways I am tough about money, but I practice self-deception too. Like I have had five pairs of Peal shoes made in the last year. They are paid for in Sterling by my London agent, and all I pay in dollars is the duty, which ranges from $2 to around $9. I therefore kid myself that I am getting a pair of Peals for $2. I had a coat made at Burberrys,[2] a cashmere topcoat. I got it for $40—the duty. In NY it would have cost me about $400. To me this all makes perfectly good sense. The money I make in England is pretend-money.

When Belle and I lived in California I always deposited New Yorker and book publishers' and such eastern cheques in my New York bank. Hard money. Real money. The money I received from the movie people I turned over to Belle to deposit in our California bank. Pretend-money, in a pretend-world. All authors ought to follow this plan when they go to Hollywood, then they wouldn't succumb to the fiscal fantasies of the place and their real earning power. I saw too many $75-a-week rewrite men convincing themselves that they were $1500-a-week authors.

Yrs,
John

¹ 25 August 1962.
² London haberdasher, originator of the trench coat at the time of World War I.

TO: Gerald Murphy

TLS, 2 pp. Honoria
Murphy Donnelly
Quogue, Long Island

30 July '62

Dear Gerald:

I imagine you and Sara will be getting a lot of letters about the New Yorker piece¹—and this is one of them. As far as I'm concerned, the piece told a few things about you both that I never knew, and left out a fair number that I thought should have been in. But it was respectful, and literate, and appreciative, and needed to be written, so I give it high marks.

I am writing you because I feel the need to sound off on the subject of the *roman a clef*, which can be pretty disturbing to me. A byproduct of my sounding off may be that you and Sara will feel a little better about TENDER IS THE NIGHT, which I love. You see, I understand exactly what Scott did, although I never discussed it with him.

When I published APPOINTMENT IN SAMARRA, people who knew me, and many who didn't, rushed to identify the Julian English character. They said it was of course autobiographical, and it did no good to point out that I had not inhaled carbon monoxide. There were others who said English was a Pottsville guy named Clinton Whitcomb Sheafer, whom I used to call the local Jock Whitney. A few said English was Edward Fox. So they had three men to work on, and 28 years after the book was published I still hear the same identifications. And they are wrong.

I could go on with the false identifications of the major characters in nearly all of my novels, but I won't. Instead I will tell you my method (which was not Scott's). Long, long before I start writing a novel I have learned all I can about the principal characters. I have determined, to my own satisfaction, what they would do in any and all circumstances. And I am pretty generally right. Why? Because they are all real people, people who are living or who have lived. I use the psychological pattern of the real people, then I put them in different locations and times, and cover them up with superficial characteristics, etc.

401

In the case of Julian English, the guy in real life was a fellow named Richards,[2] who was definitely not country-club, but had charm and a certain kind of native intelligence, and who, when the chips were down, shot himself. I took his life, his psychological pattern, and covered him up with Brooks shirts and a Cadillac dealership and so on, and the reason the story rings so true is that it is God's truth, out of life. You would be surprised to learn who some of my principal characters are—and are not. They are *not* Bob Lovett or Jim Forrestal, or Liz Altemus.[3] Gloria Wandrous, in BUTTERFIELD 8, was, of course, Starr Faithfull,[4] but that identification is unavoidable. I never pretended it wasn't she.

Now as to Scott and the Murphys, he did what all your writing friends wanted to do, which was to write about Gerald and Sara and their life. But Scott didn't have my method to guide him, and he had only the superficials to work with, with the result that Dick and Nicole were never you or Sara. Hoytie?[5]—well. And some of the minor characters, yes. But you two, no. Scott wrote the life, but not the lives. And that is true partly because Scott was always writing about the life. Sooner or later his characters always came back to being Fitzgerald characters in a Fitzgerald world. He was really quite shocked by BUTTERFIELD 8, because no matter what his own conduct was, it did not seem to belong in the Fitzgerald world. He was our best novelist in spite of this limitation. Tarkington, with a worse case of the same limitation, without it would have been much, much better than Scott. They had a fastidiousness that in my opinion should be no part of an author's equipment, at least if it makes him cheat even a little bit. The old thing about no omelet without breaking eggs, no surgery without letting blood.

But we all have our limitations and restrictions, and the lucky ones know them, and this is no criticism of Scott, really. If I had known the Murphys and been compelled to write about them, I would have started by putting them in, say, Santa Barbara, if only to get away from the very things that Scott most wanted to write about. The life, the way of life. And of course as he moved along, he got farther away from any resemblance to the real Murphys. Dick Diver ended up as a tall Fitzgerald, and you could almost see that coming a third of the way through the novel. And the sadness I felt, the pity for this great waste, was finally the real success of the novel, over and above my delight at the writing, the observations, the heat of the sun, the flowers, the nervous fun and the brutality. (To me, GATSBY is greasy kid stuff compared to TENDER IS THE NIGHT.) I'm sure Scott's dissatisfaction with TITN was due to his failure to present the Murphys, but he got his novel anyhow.

I wish the layman would stop trying to identify characters in novels. I guess they always did it, but it seems to me it became worse with the public nosiness as shown by the success of Winchells, and Time cover-stories, and New Yorker profiles. When a novel is obviously, unmistakably about a real person, okay. But it is such a bore to be asked—or, worse, *told*—that your book is about Jim Forrestal and don't you pretend it isn't. It gives us no credit for imagination. A mutual friend of ours called me up late one night to say she was horrified at what I had done to —— —— in A RAGE TO LIVE. The psychological pattern for the woman in ARTL died thirty years ago, and was never acquainted with ——, or with our mutual friend. I could have had my revenge by telling —— that her friend had so identified her, but I got troubles enough already.

I trust this finds you and Sara well and happy. Maybe I *will* write a novel about you some day. About once a year I run into Ben Finney[6] in 21, and he has all the dope about the old days in Santa Barbara.

All good wishes,

John O'Hara

[1] "Living Well Is the Best Revenge," a profile of the Murphys by Calvin Tompkins. Gerald Murphy, an expatriate painter during the Twenties, had been a close friend of F. Scott Fitzgerald's.

[2] William ("Birsie") Richards shot himself in Pottsville on 14 February 1933.

[3] First wife of John Hay Whitney.

[4] Starr Faithfull's body was found at Long Beach, Long Island, on 8 June 1931. She was twenty-five, with a history of heavy drinking and promiscuity. The case was never solved.

[5] Hoyt Wiborg, Sara Murphy's sister.

[6] Bon vivant and world traveler. O'Hara wrote the introduction for Finney's autobiography, *Feet First* (N.Y.: Crown, 1971).

TO: Charles Poore   TLS, 3 pp. PSt.
                                                      Quogue, Long Island

                                                           3 Aug. '62

Dear Chas.:

The intellectual wasteland has been reclaimed! Oh, I know it's too soon to make such sweeping statements, and I am notorious for my habit of looking on the bright side; but last night on TV there was enough concentrated bullshit to fertilize a few acres—especially around Conway, Mass. Did you permit *anything* to detain you from viewing the Dialogs of MacLeish and Van Doran?[1]

Archie was at his very best. Or one of his very bests. Naturally he was not at his sitting-on-the-floor, little-boy, it-hurts-here best. This was his Walden Pond–L. L. Bean-shirt best. Van Doran, in there as a straight-man, came on much too strong for the part he had, but the Master knew how to handle him. When the straight man gets fresh, you don't answer him; you don't even *look* at him. You set your chin like as if you were posing for a statue to be carved out of the Dakota mountains, and the upstart is left hanging with his little Plato gag, his Shakespeare funny.

Lincoln came off very well. I would not be one bit surprised to learn that the Lincoln family were old customers of Carson, Pirie, Scott.² He came off much better than God, although Archie is undoubtedly grateful to the Deity for giving him a chance to toss in a word like anthropomorphic. The Federal Communications Commission is thoroughly hog-tied when a TV performer uses the word hell as a mild cussword and on the very same program tosses in a word like anthropomorphic. (You want to know what word is like anthropomorphic? Well, I give you, for example, hermaphroditic.) MacLeish was just a little unfair to Van Doran, I thought. Van Doran attempted to get down to the people with a small, personal anecdote about Thurber, which, to those of us who knew Thurber plain, was Thurber at his pretentious worst. In such a situation all MacLeish had to do was hit the straight man with a reference to Mark Twain; but Archie brought up the heavy artillery—Lincoln. Since Lincoln embodied all the homespun humor of Mark Twain *plus* the Jesus-in-the-temple imagery, Van Doran was never able to recover, and the poor son of a bitch knew it. He introduced the Bible, which ordinarily would be an effective ploy, but in the moment's context the Bible became only a prop, a volume read by Lincoln at the log cabin fireside.

I have been listening—not without interruption—to Archie for about thirty years, and studying his techniques. I would not dream of attempting to emulate him. I am not the type, and anyway I got laid by being so different from Archie. My approach, you might say, was more nearly like that of Nonie Griggs³ than Archie's. Not exactly like, but more nearly like. Last night Archie again, as always, came out in favor of love, but of course when Archie speaks in favor of love he does so on a higher plane than I can manage to achieve so readily. Archie, approving of love, seems to be in favor of it as I would be (and am) in favor of oxygen. My trouble, obviously, is that I take breathing too much for granted, and one of these days I'm going to be sorry. Mind you, I don't take love *or* oxygen for granted, but I'll bet you that if I'd praised love publicly more than I have, people would not think that all I approve of is fucking. Archie was able to come out—rather slyly, it's true—in favor of fucking, and he was not shut off the air, but he had prepared the atmosphere with some high-level utterances on the subject of love and man. Statements on Love and Man, delivered in tones and terms that perish the thought of fucking and pederasty, automatically put the speaker among the majority of the gentlemen who attended the Last Supper. (There was, as there so often is, one shitheel to spoil even that party.) When they are made on CBS-TV by people like the author of NOBODADDY, they sound to me like rehearsals of a Nobel Prize acceptance speech, but I'm sure Archie wouldn't be caught unprepared if the Swedish academicians gave him the nod. ("It's in the bottom drawer, Ada. Brown Manila envelope.")

The only trouble I had last night was a discovery that hit me along about the first commercial, and it was a result of my study of Archie's technique. As I say, I have been listening for about thirty years, and my inability to follow everything Archie says was due, I always believed, to Archie's habit of lowering his voice to the poet's modulated delivery. But at roughly twenty past ten I realized for the first time that it wasn't how he was saying it but what he was saying that confused me. The discovery embarrassed me all through the Polaroid pitch. But when we got back to Mark and Archie I made the real discovery of the evening. All these years, when I have not quite understood Archie, I was hearing him all right. It was just that Archie has been speaking in Stengelese.[4]

Yrs
John

[1] "Dialogues of Archibald MacLeish and Mark Van Doren."
[2] MacLeish's family had owned an interest in this Chicago department store.
[3] Northam L. Griggs, a Southampton, Long Island, friend of O'Hara's.
[4] Baseball manager Casey Stengel spoke a kind of double-talk.

TO: William Maxwell

TLS, 1 p. PSt.
Quogue, Long Island
8 Aug '62

Dear Bill:

I shall answer your questions as they appear on your note.[1]

1. A half a check is a half a dollar. Slang of the Twenties. It is a curious thing that while a half a check means a half a dollar, or half a buck, I never heard anyone say "A check" for "A dollar." One of those anomalies of American speech; like two bits for a quarter, but never does anyone say one bit for 12½ cents.

2. The "tees and miss-outs" are crooked dice. The tees are also known as the tops, or tops. This is authentic gambler argot, and you usually hear gamblers refer to the tees and miss-outs together, although they are not the same. Shawn should recognize these terms. If I remember correctly, the tees, or tops, are dice so loaded that only certain combinations will come up on top. The miss-outs, if my memory is right, are simply dice which, when thrown, will not produce certain numbers, since on one die there will be no two, four, or six.

3. What ever happened to my earlier proof? I explained, or tried to explain, with a drawing, the O'Leary belt trick. You take an ordinary belt, the kind that holds up your pants; you double it and fold it a certain way, then you bet that your chump can't insert a pencil in the loop that will hold the belt. I'll have to show it to you sometime. It is old carnie stuff.

4. Jay is thinking of a long way back, and has a little trouble remembering how many straight passes he threw.

I was quite disappointed that this piece didn't run in July, as I had a special reason for wanting it to run then, and Henderson[2] led me to believe it would run. Instead, there was a piece by—Henderson.

I am glad you stayed in the saddle. However, when I went to the hospital four years ago with my bad back, the doctor, who is himself a horseman, told me that the riding I did throughout my youth was the worst thing I could have done. I was a good horseman; could, and did, ride 35 miles in a day; broke horses, schooled them, and taught kids to ride. So if you're uncomfortable riding, don't do it. You may be asking for trouble, which is what a bad back is.

J. O'Ha

[1] "The Bucket of Blood," 25 August 1962.
[2] Robert Henderson, *New Yorker* editor and contributor.

TO: Wylie O'Hara   TLS, 1 p. Mrs. Doughty
16 September 1962   Quogue, Long Island

Sunday

My dear:

Well, here we are—but not here. You at St. Tim's, Sister in Princeton, and me in Quogue, and another brand new year is about to start for you. For me, too. I always seem to approach the autumn in the frame of mind that spring induces in most people. The excitement of new things; the new plays, the new books, new clothes, etc., etc., etc. At the same time the autumn for me is a season of a sweet melancholy that is hard to explain. I love the early evenings, the leaves burning, the lights in houses.

It is the beginning of a big year for you, in many respects your biggest so far. By the time June comes around you will be 18, and graduating from school. In the past week or so I have called you "Kid" but subconsciously I have been doing that because your kid days are over, or just about. I suspect that you are going through the experience of first love, and no matter what else happens, after that experience you are never a kid again.

Most of the nice things we associate with being a kid are okay—while you are still a kid. But you gain more than you lose. You gain in understanding, in appreciation of people, in understanding and appreciation of yourself. You begin to see the wisdom in that quotation I have so often repeated to you: to thine own self be true. Every year at this time I have repeated that quotation to you, and the time is not really too far distant when you will be passing it on to your own children. It is probably the best single piece of advice I can give you, or you can give them.

You have done well, and I am pleased with you, not only for what you have done, but for what you are. As Miss Finnegan said to Sister, "Wylie has the right reactions." So good luck in your Senior Year, and always know that the old man loves you very much.

Always
Dad

TO: The *New York Herald Tribune* (19 September 1962), 24

Four or five years ago I served as a judge for the Peabody Awards, and as a result of my eloquence a prize was given to the TV program, "You Are There." I thought it a pretty good program; I like American history. I knew absolutely no one connected with the show, unless you want to go 'way back to when I was about twenty years old and had a date with one of the du Pont girls, who was visiting a friend in Pottsville, Pa. The point here is that I am not prejudiced against TV or American history, and have even signified, on that one occasion, my approval of a combination of the two.

But I am opposed to direct TV coverage of committee hearings in the House and the Senate and in sessions of court. It would be very nice to have on tape today the historic proceedings of the Constitutional Convention of 1787, as well as the first and second trials in the Hall-Mills case. Everybody would love to be able to tune in on Daniel Webster as he utters for the first time those words that have since become so tiresome when repeated by later generations of Dartmouth alumni. It might even be fun to hear again a certain worldly judge in my home county, who squelched an impertinent witness with the remark, "Don't do as I do, do as I say." Our electronically minded eggheads say, "Think how wonderful it would be if we could see and hear the Lincoln-Seward debates."[1] I'll go them one better: think how wonderful it would be if we had Lincoln. Or Seward.

But when William S. Paley says it is a shame that we don't get live coverage of Congress and the courts ("These situations are unreasonable anachronisms," he says), and supports his thesis with the argument that there are now 183 million radio sets in use, you just know that he is not fighting for the privilege of covering a tariff commission hearing on the price of tung oil.

How many times would CBS (or, for that matter, NBC) send camera crews to make a minute-by-minute report of, say, the Supreme Court listening to a complicated rate case like U.S. vs. Northeastern Southwestern Power? Paley and Sarnoff are in the entertainment business, no matter how many pious and highly intellectual statements they make about public service and the communications arts. Any programming they do will be determined on a basis of entertainment value, you can be sure of that, and not by men who are concerned with the present or future historic worth of an event. The Congressional hearings and court trials chosen for broadcasts will promise enough drama or comedy or both to make the programs attractive to sponsors. But such events will already have enough of the circus atmosphere, without the addition of the TV equipment and its paralyzing or hambo-tempting effect on the human principals. Politicians, jurists, witnesses, spectators and even the camera crews are affected by the presence of the TV apparatus. I give you, for example, the photographers who are always walking up and down behind Mr. Kennedy during a televised press conference. I give you, for another example in a somewhat different field, the Detroit photographers who are always trespassing in the third base coaching box and the third-to-home base path.

They start early nowadays. I am reliably informed that on the Dick Clark show[2] the teenagers arrive wearing brown lipstick so they will look their best on camera. Of course that's history of a sort, too.

JOHN O'HARA

Quogue, Long Island

---

[1] O'Hara had in mind the Lincoln-Douglas debates; there were no Lincoln-Seward debates.
[2] Afternoon TV show on which young people danced to popular music.

TO: The *New York Herald Tribune* (28 September 1962), 24

The spokesman for CBS News, having unburdened himself of a few sarcastic remarks about my work,[1] concludes his plea for TV coverage of Congress and the courts with the statement that I forget that the midget sat on Mr. Morgan's lap long before television.[2]

Quite the contrary. I remember the midget, and I remember Mr. Morgan's savoir-faire. And I also know that the midget never would have been there if the Pecora investigation[3] had barred newsreel cameras.

As to my appointment with the 18th century, which the CBS man says I have, the citizens of that century could at least be more confident that there would be a 19th than we can be that there will be a 21st. They also produced this nation. CBS produced the $64,000 quiz program.

Quogue, N.Y.   JOHN O'HARA

---

[1] On 25 September the *Herald Tribune* published a reply by Richard S. Salant, President of CBS News, to O'Hara's 19 September letter, in which Salant remarked that "Mr. O'Hara has an appointment with the 18th century."
[2] During a Congressional hearing, photographers had placed a midget on J. P. Morgan's lap in order to obtain a gag picture.
[3] Judge Ferdinand Pecora was chairman of this hearing.

TO: William Maxwell   TLS, 1 p. PSt.
                                                             Princeton

                                                             5 Oct. '62
Bill:
    Yes, I am bothered by Bobby and by his brother.[1] I could easily let
myself become more than bothered. I sit here in this extremely pleasant
room, surrounded by things I am fond of and loving my work; but I take
seven daily newspapers and many magazines, and I have a radio in this
room and in my bedroom and in my bathroom, and we have two televisions.
I can press a small button and listen to Moscow, and I don't have to press
anything to get an alarming view. I am revolted by the filthy treatment
they are giving Walker.[2] I have known men like Walker, and some of
them are dead and some of them are wearing high medals, for valor. I'm
sure I wouldn't get along with Walker, but I hate the evil thing they
are doing to him. The ultimate discreditation, the brand of the psycho.
And fixing bail in the same amount that Dr. Soblen[3] was held in. Soblen
and Walker? I contemned McCarthy, a slob, but they disgusted me with
their effort (which they couldn't make stick) to make lovers of him
and ——, the same thing they tried to do to Hitler. There is nothing too
vile for their enemies—but what about Sumner Welles? Acheson? Hiss?
What did Truman, no less, call Stevenson?
    Let us see what happens to Walker. But no matter what happens, we
have already seen the Kennedy brand of fascism, and there will be more.
Watch this new boy. I am told he is something. Watch John reaching
for more executive power, Bobby using Kefauver and Symington. I was
too New Deal to realize it at the time, but it all began with FDR trying
to pack the court. This tribe will make FDR seem like an ardent democrat.

                                                             John

    [1] Robert and John F. Kennedy.
    [2] General Edwin Walker had been accused of indoctrinating his troops with right-
wing propaganda and was charged with conspiracy, insurrection, and sedition in 1962.
    [3] Atom spy Robert Soblen.

TO: Bennett Cerf   TLS, 1 p. Columbia
                                                             Princeton

                                                             11 Oct 62
Dear Bennett:
    I note with displeasure the ad in The New Yorker for American Satire,[1]
etc.
    If the omission of my name was accidental, it was stupid; if it was
deliberate, that was stupid too.

                                409

As a matter of fact I have never found much to admire in the advertising department of Random House. They dirty up the ads—and ask for trouble —with their selections of quotes, and make it appear that my books have nothing to offer but sex. Then when I come up with something worthwhile, such as the Hoke Norris review of THE BIG LAUGH, or some of the reviews I have called your attention to in the past, they drag their feet. For example, I mentioned the Norris review last Spring, but when was it run? And you might ask Erskine about that one. The advertising department had forgot all about the fact that I suggested reprinting the Norris review last Spring, and had no copy of it.

It is asking too much to expect intelligence among hucksters, but when a Random House author is in a Random House anthology, he should not be buried among "61 others." That isn't good business.[2]

Yrs
John

[1] *American Satire in Prose and Verse* published by Random House in 1962, included O'Hara's "Conversation in the Atomic Age."
[2] A note by Cerf on the bottom of this letter reads "Appeased by phone."

TO: John Steinbeck
25 October 1962

Wire. *Steinbeck: A Life in Letters*
(N.Y.: Viking, 1975)
Princeton

CONGRATULATIONS. I CAN THINK OF ONLY ONE OTHER AUTHOR I'D RATHER SEE GET IT.[1]

[1] Steinbeck was awarded the Nobel Prize for Literature on 25 October.

TO: Edgar Scott

TLS, 2 pp. Scott
Princeton

5 Nov. '62

Dear Edgar:

I am more than pleased by your concern about the Brook,[1] and because I am, I hasten to give you my word that I am fully reconciled to a blackball. You have never once failed me in anything I have asked of you—

and in other things that I could not have asked, you have come through. You and Hope do not know, for instance, how much it meant to me to have those few minutes with you after Belle's funeral. On that bitter cold day the only person I talked to on my way from the car to the church was—Sister! And later, at my house, I best remember you, the Scotts. I am every bit as sentimental as our friend Dickie, who, I suspect, is going to need some sympathy this time tomorrow.[2] (I have not liked his campaign, but that is another matter.)

About the Brook. The two reasons I wanted to join it are, first, it is a prestigious club; and, second, I am disheartened by the number of creeps who have been creeping into the Century. The same kind of people, and indeed some of the same people, who ruined The Players for me have abandoned The Players and are swarming all over the Century. They will not get in The Brook, and maybe I won't either, but I had to make the try.

To be denied membership in any club is something less than a life-and-death matter. I'm a man who lost the Nobel prize. I have been up for it at least twice that I know of in the past ten years, but now that they have given it to Steinback my chances of ever getting it are gone. There won't be another American winner in the next five years, and nothing I do meanwhile will get it for me. I began pointing for it in 1948, when my work, or my attitude toward my work, underwent a change. Everything I have written since 1948 has had a secondary purpose; I have deliberately attempted to record the first half of the century in fictional forms but with the quasi-historical effect that, say, Dickens achieved. It is all there— or more of it is there than anyone else has put down or will put down. Sinclair Lewis did his share, but then he fell apart. Hemingway didn't do it, Faulkner didn't do it, Steinbeck hasn't done it. Cozzens missed his chance. Mind you, I take nothing away from what they did do that was good, but I really thought I would be judged favorably this year on the basis of what I began in 1934 and rebegan in 1948. Well, I was wrong, and now I have to create a new incentive. So you see I am not very likely to collapse as a result of a club blackball.

Work, as you know, is wonderfully soothing, and I am working harder than ever before. I have been back in Princeton a little over a month, and in that time The New Yorker has bought four stories. I have a complete novel in the safe,[3] a short one about three quarters finished,[4] a very long one about two thirds finished,[5] a completed three-act play[6] that no one has seen. In a few weeks I will publish a short story collection,[7] and I am by far the leading author in paperback sales in England. (Last year three books of mine were in the top ten.) Mr. Dickens also sold rather well, I am told, although Her Majesty did not see fit to knight him.

This might amuse you: a year ago I resigned from the Institute of Arts & Letters because they nominated Faulkner, Steinback, Katherine Anne

Porter and Kay Boyle (!) for the Gold Medal. You know who got it?
Faulkner.

Goodnight, old friend, and thank you.

Ever
John

[1] Scott put O'Hara up for this New York club. O'Hara was not elected to membership.

[2] Richardson Dilworth unsuccessfully ran for governor of Pennsylvania in 1962.

[3] Probably *Elizabeth Appleton* (1963).

[4] Possibly *Adams Landing*, which was left unfinished.

[5] Probably *The Lockwood Concern* (1965).

[6] Possibly "Far From Heaven," which was not published or produced.

[7] *The Cape Cod Lighter*.

TO: Wylie O'Hara   TLS, 2 pp. Mrs. Doughty
8 November 1962   Princeton

Thursday

My dear:

Sister and I enjoyed having you and your friends home with us. This
does not directly concern me, but as a housewife Sister was terribly pleased
by the consideration you all showed in tidying up, stripping the beds, etc.
In these days when servants are few or non-existent it is especially important
to do your share—but it was always important to have good manners,
always will be. We also got nice notes from Lorraine and Louise, and
these little things, which only take a minute or two, make life pleasanter.

Sister's friend Binkie Greene died suddenly on Tuesday. The Outerbridges were here for dinner and bridge, and Sister was notified by telephone. Binkie had very little to live for when her husband died. She had
a lot of money, but no real resources within herself, and the closest relative is a niece, a nice young woman who is married to a smoothie who
called me John as soon as I met him, although he is twenty years younger
than I. Sister is spending tonight in New York then, with Mrs. Stevens
(Anna Fay, who spent the summer before last in Quogue), driving to
Southampton tomorrow for the funeral. It is quite a push, but Sister

412

wants to do it. Only a year ago she took charge, you remember, when Orland Greene died and Binkie was helpless.

Well, you do things for old friends. Last night we went to NY to attend a dinner for my old friend Deems Taylor, who was getting a medal from NYU, his alma mater. I sat next to a woman called Ayn Rand, the author . . .[1] but we got along fine. . . .[2] Fun, actually. She started right out by telling me that she was going to have to make a report on me to a Dr. Nathan Brandon, an associate of hers in the field of psychotherapy, because Brandon reads everything I write and has said that I never make a mistake about the psychological treatment of my characters. He is not the first to say that, by the way. She asked me what my philosophy was, and that, of course, got me going. Turned out that I am diametrically opposed to her philosophy,[3] but I didn't know that till later, when Sister told me. I have never read Ayn Rand, and told her so.

Saturday, Harvard game party. It's a damn good thing, by the way, that we told Mrs. Bundy we couldn't have her daughter. Sister won't get back till tomorrow night, and we would have had to disinvite her at the last minute. I had to give up going to Atlantic City for the NJ English Teachers awards—but that was no hardship.

My friend Dick Dilworth took a pasting in Pennsylvania elections, so I wrote him a note inviting him to join the Losers Club. He lost the governorship, I lost the Nobel prize.

A good review of THE CAPE COD LIGHTER in the new Glamour, and quite by accident on the way to NY last night I read a rave review in the Philadelphia Bulletin. The book theoretically won't be out till Thanksgiving, but they don't wait any more. I turned down the NY Times for an interview, and a few minutes ago I said no to Newsweek, which wanted to take my picture. I suppose you saw this week's Life, with the picture they took last April and the snotty remarks about me and THE BIG LAUGH.[4]

I meant to make this letter a thinking out loud about your future, but that will have to wait. I have some ideas that you might want to think about on the subject of post-school jobs, etc, which may influence you in your plans for the next year.

Keep punching.

Love
Dad

[1] Nine words omitted by the editor.
[2] Twenty-one words omitted by the editor.
[3] Objectivism, which holds that man's only responsibility is toward himself ("the virtue of selfishness").
[4] The 9 November 1962 issue of Life described O'Hara as "one of the most widely disliked and widely read authors in U.S. letters."

TO: *Yale Alumni Magazine*, XXVI (November 1962), 7

Gentlemen: "The Nathan manuscripts will supplement those of many other modern American writers including John P. Marquand, Sinclair Lewis, John Hersey, Stephen Vincent Benet, Edith Wharton, Thornton Wilder and Gertrude Stein."[1]

Yes, not to mention—because you didn't—still another Friend of the Yale Library.

Grateful Yale!

JOHN O'HARA

Quogue, N.Y.

[1] The *Yale Alumni Magazine* had published an article on the American Literature holdings at the Library. O'Hara had given the typescripts of *Butterfield 8*, *The Doctor's Son*, and *Pipe Night* to Yale.

TO: Jeff Brown[1]   TLS, 1 p. Curtis Publishing Co.
                                                     "Linebrook" letterhead

                                                              12 Jan 63

Dear Mr. Brown:

Through all the changes of personnel at the Post since 1928, two things have remained constant: I always get a letter evincing interest in my stories, and the Post goes on buying the same old junk, playing it safe. Although I am not so sure that playing it safe has done much for the Post.

If you would like to come here and read some stories, you may. But I will not submit any more. It must be understood that if you take a story away with you, that means you have bought the story. In other words, you must have been given the authority to make the decision on one reading. And my minimum price is $3000; more for longer stories, of course. These conditions are not particularly inviting, but they will keep us from wasting our time.

                                                     Faithfully,
                                                     JOHN O'HARA

[1] A *Saturday Evening Post* editor. The *Post* had published "That First Husband" in 1959. The second O'Hara story to appear in the *Post* was "The Glendale People," 2 March 1963.

Dear Bennett:

I have decided on my publishing schedule for 1963.

In May I would like to bring out the novel, ELIZABETH APPLETON. This is the novel I completed about two years ago and have been holding for the opportune moment. It is a novel about a marriage in a small Pennsylvania college town. The time is the recent past. It will get me no honorary degrees—but then what has?

On Thanksgiving Day I would like to publish a collection of new stories of varying lengths. I have not decided on a title for it, but I will come up with a good one.[1] I may, and I may not, write a Foreword for it.

I have abandoned the novel I almost finished last summer, which I was calling ADAMS LANDING. Recently I reread the manuscript with a view to getting started on it again. It has a lot of good stuff in it. Some very good. But I tried to do too much in too little space and got bogged down in chronologies. There is a lot worth saving, and at some future time I will go back again and see what I want to keep. For the present, however, it is on the shelf.[2]

I have had too many interruptions of a non-literary nature in the writing of THE LOCKWOOD CONCERN. This is already a very long novel. I hope to finish it this year, for publication in 1964, probably the autumn of '64.[3] Another factor in my inability to complete this novel has been the ease with which I write and sell short stories. I sold two last week and I have three more yet unsold. This is not work for me, and I am not deceived by the praise that the stories get. I am the only man alive who could write THE LOCKWOOD CONCERN, who knows the material and how to handle it, just as I was the only one who could have written FROM THE TERRACE, etc.

George Gershwin had an assured reputation with his songs, but he also had to write the Rhapsody in Blue and the other longer pieces, and would have gone on to bigger and better ones if he had lived. You take a tune like MINE, for instance. That's like one of my short stories; it could easily (with a lot of hard work, but easily) become a long piece, but instead of a fugue we have a rich little tune that is only one of many. That is not right. When you have the mastery of your medium that George had (and that I have, let's not kid about that), you simply must not let easy popularity keep you from the big things. There is one of the basic differences between George Gershwin, the composer, and Richard Rodgers, the song writer. Rodgers has to be content with songs, and he now has a song that is almost straight Cole Porter—except that Cole Porter would have known how to hold the melodic line. I refer to THE SWEETEST SOUND, which could also have been written by Jule Styne

—and the first six notes *were* written by Vincent Youmans in NO NO NANETTE. Do you see what I mean? The pleasant little pieces become derivatives; it is only when you do something more ambitious, longer, that you display your unique artistry, your staying powers. Rodgers wrote one successful piece that was longer than a song—SLAUGHTER ON TENTH AVENUE, but even that was quasi-Gershwin, with AN AMERICAN IN PARIS ringing in his ear. I don't want that kind of success.

Yrs,
John

¹ *The Hat on the Bed.*
² O'Hara abandoned this novel after 129 pages.
³ Published in 1965.

TO: Kate Bramwell¹   TLS, 1 p. Mrs. Bramwell
                                                          Princeton

30 Jan 63

Dear Kate and Ladies of the Monday Gun Club:

Thank you one and all for your contributions accompanying the safe return of the John Steinbeck Speech.² Some of you I would like to thank personally in the privacy of my study, but I am married to a tigress who has reduced my lechery to a condition of contented timidity.

Although I am still mystified by the Strange Case of the Vanishing Pamphlet, I am pleased with the solution. As some of you may know, with better luck I might have been writing my own Acceptance Speech, since I have been nominated three times for the prize that Steinbeck got. The Pamphlet therefore is probably as close to the real thing as I'll ever achieve. They, the Nobel Committee, usually let five years pass between one award and a later award to an author of the same nationality. Five years from now I will not know what to do with $40,000. Even Dr. Pickering³ will probably be through with me by that time, and Mr. Mather's ministrations are really quite impersonal. In the words of an old Triangle Club song: "I'll be resting cold and still/while relations fight the will." So I have written myself off as a Nobel Prize winner, even though Steinbeck tells me he intends to campaign in my behalf.

In the event that I should win, I invite you all to have lunch with my tigress and me on some convenient Monday in 1968. You will have

416

to bring your own sandwiches, as I am a respecter of tradition, but we will provide coffee and aquavit.*

Sincerely,
John O'Hara

Mrs. G. A. Bramwell & The Ladies of the Monday Gun Club
*—There will be a showing of Swedish sweaters, etc., on the terrace.

[1] Kate Bramwell, Belle's closest Princeton friend, became a good friend of Sister's.
[2] Mrs. Bramwell had borrowed O'Hara's copy of Steinbeck's Nobel Prize acceptance speech for her reading club—and misplaced it. When it was found, the members sent O'Hara a gift.
[3] Donald A. Pickering, O'Hara's dentist.
[4] The Mather Funeral Home in Princeton.

TO: Graham Watson[1]　　　　　　　　　　　　TLS, 1 p. Curtis Brown
　　　　　　　　　　　　　　　　　　　　　　　　　　Princeton

7 Feb. '63

Dear Graham:

Once again this matter of title changes has come up. The enclosed clipping illustrates what I mean: apparently Blackwood's Magazine has reprinted a story of mine and in doing so has taken the liberty of changing my title.[2] I must insist on keeping my titles, even though their meanings may be obscure to editors, readers, or, as the Welsh say, whatever. Please pass the word along to people in your organization that it must be understood that my titles must not be changed: if an editor does not wish to retain my title, I do not wish him to print my story.

Editors and publishers have a fairly consistent record of opposing my titles, not only of stories but of novels. One editor at Harcourt, Brace in 1934 wanted me to change APPOINTMENT IN SAMARRA to SWELL GUY! I had to fight for BUTTERFIELD 8; and so on down through the ages. But my titles have a way of creeping into the language, like Pirandello's.

We are off to Bermuda next week for nine days. Sister has never been there, and as I have been there with my previous two wives, I am putting an end to what may have seemed discrimination against my third and final wife. If she likes the place—and the weather is not always at its best in February—we may return next year for a longer stay. I am told the cedars have succumbed to a blight since my last visit in 1946, but my dendrophilia is not that far advanced. In 1931 Bermuda was still quite British; in 1946, after the wartime invasion of our Air Force and Navy (and the Bermudians' yielding to the motor car), it was less so. If it's not British enough in 1963, we may try Victoria, B.C., which I am told is so British that T. S. Eliot might feel ill at ease there. But that's okay with me. I like the Blimps, just as long as I don't have to be one. That would be too much of a strain on my conservatism.

As I may have told you, I am publishing ELIZABETH APPLETON in May. It will get bad reviews, but not as bad as THE BIG LAUGH, and it will sell better. Then in November another collection of stories, which will get mixed reviews, not as good as THE CAPE COD LIGHTER, and will not sell as well. My honeymoon with the critics does not figure to last. We are basically incompatible, and they will soon go home to Mama. They should have recovered sufficiently, by the time I finish my next long novel, to be able to pretend that the CAPE COD LIGHTER interlude never happened. "Another monster novel, The Lockwood Concern . . ."

As ever
John

¹ Of Curtis Brown Ltd., O'Hara's English agent. Although O'Hara did not have an American agent for his books, he found it necessary to retain one for his English and European business.

² *Blackwood's* published "Trip to Sea" in October 1962. It was by-lined "John O'Hara," and O'Hara assumed that it was one of his stories with a changed title.

TO: Don Schanche¹

TLS, 1 p. Schanche
Princeton

21 Feb 63

Dear Mr. Schanche:

I just got back last night from Bermuda, hence the delay in answering your queries. As follows:

Okay. Make it AUNT ANNA.²

It is EXTERIOR:WITH FIGURE.³ In your letter you refer to it as EXTIOR:WITH FIGURE.

1. Okay, make it "one of the children."

2. Okay, spell out paying guest.

3. No, do not change that. I think if you read it over it makes sense.

I am very pleased that you would like to see some more stories. I saw the advance note in this week's Post when I was flying up from Bermuda yesterday. I hope the response will justify your confidence in the stories. At the moment I have no story (although that is not to say I won't have one by day after tomorrow.) However, about a year ago I wrote a play that I never submitted to the managers. It is about a district leader, Tammany type, who has just got out of prison and returns to his old domain. I was kind of hoping Jackie Gleason would be available for it, but he has announced that he will never do another Broadway show, so although I had a couple of conversations with him about it, I never sent it to him.

I don't think that printed plays are very successful in magazines, but this one could be edited out of the play form into story form. It is called FAR FROM HEAVEN, and I do not plan to do any more about it as far as the theater is concerned. If you care to have a look at it, I'll be glad to send it to you. I find plays hard to read, like watching a tennis match. Actually if the dialog is good you ought to be able to skip the name of the speaker of each line, but it doesn't work out that way. Those damn names in the middle of the page divert you, or they do me.

With best wishes,

Faithfully,
John O'Hara

[1] *Saturday Evening Post* editor.
[2] 23 March 1963.
[3] 1 June 1963.

TO: Wylie O'Hara

TLS, 1 p. with holograph
postscript. Mrs. Doughty
Princeton

26 Feb '63

My dear:

The Outerbridges came for dinner and bridge on Friday, but I could not see them. I got wallopped by the influenza virus and had a miserable four days; on Sunday Sister came down with it, too, although she did manage to get in the telephone call to you. Her attack was not as bad as mine. I had the doctor, Dr. Wright, but the only thing he can do is try to keep it from developing into pneumonia, which he has done. I could hardly walk, and could not walk without a cane. Temperature up to 102, etc. Can't understand why these nasty things happen to a nice feller like me. Unless, of course, the Lord is getting me ready for sainthood. But I'm not sure I wouldn't settle for a lower status and a few more creature comforts on earth. Next fall we must all get flu shots. This thing is no fun.

I am writing you now to tell you how pleased I am, we are, about Bennett.[1] I am particularly pleased because you got in without my having to search around and see where I could use my influence, if any. You got in on your record and the recommendation of Miss Watkins, which is so much better for you than to have me put the pressure on the Bennett trustees—assuming I knew them. Obviously Miss Watkins gave you the highest recommendation, to have them accept you so early in the game, and her fondness and admiration for you (which Patience mentioned to her parents last weekend) is going to continue after you leave St. Tim's. I am so glad I sent you to St. Tim's for the full four years. You would not have got much out of the extra year at Miss Fine's, and you did get a lot out of starting St. Tim's early. So did I. I got a better understanding of Miss Watkins and of the school. It has been an expensive four years, and the best expenditure I ever made (except for the money I paid Dr. Damon to bring you into the world).

Mrs. Bramwell's sister, Lydia Williams (your mother was one of her bridesmaids) was talking about Bennett last week in Bermuda. I had not realized it is acquiring a reputation in the field of Art—and neither Lydia nor we yet knew that you had been accepted. On the college level you will be able to follow your tastes and interests to a degree that is not possible in prep school. In other words, to a great extent you will be in control of your own career, and I think Bennett should be intellectually as stimulating as St. Tim's has been in the areas of human relations or citizenship. Once again I will back you in every way I can, because I believe you are finding yourself as a woman and as a citizen. The next two years should be the most exciting time of your life.

Love
Dad

See editorial in the new Sat. Eve. Post.[2]
D.

[1] A junior college in Millbrook, N.Y.

[2] "The Glendale People" appeared in the 2 March 1963 *Post* with an editorial note on O'Hara.

TO: Bennett Cerf
TLS, 1 p. Columbia
"Linebrook" letterhead

9 March '63

Dear Bennett:

I think you ought to be told that I have received an offer of $250,000, payable any way I want it, and a guarantee of $50,000 advertising appropriation, for ELIZABETH APPLETON. This is something for Random House to think about. It is especially interesting because the other publisher is making a selling point of the RH advertising campaign on my last two books.[1]

Yrs,
John

[1] O'Hara remained with Random House.

My dear:

The clipping is from the Trenton Times and does not tell all. For instance, the boys who were at the party, the invited ones, chipped in voluntarily to help defray the damages. They also were so indignant that they provided the names of the crashers whom they knew. Two boys, not one, were stabbed, and one of the hoodlums also had a gun. Your god-mother[1] is the heroine of Princeton because other parents have refused to prosecute this gang in the past, for fear of reprisals against their own kids. Good for Kate!

I have a bill here for Mrs. W. O'Hara and Mrs. Lorraine Bowan for $29.61. I am paying it as I did not take you to lunch and the theater, and you can make your own arrangements about the circus.

Your cards have been ordered and will be sent to you at St. Tim's.

I had a very successful visit from the Post editor. They are paying me a nice sum to give them first look at my 1964 novel.[2] I told him I thought you might end up a writer, that you showed promise. He said, in all seriousness, next time she writes something you think is good, send it to me. I am very pleased with this relationship with the Post. They got more letters on my story AUNT ANNA than any story since 1930—more unfavorable than favorable, but they expected that and they are in the market for everything I write. They have taken the play I hoped Jackie Gleason would be in, and are making it into a fiction story. I then may, just may, reconvert it into a play-with-music as Dietz & Schwartz[3] want me to write a show with Mary Martin as the star, and if she wants to change from those greasy kid parts, this might be it.

I hope things are going well with you. You can finish your career at St. Tim's with credit to yourself, to your mother, to Sister, and to me, and to all those people who wish you well. And they are numerous. For instance, you have a lot of really nice relations in the South whom you have never seen, but who took pride in your election as class president and always ask Winnie[4] when you are going to visit them. As for my side of the family, you must know by this time how they feel about you.

Love
Dad

[1] Kate Bramwell.
[2] O'Hara did not publish a novel in 1964; he is probably referring to *The Lockwood Concern* (1965).
[3] "Far From Heaven" was not converted into a story, and the musical project never developed.
[4] Winifred Wylie Gardiner, Belle's sister.

4 April '63

Dear Bill:

I don't think you would try to teach me to write, but I do think that if you had paused long enough to allow one more thought to come, you might not have written your letter. The one extra thought is that I am always, always, experimenting.

Because I write plain, but without the jerkiness of Hemingway-plain, most of what I do of a technical nature is not noticeable. For instance, what I do about blocks of type, or paragraphing. I have been working on that since 1930, which is the year I read A FAREWELL TO ARMS, and I still work on it in every story and all my novels. It would take too long to tell you about it, and it wouldn't make very fascinating reading, but it has to do with the technique (mine) of mesmerizing the reader, and is therefore related to the subject of your letter. I want to *control* the reader as much as I can, and I make the effort in all sorts of ways. (Punctuation is one of them.)

What you tell me about Gibbs's theories did not all originate with Gibbs. Much of it came from me to Gibbs. Much as I loved Gibbs, he had a way of telling me something I had previously told him, and the attributional theories are in that category. It began with a discussion of modifiers ("No, thank you," she said archly.), and went on to "retorted" and "chimed in," etc. Most of the time the dialog should stand on its own, but occasionally the non-modifier rule has to be broken.

The repeated use of the full name, George Denison, George Denison, is not accidental.[1] It would be a damned sight easier just to say George or Denison or he said, or said George, etc. But here again I am fixing that name in the reader's eye, and I am borrowing from, among others, the 19th Century Europeans. Ivan Ivanovitch, a Russian writer would say, every time, as the Irish, in dialog, address each other as John-Patrick, Francis Xavier, etc.

There are times when I want to slow down the reader, almost imperceptibly, but slow him down. I can do that by saying George Denison, in full. I can do it for a greater length of time with a big block of type, like the Caporetto retreat. I can make it easier for the reader by filling up that block of type with nouns—rifles, machine guns, tanks, motorcycles, ambulances, and other non-think words—but the reader is still being slowed down. He picks up the pace, is forced to, when I go back to dialog. But since most of the stories I write for The New Yorker are in dialog, I have to use other tricks, and another trick I use is to dispense entirely with the attributive tag. The full name will do that, if used sparingly. By which I mean, George Denison, but not a whole bunch of full names. One of the things that make Hellman[3] unreadable and instantly identifiable is too many proper names, too many capitalized words. Eustace Seligman, Frederick B. Adams, John Hay Whitney, et al., attending a dinner of Les Amis d'Escoffier at the John Dillinger Room of the Hotel des Artistes. I am well aware of that danger.

Finally, I prefer "said John Smith" to "John Smith said," for a number of reasons. It is easier on the eye to follow a comma and close-quotes with a small *s* than with a cap *J*. And "John Smith said" is abrupt and full-stop where I don't want it to be.

Now let us go out for a smoke.

Yrs
John

---

1 "The Locomobile," 20 July 1963.
2 Geoffrey Hellman of *The New Yorker*.

TO: The *New York Herald Tribune* (17 April 1963), 24

Tonight (April 12) on NBC a newsreader, complaining about the fact that the television apparatus are not to be allowed to clutter up the hearings on the Mayor's new tax program, used the term, "the working press," as though the complaints were coming from newspaper men.

The use of that term by NBC comes about as close to telling a lie as you can safely get. I doubt that there is a newspaper man in New York who regards the TV people as "working press." And now, more than ever, the television-radio people have been proven to have no claim to the designation. They are not The Press. They never will be The Press. The television crowd are picture-takers who augment their pictures with audible captions. They are hardly more entitled to call themselves "working press" than the man who sits in the press box at a football game and tells you, through the loudspeaker, what you are looking at.

It almost comes down to a question of whom do you trust on TV. For me there is one newsreader, McCaffery,[1] whose word I believe; one interviewer, Cronkite,[2] for whom I have any respect. I will include Red Barber[3] to make it three, and lump all the rest. But even my three favorites are not "working press."

Of course there are quite a few members of the "working press" who I think belong on TV, but that's another story.

JOHN O'HARA

Princeton, N.J.

---

1 John K. M. McCaffery.
2 Walter Cronkite.
3 Announcer of the Brooklyn Dodgers games.

TO: Albert Erskine   TLS, 1 p. Random House
                                                        Princeton

                                                       4 May '63
Dear Albert:
   Always with your best interests at heart, and mindful of an aging
father's desire to observe the miracle of a small daughter's growth, I have
sacrificed considerable time and energy of my own to enable you to get
a few days off this summer. Herewith are the stories to be included in
THE HAT ON THE BED.

   There are two dozen, and their names are:
NINETY MINUTES AWAY   JOHN BARROW ROSEDALE
THE MANAGER   N.Y.[1]   N.Y.
THE RIDE FROM MAUCH   HOW CAN I TELL YOU?
   CHUNK   *Post*   N.Y.
EXTERIOR WITH FIGURES   THE PUBLIC DOROTHY
   Post   N.Y.
THE GLENDALE PEOPLE   THE GOLDEN
   Post   TEDDY AND THE SPECIAL
AUNT ANNA   *Post*   FRIENDS
THE FRIENDS OF MISS   THE TWINKLE IN HIS EYE
   JULIA   YUCCA KNOLLS   *Show*
I KNOW THAT, ROY   THE MAN ON THE
EMINENT DOMAIN   *Post*   TRACTOR   N.Y.
AGATHA   OUR FRIEND THE SEA   *Post*
THE FLATTED SAXOPHONE   THE WINDOWPANE CHECK
   N.Y.   THE MAYOR
SATURDAY LUNCH   N.Y.   THE LOCOMOBILE   N.Y.

   This amounts to 514 pages of typescript, or what is called giving the
bastards their money's worth. I have not yet decided to or not to write
a foreword. This is as good a collection of stories as was ever published
in the United States, or anywhere else for that matter, but I am not sure
I want to say so in the book. Nor am I sure about a dedication.[2] You
can't have everything all at once, Albert.

                                                       Yrs,
                                                       J. O'H.

[1] Story locations added in holograph.
[2] *The Hat on the Bed* did not have a foreword; it was dedicated to William Maxwell.

TO: Don Schanche
4 May 1963

TLS, 1 p. Schanche
"Linebrook" letterhead

Derby Day 63

Dear Mr. Schanche:

I am sorry the play conversion did not work out. Just as well it didn't, really. A man ought to do his own work. When I will get around to doing this job myself is problematical. I am now writing another play (but not in play form), and a longish story about a rum runner, both of which you can see when they are completed.[1] The rum runner story has my complete attention at the moment because I am getting what I think is the true feeling of that time without writing another Untouchables.[2] I knew some of those people. They were plenty tough, but I am getting a little deeper than the superficial toughness. On the other hand, I full believed Gatsby until I went to NY and met some of those mob people. Gatsby would not have lasted a week with the ones I met, let alone taken control.

Best wishes,

John O'Hara

[1] The play in story form was probably "Harrington and Whitehill" which O'Hara headed on the typescript "1963 Play"—published in *Good Samaritan* (1974). The rumrunner story was "The Lawbreaker," 16 November 1963.

[2] Popular TV show about gangsters during Prohibition.

TO: William Maxwell

TLS, 2 pp PSt.
Princeton

8 May '63

Dear Bill:

"He's the kind of a guy that when you ask him how is he, he tells you." I forget who first said that. It sounds like G. K. Chesterton, or Solly Violinsky, who died the other day and was a Vine Street wit.

Well, I am better today than I was yesterday and the day before. On Monday, within one hour's time, I learned that I had *not* been given the Pulitzer prize[1] and that I *had* been given the blackball at a club. I also have other troubles, one of which was that I bet on No Robbery in the Kentucky Derby. I had him across the board and he ran out of the money. Monday night I had a nightmare that I was going crazy (possibly from rereading THE MANAGER in The New Yorker). Irving Berlin says to count your blessings instead of sheep, but I couldn't even think of any sheep, and if I had I probably would have thought of LAMB IN HER BOSOM, which got the Pulitzer prize over APPOINTMENT IN SAMARRA, the state I was in.[3]

Hank Potter is married to Lucilla Wylie, Belle's sister. Yes, I suppose he could be called an agreeable man. God knows he has had his disappointments, and I've never heard him bellyache about them. He calls himself H.C.Potter, which is such a coldly forbidding, Edith Whartonesque name, that he has been overlooked when they handed out the Hollywood and Broadway merit badges. And yet he has directed Gary Cooper, Merle Oberon, Rex Harrison, Ginger Rogers and Fred Astaire, Edward G. Robinson, Loretta Young, Paulette Goddard, Martha Raye, Olsen & Johnson, Gladys Swarthout—among others. He never got to be known to the public, and yet he played polo and hunted the fox, flew an airplane and instructed Chinese pilots, made Keys[4] at Yale and is a life member of the Racquet Club, is a grandson of a former president of the Century, had Jock Whitney as an usher in his wedding, and so many things that should have added up to celebrity. . . .[5]

Last night I finished a long short story,[6] which Shawn would not buy but I think the Post will, and now I can go back to work on my annual printemps play, which I interrupted to write the story. Every printemps I write a play, you know. But you wouldn't know it if I didn't tell you. I write plays because I haven't got the patience to train Labrador retrievers. On that cheery note I close.

Oh—it is all right to talk to Mr. Boeth of Newsweek. In fact, I suggested you as one of the men he ought to interview, since the coverstory is, I gather, to be mostly about my work.[7]

Yrs,
John

[1] O'Hara had heard that *The Cape Cod Lighter* (1962) was being considered. The prize was awarded to Faulkner's *The Reivers*.

[2] The Brook.

[3] Caroline Miller's novel, *Lamb in His Bosom* won the Pulitzer Prize for 1933 in May 1934. *Appointment in Samarra* was published in August 1934. The Pulitzer Prize novel for 1934 was *Now in November* by Josephine W. Johnson.

[4] Scroll and Key, a senior society.

[5] 104 words omitted by the editor.

[6] Unidentified.

[7] Richard Boeth wrote the cover story "John O'Hara at 58: A Rage to Write," *Newsweek* (3 June 1963).

TO: Wylie O'Hara   TLS, 2 pp. Mrs. Doughty
May 1963   Princeton

Tuesday

My dear:

Sister is off to Quogue, so I am alone for the rest of the week, and I would have been even more miserable if you hadn't telephoned. But you did telephone, and that is over. I had a particularly rough time these past few weeks. A week ago yesterday I heard on the radio that Faulkner had been given the Pulitzer prize (instead of THE CAPE COD LIGHTER, which rumor had it would or might get it); then an hour later my friend Edgar Scott telephoned to say I had been blackballed at The Brook club. The reason? Certain members of the screening committee did not like what I have written about clubs and did not want it to appear that The Brook, by making me a member, appeared to approve of what I had written. Then I also bet on the Kentucky Derby, and my horse, No Robbery, ran out of the money and I had bet him across the board (win, place, and show).

Oddly enough, Louie Gates's[1] suicide did not shock me. Saddened, but not shocked. Although she was unhappy over Geoff's death, and before that, the death of her previous husband, Harry Hopkins, I have always believed that Louie never got over her disappointment when —— —— did not marry her. (He and —— were at the funeral but I did not see them.) —— took her away from —— ——, with whom she had been in love for five years, and then he married —— —— —— instead of Louie. Almost immediately she married Hopkins and moved to the White House. Life with Hopkins was glamorous, meeting Churchill and all those people, but I never felt Louie was really in love with Hopkins. If you are ever disappointed in love, don't marry on the rebound. It seldom works. Marry *only* for love. Marriage needs love to help both parties through the tough times, and there are tough times in every marriage. Marriage also needs love to get both parties through the *good* times. Without love, the good times can be meaningless and impermanent. As you must be aware by this time, I got around quite a bit through the years: I had quite a few affairs. But those I remember most pleasantly had some love in addition to the sex and companionship, and in later years the sex recedes in importance and the affection, or love, is what makes you remember the other person. I am not knocking sex, but the power of it does not last long without love. And in your heart you always know when it is sex alone that attracts you to a person, or that attracts the person to you.

The Newsweek photographer is coming again today. They have already taken a color picture for the cover; today is black and white stuff. They are really doing a job, and I have cooperated. I will be on either the May 28th cover or the June 4th, depending on what happens with Gordon Cooper, the astronaut. Either way it works out all right for ELIZABETH

427

APPLETON, which is to be published on 4 June but is already in Double-day's windows. It is going to be a big bestseller, I think.

I have seen the graduation present Sister got you. (I don't mean your graduation dress.) It is really beautiful, and you will have it long long after the Spitfire has spat its last spit.[2] Or fire. The 5th and 14th of June will be big days for me as well as for you, because you have made them so.

Love
Dad

---

[1] Wife of special assistant to Pres. Roosevelt.
[2] O'Hara gave Wylie a Triumph Spitfire when she graduated from St. Timothy's.

TO: William Maxwell
TLS, 2 pp. PSt.
Princeton

16 May '63

Dear Bill:

I am touched by your warm partisanship, and grateful as well. My mother, I am sure, would ascribe my vulnerability to the slings and arrows as a weakness in my character and, as was frequently but not always the case, she probably would have been right. I have an additional explanation (that does not rule out hers): when I was young, right up to prep school graduation, at which I was valedictorian and class poet (!) and top man in Spanish—I got used to getting badges and ribbons and prayerbooks and certificates (at Fordham Prep the monthly honors were known as testi-monials and nicknamed testies), without trying very hard for them. I was brighter than most of my classmates, and I had a kind of Xerox memory. But from 1924 to 1952, I got nothing, and it took a revival of PAL JOEY to break that long string of defeats.[1]

Poor Fitzgerald never got nothing nohow, but he was enough older than I to have grown up before there were so many medals, etc. I imagine he must have wondered about them just a little when SO BIG got the Pulitzer for the year that THE GREAT GATSBY was published; but where he possibly could derive comfort from the contrast, I, in a similar situation, got mad. Fragile Fitzgerald had some inner resources that I haven't got, one of which is arrogance. Personal arrogance, that is. I am much more sure of myself at the typewriter than he was when he was writing; he rewrote and rewrote and polished and repolished, and he agonized. I have no such trouble. When I sit down to write a story I am sometimes only ready to write a story, but one will come. Some of the ones you like best have come that way. But Scott had a personal cockiness that in the present fashion would be said to mask his basic insecurity. I don't believe that theory, at least as it applied to him. He told me about

428

two movie stars that he wanted me to invite to a party Belle and I gave for him, implying that he had laid both of them. Well, he had laid one of them, but not the other, and the one he laid he had laid in her dressing-room but not at home. He did not have a real affair with her. The one he did not lay, —— ——, was at the time having an affair with a director named —— ——, who was a friend of Scott's and a little fellow, and I think Scott convinced himself that anything —— did he could do better. The formality of actually fucking —— ——, to her family and friends) was waived. One night in 1933, after I was divorced from Helen Petit, she and I and Scott and Dottie Parker went out together. The three got tight; I was on the wagon. Very late, on the way to Helen's apartment, Scott was making heavy passes at Helen and she was not fighting him off. We got to the apartment, which was on Park Avenue and had a doorman, and she got out and so did Scott. I couldn't, because I was not supposed to be seeing Helen and she was afraid the doorman would report me to her family. Scott followed her into the foyer as far as the elevator, then she left him. He was assisted by the doorman. Meanwhile Dottie had said to me, "He's awful, why didn't you punch him?" I said Helen seemed to like it and we were divorced (I did not see fit to tell Dottie that I was seeing a lot of Nancy). Anyway, Scott came back to the taxi and we all went back to Tony's and I'm sure Scott listed her among his conquests. Insecurity? Quite the opposite. Scott was a lot like Gibbs about sex. In time Gibbs could speak of his low vitality, but it wasn't only that. It was a kind of innocence. They both had it, really, but insecurity, no, not in matters that mattered to them, such as opinions. It could be argued that Gibbs and Scott made passes at girls out of politeness, and when I think of some of the dames Gibbs went to bed with, the argument holds up. Well, Hemingway didn't have much sense about women either, neither did Sinclair Lewis; and Faulkner's attitude toward them was so conventionally Southern that he could have written a manual. To Bill a woman was somewhere between a donkey and a princess. "Best day's wuck *yew* evah did," he said to me about my marrying Sister. I never considered that work.

I was hoping you might be at the Century yesterday. I particularly wanted you to see my hat. It is a straw hat that I bought in Beverly Hills about five years ago, but I hadn't noticed until yesterday that inside, in gold letters on the sweatband, is the name: Maxwell.

As ever
John

¹ The revival of *Pal Joey* won the Donaldson and New York Drama Critics' Circle awards for the best musical of 1952.

TO: Don Schanche   TLS, 2 pp.¹ Schanche
                                                              Princeton

18 May '63
Dear Mr. Schanche:

I am glad you are buying THE LAWBREAKER, not only for the obvious reasons but because in the modern short story there has been practically an abandonment of action—for which, I admit, I am partly responsible.
Every time I write a story I do some experimenting; it may not be apparent to the reader, but it is in there to some degree. *I* know it's there.
In the past thirty or forty years there have been very few first-rate short
stories that contained action or plot; we who wrote the stories have been
influenced by Chekhov, among others, and have been reacting against
the junky plot stories that Littauer at Collier's and Rose at the Post,²
among others, have insisted upon. That reaction was okay. The plot
stories did bear little relation to truth and life. But having been one of
the leading practitioners of the oblique and the plotless, I have recently
been putting action back into my stories. Vide, for instance, two stories
that come to mind that appeared in The New Yorker: one called THE
BUCKET OF BLOOD, about a carnival hustler who buys a speakeasy
in Gibbsville, Pa., and another called IT'S MENTAL WORK, about an
itinerant bartender in NY. I sold those stories to The NYer because the
emphasis was not on the action, but the action was there aplenty. THE
LAWBREAKER is in the same genre, but I sent it to you first because
you are entitled to first look at anyway half my stories and because I want
Post readers to be constantly surprised. I do not want them to think they
know what to expect when they see my name on a story. New Yorker
readers now know that they *don't* know what to expect from me, and
that is good. You have had a nice mixture so far, and I am going to continue to mix them up. Last week I sold a story called THE LOCO-
MOBILE to The NYer that I now wish I had sent to you, but there
will be others.

One thing you never need worry about in my stories is the dialog. Not
to go into another long lecture on The Art of John O'Hara, I may say
briefly that I *hear* the dialog before I put it down on paper. In this case,
I "heard" Beatrice Kelly. Beatrice was a maid of ours for eight years (and
I wish still was.) She was a Jamaican. . . .³ In all the West Indies and
Bermuda, etc., wherever the English were influential, you get that stilted
phraseology, as you quite aptly describe it. You doo nevvah cohnfuse it
with a white persohn's speech; you always know it is a cahlud persohn who
is speaking, enunciating carefooly, but even the totally illiterate have command of a better working vocabulary than the average US high school
graduate.

I assume that you have not Xeroxed the typescript of THE LAW-BREAKER, so I return it herewith. And herewith best wishes,

John O'Hara

[1] Part of this letter was printed in the *Post* as a headnote to "The Lawbreaker," 16 November 1963.
[2] Stuart Rose, fiction editor of *The Saturday Evening Post*.
[3] Eighteen words omitted by the editor.

TO: Wylie O'Hara   TLS, 1 p. Mrs. Doughty
"Linebrook" letterhead

28 May '63

My dear:

I wanted you to be head of school, captain of the Spiders,[1] tennis champion, and to get your classmates in a crap game in the Sixes Room and win $18,000 so that you could buy me a Rolls-Royce for Christmas.

Seriously, if you think I am in any way disappointed in you, you are out of your little pink mind. I do not want you to be any of the things you are *not* at the sacrifice of the things that you *are*: a warm, human, honorable, decent, sensitive girl. Far from being the kind of person who makes a big splash in her, or his, teens, you are entering a future that is so exciting that I believe you sense it yourself, deep down. I believe you sense it because you are having a final struggle, wrenching yourself away from the past. It is almost like giving birth to yourself. Keep this letter and in ten years, or even five, see if the old man isn't right. I'll even put the date on this letter. And don't be *afraid* of the future. You'll get what you want, if it's what you want.

Love
Dad

[1] St. Timothy's students are divided into two teams, Brownies and Spiders.

TO: Don Schanche   TLS, 1 p. Schanche
Princeton

5 June '63

Dear Mr. Schanche:

I don't remember now what I said about Littauer and Rose and their effect on the short story, but when you have selected the quote I'm sure I'll approve of it. Littauer was especially infuriating, he and his proppipe and his phony professorial manner. The first time I ever met him he said,

"When are you going to write some stories for us?" I said I had a deal with The New Yorker. He said, "Oh, I don't mean *those*. I mean *stories*." Well, as it happened, that year I had eleven stories starred in the E. J. O'Brien collection, which was more than the Collier's total for *all* authors, and more than any other author in the world. Rose was a nothing.

I am leaving for Quogue next Monday, for the summer. Maybe if I assemble a batch of stories you could take time off to come down and read them. I will provide the Atlantic Ocean for a cooling dip, and take you over to the National for a good lunch.

I want you to know that it is important to me—and not only monetarily—to help make the new Post successful. I have a quasi-patriotic feeling about the Post as an institution as do, I think, most Americans who are within twenty years of my age. You sometimes run articles that annoy me—the one on Grace Kelly was petulant and worthless, and the one on society orchestras was quite ignorant. But that isn't my province.

Cordially,
John O'Hara

TO: William Maxwell

TLS, 1 p. PSt.
Princeton

7 June '63

Dear Bill:

Herewith the proof with my usual snippy comments.

We are leaving for Quogue on Monday, the 10th, to be gone until late September. This is subject to slight alteration, as I am having a dental alteration tomorrow: one of the last remaining stalwarts must go. Dr. Pickering, with his great professional pride, and I, with my excessive sentimentality, have been waging a losing battle against the inevitable. He tells everybody I am so brave in the face of pain. I'm not, but I pretend. Philo Higley. Tuesday we drove down to Baltimore to see my daughter graduate from St. Timothy's. On the way down I kept playing tag with a $7000 Continental that had only the letters P H, no numerals, on the license plate. Paul Hollister. Philo Higley. Phil Hichborn (Elinor Wylie's son). Hollister dead, Hichborn long dead, and I have no idea about Philo. The man and woman in the car were nothing, nothing.

I was so sure I would weep at commencement that I practically didn't. I think I kept telling myself that I was better off than Fitzgerald had been in the same area. We stayed in Towson, near the school, and it was one Sunday afternoon in Towson, in 1934, that I had Scott and Zelda in my car and I wanted to kill him. Kill. We were taking her back to her Institution, and he kept making passes at her that could not possibly be consummated. We stopped at a drug store to get him some gin. The druggist would not give it to him. I had to persuade the druggist to relent, and he got the gin. But I wanted to kill him for what he was doing to that crazy woman, who kept telling me she had to be locked up before the moon came up. That was the last time I saw her.

Yrs
John

TO: Mrs. John Steinbeck TLS, 1 p. Mrs. Steinbeck
Quogue, Long Island

4 July 63

Dear Elaine:

I am so sorry to hear that John has been hospitalized and is immobilized. I telephoned the Southampton Hospital, and then through Elizabeth Otis via Henry Gross I got your Sag Harbor number and telephoned you there.

Maybe there *is* something I can do, and maybe this is it: would John like me to come and read to him three days a week for a couple of hours a day?[1] I usually get up around eleven and stall until after lunch, so I could come to Sag Harbor at half past two or thereabouts. We could arrange a fixed schedule as to time and material he would like read to him.

Except for my medical checkups and one trip in mid-August, I expect to stay put all summer, and my services are available immediately.

If there is anything else you would like me to do, please tell me. The reading job seemed like the most useful to John in the present circumstances.

As ever,
John

[1] Steinbeck had been operated on for a detached retina. O'Hara's offer was accepted.

TO: William Maxwell TLS, 1 p. PSt.
Quogue, Long Island

9 July '63

Bill:

Two things I never did; I never visited the Statue of Liberty, and I never patronized Polly Adler's.[1] I knew Polly Adler; she was a noisy bore, who looked like Mike Romanoff in drag. I once had an interesting conversation about her with Lee Francis, who was the leading madam in

Hollywood, and Miss Francis told me that Polly was no lady and out in public you gotta act like a lady in this business.

From license back to Liberty. Ever since the invention of the helicopter I have had a strange desire to charter one and go to the Statue and step out of the helicopter and down into the statue. This is strange for many reasons. I am and for ten years have been afraid of flying, although I have flown an airplane quite a few times and have had to use them to get places. I have never been in a helicopter and never expect to be in one.

It would take me a week to climb up the statue. I get out of breath at the thought of it.

My fear of flying, by the way, can be dated precisely; it came over me one day while flying in a small plane from Fishers Island to Martha's Vineyard. Three days later I was in the hospital with my big hemorrhage. The aerophobia could have been a warning that all was not well inside, because until then I loved to fly. I even flew in blimps over NY, Chicago, Miami, and LA. In 1928 a drunken pilot and I stunted over NY at night in a tri-motor Ford, and I loved it. Come to think of it, when I blimped over NY we came almost close enough to the Empire State building to reach out and touch it.

You didn't know any of these things about me, did you? Fascinating.

Yrs,
John

---

[1] New York madam, author of A *House Is Not a Home*.

TO: Bennett Cerf   TLS, 1 p. Columbia
                                    "Linebrook" letterhead

2 Nov 63

Dear Bennett:

I cannot find words to express my anger at seeing the Signet edition of APPOINTMENT IN SAMARRA, with an "Afterword" by Arthur Mizener.

I want you to go to the telephone on receipt of this letter, and tell the New American Library that the Mizener comments must be killed immediately. I don't gave a God damn whether it means killing the whole edition.

At this moment you are very close to losing an author. This is one of the most outrageous performances I have ever known, and in future, if there is to be any future, no deal is to be made for reprint of anything of mine without my being consulted in all details.

As for the present, you know what I want done. I have made myself clear. I don't care how you do it, but I want that "afterword" killed.[1]

Yrs,
John

Don't let the Signet people get the idea that they are going to have a nice little literary controversy to call attention to the book. The only controversy will be between Random House and me, and that will be very quiet indeed.

[1] Mizener had reviewed *From the Terrace* unfavorably. The Signet edition was not reprinted.

TO: William Maxwell   TLS (xerox).[1] PSt.
November 1963   Princeton

In 1922 I was in love with a girl named Gladys Suender, who was known in our set as The Creole. A real beauty, and to some extent the Natalie in FROM THE TERRACE. Her younger sister and husband were here last Saturday after the Yale game, and Jane told me that Gladys is in the hospital and may die. Kidney. Gladys has had a cruel life. A lousy marriage, ending in a desertion; family lost their dough, etc. Anyway, the Suenders lived in Frackville, up the Mountain, the second coldest town in the Commonwealth, next to Snowshoe, Pa. In 1922 the new road had not been completed (a new road which has now been abandoned, by the way) and on one side of the road there was a sheer drop of maybe 500 feet and never room for three cars abreast. So one night I was on my way back to Pottsville after a date with Gladys. If you got going right you could *coast* six miles in neutral from Frackville into the town of St. Clair. I had my old man's Buick phaeton and I got going right, all right, but half way down I discovered that while I was at Glady's house the foot brake had frozen tight. So had the hand brake, and I was moving along at about 40 m.p.h. Nothing else was on the road, but sometimes the bootleggers in their Reo Speedwagons would come through in convoy at about that hour and they didn't give a damn about anyone. The only thing I could do, I did, which was to ease the right fenders and running board against the bushes and rocks on the edge of the road, which slowed me down, until I was able to run the car up against the embankment without crashing. I got to St. Clair in second gear. The town Frackville is, of course, the town in ZERO.[2]

As ever
John

[1] The PSt copy consists of parts of two Xeroxed pages cut and pasted on another page.
[2] 28 December 1963.

435

TO: Thomas O'Hara   TLS, 5 pp. Mrs. O'Hara
                                                                   Princeton

                                                               30 Dec '63
Dear Tom:

Mother may not have told the whole story of our aunt Mrs. Gorman, and some of your report is new to me but not all of it. Catherine (I think she spelt it) O'Hara Gorman apparently was a handsome woman of the kind that Irish and non-Irish novelists are fond of depicting as the typical upper middleclass Irishwoman. I have seen pictures of her in her riding habit, and you can be damn sure she never rode astride. One picture has her in a black velvet jacket and divided skirt, with a plumed hat to match, and she is very impressive. I have no greater fondness for the Shenandoah O'Haras than you have—and I have good reason to despise Mike, Jim, and Nell. But you have to give them their due. Aunt Mollie Monahan was a pretty woman, although I didn't like her. Aunt Margaret was a funny dame, very sharp. Her name was McNamara, and I never knew her husband. She had a child who died. Aunt Nell was a sour old maid, who taught school all her life and was a town busybody. Arthur, the youngest son, was a handsome dope who got drunk and died of a broken neck in a fall.[1] He's the one who was sent to Penn and spent all his money, and the old man covered up for him. Mart is one I never knew, a stodgy type who lived in Philadelphia and I have no idea how he made his living, but it couldn't have been too profitable as he was always sending his daughter Mary to try to put the bee on the old man for money. The Marty O'Hara on WNEW is, I think, our first cousin, the son of that Mart O'Hara.

The thing about our grandfather and grandmother is that they were the top people of Shenandoah, which is top of nothing much, but top. Mike O'Hara was always known by a military title, captain or major. He owned a livery stable and he had a big farm near Brandonville with a quarter-mile track on it, and horses were always a big part of his life. But his money came from contracting. For instance, in moving houses. He also did a lot of business with James Archbald's family, who owned some mines in the Gilverton area, and our James Archbald (Margaretta's father) greatly admired our grandfather for his industry and honesty. All the O'H boys except Mart were sent to Penn, all the girls except Nell to Chestnut Hill (Sisters of St. Joseph). There was always money around, and there were always fights about money. Mike O'Hara, our grandfather, built the Shenandoah Opera House, which his sons later renamed the O'Hara Theater. Mike was one of the founders of the old Shenandoah Trust Company, but respectable old Dan Ferguson (the Ferguson House, etc.) eased him out of that. Mike was also in local politics and was Chief Burgess of Shenandoah before it became a third-class city. In short, he had his finger in many pies, and I daresay his ethics never bothered him much, in spite of Jim Archbald's family's happy experience. His sons Mike and Jim were all larceny. Mike never married, but Jim has the distinction of having been the first O'H to get a divorce. As you know, Mike and Jim studied medicine at Penn, did not get a degree, and became partners in an undertaking firm. I always suspected Jim had a bit of necrophilia in him, and I certainly suspect him of not leaving any wedding rings in the caskets. Mike, however, had a way with him. Very tall, eccentrically dressed, rather unsmiling, he was actually very popular without being much respected. Women liked him, young and old, and men liked him without trusting him. I often saw him come into saloons and roadhouses and restaurants alone, as though he owned the place, and he would sit down at a table and immediately people would flock to him, listening to his horseshit and laughing at his wry comments. What you must not forget about them is that they were half Franey, and the Franeys were of the *gentle* Irish, like the Delaneys. The O'Haras were violent and spectacular in contrast with the Franeys. But the Franeys were not flawless. Irene Franey, a little older than I, was quite a beauty and a wild one, who was the only girl I ever knew whose slipper was actually used to drink champagne out of—at a Snow Dance in the early 20s. Her sister married Dr. Gallagher, head of the Locust Mountain State Hospital, who got into some dreadful financial jam that our old man had to help him out of, but the old man was so righteous about it that the Gallaghers never spoke to him after that. Irene didn't like me much either. She called me a Pottsville snob. Actually the Franeys did not approve of the O'Haras generally, as far back as 1864, or whenever the first Mike married the first Franey. The instinct for natural selection got Mike O'Hara to marry a Franey, and his son Pat to marry a Delaney (and you a Browning and me a Wylie, etc.) but I choose to believe that however unattractive some of us may be, the stuff is somewhere there. You probably don't remember Uncle Jim, who was actually our greatuncle. He was Grandfather O'Hara's brother, and one of a generation of giants. Dark, handsome, quiet, and ineffectual, he used to come to the farm and just sit until the old man gave him some money and sent him back to Dunmore, which is where the first O'Haras settled. He was the only one of that generation I ever saw, but he helped me understand the others. He had a brother who, according to Mother, invented the air brake. Uncle Airbrake, who worked for the NY Central in Elmira or some such place, had a naughty wife who walked out on him, taking with her the drawings for the new invention, which she turned over to the ⸻ people. By a strange coincidence, Wolcott Gibbs once told me that his father invented the air brake and was screwed out of the royalties by ⸻. . . .[2] Anyway, in that generation they produced an inventor, and they also produced Sister Lucy. Mother regarded her as

437

a saint. Sister Lucy was a nun, a member of the Little Sisters of the Poor, which is a French order, originally. She and all the others were expelled from France and she ended up in Pawtucket, Rhode Island, as head of the convent there. Mother and Daddy went to see her in Pawtucket just before she died. I believe she is buried in France. Mother said she was very tall and beautiful and a fascinating conversationalist. She and Mother spoke French for three days, and I guess the old man sat there and nodded when he heard a word he could understand. Don't ask me how an O'Hara from Dunmore got to be a nun in France. That's one of those missing links, forever lost to our generation.

But I have always felt that we are something out of the usual run. The Delaney side we know about. They were pre-Revolutionary American. But I mean beyond that, on the O'Hara side. Do you remember William Wright, an old mining engineer who lived in Heckscherville and was a patient of the old man's? He had gout, was chair-ridden, and I often had the dubious pleasure of bathing his gouty foot, putting some kind of powder on it, and wrapping bandages around it. While this was going on he and the old man would talk, talk, talk. Well, he convinced the old man that the O'Haras of our line were descendants of the 9th Century kings, and he went to the trouble of authenticating our right to the coat of arms. Our papa pretended not to care about such things, but if you look in the History of Pennsylvania biography of the old man, you will find that coat of arms right there. When Sister and I were in Dublin a few years ago my friend Geraldine Fitzgerald explained to me that the gentry were not so much in awe of me as an author as of one of "the real thing," O'Hara being one of the seven or eight ancient Irish names. Well, I believe that, if only for two reasons: whenever I am in the company of the Irish (and this has been true all my life) I instantly get a feeling of being a little bit superior to the other ones—and they in turn look at me as though whatever I had to say was going to be important. There is a sort of resentful respect to them, and I have sensed it since I was a small kid. I even got it with the late JFK, and I always had it with his father. I get it with Jim Kerney, the Trenton publisher, I got it with Tim Costello,[3] and it is not mere egomania. It almost has nothing to do with me, because I watched the same thing happening between Irish men and woman and the old man. You never saw anyone get fresh with him; and do you know something? They never really got away with getting fresh with his brother Mike. If they said something fresh, he would look at them witheringly, pause, and then say something like, "Is that so, now?" and they would squirm. It was the look that did it. When Geraldine asked me if I would like to meet Brendan Behan, I said I'd already met a thousand Brendan Behans, and she laughed, because she knew exactly what I meant. Brother Jim has too much dignity, Brother Mart seems to have too little, but there's something there in both cases. And even if it exists only in my imagination, it's what I face the world with.

As ever
John
REX

¹ Family accounts of this event differ; another version is that Martin was the brother who was killed.
² Eleven words omitted by the editor.
³ Proprietor of Costello's, a New York bar.

TO: Wylie O'Hara   TLS, 2 pp. Mrs. Doughty
1963   Princeton

Sunday

My dear:

You left this cheque on the table in the livingroom. You will recall that as soon as you asked for your allowance, I went to my study and wrote out the cheque and brought it in and gave it to you, because you were going to need it the next day in New York.

This cheque is for a larger amount than my entire allowance any year that I was in boarding school. In 1963 it represents approximately the royalty after taxes on the sale of nearly 1,000 books. It is almost twice as much as I earned as a reporter on the Herald Tribune, and I supported myself on that salary. That is, I paid for all my room, board, clothes, and fun on that salary. I had no other income. I therefore take a rather dim view of your casual attitude toward a cheque for $275.

This is, I suppose, your swinging year, and I want you to have a good time. Nevertheless I want you from time to time to give mature thought to certain matters. *Every cent*, every single cent, that is spent on you, and that you spend, comes out of money that I have earned by hard, hard work. Not one single cent of your mother's or grandmother's money had been touched. Your car, for instance, cost me as much money as I have, after taxes, from the sale of four New Yorker stories. Your year at Bennett will have cost me as much as I netted, after taxes, on the sale of A FAMILY PARTY.

As authors go, I am, as I told you, a rich man. But there are not many authors who make nearly as much money as I do, and I do it because I am good and because I work very hard. In the midst of your good time I want you to stop and think once in a while about where the money comes from; not only because it has come from my hard work, but because it is absolutely necessary for you yourself to get some perspective on your

439

own financial position. When you have finished your education you are going to have to go to work, to earn a salary. I will be 59 in January, and it is just kidding myself to think that I can go on working this hard and earning this kind of money, and I do not often kid myself. At 21 you will be coming into some money, but as I have often told you, it is not going to be enough to make you Miss Richbitch or to permit you to live as Miss Richbitch. I am letting you have a good time now, because this is the time to have it, when you are young. But I would be doing you no favor if I failed to remind you of the hard realities. One of the hardest realities is money and the handling of it. Another is the fact that until you marry, and possibly even after, you are going to be a working-girl. I am very fond of most of your friends, but you must not get into the habit of taking for granted that I am as rich as some of their fathers. I'm not. I have earned as much in one year as you will inherit from your mother's estate. And you will only get the income from your grandmother's trust fund; the principal is held in trust for your children.

Now, and during the months ahead, I want you to direct your thoughts toward your own future, the kind of work you want to do, the kind of man you want to marry, the contributions you can make to your marriage, and the future wellbeing of your children. I assure you that if you do this you will enjoy yourself more than if you enjoy yourself aimlessly.

Love
Dad

TO: Don Schanche

TLS, 1 p. Schanche
Princeton

17 Jan. '64

Dear Don:

Our letters would have crossed, except I didn't write mine. But I've been meaning to the last few days.

Item: I have written most of the Women piece for the Journal,[1] and will finish it next week. I wrote most of it before 1 Jan., and could have finished it then, but I didn't want the cheque to go on my 1963 income, which was a very big year for me.

Items: Yes, I would like you to schedule the pieces in fairly rapid succession, because I want to sell you some more, and if you have too big a bank you may not want to buy. This is what was on my mind for the unwritten letter: I have written five stories and am finishing a sixth, all of which I am going to give you first look at, when next you come to

Princeton. I am not sore at The New Yorker, although Shawn sometimes turns down pieces that Maxwell wants to buy. It's just that I feel you are equally entitled to first look.

Now the thing is, we are leaving here on 3 Feb. for a three-weeks' cruise in the Franconia to the West Indies. We get back, then on 1 March we go to Bermuda (Cambridge Beaches, Somerset) for a month. I will hold the pieces until you have had an opportunity to read them, which obviously would be in the next two weeks, or in the last week of February, or early April. I am taking my portable on the cruise, and probably will write a couple of stories then; and in Bermuda I will reconstitute that play that your people did not convert into a novella.[2] That's just the right amount of work to engage me during my Bermuda vacation.

I was pleased that Butts got slapped down. The Bear must be having second thoughts, too.[3]

Cordially,
John O'Hara

[1] An article for The Ladies' Home Journal, which was not published.
[2] "Far From Heaven." O'Hara did not rework the play.
[3] Refers to the libel action brought against the Post by Georgia football coach Wally Butts as a result of an article alleging that he had conspired with Alabama coach Paul "Bear" Bryant to fix the 1962 Georgia-Alabama game. Butts won a $3 million judgment, which was reduced to $520,000. Bryant accepted an out-of-court settlement.

TO: James Gould Cozzens

TLS, 1 p. Cozzens
Princeton
27 Jan '64

Dear Jim:

I have just had a message, from me to me, that I am compelled to pass on to you. It is only and no more than the thought that you could write a hell of a play (my first thought; or novella, or novel) about inside Cuba today.[1]

I've never been to Cuba, and the only Cubans I know are what might be called White Cubans, like the White Russians we all knew in the Twenties. But nothing is coming out of that unhappy land, and nothing is going to except in the form of a work of imagination by someone like you. Those dreadful people, the TV and newspaper correspondents, have had to admit defeat by Castro's censorship, which leaves the whole lode untouched. I am not suggesting what you write, but only that you write. I get plenty of unsolicited help, and you can imagine what I do with it.

This is different, and if nothing comes of it, that's okay, too. I had a flash, and I relayed it to the proper authority.

Cordially,
John O'Hara

[1] Cozzens had worked in Cuba as a young man, and two of his novels are set in Cuba.

TO: Red Smith, *New York Herald Tribune* (28 January 1964), 26

My father was pretty good with his hands, whether he was operating on a man's skull to relieve the pressure on the brain, or breaking a Kluxer's jaw for calling him a Molly Maguire. Patrick O'Hara, M.D., could open you up with a scalpel or with a jab and an uppercut.

Thus qualified, he had credentials as an expert when he told me about the Willard-Dempsey fight at Toledo.

He, and a private carload of Pennsylvanians who were the paying guests of Philadelphia Jack O'Brien, attended that fight, and I can add his testimony to the revived controversy.[1]

He told me that when the fight was over, he helped Willard leave the arena. Willard, he said, could not see clearly, because Dempsey's fists had been soaked in plaster-of-Paris, and my old man led Willard out of the place.

In 1919 I didn't understand the plaster-of-Paris bit and so my old man hated Dempsey, really hated him, and when Dempsey fought Carpentier in Jersey City, the old man bet $1,000 on Carpentier. To make matters worse, during his absence I had sneaked the car out of the garage and wrinkled a fender. Things were not just right for quite a long while afterwards.

[1] The death of Jack Kearns, Jack Dempsey's manager, revived speculation that he had encased Dempsey's fists in plaster for the Dempsey-Willard fight.

TO: Don Schanche

Typed note on bottom of
18 February letter to O'Hara
from Don Gold.[1] Schanche
Princeton

24 Feb. '64
To Don Schanche: This is exactly why I insisted on dealing with you and not with a committee of bushers, and spineless bushers at that. I am

not going to change a word of this piece, and I want to be paid in full for it. Please return this letter for my files.[2]

J. O'H.

[1] Assistant managing editor of *The Ladies' Home Journal*.
[2] *The Ladies' Home Journal* had ordered revisions of O'Hara's article on women because of its "sexual frankness" and because it was too hard on women.

TO: John Hersey   TLS, 1 p. National Institute of Arts and Letters
"Linebrook" letterhead

27 Feb 64

Dear John:

Today, on my wife's birthday (it is also Steinbeck's), I am the one that got the best present.[1] No one can imagine the depth of my pleasure at the news you brought me, and I am delighted that you were chosen to bring it in a graceful, gracious letter.

When I got the National Book Award I broke down in the middle of my acceptance speech, and I fully expect to break down on the 20th of May, but I'll be there.* All those who hate to see a man cry are fore-warned.

This, almost thirty years after the publication of my first novel, is the high point of my professional career, and I thank you not only for your letter but for the part you must have played in bringing about this recognition.

As always,
John

*We.

[1] Hersey had informed O'Hara that he had been awarded the Merit Medal for the Novel by the American Academy of Arts and Letters.

TO: William Maxwell   TLS, 1 p. PSt.
Princeton

28 Feb 64

Dear Bill:

Here are two stories. If you don't buy them, or buy one and not the other, please hold the spurned manuscript until I get back from Bermuda. However, I would like to hear what happens to them. We leave Sunday

443

and will be at Cambridge Beaches, Somerset Parish, Bermuda, until 1 April, then return to Princeton, Mercer County, N.J. I do hope you buy MRS. ALLANSON.[1] I may change the title of that story to something more vivid, but for the time being I am more interested in putting it through the process.

It was Sister's birthday yesterday, which made the Academy recognition a special pleasure. When she read Hersey's letter, and came to the part where we are invited to the Ceremonial, she said aloud, "I accept." I burst out laughing.

In the same mail my tax man informed me that my 1963 debt to the U.S.A. amounts to $135,000, of which I have already paid only $70,000. I wouldn't mind paying $135,000 income tax if I had made $270,000, but I didn't, and that's why I'm a Republican, whatever that is, instead of a Democrat, whatever *that* is. I can remember my father's anguish when he had to pay $1500, and *he* thought *I* was a bum, the bum. Say, is that a *gold* medal they're going to give me?

Ever
John

[1] One of the stories is unidentified; "Mrs. Allanson" was declined by *The New Yorker* and published in *The Horse Knows the Way* (1964).

TO: Graham Watson

TLS, 1 p. Curtis Brown
Cambridge Beaches,
Somerset, Bermuda

8 March 64

Dear Graham:

As you see from the above, we are diligently disposing of pounds sterling in our campaign to buy British, spend British, etc. Having returned from a West Indies cruise in the M. S.—excuse me, R.M.S.—Franconia, we are now spending the month of March in this Crown Colony. Sister, as I may have told you, gets stir crazy over the long Princeton winter, and this is my effort at tender, loving care.

As I am spending sterling, I would dearly love to know how much I have to spend. Barclays Bank do not believe in regular statements, although I asked them to keep me posted. So will you please call them up and tell them that I would like them to airmail to me, here, an up-to-date statement of my wealth? Thank the Lord I have that money in London! I just got a severe jolt from my tax man in New York. I am going to have to pay $65,000 *more* than I have already paid on my 1963 income tax, thus wiping out a nest egg I had put aside. Nobody minds paying 50% tax, but this is extortion, and I am 59 years old.

444

I have had some good news. On 20 May I am to be given the Award of Merit of the American Academy of Arts & Letters. It is in the form of a medal and a cheque for $1,000, which by the way is tax free. The previous recipients of the award were Theodore Dreiser, Thomas Mann, Ernest Hemingway, and Aldous Huxley. Fast company, and it is the highest recognition I've ever got. In fact, there isn't, in my opinion, any higher in the U.S. It is for fiction, and is given every five years. I did not bother to tell you that I had already been named Author of the Year by the New Jersey Association of Teachers of English. Somehow I didn't think that would impress the boys at the Atheneum.[1]

The work goes on. I did not do a tap on the Caribbean cruise, but I am back at the typewriter here. I will publish a collection of short pieces on Thanksgiving Day. No title yet.[2] But I have also begun work on a short novel which I might possibly finish in Bermuda and publish this summer.[3] Depends on how it goes.

We will be back in Princeton on 3 April, handsomely sunburned and considerably poorer. My Mrs. and I join in best wishes to you and your Mrs.

As ever,
John

[1] London club.
[2] *The Horse Knows the Way.*
[3] Possibly "Andrea," *Waiting for Winter* (1966).

TO: Don Schanche

TLS, 1 p. Schanche
Cambridge Beaches,
Somerset, Bermuda

11 March 64

Dear Don:

The clipping from the Royal Gazette refers to a seagoing tug and to an icebreaker. The Westwind is a U.S. Coast Guard vessel used in smashing ice and taking supplies, etc., to our guys and the Canadians in the Arctic Circle. You may wonder why I am sending you the clipping.

Well, for about 25 years I have been wanting to board the first oreboat out of Duluth in the Spring and make the eastward trip. I never completed the arrangements. I have also wanted to ship out on a seagoing tug, on a salvage operation or towing a ship across the ocean. Never got very far with that either, except to have a small tangle with Admiral Moran of the tugboat Morans. Now I'll never do any of these things, and have given up trying. I have little enough time for the things I must do.

However, there are, I think, good pieces to be written about such activities, and of course they offer opportunities for photography. A man named

Jacland Marmur used to write good hack fiction in the Post about this sort of thing. I always thought he could have been a much better writer than he settled for. I don't know anything about him, but his name comes to mind, and that is the end of my tip.

We sit in the sun and read about the weather you are having. I don't mind lousy weather, but my wife does, so we are getting our money's worth.

I am writing a short novel. I will let you see it, although I doubt if you will buy it. I hope to have it finished before we return to Princeton on 3 April aboard the Queen of Bermuda, which of course puts in at Trenton. I know, by the way, that that's a misuse of the nautical term, but people misuse it all the time. When you put in it's supposed to be for repairs or something like that, which you as a seagoing man probably knew all the time. I found out about it when I was ship news reporter for the Dahlonega Nugget.[1]

Yrs,
John

[1] A joke.

TO: William Maxwell
20 March 1964

TLS, 1 p. PSt.

Letterhead of Cambridge Beaches,
Somerset, Bermuda

Friday the 20th

Dear Bill:

I am pleased that you want to buy the musician piece[1] and I want to sell it. Furthermore, if it will be bought only if I agree to the indicated cut, you may cut.

However, I do wish you and Shawn would get together to save as much of the now tentatively cut material as possible. There is humor of a characterizing kind in there. Somewhat whimsical, slightly campy. Our family magazine has been printing things that could have been cut for the same reasons you cite now. (I recall being a little embarrassed for one of your younger authors when he discovered sex a few years ago.)

What is the offensive material? My guess is the use of the word laid on Line 11, and the venereal question on Line 14. We can change laid, and we can get rid of the clap. If you agree, I will make the changes when I get back to the USA, but I would like to keep as much as possible of the interview with the doctor. When you are writing about jazz musicians you are not writing about the vicar and his wife in Melton Mowbray. As it happens the vicar is queer as a goat, and she picked up a mean dose from the green-grocer's boy.

The high winds in Jamaica have drifted this way, so I have been writing a small novel. I'll be glad to get home. (Queen of Bermuda, 3 April.)

Ever
John

1 "I Spend My Days in Longing," *The New Yorker* (23 May 1964).

TO: Don Schanche

TLS, 1 p. Schanche
Letterhead of Cambridge Beaches,
Somerset, Bermuda

23 March 64

Dear Don:

I could not be more pleased (selfishly, which is always the best kind) about your taking over at Holiday. I congratulate you while heaving a sigh of relief that Stinnett[1] didn't get the job, although he must have been drooling with desire for it.

I have a piece there now that they bought last year, and I often get ideas for non-fiction that I never write. My only other contact at Holiday, aside from Patrick,[2] was my old friend Frank Zachary, who once worked for me in Pittsburgh. But I don't do photography or draw pictures, so the contact is not very active.

It is a beautiful magazine physically, the most so in the business. Patrick sometimes bought pieces that I could not get through, and the political slant of a lot of the pieces was kind of silly; but I don't think I missed ten issues in its entire history.

Good luck. When you feel like coming to Princeton let me know. I have about four appointments during April, and will be free the rest of the time.

Best wishes,

As ever
John

1 Caskie Stinnett.
2 Ted Patrick.

TO: William Maxwell   TLS, 1 p. PSt.
26 March 1964   Bermuda

                                                            Holy Thursday
Dear Bill:

One, two, and three.[1]

"*Laid*." That can be changed to: "How long since you *did* have a
woman?"

"*Gonorrhea*." That can be changed to: nothing. Just strike out gonorrhea.
In fact let's start a movement to stamp out gonorrhea.

"*You have had intercourse, haven't you?*" We can change that to: "You
ever been married?"

* £ * £ *

Where did I get the impression that you had abandoned Yorktown
Heights? I think I know. One day you said some unfavorable things about
it that led me to *infer* that you no longer lived there. What ever happened to Peggy Sloan?

0=0=0

You can send the rejected stories to me at Princeton after next week.
They will then be stashed away until I have what I think are enough for
a book, then they all go off to the Penn State University Library, which
is where all my mss eventually will repose. A great many are there already,
crumbling to dust because I use such horrible cheap paper.

½¢½¢½¢½

I have done about 80 pages of a short novel and I am enjoying the
work. I thought I might finish it here, but it doesn't look that way. However I think I still can publish it this summer. It will add nothing to
my stature, because the people who recognize the types in the book will
think they could have done it better. The people who have never encountered the types will say they don't exist. But *I* know they exist, and *they*
know they exist. And oddly enough the English will take them in stride.
So I am having a good time. I always have a good time except when I
catch myself repeating myself. Then I worry for 24 hours and start something new.

*****

I have an interesting biographical theory about Cheever[2] that I must
ask you about some time.

⧣ ⧣ ⧣ ⧣ ⧣

                                                            Yours truly,
                                                            John

---

[1] "I Spend My Days in Longing," 23 May 1964.
[2] Novelist John Cheever.

448

TO: Bennett Cerf

TLS, 1 p. Columbia
Letterhead of Cambridge Beaches,
Somerset, Bermuda

31 March 64

Dear Bennett:

I would like you to check up and tell me when you last ran an ad for THE HAT ON THE BED. I am quite certain that you will find that you did not buy an agate line during the whole month of March and very probably not in February either. This book is not a mystery story, and it needs help. I especially want the book to be selling in May, when I get the Academy medal. The fact that I am getting the medal for my work in the *novel* is especially gratifying in the light of the success of my short story collections.

You know what I'm after. It's no secret that I am *working* to get the Nobel. I am not making speeches, or writing letters, or giving interviews, like James T. Farrell and Graham Greene. I am constantly at work, not only quantitatively but also maintaining as high standards as are within my power, and this has been going on for some time.

I have never been an author whom people made excuses for, or in whose work people pretended to see more than is there. The most disgusting recent exhibition of an author as well as his admirers on the excuse-making kick is, of course, Arthur Miller. They got tired of doing it for Irwin Shaw. They cooked Salinger and have turned against him. They will do it to Cheever and Ringo Updike, they've done it to K. A. Porter. They've never alibied for me, so when I get a badge, it means something. It means that the work has prevailed, and that's the way I want it to be. But it deserves support. I would like to see a quote ad written by a man who is not afraid to use the best quotes.

Be home Friday. May see you next week.

As ever
John

TO: James Gould Cozzens

TLS, 1 p. Cozzens
"Linebrook" letterhead

13 April 64

Dear Jim:

I guess I read the wrong papers—a pretty safe remark these days—but I have not yet come across the piece by Gore Vidal.[1] But I am delighted with your response. This —— —— is one of the many mysteries of the current crop of semi-writers. One book, or one play, and they got it made, at least to the extent that they feel free to sound off on every-

449

thing from literature to politics. *You* didn't do that, and neither did I. We went back to work.

Mr. J. Donald Adams, confessedly "tight," came and sat next to me at the Century last week and introduced himself as, "The bastard whose guts you hate," and proceeded to make a complete horse's ass of himself. So you see I got troubles from all ages. But thank God for the kind of enemies I have as well as the kind of friends.

Yrs,
John

¹ Vidal reviewed *Elizabeth Appleton* and *The Hat on the Bed* in the *New York Review of Books* (16 April 1964).

TO: John Hersey

TLS, 1 p. Hersey
Princeton

22 April '64

Dear John:

I have just received an invitation-program for the May 20th Ceremonial, and I note with pleasure that you are to make the award to me. I trust that you have no more difficulty in composing your remarks than I did in writing my acceptance. As soon as I got over the shock—and it was a shock, however pleasurable—of your letter, I immediately wrote my acceptance speech of two minutes' duration, or less, if I read it fast, so that if Anything Happened To Me before the Ceremonial, someone else could read it.

What I am writing you about now is a delicate subject: I would like very much to wangle an invitation to the luncheon for my daughter, Wylie, who is now a freshman at Bennett College. ("Oh, come on, Daddy, it isn't really a college.") She will be coming down from Millbrook for the day and will of course be at the Ceremonial, but I would like it if a point could be stretched and she could be at the luncheon as well. I think I went to two of the luncheons when I was a member of the Institute, and I just can't remember any daughters except Deems Taylor's, which is a special case as he had no wife to invite. I have a wife, who would not miss the Ceremonial, and who will be at the luncheon, so that would make the O'Hara delegation three in number. If the Academy-Institute were not so rich I would argue that since I expect to lunch off tranquilizers and coffee, Wylie could have my share of the food.

The Award continues to be an inspiriting experience for me.

As ever,
John

450

TO: John Hersey
TLS, 1 p. Hersey
"Linebrook" letterhead

21 May 64

Dear John:

Before closing the book on the adventure that began with your letter and built to yesterday's climax, let me add this final word of thanks. I am glad you said certain things in your citation, which would be valueless coming from me but are nevertheless what I strongly feel.

And I strongly feel, as I certainly demonstrated yesterday.[1] I thought I was getting by, and then my eyes lit on two words—obsolescent, and love.[2] Then I felt the effect of those thousands of nights-till-dawn, and I had no control. Well, most of the people I saw later thought I had finished anyhow.

I left out a small joke. I wanted to say, "John Hersey is a Yale man, and it would be doubly appropriate if I limited my speech to one word— bingo!"[3] I planned that on my way up in the car, then when I got to the lectern I had to rely on what I had typed out.

Sister joins me in best wishes to you and Barbara.

As ever,
John

[1] O'Hara was unable to finish reading his acceptance speech.
[2] ". . . in the context of present-day writing I am regarded as obsolescent. . . . But as long as I live, or at least as long as I am able to write, I will go to my typewriter with love of my work. . . ."
[3] Reference to Yale cheering song, "Bingo."

TO: Graham Watson
TLS, 2 pp. Curtis Brown
Quogue, Long Island

31 May '64

Dear Graham:

I would not have you think that my Buy British policy has changed, much less that I do not wish to continue to avail myself of the excellent Curtis Brown Shopping Service. Therefore . . .

I would like to have Burberry make me a jacket. (The topcoat has been a great success.) It is to be a black and white houndstooth, of cashmere or a soft woolen material. I abhor the narrow lapels that American and Italian tailors are pushing these days, and I therefore would like the jacket to be of English cut. Side vents. A little but not too much drawn in at what used to be called my waistline. Straight, as distinguished from slanting pocket flaps, and with a ticket pocket on the right (what else?) side. Skeleton-lined.

I suppose the best procedure is for Burberry to send me swatches and a measuring chart, via the C. B. Shopping Service, or direct.

We leave for Quogue (closing this house) on 10 June, to be gone until the middle of September. I would like you to urge upon Burberry the desirability of completing the work for delivery in Quogue early in September, when the weather is right for that kind of jacket, and when I shall be appearing at numerous fashionable social gatherings at which my reputation as a fashion-plate must be maintained.

To change the subject: I have delivered the typescript to Random for my next book, a collection of short stories to be called THE HORSE KNOWS THE WAY, November publication, 1964. THE HAT ON THE BED sold about 60,000 in the trade edition and can be considered a great success. It actually reached Number 1 on the bestseller list, although it did not stay there long against that British spy story[1] and Miss McCarthy's study in feminine hygiene.[2] I *was* a spy, or at least I had spy training, but I have never had any experience in the field, so I cannot compete with your English writers (among whom I include Miss MacInnes). I did not read Miss McCarthy. I met her once a long time ago and . . .[3] I don't want to read her, but I caught the reviews, etc.

I had a fine time getting the Academy Award of Merit except that I broke down toward the end of my speech of acceptance and had to leave out several deathless lines. However, I took the cheque and the medal. Next week I am getting an honorary degree from an institution called American International College, Springfield, Massachusetts.[4] I regard all this as rehearsal for my eventual appearance in Stockholm. I don't want to be caught unprepared, you know. Graham Greene would have such a lovely time if I were to make a chump of myself in front of all those Swedes.

Well, there we are, up to date. Tomorrow in New York the doctor commits certain indignities upon my person and I will not feel like sitting down for a while, but at least this year's book is on its way to the printers.

My thanks and good wishes,

As ever,
John

[1] *The Venetian Affair* by Helen MacInnes.
[2] *The Group* by Mary McCarthy.
[3] Nine words omitted by the editor.
[4] O'Hara could not attend the commencement and did not receive the degree.

TO: Graham Watson   TLS, 1 p. Curtis Brown
                                                       Princeton

                                                    2 June 64
Dear Graham:
   I have just received my copies of the Cresset edition of THE HAT ON
THE BED, and I cannot say that I am pleased with the biographical
material on the jacket. It is the same old lazy, unimaginative junk that
may be all right (though I doubt it) for an author's first book; but I have
been published for thirty years, for God's sake. (Twenty-nine in Britain.)
I did not have "innumerable occupations." They are numerable. The ship
steward, gas meter reader, and soda clerk jobs all told did not add up
to a year of my life; they were summer jobs.
   Therefore I wish you would go to Cresset and tell them I want that
jacket changed in the next printing, and hereafter to confine their biographical remarks to my writing and the hell with this other junk. I
would much prefer a simple, complete, accurate listing of my books—
and not just what Cresset has published. Incidentally, the listing in the
front matter of this book is in the wrong order and is incomplete. Returning to the jacket, I see "after his graduation," but graduation from what?
As a Borstal boy or one of Dr. Bernardo's (?) waifs? And is that supposed
to be an American-type hat on the bed? It's not like any I've ever worn.
   This jacket is lazy, tasteless, and cheap, and you may quote me as you
pound Cohen's desk. It is almost as bad as the covers on the British paperbacks, and that, my friend, is saying something. I've said it before, and
I say it again: when the British copy America they always copy the wrong
things, from hamburgers to Beatles.
   With kind regards,

                                                    As ever,
                                                    John

TO: Red Smith, The *New York Herald Tribune* (10 June 1964), 25

   Your readers may not know, so I shall tell them, that at our recent
meeting in the directors' room in what some inspired citizen has called
Payson's Place, or Chez Shea, you registered a perfectly legitimate complaint that I was behind in my letter-writing.
   As the Princeton (N.J.) representative of the Committee to Offer a
Day's Grace to an Exhausted Red Smith (CODGERS), I take my responsibility quite seriously, and my only excuse for my delinquency is that I
have been waiting for you to bring up a subject I could write about, or
in which I had more than passing interest. Recently your subject was
tennis bums, and since you mentioned my name in the column, I took
that as a strong hint for assistance.

I think it was George Lott[1] who many years ago first called wide attention to the tennis bum. I would have to check that with my acquaintance, F. Townsend Hunter, who is one former newspaper man who licked the booze problem. (Instead of just drinking it, he sells it.)

If I can't find out about George Lott from Frank Hunter, I might ask Hunter Lott, of Philadelphia, who is not related to either party but is a good tennis player. And if I can't find out from Lott, I'll ask Scott, whose first name is Edgar and who introduced me to Lott.

And if I can't find out about George Lott from Edgar Scott, I may have to ask O'Hara Watts, who used to be captain of the Navy tennis team. And if O'Hara Watts doesn't know, I may try Watts Gunn. That would be a desperate measure, as Watts Gunn is a golfer, but Pat O'Hara-Wood, the Australian Davis Cupper, is no longer available. He has departed for Tennis Bums' Heaven, which I envision as that country club in the sky where the courts are always too wet for tournament play, the members all rich and very bad bridge players, the expense accounts unlimited, and the maidens and matrons receptive and startlingly beautiful.

You risk anything from a punch in the snoot to a rap on the wrist any time you call a man a bum of any kind, especially in England, and in my present condition I would not like to take on the runner-up in the Camp Wassamaddadiddahosskikya junior boys' boxing tournament, even with the big gloves.

I think it should also be fully understood that we are discussing lawn tennis bums. There are so very few court tennis bums that any shyster worthy of the name would slap us with a suit and all that money you plan to leave to Notre Dame would vanish in legal fees.

After all, how many court tennis bums do you know? I would have a hard time thinking of more than three, and I have been in New York and vicinity much longer than you have. The scarcity of court tennis bums would make it easy for an ambulance-chaser because they are almost as readily identifiable as one-legged jockeys. However, you may know a lot of one-legged jockeys. Sports are your racket. I am just a reader who likes to help out when you want to take a day off.

So, confining ourselves to lawn tennis bums, let us examine your thesis, which is that the revival of sex around the lawn tennis courts may sufficiently revive tennis to attract the young to the game. That may be so, but who wants to revive tennis?

It was fun to play; good exercise and got you out in the sun. It was fun to watch; to go to Forest Hills and Merion, to Wimbledon and the Hamptons and the armories. I was never any good at the game; I was never really very good at any game; but I never went in for chop strokes, and as a spectator I refrained from barracking and cushion-tossing, and my tennis memories are largely pleasant.

Nevertheless, I still say that if we are going to have tennis it ought to be confined to the place where Mary Outerbridge introduced it, which is Staten Island. Cricket likewise flourished on Staten Island but did not achieve quite the degree of popularity that tennis did elsewhere. Indeed, it took the profits from tennis tournaments to enable some cricket clubs to survive.

You may wonder what I have against tennis. Well, if you read back carefully you will find that I have said nothing against tennis.

Nor did I say anything against sex. I did say that tennis ought to be limited to our local channel island, but I suggested no such restrictions upon sex, which has caught on everywhere. Sex became popular without any considerable help from tennis. In fact, I could probably cite four or five instances where heterosexual enterprise was frowned upon in tennis circles.

Therefore, if tennis is to be revived or to endure it must make it on its own. I am thinking right now of asking E. B. White to collaborate on a book to be called, inevitably, 'Is Tennis Necessary?'[2] On second thought, I recall that White is a Cornell man and so is Frank Hunter, so I probably won't make a nickel out of my idea.

Ah, well, you have your day off.

[1] Tennis doubles player, winner at Wimbledon 1931, 1934.
[2] White collaborated with James Thurber on *Is Sex Necessary?*

TO: Don Schanche

TLS, 1 p. Schanche
Quogue, Long Island

21 July 64

Dear Don:

I don't want to be pigheaded with you, but I don't agree that the Sports piece[1] should be updated. I have just reread it and I like it as is. "Last year" is now the year before last, but otherwise I think this kind of piece is better without topicality. You are the editor.

Yes, you can interest me in doing a piece on the Chaplin autobiography.[2] I despise the little bastard, and that feeling will come through in the piece, which means you will get angry letters. But I am perfectly willing to give him what I consider his due artistically.

I am off to San Francisco and a visit to the Bohemian Grove, as co-guest of honor (with, I regret to say, Bobby Kenndy as the other co). I will be back here next Tuesday, the 28th, if you want to phone or come down for a swim, etc. I expect to be here until mid- or late September, working away. The skin doctor gouged a lump out of my kisser last week and has his eye on one on my throat; but these are nothing new or very dramatic. I am slowly falling apart, but at 59½ that's par, I guess.

You should be pleased to learn that Glenway Westcott, on the radio today, described me as the modern successor to Chekhov. You and I knew it all the time.

As ever

John

[1] "Memoirs of a Sentimental Duffer," *Holiday* (May 1965).
[2] "The Wayward Reader," *Holiday* (December 1964). This article discusses three books: *Chaplin*, Hemingway's *A Moveable Feast*, and George Abbott's *"Mr. Abbott."*

TO: Graham Watson   TLS, 2 pp. Curtis Brown
                                                 Quogue, Long Island

29 July 64

Dear Graham:

Short things first: will you please ask Nuffields just what numbers they want and where I am to look for them? The serial number is C-4870. The car was purchased in 1949, at Fergus Motors, Southhampton, Long Island, and I assumed, probably erroneously, that they would report the purchaser's name, etc., to Nuffield as a matter of course.

If the Frank O'Connor who is delivering my claymore is the nom de plume of the writer Frank O'Connor, perhaps I ought to have some assurances that he is not going to stick it in me. I seem to recall that he is not a fan of mine, although the ungrateful bastard must know that I got Harold Ross interested in his work after CRABAPPLE JELLY. Fortunately I possess a small arsenal in Princeton and I know how to use fire-arms.

Yes, I daresay we have been giving you political amusement. As to our keeping you on your toes, I wonder why. Britain, and particularly the British press, are in more of a flap over a man who has not yet been elected than they have been over De Gaulle or Krushchev. Liberals like to get excited about things, and the international liberal attitude for the past ten years has been that the only fit man for president of the U.S.A. was Adlaid Stevenson. Kennedy was never really acceptable to the liberal; he was preferable only to Nixon. Now the thought that a rather ordinary, second-rate man has been chosen by the Republicans to run on a conservative ticket has the liberals sweating as though the first thing Goldwater plans to do is disconnect the hot line and push the bomb button. Britain has done not too badly under a succession of conservative governments, but the idea of our having a conservative government is displeasing even to the British conservatives. That, of course, goes back to not letting Eden have his own dangerous way in the Suez. Or it may go back to 1776 and all that. But the liberals here and elsewhere forget that Nixon

456

was beaten only by about 130,000 votes in this huge country. To demonstrate how small a margin that was, my personal friend Richardson Dilworth was beaten for the governorship of Pennsylvania by Scranton by 400,000 votes, and Dilworth is an extremely liberal Democrat, in a state that had not gone Republican in, I believe, 14 years. So Nixon almost got in, and it is cynically conceded that if the Illinois vote had been truly honest, he would have got in. So what happens to all those people who voted for Nixon against Kennedy? Do they vanish? Are they disfranchised? Did they never exist? My point is that a conservative American trend was there for all to see four years ago, and I don't believe that the Kennedy administration has done very much to make conservatism less attractive to American voters. A few more Rochesters[1]—and there will be a few more—may very easily elect Goldwater. It is already a cliche of this campaign that the incited Negro, led by the irresponsible, bloodthirsty Negro racists, may give the election to Goldwater, and my own observation is that even if Goldwater doesn't get in, the Republicans are going to be the big winners in the Senate and House campaigns.[2]

I maintain that much of the guilt for evil race situation must go to the liberals, whose conventional, strictly conformist view is that anything and everything the Negro does is right, and everything the white man does, vis a vis the Negro, is wrong. This is a gutless, irresponsible attitude, which militates against the activity of the Roy Wilkinses. Any white man who calls Wilkins—or, for that matter, Louis Armstrong—an Uncle Tom is bringing on more violence. It is so stupid of the liberals. Don't they know that the ——— ——— and the ——— ——— and the Malcolm X's are not going to stop and ask a man if he is liberal before sticking a knife in him? Martin Luther King went on the TV the other night and twice used the word murder in describing the cop who killed the kid who attacked him with a knife. This is rabble-rousing of the worst sort, because King has been playing it more cautiously. As it happens, the cop who killed the kid is a good cop, with nineteen departmental citations. The kid was six feet away from him when he shot him. Six feet. (This is the report of a Negro witness, who was testifying against the cop.) For Martin Luther King to describe that shooting as murder, and to repeat the word (I was watching the TV and heard him) is as bad as murder itself, because it is going to lead to murder. But the foreign press are clamoring for a Nobel *peace* prize for King! In liberal circles you are nothing if you don't refer to Baldwin as Jimmy these days. You are not with it. So people talk about Jimmy Baldwin, and they build him up as the spokesman for the Negro. . . .[3] I will not accept him as spokesman for the Negro—but I am not a liberal. I'm not stuck with the Jimmy Baldwins, even though I may get stuck by them.

Getting back to Goldwater: he may win, you know. There are many factors to help elect him, apart from apartheid. He is running against

457

the incumbent, it is true. But Johnson is a man that nobody loves or hates. He is a second-rater who could be demoted to third-rater if enough is made of his financial dealings. The Washington press corps possess a great deal of damaging information about him that can't be printed as news, but if the same information is reported in political speeches it becomes big news, and it aint gonna help LBJ. At the moment, however, nobody loves him or hates him; whereas there are millions of people in this country who do love Goldwater, and make no mistake about that. They are to the right of Eisenhower, of course, and my guess is that Eisenhower, though popular, was always a little forbidding, aloof. The liberals, naturally, despise Goldwater and are so zealous that they made a big thing of a line or two in his acceptance speech that I must say I considered nothing more than rhetoric. I'm talking about the extremism passages. I listened to the speech, live, and as a rather professional writer I detected the effort at phrase-making but sensed nothing sinister. The liberal attacks are going to make Goldwater a much more important figure than he is. He is no dope. He has a mind, he has certain skills (such as being able to fly a jet) that raise his intelligence rating higher than Harry Truman's. Truman, who became something of a darling of the liberals, is the man who gave the order to drop the A bomb. If you listen to the liberals you would come to believe that it was really dropped by Goldwater for practice, against the day when he could drop a bigger one and rid the earth of us all, including himself. But whether he gets in or not, the liberal movement in this country is going to have a setback. And why not? The word has lost its meaning, the movement has lost its usefulness. FDR could not have voted for that radical Eisenhower and his platform.

As ever
John

[1] Riots in Rochester, N.Y.
[2] O'Hara's predictions were wrong.
[3] Sixty-five words omitted by the editor.

TO: James Gould Cozzens

TLS, 3 pp. Cozzens
Quogue, Long Island

4 Aug. '64

Dear Jim:

Your CHILDREN & OTHERS arrived here as I was about to leave for San Francisco and my first visit to the Bohemian Grove. Thank you for sending it to me. I have read, and will only comment on EYES TO SEE, since that is all you wanted me to do. (But did I not read FAREWELL TO CUBA a long time ago in Scribner's? I liked it then and now.)

I am sorry to say I do not go along with the notion that EYES TO SEE "stands by itself as is." In my opinion it is a question of balance, or imbalance. I am willing to credit a bright boy with the observations about religion, especially since as a bright boy at that age I was deeply interested in the subject. But my criticism of the story is that the religion gets pretty far away from the boy that you are writing about, that it seems not to have much connection with him as of the time of the story. With only 42 pages to work in, you cannot successfully get that far away from the boy and back again. Also, I believe that the style is that of Cozzens the novelist rather than Cozzens the writer of short stories. We give ourselves more leisure in a novel than in a short story, but what is good for one is bad for the other. End of pontification.

I hope you are good and tough. I have been somewhat toughened by unfavorable reviews through the years, but my wife touts me off the worst of them even now. I can get very depressed by a review that is unfair, unreasonable, and totally destructive, as the one in the Times of your book was.[1] Steinbeck has been a friend of mine since 1936, and last year he was badly wounded—trying not to show it, and showing it every minute—by the attacks on him following the Nobel prize. He did not know what hit him. He had been (like you) accustomed to respectful reviews throughout most of his career, and when there was an occasion for jubilation They suddenly turn on him. Of course They are not the same identical They who were reviewing 25 years ago; but the old They did not defend Steinbeck as they could have. I happen to know that I have been up for, and passed over for, the Nobel four times. If I ever get it, I know what to expect in the way of angry protest; but Steinbeck was taken completely by surprise. As we were all surprised and outraged by the Timecoverstory on you. They wanted to do one on me, and I told Luce that after what they had done to you and tried to do for Herman Wouk, I didn't want any part of them unless Luce himself came down and did the interviewing and wrote the piece. Then, I said, I would know whom to thank.

They, the reviewers, are not us. We tend to overlook that fact when we get intelligent, understanding reviews; but they are still not us. They and we are as different as touch football and the genuine article. No training, no tackling, no risk of any kind, and no enduring skill. And, to continue the analogy a little further, no hope of ever getting a varsity letter. But they sure as hell talk big.

I like what you said about Uncle George on p. 332, whose absence of bigotry comes not so much from any broad-mindedness in admitting there may be more truths than one, as from regard for manners. While not scrupling to state or show his own beliefs, no gentleman argues about them; and he really can't urge them on others. End of quotation. Most of the people who are given books to review are as intolerant as any

Kluxer that ever lived. You go along with them, or by Christ they will try to destroy you, and not on literary grounds any more. They say quite boldly that if you fail or refuse to conform to their politics, you should not be in business. . . .[2] What "Jimmy" Baldwin says goes, and he has put himself on record as opposed to me. Before him it was Kazin and that crowd. And always it has been the academics, from Ellery Sedgwick[3] to the boys in the English department at Princeton.

I must stop this, because it could become endless and it is not good for me. But you and I and Steinbeck must go on reminding ourselves that They are not us, even when temporarily they seem to be on our side. When they knock gently on our door, we must not let them in. They will waste our precious time, and eat us out of house and home.

Best wishes,

As ever
John

[1] By Frederick C. Crews.
[2] Eighteen words omitted by the editor.
[3] Editor of *The Atlantic Monthly*.

TO: Richardson Dilworth

TLS, 1 p. Dilworth
Quogue, Long Island

5 Aug. '64

Dear Dick:

The wife and I are delighted that you and your Missus will be hereabouts on the 28th of August. It goes without saying that we will put in a good supply of eats in honor of the occasion.

As a matter of fact we had just been wondering if you and Ann were planning to be in Southampton for Bill and Cynthia Laughlin's dinner dance, and we were going to offer you sleeping accommodations. We now infer that you are passing up the Laughlin party in favor of the doings in Atlantic City.[1] *Chacun a son gout,* I always say. However, as one old-timer to another, I must caution you not to commit a certain *lapsus linguae.* I refer to the danger of referring to Lyndon B. Johnson as Nucky Johnson,[2] which would seem almost inevitable for us old Atlantic City hands.

I was recently one of the guests of honor at the Bohemian Grove, in California. One of the co-guests of honor was Bobby Kennedy, whom I met for the first time. Now *there's* a little prick for you. Perhaps when you come for lunch we ought to have a tacit agreement to stick to social scandal and lay off politics. What's new in the world of vice, in Chestnut Hill and the Main Line? Bring us some gossip about the rich—and I don't mean that broad that is mixed up in the Pottsville scandal. I can't think of her name.

Come early and stay late.

As ever,
John

---

[1] The Democratic National Convention.
[2] Enoch L. Johnson, former Republican political boss of Atlantic City.

TO: Bennett Cerf

TLS, 1 p. Columbia
Quogue, Long Island

2 Sept 64

Dear Bennett:

You caught me, as the saying goes, at a rather bad time.

On Page 50 of the current Newsweek there is an item about me that could only have come from someone at Random House, the signs pointing either to you, Albert Erskine, or Jean Ennis. My guess is Jean Ennis. If not she, some eager individual in the publicity department.

The snotnose who writes the Newsmakers page has given me trouble before, and will always give me trouble. I have refused to have anything to do with him. It is therefore particularly irritating to find that he has been given an exclusive, two-month beat on the foreword of my book.[1] The effectiveness of the foreword is now lost; reviewers and book editors will understandably take the attitude that I, or Random House, leaked the foreword to Newsweek. I owe Newsweek nothing at all (except possible a couple of punches in the nose), but someone at Random House has used me and my material to establish his or her own good will there. This has got to stop. No one at Random House is authorized to arrange interviews, quote me, or use me or my work for publicity purposes without my express permission.

I know how those things work. I have been a press agent myself. But I am in a practically unique position now, in more ways than one. By hard and good work I have advanced to that position, which is where we all ought to be, namely, aloof from the demands of the people who write about authors, the chatter writers. I am the best judge, the *only* judge, of what publicity is good for me.

I am writing you this at this time because I have been reading the new contract. Under paragraph ix of the first clause you are given the right to do just what I am complaining about now, and I am not going to give

461

you that right. There are other items in the contract that I will take up later, but this is one that by unfortunate coincidence has come up today.

As ever,
John

[1] The 7 September issue of *Newsweek* quoted passages from the foreword to *The Horse Knows the Way*, which was to be published in November.

TO: John Hersey   TLS, 1 p. Hersey
                                              "Linebrook" letterhead

5 Oct 64
Dear John:
One regrettable consequence of my resignation from the Institute of Arts & Letters was the fact that I could no longer wear the rosette in my lapel. I seem to recall, however, that Ernest Hemingway wore a rosette which certainly looked a lot like it. Does, then, my Gold Medal of the Academy make me once again eligible to wear said decoration? This is a point in protocol that you, as Secretary, can clear up for me.

I am a Hereditary Companion, Pennsylvania Commandery, Military Order of the Loyal Legion, and can wear their rosette; but that was because my grandfather was an officer in the Civil War. It is not the same as having a decoration of my own.

Congratulations on the Book of the Month.[1] I think I may have known about it before you did, but I was asked not to say anything.

Best wishes to Barbara.

As ever,
John

[1] Hersey's novel *White Lotus* was a Book-of-the-Month Club selection.

TO: John Hersey   TLS, 1 p. National Institute of Arts and Letters
                                                          Princeton

23 Oct 64
Dear John:
Many thanks for your letter, and for the trouble you have taken. Unlike J. P. Sartre, I have no fear of being institutionalized (or, for that matter, academized[1]). I therefore accept with pleasure and some alacrity your

invitation to rejoin the National Institute of Arts and Letters. Not to do so would be churlish, and anyway I made my point when I resigned. The Academy Gold Medal had the effect of binding my wounds.

Cordially,
John

---

[1] A reference to the fact that O'Hara was never elected to the American Academy of Arts and Letters. Sartre had declined election to the French Academy.

TO: Malcolm Cowley   TLS, 1 p. National Institute of Arts and Letters
Princeton

4 November 1964

Dear Malcolm:

Thank you for your note. As I told John Hersey, my resignation from the Institute (which was not capricious but was well considered) made my point. Feeling as strongly as I did, it was the only thing I could do. If I did nothing, I lost my claim to self-respect. But the Award of Merit, made freely and spontaneously and completely to my surprise, changed all that. As a friend of mine in the Institute put it, justice was done. Therefore, when John conveyed the invitation to return to the Institute fold, I would have been churlish to decline. I am glad to be back, and when I go out to dinner tomorrow night I shall wear the rosette proudly. Again as I told John, unlike J.-P. Sartre I have no fear of being Institutionalized or even Academized. (Strange sentiments from a man—meaning Sartre— who has allied himself with the most restrictive institution on the face of the earth.)

With all good wishes to you,

Cordially,
John

TO: William Maxwell   TLS, 1 p. PSt.
"Linebrook" letterhead

19 Nov 64

Dear Bill:

I wasn't snapping at you, of course, but some of those queries were so showoffy[1] . . . Kappa Beta Phi, as you said, is the drinking fraternity. I was an honorary member of the Lehigh chapter. TNE stands for Theta Nu Epsilon, a drinking fraternity that was outlawed many years ago. The ultimate in collegiate achievement was to be a Phi Bete, a Kappa Bete, and a TNE. I knew one such remarkable person. He never amounted to much, but he was fun to be with. He was also an Alpha Delta Phi at Wesleyan, and best man at my first marriage,[2] wrote one novel and the last I heard—20 years ago—was in the advertising business. I'll bet he's a bore today, if he's still alive. He'd be about 65.

I am about 60 and probably would be a bore too, but I stay home where they are used to me. If you establish a reputation as a recluse you become mysterious, and then only bores can say you are a bore. I got it all figured out, see?

As ever
John

[1] Unidentified.
[2] Lawler Hill.

TO: William Maxwell

TLS, 2 pp. PSt.
Princeton

13 Dec '64

Dear Bill:

I was rather hoping to see you at the Institute luncheon yesterday (I am a member again). Instead I was seated next to —— ——, who spits her food while talking, and when she is not spitting food, expectorates a stream of unpleasantness and untruth. She is my current candidate for the Academy of Horrible Women. On my right was a kooky woman who is related to friends of mine and whom I had never met before. She started our conversation by blaming all her troubles and her stepsister's troubles on the fact that they both attended convent schools in France, where they learned to lie and to cheat, in an atmosphere of a barbaric religion. She then asked my advice on what to do if an intruder broke into her house. She has a shotgun, she said, but did I think she would be able to hold the intruder at bay while she telephoned the police? She has not been able to sleep well recently because she lies in her bed and tries to figure out how she would deal with the intruder situation. She apparently lives alone in a New Jersey farmhouse. She keeps the shotgun in her bedroom, but would she have time to get it? I had several suggestions of an unsuitably flippant nature, but quite obviously she has had the problem on her mind and has been unable to unburden herself to anyone else. So I had to be serious with her. Her eyes sparkled as she described her peril, and I think she was a little disappointed when I said that she would not actually have to shoot the burglar; that if she pointed the gun at him—a shotgun, mind you—he could be persuaded to get the hell out.

Protect yourself, I said, and give him a chance to get away. I next suggested she buy some tear gas, but she didn't like that idea; you were just as likely to be blinded as the burglar, she argued. Then, I said, you ought to have some friend buy you a revolver, and we went into the matter of revolvers. She was much more interested in revolvers than in tear gas, and since I happen to know a lot about small arms, I was very entertaining. She found me so. I wanted very much to ask her if the French nuns had not included ballistics along with their training in lying and cheating, but she was having such a good time that I did not have the heart. She said she had been everywhere in the world and had done everything, and I realized that at age 60 she is contemplating the joys of the ultimate experience, murder. At that, she was better balanced than the —— woman, and now you see where I Get My Material.

Now as to my material, or more accurately, what I do with it: I have here fifteen stories, only one of which you have seen, and which I am planning to publish in 1966 under the title WAITING FOR WINTER. I have written the foreword, and the book is all ready to go, but first I must finish my novel for 1965 publication. Sometime after the first of the year I would like you to look at the stories and pick out those you want to publish in The NYer.[1] Then I could forget about this book and put it in my safe, or vicy versy. This would involve your coming to Princeton, an idea which may not appeal to you, but it makes more sense than my lugging the stories to New York and leaving 335 pages of MSS at the office. It would be a great favor to me if you would do it this way. I would guess that you would want to take five or four or six stories back with you for final judgment, whereas to submit the stories singly would be a lot of bother, and would take up a hell of a lot of time.

Well, think about it.

Merry Christmas. Not Season's Greetings. Merry Christmas.

Yrs
John

[1] "The Gambler," "The Neighborhood," "The Assistant," "Christmas Poem," "A Good Location," "Leonard," and "Fatimas and Kisses" appeared in *The New Yorker*.

TO: Bennett Cerf

TLS, 2 pp. Columbia
Princeton

14 Dec. '64

Dear Bennett:

Light your pipe and compose yourself. This is to be a contract discussion.

In the contracts which you sent me in August there are points on which

I could do a certain amount of nitpicking, and as you said several times over the telephone, all I had to do was scream a little and maybe twist your arm slightly, and you would yield at least some of the points.

But I know that; in recent years our negotiations have been simple and agreeable, and Random House has been reasonable—and so have I. The reason for my delay in signing the contracts has been, it might be said, a more profound one.

You and I have reached an age where we have to take into consideration what I call the terminal truth. As you know, I very nearly passed out of the picture eleven years ago, and although the years since then have been my most productive ones, I have never ceased to be mindful of the precariousness of existence. Naturally I become more, not less, aware of that fact.

The August contracts would tie me up for three books after THE HORSE KNOWS THE WAY. I do not wish to sign any such undertaking. At the moment I have the completed manuscript for a collection of stories to be called WAITING FOR WINTER, of which only two stories have been published (one in The New Yorker, the other in Sports Illustrated). I have even written the Foreword. This book, in other words, is ready to go tomorrow. But I do not plan to publish it until I have published the yet unfinished THE LOCKWOOD CONCERN, which, as you know, is a very long novel. In addition I have a short novel,[1] nearly finished (it will be around 300 pages long), and several novellas. My major concern now is the completion of THE LOCKWOOD CONCERN, which I hope to have ready for autumn 1965.

God willing, I will finish that novel, and you will publish it. But the relationship between Random House and me really comes down to the relationship between you and me. If you should die, God forbid, I may not want to continue with Random House. Random House could elect someone like Alfred Kazin in your place, and where would I be? Your heirs might find it desirable to merge with Simon & Schuster, and where would I be?

On the other hand, what if I should die tomorrow? Sister and Wylie would be committed to Random House for three books of mine, beginning with THE LOCKWOOD CONCERN. That I do not want. I want Sister and Wylie to feel free to negotiate with any publisher in the business. I do not want their hands tied by a three-book contract. Courty Barnes,[2] Sister's son, has a lot to learn about the book publishing business, and in my opinion so have his agents. Louis Auchincloss is a cousin of Sister's and a lawyer, but I am not so sure he could be depended upon for the best advice in the event of my death. Sister and Wylie are well fixed financially and can take their time in choosing a publisher, but I want them to be able to take their time, and to choose. They may choose Random House, but on the other hand they may not.

466

Therefore I do not wish to sign a three-book contract. One book at a time, from now on.

I believe that THE LOCKWOOD CONCERN is going to be very big. Possibly the biggest in sales of the trade edition, paperbacks, etc. Already I am being sounded out on a picture deal, and you can imagine what kind of money will be involved there. This brings up another problem.

You have all that money to my credit at Random House. I know, of course, that you have the use of that money while I receive $25,000 a year of it, and in effect I am receiving $25,000 of interest money. (My Wall Street people, by the way, take a dim view of this arrangement.) I have been giving a lot of thought to the idea of making THE LOCKWOOD CONCERN a separate enterprise, outside the existing arrangement between Random House and me. I have all the money I will ever need. My wants are elegant but few. I had promised myself a Rolls-Royce if I won the Nobel prize, but I am reconciled to the conviction that I will never get the Nobel, and I will have to end my days without a Rolls (I could buy one with my English money, but it isn't merely a question of the money). The point here is that I would like to have all the money from THE LOCKWOOD CONCERN made payable to Sister and Wylie while I retain control of the property rights during my lifetime. The novel would be kept separate on the Random House books, and all royalty payments would be made to Sister and Wylie direct. This is where your man Manges can earn his retainer—by suggesting the ways this might be done. Wylie, by the way, will be 21 on 14 June 1966, and her financial matters are in the hands of the U.S. Trust Company. Her legal matters are in the hands of Carter, Ledyard & Milburn, who are also Sister's lawyers.

As you see, I am trying to put my house in order. I will be 60 next month and have lived twice as long as my father said I would. I am trying to achieve peace of mind. I went in to see my father on his deathbed and my mother said to him, "John has a sore knee." My old man said (and they were his last words to me), "Poor John." Later I came to realize that he was not thinking of my sore knee but of what I, the oldest of his eight children, was going to have to face when his tangled finances were revealed. Oh, those German marks he had bought so confidently! Oh, those rows of slum houses! Oh, that failure to make a will!

Well, I daresay I've given you a few things to think about. They are the things I've been thinking about.

As ever,
John

[1] Probably *The Instrument* (1967).
[2] Novelist C. D. B. Bryan.

Dear Don:

See, I got writing paper with my name on it.[1] What I would really like is a Rolls-Royce with just my initials on it, but that may take time. Yes, I have tried to follow the palace revolution,[2] which seemed to have more fascination for the New York Times than any other publication, and I am sure there is some sinister reason for that. I did not like to see my old friend Zachary and my newer friend Schanche at odds with each other, but as a veteran of forty years in this business I have learned to expect controversy. I decided that I would withhold all judgment until the air cleared and you could come to Princeton for a conference, which I trust will be fairly soon.

Recently I have been in almost continual pain, which I thought was dental, but I went in to NY Tuesday to the Neurological Institute and had a lot of tests and X-rays. The doctor said that neurologically I am a blank, which means that I passed the tests, but he does not know what is wrong with me and will not prescribe until next week, when he will have studied the X-Rays, etc. He does not think I have an abscess or cancer or any ailment inside the cranium. I just have to wait. Meanwhile I cannot chew anything more unyielding than custard, nor sleep more than two hours at a stretch. It is fortunate for all around me that I have such a lovely disposition and am somewhat used to pain. I never complain; just scream a little when the neuralgia takes me by surprise.

Your friend Donohue[3] wrote the best review of my new book, and I would like to do something for him; but the thing he wants is out of the question. I mean the tape-recording thing. I turn down such interviews about once a week. They irritate me, and they take up too much time, whether or not the recording machine is involved.

I skimmed through the Algren book, and I kept saying to myself, Who the hell does this character think he is? I am not one to be placated by a few crumbs of dubious praise. I will not play that game. I never have. If I had been willing to, I could have assured myself a better reception among the little kazins and things like that, but that is not my way. My version of noblesse oblige is "fuck you." The work has to stand on its own, and it will. At 55 Algren has simply not gone to bat often enough to qualify as an expert. So he laid an unattractive Frenchwoman? So what? (My score in that department is also better than his.)

As to the Fred Allen book:[4] I reviewed his first Broadway show, a horror called POLLY, for Time, in the 1928-29 season, and gave him a good notice. But I met him only once, at an Information Please party, so I don't really know him. How about Frank Sullivan, who knew him quite well? I'd rather save my steam for something else.

When I have heard more about my physical condition I will write you, and we can arrange a time for your visit to Princeton. I look forward to it.

As ever,
John

[1] O'Hara was provided with a letterhead by *Newsday* for his "My Turn" column.

[2] Reorganization at *Holiday*.

[3] H. E. F. Donohue, editor of *Conversations with Nelson Algren* (1964), reviewed *The Horse Knows the Way* in the *New York Herald Tribune Book Week*.

[4] *Fred Allen's Letters*.

TO: William Maxwell

TLS, 1 p. PSt.
Princeton
10 Jan. '65

Dear Bill:

In answer to your question-mark.

I assume you meant my health, the state thereof.

After four visits to the Presbyterian[1] I can report that as a result of all sorts of tests and X-rays, I have been informed that I have not got a tic douloureux, a brain tumor, cancer, or anything drastic. The neurologist said I was a blank, but that I had symptomatic neuralgia. He then turned me over to a professor of dentistry, who, with another professor of dentistry, have figured out that I need new teeth. So I am going to get new teeth. The worst sharp pains occur less frequently; the dull pain is with me constantly and will be until and unless my new teeth correct the bone and muscle distortions. I cannot chew, and it is often hard for me to speak. As I will be 60 in a few weeks, I should not be surprised by these indications of decrepitude, but I do not welcome them. I extract some reassurance if not much comfort from the knowledge that the gnawing pain is not cancer eating away my jaw.

I will be in some day soon with the MSS, and maybe we can have a bowl of soup together. I could live on beer and liverwurst sandwiches, but I am afraid to take a glass of beer. If they had told me I had cancer I was going to be less abstemious, a word which, like facetious, contains all the vowels in their proper order.

As ever
John

[1] Columbia Presbyterian Medical Center.

21 Jan 65

Dear John:

I have been reading reviews of your book.[1] I have not read the book; I haven't even read my stepson's book.[2] It takes me a long time to read any work of fiction. The reading of fiction is for me an analytical process, and as I proceed I go over every paragraph twice: once to see what is said, then immediately a second time to try to see why the good was good and the bad was bad. I began reading Henry Adams's DEMOCRACY before Christmas and I am only half way through it. Non-fiction, on the other hand, is easy, even a book like Calverton's THE MAKING OF SOCIETY, which includes everyone from Plato to Hitler. The reason for that, of course, is that what they say is important rather than how they say it—and how badly most of them said it!

Anyhow, as the holder of about 15 literary Purple Hearts I thought I would commiserate with you. It is fairly obvious that you write exactly what you want to write, but as a member of the human race you cannot be overjoyed with those reviews. Oddly enough, too, there are some parallels in our literary careers. We both got off to a good start, and the Cyril Connolly's enemies of promise—he is one of the worst—began to take over. They have always been more violent in my case than in yours, but the two graphs are similar. They use the more or less universally accepted good work of the past to demonstrate how bad the work at hand is. For instance, when I published BUTTERFIELD 8 in 1935, they expressed their indignation as though the author of APPOINTMENT IN SAMARRA had betrayed them. Then as I kept writing away, BUT-TERFIELD 8 receded into my personal literary history and was lumped with SAMARRA, to the discredit of A RAGE TO LIVE. My best novel is FROM THE TERRACE, but over and over again it was unfavorably compared (and so was I) to the writing I had done 24 years earlier. But in 1964 Timetheweekly rapped THE HORSE KNOWS THE WAY and cited FROM THE TERRACE etc. as examples of the kind of work I ought to be doing, forgetting that the reviews of those earlier books had been destructive and somehow vindictive.

This, of course, is the experience you are enduring now. I am older and probably tougher than you, toughened by those people because it was either fight them with work or give up. I believe they have destroyed Jim Cozzens, because they left him unprepared for the latter-day attacks. You must not let that happen to you, and there is some danger of it. They have always *liked* you, as they always *liked* Cozzens. But as I said to Cozzens, they are not us. Look what they did to Steinbeck after he got the Nobel. Instead of rejoicing that an old favorite of theirs had got the top badge, they turned on him with savage and senseless ferocity. On the other hand, they destroyed Fitzgerald, who needed no help in that direction, and when they had their posthumous second guesses about him, they went too far the other way. I am inclined to believe that Hemingway was destroyed by his own conscience, not by them, but that did not keep them from celebrating his destruction as though it had been their victory. The only one who really escaped them (except for the sniping by that —— Fadiman) was Faulkner, but he was made invulnerable by his genius. You cannot hurt a genius, even with a silver bullet. I am not a great fan of Faulkner's, but I know genius when I see it, in a writer or in a drinking companion, and he was it. For me he had the same intangibility, elusiveness, that Robert Oppenheimer has. You don't suppose that when I am with Oppenheimer we chat about the quantum theory? We are friends, and I warm to him as I did to Faulkner, but I would not be that lonely for anything in the world. To go through life as Faulkner and Oppenheimer have, untouched, like Sunshine biscuits, by human hands, is not my desire. A little late for that anyway.

The only reply to the critics is, curiously, the same reply to the hostile and to the friendly. It is work. I have repeatedly told my stepson to be *engaged* in work at the moment of publication of his novel. Do anything —a play, short stories, another novel—but be doing something. In recent weeks I have had a lot of physical pain, a pinched nerve in my jaw, they think, and so I have been writing a play, to take my mind off the misery. The pain comes back, as I know it will, but for several hours a day it is not the most important thing in the world. I am not so sure that amor vincit omnia, but work keeps us going. It is a reply and an answer.

As ever,
John

1 *White Lotus.*
2 *P.S. Wilkinson* by C. D. B. Bryan.

TO: Bennett Cerf
c. January 1965

TLS, 1 p. Columbia
Newsday letterhead

Dear Bennett:

Have a look at my business stationery.

I have been giving some thought to a collection of my columns, to be called, inevitably, MY TURN. I happen to know that even before I signed the contract, a publisher offered Harry[1] $25,000 for the paperback rights, and now that the column is established and reasonably successful, the $25,000 figure seems even smaller than it did last summer.

What I would like to do is put the first 50 columns in a book, to be published on Thanksgiving Day. A small but not insurmountable problem would be the time element: the last say four columns would have to be written in advance, etc. The first year, or 52 columns, will be up around the first of October.[2]

I was not exactly pleased with the way you let SWEET AND SOUR[3] languish, but as I have sold several million books since then, I feel you may be more energetic on this one.

I am anxious to hold on to the Thanksgiving Day publication date, which has become a minor tradition in the trade. I have resumed actual writing on THE LOCKWOOD CONCERN and am full of enthusiasm for it, but I know it will not be ready for Thanksgiving 1965.[4] I have the material for a collection of short stories called WAITING FOR WINTER (I just sold four of the stories to The New Yorker last week), which *could* be published in November 1965, but I do not want my next book to be short stories, and I have abandoned the play I told Erskine about in order to get back to THE LOCKWOOD CONCERN.

It is impossible to say how much longer I may continue writing the column. I love doing it; it is easy and fun to do, and I have reached a new audience; but now that I am sixty I admit that there are hazards and vicissitudes to be considered, and if I have to ration my energy, I would give up the column in favor of fiction-writing. THE LOCKWOOD CONCERN will be my final long novel. I can stay at the typewriter for four hours, but not six, and never again eight. I have to decide what is important, and from the standpoint of what I have to offer, novels and short stories and novellas get priority.

You looked very healthy on WML.[5] I, the worker, and [sic] quite pale, except my nose, but booze did that a long time ago.

As ever
John

[1] Harry F. Guggenheim, publisher of *Newsday*.
[2] "My Turn" ran from October 1964 to October 1965. The book, published in 1966, was not a success.
[3] *Sweet and Sour*, a collection of O'Hara's columns in the *Trenton Sunday Times-Advertiser*, published by Random House in 1954, sold poorly.
[4] *The Lockwood Concern* was published on this date. O'Hara shortened it from what was planned as a longer novel.
[5] *What's My Line?*, a television game show on which Cerf was a panelist.

                                                    17 April 65

Dear Don:

I trust that you will have returned from Vietnam without a tapeworm
or other unpleasant mementoes of your trip.

Next time you come to Princeton I shall meet you in style. I have
gone and done it: I have taken the plunge; I am now the owner of a
brand new Rolls-Royce automobile, and nothing in my vast automotive
experience had prepared me for this pleasure.

If I have no other distinction—a point I am likely to argue—I probably
am the only author in the world who owns four British cars. The British
Fleet, I call it. A Rolls, a Jag, a TC-MG, a Spitfire. At least they are
legally mine at this writing.

Naturally I am full of observations and comments that are convertible
into printed prose. Come over and discuss them when you can.

                                                    As ever
                                                    John

                                                    1 May '65

Dear Don:

Inasmuch as you cannot get here before the fortnight is ended, I wonder
if it would be possible for you to straighten me out on the terms of that
advance I took from The Post, which gave The Post some kind of reading
option on a novel of mine.[1]

The reason I would like to get that clarified is that much to my surprise
and delight, I expect to finish THE LOCKWOOD CONCERN in a few
more weeks. This is the novel we discussed when you took the option.
It is quite long; will probably run to about 700 pages in MS.[2] I have had
a feeler from another magazine. I am not at all eager to run it in any
magazine before book publication; it is all but signed up for a movie
sale,[3] and I suspect it will be a big best-seller in the trade edition. And
the paperback rights—oh, dear! When I think of all that beautiful money
being spent by Lyndon Johnson.

So I am not worried about the financial aspects of our agreement or
the financial future of this novel. But as I have often told you, I *am* interested in reaching the widest possible public. That factor may influence
me in publishing a serialization in The Post. On the other hand, I plan
to publish two books in 1966; one of them a collection of short stories,

already ready to go, and the other a collection of columns that I will have written by the end of this year.[4] I may decide that this is the moment to call a halt somewhere. My column is syndicated in 40 papers, big and little, and with books, paperbacks, and magazine publication, it becomes less and less easy to avoid me in print.

So in the next couple of weeks will you please look into the agreement between The Post and me? The terms, I believe, were left vague and the agreement was really between you and me, with the dough being put up by The Post. Oh, hell, we can iron it out when you get here.

As ever
John

[1] *The Lockwood Concern* was not serialized, nor were any of O'Hara's novels.
[2] *The Lockwood Concern* typescript was 608 pages.
[3] The novel was not sold to the movies.
[4] *Waiting for Winter* and *My Turn*.

TO: Graham Watson

TLS, 1 p. Curtis
Brown
Princeton

12 May 65

Dear Graham:

I am glad that you concur on the Cresset contract.

I have completed THE LOCKWOOD CONCERN, and will take it in to Random House next week, after Dave Brown has seen the ms. The publication date here will be 25 November. The ms is 608 pages long, double spaced on the kind of paper you hold in your hand. It was going to be longer, but I decided that the extra length would in effect deprive me and my eager public of a sequel,[1] so I ended it where I ended it. Artistically it is better this way.

. . . .[2]

All the best,

As ever
John

[1] There was no sequel to *The Lockwood Concern*.
[2] Three hundred sixty-six words about travel plans omitted by the editor.

TLS, 1 p. with holograph
postscript. Hersey
Princeton

26 May '65

Dear John:

Congratulations on your appointment as Master of Pierson College.[1] If my early life had been a bit more orderly I would have striven for just such a berth. There have been a lot of jokes about my youthful preference for Yale, which grew tiresome as the years went by, but they were based on a simple truth.

I have the honor to present to you this Pierson College tie, and with it goes a tale. I made several appearances at Yale. Once at the Lizzie Club. Once as Bergen lecturer. Etc. To digress a moment, after one of my appearances a party was given me by and at the home of a man named (I think) Liebert, of the Yale Library staff. That was around 1948. He asked me if there were any faculty people I would like him to invite, and I said Whit Griswold and Mary were old friends of mine. Liebert did not know the Griswolds, and I said, "Well, you'd better start getting to know him, because he's going to be president of this place some day." I had been saying that, by the way, since 1935. Bob Lovett was the first big Eli I ever said it to, and that was curious because Yale offered Lovett the presidency before they gave it to Whit.

Anyway, among my Yale appearances was one at Pierson College. Gordon Haight was then master. I talked to the members of the college and got a little drunk. Instead of an honorarium, I suggested they give me a Pierson College tie, and by God some kid went down to J. Press and got me one. Some time later, in Princeton, Thornton Wilder referred to me as an honorary Fellow of Pierson. I said I didn't know that, and he said, "Oh, yes. You are." But on a subsequent visit to the Haights I learned that I most definitely was *not*. So the tie has been worn once—the night at Pierson when they gave it to me. Wear it, as the old Jewish expression goes, in good health.

I have another, somewhat tenuous connection with Pierson College. Old Alexander Pierson was an ancestor of my daughter Wylie. My nephew, John Wylie, and another nephew, Earl Potter, who are now at Yale, are not members of Pierson, but the old boy is somewhere on their family tree. My father went to Penn, as did three of his brothers, so all my Yale connections are by marriage. My first father-in-law was a Princeton man, and that marriage was a minor catastrophe; but when I began marrying Yale daughters I did much better: sixteen years with the daughter of Dr. Robert H. Wylie, and already ten with the daughter of Courtlandt Dixon Barnes. I am going to quit while I'm ahead. No more marriages.

Tell Barbara that I finally took the plunge: I bought myself a brand new Rolls-Royce. There too I'm going to quit while I'm ahead.

As ever,
John

I disagree with your remarks as quoted in the Trib.[2]

¹ At Yale.
² In the article announcing Hersey's appointment as Master, he was quoted as saying that the best students "have just about usurped from novelists their traditionalist gift, that of being able to remind everyone that life doesn't have to be as dull and stupid and degrading as it so often seems."

TO: Graham Watson
TL, 2 pp. Curtis Brown
Quogue, Long Island

23 June 65

Dear Graham:

A situation has arisen here that is going to require our consideration. I do not believe it wise to postpone such consideration until my visit to London in September.

To begin with, New American Library has signed the contract for the U.S. paperback rights to THE LOCKWOOD CONCERN. They are shelling out $500,000, which is pretty good shelling, particularly at this moment when so many people over here are baffled by the behavior of the stock market. This contract has been followed by a letter from Gareth Powell,[1] whom you undoubtedly know and who is over here now. He wants to come and talk to me about the British and Commonwealth rights, but I do not want to talk to him. I prefer to have all such negotiations go through you. So when he telephones me this afternoon, I shall tell him exactly that.

However, it is important that you have this information, obviously, so that you can give the whole matter your best thought. It does not seem to me that Cresset is our best bet. Cerf tells me that Dennis Cohen, whom I rather like, is just about out, there, and the only other person I know there is Howard,[2] whom I really don't like. Not to go into details, he just rubs me the wrong way, and I really dislike his wife. Therefore, if Dennis should retire, or die, I would not be at all comfortable with Cresset, and to continue that line of reasoning, neither would my wife. I am very hard to please sometimes, which is why I finally settled for a Rolls-Royce.

THE LOCKWOOD CONCERN is going to be, in the special argot of American publishing, a blockbuster.[3] Dave Brown and Zanuck did not buy it for Fox, but they have not removed themselves from the bidding, when it starts. Swanson this week is sending Xerox copies to four movie

476

producers who have requested them. The requests came from the top guys, and no one else is going to get copies. Brown told me that Fox are worried about Warners, but obviously not yet worried enough to make a freezeout bid of their own. There will be plenty of time for all that, even if I decide not to sell in advance of publication.[4] My price now is $750,000; my bottom price is $600,000. I do not want to die poor.

While I think of it, Swanson tells me that Metro are going to rerelease BUTTERFIELD 8, which should stimulate paperback sales in the U.K. My father had a friend in Pottsville, Pa., who had two Rolls-Royces; one for Pottsville, and one for New York. . . . And my father's friend was a bachelor and could not drive a car, and I have a wife and daughter who can drive and so can I. . . .

LATER. Powell telephoned, eager to come and talk, but I put him off. He managed to get his points across. He is talking in terms of $100,000 for the paperback rights to THE LOCKWOOD CONCERN, plus a program of publicity and advertising. I told him I would see him in London in September, with you. I made it clear that I would not move without you, which he understood. Therefore you may, if you like, get in touch with him this summer and discuss the preliminaries. He seemed to think I had not heard of the new publishing arrangements, whereby a book is put out first by the paperback people, with all paperback rights to go to the author.

Well, that is the trend here as well as in Europe, as I believe I mentioned in a previous letter. I am inclined to follow it, at least in Europe. If the critics for the London journals are more concerned with the bindings of books than with the contents, a paperback of THE LOCKWOOD CONCERN will not get reviewed. But if the book sells as everyone here believes it is going to, the critics will have to review it or look silly. I am certainly no better off by having, say, John Davenport make his usual announcement that APPOINTMENT IN SAMARRA is the only worthwhile thing I have written, and that my latest hardback does not measure up to it. The highbrow critics are not going to get me the O.B.E. or anything comparable to it. I am somewhere between Willie Maugham and Theodore Dreiser, critically speaking. Therefore I must console myself with vast circulation, and go without the badges of honor. This is the only life I am given to live, and if it ends tomorrow I will have reached my share of readers; but I want to reach more. I went to a function at the White House last week, at which the President gave the presidential scholarship medals to 115 high school graduates, from the 50 states and a few foreign countries. I was amazed to see how many of them knew me, as I had not thought high school people read me. But they do. Of course these were the *bright* ones.

My steamer tickets have arrived for wife, self, and car. It now appears that Wylie may be going with us, unaccompanied by friend. When we are more certain of her intentions, I will let you know, but apparently she will fly over and back and go with us on the motor trip, from London to Dublin. Knowing the young, I am putting off her reservations for the time being.

All the best,

As ever

Will I need a gun in London? We are getting some rather disturbing reports of your fair city's crime rate. Put me down for a .32 Webley.

[1] Managing director of the New English Library, a London paperback publisher.
[2] John Howard, a partner in Cresset Press.
[3] The novel required three Random House printings and sold about 75,000 copies in cloth.
[4] Movie rights were not sold.

TO: Graham Watson
TLS, 1 p. Curtis Brown
Quogue, Long Island

6 Sept 65

Dear Graham:

And so, tomorrow, we close up Quogue and leave for Princeton, and next week we set sail for The Solent.

The Cunard people have promised me that they will stow my Rolls-Royce in such a way as to make it most accessible at Southampton, and unless the Queen Mary should arrive at the dock after 8 p.m., we will be able to proceed to London shortly after arrival Monday night, the 20th.

My daughter Wylie arrives in London by plane on Tuesday evening at 9. (Tuesday the 21st.) That means no theater that night. I have written some English friends about having lunch with us Thursday, the 23rd. Otherwise, we have no fixed dates.

Except for some shopping, I will be free for any and all business dates you may wish to make. I would like you to take me to Barclays Bank, if convenient, the first day, Tuesday, so that my pockets will be lined with sterling. The other items of importance are, of course, our getting together on the New English Library deal and the hard-cover deal, if any. While in London I rather hope to be able to get something going on one or more of the five plays in my book, FIVE PLAYS. Freedman seems to have done little or nothing, and I am quite eager to get a West End production for at least one of the plays.[1] PAL JOEY did fairly well in London, despite the strange ethics of the late Jack Hylton and the still living Jule Styne and that saintly character Richard Rodgers. So I have remotely participated in London theater; but I am hopeful that some of my straight plays would play there during the next few years. I realize, of course, that I cannot expect to make a great fortune in the London theater, but that is not my objective. One London success, even a moderate one, will lead to Broadway, and Broadway leads to movie money, so it isn't just vanity that inspires me. I am not much troubled by vanity. And as Dave Brown is fond of pointing out, no O'Hara enterprise has ever lost money for the producers, not even a movie called THE DESPERA-DOES that you never heard of and that I never saw, but for which I got $75,000 for the original. (That was under an old Fox contract.) It would suit me fine if I had a good excuse to go to London every year and that excuse were a play in rehearsal. I really don't like New York, and I do like London.

By the way, is there anything you or your wife would like me to bring you from the U.S.A.? There will be time to cable us before we leave, and we will be in New York for 24 hours before we sail.

As ever,
John

¹ None of these plays was produced in London or New York.

<table>
<tr><td>TO: Albert Erskine</td><td align="right">TLS, 1 p. Random House
Princeton</td></tr>
</table>

8 Nov '65

Dear Albert:

Here, with eight columns missing, are the tearsheets for MY TURN. I have written to Harry Guggenheim asking him to supply the missing columns. According to my tally, the dates are: 24 Oct, 31 Oct, 7 Nov, 5 Dec, and 26 Dec in 1964, and 13 Feb, 14 Aug, and 21 Aug in 1965.

Guggenheim, or Newsday, will send the missing columns to you direct.

Meanwhile I shall be preparing a foreword that ought to get me expelled from Sigma Delta Chi, the National Press Club, and the Holy Name Society.

I shall also give some thought to the publication date.

Remind me to join the Holy Name Society so that I can be expelled. I never was a member, although I did belong to the St. Aloysius Society, which was for altar boys. No other Random House author can make that statement. Truman Capote looks more like an altar boy than I do (or, possibly, did), but I just bet you he never was one.

So here we go again.

As ever
John

TO: Kate Bramwell

TLS, 1 p. Mrs. Bramwell
Linebrook stationery

3 Jan '66

Dear Kate:

If trouble could get us used to trouble, you would be used to it now, but it doesn't work out that way. How do your friends lessen your sorrow? They don't, except by wishing they could.

Many years ago I made a study of suicide for my first novel, and I have never stopped studying it. Of one thing I am convinced: from Julian English to Jim Forrestal, from Louie Macy Gates to young Jerry Bramwell, no one who committed suicide could have done anything else.[1] There is an inevitability to it that has a logic of its own, so powerful as to prevail over self-preservation, therefore more powerful than the most fundamental of our instincts.

We are sorry for the sadness to you and Jerry and the girls, but who can argue with the power of the inevitable?

Affectionately,
John

[1] Mrs. Bramwell's son had Hodgkin's disease and committed suicide.

TO: William Maxwell

TLS, 2 pp. PSt.
Princeton

4 Jan '66

Dear Bill:

I rather figured that 100 miles of captivity in a motor car, while listening to the competitive monologs of BC and TC,[1] would not be your idea of how to spend Sunday. By the way, my favorite Goldwyn joke, a true one, which you may never have heard. Sam went out on the beautiful terrace of his beautiful place in Beverly Hills, took a deep breath, looked about him and said, "Vot a beautiful day to spend Sunday!"

About the secret staircase.[2] First, what you remember is, I believe, an old thriller by Mary Roberts Rinehart called THE CIRCULAR STAIRCASE. She also wrote THE BAT, hence the association.

Second—and not as easy to answer. THE LOCKWOOD CONCERN is an old-fashioned morality novel, as are all my longer novels. I have a theological theory that God is, among other things, the Supreme Ironist; that no matter how long or short a time you spend in this life, it all evens up in the end. My mother, for instance, was a terribly *good* woman, guided by high principles all her life and extremely proud of her goodness. She took great pride in her ability to cope with adversity.

480

She was not a stupid woman; she had brains and ability, she was well educated and she kept up with things. A musician of professional calibre, a woman who, for relaxation, used to get out my prep school trigonometry books and do trig problems. A great admirer of Eleanor Roosevelt, by the way, but at the same time a devout Catholic, an almost daily communicant. She never met my first wife, and refused to receive her and me until after we were divorced. She bore six sons and two daughters, and the only thing I ever heard her say about that was, "Thank heavens all my children have well shaped heads." Now the point about this strong character was that in the period between my father's death and my first success she had very rough going, but she enjoyed it. She baked cakes and sold them for $5, she gave French lessons and did crocheting, and she was also president of the Shakespeare Society, active in the D.A.R., gave recitals with The First Piano Octette of Pottsville, Pa., and not too humbly heard herself described as "Katharine O'Hara is a remarkable woman." She loved it. But when she was eighty-three she died of cancer, quite horribly, including what I now regard as unnecessary surgery. Life was fine, death was horrible, it all evened up in the end. The Supreme Ironist at work.

The same with George Lockwood. Completely self-centered, enormously selfish, enjoyed life, in his way, as my mother did hers in her way. It does not matter that he was evil and she was good. The Almighty system of checks and balances and compensations operated with both.

I, of course, playing God, invented the secret staircase device to use as a symbol of Lockwood's secretiveness, withdrawal, superiority complex, and to provide myself with the instrument of retribution. It is not supposed to be a bigger symbol than that, with more general applications, but if it works in the case of George Lockwood, it has served its purpose.

But I must also tell you something else. The late Herbert Langfeld, a friend of mine who had been head of the psychology department at Princeton, told me one day that he had just gone through *all* of my writings, and that it might please me to know that from his point of view as a psychologist, everything I wrote was sound. I then told him that one reason for that was that I always used the psychological patterns, as I knew them, of real people. I have, of course, a psychological pattern of a real person for George Lockwood. He is still alive, but you don't know him. I shall be very curious to see how he turns out in real life, and in death. The oddest thing, however, is that. . . .[3] He is a horse's ass, and I would not devote a novel to a study of him. Nevertheless, —— is a lot like Lockwood in many respects, and here is life mirroring art: at the very moment that I was struggling with the galley proofs of THE LOCKWOOD CONCERN, —— —— was erecting a fence around his estate! It always amuses me when some bush league critic says that the kind of people I write about no longer exist.

Emmy probably knows how the Supreme Ironist is at work on the lives of Nick and Min Ludington.[4] It is brutal. But if I wrote it it would never get past Shawn. It might not even get past me, it is so brutal and incredible.

See you soon.

As ever
John

[1] Bennett Cerf and Truman Capote.
[2] In *The Lockwood Concern.*
[3] Twenty-one words omitted by the editor.
[4] Nicholas Ludington, an aviation pioneer, was terminally ill.

TO: William Maxwell

TLS, 2 pp. PSt.
Princeton

7 April '66

Dear Bill:

1. Just confront the checker with "Balls!"[1]

2. The Pre Cat? Ah, if Gibbs were still around! Isn't Weekes[2] at The New Yorker any more? The Pre Cat, or Catalan, was a night club on West 39th Street, presided over by one Helen Smith. To my generation and the half generation preceding it, the Pre Cat was the glamor spot for collegians and prep school types from Charlottesville to Cambridge. Just for fun, ask Weekes if he ever heard of a night club character named Helen Smith, and he will immediately say "Pre Cat." Even Andy White and Katharine would have *heard* about the Pre Cat.

3. You have no query numbered 3 on the proof, but I guess you mean the one on Galley 16. "He's an altogether different one." "He's" is a dialogical contraction for "he has."

4. I know that thing about "No comma thanks," but it isn't spoken that way.

***I had Burberry of London make me a houndstooth cashmere topcoat a couple of years ago. It cost plenty, around $300. If you want to spend less for something readymade (you would be easier to fit), you can get one at Burberry's, Austin Reed's, Fortnum & Mason's, or Simpson's, and you won't go wrong either place. In London, for $100, you will get a topcoat you'd pay $200 for here. I got the cashmere job because it was sheer luxury; tweed, of course, will cost you a great deal less. My coat is too loud to wear in town; here, playing squire, I go all out. A tip for Emmy: if she has in mind getting any suits, it would be worth her while to fly over to Dublin to Sybil Connolly's. I talked Sister into buying a suit there, and she was so delighted with the style, workmanship, etc., that she now has four or five of S. C.'s suits and two or three coats. They are, of course, tailor-made; but Sister, who had been paying around $400 for a suit in NY, gets Connolly suits, including duty, for less than $200. She even wrote Connolly a fan letter. Emmy could fly to Dublin, be measured, back in London the same day, and would actually save money. Of course if my name were Maxwell, for tweeds, etc., I would head straight for Home Industries, in Edinburgh. Indeed, my name is O'Hara and I headed there anyway, last fall, bought some material for a pair of slacks, and the material has somehow metamorphosed into a jacket and skirt for Sister. She said the material was too daring for a man's slacks. I was going to call them trews.

The umbrellas for Sister and Wylie have arrived from Swaine, Adeney & Brigg. Now there's a place to stay out of if you are trying to keep inside a budget. Makes the modern Mark Cross seem like Bloomingdale's, which it practically is. I very nearly bought a folding cane that is used for measuring things like the distance in feet and inches between Buckingham Palace and St. Paul's or Westminister when they have a royal funeral march. No home should be without one, and if it's still there next time I go to London, I'll get it. After all, in my study I have a bugle that was blown on Everest by a Belgian member of Hilary's expedition. Not to mention the cup I won for rifle shooting on the Conte di Savoia in 1935, and Robert Benchley's banjo-mandolin, and two John Held Jr. original drawings, and the 100th anniversary edition of the Pottsville Journal.

Yrs,
John

1 "Fatimas and Kisses," 21 May 1966.
2 Hobart Weekes.

TO: Graham Watson   TL, 2 pp. Curtis Brown
                                                     Princeton

18 April '66

Dear Graham:
Herewith the signed and initialed copies of the various contracts you sent me on 12 April. I trust that international amity and prosperity will now ensue.

Over here, I seem to have a flop with MY TURN. Quite obviously the liberals have agreed to pretend the book does not exist: no reviews in Time, Newsweek, daily and Sunday Times and Herald Tribune, and that's no unplanned coincidence. I am waiting to see what happens outside New York, where the book should have its widest appeal. The liberals' treatment of the book is positive corroboration of my statements in it about liberal conformism. I am so glad I switched when I did.

Random House have prepared an ad based on the Braine[1] quote, but it has not yet appeared. THE LOCKWOOD CONCERN is now off the bestseller lists here, having sold around 75,000 in the trade edition. I rather expect it will do well in the New American Library paperback, and of course I am counting on good sales in the U.K.

Proceeding to more vital topics, I plan to visit the Century soon to have a look at the Garrick roster. The name that comes to mind is Cedric Hardwicke, but he won't be much help now. The stairs at the Garrick are rather steep for my aging bones, but as I hope to be spending more time in London, I feel the need of a club, as member and not as guest. The Scottish neckties have not yet arrived, but if they have sent them to you already, that's quick action for them. In spite of the various badges on my Rolls, I got my first ticket for speeding in—mirabile dictu!—thirty-one years, and have to appear in court as I was going 64 in a 50 zone. I believe my driver's license will be suspended for several weeks, plus a fine. Three such penalties and I lose my license entirely, in which case I will leave the U.S.A. and take up residence in the U.K. or Ireland. I have joined the Royal Automobile Club of Canada, which has a maple-leaf badge, making five badges in elegant symmetry for the front of the Rolls, so I obviously am making preparations against the day when I have to abandon this country in order to enjoy my car. Conceivably I could end up in County Mayo, the birthplace of my paternal grandfather. Sister has become such a good customer of Sybil Connolly that she has nothing to fear from the climate. Oh, we are getting ready to make the move, all right.

It was a British invention, radar, that caught me speeding.

As ever,
John O'Hara

[1] Novelist John Braine.

TO: Richardson Dilworth   TLS, 2 pp. Dilworth
                                                              Princeton

31 May 66

Dear Dick:

I don't think I will go quite so far as to reserve a place for you on the roster of us disillusioned liberals. You have had too much fun putting the blast on the conservatives. So did I, and then I made my switch and am having as much fun, if not more, by commenting on the liberal mess. However, I would be glad to welcome you aboard.

From time to time I have seen the liberals go to work on you since you became President of the School Board, and I probably was less surprised than you were. Seventeen years of residence in the Groves of Academe, a year in my youth as a student at a normal school (Kutztown, Pa.), and God knows how many professional contacts with teachers have made me familiar with the breed. We all have a tendency to respond automatically to the word teacher by thinking of favorites of our own in a sentimental way, forgetting about the incompetents, the sadists, the envious, the venal, the ignorant ones. I had a favorite at each of the three schools where I was presumably being prepared for college, but three men out of twenty is not a very good average. Although I did not go on to college, I have had those seventeen years to observe the members of an Ivy League faculty more intimately than if I had been an undergraduate, and if I were God I would keep them out of heaven.

As a group they may be the most offensive devotees of liberalism. They are protected by their quasi-clerical standing in the community, but they are no better than bus drivers or those arch crybabies, the farmers. I make little distinction between private and public school teachers, on the grade, high school, or college levels. They fall into the habit of despotism, with the power to flunk, and any kid who wants to get anywhere had better play it their way. You don't suppose for one minute that a student who stood up to a New Deal economics professor is going to get as good marks as another student who is anti-conservative?

In New Jersey we are about to embark on a big education program— as soon as Hughes[1] gets Big Labor and some other dissidents together on a tax program. I shudder to think of the money that is going to be wasted on that, but as frightening as the money waste is the *kind* of educational program we are going to get from those boys at Rutgers. They are making a valiant effort to outdo the gang at Berkeley, Calif., and they'll get there soon.

There is a theory that the decline of France is due to long overindulgence in wine, and I subscribe to the theory. The things that are happening to this country are not as easily accounted for, but when you see our educators trying to laugh off marijuana and make narcotics readily available to all users (a scheme which failed in Britain) and fight against the control of LSD—you know where some of the blame for our decline can be placed.

On the pleasanter side, Wylie has announced her engagement to Ensign Dennis Holahan, USNR, Andover '61, Yale '65. He just finished Officer Training at Newport; they will be married in September, and then will go to Guam. I am very pleased that they are both private-school educated, and I hope their children will be.

As ever
John

[1] Gov. Richard Hughes.

TO: Graham Watson

TLS, 1 p. Curtis Brown
Curtis letterhead[1]

20 Sept. '66

Dear Graham:

How good is the real estate division of the Curtis Brown Service? Shall we put it to a test?

I have been thinking of taking a house in Ireland, in the neighborhood of Ballina, County Mayo, for next May, June, July, August and September.[2] It must not be in town, but it should have electricity, etc. It should have three master bedrooms and two baths. I would like it to have a view of the land or of the sea, or both! A garage for my Rolls. A live-out servant, and a gardener if necessary. It would be for Sister and me, with one of the bedrooms to serve as a guest room. As we live very quietly, and I am always working on something, privacy is essential, and we are not looking for anything grand.

I am not committed to the immediate vicinity of Ballina, which my Rand-McNally tells me is about equidistant from Dublin and Belfast. But I want to use Ballina as the basis of certain operations, and the house I rent should be in a twenty-mile radius.

This would be a trial run; if it works out, we might well go back to Ireland every year. I assume that the renting agent you find will offer several possibilities, in which case we would fly over and have a look at them, ahead of time.

Wylie's wedding went over nicely; she is still on her wedding trip before her husband goes back to the Navy and, in due course, Guam.

The sojourn in Ireland, by the way, could be tied in with the visit to the U.K. in connection with my book publication. What's new?

All kind thoughts,

As ever,
John

[1] O'Hara was writing "The Whistle Stop" column for *Holiday*, a Curtis publication.
[2] This plan never materialized.

TO: Finis Farr

TLS, 2 pp. Boston U.
Princeton

19 Nov. '66

Dear Finis:

It is nice to be able to get the eyes open with that first cup of coffee and revive the spirit with a good letter. Thank you for your contribution to the ceremony, which arrived today.

The day before yesterday I was having the coffee and in among the mail was a large envelope from the National Institute of Arts and Letters, of which I am a member. It had my name and address stenciled on it, and I figured it was some announcement of some function that I had no intention of attending; but I had enough curiosity to open the envelope, and imagine my pleased surprise to find that it contained, among other things, a ballot. On the ballot were three names: Vladimir Nabokov, John O'Hara, and Katherine Anne Porter, in that order. These individuals were the nominees for the Institute Gold Medal for Fiction. So I marked the second name and sent the ballot off. I will know the results late in December.[1] As the parent body, the American Academy of Arts and Letters gave me their Gold Medal of Merit two years ago "for distinction in the art of the novel," the members may think they have done enough for me. On the other hand, my competitors haven't done much. The Nabokov citation was written by John Cheever, mine was by Lionel Trilling, and the Porter was written by Glenway Westcott, and of the three I'd rather have Trilling. Well, we'll see. This medal won't be awarded again for five years, and I don't care to wait for the next time around. Literary politicking being what it is, if I get this medal I might get the Pulitzer, which I don't think much of but you can't rap it with impunity unless you have it; and I might also get my second National Book Award. The Nobel is now out of the question for me. I am told that the Nobel Committee no longer maintains communication with the American Academy, and frankly if they said to me, "Give up your Rolls-Royce and we'll give you the medal," I'd tell them to go fuck.

Without knowing all the facts, I concur in your decision to abandon the Tilden project. Did you ever get to see my friend Miriam Tilden Ambrose? She is the niece who married a British brigadier, now retired. I never spoke to her about Big Bill[2] so I don't know what, if any, traumatic effects she experienced as a result of her uncle's misbehavior. The kind of reckless, compulsive homo that Tilden was would have to have a lot more in his favor than his greatness at a game, and it is at least arguable whether he allowed his appetites to do a great deal of harm to the sport that gave him a kind of protective prestige. I look at it another way: that he *was* great, and that his life was a tragedy; but I would not like to undertake to convince the world of that. I'm not even sure I would end up convincing myself.

Our Harvard game party was smaller this year, and the average guest was older. I find that as I get older the people I want to be with are older too. And fewer. When I go to parties I nearly always sit and talk to my wife. I like to put on my country-squire uniforms and watch people for a little while, but very few people can hold my attention for long. The ones who interest me most are those that are waiting to be put down on paper.

I want to punch that fellow in the nose that snaps his fingers in the Chesterfield commercials.

As ever
John

[1] The medal went to Katherine Anne Porter.
[2] Tennis player Bill Tilden.

TO: Richardson Dilworth

TLS, 1 p. Dilworth
Curtis letterhead

11 Jan 67

Dear Dick:

I am in complete agreement with your friend Mr. Randall: you deserve the Bok Award[1] and should have had it long ago, and I am all in favor of my getting the Nobel Prize for literature. If they don't give you the Bok prize, they might as well abandon it, because it will be meaningless.

As for my getting the Nobel, that will never happen. I have been up for it three times, maybe four, but I am told that the Swedish Academy no longer replies to communications from the American Academy of Arts & Letters, with whom they are supposed to consult on literary matters. The bad press that Steinbeck got when he won the Nobel—starting with the New York Times and Newsweek—makes it fairly certain that no American is going to be considered in the near future. Also, I personally have about as much chance of getting the Nobel as I have of being made chairman of the Sniff Committee at the Philadelphia Club, or getting an honorary degree at Yale.

Sister and I are off to Palm Springs for a fortnight on the 23rd. She has never been there and I haven't been since before the war. Any chance that you and Ann will be there then? My son-in-law is momentarily at San Diego, waiting to ship out in his LST, and Wylie is with him, so we'll see them. As Dennis is probably the most junior ensign in the U.S. Navy, Wylie is Number 40 on the waiting list for housing at Guam. If Jim Forrestal were still alive we'd soon fix that all right all right.

Yes, let's get together soon after we return from California. We spent a night with Gee Marvel when Bill Marvel's daughter came out, but saw no Philadelphians except the Scotts, who came for Sunday lunch. That was the week we touched all bases: Saturday, the Marvel debut; Monday, the Capote party; Wednesday, dinner with Dick and Betty Hughes at the governor's mansion; Saturday, a real swinger at the Wilmerdings. Since then we have been living retired.

Our fond greetings to Ann and to you,

As ever,
John

[1] Annual public service award to a Philadelphian; Dilworth received it in 1968.

TO: Richardson Dilworth

TLS, 1 p. Dilworth
Curtis letterhead

17 Jan '67

Dear Dick:

I just read a pretty good piece about you in PHILADELPHIA magazine. In fact it was better than pretty good; it was the best I've ever seen on you. By a coincidence I have also been reading a privately printed autobiography by Jack Parkinson, whom you no doubt know. He, too, is quite a guy. I only know him through my friend Pat Outerbridge (whom you spoke to at the Barclay a few weeks ago and whom you have met here) who has crossed the ocean with Parkinson and been in six Bermuda races with him, was his classmate at Harvard, etc. The coincidence lies in the fact that the American gentry goes on producing some high type men, as alike and as different as you and Parkinson. Fortunately for the self-esteem of us middle class individuals, St. Paul's and Yale can also produce such silly jerks as that character who is now mayor of New York— *if* he's mayor of New York.[1] My guess is that he's afraid to take a leak without raising his hand and asking Javits[2] for permission. "Please, Jake, may I do Number One?" To which, of course, Javits would reply: "Well, now let's look at it this way, Lindsay. Any precipitous action on our part at this time could lead to dire consequences, whereas on the other hand I recently introduced a bill in the Senate, S. 1234, that covers the whole problem of air pollution and flood control . . ." and meanwhile Lindsay pees his pants.

By another coincidence, I just lost out on the Medal for Fiction of the Institute of Arts & Letters. There was a tie between Vladimir Nabokov and Katherine Anne Porter. So if you don't get the Bok Award, you have company.

As ever,
John

[1] John V. Lindsay.
[2] Sen. Jacob Javits.

TLS, 1 p. Curtis Brown
                                    Letterhead of the Racquet Club
                                      of Palm Springs, California

                                                          27 Jan 67
Dear Graham:

Yrs of 19 Jan rec'd and contents noted.

Tuesday 2 May: five interviews on one day is spreading it too thin and would be too exhausting. It is all very well for the publicity people to say we'll go here for an hour and there for an hour, etc., but they forget that an interview is hard work—harder than writing, and a lot harder than arranging the interviews. I suggest one interview on Tuesday morning, elevenish; lunch-cum-interview, followed by another interview before tea-time. I then sack out. I am a little apprehensive about the NEL[1] idea of dinner with "half a dozen selected members of the book trade," if that means interviews. If it only means having dinner with a very few of the top booksellers, okay. I will show them how Americans hold their forks in their right hand, tines up.

The Wednesday program: I will see an "evening paper diarist," but not before 11 a.m. The Foyles luncheon[2] is probably a necessary evil, which I have always avoided in this country, but it is probably the raison d'etre of the trip. It should be understood that there is to be no TV or radio at this luncheon. My "speech"—well, what about that? That word *speech* means, or could mean, a lot of work for me. I could write something brilliant that I would read to the multitude and then publish in an American magazine such as The Post or even in my column in HOLIDAY. This is the lousiest type writer I've come across in a hell of a while, by the way. Anyway, please let me know how long I am expected to sound off.

Thursday: cocktail party, okay; dinner, no. Cocktail parties are the same the world over. A woman with bad breath grabs hold of your lapel and clings. But if you're strong enough and rude enough, you can knock her down and break away. At dinner you may be stuck for two hours. As we are leaving the next day, I can always leave a cocktail party unnoticed. (In 1938 I was frightened by Mrs. Belloc-Lowndes,[3] a traumatic experience.)

If I seem to be "uncooperative" it's because I tire easily and do not wish to end up at Guy's.[4] In that connection, I am depending on you to be present as much as possible. I have seen the adroit and tactful way you have in dealing with the English vis-a-vis an American author, and I am relying on you to keep me out of trouble. I have no desire to see Walter Allen or John Davenport,[5] for instance; on the other hand I would be charmed to see Margaret Lane.[6] And put us down for dinner with the Watsons any night.

We are lunching with Mrs. Eisenhower on Sunday.[7] I mention that because I don't want you to think we are carousing. The temperature is 63F, sunny.

As ever
John

[1] New English Library.
[2] O'Hara spoke at a Foyles Bookstore luncheon in London marking publication of *The Lockwood Concern* by the New English Library, 3 May 1967. His speech is reprinted in *"An Artist Is His Own Fault": John O'Hara on Writers and Writing* (Carbondale: Southern Illinois University Press, 1977).
[3] Author of *The Lodger*.
[4] London hospital.
[5] English critics.
[6] English novelist and biographer.
[7] Mrs. Eisenhower invited the O'Haras to meet her husband. See "Hello Hollywood Goodbye," *Holiday* (May 1968).

TO: Alfred Wright

TLS, 1 p. Wright
Curtis letterhead

11 March '67

Dear Al:

Thank you for sending TIME to Wylie. Denny is now out on a nine weeks' tour, and in anticipation of the dreariness she has even asked us to send her some catalogs from the shops.

I know so little of Inside TIME these days that I can't begin to guess what's going to happen there. I'm sure Harry anticipated anything but dreariness on his departure, and it will be interesting to observe the intramural power struggle. My personal spy has not been in the organization in recent years. The last time I talked to Harry was at a party at Jock and Betsey Whitney's, when he and I got together after dinner for a half hour or so, and that was three years ago. I made some long-range guesses about race relations and most of them have come true. On that basis Harry and I always got along, but otherwise he always gave me what I call That Protestant Look. He was only too well aware that he acted chicken when Johnny Martin insisted on firing me, and he did not like having that on his conscience.

Welcome aboard the wagon. You are getting aboard at just about the same age I was when I stopped drinking. The only way to do it is completely, and the only way to do it completely is to do it one day at a time. After 13 years I can still taste Scotch and beer, and I still have a recurrent dream about Scotch, in which I am at the bar at 21, order a St. James,[1] am just reaching for it, and Emil[2] takes it away. I have another dream in which I belong to three non-existent clubs, two in NY

491

and one in Philadelphia, to which I go for a sneak drink, but when I get to the clubs they are all closed. I still have trouble when I travel abroad, especially if I go by ship.

You are going to find that no one, absolutely no one, who has passed 40 can remain unaffected by two Martinis. There will be constant demands on your tolerance and patience. But there will be no more hangovers, and you will still be alive, be able to sleep better, and your capacity for work will increase. I have often suspected that you have been putting off a book about your wartime experiences. If I am right, now is your chance. You have had a full and rather unique life, you are not a kid any more, and you were not cut out to be one of those amiable halfwits at the Racquet Club bar.

As ever
John

---

¹ O'Hara's favorite brand of Scotch.
² Barman at "21."

TO: Wylie O'Hara Holahan

TLS, 1 p. Mrs. Doughty
Princeton

23 March '67

My dear:

Herewith some reading matter. The catalogs are not up to date, but they may give you some ideas. The book, COLLEGE OF ONE,¹ may also give you some ideas. Miss Graham is not too accurate; in this book and in an earlier one she seems to be trying to create the impression that she and I were A Thing. We were not. But apart from that, I thought you might be interested in seeing what Fitzgerald recommended for reading. His recommendations are very sound, I think, and when time weighs heavily on your hands, you can be guided by his taste.

It has been snowing all week and I have started work on a new novel.² I have one half finished that I will return to in Quogue and finish by the end of summer,³ then in the fall I will get back to work on this one. No hurry, as I have a completed one at Random House to be published on Thanksgiving Day '67,⁴ and next year another book of short stories. Katharine Gates⁵ has been here all week, and the kitchen takes on the look of a Southern plantation, with Thelma, Frances, Willard, and Mary, all vying for Katharine's favor. At my nap time she takes me by the hand and leads me to my bedroom, to "tuck John in." Willard made her a snow man and a snow house.

Kate Bramwell was here for lunch Monday. She and Gerry had your note about young Gerry photostated, and gave me a copy.

Benny Goodman asked me to write the liner notes for his new album, and he is coming here next week to talk about it.[6] I probably will do it, as I have quit my HOLIDAY column and will have time. Speaking of TIME, Al Wright is giving it to you for two years as an additional wedding present.

Now keep those letters and postcards coming in . . .

Love
Dad

[1] Sheilah Graham's account of her education by F. Scott Fitzgerald.
[2] Possibly *Lovey Childs* (1969).
[3] "The Indiana Story" (unfinished).
[4] *The Instrument.*
[5] Sister O'Hara's grandchild.
[6] O'Hara did not write the Goodman notes.

TO: Graham Watson

TLS, 1 p. Curtis, Brown
Curtis letterhead

4 April '67

Dear Graham:

As the time draws nigh for my descent upon London I have been making lists of Buy British items. One item is not British, but I'm sure it can be obtained in London (Asprey's, I think). I want a Louis Vuitton briefcase, with or without straps, and stamped "J. O'H." (Not an attache case; I have one of those.) Can the Curtis Brown Shopping Service buy one for me so that I will have it there when I get to London? You can bring it to the Airport, if you still plan to meet us; or to Claridges next day. It should be of a size to hold MSS of novels, etc., and I will reimburse the C.B.S.S.

The other items on my list will give Sister something to do, but this one might take a little time.

A packet of reviews of WAITING FOR WINTER arrived from Hodder, and I must say they are pleasing, by and large.

I have done 80 pages of a novel for 1969, and it is going very well. It will be a long one. As you know, THE INSTRUMENT comes out here in November, and I am well along in still another novel, tentatively called the Indiana Story, which I'll finish this summer in Quogue. Somewhere I must find room for another collection of stories, too. The boys and girls are being patronizing toward Thornton Wilder, who hasn't published a novel in 20 years,[1] so you can't win, work or loaf; and they are being unmerciful toward James Jones, but I hear his book[2] deserves a pasting. The disheartening thing is that Wilder, the most truly intellectual man we have, is getting it from the intellectuals.

John

[1] *The Eighth Day.*
[2] *Go to the Widow-Maker.*

TO: Graham Watson   TLS, 1 p. Curtis, Brown
                                                               Princeton

10 May '67

Dear Graham:

Dear, blessed sleep has been claiming the larger share of my attention since Friday evening. I figure it will take the same time to recuperate as I was on the go, so tomorrow I ought to begin to get back to my usual vigorous self.

Sister and I agree that you and Dorothy were the lifesavers, and she joins me in thanking you. It was foolish of me to overestimate my resources, especially since I know damn well that a single interview is so taxing that I stopped giving them here. I like to go to London, spend an evening as we did Thursday, and get in some shopping and riding about in taxis.

I have written Asprey's about the keys to my briefcase, which I did not find, and which I assume were also missing from your case. You should be hearing from them.

We—you and I—did not get much chance to go into the situation regarding the NEL, about which I am understandably curious. If you have time, will you extend your remarks on that subject? The collapse, on the day of our return, of the World-Journal-Tribune is disconcerting for many reasons, not the least of them being the fact that one of my brothers[1] was the political writer for it. He has had offers of other jobs, but the field is narrowing down. Imagine New York City with only three newspapers, neither of them very good. I am counting on vast sums from the trade and paperback editions here and abroad of THE INSTRUMENT, and I am not really worried, but the overall picture of Communications is pretty dismal, financially and otherwise. The power play that is going on for thought control is alarming, and I am alarmed.

Naturally I expect to go on with my work—the two novels besides THE INSTRUMENT—and adhering to my schedule. For that reason the exhausting experience in London may turn out to be valuable. I shall hoard my strength for creative purposes, and waste no more time and energy in promotional activity. The announcement about the Queen Mary and the Queen Elizabeth,[2] the death of Henry Luce, the death of John McClain, the collapse of the World-Journal-Tribune, the sudden illness of another brother of mine, the illness of my neighbor Bernard Kilgore (editor of the Wall Street Journal), etc., etc., etc., are compelling reminders of one's own fragility. Why, a friend of mine had a horse running in the Kentucky Derby last Saturday, a 3-1 shot, and if finished out of the money. I certainly could use some good news. If you hear any, please pass it on.

As ever
John

[1] Tom O'Hara.
[2] Both ships were removed from service.

TO: Graham Watson

TLS, 1 p. Curtis, Brown
Quogue, Long Island

10 July 67

Dear Graham:

Yes, we are in Quogue, away from the heat of Princeton and New York. We plan to remain here well into September. Then we may go abroad for a more leisurely visit than the last one. John Moore[1] has kindly proposed me for a temporary membership in the Savile Club, which I hope will develop into a full membership; and, if I have my way, a sojourn in London that can be extended indefinitely.

On the N.E.L. proposal, I am not in favor of combining A FAMILY PARTY and SWEET AND SOUR. I cannot imagine how that idea came into being, since one is one thing and the other is so very much something else, but without any reason or purpose for linking the two except for the dubious advantage of having a title bearing my name. I say forget it.

My big news concerns THE INSTRUMENT. It has been taken as the Literary Guild book for December, and it has been sold to Bantam for $250,000. At the moment I have the galleys to read, which means that no movie company has had a chance at it, but I feel sure there will be a movie sale,[2] as well as a considerable sale in hardbacks. I won't be surprised if this book gets to be Number 1 and stays there for six months. Maybe my slightly fantastic notion of having a right-hand drive Rolls for use in the U.K. may come true. Why not? Why the hell not? I might as well have the fun out of it before they take my driving permit away from me. I might even have Mulliner build a body that would be convertible into a hearse. With or without the Duke of Norfolk I may yet make you the proudest literary agent in London. What an incentive!

You may be hearing from Mr. Peter McN. Gates, of the legal firm of Carter, Ledyard & Milburn, Wall Street, New York. He is Sister's son-in-law, recently prepared my last will and testament, and is presently occupied with the task of estate-planning against the day when I'll need that hearse. You can feel free to give him any information he seeks. Also, f.y.i., Julius Winokur has retired and my income tax business is in the hands of Miss Alice Braveman, 1 Palmer Square, Princeton. She too will be asking for information. She has been my non-tax accountant for the past twelve years.

All the best to you,

As ever
John

¹ English novelist whom O'Hara met at the Foyles luncheon in May 1967.
² There was no movie sale.

TO: William Maxwell   TLS, 1 p. PSt.
                                        Quogue, Long Island

                                            11 Aug. '67

Dear Bill:

One of the things I count on in this life is a continuing cordial relationship with you, quite apart from whatever my relations with The New Yorker may be at any given moment. As it happens, I am a little pissed off at Shawn for ignoring my letter about St. Bartholomew's School, but that has nothing to do with my not having sent in any pieces all that time. I was working, I was traveling, and I was in delicate health, besides which it is much easier (and much more profitable) to sell pieces to the Post.

It is quite true that I believe that many times you will like a piece and then Shawn will capriciously turn it down. At the Post my arrangement is that the fiction editor comes to my house two or three times a year, reads what I have to offer, and then and there decides to buy or not to buy. No judgment by committee; one man, instantly. Consequently the Post sees pieces that Shawn never sees—and buys them, as many as six at a time.

I am sorry you have had illness to contend with. It is tough enough to struggle along in the best of health. For three years I had pain that five doctors could not diagnose. Two months ago it was cured, by accident, when one of my medicos suggested that I have the wax taken out of my ears. It had been there for 52 years, according to my recollection. I am not going to wait that long again.

All the best to you,

As ever
John

TO: Richardson Dilworth

TLS, 1 p. Dilworth
Quogue, Long Island
24 Aug 67

Dear Dick:

Thank you for letting me see the story in The Bulletin,[1] which I return herewith. I hope it inspires some of those deadheads to see that you get the Bok award, but if they haven't given it to you so far, they have their own insufficient reasons. It is not enough to do good work, as I have found. You also have to make yourself pleasing to the last son of a bitch that you want to please. One slight consolation is that awards are cheapened by the people who give them. When Yale gave Duke Ellington[2] an honorary degree the citation was so patronizingly juvenile that Ellington could have been forgiven if he had tossed the parchment back in Kingman Brewster's[3] kisser.

All the best to you and Ann,

As ever,
John

[1] The *Philadelphia Bulletin*.
[2] Orchestra leader and jazz composer.
[3] President of Yale.

TO: Graham Watson
Fall 1967

TLS, 1 p. Curtis Brown
Collier's letterhead

Dear Graham:

I can't throw anything away. Hence this historic letterhead.

Very good news about the N.E.L. and THE INSTRUMENT. I trust that this presages wide sales for the Hodder & Stoughton version of the book as well. As I may have said before, this book gives every indication of a vast circulation, which the Irish would say is better than a poke in the eye with a sharp stick. Incidentally, it is my first book club selection only because I refused to consent to one in the past. I still would not consent to a Book of the Month selection so long as Clifton Fadiman is with them. I despise the fellow and everything about him, and I enjoy rubbing his nose in it.

Thank you for attending to the Savile Club and the Royal Scottish Automobile Club matters. I am also indebted to the A.A., the R.A.C., the Royal Irish Automobile Club, and the Royal Canadian A.C., in case you get bills from them. I now have designs on the Garrick Club, which in spite of the steep stairways is an attractive institution. As I am constantly torn between living out the remainder of my life in the U.S. of A. and the U.K., and clubs don't cost very much, I can justify these smaller extravagances. Actually I can justify larger extravagances too, don't think I can't. Upon meeting J. Paul Getty at the Foyle's lecture I was very pleased to discover that I felt just as rich as he is, totally lacking in awe of his wealth for that reason. This is a very good attitude for a man to have who writes about rich people. You do not have to be a general to write about generals, but you are probably going to have a better understanding of generals if you have been a captain than if you have never risen above N.C.O.

You may be sure we will not plan to go to London during the Watsons' absence.

As ever
John

———◆◆———

On 30 October 1967 Bennett Cerf wrote to O'Hara pretending to be Otto H. Claridge, president of Claridge's Hotel in London, and claiming it had come to his attention that O'Hara had been "hooking scratch pads" from the hotel. O'Hara replied to Cerf, at the bottom of the letter, extending the gag.

Dear Mr. Claridge:

At the prices you charge you are damn lucky I didn't come away with at least a bidet. When I think of the prestige I bring to your fleabag, I am ashamed of your stinginess. You ought to ask my good friend Bennett Cerf, the retired TV personality, how much my name on your registry can mean. Good old Bennett would tell you off good and proper. Wait till you see all the ads good old Bennett is going to take to get the full advantage of my name. So you go fuck yourself, Claridge Smarridge.

> J. O'H
> (You don't even get my autograph!)

Dear Executive Vice-President:[1]

Here is the glossy that I liked best of those sent me by Alden Whitman.[2] It not only shows me as the rich and stylish country squire, but it also shows me in an act of defiance to the anti-cigarette-smoking bluenoses. Incidentally, the device on my necktie is a ruffed grouse, which is the official bird of the Commonwealth of Pennsylvania. The jacket and waist-coat came from Trimingham's, in Bermuda; the shirt from Brooks and the cap also from Brooks. The station-wagon is of domestic manufacture, the only non-British rolling stock on the premises.

A great character study, of a great character. Make a nice full-page ad in the Sunday Times book section; the Random House answer to McCall's ad for Capote.[3]

Yrs,
J. O'H

[1] Erskine was Vice-President and Executive Editor of Random House.
[2] *New York Times* reporter who interviewed O'Hara.
[3] Photo of young Truman Capote at the time of *Other Voices, Other Rooms* which attracted considerable attention.

TO: Graham Watson

TLS, 1 p. Curtis Brown
Princeton

14 Nov. '67

Dear Graham:

As I also had a note from John H. Perry, your theater man, in the mail with yours of 9 November, this letter can be shared by both of you.

The play do move. I am on Page 46, this size paper, and if an audience gets half the fun out of attending the play that I am with the writing of it, it should run for years.[1]

I am not going to say much about the content of the play now; it's too early. But I will say this now: it is what they call a vehicle. I always said I'd never write a vehicle for any actor or actress, but this is a vehicle for Robert Morley. The more I write, the more I am convinced that Morley is the man for this play, and already he has taken it out of my hands. I make this admission now because I'm sure Morley is a busy man, and I don't want to do a play for Morley and then have to settle for George Sanders (who could also play it, but not nearly as well). The character is a rascal, a rogue, who has funny lines that are not gag lines but are the expression of his point of view and his attitude toward life and people. He is best friend and secretary-companion to a movie star. They are in London because the movie star has signed to do a play in London, and for both of them it is London revisited after many years in Hollywood. In my play the movie star never actually appears onstage. We don't need him; he'd only get in the way. So if either of you knows Morley, please tell him to take good care of himself.

Universal sent me Hitchcock's outline for the film he wants me for,[2] but I am not reading it until I get all the details of his offer. Hitchcock knows that a lot of money must change hands if I am to work with him, but I also have to know about working conditions, etc. Hitchcock, as you know, wanted me to come out to Hollywood last August, and I told him I couldn't because I was getting ready for a trip to London. Only now has he got around to sending me his story outline. That's no way to treat old John. Old John has plenty of other things to do, and is doing them.

As ever
(Old) John

This is not the Merioneth play.[3] I need more time for that.

---

[1] The play was never produced; a 152-page draft of "London Play" is among O'Hara's literary remains.

[2] This movie project has not been identified.

[3] Unidentified.

TLS, 1 p. Curtis Brown
Princeton

30 Nov. '67

Dear Graham:

A piece of good news about THE INSTRUMENT that may delight Hodder and the NEL. Cerf called me yesterday to inform me that the subscribers to the Literary Guild have already made THE INSTRUMENT a record-breaker; more subscribers have ordered the book than have ordered any other book in the history of the Literary Guild, by something like 19,000 copies over the previous high. In the Random House trade edition the book has gone out to 46,000, which, with the Guild orders, places the total yesterday at about 220,000, within a week of publication. How about another floating picnic up the Thames?

I am not sure that I will have the Robert Morley play finished by Christmas, which is nearer than I realized. However, it certainly should be ready for the typists by the time you stop here on your way back from Down Under. You can then take the script back to London with you, and I'll follow you to London when it's necessary/convenient. When do you expect to be here, by the way? I want to be sure we have your dates right so that we won't be skipping off to distant points.

Sister's Jaguar has been retired, and I gave her a Thunderbird, which I trust will not be in the garage as much as the Jag has been. I have been having a little trouble with my Rolls, and I may have to take it over to Coventry with me next time I go to England.

To return, for a moment, to my play: I've never met Morley—the closest was when his son interviewed me on the telly in London last spring. But I am not averse to letting him know what I am doing. I know actors and show people, and it might not be such a bad idea to start getting Morley steamed up ahead of time. Peter Ustinov is repulsive to me, and without having any notion of what his play is about, I am pretty damn certain that anything I write would be completely different from the Ustinov piece. Morley, therefore, would have that to look forward to. So I suggest that your theater department put a bee in Morley's bonnet now, before he has a chance to get committed to something to follow the Ustinov play.

It is snowing here, the first real snowfall of the year, and the roads are so bad that we are momentarily marooned. I love it.

As ever
John

TLS, 2 pp. Curtis Brown
                                                   Princeton

                                                 1 Dec. '67
Dear Graham:

Your reply to Robin Denniston[1] on the subject of reducing the advertising budget for my books seems to take care of the problem for the moment.
However, I must say I am disappointed in Hodder/Denniston for trying
so soon—much too soon—to cut down advertising expenditures. My deal
with Hodder is not yet two years old. More or less in that connection, I
am somewhat amused at Denniston's saying "We are, as you know extremely anxious to put John O'Hara across." They were not buying a
pig in a poke when they signed to publish me. From what I have seen
of Hodder & Stoughton I would say they are an extremely business-like
operation, who know what they are doing all the time, and one thing
they knew they were *not* doing was introducing a promising unknown
author.

No author, of course, is ever satisfied with his publisher's advertising
budget (where it concerns the author's books). Faber and Cresset were
completely dormant in that respect, but I was led to believe that Hodder
would be an improvement.

I don't know that I agree with you on the subject of the efficacy of
advertising. In fact, I disagree, and curiously enough in my case I believe
advertising is very important, for the very reason that I am not unknown.
I put out so many books, with such regularity, that the public are liable
to become increasingly familiar with my name while losing sight of the
fact that my output is not one continually selling book. Each new title
has to be publicized. I am what they call a brand name, but I bring out
a new and different product once a year. The only way to make the
public aware of the new product is to advertise it, identifiably in connection with the name they already know. The most recent proof of this
is contained in the letter I wrote you yesterday about the record-breaking
orders for the Literary Guild edition of THE INSTRUMENT. The brand
name and the new product were advertised to the Guild subscribers, and
the response was immediate and gratifyingly large. Next year there will
be a book of short stories, the new product, which I daresay the Literary
Guild will want to publish if only because they will hope to capitalize on
the popularity, among Guild subscribers, of THE INSTRUMENT.[2] The
many millions of books I have sold throughout the world make it impera-
tive that each new book be given its own identity.

I enjoy talking about myself as a brand name. It is a harmless conceit
so long as I know that when I return to this typewriter to do my work,
I must rely on my skill. A blank page can quickly restore one's modesty,

although I know some authors who have spent years looking at blank pages with no discernible resurgence of humility, poor dears.

As ever
John

[1] Managing director of Hodder & Stoughton.
[2] The Literary Guild did not take *And Other Stories*.

TO: Graham Watson

TLS, 1 p. Curtis Brown
Princeton

6 Jan. '68

Dear Graham:

We were wondering today when you expect to come to Princeton. We want to have some people in to meet you, and naturally we will invite anyone you say, if I'm on speaking terms with them. That condition practically excludes the entire personnel of Princeton University, but there are exceptions.

My play is now on p. 131, and it is a wild, undisciplined thing with which I am having great fun. In about a month I would like to take it to London and let Morley read it while I am there (though not, of course, in my presence.) I am reasonably sure he will know from one reading whether he wants to do it or not. If he doesn't, I'll bring it right back to New York and give it to Random House for publication next summer (1968) so that the copyright will be established and I can forget about the whole project and get on with something else, namely, my long novel.[1] I regard the play as a Fun Project and the novel as very serious work since I think it will be my final long novel. (One never knows, of course; PAL JOEY was a Fun Project too.) It really all depends on Morley's enthusiasm for the play, which would be a field day for him, so much so that even if he doesn't do it, everyone reading the play in book form will see him in it. I still have no intention of showing it to a Broadway manager unless it is done first in London.

I am rather enjoying this winter. I haven't been to New York at all, but we went to Pottsville, Pennsylvania, for a party of my oldest friends,[2] not having been there to a party since 1935, and it was very pleasant. We do a social thing about once a week, and I have my play, and it's good weather for sleeping. At 63 (on the 31st) what more can a man ask?

As ever
John

[1] The play was never completed. The novel O'Hara refers to is probably *The Ewings*, published posthumously in 1972.
[2] Mr. and Mrs. Edward Fox were the hosts.

Dear Graham:

Herewith the Agreement between the Dutch and me on A RAGE TO LIVE. Six thousand florins is not going to get me another Rolls-Royce, but maybe THE INSTRUMENT will do that. Robin Denniston passed on the news that the Book Club chose Lawrence Durrell over me, which is odd chauvinism. How many Rolls-Royces and Jaguars and Triumphs does Durrell buy?

I do not wish to lower the royalty rates for the Cresset successors.

We are delighted that you and Dorothy will be with us for the night of 19 March. Although you may be exhausted after marching in the St. Patrick's Day Parade, we plan to have a dinner party for you, so do let us know if there is anyone in this area you'd like to see. Also, I recall that Brooks's Club has an arrangement with the Knickerbocker, which is a very prestigious tong in a prestigious sort of way (it is supported by the Rockefellers), but you may want to use the Century, of which I am a member. If you let me know the dates you will be in New York, I'll fix you up with a guest card for your stay. The Century, as you may know, exchanges privileges with the Garrick, but is actually more like the Athenaeum. If you are going to be in Philadelphia (I can't imagine why), I'll fix you up at the Racquet Club, another of my clubs. There is a club here in Princeton called the Nemderoloc Club, of which I am not a member. If you study the name carefully you can see why I would be blackballed, but I have some influence with some of the members and might be able to fix you up.

Speaking of clubs, I told Denniston that I had not yet received official notification of my election to the Savile Club. He checked, and they told him I am a member, but I have not been billed for dues. When I get the bill I'll send it on to you for payment.

My crazy play, which I am calling KNOCK ON WATER, should be good and ready by the time you get here so you can take it back to London with you. Has your theater man spoken to Robert Morley?

As always,
John

TO: Albert Erskine

TLS, 1 p. Random House
Princeton

6 Feb '68

Dear Albert:

The title of the forthcoming collection is AND OTHER STORIES. Here is the Foreword. The stories will be along later.

I think the title is so good that maybe it would be a good idea to institute a title search in case someone else has used it.

I am going to dedicate it to Bennett, as follows:

To Bennett Cerf
An Amiable Man

I will let you convey the news to him. I can't bear to see a grown man cry.

Yrs,
John

TO: Albert Erskine
March 1968

ALS, 1 p. Erskine
Princeton (Claridge's notepaper)

Albert—

Here is the map that takes you to the buried treasure.[1]

— — —

Lincoln Tunnel to N.J. Turnpike.
Turnpike to Exit 9 (New Brunswick).
Take U.S. ① South to Princeton.

Yrs
John

[1] The Erskines attended the dinner party the O'Haras gave for the Watsons on 19 March.

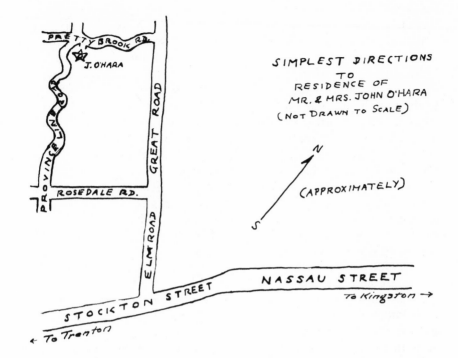

Map labels: PRETTY BROOK RD., J. O'HARA, PROVINCE LINE, GREAT ROAD, ROSEDALE RD., ELM ROAD, STOCKTON STREET, NASSAU STREET, To Kingston →, ← To Trenton

SIMPLEST DIRECTIONS
TO
RESIDENCE OF
MR. & MRS. JOHN O'HARA
(NOT DRAWN TO SCALE)

N
(APPROXIMATELY)
S

TO: Alfred Wright

TLS, 1 p. Wright
Princeton

21 March '68

Dear Al:

Thank you for the Grant-Frost Report.[1] Meanwhile I had learned that Grant's father apparently offered to make the bet in various forms, depending on the recklessness induced by alcohol and probably by the fact that no one ever offered to take the bet. It occurs to me, rather late in the day, that we might have made a fast buck by taking the bet and naming Jackie Gleason as our man.

Of more interest is your news about moving to California. You say reluctantly, but it may be a lucky break for you. It is first of all where your roots are, and you are approaching the age where roots become important. Since Yale you have had thirty years of a peripatetic existence, which is fine as long as you enjoy it; but it takes its toll in more ways than one. And even while you were at New Haven you were not exactly leading the monastic life during those four years. The point is you are—mirabile dictu—you are a middle-aged man. In seven years I'll be seventy,

507

and even if I don't reach it, the fact that I have come that close is incredible. Apart from the annoyances of my infirmities, I like being a senior citizen. I certainly would not like being young today, and you are about at the age when my present frame of mind came into being. True, I have had better luck than you in two respects: sixteen years with Belle, and already thirteen years with Sister. My first marriage lasted two years to the month, and was followed by nearly five years of extremely active research before I married Belle. Chacun a son gout, to be sure. I could not land an airplane on a flight deck or beat Gilbert Roland at tennis, although I *have* landed an Aeronca at the old Westhampton Airport and I *have* aced Alice Marble.[2] What man has done, man can do, theoretically. Theoretically, it comes down to a question of determination, and one's determination is largely influenced by what one wants to do. So if that be true, what you do with your life in California will be largely influenced by what you want to do. However, it does seem to me that the circumstances created for you by the SI[3] people can turn into a great break for you. In December I went back to Pottsville to a party which was attended by the people I have known all my life, in a club where my father once lived, on the street where I was born. For the first time since 1927, when I left Pottsville, I had a good time there, recalling people's middle names and old sweethearts and so on. On our way back to Princeton I said to Sister that I enjoyed the feeling of rediscovering my roots, indeed of really discovering them for the first time. At twenty-two I was too young to have anything but roots; at sixty-two the tree that I had become (I fancy myself as a sturdy oak type) was something more than a stick pushed haphazardly into the ground. I have no intention of moving back to Pottsville; we are settled here; but it is nice to know that 130 miles away I have roots some of which were planted two centuries ago.

These random observations are meant to stimulate you on your return to the Southland. Before you go you might come here for a night or maybe we can have a meal in town. We will not be opening Quogue before June as I am hoping to finish up some work.

All the best
John

1 Unidentified.
2 Women's amateur tennis champion.
3 *Sports Illustrated.*

TO: Graham Watson

TLS, 1 p. Curtis Brown
Princeton?

23 May '68

Dear Graham:

Herewith the signed contracts, the Droemer ones for THE INSTRU-
MENT.

In future I wish you would translate the money into English or American terms, so that I can make a guess about the amounts I can count on.
As you know, I am terribly interested in money that relates to me. This
concern is not likely to decrease as I have just heard, yesterday by overseas
telephone ($127.00), that my daughter Wylie, with the active coopera-
tion of Lt. (j.g.) Dennis Holahan, USNR, is making me a grandfather
on or about 13 October. Splice the main brace! The baby will be born
at the U.S. Navy Hospital on Guam, since Denny has still a year to go.
Me a grandfather at 63! Sister has five grandchildren, who have given me
some basic training in the role, but their actual grandfathers are all
alive and this child will be my first.

Albert Erskine has already been in touch with Roger Denniston about
AND OTHER STORIES, so all is in the clear there. As this book includes
a story of novel length[1] it should be a nice package for the paperback
market. Let us all make money and lots of it.

As ever
John

[1] "A Few Trips and Some Poetry."

TO: Don Schanche

TLS, 1 p. Schanche
Quogue, Long Island

19 July '68

Dear Don:

It was nice to hear from you again.

I am in favor of your doing a piece about me for LIFE,[1] and you can
come to Quogue any time you like. From my point of view, it is a good
idea because I respect and trust you, and at 63 it is time I got a piece
written about me that the obit boys can be guided by.

Be sure and make them pay you a fat sum. I have turned them down
two or three times before, and twice I refused to "cooperate" for a TIME
cover story.

My conditions are fairly reasonable. No tape machine, and no checker
present or coming to see me later. I have seen Lucedom operate, and this

is between you and me, not Lucedom and me. As to photographs, any good photographer can take all he needs in less than two hours.

Yes, I will be having a book out on Thanksgiving Day as usual. It is a collection of short stories called AND OTHER STORIES. I have been very hot on the short story this summer, doing new things with it and enjoying myself. Bantam Books just yesterday bought the paperback rights to AND OTHER STORIES, which will be released a year after the Random House publication. There is also pretty far along a deal for the TV production of FROM THE TERRACE by the Fox TV outfit.[2] A year hence, a long novel, now about a third finished.

We'll be here till September 15 or thereabouts. My daughter is having a baby on Guam in October, my first grandchild.

That about brings you up to date on me.

All the best,

As ever
John

[1] Schanche's article, "John O'Hara Is Alive and Well in the Twentieth Century," appeared in *Esquire* (August 1969).
[2] The TV movie was not produced.

TO: Graham Watson   TLS, Curtis Brown
                                                     Quogue, Long Island

                                                     20 Aug 68
Dear Graham:

The piece of paper herewith is for forwarding to Who's Who after you have checked with Robin Denniston about my status in the Savile Club. I still don't know whether I am a full-fledged member or not, as I have had no word from you or Robin or the club. It was my understanding that the club was to send you the bills for dues, which apparently they have not done. Will you call Robin on this?

Our plans eastward are, as you may know, very tentative and depend upon what happens with Wylie and unborn child. The baby is due in October, and our plans eastward and/or westward are not up to us. However, I am counting on a visit to London if only to show off Sister's new luggage, which finally arrived from Asprey's, and very handsome it is, too: two matching pieces of Asprey's answer to Louis Vuitton.

We have been here all summer, and I have been working on a book of stories, now nearly finished, for 1969 or 1970.[1] Bantam bought the paperback rights to AND OTHER STORIES, which Random bring out in November '68, and I have had a fine time writing this new book. My long novel has to wait. At this point in my career the writing of stories is more fun, and I won't be ready for work on my novel until I know about Wylie. The fact is that any and all work I do now should be done for fun. I can make more money, but for whom? I saw in the paper that Steinbeck had had a heart attack, and today I was sent a copy of Cozzens's new novel[2] (which is not so good), and these are two reminders of the impermanence of the stage I have reached. Willie Maugham bored everybody with his frequently announced retirements, and I'm not going to do that, but henceforth my efforts will be to amuse myself, not to sweat when a book doesn't sell. There's nothing I can do about that anyway, but I did sweat.

I'll let you know when we have more definite plans about London. Meanwhile, our best to Dorothy and to you,

As always
John

[1] O'Hara did not complete this story volume.
[2] *Morning Noon and Night*.

TO: Finis Farr[1]

6 Sept '68

Dear Finis:

In September 1927, having recently returned from a trip to Germany (I was a steward in the old Washington of the U.S. Lines), I went up to Penn State to visit a friend of mine and go to a football game. This friend was half owner of a restaurant, and fed me, and was a member of Phi Gamma Delta, which gave me a bed. One word led to another and I found myself headed for the Great West with $5 in my kick, thumbing my way and sponging off people until I landed in Chicago. There I took a room at a fleabag at 600 West Madison Street and began looking for work. I got no work. I hung around Chicago until it got too cold—me without an overcoat—and I thumbed my way back to Pottsville, Pa., having spent my $5 and another $5 my mother sent me, and forming a lifelong impression of Chicago as a very cold place to be without an overcoat. Later that winter I got a job on the Herald Tribune, and the rest is history, but the low point was Chicago. I even applied for a job as a groom, and the guy who had the job to give said, "What's a young fellow in a Brooks suit trying to get a job as a groom for?" "To eat," I said. He didn't believe me, and wouldn't hire me. The only friend I had in Chicago was in the insurance business, and he was no help except that he and his wife supplied the free booze. It was fun, but no fun, if you know what I mean. I was just as broke in New York a year later, but

511

Chicago was a totally unfriendly place to me, and it was awfully cold. In New York I once went three days with nothing to eat, but I didn't lose hope. In Chicago I never had any hope, and though I have often been there since, in the chips, it is not my town. I am too much of an Easterner for it.

All the best,

As ever

John

---

¹ Farr was working on *Chicago* (New Rochelle, N.Y.: Arlington House, 1973), in which part of this letter was used.

TO: Richardson Dilworth

TLS, 2 pp. Dilworth
Princeton

9 Oct. '68

Dear Dick:

From what I have been able to gather, they have been giving you a bad time. The question is, could that job ever offer you a good time? When you were the d.a. and the mayor, and potentially the governor, you were dealing from a position of strength; but that is not so now. As president of the board of education it does not strike me that the job is prestigious enough for you. I think it was John Quincy Adams who, after serving a term as president of the U.S., got himself elected to Congress, but he was the exception. I always wondered why you took the board of education job. To keep in the public eye, no doubt, but you were not going to be forgotten, and I think you'd have done better to have engaged in the practice of law and let the people (and the politicians) miss you. The education job is a thankless job and would be one even if you had thirty years to devote to it, and were just starting out.

Six years from January I will be 70 and that makes me 6½ years younger than you but not 6½ years more vigorous. Writers don't retire (except Carl Van Vechten, who switched to photography), and so I will go on while I can. But the fact remains that time is running out. Three acquaintances in Princeton died in less than a week, and two of them were younger than I, so all I have to do is read the obit page to be reminded of that fact. Then too, I will be a grandfather in a few days from now; Wylie is having her first child on Guam. A man is writing a piece about me for the Satevepost,¹ and I have had to live my life over again for him, as much as can be printed, in the hope of getting it down right. So you see I am conscious of the passage of time passing and of having passed. I don't really mind getting old; I rather enjoy taking it easy, since I have enough money to do pretty much as I please. I am reconciled to my failure to win the Nobel prize, since there is nothing I can do about it anyway. I doubt that I shall produce anything so earth-shaking that the Swedish Academy will have a change of heart.

I'm ready to go quietly, officer.

As ever, kind thoughts
John

[1] Don Schanche's article, which appeared in *Esquire*.

TO: Wylie O'Hara Holahan
TLS, 1 p. Mrs. Doughty
Princeton
29 Oct '68

My dear:

This letter is really to both you and Denny to congratulate you on your joint effort in making me a grandfather, a laudable enterprise. When a man is almost 64 he ought to be able to speak of his grandchild, his grandson. I have the grey hair and the pot belly and the sedentary habits, so the grandson completes the picture of the aging author. Among the thoughts I had after Denny called on Saturday was the idea that I ought to send a telegram to Yale, to enter Nick[1] tentatively with the Class of 1992, but I dismissed the idea as rather impertinent. After all, Nick's father and other grandfather have priority. It did occur to me that Nick would be in a class that is exactly 100 years later than his great-grandfather O'Hara's class at Penn. I also thought of putting Nick up for one of my numerous clubs, but the way things are going who knows what club, if any, will be in existence 25 years from now? My now three-day-old grandson, who probably will never know me, belongs to the present only to the extent that he signifies the existence of your happy marriage; but for that I am grateful to him and to you two. We have had a very full life together, beginning on that hot, hot day in June, Wylie, when you were born, and climaxed on that warm September day two years ago when you and Denny were married.

I congratulate you on this baby, and I thank you for having him.

Love
Dad

[1] O'Hara's first grandchild was christened Nicholas Drew Holahan.

15 Nov. '68

Dear Hope and Edgar:

I gather you have not heard what happened to me the morning after the Dilworths' dinner. I took a spill on the ramp leading to the garage and ended up in the Pennsylvania Hospital, with six stitches in my eyelid; a slightly fractured elbow, and various other contusions and abrasions that shouldn't happen to a non-drinking man. My arm is in a cast, and I think I had better bow out of your invitation for the concert on 25 January, in time for you to get a substitute. I was pretty badly bunged up, spiritually as well as physically. I didn't know I was so fragile, but such apparently is the case.

Thank you for asking us. It would have been fun.

Love to you both,

As always
John

TO: Graham Watson

1 Feb '69

Dear Graham:

I assume that the Curtis Brown Service has bought our tickets for the TWA passages back and forth between New York and London, and that our reservations were made at Claridge's Hotel. You didn't say anything about these details, and I am literal-minded.

We would love to have dinner with Dorothy and you on the 25th and go to the theater with you. On the other hand, we'd just as soon dine chez vous with your friends. We have made no plans, and we'll have six evenings for the theater.

There is no spare typescript of LOVEY CHILDS.

I might as well tell you that I have gone half blind in the upper half of my right eye. It happened a week ago. I went to my oculist in New York, was thoroughly examined, and got the final news right away: I am stuck with the blindness. Apparently a block occurred that is inoperable (which I don't really regret), and I have to live with it the rest of my life. It happened a few days before my 64th birthday. As I had completed LOVEY CHILDS a fortnight before, I can take it easy now and maybe forever, while making up my mind what to do next. My father went blind in the same eye at about fifty, and continued to perform surgical operations for several years thereafter, but there is a difference between fifty and sixty-four. I don't think I told you about a fall I took in Philadelphia in November, which landed me in the hospital for four days with a cracked elbow, a concussion, and six stitches near the other eye, and left me unsteady on my pins; but having had two warnings, I don't look forward to a third, so be prepared to greet a semi-invalid in London. I thought I'd alert you.

Love to Dorothy,

As ever
John

"And Other Stories" has passed 50,000.

J.

TO: Albert Erskine   TLS, 1 p. Random House
                                             Quogue, Long Island
                                             1 Sept 69
Dear Albert:

I need some information. There was a car called a Lozier, which existed about 1915. I used to go for a ride in a Lozier, but it was chauffeur-driven (by a man named Norman Hipple) and I sat in the back with Augusta Yuengling, whose father owned the car. Consequently, my recollections of the Lozier are dim, dimmed by the beauty of Augusta Yuengling.

I want to know the exact years of the existence of the Lozier; and (b) did it come equipped with a self-starter? Is there a book which contains this information? Can you get it for me? I figure you ought to know this, as the Erskine, made by Studebaker, would be mentioned in such a book, although the Erskine was a much later car.

Lack of this information is holding up my 1971 novel,[1] and time is of the essence, whatever that means. I am coming along with LOVEY CHILDS,[2] and should finish reading it this week.

Regards,
John

[1] *The Ewings.*
[2] O'Hara was reading proof; the novel was published on Thanksgiving 1969.

TO: Graham Watson   TLS, 1 p. Curtis Brown
                                                            Princeton

                                                          17 Oct. '69

Dear Graham:

The intelligence from Mr. O'Hara . . . I went to the hospital for 11
days and let them confirm the diagnosis that I have diabetes, but insulin
is not necessary at this point. The doctor stuck six things down my throat
—not simultaneously—and reached the inside of my stomach, where he
dislodged a piece of meat loaf that had been stuck there, and I felt better.
I had not eaten anything in three days. I also have a hiatus hernia.

I am on Page 104 of my 1972 novel, which I am pleased with and
which probably will take at least another year to finish.[1] No title.

Sister is now in Aspen, Colorado, where on 30 Sept. my daughter gave
birth to my first granddaughter, Belle Wylie Holahan. It was premature,
but it is all right. Sister will be there a week.

Which leads me to our London plans. Will you please reserve rooms
for us at Claridge's from 22 February to 29 February, which covers Sister's
birthday, the 27th? Also, will you buy our TWA tickets back and forth on
the 22nd and the 29th, the same flights we took last February? Make
that 1 March, not 29 February, as there will not be a 29 February in 1970.

I expect to buy a new hat at Lock's, and to go to the theater while in
London. Otherwise I have no desire to do any squandering, but who
can tell? My wife will take care of that anyway. It's her birthday and we'll
have been married 15 years on my birthday, 31 Jan. My Rolls-Royce is only
five years old and shows hardly a sign of wear. In fact, it won't be five
years old until April.

I trust all goes well with you and Dorothy, whom we look forward to
seeing.

                                                          As always,
                                                          John

---

[1] *The Ewings* was dedicated to Watson.

TO: Graham Watson   TLS, 1 p. Curtis Brown
                                                            Princeton

                                                          5 Nov. 69

Dear Graham:

Under separate cover I am sending you two copies of LOVEY CHILDS;
A PHILADELPHIAN'S STORY, one for you and the other for the New
English Library. The other reprint people will have to wait for the English
edition. It is a long way off to 22 February. The purpose of the trip, of

course, is to give Sister a birthday present on 27 February, a week in London. I, to be sure, am still very fond of London and I expect to go to the theater a lot. But I am on a diabetic's diet, which restricts my food intake, and my drink intake has been restricted for 16 years, and I'm used to that, if one ever gets used to it. I drink a lot of coffee, sweetened by Crystallose, a sugar substitute, and I smoke a lot of cigarettes, against my doctor's orders. And I do a lot of writing. It sounds like a pretty dull life, but what is the alternative? I am on Page 156 of my new book, which I like, and which probably will take me another year to complete, and then, like Willie Maugham, I'll announce the first of several retirements. I'll be 65 in January, time to start retiring.

Yours,
John

TO: Graham Watson TLS, 1 p. Curtis Brown
Princeton

16 Nov. 69

Dear Graham:

A chore for the Curtis Brown Unlimited Service.

I have at home a stationary bicycle, which I have been pedalling a mile every day and thereby have taken off ten pounds in a month. I wrote to Claridge's, asking them to instal one in my suite from the 22 February to 1 March, as this exercise is very essential to my well-being. Claridge's wrote back and said they couldn't do that, giving no reason, and I don't think they tried very hard. Do you suppose the CBUS could have one installed on Monday, 23 February? I imagine that Lillywhite's would be the place to get one. (I don't want to purchase one, as I will be using it only a week.) I don't wish to be a nuisance about this, but it is important that I get this exercise without interruption.

I had Random House send you four extra copies of LOVEY CHILDS, in addition to the two I'd already sent you. Bantam Books paid $200,000 for the paperback rights, so I can afford the four extras. Robin Denniston is quite enthusiastic about the book. Sister is not. She doesn't like Lesbians. But they're part of life, especially life in the upper crust.

Thanks and regards,

As ever
John

Index

---•••---

Crowell, W. G., 126
Crown, Mr., 321
Crozier, Emmet, 187, 189
Cruise, Michael J., 42
Cukor, George, 380–81, 381n
Cummiskey, Joe, 188, 189n
Curtis Brown Ltd. (agency), 162, 418n,
    493, 514, 517
Curtis Publishing Company, 128, 128n
Curtiss, Glenn, 159
Cushing, Mrs., 176
Cutler-Hammer, 126

Daily Worker, 232
Daley, George, 105
Damon, Dr. Virgil G., 387, 388
Dark, Joe, 99, 99n
Dartmouth College, 5n, 16, 18, 37, 40,
    60, 391, 407
Dashiell, Alfred, 65, 65n, 78, 78n, 86
Daughters of the American Revolution,
    481
Davenport, John, 477, 490, 491n
Davis, Norman, 180
Dawson, 352
Day, Clarence, 154n
"Days" (O'Hara), 127, 127n
Deaver, Dr. John B., 76n
Debussy, Claude, 307
"Decision, The" (O'Hara), 197, 198n,
    221, 222n
De Gaulle, Charles, 456
Deisher, George ("Deacon"), 4, 5n, 6,
    10, 11, 12
Delaney, Eugene, 392
Delaney, Israel, 76
Delaney, Joseph I., 76, 87n, 392
Delaney, Mrs. Joseph I., 41, 43n
Delaney, Liza, 76
Delaney family, 20n, 383, 437
Democracy (Adams), 470
Dempsey, Jack, 150, 151n, 442, 442n
Denniston, Robin, 503, 504n, 505, 510,
    517
Denniston, Roger, 509
Dere Mable (Streeter), 154n
Desperadoes, The (motion picture), 479
De Sylva, Brown, and Henderson (song-
    writing team), 244n
Devil's Advocate, The (Caldwell), 326
Devil's Disciple, The (motion picture),
    306
Devitt, Joe, 4
Dewey, Thomas, 216
Dezell, Paul, 220
Dickens, Charles, 411
Didrikson, Mildred "Babe"), 160, 161n
Dietz, Mrs. Betty, 32, 71
Dietz, Howard, 32, 71, 176–77, 421

Diller, Mrs., 7
Dilworth, Mrs. Ann, 460
Dilworth, Richardson, 260, 260n, 352,
    363, 363n, 411, 412n, 413, 457, 460–
    61, 484–85, 488–89, 489n, 497
DiMaggio, Joe, 283
Dinneen, Joseph, 122
Disorder and Early Sorrow (Mann), 116,
    117n, 118
Dobson, Zuleika, 328
"Doctor and Mrs. Parsons" (O'Hara),
    196, 221
"Doctor's Son, The" (O'Hara), 59n,
    65n, 71, 73n, 114, 118, 131, 133, 234,
    414n
The Doctor's Son and Other Stories
    (O'Hara), xvi, 56, 56n, 129, 131
Dolan, Ned, 24, 46
Dolan, Red, 263, 264
Doll's House, A (Ibsen), 315
Donaldson Award, 429n
Donohue, H. E. F., 468, 469n
Donovan, Gen. William, 180, 182n
Donovan Committee, 166
"Don't Say It Never Happened"
    (O'Hara), 393n
Dos Passos, John, 117
Dostoevsky, Feodor, 325
Doty, Bennett, 28
Doubleday, Doran & Company, 133
Doubleday, Nelson, 288
Doubleday & Company, 288, 337, 428
Dougherty, 95
Doughty, Mrs. Wylie O'Hara. *See*
    O'Hara, Wylie Delaney
Downey, Morton, 155, 156n
"Do You Like It Here?" (O'Hara), 143,
    146n
Dreiser, Theodore, 445, 477
Dubliners (Joyce), 357
DuBois, J. J., 321, 322n
Du Bois, William, 267, 267n
Duel of Angels (Giraudoux), 335n
Duell, Sloan and Pearce, xiii, xvii, xviii,
    102n, 206n
Duffield, Eugene, 187, 187n, 193
Dunne, Philip, 167–68, 170n, 270, 272n
Dunning, 223
Durrell, Lawrence, 505
Duschnes (appraiser), 353
Dystel, Oscar, 361, 361n

Eagels, Jeanne, 380
"Early Afternoon" (O'Hara), 63, 65n
Eastman, Max, 125, 208
Eaton, Alfred, 292
Eden, Sir Anthony, 456
Edison, Thomas A., 291
"Editorial Musings" (column), 362n

"Joey on the Cake Line" (O'Hara), 154n
"Joey and the Calcutta Club" (O'Hara), 154n
"Joey in Herta" (O'Hara), 152n
Johannsen, Miss, 314
"John Barrow Rosedale" (O'Hara), 424
John O'Hara on Writers and Writing, 491n
Johns, Brooke, 152
Johnson, Enoch L., 460, 461n
Johnson, Lyndon B., 458, 460, 473
Johnson, Nunnally, 94, 95
Johnston, Alva, 53, 53n, 66, 123, 124, 253, 263
Jones, James, 494
Jones, Jennifer, 265-66
Josephson, Matthew, 66, 67n
Joulwan, Mike, 370n
Joulwan, Sol, 370, 370n
"Just a Twirp" (O'Hara), 56, 56n

Kafka, Franz, 399
Kahane, Ben, 124
Kahn, Gordon, 263
Kanin, Garson, 371, 372, 372n
Katz, Sam, 262, 263n
Kaufman, George S., 294n
Kazan, Elia, 399, 399n
Kazin, Alfred, 293, 294n, 392, 393n, 460, 466
Kearns, Jack, 442n
Keeney, Doc, 4
Kefauver, Estes, 409
Keiter, Beulah, 391
Keiter family, 392
Kelly, Beatrice, 430
Kelly, Grace, 245, 246, 432
Kemp, Townsend, 356
Kennedy, John F., 254, 352, 397, 398, 398n, 409, 409n, 438, 457
Kennedy, Robert F., 398, 409, 409n, 455, 460
Kennerley, Morley, 130n, 133, 141
Kerney, Jim, 438
Kew-Teddington Observatory Society, 276, 278n
Keystone State Normal School, xv, 5n, 6n
Khan, Aly, 312
Khrushchev, Nikita, 456
Kibler, Barbara, xvii, 109-10, 110n, 113n
Kieran, 105
Kierkegaard, Søren, 399
Kilgore, Bernard, 495
Killers, The (Hemingway), 380
King, Martin Luther, 457
King Features, 182n

Kirsch, Robert, 282-83, 283n, 379, 381n
Klinger, Harry, 255, 257
Klopfer, Donald S., 214, 215n, 234, 235, 236-37, 359, 360
Klopfer, Sonya, 234
Knapp, Clarence, 188
Knickerbocker, Cholly (Maury Paul), 259, 260n
"Knock on Water" (O'Hara), 505
Knowlton, Percy, 232, 232n
Kober, Arthur, 115, 115n, 266, 267n
Kon-Tiki (Heyerdahl), 237n
Korda, Alexander, 130n
Kroll, Mrs. *See* Archbald, Margaretta
Kronenberger, Louis, 282, 337
Kungsholm (liner), xvi, 90

LaCava, Gregory, 233, 233n
Ladies' Home Journal, The, 440, 441n, 443n
Laemmle, Carl, Jr., 119, 119n
Lamarr, Hedy, 145
Lamb in His Bosom (Miller), 436, 436n
Lane, Margaret, 490, 491n
Lantern Club, 193, 194n, 203
Lardner, Ring, 78, 79, 160, 400
Larsen, Roy, 36, 38n
Lash, Don, 126
"Last of Haley, The" (O'Hara), 222, 222n
Latone, Tony, 183
Laughlin, Bill and Cynthia, 460
"Lawbreaker, The" (O'Hara), 425, 430, 431, 431n
Lawrence, Gertrude, 140
Lazar, Irving, 249, 250n
Leacock, Sir Robert and Lady, 311
League of Decency, 95, 97n
Leash Club, 256
Lee, Rensselaer, 327
Legion of the Damned, The (Doty), 28
Lehman, Ernest, 295, 297n, 309n
Lehman, Herbert, 253
Lemmon, Lenore, 231, 231n
"Leonard" (O'Hara), 465n
Lesher, 71
Levant, Oscar, 290, 320, 321
Levathes, Peter G., 369, 369n
Levien, Sonya, 262, 263n
Lewis, Ed ("Strangler"), 87n
Lewis, Jerry, 290
Lewis, John L., 156, 179
Lewis, Sinclair, 44, 50, 83, 85, 87n, 226, 227, 251, 262, 288-90, 299, 300n, 358, 371, 380, 399, 411, 414, 429
Lewis, Wilmarth S., 363, 363n
Liagre, Alfred de, 335
Liberty, xviii, 65n, 172n, 187n
Library of Congress, xix, 347

534